Knowing Future Time In and Through Greek Historiography

Trends in Classics – Supplementary Volumes

Edited by
Franco Montanari and Antonios Rengakos

Scientific Committee
Alberto Bernabé · Margarethe Billerbeck
Claude Calame · Philip R. Hardie · Stephen J. Harrison
Stephen Hinds · Richard Hunter · Christina Kraus
Giuseppe Mastromarco · Gregory Nagy
Theodore D. Papanghelis · Giusto Picone
Kurt Raaflaub · Bernhard Zimmermann

Volume 32

Knowing Future Time In and Through Greek Historiography

Edited by
Alexandra Lianeri

DE GRUYTER

ISBN 978-3-11-057821-8
e-ISBN (PDF) 978-3-11-043078-3
e-ISBN (EPUB) 978-3-11-043082-0
ISSN 1868-4785

Library of Congress Cataloging-in-Publication Data
A CIP catalog record for this book has been applied for at the Library of Congress.

Bibliographic information published by the Deutsche Nationalbibliothek
The Deutsche Nationalbibliothek lists this publication in the Deutsche Nationalbibliografie; detailed bibliographic data are available on the Internet at http://dnb.dnb.de.

© 2016 Walter de Gruyter GmbH, Berlin/Boston
This volume is text- and page-identical with the hardback published in 2016.
Logo: Christopher Schneider, Laufen
Printing and binding: CPI books GmbH, Leck

♾ Printed on acid-free paper
Printed in Germany

www.degruyter.com

Table of Contents

Preface —— VII

Alexandra Lianeri
Introduction: The Futures of Greek Historiography —— 1

Future Times and the Poetics of Greek Historiography

Jonas Grethlein
Ancient Historiography and 'Future Past' —— 59

Emily Greenwood
Futures Real and Unreal in Greek Historiography —— 79

Antonis Tsakmakis
Between Thucydides and the Future: Narrative Prolepsis and Xenophon's Concept of Historiography —— 101

Emily Baragwanath
Knowing Future Time in Xenophon's *Anabasis* —— 119

Nikos Miltsios
Knowledge and Foresight in Polybius —— 141

Christopher Pelling
Preparing for Posterity: Dionysius and Polybius —— 155

Temporalities of the Future and the Times of Historical Action

Catherine Darbo-Peschanski
The Future and the Logic of Closure in Greek Historiography —— 177

Katharina Wesselmann
No Future? Possibilities and Permanence in Herodotus' *Histories* —— 195

Karen Bassi
Fading into the Future: Visibility and Legibility in Thucydides' *History* —— 215

Nicolas Wiater
Shifting Endings, Ambiguity and Deferred Closure in Polybius' *Histories* —— 243

Paolo Desideri
Plutarch on the Future of an Ancient World —— 267

Luke Pitcher
Future's Bright? Looking Forward in Appian —— 281

Melina Tamiolaki
Writing for Posterity in Ancient Historiography: Lucian's Perspective —— 293

Toward the Modern Futures of Greek Times

Dennis Pausch
On the Shoulders of Greeks? Future Time in Livy's *Ab urbe condita* —— 311

Antonis Liakos
Constituting the Modern World as the Future of Greek Antiquity —— 329

Tim Rood
Horoscopes of Empires: Future Ruins from Thucydides to Macaulay —— 339

Aviezer Tucker
Historiographic Ancients and Moderns: The Difference between Thucydides and Ranke —— 361

Oswyn Murray
The Western Futures of Ancient History —— 385

Bibliography —— 401

Notes on Contributors —— 431

Index —— 435

Preface

Bringing a collaborative publication to completion is invariably dependent upon the contributions of many individuals and the support of many institutions. This is all the more true for this specific edited volume, as it is based on a conference organised at the Aristotle University of Thessaloniki in 2013 which was itself part of the conference series 'Trends in Classics', which goes back to 2007.

I am grateful to the 'Welfare Foundation for Social and Cultural Affairs' and particularly to Manos Dimitrakopoulos, whose generous funding in a period of financial crisis sustains the 'Trends in Classics' series.

Co-organising the conference with Jonas Grethlein and Antonios Rengakos provided a framework for intellectual debates that is rarely found, but also help with numerous practical problems; I would like to thank them for having listened, read and discussed with exceptional acumen, for their insightful critiques and for subtly reminding me of the value of close readings of ancient historians. Delegates who participated in that event made it one of remarkable intellectual stimulation; I am grateful for the lively debates, especially those that appeared at the time to take us off the main paths of the topic. Finally I would like to acknowledge the invaluable contribution of graduate students to the conference.

The opportunity to work with the contributors to this volume has been one characterized by high standards of learning, collaboration and collegiality; I thank them for their insights, meticulousness and commitment to the critical reading of concepts through which we understand antiquity. While Jonas and Antonios were not formally involved in editing the volume, they generously followed my attempts to trace connective webs and formulate a certain argumentative coherence. Discussions with Yorgos Avgoustis, Robin Osborne and Kostas Vlassopoulos have been central to my understanding of concepts underpinning this study long before I began to conceptualise it. Finally, I am more grateful than I can say to my family and especially my son Alcibiades who valiantly came to a conference about Greek temporalities at the age of two months.

Alexandra Lianeri
Introduction: The Futures of Greek Historiography

τὸ δὲ ἀστάθμητον τοῦ μέλλοντος ὡς ἐπὶ πλεῖστον κρατεῖ.
It is the uncertainty of the future that has the biggest influence on events.
Thucydides, *Hist.* 4.62.4, tr. J. Mynott

1 Knowing the future in and through Greek historiography: Concepts and questions[1]

In a famous passage in book 1 of his history, Thucydides made a remarkable assertion about the future of his work:

> καὶ ἐς μὲν ἀκρόασιν ἴσως τὸ μὴ μυθῶδες αὐτῶν ἀτερπέστερον φανεῖται· ὅσοι δὲ βουλήσονται τῶν τε γενομένων τὸ σαφὲς σκοπεῖν καὶ τῶν μελλόντων ποτὲ αὖθις κατὰ τὸ ἀνθρώπινον τοιούτων καὶ παραπλησίων ἔσεσθαι, ὠφέλιμα κρίνειν αὐτὰ ἀρκούντως ἕξει. κτῆμά τε ἐς αἰεὶ μᾶλλον ἢ ἀγώνισμα ἐς τὸ παραχρῆμα ἀκούειν ξύγκειται.[2]

> Perhaps the absence of the element of fable in my work may make it seem less easy on the ear; but it will have served its purpose well enough if it is judged useful by those who want to have a clear view of what happened in the past and what – the human condition being what it is – can be expected to happen again some time in the future in similar or much the same ways. It is composed to be a possession for all time and not just a performance-piece for the moment.[3]

The vision of the future put forth in the passage is consciously indeterminate. As Emily Greenwood points out, while it is possible to argue that the instances of the future tense are non-specific and may refer to Thucydides' contemporaries in the immediate or near future, the addition of the phrase κτῆμα ἐς αἰεί, possession for all time, makes the assertion deliberately open-ended. The text states its

---

[1] I am grateful to Yorgos Avgoustis, Jonas Grethlein, Robin Osborne and Antonios Rengakos for their critical and insightful comments on previous versions of this introduction.
[2] Thuc. 1.22.4.
[3] Mynott 2013, 15–16.

relevance to both the immediate readers of the history and its ongoing, long-term reception.[4]

This was a very radical and very sophisticated contention. Studies of Thucydides' deployment of writing as a new medium in a predominantly oral culture indicate the originality of his enterprise.[5] Thucydides not only proclaimed the invention of "a new kind of book, a book to take home and keep, rather than a piece making its effect in performance", as James Redfield puts it;[6] he also delimited a novel time-frame associated with the indeterminate horizons of readings which this book could enter. By reflecting on his work's long-term reception, Thucydides appropriated the Homeric κλέος ἄφθιτον, everlasting glory. The intertextual reference is pointed out by Gregory Crane,[7] and qualified by Jonas Grethlein who cogently pointed out that "whereas poetic works define their own eternity via their objects, Thucydides claims eternity in relation to his readers. Fame has been replaced with usefulness".[8] But this new claim refashioned the temporal horizon of the epic by intertwining the object of the historical narrative, which was the present and past, with an elusive temporal horizon of the future. At the most immediate level, this intertwinement was distanced from epic temporalities by means of escaping the finite horizon of the author and his world, and acquiring the potential to explode this horizon.[9] Unlike epic heroic deeds, whose glory remained stable, as it did not depend on narrative, but rather itself bestowed fame on the narrating text, historiography's movement towards its readers was subjected to the temporal structures of change. By replacing fame with everlasting usefulness and thereby meaningfulness, Thucydides' text entered the shifting horizon of its reception.[10] On a second level, this horizon was also moved into the text. Thucydides' claim brought the future to the centre of the *métier d'historien* insofar as history writing was considered to take its form in the light offered by subsequent readers. It was the future, he says, that provided the best criterion for separating history from other narratives, and especially those narratives with which the historian first had to compete, stories composed with a focus on the present.

---

4 Greenwood 2006, 8–9; Greenwood 2012, 163.
5 Loraux 1986; Darbo-Peschanski 1987.
6 Redfield 2000, 91.
7 Crane 1996, 211–215.
8 Grethlein 2010, 214.
9 Ricoeur 1981.
10 Cf. my discussion of this passage in section 1.2. I am grateful to Jonas Grethlein for his critical disagreement which helped me qualify this argument.

The peculiar entailment of this contention is that the past and the present cannot be known historically when they are studied in their own terms. A key principle of historical investigation lies in a certain synthesis between history and the future. There is an anticipatory voice sustaining the definition of history in opposition to delightful stories, since only the former can remain meaningful and maintain a relation to future readers. But there is, at the same time, a historical voice sustaining the possibility of engaging with the future; for it is this voice that offers a clear view of what once happened (τῶν γενομένων) and through it a prognosis of what may happen in the future (τῶν μελλόντων). Without the future there would be no way of separating history from stories; but there would also be no future, no possibility of foreknowledge or anticipation, without a historical knowledge that makes it possible to see into what may happen outside the perspective, the experience, and the needs of the present.

This volume approaches this relation both in the context of antiquity and from the viewpoint of the relation between ancient and modern historiography. In doing so, it pursues a double aim. First, it seeks to identify and, to an extent, codify concepts of the future and corresponding temporal relations of 'before' and 'after' in the writings of Greek historians. This involves the diachronic account of ideas about the future in different historians, from Herodotus and Thucydides through Xenophon to Polybius, Plutarch, Diodorus and Appian. But it also involves exploring diverse articulations of the future which are at work in the same text, the anticipatory voices constituting what we shall describe in this introduction, deploying Mikhail Bakhtin's term polyphony, as a polyphonic temporality: a discourse about future time formulated when the historian's voice takes shape in a dialogue with other voices, such as those of historical actors including characters, voices associated with other discursive forms, such as myth, philosophy and literature, but also those of ancient and modern readers, including historians.[11] These two levels invite reflection about *some* level of unity underpinning considerations of the future in specific contexts and periods, establishing relations of continuity and discontinuity among these periods, and engaging in the comparative study of Greek historiography and other historiographical traditions with a special focus on the modern. What, for instance, was the relation between Thucydides' appeal to future readers and Xenophon's response to it, when he began his account of Greek history at the end of Thucydides' narrative? What was the meaning of the future posited by metahistorical notions used throughout Greek historiography, such as 'change of fortune',

---

11 I am grateful to Vassilis Argyris for suggesting that I investigate Bakhtin's concept of polyphony in order to discuss this issue.

'good' or 'bad fortune', 'necessity' or 'causality'? What was the role of other anticipatory voices, such as those articulated by oracular, medical, poetic or philosophical discourses? How can we identify the ideological dimension and political implications of historiographical discourses about the future?

Second, the book combines the study of ancient cases with a theoretical reflection on time and history. It does so by investigating the future trajectories of Greek concepts of time and the future in the context of modern temporalities. One of the implications of this investigation is that we, as readers of Greek historiography, do not stand outside time and the temporal categories of our age, which are the legacy of the modern confrontation with antiquity. We reflect on time while standing in time. So the concepts we use to analyse ancient temporalities are conditioned by the modern categories, and especially by the exclusive claim to the future made by European modernity. The idea that modernity's break with *historia magistra vitae* constituted a new category of the future as different from the present and past is not based on an opposition between ancient and modern temporalities that is external to those who observe these periods. Rather, the 'atemporal paralysis'[12] it attributes to premodern times indicates more the self-definition of modernity, rather than the absence of reflection on time that recognises the difference between past, present and future.

Ever since antiquity, historians have acknowledged that time is central to history writing. Greek historians reflected profoundly upon time and the future, even though this reflection was not always direct and explicit, but needs to be inferred from their account of events. In an inaugural gesture, Herodotus separated his enquiry from local narratives by stating that his work concerned change in the loci of power, implying that this change is brought about by the course of time. Unlike the existing *logoi* of both Greeks and barbarians, he promised to account equally for small and powerful cities, insofar as many of those which were large subsequently became small and many of those that were currently small used to be commanding and strong.[13]

For Thucydides, the uncertainty about what the future might bring about became a key historical force: people, he wrote, decide about the present on the grounds of anticipations that are characterised by vagueness and uncertainty: hence it is the future that has the biggest influence on most things.[14] Hellenistic historians reflected on the different temporal modes and rhythms of change. Polybius approached this subject with the intention to construct models for

---

12 For the term see section 3.
13 Hdt 1.5.
14 Thuc. 4.62.4.

knowing and controlling the future by especially drawing attention to how things turn out παρὰ τὴν προσδοκίαν, contrary to expectation.¹⁵ Diodorus' universal temporality constructed the future as part of a long-term time-frame: in attempting to account for all known history in a continuum it implied that the distant past was needed in order to illuminate all future phases of history up to the present.¹⁶

Seeking to explore these considerations, contributors to this book were invited to combine a close reading of ancient texts with a reflection on time in Greek historiography. Their contributions configure a web of interconnected fields and concepts, on which this book builds. A primary field is the poetics of historical time, as formulated mainly in narratological studies of Greek historiography and other contemporary genres. Based on wider philosophical and historiographical debates on historical time, poetics and narrative,¹⁷ this field has offered fruitful research in the field of classics.¹⁸ Focusing on the inherently narrative dimension of history writing, relevant studies identified poetic modes of articulating time as central to the antagonistic relation between the historian-narrator and the experience of historical actors, to the diverse modes of focalisation and organisation of events included in the narrative, to the relation of historiography to legendary traditions and other genres, such as epic poetry, elegy and tragedy, as well as to questions of delimiting historical truth and knowledge.¹⁹ What these studies have shown is the constitution of Greek historiography as a mode of knowledge entertaining a dual relationship to narrative on the one side and to methodological or 'scientific' objectivity,²⁰ on the other. It is thus a mode of knowledge which, in virtue of its claim to 'science', as Ricoeur writes, "tends to forget

---

15 See 4.22.6 among many other instances of the phrase in Polybius pointed out by McGing 2013, 188.
16 Clarke 1999.
17 Veyne 1984; de Certeau 1988; Ricoeur 1980; 1984–1988, 2004; Rancière 1994; 1994a.
18 For an overview of recent bibliography see de Jong 2014.
19 Extending the seminal work of writers such as Simon Hornblower (1994), Tim Rood (1998), narratological approaches to Greek historiographical time are found in I. de Jong and R. Nünlist's seminal *Time in Ancient Greek Literature* (2007) (Cf. De Jong / Nünlist 2011); Jonas Grethlein's *The Greeks and their Past* (2010), which posits time in the field of literary memory; articles in *Narratology and Interpretation* by Grethlein and Antonios Rengakos (2009); Grethlein's recent *Experience and Teleology in Ancient Historiography* (2013) which examines the intertwining of the experience of historical actors and the teleological discourse of historians (Cf. Grethlein 2011; 2014 and Grethlein / Krebs 2012); and Emily Baragwanath and Mathieu de Bakker's *Myth, Truth and Narrative in Herodotus* (2012) exploring the force of myth in shaping Herodotus' narrative organisation and consideration of historical truth.
20 On the emerging constitution of the concept, methods and problems of 'science' see Lloyd 1993.

this line of derivation which continues nevertheless tacitly to preserve its specificity" as a historiographical discourse.[21]

Ricoeur discerns in W. B. Gallie's *Philosophy and Historical Understanding* a thesis that sustains the derivative character of historical narrative while simultaneously raising the problem of linking narrative time to the wider discursive and social conditions of its constitution. This connection delimits the second field on which this volume builds. According to Gallie, it is the historian that makes it possible for the reader to understand what may have otherwise appeared as an incomprehensible or even meaningless succession of events. The historian establishes the 'followability' of the story which formulates the succession of events into a meaningful whole by means of emplotment.[22] The followability of the story links Greek historiography to other contemporary genres, as it calls upon the reader to recognise already established narrative paradigms – for instance in epic poetry or tragedy – which also invite readers to understand actions, thoughts and events as a coherent whole.[23]

These patterns or schemas have further been studied as articulations of the social function and ideological constitution of Greek historiography. It is in this respect, rather than as an advocacy of specific political positions, that scholarship has approached Greek historiography's manifest focus on the present. Thus Christian Meier argues that the Greeks' focus on contemporary history posited the present as both an achievement and "a limit that was hardly ever transcended."[24] Francis Dunn explored this shift to a present-centred temporality in the fifth century as the experience of a "present shock" produced by a "radical disorientation at living in the present no longer shaped and given meaning by the authority of the past".[25] Charles Fornara has read Herodotus as writing for his contemporary Greek public, rather than posterity, capitalising on analogies

---

[21] Ricoeur 1984–1988 v. 1, 91.
[22] Ricoeur draws the idea of followability from Gallie 1968 and relates it to the operation of narrative emplotment. Cf. Ricoeur 1984–1988 v. 1, 149–152.
[23] On this issue see Grethlein 2010; Loraux 1986a; de Romilly 1968. For a study of conceptions of time beyond historiography see Marincola 2012. For considerations of tragic time and their implications for understanding historical/human time see Vidal-Naquet 1986. Considerations of time are present throughout Loraux's writings, as for instance in Loraux 1993, 6–7, 101, 113, 218. See also Sean Kirkland's (2014) significant reconsideration of tragic time as formulated in the transition from a temporality of racing or speeding (dromoscopic time) to a temporality of waylessnessness and hesitation (aporetic time). On the temporality of epic poetry with a focus on the *Odyssey* see Bergren 1983.
[24] Quoted in Csapo / Miller 1998, 123.
[25] Dunn 2007; cf. D'Angour 2011.

between his time and the remote past.²⁶ Phiroze Vasunia has further argued that Herodotus' engagement with the present implied a certain valorisation of fifth-century Athens as a particular *telos* through which his historical account entered into the history of otherness: the presumably static temporality of the Egyptians and the despotic past linked to this temporality.²⁷ From a different perspective, scholarship on Greek historiography has explored the interlinking of the focus on the present with the operation of memory²⁸ as well as temporalities of pattern and process, and their implications for forms of self-identification of the Athenian community in relation to the past and future. ²⁹

A third field arises when we move out of Greek history both geographically, through comparisons with other ancient historiographical traditions, and temporally, through the juxtaposition of ancient and modern temporalities. The predominant theme here is the way in which different cultures configure distinct modes for dividing time and attribute to them distinct rhythms and orientation.³⁰ The question of identifying distinct historiographical temporalities becomes especially perplexing in the juxtaposition of ancient and modern temporalities attempted recently in studies by Reinhardt Koselleck and François Hartog.³¹ As will be argued later, the difficulty with regard to such comparisons arises from the impossibility of disentangling the objects of study that are juxtaposed to one another from the theoretical frame that enables their identification and mutual interlinking. Still, to consider articulations of the future in Greek historians draws on wider theorisations of the ways in which time was configured in antiquity; on exploring the meanings and orientation of time and the wider relation between time and texts;³² as well as on the reflexive question of how to identify conceptions of time as distinctions that are not given but involve a more active stance through which historical actors 'break up' time.³³

The notion of the future posed by this book raises some difficult questions. One of these concerns a conflict of temporalities: on the one side is the sequen-

---

26 Fornara 1971; see also Strasburger 1955.
27 Vasunia 2001, 133–135. Cf. Csapo / Miller 1998; Boedeker 1998; Clarke 2008; Foxhall et al. 2010; Steinbock 2013.
28 Grethlein 2010; Morrison 2004.
29 Edelstein 1967; Meier 1990.
30 Rosen 2004; Raaflaub 2014; Miller 2008. Geoffrey Lloyd has done much to enhance our comparative perspective on ancient Greece and China. See Lloyd 2004. Also see Shankman / Durrant 2000; Foxhall / Gehrke / Luraghi 2010; Konstan / Raaflaub 2010.
31 For both Koselleck's and Hartog's consideration of this issue see the discussion in section 3 of this introduction.
32 In addition to Koselleck's and Hartog's works, to be discussed below see Kennedy 2013.
33 Lorenz / Bevernage 2013, 9–10.

tial ordering of time in the historical narrative that claims to accommodate (or at least interpret) what is to come, and, on the other, the interruption of this sequence by the acknowledgement of the temporal volatility and radical unpredictability of the future. In his analysis of narrative time, Gérard Genette argued that the sequential, forward-looking narrative time of events and actions presented in a text metonymically "borrows" the temporality of reading – what he calls the 'pseudo-time' of the text. Yet the structure of the narrative, according to Genette, follows a "retrograde movement": a temporal reversal by means of which each element of the story is accounted for by subsequent ones – from which it is entailed that the last element commands all previous ones, but also that nothing commands. According to Genette, the arbitrariness of narrative time lies precisely in this reversal: the construction of the story through a backward-oriented temporality, in accordance with which the narrator makes meaningful a web of events and actions by going from effects to the causes that explain them, from ends to means.[34] This structure makes the future an inescapable dimension of narrative. While Genette's analysis is mainly focused on literary texts, this role of the future can be applied to historical narrative insofar as the historian – even the contemporary historian insofar as she does not merely chronicle a web of events – attributes coherence to the whole by means of this movement from the future to the past, from effects (e.g. the outbreak of a war, the collapse of a city) to causes.

Greek historians' claims to instruct readers with regard to the future, as we shall see, lay precisely in this relation. Theirs was not the knowledge of foretellers, but of interpreters constituting causal and temporal relations with regard to what would otherwise appear as an incomprehensible set of events. In claiming this knowledge Greek historians inaugurated a twofold limit for historical discourse drawn in opposition to other forms of knowledge of time pursued, for example, by philosophy or poetry, and in opposition to alternative understandings of the temporalities of historiography's object, such as those formulated by historical actors and communities. The retrospectivity of historical narrative offered a signifying whole that excluded other interpretations of time. However, the future also entered this narrative as a realm that disrupts this coherence and unhinges certain relations of 'before' and 'after', a realm whose determination by sheer fortune rather than necessities, accident rather than determinable causes, and opinion rather than truth and reason, questions historical knowledge as such. In Greek historiography this disruption was formulated through a polyphonic narrative in which the voice of the historian determining time was juxta-

---

34 Genette 1969; 1980, 33–85.

posed to those of historical actors and communities included in his text, but also through a serial canon of historians-narrators extending the endpoints of the same story and thus rewriting the beginnings and middles of it.

1.1 What was future time?

There is, at the outset of this book, a contradiction pertaining to the very object of our enquiry: considerations of the future in Greek historiography. On the one hand, the explicit focus of Greek historians on present and past history makes this object appear as counter-intuitive: why would one investigate the future in a discourse whose writers and contemporary readers engage with the present and past?[35] For example, Thucydides organises his narrative by following the development of the Archidamian war formulating "a strongly paratactic sequence", in which "unit follows unit within the season as, on a larger scale, season follows season and year follows year."[36] Moreover, with the exception of the prolepses looking ahead explicitly to the defeat of Athens in 2.65, 5.26 and 6.15.3–4 Thucydides' work is focused on the present, and deploys no prolepses, especially no prolepses looking beyond this final defeat.[37] As Grethlein argues, Thucydides' reader is then by and large limited to the perspective of contemporary history, as formed by the tension between the backwards gaze of historiography and that of historical agents.[38] Likewise, Dunn studied both Thucydides and other contemporary writers in order to identify what he called a 'present shock' in Athens at the end of the fifth century: a condition of cultural change that severed ties with the authority of the past and the perspective of the future: rather than "future shock", he argues, these changes produced "present shock," whereby changes immerse individuals in a disorienting present, they command "special attention in some way to the here and now, to a present that is not understood by reference to past (or future)."[39]

The contradiction becomes more evident if we compare Greek historiography to other Greek discourses that address the future more explicitly, such as those formulated in philosophy, tragedy and epic poetry, or to other historiographical traditions. As Arnaldo Momigliano notes, "the future did not loom large in the

---

[35] I owe this question to a conversation with Rosalind Thomas.
[36] Dewald 2005, 46.
[37] On the rarity of prolepses in Thucydides see bibliography in Grethlein 2010, 242, n.127. On the absence of prolepses beyond the final defeat of Athens see Rood 2007b, 145–146.
[38] Grethlein 2013a, 93; Cf. Grethlein 2013, 29–31.
[39] Dunn 2007, 2, 36.

work of Greek historians", especially in comparison with Roman, Judeo-Christian or modern historiography.[40] Developed in a context wherein interpretations of oracles and divine signs posited prognosis at the heart of cultural conceptions of time, while literary, philosophical and mythical discourses offered multiple configurations of the apocalyptic voice, historiography may be seen as establishing a critical distance from narratives of future time, of foreknowledge, anticipation and prediction. At the same time, both the idea of addressing the future and specific claims to knowing it were far from banished. As Momigliano writes, modifying his previous statement, "the Greek historian almost inevitably thinks that the past events he tells have some relevance to the future." The events would not have been chosen as important if they did not teach something to the readers of histories. Stories would then "provide an example, constitute a warning, point to a likely pattern of future developments in human affairs."[41]

Two sets of questions need to be posited with regard to the above contentions. The first concerns the meaning of the concept of the future deployed by different discourses on Greek historiography. Does Momigliano use the same concept when he both denies and affirms the presence of the future in the writings of Greek historians? Likewise, is the tension between the historiographical gaze and that of historical agents dissociated from considerations of future time? As Grethlein argues in this volume and elsewhere, this tension is itself grounded in a dual temporality of *telos*, a final viewpoint in the light of which the events narrated are envisaged, a viewpoint which is still future for the historical agents, but already past for the historian and her readers.[42] Thucydides' narrative builds on this tension: at the outset of his work, as Simon Hornblower notes, Thucydides informs his readers that he "sat down to record a set of events which were still in the future"[43] pointing at once to the unfolding of his history alongside the events of the war and the position from which he could see the end of it. Finally, are historiographical articulations of a radically shifting present devoid of appeals to the future? As Dunn observes, Thucydides' work voiced a striking reversal of cultural values hitherto centred on tradition, age and proven worth by claiming that present events are not to be seen as ephemeral, but as great and noteworthy as events in the past.[44] But is not this claim dependent on envisioning the future as a perspective from which both the value and the longevity of the present can be recognised? Finally, if, as we saw, any sequential narrative pre-

---

40 Momigliano 1966.
41 Momigliano 1990, 18.
42 Grethlein, this volume; 2013.
43 Hornblower 1991–2008 commenting on Thuc. 1.1.1.
44 Dunn 2007, 112.

supposes a backward-looking move from effects to causes, does not Thucydides' paratactic structure accommodate the future by depending on endpoints – and the final endpoint of the defeat of Athens – for its meaning?

To ask these questions is not only to challenge the familiar meaning of the future as something that simply comes after the present. It is also to challenge the familiar meaning of time as moments that follow one another in an orderly fashion. The possibility that the future, as a temporal dimension of historical thought, can be understood differently also means that time in Greek historiography cannot be understood as a given relation between past, present and future, but, rather, that this relation needs to become the object of our enquiry. As C. Lorenz and B. Bevernage point out, to ask how the temporal dimensions of past and future are related in a given present means to enquire about how both these dimensions and temporality itself – the order of relations posited by our concepts of time – become relative to those who identify them.[45] This means that temporalities are relative not only to the cultural position and conceptual tools of Greek historians, but also to our own readings of Greek historiography through the temporal categories of the modern age. So our second set of questions pertains to the dimensions of historiographical concepts that construct relations between past, present and future in specific historical contexts. These include, for instance, the concept of progressive orientation of the present towards the future; the notion of exemplarity through which the future inscribes itself into the present as a moral law or necessity; the ideas of hope and expectation implicit in eschatological approaches to time; the constitution of historical breaks underlying the temporality of revolutions from antiquity to the present; or the temporality valorising present time as the source of both future and past times. So to deny the presence of the future in Greek historians in comparison with Judeo-Christian or modern historiography would presuppose identifying the absence of a certain eschatological viewpoint through which the future enters historical narratives as the intertwinement of secular and sacred time – the hope and expectation of the historical arrival of doomsday. It would also presuppose identifying the absence of the modern notion of the future as open for the new and without limit. Yet it does not necessarily follow from these identifications that concepts of future were absent from the discourse of Greek historians.

Stating that Greek historians deployed no category of the future evokes a specific notion of the future formulated outside the Greek historical context and deployed as an imaginary model enabling us to discern the absence in ques-

---

45 Bevernage / Lorenz 2013.

tion. Yet the terms in which this comparison is conducted fail to account for the variety of ways in which different communities of historians and broader cultural groups have defined the future and linked it to the present and past. Indeed, as Peter Burke points out, the very notion of the future entered the historian's agenda with regard specifically to modern temporalities, since it was only recently pioneered by Reinhart Koselleck as a characteristic of modernity.[46] This notion was therefore inordinately embedded into modern conceptual networks. We begin our enquiry about the Greek past with theoretical postures about time and the future inherited by the modern tradition. Moreover, this starting point implicitly privileges modern temporalities and the social and political values associated with them. This is so because concepts of the past, present and – perhaps especially – the future entail forms of periodisation which valorise and evaluate certain periods in terms ensuring the effective control of the political life of a community. These values mean, for instance, the authorisation of a vision of the modern present as uniquely capable of moving toward a better future, with the concomitant exclusion of alternative political, economic or cultural possibilities.

Yet the future, as a concept, has been understood in too many ways to be reduced to a single definition, period and history. Anthropological research has identified diverse 'cultures of the future' associated with different historical communities.[47] Moreover, differences pertain to the distinct contexts of a culture in which conceptions of the future are formulated. In ancient Greece, for instance, as elsewhere, religious time is not identical with civic time, while diverse cultural communities, such as women, experienced time differently. Richard Sorabji's seminal *Time, Creation and the Continuum* shows that concepts of time and the future further change in diachrony. Focusing on shifting philosophical traditions, Sorabji traces changing concepts and questions, and perspicaciously suggests that the ancient discussions of time were fuller than the modern ones: the sheer range of arguments and possibilities considered was greater.[48]

The future, as the next section suggests and several essays in the volume contend, was formulated and considered in antiquity by evoking the plurality of its meaning. Even – or particularly – when we study a single historian, it was constituted by a dialogue which not merely resisted, but radically uprooted, the establishment of a unified concept. This was so even when historians ap-

---

46 Burke 2004, 617–626, 620.
47 For an anthropological overview see Maruyama / Harkins 1978; Tiemersma / Oosterling 1994.
48 Sorabji 1983, 3.

pealed to such singularity; for this assertion was made possible by taking the risk of a "repetition in alterity,"[49] the risk of surviving one's time by means of a dialogue with others, which is ultimately the risk of moving towards the future, the risk of translation, transformation and polyphony.[50] Taking this multiplicity as our starting point entails studying the depth and complexity of Greek historiographical temporalities, rather than attributing to antiquity a unifying absence of reflection about the future.

1.2 A polyphonic future

In her pioneering reading of Thucydides' narrative, Carolyn Dewald deployed Bakhtin's concept of polyphony in order to explore the profoundly dialogic constitution of the text. As she argues, the emphasis Thucydides "puts on the decisions and actions of the actors within the account ... links their rational behaviour, as people whose actions are under narration, to the corresponding rationality of the narrating historian." In other words, the thinking of the historian and that of historical actors leading to actions and events "are conveyed simultaneously to the reader, through the way the narrative structure is organised".[51] The story "allows both the decisions and actions of people in the past and the historian's own understanding of them to emerge, in tandem with one another, as coherent and credible for the reading audience."[52] Drawing on both Dewald's analysis and Bakhtin's writings, this section discusses Thucydides as a case study exemplifying the polyphonic articulation of the future in Greek historiography. The dialogic constitution of Thucydides' narrative involves a specific consideration of time: a plural sense of the future as the outcome of both diverse 'authorial' voices engaging with the present and past, and a certain openness and unfinalisability attributed by these voices to historical events. There are, in other words, two interconnected levels on which the future manifests polyphony. The first is that of the historiographical work, which involves a dialogue not only with historical actors and readers, as Dewald aptly suggests, but also with other authorial voices, such as those of the poet and the philosopher, and those of subsequent historians. The second level is that of the relation between poetic or narrative temporalities and the temporalities of action and

---

49 Bennington / Derrida 1993, 86.
50 On the notions of translation and transformation see Derrida 1985.
51 Dewald 2005, 15.
52 Dewald 2005, 15.

events, which, in turn, entails the 'potential' and unfinalisability of the historical event as such.

According to Bakhtin, polyphony is not to be understood as synonymous with heteroglossia – the mere diversity of speech styles in a language. It rather has to do with a dialogic sense of truth pertaining to the position of the author within a text.[53] As Gary Morson argues, Bakhtin's concept is not merely stylistic. It depends on content and the handling of diverse authorial voices in it. This must not be understood as the annihilation of an authorial perspective. Bakhtin rather speaks of this perspective as different in kind and method of expression from its monologic counterparts, insofar as it is constituted by means of dialogic interaction through which a unified sense of truth is constituted as "voice-ideas" confronting one another. As he writes,

> It is quite possible to imagine and postulate a unified truth that requires a plurality of consciousnesses, one that in principle cannot be fitted within the bounds of a single consciousness, one that is, so to speak, by its very nature *full of event potential* [*sobytiina*] and is born at a point of contact among various consciousnesses.[54]

The dialogic sense of truth then requires an open unity in dialogue, which Bakhtin further describes as the open-ended unity of the event. On both levels, that of dialogic authorship and that of events, the object in question is neither static, nor is it to be seen as developing in a predetermined way. It is rather open-ended, productive, full of potential and 'event potential', since it takes shape on the 'threshold' of several interacting consciousnesses – a plurality of existing and unmerged voices.[55] It thus itself manifests an unfinalisability through which the polyphonic constitution of authorial discourse and the polyphonic potential of the event acquire a future-oriented temporality. Both are open-ended and both include the potential for exploding the present.

In Greek historiography, as will be argued, this polyphony is formulated on multiple levels, including the voice of historical actors incorporated into the text, the dialogue with other discourses as well as ancient and modern readers. We may begin to grasp this polyphony in relation to Greek historians if we go back to Thucydides' vision of history in 1.22.4. In this formulation there is, first, a plurality of authorial consciousnesses delimiting the future. This enters the text once Thucydides' projection of his writing into the future confronts

---

53 Bakhtin 1993; 1981. For my reading of Bakhtin I draw on Morson 1990. For a wider reflection on Bakhtin and the classics see Branham 2002.
54 Morson 1990, 236.
55 Morson 1990, 228, 236.

the temporality of the particular according to which the object of historical enquiry is posited in the present and past. In the *Poetics* 1451a36-b11, Aristotle codified the opposition between historiographical practice on the one hand and poetry and philosophy on the other. According to his formulation, poetry does not engage with what happens (γενόμενα), but with what might be expected to happen and what can possibly happen (οἷα ἂν γένοιτο καὶ τὰ δυνατά) according to what is usual (εἰκὸς) or necessary (ἀναγκαῖον). It is thus more philosophical and valuable than history, because it deals with universals (τὰ καθόλου), rather than particulars (τὰ καθ' ἕκαστον) – with "what Alcibiades did or what happened to him",[56] as Aristotle says, implying that these deeds and sufferings acquired their meaning within their specific moment in time. The opposition was blurred in the *Poetics* itself. As a historical fact, Alcibiades' deeds and sufferings were understood as the object of interpretations long before Aristotle's time. Consequently, history's focus on the particular as mediated by interpretation stood uncomfortably close to Aristotle's approach to the tragic plot which also mediated deeds and sufferings, human πρᾶξις and πάθος.[57] Thucydides' appeal to the future temporalised this link between historical facts on the one side, and poetry's and philosophy's δυνατά on the other. As the striking conjunction of γενόμενα and μέλλοντα suggests in the above passage, history could remain useful in the long term because of its dual capacity to focus on and, at the same time, transcend the particularity of what happened at a given moment in time.

This conjunction of the particular and the possible meant that the emerging voice of the historian inaugurated a dialogue with the anticipatory voices of the poet and philosopher. Thucydides promises to record what happened in a form that will survive time as a monument – an inscription, as Moles cogently put it, whose survival is achieved by means of its detachment from a certain time.[58] In this promise we may read the voice of the poet – especially the epic poet – whose words were unchanging and projected into the future due to their detachment from time and their relation to divine things,[59] and the poet who gives discursive form to divine foreknowledge, precisely as the prophet puts into words the vision of the mantis and the oracle.[60] But we also discern the voice of the philosopher considering a possible future, one that has not already been fulfilled as a modality of the present. One thinks, for instance, of Gorgias' reference to *logoi* as the medium for knowing the future, which bears the possibility of both truth and

---

56 On Aristotle's concept of history see de Ste Croix 1992.
57 Wohl 2014, 142–159, 145. Cf. Frede 1992.
58 Moles 1999.
59 Bakker 2002, 23.
60 Nagy 1990.

false knowledge;[61] Plato's contention in the *Theaetetus* that present legislation and judgment are formulated on the grounds that they will continue to be beneficial in later times and carry implications for the future;[62] but also Aristotle's emphasis on the now (νῦν) as the notion of the present which links (συνέχει) what has happened and what will happen.[63] The statement also echoes wider motifs concerning the future, such as the continuing importance of truth and the long-term usefulness of a work's subject-matter, which were deployed in both poetry and philosophy.

Secondly, this polyphonic historical consciousness is linked by Thucydides to the temporality of action through the complex notion of κατὰ τὸ ἀνθρώπινον. As Katherine Harloe and Neville Morley point out, debates over the meaning of the phrase skate over issues of translation. Renderings which deploy the phrase 'human nature' imply that Thucydides had a clear sense of an unchanging human nature and use this translation to reinforce their interpretation of human action as revealing timeless or universal principles.[64] Yet, this translation can be countered on the grounds that it evokes anachronistic assumptions pertaining to modern categories of humanity. Alternative renderings as 'human condition', 'human situation' or 'humanness' are more prone to stress the diversity and contingency of experience and action under conditions of ignorance and uncertainty (though they are not themselves free of anachronistic premises).[65] Momigliano usefully accentuates the temporal dimension of the phrase by opting for Charles Foster Smith's translation: "whoever shall wish to have a clear view both of the events which have happened and of those which will some day, *in all human probability*, happen again in the same or similar way."[66] As he explains, the passage contains no reference to some eternal return. Thucydides only suggests that, in the future, there will be events that are either identical with or similar to those he is going to narrate. But he does not specify a certain kind of identity, nor does he explain whether similarity between present and future is meant to refer to specific parts of the narration or the

---

[61] Gorg. Hel. 10–11.
[62] Plat. Theaet., 178a. See Burnyeat 1990, 41–42.
[63] Arist. *Phys.* 4.13, 222a10–11. See Roark 2011.
[64] It has even been argued that, according to Thucydides, *nomos* in the sense of human convention was to human nature "as the contingent to the necessary and the mutable to the unchangeable". Sahlins 2004, 120.
[65] Harloe/Morley 2012, 14–15. Cf. Pires 2006. On τὸ ἀνθρώπινον in Thucydides see the scholarly literature in Harloe/Morley 2012.
[66] Momigliano 1966, 11.

whole of his subject, the Peloponnesian War.[67] To ask what is probable for humans does not thrust human nature entirely out of sight, since what makes something probable for humans has to do with what humans are like. However, unlike human nature, the concept of probability conveys the idea that things which are probable may also turn to be otherwise. In other words, it refocuses attention on the condition of humans (rather than nature), which is a condition of affairs that may or may not be achieved, may or may not happen, that is to say, a historical condition.[68]

So human probability operates here as a metahistorical category deployed to account for and unify the temporality of the work's subject-matter: the human historical condition. The events described as historical facts (γενόμενα) can be chosen and organised as such by the historian on the basis of a common characteristic, element or occasion, which is represented as a specific instance of the probable: what individuals or communities have done and could do in the future when they are faced with the same or similar circumstances. Reversing an eloquent contention in the preface to the *Cambridge Ancient History*,[69] we may say that Thucydides constitutes here the category of *kata to anthropinon* as the principle that allows *him* to draw together the innumerable dimensions and infinite implications of an occurrence – from the diverse individual experiences to the countless elements of historical reality constituting this occurrence – in order to transmute it into an event in his military and political narrative. This 'transmutation' imposes a narrative organisation and closure on the time of historical action. In this sense, Thucydides and his interest in *to anthropinon* constitutes a poeisis which fully falsifies Aristotle's distinction between history and poetry.

However, as the notion of the probable indicates, the poiesis that is history writing does not organise a narrative in terms of a single temporality. On one level, such a temporality is formulated as the account of events through which Thucydides reconfigures the diverse temporal experiences and visions of historical actors by subjecting them to a narrative mode linking causes and effects, and moving forward to ends that determine the whole as representative of human probability. By distinguishing his narrative from that of historical actors, as we shall further see below, Thucydides constructs this temporality as trans-

---

[67] Momigliano 1966, 11–12.
[68] This distinction between human nature and human condition was formulated as a response to an insightful critical comment by Robin Osborne.
[69] "[Thucydides'] most remarkable achievement was to transmute even military narrative into a commentary on the human condition," Lewis *et al.* 1992, xiv.

historical and beyond the processes of historical time.[70] Still, on a different level, the notion of the probable allows the experiences of historical actors to enter the narrative and shape its temporality. There is, in this sense, a constant tension between the temporality through which the author narrates the events and that associated with human experience and action. The voice of historical actors reflecting on the probable is prominent in Thucydides. Particularly in speeches, but also when he reports on collective decision making, Thucydides "not only adopts the perspective of the protagonists", as Grethlein observes, "but also lets them speak in their words." Only rarely does his voice intervene to reconstruct this temporality and remind the reader of its distinct mediating function.[71] No doubt the actors' expectations about the future are finally often proved to be wrong by the course of events. Yet this is the condition of probable knowledge, which also determines Thucydides' engagement with the future. While his authority over past times cannot avoid the benefit of hindsight, the rare use of prolepses in his text, noted above, indicates that he does not secure for himself a discourse beyond the condition of probable knowledge. Moreover his constant use of retrospective narrative shedding light on historical actors' expectations[72] registers the diversity of temporal experiences of events and the potential explosion of a single account of them. This almost uninterrupted presence of actors' voices and experiences, the author's silence about the future at key points in the narrative, as well as the organisation of the narrative as running parallel to the war, all suggest an uncertainty surrounding human probability as a metahistorical category. Thucydides displays his knowledge about the war with the mere promise that people may act in a similar way when they find themselves in similar circumstances. But there is already a variety of voices about these circumstances to remind the reader that different people view things differently and act differently. This multiplicity underlies the varied faces of the historian-narrator in the narrative, which, according to Dewald, include the overt narrator, who has privileged access to the thoughts and emotions of the actors; the organiser-narrator explicitly positing the orientation and time-frames of the text; the knowledgeable narrator, importing, either in the first person or in neutral third-person description, supplementary background information; but also the

---

70 I owe this formulation to a conversation with Jonas Grethlein who further discusses the transhistorical temporality of Thucydides as distinguished from that of historical actors in Grethlein 2010, 213f.
71 Grethlein 2013, 21. Cf. Hornblower 1987; Morrison 2006a.
72 Grethlein 2010, 242.

modest or hesitant narrator, acknowledging the limitations of his knowledge and visions of time and the future.[73]

The articulation of diverse visions of the future can then be understood as constructing a unity of a higher order which, as we shall see, both sustains and exceeds the conflict between the perspective of the historian and that of historical actors. This is a kind of unity which consists of a variety of competing voices, voices which enter the text even as the historian explicitly dismisses them. As we shall further see below, all Thucydidean speeches beg the reader to look forward and compare what is said and predicted to what happened. Likewise, the fact that Thucydides' actual point and the implied endpoint are different accentuates divisions in the readers' understanding of the whole history. This 'whole' manifests a unity grounded in polyphony and indicating, at one and the same time, the distinctness of the historian's claim to a narrative endpoint commanding the whole and the very absence of a commanding voice, to return to Genette's argument, insofar as this claim stands in a continuum with those of historical actors and readers.

2 Future time and the sense of history in Greek historiography

Throughout Greek historiography and beyond the realm of the ancient world concepts of time have been central to the constitution of the sense of history. As Jörn Rüsen writes, the ways in which these concepts are related to the human world and to the precarious balance between the experience of the past and the expectation of the future perform "any sense and meaning of the past as history." This is so because historical consciousness enlarges the concept of the temporal dimension of human life "into a temporal whole which goes far beyond the lifetime of the people who do the historical work of recollection."[74] Thucydides' notion of history as 'possession for all time' not only presupposed this expansion as a condition of historical enquiry, but also performed the movement outside one's time and consciously opened the work to the perspective of future readers. He and other Greek historians deployed both this and other categories to serve the same purpose: set the limits for the historical irreversibly wide in time, moving them both toward the past and toward the future.

---

73 Dewald 2007, 97.
74 Rüsen 2005, 116.

The book seeks to explore this relationship between future time and the historical on the basis of a threefold structure, which will also be used to organise the following sections of this introduction. The first section of the book, 'Future times and the poetics of Greek historiography', presented in the introduction with the subtitle 'or, the elusive temporality of historical knowledge', discusses the constitution of the future through poetic operations, such as narration, description and so on, with a special focus on the polyphonic tensions of historical works. The second section, 'Temporalities of the future and the times of historical action', which bears the subtitle 'or, Greek historiography between poiesis and praxis' recalls the etymological force of the Greek term *poiein* to relate poetics to the times of historical praxis. Its aim is to discuss how the closures and endpoints constituted by Greek historiographical poetics relate to the times of action. Essays in this section reflect specifically on representations of this relation as a confrontation of poetic closure with the infinite nature and potential of the time of events and praxis. Finally, the third section, 'Toward the modern futures of Greek times', with the subtitle 'or, toward a monologic poetics of history writing' in the introduction, discusses the narrative constitution of modern historical knowledge as the future of Greek historiography. The enterprise critically examines how this narrative reconfigured Greek conceptions of time as presumably circular or exemplary through their opposition to the future-oriented time of modernity. Arguing against the "atemporal paralysis" attributed to ancient historiography, the section suggests focusing on the polyphonic poetics of the ancient tradition as accommodating alternative constitutions of time which were wiped out in the more monologic discourse of modern historiography.

2.1 Future times and the poetics of historiography, or, the elusive temporality of historical knowledge

In the sixth book of Thucydides, two rival statesmen, Nicias and Alcibiades, deliver their speeches before the Athenian assembly regarding the proposed Sicilian expedition.[75] Many of Nicias' warnings about the forthcoming military disaster in Sicily are confirmed by the events of the next two years, while Alcibiades' predictions are falsified. Yet, as Marincola points out, Nicias' vindication coexists in the narrative with the sense that different actions were possible – from his

---

[75] Nicias' two speeches are presented at 6.9–14.1 and 6.20–23.4. Alcibiades' speech is at 6.16–18.7.

side as well – which might have led to different results. Thucydides is consistently complicating matters for the reader as the text stresses the interlinking of expectation, anticipation and informed action with irrational behaviour and chance as the decisive elements of historical processes and action.[76] Building on Marincola's suggestion, I will discuss the Sicilian Debate in order to examine Thucydides' polyphonic narration of the future, highlighting the gap among diverse voices of historical actors and between them and the voice of the historian. In doing so I will seek to a) elaborate on a notion of elusive temporality manifested in the poetics of Greek history writing; and b) deploy this notion as a starting point in order to present the contributions to the first section of this volume dealing with the configuration of future time through a poetics of historical knowledge.

The notion of elusive temporality has been fruitfully applied to Greek tragedy, and specifically to the conflict between two orders of time, the time of gods and the time of men. Vidal-Naquet and Jean-Pierre Vernant have examined these two orders as coming together in the tragic stage in a form that eludes the temporal experience surrounding human action.[77] As Vernant writes, because the actions of the tragic hero "take place within a temporal order over which he has no control and to which he must submit passively, [these] actions elude him; they are beyond his understanding" even though it is the self of the protagonist that lies at the core of decisions leading to these actions. As the Greek artists who produce their works through their *poiesis* embody in matter some preexistent form and thus their work is more perfect than the worker, likewise, with regard to practical action, to the praxis of the tragic hero, "man does not measure up to what he does."[78] Taking his cue from Vernant and Vidal-Naquet's thesis, Sean Kirkland recently theorised tragic time as being constantly in excess. In Greek tragedy, he argues, decisions and actions contain something that exceeds the actors' understanding and power precisely because of the obscurity of the past on the basis of which people act and the obscurity of the future toward which they act.[79]

In the Sicilian Debate, historical actors are equally set in a temporal order that eludes them even though they are actively engaged in anticipating its unfolding. The scene is set in terms which undermine the ability of the protagonists to foresee the future, however correct isolated predictions may be. Thus Nicias evokes explicitly forethought (πρόνοια) as what is best for the city in opposition

---

76 Marincola 2001, 101.
77 Vidal-Naquet, 1986.
78 Vernant 1988, 82.
79 Kirkland 2014, 52.

to desire which represents what is worst.⁸⁰ But despite his wisdom and foresight, and despite his personal qualities and expertise, he proves unable to persuade the assembly and prevent the disaster. This is not only a matter of the Athenians taking the wrong decision. As in tragic plot-lines,⁸¹ the course of events takes shape also through Nicias' actions attempting to change its direction. According to Josiah Ober, Thucydides' narrative underlines the incapacity of the speakers' intention to determine outcomes in post-Periclean democratic Athens and clearly implies that both Alcibiades' and Nicias' speeches – especially his second speech – were responsible for much for the general eagerness to initiate the expedition. Before the speech contest, the Athenians were not especially mad for the expedition; it was Nicias who willfully rekindled the debate; whose first speech described the Athenians as 'eager to initiate' the expedition; and made them 'much more eager' after his second speech.⁸² Moreover, Nicias is himself compelled to admit that his words are weak and unlikely to dissuade his audience from risking what they have already for things that are still obscure and lie in the future (περὶ τῶν ἀφανῶν καὶ μελλόντων). Rather, as he says, the speech can only show the Athenians how their eagerness for the expedition is untimely and their ambition not easy to accomplish.⁸³ But these qualifications inscribe into Nicias' words the expectations and workings of the Athenian assembly, so that Nicias, as Sarah Brown Ferrario argues, functions both as an individual historical agent and as an enacting arm of Athens' collective, group historical agency.⁸⁴

On the other hand, Alcibiades' triumphalism proves to be misleading not only with regard to privileging desire over forethought, but also concerning the mode in which he seeks to anticipate the future. So after presenting a series of arguments evoking historical probability,⁸⁵ Alcibiades appeals to the unity of the Athenian voice. He encourages the Athenians to be of one mind in responding to any proposal (μιᾷ γνώμῃ ἀκροᾶσθαι) and act with a common purpose

---

80 Thuc. 6.13.1.
81 For the tragic dimension of Thucydides' narrative see Cornford 1907; Macleod 1983; Moles 1993; Lebow 2003, 135–137.
82 Ober 1998, 115.
83 καὶ πρὸς μὲν τοὺς τρόπους τοὺς ὑμετέρους ἀσθενὴς ἄν μου ὁ λόγος εἴη, εἰ τά τε ὑπάρχοντα σῴζειν παραινοίην καὶ μὴ τοῖς ἑτοίμοις περὶ τῶν ἀφανῶν καὶ μελλόντων κινδυνεύειν· ὡς δὲ οὔτε ἐν καιρῷ σπεύδετε οὔτε ῥᾴδιά ἐστι κατασχεῖν ἐφ' ἃ ὥρμησθε, ταῦτα διδάξω. Thuc. 6.9.3, translated by Mynott 2013, 399.
84 Ferrario 2014, 124.
85 He states, for instance, that empires have been won by a constant readiness to support all; that keeping quiet or picking and choosing whom to assist would entail risks for present conquests and so on Thuc. 6.18.2–7.

(ἐς τὰ ἔργα κοινῶς τρέπεσθαι):[86] do not let Nicias' words deter you from your purpose and his divisive attempt (διάστασις) set the younger against the older, he says; but rather hold to your traditional good practice whereby the city blends together all of its elements including the poorer, the average and the finer members in a powerful combination.[87] But it is precisely the unity of the polis on this matter that is retrospectively cast by Thucydides as the cause of the Sicilian tragedy. The future prospects of the polis voting for the expedition elude both the speakers and the Athenian community itself.

As in tragic time, decisions and actions pertaining to this decision contain a temporal element that exceeds the actors' understanding and points toward the narrative's future time. As the story unfolds and this future becomes present, it does not resemble what historical actors thought about it in the past. More perhaps than in other parts of his work, Thucydides emphasises here the tension between his backward-oriented temporality moving from effects to causes and the future-oriented gaze of historical actors, so that the tragic outcome of the Sicilian debate is narratively prefigured. In doing so Thucydides establishes the limits of historical knowledge not only against other poetic modes, such as those found in poetry, but also against alternative temporalities, such as those of historical actors. Seen in these terms his text does not merely reflect a consciousness of time in the sense that it accounts for events that take place in time; it creates time by constructing an excess of meaning implying that actions and events narrated by the historian can only be understood retrospectively through relations of effects to causes, of ends to means. This operation thus sustains what Jacques Rancière defined as a poetics of knowledge: the literary procedures by which the historical discourse escapes literature and gives itself the status of a science; the rules according to which this knowledge is written and read as a specific genre; and the ways these procedures and rules constitute a mode of truth to which such knowledge is devoted.[88] The future-oriented meaning entailed by the narrative gap between Thucydides and participants in the Sicilian debate is central to the constitution of the poetics that delimit and legitimise the emerging discourse of history.

---

86 Thuc. 6.17.4.
87 καὶ μὴ ὑμᾶς ἡ Νικίου τῶν λόγων ἀπραγμοσύνη καὶ διάστασις τοῖς νέοις ἐς τοὺς πρεσβυτέρους ἀποτρέψῃ, τῷ δὲ εἰωθότι κόσμῳ, ὥσπερ καὶ οἱ πατέρες ἡμῶν ἅμα νέοι γεραιτέροις βουλεύοντες ἐς τάδε ἦραν αὐτά, καὶ νῦν τῷ αὐτῷ τρόπῳ πειρᾶσθε προαγαγεῖν τὴν πόλιν, καὶ νομίσατε νεότητα μὲν καὶ γῆρας ἄνευ ἀλλήλων μηδὲν δύνασθαι, ὁμοῦ δὲ τό τε φαῦλον καὶ τὸ μέσον καὶ τὸ πάνυ ἀκριβὲς ἂν ξυγκραθὲν μάλιστ' ἂν ἰσχύειν. Thuc. 6.18.6.
88 Rancière 1994.

This gap is astutely studied by Grethlein in the frame of the tension between historical actors' experience of the past and the teleological viewpoint from which the historian organises the narrative with the benefit of hindsight.[89] Appropriating Koselleck's concept of 'future past',[90] Grethlein defines this concept as the historiographical *telos*, the point in the light of which the events narrated are envisaged by the historian (which is to be distinguished from the historian's own context). The temporal asymmetry implied by this *telos* is, according to Grethlein, at the core of all historiography: "it is crucial for historians to go beyond the perspective of their characters and view the past from the *telos* of events still anterior to them."[91] In this volume, Grethlein elaborates on this thesis to explore different narrative configurations of the *telos* in ancient historiography: the salience of the *telos* from which Thucydides narrates the Peloponnesian war – the capitulation of Athens in 404/3; the shifting *telos* of Polybius' history; Herodotus' multiple *telê*; as well as Sallust's diverse vantage-points; and Tacitus' asymmetrical relation between the historian and his characters. The investigation of these 'futures past', Grethlein argues, implies that historiography is also an engagement with temporality as well as an attempt to counterbalance the rule of time over human experience. Looking back, we see this rule over human beings without being exposed to it ourselves and thus hindsight allows us to overcome our experience of contingency. "Unlike the historical agents we know where history is headed and can see the past in the light of its future. Hindsight lets us replace the fragility of our lives with sovereignty."[92]

One consequence of this approach is that history writing is construed as an operator of power: the power claimed by the historian and his readers over the temporality of historical actors. This is a power that is intertwined with the status of historiography as mode of knowledge as well as the poetic rules that sustain this status – what has been defined above as a poetics of knowledge. It must be noted, however, that the historian's appeal to this power, as Grethlein's study also indicates, is not stable. It is undermined first by the narrative presence of multiple or shifting *telê*, which either coexist in the historical work itself, as in the cases of Herodotus and Polybius, or emerge through its confrontation with other genres, as in the case of Thucydides. Moreover, with regard to ancient historiography in particular, the constitution of a serial temporality, wherein a historian's narrative begins where a previous one ended, anticipates its own continuation, or goes back in time taking another history as its endpoint; all suggest a

---

[89] Grethlein 2013. See also Grethlein/Krebs 2012.
[90] Adapting Koselleck's concept of the 'Vergangene Zukunft'; Koselleck 2004 [1979].
[91] Grethlein 2013, 6.
[92] In this volume, 76.

shifting future element that commands the story. Greek historians self-consciously challenge the *telos* envisioned by their predecessors. In so doing they create a polyphony of narrative temporalities wherein the absence of an ultimate *telos* indicates, to return to Genette's words, that nothing commands.

The historian's mastery over time is both strengthened and challenged by the task of knowing the future through the investigation of the past. As Emily Greenwood argues, this task is centred on the opposition between the real future lying ahead of the historian's time and what she calls the "the unreal, diegetic future": the prospective future significance of historical accounts of the past, in other words, a past with a strong future orientation, which is predicated on the relay of past-present-future. This prospective past is shown to pervade Greek historiography, firstly as tense, in both narratorial and actorial voices, and secondly, in narratological terms, as the proleptic future, through which the intimations of events and information that is available to the historian is still future for historical actors. Considering the tension generated by this prolepsis as central to the poetics of knowledge in the fifth and fourth centuries BCE, Greenwood, explores how the description of the future was an area of inter-generic comparison. This was particularly so in contexts where there was intense competition among different technologies of knowledge. Starting from a study of Thucydides, she foregrounds analogies between historiography and the future-oriented 'genre' of sumbouleutic oratory as well as historiography and Hippocratic medical treatises. On this basis the essay contends that inter-generic comparison unpacks the implicit futurity of Greek historiography and the ways in which the future was conceptualised in terms of prognosis and time-(self)consciousness. Utility becomes a fundamental basis for comparing different technologies of knowledge in this period. Greek historiography was informed by an implicit futurity that stemmed from a sense of the prospective relevance of the past as a practical resource for political decision making in conversation and competition with other genres over their respective advice for/visions of the future.

The inter-generic comparison which Greenwood perceptively discusses raises a fairly clear analytical question: was there a specificity attributed to Greek historiography as a mode of knowledge? While on one level the answer she gives to this question evokes the configuration of a specific historiographical poetics, on a more radical level of analysis, the essay asks about the ways in which the constitution of historiographical discourse functions in the field of praxis and therefore how the narrative of historiography (among other genres) functions politically. Focusing on the interlinking of these levels, the essay renders different discourses on the future comparable by viewing them as articulations of mutually interacting and antagonistic appeals to knowledge; or, to use Rancière's vocabulary – which Greenwood evokes explicitly – by setting these discourses within a shared horizon of knowledge within which they compete over modes of truth. The poetics of this operation thus make these discourses distinguishable not by reference to their object, but rather by modes and devices through which they constitute the temporality of objects and thereby transform them into a practical recourse for political decision-making concerning future action.

The specificity of historical narrative as it pertains to temporalities of the future is also a key theme in Antonis Tsakmakis' study of Xenophon's *Hellenica*. The essay engages with Xenophon's concepts of history and temporality as they are constituted through the opposition between worldly and textual futures. It examines narrative anticipation in historiography as a technique that both distinguishes and complicates the historical narrative. In comparison with fiction, the narrative of historiography not only instigates an internal future that is gradually disclosed; it also avails of an external future, in which the reader and author are involved. Internal and external futures are interdependent insofar as they form contiguous segments of historical time. Xenophon's *Hellenica* demonstrates this interdependence through narrative anticipations suggesting: a) a textual continuity between his own work and that of his predecessors and successors; and b) a worldly continuity linking past, present and future time, first through a succession of historical narratives, and secondly through statements prompting readers to wonder whether historical conditions of the past were still present or pertinent in their own time. Xenophon invented not only continuous history by starting his work where Thucydides' history ended, but also his predecessors: using cross-textual references he suggested that the works of Herodotus, Thucydides and his own *Hellenica* formed a continuous narrative dealing with what was later to be labelled as the history of "classical Greece". On a different level, proleptic parts of his narrative link this history to the real world of the author's ultimate present. This narrative continuum significantly attests to the insecurity of human attempts to predict the future and the historian's acknowledgement of his inability to foresee what was coming next.

Xenophon also becomes the focus of Emily Baragwanath's essay, which engages with the *Anabasis* as a work signaling the future of new forms of historical narrative focusing on individuals, whose agency becomes key in shaping the world of the fourth century and beyond, and whose success or failure depends on their ability to interpret the future. In this narrative the future is configured as a site of tension and obscurity: it confronts human beings with the distance between probable, ideal or aspirational versus actual futures. The best one can do is to rely on probabilities, on the *eikos*, but this may be misleading: on occasion all sources work in tandem to construct a sustained picture of a probable, and yet incorrect future. The emphasis on the uncertainty of the future fits the extreme political insecurity of the Greek world in the decades after the Peloponnesian war. In this context Xenophon constructed an idea of time that was centred upon the volatility of human affairs and the notion of change as central to human history. While this idea was also present in his predecessors, in the *Anabasis* the consciousness of mutability is applied more forcefully to the relationship between present and future. Consequently, the challenge of knowing future time appears to overshadow the emphasis found in earlier historians on the challenge of knowing the past. Xenophon forged a new sort of historiography that was oriented forward more than backwards. It was this complex and obscure knowledge that was posited as a task for an aspiring leader: far from offering a quick route to the future, historiography held out the promise of making readers better *interpreters* of their future worlds.

Drawing on both Tsakmakis' and Baragwanath's essays we might take Xenophon's narratives of the future to signal something more than history as a form of knowledge aiming at the possession of the past and the self-recognition of the present and future. In all levels of Xenophon's narrative, the future is a site that radically exceeds historical probability; and yet one that remains at the centre of historiographical enquiry. Both with regard to the continuum of histories of Greece and with regard to political leaders' visions of the future depicted in the *Anabasis*, historical knowledge offers no safe route to foresight and prediction. While Thucydides' narrative, as we saw, attributed this insecurity to historical actors and generally conveyed only implicit recognition of the limits of the historian's voice, Xenophon was less confident. Tsakmakis and Baragwanath fruitfully explore his hesitation as formulated in a time of transition offering no secure grounds on which to approach either the past or the future. We may then raise the question of whether the new narrative they discuss reformulated the relationship between historical knowledge and the future by introducing into it the element of the unexpected, the condition of absolute surprise.

The immensity of this question makes it impossible to engage with it here. Yet by raising it we may begin to disentangle the unexpected from the temporalities of Western modernity and discern its presence in other discourses on time. Xenophon engages with the unexpected not as the outcome of the future's radical difference from the present, but through the aporetic confrontation of narrative temporalities with the historical time of the narrating subject. This confrontation enfolds the question of whether Xenophon's history posits a concept of the future with a question concerning the subject which constitutes itself, at one and the same time, in anticipating its teleological development and in absolute surprise.[93] If, as Jacques Derrida writes, there would be no more future, no possibility of the event and the new without a certain conjunction of these elements, that is, on one side, the possibility of absolute surprise (without seeing into the future blind to all anticipation) and, on the other, the formulation of some historical link, memory, retention or tradition seeing the teleological development of itself in the future,[94] then Xenophon's ending may be read as positing such a conjunction. In it the future stands beyond the question of its identity or difference from the present and past, but is nevertheless inscribed in the antagonistic synthesis of the necessity of a *telos* and the subject's confrontation with the unexpected, the future beyond the realm of historical knowledge.

In the following essay, Nikos Miltsios moves forward in time to examine the theme of foresight in Polybius. His starting point is the observation that the Polybian narrator interrupts his narrative in order to addresses future readers; explain how useful his account might be; and emphasise that the situations he is describing are likely to be repeated. The essay argues that Polybius is aware of an element of uncertainty regarding anticipation and recognises that even the best-laid plans about the future can fail due to uncontrollable and unforeseeable factors. Yet this awareness is reconciled in the narrative with an optimism about the ability to gain insights into future possibilities. For Polybius the usefulness of history resides in the fact that those who study it can deal with situations similar to those they have read about more effectively. Uncertainty about the future plays a key role in this enterprise: it is the incalculable element in life that makes it more imperative to engage with history and its lessons. Hence Polybius' work sets out to educate readers on how to cope with future uncertainty. This is achieved through the examples it includes, but also through the method deployed to analyse these examples. By attempting to trace the causes of events, even when these appear at first to be strange or inexplicable, he offers a method for analysis intended to help readers think about the future. The *Histories* do not guarantee an ability to foresee the future, but promise to provide readers with a valuable assistance in their attempts to understand it.

In Christopher Pelling's reading, Polybius becomes the centre of an intertextual relation focusing on the future, a relation constituted by his successor Dionysius of Halicarnassus. This is first manifested in Dionysius' time frame which spans Roman history from the earliest times to just before the First Punic War in 265 BCE, when Polybius' history started. This choice not only transformed the practice of the serial historiographical canon by engaging with an earlier historical period

---

93 For the formulation of this question I draw on Derrida 2005, xiii.
94 Derrida 2005, xiii.

than that of Polybius; it also reflected a fundamental disagreement. Dionysius, unlike Polybius, set Rome's march to Mediterranean primacy in a temporal perspective that stretched many centuries back. But his narrative refrained from projecting this perspective onto the future through the idea of *Roma aeterna*. Rather, Rome's was for him a practical future based on diverse experiences included in the past. At the same time future greatness and future problems became something that already pervaded the past, as if the future was already there and was constitutive of the historical narrative. Pelling interprets this presence as a narrative achievement of immediacy and plausibility intended to enable Dionysius' audience to picture the past clearly, acknowledge its relevance and consider it plausible. Yet Dionysius' distant past also pointed to a counterfactual history, to alternative futures that could have happened along the way. These highlight the principle of responsibility underlying Dionysius' historical temporalities and the question of preparing for posterity's judgment, already posed by Polybius in relation to Rome's destruction of Carthage. In the proem Dionysius calls on the present and future descendants of his protagonists to do nothing unworthy of their ancestors and suggests that the road to favourable verdict is still open to them, if only they learn the right lessons from the distant past.

Writing in the context of Roman domination, which he described as absolute throughout the *oikoumenê* after the Roman victory at Pydna,[95] Polybius' narrative, in Miltsios' reading, is optimistic as regards the historian's ability to instruct readers as to an effective understanding of the future (We shall see a less secure Polybius in Nicolas Wiater's essay in the next section). Both the method of analysis and the organisation of events promise to help readers think about the future at least more clearly than historical subjects failing dismally to attain foreknowledge. Dionysius' perspective, in Pelling's approach, is more ambiguous. Not only does the time-frame going back to antiquity imply the existence of diverse historiographical temporalities for interpreting Rome's march to dominance; by refraining from the contemporary idea of *Roma aeterna* Dionysius admits to the obscurity of the future, while his warning about posterity's judgement entails a further revision of Polybius' engagement with the same question. As a case of the serial canon established by Greek historians this dialogue between the two historians hints at the polyphonic dimension of Greek history writing, in which poetics undermines the security of the historian's knowledge and his mastery of time.

The same effect of polyphony can be discerned in Greek historians' use of speeches creating a tension between the authorial voice and the voices of histor-

---

95 Plb. 3.4.1–8.

ical subjects. As they deal with this tension from various perspectives on future time the above essays invite reflection on the power of historiographical poetics to impose a temporal order, but also to shed light on the dialogic constitution of historical time. In his reading of Tacitus' account of the speech of the soldier Percennius in the *Annals* – given as reported speech rather than as a direct quotation[96] – Rancière observes how Percennius "speaks without speaking ... expressing the value of the information without deciding on the value of this information ... The indirect style cancels the opposition between legitimate and illegitimate speakers". By the same token, he goes on, Tacitus by using the speech to express the soldiers' position in his narrative "creates a model of subversive eloquence for the orators and simple soldiers of the future."[97] In other words, the poetics of the text both silence those who have no place to speak and, at the same time, allow them to take hold of words and phrases, of argumentations and maxims which may amount to a new and subversive discourse.[98] As this section suggested, to emphasise the dialogic poetics of Greek historiography is both to discern the operation of silence by which the historian authorises his language and at the same time to emphasise the multivocal constitution of historiographical discourse on time. The poetics of the discourse of Thucydides undermining Nicias' and Alcibiades' claim to foreknowledge, with which we began this enquiry, is different from the poetics of the language by which the two orators attack one another. But both equally signal the elusiveness of historical temporalities and thus the possibility for historiographical knowledge to be appropriated by both future historians and historical subjects.

2.2 Temporalities of the future and the times of historical action, or, Greek historiography between poiesis and praxis

The polyphony of Greek historiographical poetics indicates an underlying kinship among different considerations of the future. The historian, as we saw, becomes the privileged interpreter of a community's futures by means of a poetic reconfiguration of events and action, including a narrative undermining of this community's ability to understand its actions as located in time. However, the rhetorical dimension of Greek historiography also involved the critical return

---

96 Tac. *Ann.* 1.16.
97 Rancière 1994, 29.
98 Rancière 1994, 29–30.

of historical subjects through a polyphonic narration of future time. The question then arises as to how this narrative relates to the time of historical action or, to put the same question in different terms, how the poiesis that was Greek history-writing related to the time of past, present and future praxis.

Poiesis, in its most general sense, refers to the manufacturing or making of a work, whereas praxis or action produces an event.[99] The poiesis that was Greek historiography, this section suggests, signals, simultaneously, the temporal necessity and unfinalisability or event potential enfolded in praxis. Temporal necessity is the outcome of the historian's consideration of the future in the sequential temporality of the narrative, in which elements, as we discussed in relation to Genette's analysis of narrative time, are explained in terms of what follows. As Meir Sternberg writes, historians "have been concerned to fill out and weld the chronological series of events into chronological, hence meaningful, plot".[100] By explaining why what happened had to happen the way it did, the historian constructs historical time as the most salient characteristic of a causal concatenation of events, a directional force bound by necessity. In this narrative the future emerges as a range of possibilities reflecting the determination of causal and temporal relations linking it to the present and past. It is the extension of a logic that not only relates events to one another, but also separates them through the suppression of the past. Historiographical poiesis operates by means of restriction and suppression, even though it is the denial of such a loss that frames both Greek and modern historiography. By positing his enquiry as a work standing against loss and forgetting, Herodotus inaugurated a discourse which, as Michel de Certeau writes, denied the diverse stages of the historian's loss "by appropriating to the present the privilege of recapitulating the past as a form of knowledge." History then stood as "a return of the past in present discourse", a return "within the work whose postulate was [the] disappearance [of the past].[101]

Historiographical poiesis is formed by temporalities that veil absence – above all, the absence of events and voices with a potential that exceeds the voice of historians. Yet unlike modern historiographical poetics, wherein history writing, as de Certeau notes, is destined to speak the otherness of the past in a mode through which the voices of subjects vanish under the authority of the historian's writing,[102] Greek historiography is constituted by these voices. The tension between them and the voice of the historian does not simply authorise

---

[99] Acton 2014; Thomson 2011, 212. Cf. Volpi 1999, 13–14.
[100] Sternberg 2004, 105.
[101] De Certeau 1986, 214; 1988, 78–79.
[102] De Certeau 1988.

the latter; it also constitutes an idea of the future as constituted by a potential that is both contained in and remains irreducible to the present. The relation between the multivocality of historiographical poiesis and future praxis is determined by the tension between on the one hand the future as that which lies ahead of us and we can see coming; and, on the other, the future as that which no mode or depth of knowledge could possibly foresee, that which cannot be formulated through the predictions and anticipations of the present.[103] The former of these concepts is then a future that can be derived from the knowledge of the present and past. The latter is a future that uproots both present historical knowledge and the worldly experience of time with which this is associated by taking account of the unexpected and unfinalisable, that which uproots the temporality of events and moves the events themselves into another orientation and direction.

Catherine Darbo-Peschanski approaches the tension between historiographical poiesis and future praxis by studying the operation of the future in the *historiai* through the intertwinement of the external organisation in which these works take place as discrete units of time and the internal organisation of their temporality. This study entails a fundamental distinction between *logos* and *chronos*. Drawing on Aristotle's *Poetics* Darbo-Peschanski notes how the narrative discourse of *logos* manifested in poetry comes with internal temporalities belonging to the plot line(s). By contrast the temporality of *historia* is delimited by a portion of time (*chronos*) in a given calendar and does not bring with it consistency either in terms of plot line, or in terms of internal temporal connection. The *historiai* must create a plot line themselves; in so doing, they must create an internal temporality connected to that plot. The essay identifies three main drivers of temporality: justice, human nature and the dialectic between a force at work organising events and human actions (*praxeis*). All of them, it contends, include the future by means of imposing closure on its unbounded infinity. This is achieved on the basis of four principles. The first, exemplified in Herodotus, concerns the role of divine sanction putting an end to a series of injustices and transgressions through punishment. The second, which returns to the question of the meaning of *anthropinon*, is a principle of 'continuity' which is studied in Thucydides and Polybius as derived from the notion of human nature. This enables at once the comparison of historical events – such as wars – and their opening up to the future. Polybius and Plutarch provide the third principle, described as "the spatialisation of time" and evoking a concept of geometrical

---

[103] The distinction appropriates Derrida's definition of the term *à-venir* ['to-come'] in Derrida 2005.

parallelism that remains irreducible to similarity. Plutarch's temporal parallelism, according to this argument, summons a spatial (geographical) parallelism, which is the spatial parallelism of cartography retaining a technical geometric value. The fourth principle moves beyond parallelism to universal identity involved in philosophical systems and pervades, to a varying extent, historiographical works aiming to tell of the world and the course of events. All of these shapes of the future and closures of time cause the "makers of *historiai*" to come face to face with the problem of the infinite and indeterminate nature of the particularities of human action.

Starting from a perspective that challenges the idea of infinite time, Katharina Wesselmann examines Herodotus' confrontation with the time of praxis by focusing on what she describes as 'mythical temporalities'. The essay puts forth an argument with which other contributors to this volume are likely to disagree to varying degrees, but whose inclusion in the book not only enables a fruitful dialogue, but also introduces considerations of Greek temporalities that underlie comparative studies of ancient and modern traditions, discussed in the book's last section. Wesselmann distinguishes Herodotean temporalities which include the future and concern a) the fate of individual protagonists; and b) Herodotus and his contemporary audiences. But there is a second type of temporalities which Wesselmann calls 'mythical' and excludes the future. These are narrated as a traditional pattern of events, stories that happen repeatedly to different people and present "no concept of the future in a progressive sense, no true change or perfectability". These stories rather convey a sense of permanence, a *perpetuum mobile* or "eternal return of the same", wherein variations are not differentiating but construct a continuous system of plot rules. Significantly, the essay does not say that nothing new ever happens in the *Histories*, but rather that repetitiveness is included in the plurality of Herodotean concepts of the future. In seeking to categorise these concepts, mythical temporalities represent a certain absence of future time – at least, from the viewpoint of the historian insofar as the protagonists are not usually aware of the timelessness of their fates. In this poietic configuration, the future is established as an "omnitemporal continuity of repetition" setting mythical temporalities on the opposite side of historical time. This tendency, as Wesselmann notes in her conclusion, concerns the entirety of history writing, insofar as the main function of the genre is 'making the past present' – eliminating the boundaries of time; but it is especially visible in Herodotus because of the close intertwinement of historiography and tradition.

In order to discuss Wesselmann's thesis we may return to two books, Mircea Eliade's classic study of myth and ritual, *The Myth of the Eternal Return*, which asked how "the man of the archaic societies" according to the image formed by himself differs from the image of the "historical" or "modern" man and attributed the 'cyclic' vision of time in ancient thought to belief in the 'eternal return';[104] and Nietzsche's *Birth of Tragedy* which proposed a critique of modernity based on an appeal to the temporality of myth.[105] According to Eliade's argument, which is largely confirmed by Wesselmann's essay, the man of archaic societies explains contingency as a function of fury or fate and confronts it by imitating or recounting the exemplary acts of gods or heroes through myth and ritual – an operation which enables his dissociation from profane time and his entering into sacred time, where 'real' events take place. As Eliade argues, this operation is demonstrated by the Greeks in the myth of eternal return and exemplifies a need for regeneration through the repetition of an archetypal act: "the need of archaic societies to regenerate themselves periodically through the annulment of time".[106] Eliade's thesis pertains to Wesselmann's argument through their identification of mythical approaches as ahistorical and atemporal, and thus as unable to accommodate conceptions of the past, present and future. Critics of Eliade, including personal friends and colleagues Ricoeur and Momigliano,[107] have pointed out the problems involved in this opposition of myth to history, among which was the coexistence of several temporal values and qualities in "archaic" temporalities challenging their reduction to some "eternal return of the same". This plurality accentuates the complexity of archaic conceptions of time and the future and renders their characterisation as ahistorical problematic and dependent on privileging modern considerations of historical time. As Dewald argues, Herodotus brings into the narrative divine temporalities only as a component of the logoi he is retelling and professes doubt about their ultimate purposes: "they are as mysterious as the shape of history itself as it unrolls; only afterward ... can we look back and see what it was all about".[108]

From this view, Wesselmann's meticulous analysis of Herodotus' evocation of patterns and repetitions may be read in terms of a specific vision of history and the future, which stands in tension with other visions inscribed in Herodotus' logoi. This seems to classify Herodotus in terms of Darbo-Pechanski's fourth category of temporality involved in universal philosophical systems. We shall re-

---

104 Eliade 1971.
105 Nietzsche 1999. For reading the *Birth of Tragedy* with a view to the temporality of myth see Hammer 2011.
106 Eliade 1971, 81.
107 See Ricoeur 1985, 13–30; 1987; 1995, 52ff. Momigliano 1966; Smith 1991, 73–76. On this question cf. Vansina 1985 and Robert Fowler's introduction to commentary on texts of early Greek mythography in Fowler 2013.
108 Dewald 2007, 96.

turn to this temporality in the last section from the viewpoint of the juxtaposition of ancient and modern temporal frames. At the moment let us note that Nietzsche's argument in *The Birth of Tragedy* critically reverses the conventional attribution of stability to ancient temporalities and identifies instead a monotonous existential blankness and a tremendous loss of meaning in modern conceptions of time and the future, which can be overcome only by returning to myth.[109] Moreover, this category of temporality does not exhaust Herodotus' constitution of historiographical time. Grethlein's discussion of Herodotus' use of multiple *telê* in this volume as well as his analysis of the pluralism of concepts used in the *Histories* attest to the difficulty of mastering contingency in a coherent system even in retrospect.[110] They thus indicate a stronger awareness of the historian's own historicity and of the subjection of his narrative to the flux of time, precluding the stability of historical perspective.

The tension between the times of historiographical poiesis and action is further elaborated by Karen Bassi in her discussion of Thucydides' constitution of the relationship between the past as prior reality and the future as possibility. The essay explores how the interlinking of visible, material remains and historical narrative position the historian and reader of history between the past (in the remains' association with historical events) and the future (as remains become objects with evidentiary value – a value that becomes more important with the passing of time). Deploying the term 'historical future', Bassi argues that past and future are mutually productive and dialogic temporal categories. The study of this dialogue in Thucydides indicates not only the invisibility of the future in the *History*, but also, paradoxically, the limits of what can be known about the past: for the historical future that sustains this dialogue is a measure of the extent to which the historical past is itself dependent on linguistic representation. Metaphors of visibility and invisibility express the gap between historical events and the language used to represent them. This gap is traced in the mutually constitutive relationship between the past as prior reality and the future as pure possibility. Thucydides' significant methodological description of his work as a possession for all time extends the concept of history into a future that never ends, and thus resists the invisibility of what is to come by proclaiming the eternal legibility of the text. Yet, even at this point, according to Bassi, Thucydides contributes to the conclusion that the future is itself the limiting factor of what can be known about the past, as his narrative suggests by

---

[109] Hammer 2011, 142.
[110] Grethlein 2010, 195.

ultimately failing to foresee correctly the future ruins of its main protagonists, the cities of Sparta and Athens.

Bassi's essay configures a concept which informed Darbo-Peschanski's approach: the poetic imposition of limits on the unbounded infinity of the historical time of praxis. In both readings, the shapes of the future articulate the tension between the time of historical events and the language used to represent them. For Darbo-Peschanski this is a tension between on the one side the internal organisation of historical temporality as plot-lines involving certain poetic drivers and principles of closure and, on the other, the infinite and indeterminate nature of human action. Bassi's argument evokes the same tension from the viewpoint of the relation between the visibility of remains of the past and the invisibility of the future. On the one side, the visible remains attest to the dependence of the past on narrative representation, since the remains have no meaning without a narrative. On the other side, the remains indicate the independence of the past from narrative: the remains are there whether we can tell a story about them or not. This independence indicates the temporal excess of events associated with visible remains. The irreducibility of remains to narrative implies that their meaning must be understood as open-ended: the remains can become meaningful in different stories about their building and different future claims to the events associated with them.

Finally both essays invite reflection on the ethics involved in the historian's engagement with the unfinalisable or excessive temporality of events or praxis. The temporal horizon linking past, present and future, as they suggest, imposes a temporality on the infinite experiences and possibilities associated with human action. The recognition of this operation as a limit of historical knowledge, in the sense that Bassi defines it, but also as a pragmatic dimension of historical sense-making posits an ethical imperative for historical poetics to acquire counter-factual qualities.[111] These are qualities of a temporality going beyond the representation of the visible and doing justice to latent and excessive time, that is, a historiography with a "critical potency".[112]

Nicolas Wiater also deals with the question of poetic closure that is imposed on the time of action through a refreshing reading of Polybius. He argues that Polybius consciously denies his readers a "sense of an ending" and the narrative closure that would go hand-in-hand with it. Rather, he presents his work as part of a *historia perpetua* not only with regard to the past, as a continuation of Timaeus' account, but also towards the future. According to Wiater, by leaving

---

111 Rüsen 2006a, 60.
112 For the term see Rüsen 2006.

his own narrative open-ended and to be continued by the narratives to come, Polybius invites his readers to take over where he leaves off. This open-endedness is first achieved by the revision of the existing narrative and explanatory unity of the work at the beginning of book three, wherein the addition of ten books introduces a new narrative design and *telos* going down to 146. Polybius specifically describes the last part of his work, the account of the period of ταραχὴ καὶ κίνησις, as 'a new beginning'. According to Wiater, this is a deliberate refusal to provide closure. In the final part of the *Histories* beginning and end are conflated; just as beginnings spawn ever new narratives into the past, endings defer the end further into the future and as such constitute new beginnings: choosing 168/7 as the original ending point deferred the narrative end to 146, and 146 opens it up to the future in a story that stops, but never ends. Readers, according to this approach, are prompted to supply an ever-renewed end to the "new beginning" of the last part of the *Histories* – a gesture which also constitutes an assessment of the state of events after 146. The text conveys the idea that the spatial stability of the *oikumenê* achieved by the rise of Roman power and the future of the political structure of the Mediterranean had become, once more, an open question. Whether the end will tell the story of Rome's recovery from the ταραχὴ καὶ κίνησις or the continuing demise of Roman power is in his readers' hands. This openness also underpins one of the endpoints of the *Histories*, the destruction of Carthage. It was up to future generations to actively confront, create and record this new condition for which the historian offers no closure.

Wiater's reading of Polybius evokes Xenophon's implication of the *Hellenica* in ταραχὴ καὶ κίνησις. Still, one of the differences that needs to be noted is that in Xenophon ταραχὴ καὶ κίνησις stands in the future of the story he narrates, while in Polybius it is part of the story, in the sense that it refers to the events of the period from 151 down to 146. By attributing ταραχὴ καὶ κίνησις to the temporality of events and action Polybius points to their temporal potential, to the open-ended time of the historical scene outside his narrative. This is partly reflected in the tension between the shifting narrative closure and the final endpoint of the story he begins to tell. It is this tension that invites readers both to decide on his chosen closing point and to reflect on the impossibility of finally closing the temporality of action. Both the scene of Carthage and the shifting design of the narrative interrupt the sequential temporality of historical narrative. They thus accentuate a lack of *telos* pointing both to further readings of the past and the continuing expansion of event potential in the realm of historical action.

Turning to Plutarch, Paolo Desideri examines conceptions of the future formulated in the intersection of historical and biographical writing. For Plutarch studying the biographies of great men of the past offered a framework for approaching contemporary decline and actively shaping a new possible future.

Starting from a rejection of the Augustan and post-Augustan interpretations of history in terms of a progressive evolution, Plutarch saw the Empire as the outcome of the combination of fortune and a certain sense of divine design, which was not the ultimate accomplishment of history. His task was then to rethink the past as a whole made up of biographical experiences that could demonstrate intervention into the lives of entire cities and peoples with a view to the future. This new role of historiographical biography underscored a condition of diversity and the openness of the future. It was not only that lives formed "a kaleidoscope of experiences" indicating new possibilities; it was also that these lives were associated with a plurality of worlds acting to relativise the value of the present. Plutarch's extensive consideration of this plurality rejects the hypotheses of necessity, let alone progress, through which it was possible to construe the sequence of the historical events in his world. It was rather the idea of plurality that enabled him to posit diachronic temporal relations between worlds and, at the same time, show how these relations allowed men to struggle with their times and transform their worlds.

In this reading the relationship between poetic temporalities and the time of historical action acquires a new and radical meaning. By treating the time of history as prior to future action, Plutarch makes two fundamental contentions. The first attests to the ability of historical-biographical discourse to reach and merge the times of action. Plutarch's *parallel* lives brought together pairs of different individual lives lived at different periods for which parallelism is nevertheless claimed. Historiographical language plays a key role in constructing this parallel by joining the times of historical events and worlds. The second contention pertains to his idea of readers as capable of mediating the gap between words and action, that is, as capable of mediating the excess of events by means of imitation or repetition, which is what he foresees as future action. It was the latter attribute that made Plutarch significant for Nietzsche who, as Desideri notes, made explicit reference to the Greek author in his *Vom Nutzen und Nachteil der Historie*, the second of his *Unzeitgemässe Betrachtungen*. In a critical passage Plutarch became for Nietzsche an ally in his critique of Hegelian historicism as causing the suffocation of any impulse to action and the lifeless acceptance of the present; in so doing he advocated the usefulness of historical writings and especially those proposed in biographical form.

A distinct approach to the tie between words and action is further elaborated in Luke Pitcher's study of Appian's treatment of the future in the *Rhomaika*. The essay discusses elements of continuity with previous historians, but also some crucial differences. Appian shows little explicit interest in the future of his work and, even though he sometimes anticipates possible responses, his focus is more in controlling his reception, rather than its actual occurrence in the future. His use of narrative prolepsis, even though limited, is effective, especially where it has some impact on contemporary practices and must be understood as part of the temporal movement of the work towards a mid-second century CE present. But his most compelling futures are those found in the visions of historical actors in the face of contingencies. The *Rhomaika* configures the future as the manifestation of contingency that human beings seek to control. Appian shares with prior historians a sceptical view of this activity and actors who make prophecies or assumptions about their prospects tend to be falsified. As in other historians of antiquity the future in Appian represents the unexpected. Yet, unlike most previous historians, the lesson to be drawn from this can be, within limits, also a hopeful one: the potency of the unexpected in human affairs can have good consequences as well as bad. So, especially *in extremis*, looking for an unexpected fulfillment of expectation, as unlikely as it may be, is a more rational plan than simple despair. In this reading, Appian moves away from the future as a line of historical narratives and readings and he further distances himself from the tension between events and representation. While he conceded that the future (also) consists of the unexpected and the unknown, his pragmatic interest in action constructed a time of expectation as the rational man's defence against contingency.

In the last essay of this section, Melina Tamiolaki focuses on Lucian's *De Historia Conscribenda* in order to explore the work's multifold approach to the topos of posterity. Lucian distances himself from the conventional view that teaching and instructing is the main purpose of aspiring to posterity. Rather, he establishes a distinction between writing for the present and writing for the future, identifying the former with flattery and lies, and the latter with truth and posterity. In so doing, Lucian transforms the traditional topos into a methodological statement involving a reflexive definition of history writing. The idea that historians should aspire mainly to the future challenges the established practice of contemporary history and Lucian explicitly questions Thucydides' historiographical focus. Moreover, his idea of posterity contains original characteristics which render it radical not only for antiquity but also for modern concepts, such as the idea of historical distance as a prerequisite for impartial history writing. But his insistence on the future also undermines modern definitions of historical distance as the vantage point from which the historian observes the past and which can guarantee his impartiality: for Lucian it is the future that constitutes the ultimate scope to which the historian should aspire. Unlike modern considerations of the historian as looking *backwards from* his "future", for Lucian the historian should look only *onwards, to the future*. He does not therefore limit historical distance to the temporal gap between the historian's time and the time of the events narrated, but rather amplifies this gap by stressing the open and indefinite future which the historian must have in mind.

By positing this distance Lucian reversed contemporary attempts to bridge the gap between events and historical investigation suggesting instead that the historian should both widen and embrace this gap. As Tamiolaki points out – aptly quoting Koselleck's remark that Lucian was the first to introduce the term apolis for the ideal historian – for Lucian the historian should not be attached to his own time and place. This perspective on temporal distance had a crucial self-referential quality evidenced in Lucian's reflexive engagement with historiography's relation to rhetoric – a subject that was also debated at the time in the context of the second sophistic. At the same time, his contribution may be considered in the context of the genre of the theory of history. Lucian's quest for historical distance is not limited to the historian's relation to the time of events he is narrating, but also includes moving his narrative out of his time to confront future readings and events. His is thus a theory of history that accounts for the unfinilisable character of historical writing, reading and action.

This appeal to the future concludes a section that invites the consideration of future time by means of the twofold affiliation of historical knowledge to narrative and action. The narrative basis of history writing, as was argued throughout this introduction, means, in Ricoeur's terms, that the significance of temporal constructions that historians attribute to their objects is borrowed: it derives from specific narrative configurations. Yet, by way of this process of derivation historiographical constructions of time are also rooted in the temporality of the world of action.[113] According to the above essays, Greek historiographical poetics offers a temporal perspective on action that renders it, at one and the same time, completed and unaccomplished, closed and essentially unfinalisable – or, to make the same point in different terms, full of event potential. Equally significant is the imperative to use historical knowledge in order to intervene in the time of events and action. As most essays argued, this quest was not circumscribed by an exemplary temporality projecting onto the future a reserve of examples provided by the past. Rather than following examples, readers of Greek historiography are called upon to interpret a multivocal narrative, in which the historian's attempt to construct models for action is complicated not only by protagonists who variously fail to predict the future, but also, as Darbo-Peschanski's, Bassi's and Wiater's essays contend, by the historian's recognition of his own limited foreknowledge.

---

113 Ricoeur 1984–88, v.1, 91–92.

In a discussion of the exemplarity of Greek historiography, Marcel Detienne claimed that Thucydides constructed his work as "a model for political action, an understanding of future possibilities, with the historian regarded as an ideal political reader". His aim was not therefore to recount what happened, but "to convey the truth in discourse made up of arguments that ... indicated how best to behave within the space of the city, both in the present and in the future."[114] According to the argument suggested here, this model was neither secure nor unitary, but rather confronted the readers of histories with the infiniteness of future possibilities and the potential of events to explode the knowledge of historians. Such a contention is thus closer to Geoffrey Hawthorn's recent reading of Thucydides as a political writer who "has no conceptual ambition, favours no one kind of explanation, harbours no *telos*, evinces no one opinion, and is neither a cynic nor a moralist";[115] with the proviso that the diversity of anticipations and opinions about the future is to be traced between the lines of a text which, simultaneously, confines the infinite potential of events in the frame of narrative sequence and necessity.

3 Toward the modern futures of Greek times, or, toward a monologic poetics of history writing

Xenophon ended his account of Greek history with the battle of Mantinea. This was not a random closing point, but a battle expected to resolve the state of confusion and disorder in Greece, either by restoring Sparta's power or by establishing Theban domination. Yet, in contrast with all expectations, including his, Xenophon declared the result of the battle inconclusive:

> Τούτων δὲ πραχθέντων τοὐναντίον ἐγεγένητο οὗ ἐνόμισαν πάντες ἄνθρωποι ἔσεσθαι. Συνεληλυθυίας γὰρ σχεδὸν ἁπάσης τῆς Ἑλλάδος καὶ ἀντιτεταγμένων, οὐδεὶς ἦν ὅστις οὐκ ᾤετο, εἰ μάχη ἔσοιτο, τοὺς μὲν κρατήσαντας ἄρξειν, τοὺς δὲ κρατηθέντας ὑπηκόους ἔσεσθαι· ὁ δὲ θεὸς οὕτως ἐποίησεν ὥστε ἀμφότεροι μὲν τροπαῖον ὡς νενικηκότες ἐστήσαντο ... ἀκρισία δὲ καὶ ταραχὴ ἔτι πλείων μετὰ τὴν μάχην ἐγένετο ἢ πρόσθεν ἐν τῇ Ἑλλάδι.[116]

> When these things had taken place the opposite of what all believed would happen was brought to pass. For since nearly all the people of Greece had come together and formed

---

114 Detienne 2007, 32.
115 Hawthorn 2014, x.
116 Xen. *Hell.* 7.5.26.

themselves in opposing lines, there was no one who did not suppose that, if a battle were fought, those who proved victorious would exercise rule and those who were defeated would be their subjects; but the deity so ordered it that both parties set up a trophy as though victorious ... In fact, there was even more uncertainty and confusion in Greece after the battle than there had been previously.[117]

Then, in one of the most ambiguous closing sentences of history writing, Xenophon denied his readers an endpoint: ἐμοὶ μὲν δὴ μέχρι τούτου γραφέσθω· τὰ δὲ μετὰ ταῦτα ἴσως ἄλλῳ μελήσει. "Let this then, be the end of my narrative. Someone else perhaps will deal with what happened later."[118]

The use of the term 'narrative' is a modernising translation concealing the fact that Xenophon words – "I am going to stop writing here" or "I have written up to this point" – stress further the tension between the temporality of events and the temporality conveyed by his story. Indeed, the very claim that he, among all others, also failed to foresee the future, accentuates this tension. Even though he, as writer, could potentially be excluded from the sentence denoting this failure, he becomes part of it. By inviting a successor, Xenophon leaves in the starkest dispute the historian's claim to an authoritative knowledge of time. His call for possible successors invites or at least considers subsequent perspectives on what appears as an obscure course of affairs. "But the deity so ordered it" offers no definitive temporal scheme of explanation: as with certain articulations of tragic time, the sentence registers only an inexplicable necessity of the human failure to foresee the future and thereby the necessity of human frustration – a necessity which, as Bernard Williams wrote in relation to tragedy, may perhaps be ascribed to the gods, but if so, to gods who do not explain themselves or account for the consequences for humans of what they bring about.[119] In other words, Xenophon offers here no authoritative voice – either divine or authorial – on historical temporalities linking past, present and future.

The battle of Mantinea was also chosen as the narrative end of a different account of Greek history stretching from 406 to 362 B.C., the *Commentarium rerum grecarum* written by Leonardo Bruni (1369/70?-1444) in 1439. While Bruni's work was clearly based on portions of the *Hellenica* and was for this reason often relegated to the status of a translation,[120] his assessment of Mantinea differed radically from Xenophon's in that it proclaimed the unqualified success of the Thebans: "The result was nevertheless a clear Theban victory, and as a conse-

---

117 translated by Warner 1966.
118 translated by Warner 1966.
119 Williams 2006, 58.
120 Ianziti 2012, 239.

quence Sparta lost her hegemony, and all power and authority in Greece was transferred to the victorious Thebans."[121] The book's closing statement elaborated on this view by explaining the historical meaning of the battle: "Thus did hegemony in Greece pass – through the marvelous workings of fortune – from the Athenians to the Spartans, and then again from the Spartans to the Thebans."[122]

The difference between the two histories relates, among other things, to their respective approach to time. For Bruni, as Gary Ianziti notes, the battle confirmed the overall theme of the *Commentarium* set forth in the preface: "to chronicle the transfer of hegemony in Greece from one power to another."[123] This enterprise evoked the educational function of history and the power of the past to offer lessons for the future: Bruni sought to make Greek history useful by forging new cultural and political tools for Florentine leadership. Modifications of Xenophon's legacy thus served the attempt to fashion a narrative illustrating certain truths about the questions of peace, war and political decision-making.[124] At the same time, Bruni's interpretation was part of the wider preoccupation with the topos of the rise and fall of cities taking shape in the background of the replacement of the former *regnum italicum* by contests between cities over territorial domination in which none could hope to achieve empire.[125] J.G.A. Pocock's *Machiavellian Moment* has shown how the awareness of a city's forthcoming moment of fall attested to a modern secular consciousness of temporality defined by the tension between the recognition of contingency and the universal values that would extend survival.[126] Bruni's narrative end offered a model for perpetuating the city's power and postponing its collapse. But in doing so, Bruni overwrote Xenophon's recognition of the finite historical knowledge available to cities and their leaders. Unlike Xenophon's self-identification with the puzzlement of historical actors, Bruni distinguished his voice from the state of confusion prevailing in the historical scene. He thus put forth a historiographical temporality claiming to encompass and supersede diverse considerations of time associated with historical experience and action.

---

[121] "Victoria tamen manifestissime parta, Lacedemoniis principatu adempto et auctoritate potentiaque omni ad Thebanos victores traducta". Quoted in Ianziti 2012, 249. My comparison draws on Ianziti's (2012) discussion of Bruni's work in the context of the Renaissance engagement with ancient history writing. The edition of Bruni to which this work refers is Bruni 1993.
[122] Ianziti 2012, 239.
[123] Ianziti 2012, 249.
[124] Ianziti 2012, 239–240, 248.
[125] Pocock 2003a, 159–160.
[126] Pocock 2003.

In doing so, as we shall see, he positioned his work on the verge between ancient and modern histories of antiquity.

Bruni's take on Xenophon exemplifies a long process of inscribing the ambivalence of Greek polyphonic configurations of the future into a more monologic modern historiographical discourse on time. By translating a narrative juxtaposing diverse temporalities into a historiographical discourse claiming to encompass the time of events Bruni (pre)figured what we shall describe, following Koselleck, as the singularity of the modern concept of history, which collapsed the division between *res gestae* (the things that happened) and *historia rerum gestarum* (the narrative history of the things that happened). Bruni was premodern in his willingness to accept the exemplary operation of the past; but modern with regard to a poetics of self-authorisation through which he legitimised his ordering of historical time. The modern concept of history, according to Koselleck, involved the end of exemplary historiography and the emergence of modern temporalities proclaiming the singularity of both historical narrative and the events of the past over the eighteenth century.

This section explores how this concept formulated two contentions for understanding antiquity, which I shall further use for introducing the essays in the last part of the book: a) the constitution of modern historical knowledge as the future of Greek historiography by placing both traditions within a scheme of predecessors and successors; b) the refiguring of Greek articulations of time through the temporalities constituted by this scheme, and particularly the opposition between the linear, future-oriented time of modernity and the cyclical or exemplary time of antiquity. Both of these contentions entailed the suppression of the polyphonic times of antiquity; the constitution of a monologic temporality centred on the historian's knowledge; and the exclusion of alternatives to the dominant relation between a European antiquity and modernity.

According to Koselleck, modes of knowing the future based on the exemplarity of the past – the topos of *historia magistra vitae* – dissipated in modern historical consciousness. Hence evocations of the ancients as a model, having rested on the structural similarity of all possible past and future, declined: "the singularity, that is to say, the absolute newness of events, gradually fills out the space of experience."[127] This process further involved a transformation of the concept of the future. For modern historians an appeal to the future which anticipates what has always been possible so far constitutes no knowledge at all. The modern age was characterised by the broadening distance between experience and expectation, and thus the assumption that the future would be dif-

---

[127] Koselleck 2002, 166.

ferent from the past. Koselleck draws on Kant to illustrate this thesis. As he notes, Kant assumes that the future will be different from the present because it is supposed to be different. He is thus concerned to surpass previous experience and open up the possibility for a new future, for instance by advocating a league of nations which had so far been unprecedented.[128]

The possibility of thinking the future as different from the present and past was intertwined with a shift in the concepts of history and historical time. In *historia magistra vitae* the past, according to Koselleck, was a reservoir of multiple experiences from which readers of history could learn in order to act upon their present and future. By contrast, modern historical consciousness construed past events as unique and brought them together under a unifying category of linear time and a corresponding concept of history as a singularity. In his seminal essay "Geschichte, Historie", Koselleck identified this concept as the substitution for a master category of history itself (*Geschichte selber*) for plural forms like *die Geschichten* or *die Historien*.[129] Johann G. Droysen offers an illuminating example of this shift in his statement that "even the narrow, the very narrowest of human relations, strivings, activities, etc., have a process, a history, and are for the person involved, historical. So family histories, local histories, special histories. But over all these and such histories, there is History."[130] Significantly, this abstract, master category, now encompassing all events and experiences of time, underpinned the uniqueness of the three dimensions of time, the past, present and future. The modern recognition of temporal difference was profoundly rooted in the constitution of a singular concept of history. The unique times of history existed on the condition that one single history also existed.[131] This condition entailed that the term *Geschichte* would then begin to interweave *res gestae* and *historia rerum gestarum* so that the two fields were no longer differentiable, but products of a metahistorical category which not only superseded diversified accounts of events, but also accounted for the conditions of their possibility, that is to say, for historical time in its dual dimension of words and action. Through this shift, history became universal in its scope and narrative in its form of articulating time.[132]

Confronted with ancient historiography this singular narrative was involved in a twofold challenge: first the need to appropriate Greek and Roman historical times as a predecessor of modernity within a unified scheme of linear succes-

---

128 Koselleck 2002, 112–113.
129 Koselleck 1975, 647–658.
130 Droysen 1893, 44.
131 Koselleck 1975. Cf. Lianeri 2011a.
132 Koselleck 1975.

sion;[133] and second, to reconcile the modern temporalisation of antiquity with the temporalities offered by Greek and Roman historians. The former of these tasks was inscribed in the Eurocentric narratives of world history and philosophies of history, in which Greek and Roman antiquity offered an inaugural moment.[134] The latter task was articulated in the new narrative histories of antiquity which reconfigured the temporalities of ancient historians: over the eighteenth century, the emergence of the new genre of modern histories of Greece by Temple Stanyan, Thomas Hind, Charles Rollin, John Gillies and William Mitford used ancient historians as sources to be structured in new chronological narratives.[135] The configuration of modern temporalities for studying ancient history, both in relation to wider temporal structures linking ancient and modern times, and in relation to the temporalities of Greek and Roman historians is a story that remains to be told, but lies beyond the scope of this introduction. For our purposes, we may observe that this enterprise subsumed the poetic polyphony of ancient historians under a monologic and singular discourse on antiquity which posited the identity of the times of things and times of words, of *res gestae* and *historia rerum gestarum*. Intertwined with this monologic reconsideration of ancient history was the configuration of the opposition between cyclical or exemplary and modern progressive and future-oriented time.

A claim to the identity of the times of words and things was also made by Greek historians; yet this claim, as we saw, was simultaneously interrupted by the rhetorical and intersubjective poetics of their narrative. The Roman engagement with Greek historiography constituted an equally complex temporality to be bequeathed to modern historians. In his essay on conceptions of the future in Livy's *Ab urbe condita*, Dennis Pausch configures a multifold relation with the legacy of Greek historians, and especially Polybius. The essay identifies four forms of anticipation. The first, knowledge of the future presented in the form of previews by the primary narrator, was an established technique in Greek historiography and Polybius in particular. Livy rarely makes use of it outside the proems, and when he does, he expresses a high degree of emotional commitment. More common are references to the future in speeches deployed by historical figures, which was also common in Greek historians. Two further techniques are more specific to Roman historiography, even though they were not unfamiliar to Greek historians. One is the way of looking into the future by means of supernatural occurrences that the historian reports. The last strat-

---

[133] Cf. Lianeri 2011a.
[134] Cf. Vlassopoulos 2011.
[135] Ceserani 2011.

egy, which is the most distinctly Roman one, occurs in reports on the assignment of duties to the newly elected magistrates, which offers an opportunity to preview imminent military conflicts and domestic problems. The comparison suggests that Livy appropriated not only parts of Polybius' *Histories* that would be useful in his narrative, but also elements of the work's narrative techniques and especially those concerning time and the future. Yet whereas Livy used more indirect and literary devices as well as those aiming at an open-ended anticipation, Polybius mainly deployed direct interventions of his primary narrator – a difference attributed to the shifting historical context of Roman domination, which was an open question in Polybius' time, but had become a historical reality in Livy's time.

According to this argument, both Polybius and Livy claimed their authority as regards the question of the Roman future of the Mediterranean world. Polybius did so in an attempt to convince his readers that his version of the future was the correct one – hence it was conveyed by the narrator himself. For Livy what was future for Polybius – Roman domination – was an established historical reality, which allowed him to make prediction in a more general and emphatic language. However, none of their texts was formulated as monologic. Polybius, as was argued, already achieved polyphony through a shifting *telos* or even a denial of a sense of closure. In Livy, the continuation of the sense of dialogue with one's predecessors and the restricted role of the historian's voice in predicting the future constantly remind his readers of a poetics that challenges the text's evocation of authoritative knowledge and mastery of time. Even in their strongest claims to authority, Greek and Roman historians did not produce a monologic discourse on time, nor a singular idea of history.

The modern reception of the Greco-Roman historiographic tradition involved the positing of a unifying temporal frame encompassing both antiquity and modern times. Antonis Liakos' essay explores this shift by taking its cue from an image representing antiquity engraved by Rubens. Liakos construes this engraving as evidence of a transition from one temporal order or regime to another: one which constituted the Renaissance and the modern world as the future of the Greek and Roman pasts. The essay refers to the shift in seventeenth-century European thought from conceptions of the history of the world as the succession of four empires – the Median, the Persian, the Macedonian and the Roman – to a model positing antiquity, the Middle Ages and the Renaissance as a genealogical succession of periods leading to modernity. In the former regime, wherein the idea of the four empires was derived from an interpretation of a dream by the prophet Daniel, Greek antiquity was effaced. It was not only that the Greek past stood in the margins of empires; it was also that this temporal framework constructed a notion of the future derived from a predominantly cyclical model, in which divine intervention was represented as the future and the inevitable end of the world. The shift to the new temporality constructed modernity as the future of antiquity by substituting for a linear succession of heterogeneous historical frameworks the homogeneous times of empires. This sequence posited the Renaissance and the modern world as a new kind of future, which presupposed antiquity as its past. Within this regime, temporal predicament did not involve sticking with the tradition, but anticipating the future. Rubens's engraving was a description of this transition that was happening during his time, but also an imperative directing this change. Hence in the engraving the two figures pushing to oblivion the symbols of the empires are Time and Death.

The concept of Liakos's essay illuminates a key step in the constitution of the temporality of succession linking antiquity and modern times: it was the transition from the cyclical temporal scheme of the four empires to the linear temporality represented by Rubens that made it possible to identify the modern world as the future of antiquity. Moreover, this essay allows us to note a peculiar historical irony. Daniel's story, as Momigliano writes, can be traced back to Roman and Greek sources: the theory of successive empires first appears in Herodotus who speaks of the Medes succeeding the Assyrians in Asia (1.95) and then the Persians succeeding the Medes. The idea is used by Ctesias (deploying Herodotus' model); then, after Alexander, by Demetrius of Phalerum who described the Macedonians as successors to the Persians in ruling over the world, and then others including Polybius.[136] This means that the destruction of the temporal frame that was formulated in and handed down by the Greek tradition – the scheme of successive empires – sustained the reconstitution of this tradition in the genealogical temporality of successive periods from antiquity to modern times. The irony behind the effacement of this temporality points to the ideological dimension of both perspectives on the ancient past and the futures implied by them. The story of the succession of the empires, as Liakos's essay suggests, related history to eschatology: historical time was construed as the unfolding of a deeper text written by God, according to which the last empire was to be replaced by the kingdom of God. The story of successive periods leading to modernity offered an antagonistic reading of antiquity, whose victory over a previous genealogy of readings (Daniel's reading of Roman and Greek historians) is represented in the painting through the figure of Athena whose torch illuminates the attempt to recover the knowledge of the ancient past.[137] While the presence of

---

[136] Momigliano 1994, 29–35.
[137] This volume, 330.

Athena points to the demise of the cyclical scheme of empires as the outcome of a new historical awareness of the ancient past, the figure of antiquity and its relics remain a historical construct: the contingent outcome of an antagonism over specific readings of antiquity and its (modern) futures.

Shifting from wider temporal frames to specific considerations of the future Tim Rood advances a comparative reading of Thucydides' glimpse at the hypothetical future ruins of Athens and Sparta. His essay juxtaposes this perspective to anticipations of future ruins in European (especially British and French) art, literature and historiography after the mid-eighteenth century. Through comparative analysis, including writers such as François-René de Chateaubriand, Thomas Smart Hughes, Constantin-François de Volney and Thomas B. Macaulay, Rood advances a critical reflection on the opposition between ancient and modern temporalities, wherein the former represent the Ciceronian doctrine of *historia magistra vitae* (grounded in a view of universal human nature) and the latter focus on historical difference. Rood starts with a contradiction: considerations of Thucydides' history as an exemplary expression of the idea of a universal, transhistorical nature cannot accommodate his sense of ruins of Athens and Sparta. Thucydides' glimpse to the future in this case indicates a greater sensitivity to the idea of historical difference, associated with the modern regime of historicity. Rood's comparative study juxtaposes Thucydides to historians of ancient Greece and travellers to modern Greece who responded most to Thucydides' anticipation of the future ruins of Athens and Sparta. He argues that Thucydides' exploration of these ruins differs from modern uses of the motif. He approaches monuments as a potentially deceptive index of power and his anticipation of a future viewer ensures that ruins are themselves endowed with a historicity, rather than being an ahistorical emblem of either the decay or the permanence of the past. By contrast, modern writers have been more concerned with memorialisation and historical stature, while also inscribing into the sight of ruins more complex historical patterns than Thucydides. Thucydides' and modern temporalities nevertheless share a consideration of future ruins that reflects the idea of historical rupture – and it is precisely this idea of rupture that explains why Thucydides looks into the future at all. Moreover, Thucydides resembles modern writers in being interested in the future as a way of thinking about the present. On the basis of this comparison as well as other examples of Thucydides' references to the temporal gap between past and present, Rood argues against viewing the ancient historian as conforming to a simple model of exemplary historiography. He suggests that a certain 'modernity' of Thucydides is evidenced in the dialectic between historical difference and similarity as well as awareness of rupture that shapes his idea of future ruins. The continuing homage paid to the 'modernity' of Thucydides, the essay concludes, shows how his ('modern') sense of the past as a foreign country remained irreducible to the idea that history offers lessons.

Aviezer Tucker's essay argues against this contention. Focusing on Ranke's relation to Thucydides, it considers the modern historian's homage to his predecessor as merely rhetorical and aiming at making acceptable by his contemporaries his radical revision of *historia magistra vitae*. According to Tucker, Rankean historiography differs from its ancient predecessors mainly with regard to its methodological approach to evidence, which enabled scientific historiography to generate probable knowledge of the past. The probabilistic inference from multiple sources and forms of evidence (testimonies, texts and so on) allowed modern historians to constitute new knowledge of the past. Ranke was the first to successfully apply this probabilistic method to historiography. By contrast, according to this argument, Thucydides, among other ancient historians, even though he was critical of his sources, did not infer from multiple testimonies. His method was centred on finding the reliability of witnesses, but did not seek to produce new historiographic knowledge from testimonies of various reliabilities. Despite his own references to Thucydides, Ranke, Tucker concludes, founded scientific historiography in opposition to ancient historical methods and within the background of a wider paradigmatic shift in biblical criticism, classical philology, and comparative linguistics. His approach exemplified the methodological difference between the contemporary historiography practised in antiquity and the modern, past-oriented scientific history. Historical distance was deemed necessary for the collection and comparison of multiple evidential sources that were not available to contemporaries as well as the ability to colligate events in the context of longer processes. On these grounds, the Rankean paradigm could generate historical knowledge that remained unavailable to contemporaries or observers.

The dilemma arising from the juxtaposition of Rood's and Tucker's arguments as to the relation between ancient and modern temporalities is insoluble, since both hypotheses can be justified by almost the same historical evidence. Strictly speaking, Tucker's thesis about a distinct modern historical sense grounded in a) the comparison of evidential sources aiming to produce new historical knowledge, and b) the colligation of evidence in the context of longer processes constituting what we described as a singular temporality of history, is correct. This is so even if we seek to qualify the identification of this shift with Ranke (whom Tucker also considers as part of wider intellectual developments) and trace its roots in the eighteenth century or Renaissance historiography.[138] Tucker's thesis is further sustained by the modern historiographical engagements with ancient historians, which were centred on the quest for producing new historical knowledge, that is, knowledge going beyond Greek and Roman historical narratives. Momigliano appraised George Grote as the first modern historian of Greece, on the grounds that he juxtaposed the ancient sources to corroborative evidence in order to produce a new account of Greek history; Giovanna Ceserani traced this shift in the emergence of the genre of history of Greece over the eighteenth century; while Kostas Vlassopoulos has further associated modern histories of Greece to Koselleck's thesis about a broader transformation of historical consciousness over the eighteenth century.[139]

At the same time, debates over periodisation in the history of historiography, and especially over the demarcation of antiquity and modernity, are as susceptible to a politics of time, to use Johannes Fabian's term, as are political and other forms periodisation. In his seminal critique of anthropology, in *Time and the Other*, Fabian sets out this contention: "If it is true that Time belongs to the political economy of relations between individuals, classes, and nations, then the construction of anthropology's object through temporal concepts and devices is a political act; there is a 'Politics of Time'".[140] Drawing on this thesis Kathleen Davis has criticised characterisations of the modern historical sense as scientific, secularised and aware of historical difference, on the grounds that they "operate on the basis of such sweeping assumptions that they easily rationalise and absorb contradictory empirical evidence".[141] In particular, Davis observes the "atemporal paralysis" that such concepts attribute, for instance, to the Middle Ages and the oppositional logic through which they exclude 'medieval' time from the realm of history, on the grounds of a politics of periodisation that sustains the philosophical and political claims of modernity.[142]

In line with this criticism, the reduction of antiquity to a paradigm of exemplary history, is profoundly problematic, as Rood's critical reading also suggests. As we have seen in this introduction and several essays in the book contend, the idiom that Cicero designated as *historia magistra vitae* is far from straightforwardly entailing the collapse of past, present and future. To consider Greek temporalities as oriented toward a reservoir of past examples that can straightforwardly be applied to the present and future only makes sense in the context

---

[138] See for instance Peter Burke's seminal *The Renaissance Sense of the Past* (1969). Cf. Burke 2001.
[139] Ceserani 2011; Vlassopoulos 2011.
[140] Fabian 1983, x.
[141] Davis 2008, 87–97; 2010, 50. Cf. Kontler 2008.
[142] Davis 2008, 90.

of a binary opposition confronting this 'atemporal paralysis' of antiquity with the modern historical awareness of temporal difference. Indeed, such theses have been consistently formulated on the grounds of this opposition with modern temporalities: for instance Hartog drew on Koselleck to oppose what he calls the pre-modern regime of historicity on the one hand to a modern regime, which, after the late eighteenth century focused on the qualitative difference of the future from the present and past; and, on the other, to our contemporary time centred on an undifferentiated and self-perpetuating present.[143] Yet the contention that history will always be made different from the present and past is no less the product of a specific historiographical and political imaginary – one providing western imperialism with a vision to impose on the world – than any other conception of time and history. Moreover, modern engagements with Greek historians as sources for the production of new historicities of antiquity were equally implicated in this political imaginary: both the eighteenth-century historical narratives of ancient times claiming a new scientific status and the invention of specific relations between ancient and modern historians were the contingent articulation of political temporalities, in which the slippage from a historical to a purportedly universal narrative – from Greece in its historical specificity to Greece as the inaugural moment of a paradigmatic European temporality – served to sustain imperialist discourses and relations of the period.[144]

Oswyn Murray's essay focuses precisely on how the western perspective on ancient history has centred around the concepts of imperialism and liberty through which western modernity recognised itself as the future of antiquity. The former concept is manifested in the fundamental importance of Roman history. The latter includes the history of political liberty and democratic forms of government, together with personal or individual liberty. The essay invites the juxtaposition of these conceptions of history with non-Western traditions, but also the recognition of alternatives in western constructions of the ancient past, such as those formulated in the Jewish historiographical tradition. It discusses Josephus' *Jewish Antiquities* as the first attempt to align the Jewish historical tradition with classical historiography, characterising the author as an ancient historian who shared many of the political and rational attitudes of the canon of Greek and Roman historiography. Writing outside the frames of the holy texts, Josephus made it possible for future historians to compare the Jewish historical tradition with those of Greece and Rome. Hence his work was met with

---

[143] Hartog 2003. Cf. also Hannoum 2008 for a critical review of Hartog 2003, and Tamiolaki in this volume.
[144] Lianeri 2014; Vlassopoulos 2010.

a long strand of translations produced up until the early nineteenth century and aimed to provide a complete history of Judaism going back to antiquity. In this period, the emergence of modern Jewish histories with H.H. Milman was intertwined with the new German scientific histories of the ancient world. This link allowed for the insertion of Jewish history into contemporary ideas of progress as well as comparisons such as between Moses and Solon. While recognising differences, such as those associated with divine dispensation, Milman presented classical history and Jewish history as flowing together, and comparison was simply a question of selection from tradition. Murray finally turns to Heinrich Graetz's novel interpretation of Jewish history arising out of the needs of the Jewish people to understand its past in its own terms. Graetz's use of the concept of Diaspora indicated differences from the histories of other peoples, but he nevertheless also acknowledged, on the completion of his work in 1874, the twin legacy of Western history consisting of Hellenism and Hebraism. The essay concludes by discussing the roots of Western histories of antiquity in the eighteenth-century conditions of European imperialism, emerging democracy and the free-market; yet, it also observes the existence of alternatives, such as Graetz's history, and invites reflection on the way dominant traditions of interpreting antiquity in the West were established and challenged.

Murray talks about traditions in a very specific sense. It is not traditions in the sense of handing down to future generations something that was already produced in the past, but as genealogical reconstructions of time positing themselves as the future of antiquity. The essay further argues that this future must be understood in the plural, as futures, rather than 'future', even though each genealogy presents the uniqueness of its *telos*. These futures, Murray suggests, are not only embedded in their concrete historical contexts, but are themselves only one product of this context: the historical account that dominated over alternative views of the ancient past and its links to the present. Building on this concept we may ask about the alternatives suppressed by the modern reduction of ancient temporalities to the topos of exemplarity. One of these alternatives might then be identified as the concept of history writing offered by the poetic polyphony of the Greek and Roman traditions.

What was identified in antiquity as historical example had no autonomy and signified no 'atemporal paralysis'. Rather, it was formulated as part of a complex historical whole in which, as we saw, competing temporalities and visions of the past, present and future encountered one another. The very notion of example denoting a part taken out of some whole and standing for the whole, as Alexander Gelley argues, suggests the relation of specific cases (examples) with a wider temporality: the example stands – but *how?* And for *what whole?*[145] This introduction suggested that Greek historians constructed this whole and its links to historical cases through a poetic polyphony, a competition of voices about historical time and the future. Even though it asserted the authority of the historian, this poetics not only prefigured subsequent revisions of this authority by other historians, but also allowed for the alternative time of historical actors to sustain its constitution. The polyphonic poetics of Greek historiography thus highlighted the political questions underlying conflicting historical understandings of time. By contrast, the quest posited by modern historians to infer new knowledge from evidence was a quest for a monologic discourse; one in which all other voices and perspectives on time were subsumed under the voice of the historian. Indeed, the modern writing of ancient history and temporality depended on this silence: on the modern historian becoming the privileged interpreter and organiser of ancient time. But this privilege was claimed on the grounds of a scientific method that effaced its own dependence on poetics and suppressed the politics of a temporality that returns to the past only in terms that identify its unity as an epoch.

Momigliano has long warned us against generalisations contending, for instance, that time was a circle to the Greeks, whereas the Hebrews and the early Christians conceived it as a progression *ad finitum* or *ad infinitum*, while modern historians appropriated and inverted the Judeo-Christian notion. As he states with admirable clarity, "if one wants to understand something about Greek historians and the real differences between them and Biblical historians, the first precaution is to beware of the cyclical notion of time"[146] – in other words, the notion of time which either precludes the future or reduces it to a modality of the present. To deny the reduction of Greek historiography to a single model of cyclical or exemplary time is first to deny the monologic unity of this discourse. In the light of Momigliano's warning that generalisations introduce "too much coherence" into Greek conceptions of time,[147] this volume seeks to approach Greek considerations of the future not with a view to identifying an absence of unity, but in search of a unity of a higher order, a kind of unity through which competing voices and traditions about historical truth and knowledge, including our own, confront one another. It is by way of this polyphony that Greek historiography relates to human praxis. Hence its conflicts confirm that the his-

---

145 Gelley 1995, 2.
146 Momigliano 1966, 10.
147 Momigliano 1966, 12, n.26.

torians' engagements with knowing their object, as Constantin Fasolt put it, cannot be separated from the (mutually conflicting) actions a community takes to change its fate.[148]

---

[148] Fasolt 2004, xiii.

Future Times and the Poetics of Greek Historiography

Jonas Grethlein
Ancient Historiography and 'Future Past'[1]

1. 'Future Past'

It is common sense that historians deal with the past, and yet, they also engage with the future in manifold ways. Time and again, historians refer to the future, directly as when Thucydides hopes that his work will be a 'possession forever', and indirectly, for example when Polybius has Scipio muse about the fall of Rome. It has recently been claimed that the methods by which historians explore the past are apt tools for making scenarios about the future.[2] From a different angle, Lucian Hölscher demonstrated that the future is a construct which closely corresponds to the idea of history.[3] Our notion of the future as a realm open to unprecedented developments, he shows, emerged together with the modern historical awareness around 1800.

In this article I will elaborate on yet another way in which the future comes into play in historiography. The past as narrated by the historian is, I argue, essentially constituted by the future. To be more precise: historiographic works are shaped by the future of the events narrated. Danto's analytical philosophy of history can illuminate this point. Danto observes among historians a predilection for a certain type of sentences that he labels 'narrative sentences': 'Narrative sentences refer to at least two time-separated events, and describe the earlier event.'[4] The statement 'The Thirty Years' War began in 1618',[5] for example, is about an event in 1618 that is seen against the horizon of a later event, the year 1648. Danto limits his analysis to single sentences, but I contend that the structure of 'narrative sentences' also defines narratives of the past as a whole: retrospect makes historians view the past in the light of subsequent events. The vantage-points chosen by historians influence the selection of the material as well as its arrangement and thereby give historical narratives their specific character. The later event against which the earlier event is described

---

1 I wish to thank Aleka Lianeri for her comments on this paper as well as many stimulating conversations about the history of theory over the course of the last years.
2 Staley 2002; 2007. For a critical assessment, see Bonneuil 2009.
3 Hölscher 1999.
4 Danto 1985, 159.
5 Cf. Danto 1985, 152.

in Danto's narrative sentences recurs *mutatis mutandis* as the *telos* in a historiographic work.

The kind of future on which I will focus can be labelled 'future past':[6] the *telos*, the point in the light of which the events narrated are envisaged, is still future for the historical agents, but already past for the historian and her readers. The term 'future past' thus highlights the temporal asymmetry between historian and historical agents that is at the core of historiography. A simple thought experiment illustrates the great impact that the choice of a *telos* has on the selection and arrangement of historical material: think about how to write a history of Germany in the 1920s. If we choose 1945 as *telos*, then our history will be very different from an account that is given from the perspective of 1930. The Beer Hall Putsch, Hitler's arrest in Landsberg and the publication of 'Mein Kampf' will be prominent events in the former history. In a history that does not look beyond 1930, however, they will figure, if mentioned at all, as minor incidents in a period rich in activities of extremists. Shifting the *telos* results in a very different account of the same events. It is hard to overestimate the significance of the point from which history is envisaged, past for us, future for the historical agents.

This example also drives home that, the case of *Zeitgeschichte* left aside, the *telos* is distinct from the present of the historian. Forming the hermeneutic horizon, the present of course shapes the historian's understanding of the past. Experiences with the financial crisis erupting in 2007, for example, may prompt contemporary historians to pay closer attention to the economic issues in the 1920s. Differently from this, the *telos* signifies the point towards which the events narrated are said to move, in our case the crash of the stock-market, the rise of Hitler or the emergence of new political blocs. Often this point simultaneously constitutes the closure of the account, but this is not necessarily so. While ending with 1930, our narrative may envisage the 1920s from the point of view of WWII for example. If I use the spatial metaphor of vantage-point to describe the *telos*, then I do not mean the horizon of the historian's present, but the point in the past from which she views the course of events. While belonging to the realm of hermeneutics, 'future past' signifies the distinct temporal poetics of historical writing.

---

6 My use of 'future past' is distinct from Koselleck's. His 1979 book bears the main title *Vergangene Zukunft* that is rendered as *Futures Past* in the title and as 'former future(s)' in the text of the English translation (cf. the translator's note in Koselleck 1985, xi n. 13). While Koselleck is interested in the future as seen in the past, an aspect that proves fundamental for his take on *Neuzeit*, I focus on the temporal asymmetry of agents and historians in the sense outlined above.

In another paper, I elucidate the concept of 'future past' from a more theoretical point of view, weighing the benefits and problems of teleological constructions.[7] Teleology can become a snare, as it easily tricks us into ignoring that the past was open to various developments. Focusing on the large lines of history, we tend to lose track of the experiences of the historical agents. This danger notwithstanding, it is hard if not impossible to shun teleology fully. The teleological tendency of historiography is rooted in hindsight. Historians can of course try to adopt the perspective of eye-witnesses, but entirely suppressing hindsight is a challenge that is hard to meet. Moreover, retrospect is a central asset that has been called 'l'arme secrète de l'historien'[8]. Since Tacitus, historians have not tired of stressing that only temporal distance permits balanced judgement. In particular historical explanation hinges on links still invisible to contemporaries: the historian needs to know where history is headed.

In this paper, I will use select ancient historians to illustrate the significance of 'future past' and tease out some of its ramifications. The dynamics of 'future past' is pervasive in any kind of historiography, but it is more tangible in the strongly narrative works of ancient historians than in historical writings that favour analysis. I will start with Thucydides whose account of the Peloponnesian War drives home the salience of the *telos* for our understanding of the past. We tend to take Thucydides' view on the Peloponnesian War for more or less granted, and yet as Dionysius' critique of the ending of his account shows, Thucydides' account is a specific take that hinges on the choice of *telos*. Concerning 'future past', Polybius proves to be more than an epigone of Thucydides. I will argue that his decision to extend his work beyond the intended endpoint is carried by profound reflections on the temporal dynamics of writing history. While Polybius shifts the *telos*, Herodotus' *Histories* illustrate that historians can operate with more than one *telos*. In order to elucidate further aspects of 'future past' as well as to show its significance beyond Greek historiography, I shall also touch on two Latin authors. I will argue that in Sallust's *Bellum Catilinae* the evocation of several vantage-points challenges its straight-forward account of Roman decline. Tacitus' *Annals*, finally, intimate that the temporal relationship between historian and his characters may be more complex than it appears at first sight. It is definitely asymmetrical, but the orientation of humans to the future embeds in history a structure that prefigures the historian's 'future past'. I will close with a broader reflection on time and historiography.

---

[7] Grethlein 2014a. For a more extensive exploration of the ancient works discussed here, see Grethlein 2013.
[8] Hobsbawm 1993, 98.

2. The salience of the *telos*: Thucydides

Thucydides, it may seem, is not a good starting point for an investigation of teleology in ancient historiography. Besides writing annalistically, he is at pains to restore presentness to the past. As several scholars have shown, the temporal orchestration of the narrative, the use of speeches and focalisation as well as narratorial reticence and linguistic features all contribute to rendering the narrative mimetic.[9] Commenting on the description of the battle in the Syracusan harbour, Plutarch notes (*De glor. Ath.* 347a): 'Thucydides is always striving for this vividness in his writing, since it is his desire to make the reader a spectator, as it were, and to instil into readers the emotions of amazement and consternation felt by eyewitnesses.' Even in the main bulk of his narrative, which is less vivid than the account of the Syracusan harbour battle, Thucydides tends to limit the view of his reader to the perspective of a contemporary.

That being said, Thucydides' experiential narrative is built on a firm teleological scaffolding. The fragmentary status of *The History of the Peloponnesian War* makes it difficult to comment on its narrative trajectory, and yet a few references grant us a glimpse of the *telos* from which the Peloponnesian War is envisaged. In the appraisal of Pericles in 2.65, for instance, Thucydides surveys Athens' course after the death of Pericles: Athens would survive the disaster of the Sicilian episodes and also brave new enemies such as the Persians, but finally, 'coming to grief through individual disputes, they brought about their own overthrow'. In 5.26, to adduce another incisive passage, Thucydides mentions the length of the war and muses on the process of his writing. We of course do not know where Thucydides' narrative would have ended or where, in case the end has been lost, it ended, but the passages mentioned leave no doubt that the capitulation of Athens in 404/3 forms the *telos* from which Thucydides views the Peloponnesian War.

Thucydides' work has proven so powerful that we take its reconstruction for granted, but alternative views of the Peloponnesian War are possible and have indeed been voiced. Unimpressed by Thucydides' argument for the coherence of the military encounters at the end of the 5th century, fourth-century orators distinguish between several wars (Andoc. 3.3–9; 29–31; Aeschin. 2.173–6). The critique that Dionysius of Halicarnassus levels at the ending of Thucydides' work is particularly instructive. Dionysius ignores its fragmentary status and obviously assumes that 411 is the intended endpoint, and yet his invective illus-

---

9 For a survey, see Grethlein 2013, 91–3.

trates an interpretation of the Peloponnesian War that is at odds with the one we find in Thucydides' work (*Pomp.* 3.10):

> It would have been better, after going through all the events, to end his history with a climax, and one that was most remarkable and especially gratifying to his audience, the return of the exiles from Phyle, which marked the beginning of the city's recovery of freedom.
>
> κρεῖττον δὲ ἦν διεξελθόντα πάντα τελευτὴν ποιήσασθαι τῆς ἱστορίας τὴν θαυμασιωτάτην καὶ μάλιστα τοῖς ἀκούουσι κεχαρισμένην, τὴν κάθοδον τῶν φυγάδων τῶν ἀπὸ Φυλῆς ἀφ' ὧν ἡ πόλις ἀρξαμένη τὴν ἐλευθερίαν ἀνεκομίσατο.

Whereas the *telos* of Thucydides' account creates a sombre picture of Athenian history, the vantage-point favoured by Dionysius would have it end on an upbeat note.[10] Instead of being the story of a mighty polis brought down by a corrupt political system, the Peloponnesian War would reveal the pertinacity of the Athenian democracy through a host of hardships and trials. The shift of the *telos* would result in a very different account. Thucydides' account highlights that even a strongly experiential narrative is essentially shaped by its telos. The *History of the Peloponnesian War* is a prominent example that proves how a shift of *telos* can make us see the same events in new light.

3. The *telos* deferred: Polybius

Recent scholarly efforts notwithstanding, Polybius is still in the shadow of Thucydides and counts as an epigone who tries hard, but cannot hold a candle to his model. In many regards this may be correct, if not always fair; concerning the temporal dynamics of historiography, however, Polybius easily outstrips Thucydides. Polybius, I will argue, was highly aware of how crucial a role the *telos* plays for how history is written.

To start with, in universal historiography, the *telos* is particularly delicate. While the death of kings and the fall of empires provide historiographic monographs with apt vantage-points, *telê* are harder to identify in the vast and disparate field of world history. Polybius, however, could consider himself lucky. As he sees it, the course of world history itself requires a teleological account (1.4.1):

> For what gives my work its peculiar quality, and what is most remarkable in the present age, is this. Fortune has guided almost all the affairs of the world in one direction and has forced them to incline towards one and the same end; a historian should likewise

---

10 Cf. Marincola 2005, 305; Fromentin 2008, 61.

bring before his readers under one synoptical view the operations by which she has accomplished her general purpose.

τὸ γὰρ τῆς ἡμετέρας πραγματείας ἴδιον καὶ τὸ θαυμάσιον τῶν καθ' ἡμᾶς καιρῶν τοῦτ' ἔστιν ὅτι, καθάπερ ἡ τύχη σχεδὸν ἅπαντα τὰ τῆς οἰκουμένης πράγματα πρὸς ἓν ἔκλινε μέρος καὶ πάντα νεύειν ἠνάγκασε πρὸς ἕνα καὶ τὸν αὐτὸν **σκοπόν**, οὕτως καὶ <δεῖ> διὰ τῆς ἱστορίας ὑπὸ μίαν **σύνοψιν** ἀγαγεῖν τοῖς ἐντυγχάνουσι τὸν χειρισμὸν τῆς τύχης, ᾧ κέχρηται πρὸς τὴν τῶν ὅλων πραγμάτων συντέλειαν.

The visual metaphor deployed in the *skopos* to which 'all the affairs of the world' are 'inclined' helps to close the gap between the events and their 'synopsis' through the historian. The *skopos* in which all threads come together is the hegemony of Rome (e.g. 1.1.5–6). In diction reminiscent of Aristotle, Polybius claims that this development of history has a recognisable beginning, a limited duration and an uncontroversial end (3.1.4).[11] That being said, neither beginning nor ending of Polybius' *Histories* are clear cut. He first announces the year 220 as his starting point (1.3.1), but then devotes two full books to the years 264–220. Embedded in this *prokataskeue*, we find yet another review providing a synopsis of the years 386–264 that is intended to clarify why Rome crossed over to Sicily (1.12.5). The instability of the beginning is highlighted by the fact that Polybius alternatively calls 264 and 220 the beginning of his history.[12]

The oscillating starting point is mirrored by the deferral of the endpoint. In the proem, Polybius proclaims the Roman triumph over Macedonia as *telos* of his *Histories*. Pydna seals Rome's rule over the world. The events up to Pydna, however, fill only the first 30 books; ten more books covering Rome's history until the destruction of Carthage in 146/5 follow. At the beginning of book 3, Polybius muses on this temporal extension of his investigation. His reflections have not been received favourably in modern scholarship. The most prominent Polybius scholar, Walbank, condemns them as 'singularly confused'.[13] The argument, he claims, is muddled and barely conceals Polybius' real motive, namely integrating into his work the material that he collected while accompanying Scipio to Spain and Africa.

---

11 For a comparison of Polybius' reflection and Aristotle's idea of plot, see Grethlein 2013, 227–30.
12 For 264 BCE, see, e.g., 1.5.1; 1.12.5–6; 39.8.4; for 220 BCE, see, e.g., 1.3.1–4; 2.37.2; 3.5.9. Cf. Rood 2007, 172–3.
13 Walbank 1977, 159. Besides the extensive argument in Walbank 1977, see also Walbank 1972, 182–3; 1974, 22–7. Walbank 2002, 21 is inclined to consider Polybius' reasoning as more than a 'smoke-screen' for his desire to integrate his personal story, but does not elaborate on this. Ferrary 1988, 289–90 takes Polybius' reflections seriously, but runs into new problems. For a critique of Walbank's reading, see also Shimron 1979/80, 104–11.

I do not dare to make claims about Polybius' real motives, but a careful reading of the first chapters of book 3 reveals that they are anything but 'singularly confused'.[14] They feature a profound reflection on the role of retrospect in historiography. Polybius notes that his *Histories* could stop with 168/7, as initially planned, if an account of Rome's military triumph sufficed as the basis for an evaluation of Rome's hegemony (3.4.4–5):

> But since judgments regarding either the conquerors or the conquered based purely on performance are by no means final – what is thought to be the greatest success having brought the greatest calamities on many, if they do not make proper use of it, and the most dreadful catastrophes often turning out to the advantage of those who support them bravely …
>
> ἐπεὶ δ' οὐκ αὐτοτελεῖς εἰσιν οὔτε περὶ τῶν κρατησάντων <οὔτε περὶ τῶν> ἐλαττωθέντων αἱ ψιλῶς ἐξ αὐτῶν τῶν ἀγωνισμάτων διαλήψεις, διὰ τὸ πολλοῖς μὲν τὰ μέγιστα δοκοῦντ' εἶναι τῶν κατορθωμάτων, ὅταν μὴ δεόντως αὐτοῖς χρήσωνται, τὰς μεγίστας ἐπενηνοχέναι συμφοράς, οὐκ ὀλίγοις δὲ τὰς ἐκπληκτικωτάτας περιπετείας, ὅταν εὐγενῶς αὐτὰς ἀναδέξωνται, πολλάκις εἰς τὴν τοῦ συμφέροντος περιπεπτωκέναι μερίδα …

For this reason, Polybius notes, he has decided to continue and to report the behaviour of the victors, the views of the others and the further efforts of both sides (3.4.6). This will permit contemporaneous readers to decide whether or not to accept Roman rule and later readers to arrive at sound judgments on Roman hegemony, the greatest use that Polybius assigns to his *Histories*.

Nothing of this is noted by Walbank. He claims that the reflections on changes of fortune do not pertain to Rome and therefore fail as an explanation for the extension of the *Histories*. Indeed, there is no downfall, Rome succeeds in sustaining its hegemony. However, Walbank misconceives the train of thought: Polybius' argument does not require an actual reversal, its point is an evaluation of Rome's rule. Polybius covers the history subsequent to Pydna not to narrate Rome's loss of its rule but to check whether or not she would lose it. A change of fortune is merely a potential development.

The argument that Walbank considers to be 'singularly confused' is not only fully consistent, it also contains a profound reflection on 'future past' and its significance for historical judgments. The continuous flow of time creates new vantage-points from which the past can be seen in a new light. Were Rome's hegemony to turn out to be unstable, the evaluation of her military triumphs would have to be revised. The impact of the future on how we view the past renders historical judgments notoriously unstable. Every new *telos* that the course of his-

---

14 I also disagree with Walbank's interpretation of ταραχὴ καὶ κίνησις (3.4.12). See Grethlein 2013, 237–40.

tory generates may bring events to the fore that were ignored before and construe links hitherto invisible. Polybius only notes that the events immediately after Rome's victories may yield perspectives that force us to reconsider the military triumph, but his observation opens up a *regressus ad infinitum:* in the further course of history, the verdict on the aftermath of the victory may have to be revised, which in turn could affect the view on the original triumph and so on. The instability of historical meaning and of historical judgment is encapsulated in the flux of time to which also the historian is subject.

Most philologists despise Polybius, historians tend to revere him. While Polybius' awkward style makes philologists shudder, historians praise him for his methodological rigour and consider his work an important source for Hellenistic history. However, Polybius is more than an old warhorse that is honest but intellectually limited. I hope to have shown that he is to be taken seriously as a theoretician of history. In addition to flying the flag of Thucydides' methodological standards, he engages in piercing reflections on the teleological structure of historiography. As the first chapters of book 3 show, the extension of the *Histories* by ten books is the product of a keen sensitivity to the temporal dynamic of writing history. By moving the *telos* from Pydna to the destruction of Carthage, Polybius tries to do justice to the dependence of historical judgment on the vantage-point. He is fully aware of the instability of historical meaning.[15]

4. Multiple *telê*: The ending of Herodotus' *Histories*

The works of Thucydides and Polybius, as interpreted above, drive home the salience of 'future past' in historiography. Shifting the *telos* can result in very different views of the same events. I will now turn briefly to Herodotus' *Histories* in order to illustrate that historians are not bound to a single *telos*, but can deploy more than one *telos*. This point will then let us take a fresh look at Sallust's *Bellum Catilinae*. The passage in the *Histories* upon which I will touch is the ending.[16] As pointed out above, the historian's *telos* is not necessarily identical

---

[15] To avoid misunderstanding, let me emphasise that this does not make Polybius a Derridean *avant-la-lettre*. Polybius comments on the temporal dynamics of historiography, not on language as a precarious sign-system.

[16] My argument builds on a number of articles on the *Histories*' closure that have elucidated its resonances with the preceding narrative and its ambiguous presentation of Persia and Greece: see especially Boedeker 1988; Dewald 1997; Welser 2009.

with the point where her account ends: a narrative of the 1920s may end in 1930, but view this period in light of later events. If however a historian chooses to close her narrative with the event that has provided its *telos*, then both can reinforce each other. In Herodotus' *Histories*, for instance, the closure gives prominence to the *telos* of the narrative. At the same time, it opens up a new vantage-point from which the events narrated can be seen.

On the one hand, the ending of the *Histories* helps to cement the failure of Xerxes as the *telos* of Herodotus' report of the encounters between East and West since Gyges. In particular the Artayctes episode provides the narrative with closure. Strikingly, Artayctes is executed at the very place where Xerxes crossed the Bosporus to get to Europe.[17] The desacralisation of the Protesilaus temple evokes the proem of the *Histories* where the rape of Helen is mentioned as well as the beginning of the most famous war between Greeks and barbarians. Reinforced by the ring-composition, the restoration of the boundary between the continents underlines that Xerxes' failure brings the conflicts between Greeks and barbarians to an end. That the final disaster provides the vantage-point from which Herodotus narrates Xerxes' expedition is tangible in the Persian Council scene at the beginning of book 7: several of the objections against the invasion advanced by Artabanus anticipate key reasons for its actual failure.[18]

On the other hand, the Artayctes episode destabilises the closure and prompts the reader to look beyond this *telos*. The extraordinarily cruel execution of Artayctes raises the question of requital. The phrase καὶ κατὰ τὸ ἔτος τοῦτο οὐδὲν ἔτι πλέον τούτων ἐγένετο ('Nothing further happened for the remainder of the year.' 9.121.3) makes it hard not to think ahead and wonder what the Athenians still had in store. The ending thus adds to the network of passages that adumbrate the later course of events, especially the history of Athens, which, Herodotus insinuates, would be the next empire to enter the cycle of rise and fall.[19] Herodotus thus deploys more than one *telos*: he casts the defeat of Xerxes as *telos* for the military encounters between East and West and simultaneously projects the Persian Wars against the backdrop of the history of Athens in the second half of the fifth century.

Elsewhere, I argue that Herodotus' subtle juxtaposition of Athens and Persia ought to be seen in the light of his insight into the significance of retrospect for history.[20] Herodotus obviously takes a strong interest in contemporary politics,

---

[17] Cf. Boedeker 1988, 41–42.
[18] Cf. Grethlein 2009, 201–202.
[19] Cf. Strasburger 1955; Fornara 1971; 1971a; Raaflaub 1987; Stadter 1992; Moles 1996; 2002.
[20] Grethlein 2013, 185–223.

and yet he does not dare to comment explicitly on history still in flux. He therein heeds the wisdom voiced by Solon programmatically at the beginning of the *Histories:* 'We must look to the conclusion of every matter, and see how it will end' ('σκοπέειν δὲ χρὴ παντὸς χρήματος τὴν τελευτὴν κῇ ἀποβήσεται.' 1.32.9). If my argument is correct, Herodotus' deployment of multiple *telê* owes much to a specific philosophy of history: it permits him to shed light on contemporary events without having to commit to explicit comments on what is still in flux.

This said, the introduction of multiple *telê* also lends itself to other functions. Envisaging the past from more than one vantage-point is an apt response to the 'Gleichzeitigkeit des Ungleichzeitigen' to which Reinhart Koselleck devoted some considerations.[21] The same time sees processes that, while possibly linked to each other, follow different temporalities. Koselleck coined the spatial metaphor of 'Zeitschichten' to account for such parallel developments that progress at different speeds.[22] The use of multiple *telê* is a narrative means of representing such disparate processes, permitting the historian to do justice to their individual dynamics.

5. Sallust: *Telos* without alternative?

The boundary between Greek and Roman historiography is hard to maintain. Beginning with the Hellenistic Era, Greek authors such as Polybius felt the need to write the history of the Roman Empire. At the same time, Latin historians are much indebted to their Greek predecessors. It thus seems to be fitting to add to my discussion of Greek historians two Latin authors whose works will permit me to elaborate on further aspects of 'future past'. The deployment of more than one *telos* makes Sallust's *Bellum Catilinae* more complex than is generally assumed.[23] But before elaborating on Sallust's use of multiple vantage-points, it is worth commenting on another point about 'future past' that plays out in the *Bellum Catilinae:* the choice of a *telos* defines not only our understanding of the preceding events, but also our view on the event figuring as *telos*.

Together with Cicero's *Catilinarian Speeches*, Sallust's *Bellum Catilinae* had a huge impact on how Catiline was viewed subsequently, and yet, it did not escape the notice of ancient historians that their assessment of the conspiracy may have been inflated. Cassius Dio for one remarks (37.42.1):

---

[21] Koselleck 1979, 323–39.
[22] Koselleck 2000, 19–26.
[23] The *Bellum Jugurthinum* can also be read as an engagement with the temporal dynamics of writing history. Such a take could build on Levene's interpretation of it as fragment (1992).

Such was the career of Catiline and such his downfall; but he gained a greater name than his deeds deserved, owing to the reputation of Cicero and the speeches he delivered against him.

Κατιλίνας μὲν ταῦτ' ἐποίησε καὶ οὕτω κατελύθη· καὶ ἐπὶ πλεῖόν γε τῆς τῶν πραχθέντων ἀξίας ὄνομα πρὸς τὴν τοῦ Κικέρωνος δόξαν καὶ πρὸς τοὺς λόγους τοὺς κατ' αὐτοῦ λεχθέντας ἔσχε.

Modern historians too have been cautious in their use of Sallust as a source for Catiline. While some even doubt that there was a conspiracy at all, a more moderate position prevails:[24] Catiline, scion of an old aristocratic family fails twice in his application for the consulate and then embarks on a *coup d'état*. He not only attacks the Republic, but, in trying to defend his *dignitas*, is concerned with one of its core values. Ultimately, Catiline's attempted overthrow is not that different from Caesar's decision to cross the Rubicon.[25] He is not so much an evil threat to Rome as a failed politician desperately clinging to a central value of its elite. The importance of the Catilinarian conspiracy is not ranked very highly. It is for example not even mentioned in Alfred Heuß's Göttingen inaugural lecture on the decline of the Roman republic and the problem of revolution.[26]

Sallust makes a footnote, a conspiracy that was uncovered in time, a key moment of Roman history. Teleology is crucial to this take on Catiline: Sallust endows his conspiracy with weight by making it the *telos* of Rome's decline. While not necessarily the ultimate endpoint, Catiline appears as the peak of a deterioration that for Sallust starts with the capture of Carthage in 146 and receives a strong push from Sulla. *Avaritia* and *ambitio*, the central vices triggering the decline, come to a head with Catiline. Sallust thus charges Catiline's conspiracy with significance by carefully presenting it as the *telos* of a development that reaches far back. Making an event *telos* defines our view not only of preceding history but also of the event itself. It gains weight and is strongly defined by the course of events which it caps. A simple example corroborates this observation: The exile of Romulus Augustus in 476 was only one deposition among many in an instable period. If we follow however Marcellinus Comes, as many histor-

---

[24] For the radical position, see Waters 1970; for the more moderate assessment of the conspiracy, see, for example, Hoffmann 1959; Schmal 2001, 51–4. Against the tendency to relativise the importance of Catiline, see recently Odahl 2010.
[25] On the central role of *dignitas* for Caesar, see Morstein-Marx 2009, 122–35.
[26] Heuß 1956.

ians did, and consider the flight of Augustus the end of the Roman Empire, then it becomes a turning point in world history.[27]

Despite its strong teleology, the *Bellum Catilinae* demonstrates that the same events can be seen differently from different vantage-points. While Polybius defers the *telos* of his account, Sallust integrates into his work the seed of an alternative narrative.[28] We find this counter-narrative in the speech duel between Caesar and Cato (50.4–53.1). Caesar makes a plea for clemency towards Catiline's followers, Cato insists on execution and carries the day. The *synkrisis* notwithstanding, it is still controversial whose position Sallust favours.[29] The juxtaposition is too complex to reveal a simple authorial bias. In my interpretation, I would like to show that Caesar's speech contains the elements for an alternative take on both Rome's history and the events of 63. Echoes of Sallust's proem and historiographic *topoi* invite the reader to compare Caesar's speech with Sallust's narrative (51.1–4):[30]

> Fathers of the Senate, all men who deliberate upon difficult questions ought <u>to be free from hatred and friendship, anger and pity</u>. When these feelings stand in the way the mind cannot easily discern the <u>truth</u>, and no mortal man has ever served <u>at the same time his passions and his best interests</u>. When you apply your intellect, it prevails; if passion possesses you, it holds sway, and the mind is impotent. I might <u>bring to remembrance</u> many occasions ...

> *Omnis homines, patres conscripti, qui de rebus dubiis consultant, <u>ab odio amicitia, ira atque misericordia vacuos esse</u> decet. Haud facile animus <u>verum</u> providet ubi illa officiunt, neque quisquam omnium <u>lubidini simul et usui</u> paruit. Ubi intenderis ingenium, valet; si lubido possidet, ea dominatur, animus nihil valet. Magna mihi copia est <u>memorandi</u>* ...

Omnis homines ... decet cites the beginning of the *Bellum Catilinae*, in which Sallust also muses on the capacity of *animus*, here opposed to *corpus*. The claim to impartiality and truth are prominent *topoi* of historiography that also figure in the *Bellum Catilinae*'s proem. The verb *memorare* further signals that Caesar moves into the field of the historian. The comparison that is provoked by the his-

---

[27] See the note on the year 476 CE in Marcellinus' chronicle in Croke 1983. For a survey of different approaches to the end of Rome, see Demandt 1984; on more recent contributions, see Marcone 2008.
[28] In Grethlein 2013, 283–9, I argue that besides Caesar's speech also Catiline's letter (35) encapsulates a deviant interpretation of the conspiracy.
[29] Scholarship on the two speeches is abundant: see, for example, Syme 1964, 103–20; Pöschl 1981; Drummond 1995; Sklenář 1998; Feldherr 2012. On the *synkrisis*, see especially Batstone 1988.
[30] See Sklenář 1998, 206–7; Feldherr 2012, 98–102.

toriographic and specifically Sallustian colouring yields striking differences. Caesar refers to two corner stones of Sallust's archaeology, to Carthage (51.6) and Sulla (51.32–4), but assigns them an entirely different significance. As we have seen, Sallust connects the destruction of Carthage and Sulla and the culmination of Rome's debasement with Catiline. Caesar, on the other hand, adduces Carthage and Sulla as two *exempla* that shed light on the current situation without being linked to each other. Carthage is not the beginning of Rome's decline, but a positive example of Roman clemency.[31] The senate should now be merciful with the Catilinarians just as Scipio treated Carthage clemently. Sulla, together with the rule of the thirty in Athens, serves as a negative paradigm. In contrast to the archaeology, however, Sulla is not connected with the present. Caesar even emphasises the gap between the current situation and the age of Sulla: '... and the massacre did not end until Sulla glutted all his followers with riches. For my own part, I fear nothing of that kind for Marcus Tullius or for our times ...' (... *neque prius finis iugulandi fuit quam Sulla omnis suos divitiis explevit. Atque ego haec non in M. Tullio neque his temporibus vereor ...*, 51.34–5).

Caesar does of course not present a linear account of Rome's history and evokes only select *exempla*. Nonetheless, the historiographic and Sallustian echoes draw our attention to the deviant view on the central events of the archaeology. Caesar's speech encapsulates an alternative panorama of Rome's history, a view that is much more benign than the main scenario in the *Bellum Catilinae*. Sallust 'might bring to remembrance the battlefields on which the Romans with a mere handful of men routed great armies of their adversaries, and the cities fortified by nature which they took by assault' (*Memorare possum quibus in locis maxumas hostium copias populus Romanus parva manu fuderit, quas urbis natura munitas pugnando ceperit*, 7.7), but he prefers not to do so. Caesar remarks that he 'might bring to remembrance many occasions, Fathers of the Senate, when kings and peoples under the influence of wrath or pity have made errors of judgment; but I prefer to remind you of times when our forefathers, resisting the dictates of passion, have acted justly and in order.' (*Magna mihi copia est memorandi, patres conscripti, quae reges atque populi ira aut misericordia inpulsi male consuluerint; sed ea malo dicere quae maiores nostri contra lubidinem animi sui recte atque ordine fecere*, 51.4). Caesar elaborates on the very elements that are glossed over in the main narrative. Where Sallust scents moral depravation and decline, Caesar finds a story of generosity and clemency.

---

31 On the Carthage *exemplum*, see Levene 2000, who argues for an intricate intertextual engagement: In referencing the destruction of Carthage and the Rhodians, who had betrayed the alliance with Rome in the Perses War, Caesar invokes the two most famous political interventions of Cato Censor whom he thereby contrasts with his opponent, the Younger Cato.

In addition to outlining a deviant history of Rome, Caesar's speech also intimates an alternative view of the Catilinarian conspiracy. We have seen that Sallust assigns importance to Catiline's failed putsch by casting it as the *telos* of Rome's decline. Caesar, on the other hand, envisages Catiline against the backdrop of later possible developments. He invokes not only the verdict of future generations, but also the political consequences of the trial. Sulla and the Thirty in Athens are, Caesar points out, instructive examples (51.27):

> All bad precedents have originated in cases which were good; but when the control of the government falls into the hands of men who are incompetent or bad, your new precedent is transferred from those who well deserve and merit such punishment to the undeserving and blameless.
>
> *Omnia mala exempla ex rebus bonis orta sunt. Sed ubi imperium ad ignaros eius aut minus bonos pervenit, novom illud exemplum ab dignis et idoneis ad indignos et non idoneos transfertur.*

This, Caesar claims, is relevant to the present situation. He does not expect problems with Cicero as consul, but he is worried about how an execution of the Catilinarians could be abused later in a different political constellation (51.36):

> It is possible that at another time, when someone else is consul and is likewise in command of an army, some falsehood may be believed to be true. When the consul, with this precedent before him, shall draw the sword in obedience to the senate's decree, who shall limit or restrain him?
>
> *Potest alio tempore, alio consule, quoi item exercitus in manu sit, falsum aliquid pro vero credi. Ubi hoc exemplo per senatus decretum consul gladium eduxerit, quis illi finem statuet aut quis moderabitur?*

Arguing that an execution may be abused as precedent, Caesar views the trial in anticipated retrospect; he historicises the present. Commentators have found here an allusion to actual later events. Besides Antonius, particularly Octavian with the proscriptions in 42 BCE has been discussed as the target of Sallust's veiled critique, but it has also been noted that the latter case does not exactly match the prediction.[32] While it is hard to find a single event that makes Caesar's concern a prediction, it cannot fail to adumbrate in general the extreme violence

---

[32] For a critique of Antonius, see Havas 1990, 220–1; of Octavian, see Syme 1964, 121–3; Vretska 1976, 552; Pöschl 1981, 385; of both, Perl 1969, 204. Against the critique of a specific person, see Drummond 1995, 33–6, who suggests a reference to the 'violent atmosphere of 44–3' (35), and Levene 2000, 189–90, who persuasively lists transgressions from the 40s before the triumvirate that resonate with Caesar's warning.

and abuse of power under the triumvirate and already in the preceding years. The shift of perspective, the anticipation of retrospect, is crucial to my interpretation. In viewing Catiline not as the *telos* of Rome's decline but by projecting him against the backdrop of future developments, Caesar arrives at a very different picture of 63. In the main narrative, Catiline is the climax of Rome's deterioration that starts with the capture of Carthage. For Caesar, however, a senatorial verdict that ignores the exemplary clemency towards Carthage leads to the excesses of violence against citizens in the 40s. In this scenario the heir of Sulla is not Catiline, but Cicero, who pushes the door open for the proscriptions.[33]

The main narrative of *Bellum Catilinae* and the alternative history that is encapsulated in Caesar's speech are not mutually exclusive. While the former puts the conspiracy centre stage, the latter focuses on the execution of the conspirators. We can consider the conspiracy a result of Sulla's policy and simultaneously align the execution of the Catilinarians with Sulla's proscriptions and the violence of the triumvirs. And yet, the difference between the two story lines is glaring and highlights to what extent our understanding of the past hinges on our vantage-point. Catiline's *coup d'état* looks very different when seen against the foil of later civil war or as *telos* of Rome's decline.

The subtle play with historical perspective shows us a new facet of Sallust. Batstone, Levene and Gunderson have started elucidating the complexity of Sallust's moralism.[34] Far from being a maverick thinking in black and white, Sallust gives us a nuanced portrait of Roman society. My reading ties in well with such attempts to reconsider Sallust. The presentation of Rome's history in the *Bellum Catilinae* is less monolithic as it may seem at first sight. There is space for more than one version. The archaeology describes the development after 146 as one of decline, but the alternative version embedded in Caesar's speech undercuts this narrative. For sure, the decline narrative is the main story line, which, however, does not go unchallenged. Crucial for this historiographic form of polyphony is Sallust's take on 'future past'. Like Polybius, Sallust is highly sensitive to the significance of retrospect. While Polybius responds to the instability of historical meaning by deferring the *telos* and extending his narrative, Sallust introduces an alternative *telos* that opens up an alternative view to the perspective of the major story line.

---

[33] Though such a view may be surprising at first sight, it is not unattested in antiquity. See, for example, Cassius Dio 46.20; (Sall.) *inv. in Cic.* 5–6. Cf. Grethlein 2013, 297–8.

[34] Cf. Batstone 1988; Levene 2000; Gunderson 2000.

6. The prospect of retrospect: Tacitus

Sallust has his Caesar worry that later, under different circumstances, an execution of the Catilinarians may serve to legitimise an abuse of executive power. Caesar thus anticipates the retrospective stance from which the present will be viewed as a past. Tacitus engages with a similar temporal construction and applies the prospect of retrospect specifically to historiography. That future historians are a force to be reckoned with by historical agents is pointed out in Tacitus' reflection on the use of history in *Annals* 3.65.1: [35]

> Recounting proposals has not been my established practice, except those distinguished by honourableness or of noteworthy discredit, which I deem to be a principal responsibility of annals, to prevent virtues from being silenced and so that crooked words and deeds should be attended by the dread of posterity.
>
> *Exsequi sententias haud institui nisi insignes per honestum aut notabili dedecore, quod praecipuum munus annalium reor, ne virtutes sileantur utque pravis dictis factisque ex posteritate et infamia metus sit.*

As observed by Luce, Tacitus here gives the *topos* of history's usefulness a special twist.[36] Historiography helps to shape the present not only through the evocation of an exemplary past, but also through anxiety about future records of the present.

This agenda becomes flesh and blood in the person of Cremutius Cordus who was put on trial and killed himself under Tiberius. Our evidence suggests that the trial concentrated on Cremutius' rhetorical invective against Seianus. As Tacitus presents it, however, Cremutius was driven to suicide on account of his Annals, which praised Brutus and called Cassius the last Roman (4.34–5). The trial of Cremutius forms part of a 'triptych on memory' in the *Annals*.[37] It is preceded by two chapters in which Tacitus discusses his own work by juxtaposing it with records of the Republican past (4.32–3) and followed by a speech in which honours offered by Farther Spain prompt Tiberius to ponder on memory (4.37–8). The three parts of the 'triptych' resonate with each other and yield a multifaceted reflection on memory. For the purposes of my argument here, I will confine myself to the last sentence of Cremutius' defence speech (4.35.3): 'Posterity pays to every man his due repute; and, if condemnation is closing

---

35 The syntactic construction of the sentence is debated, see Woodman 1998, 86–103.
36 Luce 1991.
37 Cancik-Lindemaier / Cancik 1986, 17. See also Grethlein 2013, 172–7 with further bibliographical references in 173 n. 123.

in on me, there will be no lack of those who remember not merely Cassius and Brutus but also myself.' (*suum cuique decus posteritas rependit; nec deerunt, si damnatio ingruit, qui non modo Cassii et Bruti, sed etiam mei meminerint.*).

Invoking future records of the present, Cremutius illustrates Tacitus' meditation on the usefulness of history in 3.65.1. What is more, as noted by commentators, Tacitus' presentation of Cremutius serves his own self-fashioning.[38] Cremutius is a mirror image that underscores the danger which he himself runs with his critical account of the principate. At the same time, Tacitus' *Annals* can be read as the very work that helps preserve the memory of Cremutius. Metaleptically, Tacitus makes his retrospect the object of prospect within his narrative. He thereby not only enmeshes past, present and future, but also blurs the boundary between *res gestae* and *historia rerum gestarum*. Cremutius is a historian, but nonetheless his and in analogy also Tacitus' work is ascribed the same political relevance as the actions of Cassius and Brutus. Writing history, it appears, is as dangerous as making history.

Tacitus' intriguing entwinement of prospect with retrospect reveals a new facet of 'future past'. The notion of 'future past' captures the temporal asymmetry between historian and historical agents. The former records the experiences of the latter from a vantage-point that was still unknown to them. At the same time, historical agents can anticipate the stance of future historians whose perspective is thereby integrated into the *res gestae*. While still asymmetrical, the relationship between *res gestae* and *historia rerum gestarum* has become reciprocal.

More generally, it can be said that even if not anticipating specifically the future verdict of historians, the expectations of historical actors prefigure the dynamic of 'future past'. Of course, the goals pursued by acting individuals do not necessarily become the *telê* from which historians envisage their deeds, but the prospects of historical agents embed in history a structure that is homologous to the retrospect on which historiography is predicated. Polybius seems to have been aware of this: in order to justify the extension of his narrative, he also comments on the intentionality of human action. He cannot end with Rome's military triumph, but has to check whether or not it proves stable: 'For nobody with reason wages war with his neighbours for the mere sake of defeating the opponents nor does he sail the oceans only to traverse them, and he does not acquire arts and crafts only for the ability. All do everything for the sweet, good and useful they derive from the activities.' (οὔτε γὰρ πολεμεῖ τοῖς πέλας οὐδεὶς νοῦν ἔχων ἕνεκεν αὐτοῦ τοῦ καταγωνίσασθαι τοὺς ἀντιταττομένους, οὔτε πλεῖ τὰ πε-

---

[38] See Sailor 2008, 291–305; McCullough 1991: 2932–3.

λάγῃ χάριν τοῦ περαιωθῆναι μόνον, καὶ μὴν οὐδὲ τὰς ἐμπειρίας καὶ τέχνας αὑτῆς ἕνεκα τῆς ἐπιστήμης ἀναλαμβάνει· πάντες δὲ πράττουσι πάντα χάριν τῶν ἐπιγινομένων τοῖς ἔργοις ἡδέων ἢ καλῶν ἢ συμφερόντων, 3.4.10). In aligning his *telos* with the intentions of the historical agents, Polybius drives home that the historian's view of the past in the light of later events is prefigured in the orientation of historical agents towards the future.

7. Future past and the rule of time

The last two decades have seen major re-assessments of ancient historiography. With the help of narratology, scholars have examined how Greek and Roman historians convey their interpretation of the past through the form of their accounts.[39] Focalisation, narratorial persona and temporal organisation are powerful tools in the hands of Thucydides & Co. Historical meaning is often constructed less in explicit comments than in narrative form. It has also proven fruitful to investigate the political dimension of ancient historiography. Herodotus writes not only the history of the Persian Wars, but also scrutinises, if obliquely, contemporary Athens.[40] Tacitus' writing can be understood better if seen as part of his political career.[41]

My investigation of teleology homes in on a new aspect that may be no less fundamental. Historiography, I contend, is also an engagement with temporality.[42] Life confronts us with an open future. What will be depends on many factors that are beyond our control. The past, however, is free of this insecurity. Looking back, we see the sway of time over humans without being exposed to it ourselves. Retrospect lets us overcome contingency to which we are subject in our own lives. Unlike the historical agents we know where history is headed and can see the past in the light of its future. Hindsight lets us replace the fragility of our lives with sovereignty. Thucydides claims to write history while it is happening, but despite its annalistic structure and experiential appeal, his *History of the Peloponnesian War* clearly takes its cue from Athens' downfall in 404 BCE. Herodotus' oblique comments on contemporary politics bespeak, I think, the insight that history can only be written in retrospect.

---

39 See, for example, Hornblower 1994a; Marincola 1997; Rood 1998. The emphasis on the rhetorical character of ancient historiography by Wiseman 1979 and Woodman 1988 was seminal for works focusing on historiography as narrative.
40 See the titles listed in n. 19
41 Sailor 2008.
42 See Grethlein 2013; 2014b.

And yet, as Tacitus' play with the prospect of retrospect intimates, the wall between *res gestae* and *historia rerum gestarum* is more porous than it may first seem. Tacitus makes a case for the salience of historiography as part of history. On the other hand, the vagaries of historical time also infiltrate the seemingly closed world of historiographic reconstruction. Especially the works of Polybius and Sallust reflect the continuous proliferation of new vantage-points that make us see the past anew. Viewed from the *telos* of Roman hegemony, the events of the third and second centuries BCE yield a coherent picture, but what remains of this picture once the rule of Rome crumbles? Seen as the peak of Roman decadence, Catiline's *coup d'état* appears as the ultimate threat to the Republic, but the proscriptions of the 40s let us reconsider the execution of the Catilinarians as the trigger of even greater evil. As narrators of the past, we are able to control time in a manner not possible in our own lives, and yet this control is not without limits. The openness of the future that makes our lives so hard to control survives in the form of 'future past', in the significance of the future of the past for our understanding of the past. The flux of time to which historians as well as historical agents are subject precludes historical meaning from being stable. Historiography calms the flow of time, but is unable to arrest it fully.

Emily Greenwood
Futures Real and Unreal in Greek Historiography

Unsurprisingly, the real future – events that have yet to occur at the time of writing – tends to lose out to the past in the writing of history. 'Historians deal with the past', as the editors of a recent volume on the plupast in Ancient Historiography remind us.[1] From the point of view of ancient Greek historiography, the extra-textual future is a fiction, like the term 'speculative fiction' that is increasingly used to describe science fiction. And yet, another mode of the future, what I call 'the unreal, diegetic future', is omnipresent in the writing of history. Firstly, the future is present as tense, in both narratorial and actorial voices: Herodotus telling us how his narrative will proceed at 1.5.3, or Croesus advising Cyrus in Herodotus that, 'if you lose the battle [against the Massagetae] you will lose a whole empire' (1.207.3). Secondly, in narratological terms, the proleptic future is fundamental to the very structure of historical accounts, where the intimations of events and information that is present to the historian but in the actors' future is vital to the flow of knowledge, or what Rancière calls the 'poetics of knowledge' in history.[2] Again, Herodotus furnishes us with an apt example:

> However, the oracular pronouncement was favourable and so Gyges became king of Lydia. However, the Pythia qualified her declaration by saying that for the Heraclidae vengeance would come on the fourth in descent from Gyges. But neither the Lydians nor their kings took any notice of this prediction until it was fulfilled.
>
> (*Histories* 1.13.2; transl. Waterfield 1998: 8)[3]

Alternatively, we might think of a more striking extra-diegetic prolepsis like the authorial remark that the Athenians capitulated to their Greek allies so as not to risk internal dissension, 'but, as they later demonstrated, only for as long as they badly needed the rest of the Greeks' (*Histories*, 8.3.2). Prolepsis and other narratological devices in Greek historiographical narratives have been the subject of fruitful research.[4] Recently Jonas Grethlein has argued for an approach to temporality in historical narratives that combines narratological analysis with an

---
[1] Grethlein and Krebs 2012a, 1.
[2] Rancière 1994 [1992].
[3] Unless otherwise stated, all translations from Herodotus cited in this essay are from Waterfield's translation (published in the Oxford World's Classics series).
[4] See Hornblower 1994a, Rood 1998, de Jong 2001.

awareness of the work that narrative structures do in recreating historical experience.[5] In this analysis, a narratological approach that focuses on the posterior, teleological perspective of the historian is balanced by consideration of the ways in which historical narratives attempt to capture the present and future of historical experience including past futures or 'futures past' (the future as experienced by historical actors in the past).[6]

In contrast to the various narrative futures studied in narratology, the 'real' future, which is still in the future for the author and therefore genuinely unknown or known only speculatively, is much rarer. An example is Thucydides' speculation at 2.54.3–4 that 'I fancy at any rate that if another Dorian war should visit them after this one (τοῦδε ὕστερος) and if that were accompanied by a famine they will probably recite the verse (ᾄσονται) that way.'[7] While in historiographical terms to speak of 'the real past' or 'what really happened' is to naively overlook the inextricable narrativity of his past,[8] I submit that the 'real future' is a less problematic concept since, by definition, it lies outside of the scope of the narrative and the historian's experience.[9] Paradoxically, it is its very unreality at the time of writing that guarantees its reality.

Although the real future is rare, the prospective future significance of historical accounts of the past pervades ancient Greek historiography. This prospective past – a past with a strong future orientation – is neatly articulated in Michael Oakeshott's pragmatic philosophical account of 'the practical past' – a conception of the past predicated on the relay of past-present-future:

> Here, time is a relation between a present and an imagined future condition of things relative to ourselves. Thus, the present we occupy in practical understanding evokes future. Indeed, it evokes a variety of futures: a conjectural future, a future foreseen, one which (in addition) evokes fear or in which we have invested our hopes, an intended and sought-for future etc., but always a future related to and of the same kind as this present. With every want we evoke a future, and in every action we seek a future condition of things,

---

[5] See Grethlein 2013, ch.1, "Introduction: 'Futures Past': Historiography between Experience and Teleology".

[6] Redeploying and adapting Koselleck's concept of the 'vergangene Zukunft' ('future past', or 'former future'), Koselleck 2004 [1979].

[7] Transl. Mynott 2013, 123. Unless otherwise stated, all translations of Thucydides cited in this essay are taken from Mynott's translation.

[8] From among a vast literature, I am thinking here of Paul Ricoeur's critique of the complex epistemological challenges that historiography poses for any analysis of the 'reality of the historical past' – Ricoeur 1984.

[9] Which is not to say that the 'real' future lies beyond narrative strategies of representation; after all, it can only have meaning for us as a result of narrative. See Abbott 2005.

uncertain of achievement and sure only of its transience. In short, this present of practical engagement is not merely intermittently related to future; it is itself a present-future.[10]

Oakeshott's formulation helps to explain the trend in recent scholarship to analyse the prospective, future-oriented significance of Thucydides' historical narrative. I cite three examples of this trend. Tim Rood's 1998 book *Thucydides: Narrative and Explanation* ends with a chapter entitled 'The Ends of History', which caps the preceding analysis of the explanatory work that Thucydidean narrative does (with its point of view, selection, omission and temporal structure) with the argument that, 'Thucydides does not just try to make the past comprehensible by the way he tells his story, he also tries to make the future comprehensible by the broader categories to which he appeals'.[11] Similarly, Lisa Kallett has argued that Thucydides' statement of the utility of his work at 1.22.4 suggests that, 'understanding the text is merely the means to an end, namely the understanding of events other than the Peloponnesian War'.[12] In a study of Thucydides' shaping of his readers, James Morrison suggests two types of reader, the 'engaged' or 'participatory' reader, who projects himself into the situations Thucydides presents, and the 'retrospective' reader, both of whom learn not only how to read Thucydides' text with discernment, but also how to compare events in the past and present and thereby anticipate the likely course of future events.[13] In this respect, recent scholarship on Thucydides sees a close relationship between unreal, diegetic, futures (specifically the chronological progress of the narrative where the reader reads forward into time) and real futures that transcend not only narrative time, but the author's and reader's temporal horizons as well.

In this essay I hope to build upon existing work on the relationship between real and unreal futures in Greek historiography by suggesting that the description of the future was one obvious area of inter-generic comparison, particularly in contexts where there was intense competition among different technologies of knowledge in the Greek world in the fifth and fourth centuries BCE.[14] Utility is

---

10 Oakeshott 1983, 13.
11 Rood 1998, 286.
12 Kallett 2006, 336–7.
13 Morrison 2006, 14–17. More recently still, Morrison's approach is endorsed by Grethlein 2010, 277, who has a section on 'The Usefulness of the *History*' (*ibid.*, 268–279).
14 The phrase 'inter-generic comparison' is indebted to the phrase 'inter-generic competition', which Nightingale applied to the intellectual context of the Platonic dialogues (Nightingale 1995). I use the phrase 'technologies of knowledge' to signify the circulation of different branches of knowledge, based on *logoi* and / or *technai* that were in circulation in this period and which offered rival accounts of history, society, culture, human nature, natural science and theories of knowledge.

the fundamental basis for comparing different technologies of knowledge in this period, and since the criterion of usefulness is inescapably future-oriented (how will *x* help to do *y?*), genres and types of knowledge were competing over their respective advice for, and visions of, the future.

Recent scholarship has rightly stressed the trans-generic nature of the commemoration of the past in ancient Greek cultures, and in extant Greek literature.[15] Prose genres were preceded by a rich tradition of remembering the past in poetry and song, and historiography did not have a monopoly on history, in the sense of the events of the past and its remains.[16] If historiography did not have a monopoly on the past, ostensibly it had even less of a monopoly over the future than other genres, including those in prose. Rosalind Thomas's *Herodotus in Context*[17] demonstrated the extent to which Herodotus' *Histories* were part of a larger, competitive intellectual scene in which experts offered lectures, treatises and longer works on ethnography, anthropology, natural philosophy and medicine. I argue that it is this very consciousness of alternative technologies of knowledge that explains historians' concern with future and futurity: with identifying specific ways in which the critical analysis of the past that we find in history might help in the present-future of the readers. The discussion of the potential futurity of Greek historiography has tended to focus on analogies with early Greek science and with medicine – specifically the *technē* of prognosis,[18] but here I want to foreground analogies between Greek historiography and the future-oriented 'genre' of sumbouleutic oratory, taking Thucydides' *History* as a case-study. Other scholars before me have argued for the political significance of Thucydides' work; I propose to strengthen and supplement this argument with a focus on the prospective, practical past and by pointing to some forceful parallels between Thucydides' text and extant sumbouleutic oratory. I will turn to potential analogies between historiography and Hippocratic medical treatises in the second part of my argument to offer a fresh account of shared attitudes to time-rich inquiry in Greek medicine and historiography.

---

15 On commemorating the past in local history, see Clarke 2008, and on the inter-generic commemoration of the past in archaic and classical Greek literature see Grethlein 2010.
16 An argument made comprehensively in Grethlein 2010.
17 Thomas 2000.
18 See Rutherford 1994.

Real and unreal futures in Thucydides

Of the extant ancient Greek historians, Thucydides offers us the most fertile text for thinking about real and unreal futures, because both figure prominently in the self-presentation of his *History*. The subtlety of the temporal nexus that underwrites Thucydides' ambitious historical project is already apparent in the first sentence of the *History*, in which the work that we are now reading is presented as the product of a past and finite process of recording (the aorist ξυνέγραψε), motivated by Thucydides' expectation, at a certain point in the past, that it would be a great war (ἐλπίσας μέγαν τε ἔσεσθαι), and more worthy of account than any previous conflict. The aorists ξυνέγραψε and ἐλπίσας signal a past projection of the future (ἔσεσθαι) and record the temporal horizons at the outbreak of the war when its future was unknown. And yet this anticipated future is a diegetic, unreal future: constructed by a narrator for whom that future was in the past by the time he was writing up the *History*.[19] This is not to deny that Thucydides, the general and author, could have had a strong grasp of the magnitude and probable historical significance of the war at its outbreak in 431 BCE, but rather to point out that we have no unmediated access to that forecast of the future as a historical testimony. In its place we have a diegetic future where a narrator looks back on past projections of an unfolding war from the benefit of hindsight. In one sense all presentiments and forecasts of the future in narrative are 'diegetic', but in the sense in which I intend it here, a 'diegetic future' is a future that is a construction of narrative because it is already past at the point of narration.

The difference between a real prediction for the future and an unreal, diegetic future is evident if we compare the first chapter of Thucydides' *History* with Vera Brittain's account of another 'great' war during which she kept a daily diary and about which she subsequently wrote a retrospective memoir, *Testament of Youth*, reflecting on her war-time experiences. The diary was not published in the author's lifetime (1893–1970), but instead furnished excerpts for her memoir *Testament of Youth: An Autobiographical Study of the Years 1900–1925*, which was published in 1933, some fifteen years after the end of the First World War. Brittain's diary entries in early August 1914 convey a sense of excitement, uncertainty and foreboding in view of the scale of the imminent war:

---

19 I use a past continuous tense here to acknowledge the incompleteness of the *History*, which he never finished 'writing up'.

> To-day has been far too exciting to enable me to feel at all like sleep – in fact it is one of the most thrilling I have ever lived through, though without doubt there are many more to come. That which has been so long anticipated by some & scoffed by others has come to pass at last – Armageddon in Europe![20]
>
> Late as it is & almost too excited to write as I am, I must make some effort to chronicle the stupendous events of this remarkable day. The situation is absolutely unparalleled in the history of the world. Never before has the war strength of each individual nation been of such great extent, even though all the nations of Europe, the dominant continent, have been armed before. It is estimated that when the war begins *14 millions* of men will be engaged in the conflict. Attack is possible by earth, water & air, & the destruction attainable by the modern war machines used by the armies is unthinkable & past imagination. [...] (p.87) Stupendous events come so thick and fast after one another that it is impossible to realize to any extent their full import. [...] To sum up the situation in any way is impossible, every hour brings fresh & momentous events & one must stand still & await catastrophes each even more terrible than the last.[21]

In this case, the future projection of the war and its anticipated course is a real future, in that it is written at the outbreak of the war and the writer, writing synchronously with the events that she is narrating, has no knowledge of their outcome. In that sense the diary offers us an historical account of a future imagined and anticipated.[22] In her autobiographical memoir, written with the benefit of hindsight and with undisguised disillusionment about the war, the emphasis that Brittain places on the days described in the diary entries above, and her state of mind during them, is rather different. In fact, she plays down the testimony of the diary entry for August 3rd and the following days, choosing instead to strike a more meditative tone and to focus on the tragic loss of life in war. Tellingly, Brittain splices diary entries from different points of time in order to present a less ephemeral and impressionistic response to the unfolding war:[23]

> My diary for those few days reflects *The Times* in its most pontifical mood. "Germany has broken treaty after treaty, and disregarded every honourable tie with other nations ... Germany has destroyed the tottering hopes of peace. ....." I prefer to think that my real sentiments were more truly represented by an entry written nearly a month later after the fab-

---

[20] Extract from Brittain's diary entry for Monday August 3rd 1914: Brittain 2000 [1981], 84.
[21] Extract from Brittain's diary entry for Monday August 3rd 1914: Brittain 2000 [1981], quoting from pp. 85 and 87.
[22] This is not to imply that diaries offer simple windows onto past futures, since diary writers can play all kinds of elaborate tricks with time, address future audiences, and engage in prospective hindsight. However, so long as diaries remain unedited, projections of the future involve a future that is real and unknown.
[23] Of her diary entry for August 3rd Brittain writes, 'My diary for August 3rd, 1914, contains a most incongruous mixture of war and tennis' (2005 [1933], 94).

ulously optimistic reports of the Battle of Le Cateau. I had been over to Newcastle-Under-Lyme to visit the family dentist, and afterwards sat for an hour in a tree-shadowed walk called The Brampton and meditated on the War. It was one of those shimmering autumn days when every leaf and flower seems to scintillate with light, and I found it "very hard to believe that not far away men were being slain ruthlessly, and their poor disfigured bodies heaped together and crowded in ghastly indiscrimination into quickly provided common graves as though they were nameless vermin … It is impossible," I concluded, "to find any satisfaction in the thought of 25,000 slaughtered Germans, left to mutilation and decay; the destruction of men as though beasts, whether they be English, French, German or anything else, seems a crime to the whole march of civilization."[24]

In the Foreword to *Testament of Youth*, reflecting on the diary from which the extracts quoted above were taken, Brittain acknowledges the cognitive gap between the perspective of her diary entries and the retrospective reflections in her Memoirs.[25] Whether one regards the contemporary reactions of the younger Brittain, recorded in her diary, or the jaded testimony of her Memoirs almost two decades later, as a more 'accurate' account of the War and what it meant to those who lived through it, is a matter for serious and ongoing historical debate. A deep, representative account of British attitudes to the First World War should include both contemporary sources that reflect the complex range of attitudes to the war on the part of civilians and retrospective accounts that show how these attitudes shifted over the course of the war. In terms of 'past futures', Vera Brittain as autobiographical narrator of the *Testimony* edits the future as perceived by her younger self, Vera Brittain the diary writer. In the *Memoirs*, the result is an edited, strictly diegetic, elapsed future and therefore an unreal future.

The comparison with Brittain's diary brings out the conceit in play at the beginning of Thucydides' narrative where he is simultaneously diarist (starting to write up the war as soon as it started) and retrospective historian, presenting us with an edited account of the war. The contemporary perspective is reiterated at 5.26, where Thucydides defends his temporalisation of the war as a single conflict lasting twenty-seven years, as opposed to a series of related conflicts. In support of his judgment he cites the fact that he lived through the war in its entirety, was of an age where his powers of perception were sharp, and focused his attention on the war continually (5.26.5):

---

24 Brittain 2005 [1933], 96–97.
25 Brittain 2005 [1993], 12 'I have also made as much use as possible of old letters and diaries, because it seemed to me that the contemporary opinions, however crude and ingenuous, of youth in the period under review were at least as important a part of its testament as retrospective reflections heavy with knowledge.'

> ἐπεβίων δὲ διὰ παντὸς αὐτοῦ αἰσθανόμενός τε τῇ ἡλικίᾳ καὶ προσέχων τὴν γνώμην, ὅπως ἀκριβές τι εἴσομαι·
>
> I lived through the whole of it when I was of an age to appreciate what was going on and could apply my mind to an exact understanding of things.

In the Greek, two present participles underscore this sense of Thucydides' observation of the war in real time: αἰσθανόμενος and προσέχων. In fact, to bring out the vivid, continuous present, the participles should perhaps be translated as 'being of an age to perceive what was going on' (αἰσθανόμενος τε τῇ ἡλικίᾳ), and 'paying attention from moment to moment' (προσέχων τὴν γνώμην). The cumulative effect of these present continuous participles is to remind us of the opening sentence of the work and Thucydides' claim that he started writing as soon as the war began, with the implication that he wrote it up in real time. Although this self-presentation is later modified when we read, at 1.22.1–3, about Thucydides' historical research, his interviewing of various informants, the inevitable reliance on memory, and the need to review and edit different sources of information, there is still a powerful impression of contemporary history that is synchronous with the events described and which faces an unknown future.

The play on tenses that belies the intricate temporal layering of the *History* is also evident in the well-known statement at 1.22.4, where Thucydides expresses the hope that future readers[26] who want to gain a clear perspective on past events and future events will consider his work useful: 'τῶν μελλόντων ποτὲ αὖθις κατὰ τὸ ἀνθρώπινον τοιούτων καὶ παραπλησίων ἔσεσθαι'.[27] But a pertinent question, and one which is too seldom asked, is *whose* future events? The combination of a futuritive verb (μέλλω) and a future infinitive distracts us from the indeterminacy of the future in question. Does Thucydides mean the future from his point of view: i.e. readers of the future will consult his history to get a clear perspective on events that are in the present for them, but in the future for Thucydides? Or will they also use his *History* to gain an insight into the likely outcome of events in their futures? Arnold Gomme tackled this question head on:

> It should not be necessary, but it is, to explain that is future to Thucydides, not to his readers: the latter will not find his work useful in order to divine what will happen in the future, as though it were a sort of horoscope, but for the understanding of other events besides the Peloponnesian War, future to Thucydides, but past or contemporary to the reader.[28]

---

26 The future is contained in the tense of the verb: 'As many as will want' (ὅσοι δὲ βουλήσονται).
27 '[have a clear view of] what – the human condition being what it is – can be expected to happen again some time in the future in similar or much the same ways'.
28 Gomme 1956, 149.

As Gomme notes, while the famous phrase κτῆμα ἐς αἰεί suggests that the work will not expire and that successive generations of readers will find that it contains material that is relevant for their own time, this is not the same as saying that readers will be able to get a sense of plausible futures from reading the *History*.[29] The most recent challenge to Gomme's objection has come from Roberto Nicolai, who has used a study of the fourth century reception of Thucydides to make a convincing argument for the political application of the *History* as a practical resource for political decision-making.[30] Building on Nicolai's arguments, I adduce specific parallels with extant sumbouleutic oratory to make a robust case for the futurition of the *History*. I submit that Thucydides deliberately sketches an open, indeterminate future, which projects the usefulness of his *History* not just for future generations of readers as they contemplate contemporary history, but as they contemplate potential futures as well.

Thucydides' temporalisation of history is characterised by a subtle blurring of real, as yet unknown futures on the one hand, and unreal diegetic futures on the other hand. In what follows, I argue that the strong accent on the future at 1.22.4 is to be explained through recourse to the intellectual culture of late fifth-century Athens, in which practical usefulness was an important criterion for evaluating knowledge and for comparing rival claims to expertise. When evaluating knowledge on pragmatic grounds, prospective advice about the future was deemed especially useful for civic communities. Recall Thucydides' obituary for the Athenian general Themistocles, which dwells on his native intelligence and underscores his capacity for accurately assessing the outcome of future events (1.138.3):

> καὶ τῶν μελλόντων ἐπὶ πλεῖστον τοῦ γενησομένου ἄριστος εἰκαστής … τό τε ἄμεινον ἢ χεῖρον ἐν τῷ ἀφανεῖ ἔτι προεώρα μάλιστα.
>
> [Themistocles was] supremely good at envisaging future events very fully … and he could always see in advance the better and worse options in a still uncertain future.

The phrase 'τῶν μελλόντων' echoes Thucydides' framing of the value of his own work at 1.22.4. In this instance, the extraordinariness of Themistocles' ability to envisage or conjecture the future is stressed by what we might call a 'double future' construction: Thucydides describes Themistocles as the best conjecturer of 'what

---

29 *Ibid*. On κτῆμα ἐς αἰεί, see Bakker 2006, 122: 'the modifier ἐς αἰεί suggests a more dynamic permanency as well. The work is presented as an asset for each new generation of readers, thus conveying the idea of an eternal process no less than the idea of an eternal materiality: Thucydides' bond with his readership is renewed across generations.' In an accompanying note (*ibid.*, n.38) Bakker suggests an analogy with the phrase τῶν αἰεί παρόντων at 1.22.1.
30 Nicolai 2009, 390–391 and *passim* (this article was first published in 1995).

would happen' (*tou genēsomenou*), which is itself a dependent genitive of *tōn mellontōn* – (of) things to come. This is to construe the neuter plural participle *ta mellonta* as a substantive: 'things to come', 'the future', which is the meaning that the standard lexicon suggests for this passage.³¹ But the participle may also retain the sense 'to be likely / probable', in which case the translation of this double future construction would be something like, 'with regard to probable future events he was the best conjecturer of what would actually happen'. The point is that, while all political leaders were expected to offer informed projections of the future (the kind of probabilistic reckonings implied by 'τῶν μελλόντων ... εἰκαστής'), Themistocles had a more refined instinct for envisaging what would actually happen. Jeremy Mynott hints at this with the phrase 'very fully': 'supremely good at envisaging future events very fully'; but Martin Hammond's translation best captures Thucydides' precise point, 'supreme in conjecturing the future, more accurate than any in his forecast of events as they would actually happen'.³²

Thucydides highlights foresight in his depiction of other political leaders in the *History*, reflecting a broader conception of political intelligence in which the ability to offer reliable projections of the future in speeches was integral to the politician's role of advising the city. Hence Diodotus' rejoinder to Cleon's critique of speechmaking in the Mytilene debate: 'As for words (*logoi*), anyone who argues seriously that they should not guide our actions is either stupid or has some personal interest at stake: stupid, if he thinks there is any other way to explore the future (*to mellon*) in all its uncertainty; ...' (3.42.2).³³ This pragmatic, political conception of knowledge influenced Thucydides' case for his *History*: his work will suffice if it is judged useful by those who want a clear insight into past events and events that are likely to happen in much the same way in the future. Readers have noted an allusion to the formulae for the public scrutiny of inscribed decrees in democratic Athens in the phrase *hosoi boulēsontai skopein* at 1.22.4, but the stress on the likely course of future events also recalls the preoccupation with the future in assembly debates both in Thucydides' *History* and in extant sumbouleutic (deliberative) oratory from the fourth century BCE.

Demosthenes' *First Olynthiac* begins by acknowledging that what Athenians most want from their political leaders in the present crisis is a reliable forecast of

---

31 LSJ – Liddell, Scott, Jones 1968, s.v. μέλλω IV.
32 Hammond 2009, 67
33 τούς τε λόγους ὅστις διαμάχεται μὴ διδασκάλους τῶν πραγμάτων γίγνεσθαι, ἢ ἀξύνετός ἐστιν ἢ ἰδίᾳ τι αὐτῷ διαφέρει· ἀξύνετος μέν, εἰ ἄλλῳ τινὶ ἡγεῖται περὶ τοῦ μέλλοντος δυνατὸν εἶναι καὶ μὴ ἐμφανοῦς φράσαι ...

future events.³⁴ In this instance he suggests that his audience in the Assembly would pay a large sum of money in return for the most advantageous policy to be made visible:

> Ἀντὶ πολλῶν ἄν, ὦ ἄνδρες Ἀθηναῖοι, χρημάτων ὑμᾶς ἑλέσθαι νομίζω, εἰ φανερὸν γένοιτο <u>τὸ μέλλον συνοίσειν τῇ πόλει</u> περὶ ὧν νυνὶ σκοπεῖτε. ὅτε τοίνυν τοῦθ᾽ οὕτως ἔχει, προσήκει προθύμως ἐθέλειν ἀκούειν τῶν βουλομένων συμβουλεύειν.³⁵

As he proceeds to tell them, in the circumstances, the next best thing is to listen to those who would advise them (συμβουλεύειν). This language is echoed at the close of the *Third Olynthiac*, where Demosthenes concludes that he has said what he considers to be in the city's interest (ἃ νομίζω συμφέρειν) and entrusts the decision about what will benefit the city to his audience: ὑμεῖς δ᾽ ἕλοισθ᾽ ὅ τι καὶ τῇ πόλει καὶ ἅπασι συνοίσειν ὑμῖν μέλλει.³⁶ The implication is that his three speeches have revealed to the Athenians what will benefit the city in the future, as implicitly promised at the beginning of the first *Olynthiac*.

Turning back to Thucydides, there are clear parallels with 1.22.4, with its stress on useful knowledge and on the relevance of Thucydides' account for giving readers a clear insight into both past events and probable future events. Thucydides has the adjective ὠφέλιμος (useful, beneficial), where Demosthenes has the verb συμφέρειν (to be beneficial for / to, to be in one's interests), and both tie the usefulness of their account / advice to its ability to offer a projection of the future.

The strong association between prospective knowledge about the future and sumbouleutic rhetoric in contemporary Greek thought is clearer still in Aristotle's *Rhetoric*. One of the ways in which Aristotle distinguishes between the different species / types (εἴδη) of rhetoric — in addition to different categories of audience – is in respect of their orientation to past, present and future time (χρόνος):³⁷

> χρόνοι δὲ ἑκάστου τούτων εἰσὶ τῷ μὲν συμβουλεύοντι ὁ μέλλων (περὶ γὰρ τῶν ἐσομένων συμβουλεύει ἢ προτρέπων ἢ ἀποτρέπων), τῷ δὲ δικαζομένῳ ὁ γενόμενος (περὶ γὰρ τῶν πεπραγμένων ἀεὶ ὁ μὲν κατηγορεῖ, ὁ δὲ ἀπολογεῖται), τῷ δ᾽ ἐπιδεικτικῷ κυριώτατος μὲν ὁ παρών (κατὰ γὰρ τὰ ὑπάρχοντα ἐπαινοῦσιν ἢ ψέγουσιν πάντες) ...

---

34 The crisis in question is the Athenians' response to Philip of Macedon's attack on the allied *polis* of Olynthus in Northern Greece in 349 BCE.
35 Demosthenes *Olynthiac* I.1, 'You would, I expect, men of Athens, accept it as the equivalent of a large amount of money, if it could be made clear to you what will prove our best policy in the matters now under discussion'.
36 Demosthenes, *Olynthiac* III.36, σχεδὸν εἴρηχ᾽ ἃ νομίζω συμφέρειν· ὑμεῖς δ᾽ ἕλοισθ᾽ ὅ τι καὶ τῇ πόλει καὶ ἅπασι συνοίσειν ὑμῖν μέλλει ('I have now said almost all that I consider suitable. It is for you to choose what is likely to benefit the city and all of you').
37 *Rhetoric* 1358a36.

Each of these has its own "time": for the deliberative speaker, the future (for whether exhorting or dissuading he advises about future events), for the speaker in court, the past (for he always prosecutes or defends concerning what he has done); in epideictic the present is the most important; for all speakers praise or blame in regard to existing qualities ...[38]

Prior to this passage, when distinguishing between different categories of listener, Aristotle identifies the member of an assembly meeting as 'an example of one judging about future happenings' (ἔστιν δ' ὁ μὲν περὶ τῶν μελλόντων κρίνων ὁ ἐκκλησιαστής), while the juror is an example of one judging the past (περὶ τῶν γεγενημένων).[39] In staking out the temporal span of his *History* as offering a clear picture of both past events and future events, Thucydides likens the content of his work to two major sources of contemporary political knowledge, namely deliberative and judicial rhetoric. At the same time, Thucydides' reader / listener is cast in the role of a judge through the use of the vocabulary of *krisis* (ὠφέλιμα κρίνειν αὐτὰ – 1.22.4).[40] The implicit charge to the reader is to read / listen to this work and then deliberate about its usefulness for developing a clear, accurate understanding of the past, a reliable guide to present events as they unfold, and to probable future events.

In spite of the significant gap between the composition of Thucydides' *History* (431 – ca. 404 BCE), Demosthenes' *Olynthiac* orations in 349 BCE, and Aristotle's *Rhetoric*, these parallels suggest that Thucydides envisaged the value of his history in political terms, through analogy with the kind of information that benefits the *polis* in sumbouleutic oratory. Aristotle's analysis of sumbouleutic rhetoric is particularly pertinent here, because its normative classification of modes and techniques of rhetoric is culled from the fullest possible study of the practice of different types of rhetoric in Greece, including rhetoric as it was practised in Thucydides' day.[41]

The major difference between Thucydides, Demosthenes and the political orators whom Aristotle has in mind in his analysis of sumbouleutic rhetoric is that in 1.22.4 the future is actually visible to Thucydides the writer in ways in which it is not visible to the politician speaking in the assembly, because Thucydides has

---

[38] *Rhetoric* 1358b13–18, transl. Kennedy 1991.
[39] *Rhetoric* 1358b2–5.
[40] Listener – cf. the verb ἀκούειν at 1.22.4. While I understand Thucydides' *History* as a work primarily to be read, rather than performed, I also imagine that this reading had a strong acoustic dimension (see Greenwood 2006, 14–17).
[41] See, recently, Pelling 2012, for a careful discussion of the *Rhetorica ad Alexandrum* and Aristotle's *Rhetoric* as works that arguably engage with Thucydidean speeches and provide valuable independent evidence for the context of fifth century political oratory on which Thucydides drew.

seen how the war plays out.⁴² As to the question of how the war might have played out differently and how the Athenians might have avoided their most costly mistakes, Thucydides has suggestions, which further contribute to the deliberative texture of his *History*.⁴³

Enduring knowledge in history and medicine

The argument that I have presented here about the close relationship between the futurity of Thucydides' *History* and the practical, future-oriented political counsel that survives in sumbouleutic oratory does not entail the assumption that Thucydides subscribed to a positivistic, quasi-scientific conception of history or that he imagined that the insights of his *History* would easily translate into other scenarios that followed set, historical patterns.⁴⁴ Instead, the minimal assumption — and one that I think has been ably demonstrated by James Morrison and others — is that Thucydides expected readers to learn critical historical analysis from reading and studying his *History*.⁴⁵ In revisiting intellectual affinities between Thucydides and the Hippocratic Corpus I do not wish to imply that Thucydides conceived of history in terms of medicine, but rather that there are two-

---

42 This apparent difference raises interesting questions about the revision and publication of sumbouleutic speeches, like Demosthenes' *Olynthiacs*, by their authors. In the case of revised, published speeches, orators would have the benefit of hindsight. For the argument that deliberative speeches were not revised and published by their authors, see Trevett 1996.
43 See Grethlein 2010, 250–251 on Thucydides' use of 'sideshadowing' devices that help to tease out contingency in history and the openness of the past. Grethlein 2013 revisits side-shadowing in the context of the experiential historical narrative, where 'side-shadowing' enables readers of historical narratives to re-experience the past and to consider alternative, counterfactual outcomes (see, especially, Grethlein 2013, 13–14, and 45).
44 Stahl 2003, 15 ff. provides a helpful critique of this scientific, positivistic tradition of Thucydidean criticism, which he traces to a 'utilitarian interpretation' of 1.22.4. See *ibid*, p.16: 'All such interpretations – even when they do not expressly begin from the positivist thesis – share the assumption that Thucydides, on principle, considered the forces at work in political events rationally comprehensible and therefore was able to pursue a more or less practical goal with his work.' However, I would disagree with Stahl on the grounds that one can argue that Thucydides had ambitions for the practical, political utility of his work without subscribing to the idea that he believed in rational laws of history and human nature. Hawthorn 2012 offers a refreshing discussion of the enduring political significance of Thucydides' historical account which gives due attention to his history of 'political unreason': 'We can come away from his story with the conviction that what will happen in his future – our present, and our future also – will be as unreasoned as what happened in his time' – Hawthorn 2012, 225.
45 See Kallett, Morrison, and Rood, quoted on p. 81 above.

way analogies to be drawn between the ways in which both intellectual disciplines ground arguments for their useful expertise in time-intensive research, the fruits of which they expect to last.

Comparison with the Hippocratic corpus brings the trans-generic preoccupation with the future benefits of past and present knowledge and expertise into sharp focus. The early works in the Hippocratic corpus, dating from the mid- to late fifth century BCE, are contemporary with the composition and circulation of the Histories of Herodotus and Thucydides. One does not have to look far to find the future in the Hippocratic texts. Medicine is an inherently prospective science: in the Hippocratic corpus all of the diagnosis and collection of information about the past (the patient's lifestyle and the 'history' of the disease) is in the interest of anticipating the course of the disease and likely outcomes for the patient. In the corpus that has been transmitted there are three authentic prognostic works ('authentic' insofar as they are confidently attributed to the School of Cos); these are *Prognostic* and *Prorrhetic I* and *II*, which date from the middle and the second half of the fifth century BCE.[46] The later 'prognostic' work, *Precepts*, thought to date from the Hellenistic age, is also admissible in this context because it culls material from other works in the corpus and thus reflects diachronic teaching about prognosis in different medical schools. The importance of the language of prognostication and prediction for Herodotus and Thucydides is well known, including the use of signs / evidence to make inferences about probable outcomes.[47] However, here I want to argue for another analogy between Greek historiography and Greek medicine; instead of focusing on the influence of the latter on the former, I will point to similarities between the way in which each field of expertise represents the connection between past research and future knowledge.

In addition to the prognostic works, all of the works in the Hippocratic corpus are acutely time-conscious. Consider the famous beginning of the treatise *Aphorisms* (1.1):

Ὁ βίος βραχὺς, ἡ δὲ τέχνη μακρὴ, ὁ δὲ καιρὸς ὀξὺς, ἡ δὲ πεῖρα σφαλερὴ, ἡ δὲ κρίσις χαλεπή.[48]

Life is short, the Art long, opportunity fleeting, experiment treacherous, judgment difficult.

---

46 Following Jouanna 1999, who argues for the probable attribution of *Prorrhetic* II, rejected by Littré, to the author of *Prognostic*.
47 For the latter, see Hollmann 2011, 253, who draws an analogy between the language of Herodotus and the author of *Prorrhetic* II.
48 Littré Vol. 4; transl. W.H.S. Jones 1931, Loeb Hippocrates Vol. IV.

Here we have a succinct statement of what is at stake in the *technē* of Greek medicine: the laborious and time-consuming study of cases – both those that the physician has seen with his own eyes and those that he has read about in treatises. These cases are a necessary propaedeutic for the physician's encounter with the disease or with the patient, which is characterised by a lack of time and, indeed, is time-critical: the right treatment must be administered at the right moment. The beginning of the treatise *Precepts* has a similar message:

> Χρόνος ἐστὶν ἐν ᾧ καιρός, καὶ καιρὸς ἐν ᾧ χρόνος οὐ πολύς· ἄκεσις χρόνῳ, ἔστι δὲ ἡνίκα καὶ καιρῷ. Δεῖ γε μὴν ταῦτα εἰδότα μὴ λογισμῷ πρότερον πιθανῷ προσέχοντα ἰητρεύειν, ἀλλὰ τριβῇ μετὰ λόγου.[49]

> Time is that wherein there is opportunity, and opportunity is that wherein there is no great time. Healing is a matter of time, but it is sometimes also a matter of opportunity. However, knowing this, one must attend in medical practice not primarily to plausible theories, but to experience combined with reason.

The time-pressures that make the treatment of difficult diseases doubly difficult necessitate time spent amassing experiential knowledge[50] – τριβῇ μετὰ λόγου in the words of *Precepts*. Seen in this light, the statement in *Prognostic* that the *technē* of medicine is long has a double sense: long to acquire, but also capable of maximising time, both by identifying and taking advantage of the *kairos* and, ideally, prolonging human life. The time invested in the art yields future benefits (including monetary benefits: *Precepts* includes a section on the professional etiquette of charging fees).

Prediction of the future course of the disease is only possible because of the time that one has put into study in the past. The treatise *Prorrhetic II* begins with a sceptical discussion of the doctors who are reputed to have great success in making predictions, with unfeasibly impressive degrees of precision (*Prorrhetic* 2.1):

> There are reports of physicians making frequent, true and marvelous predictions (προρρήσιες), predictions such as I have never made myself, nor ever personally had anyone else make. Here are some examples ... This is how precise all these kinds of predictions are reported to be (οὕτως ἐξηκριβῶσθαι οὗτοι πάντες οἱ τρόποι λέγονται τῶν προρρησίων).[51]

---

49 Littré Vol. 9; transl. W.H.S. Jones 1923, Loeb Hippocrates Vol. I.
50 I use the compound term experiential knowledge advisedly, to acknowledge debates in the scholarship on the Hippocratics about the relationship between experience and knowledge in the corpus.
51 Littré Vol. 9 [Littré assigned *Prorrhetic* 1 to Vol. 5, and *Prorrhetic* 2 to Vol. 9] – see n.38 above; transl. P. Potter 1995, Loeb Hippocrates Vol. VII.

Conversely, the author advises readers that they should only attempt making predictions in medicine after thorough study: 'But anyone who desires to win such successes should make predictions only after [thoroughly] learning about all these details (ἀλλὰ χρὴ προλέγειν καταμανθάνοντα πάντα ταῦτα, ...' (*Prorrhetic* II.2).

When we turn to Thucydides' account of the plague at 2.47–54, we note that Thucydides' statement about the doctors' helplessness when faced with the plague (2.47.4) does not pit his descriptive historiographical acumen against medical knowledge.

> οὔτε γὰρ ἰατροὶ ἤρκουν τὸ πρῶτον θεραπεύοντες ἀγνοίᾳ, ἀλλ' αὐτοὶ
> μάλιστα ἔθνησκον ὅσῳ καὶ μάλιστα προσῇσαν, ...
>
> The physicians were not able to help at its outset since they were treating it in ignorance, and indeed they themselves suffered the highest mortality since they were the ones most exposed to it.

Instead, Thucydides states that initially (τὸ πρῶτον) the doctors were at a loss because they had to treat patients in ignorance; that is to say, without any experience of the disease. The temporal adverb implies that with time they gained relevant experience, if not a cure. What is more, a large number of them died through contact with patients. By contrast, having suffered from the plague and survived, Thucydides offers an account in lieu of the ones that doctors might have written to ensure that readers of the future (doctors and lay people) would not be similarly ignorant when confronted by an epidemic of this nature. Hence these chapters read like a detailed and technical case history.[52]

In this sense the characterisation of the physician's necessary knowledge is reminiscent of Thucydides' authorial persona: the emphasis on the enormity and difficulty of the research that lies behind his historical account:

> τὰ δ' ἔργα τῶν πραχθέντων ἐν τῷ πολέμῳ <u>οὐκ ἐκ τοῦ παρατυχόντος πυνθανόμενος</u> ἠξίωσα γράφειν, οὐδ' ὡς ἐμοὶ ἐδόκει, <u>ἀλλ' οἷς τε αὐτὸς παρῆν καὶ παρὰ τῶν ἄλλων ὅσον δυνατὸν ἀκριβείᾳ περὶ ἑκάστου ἐπεξελθών</u>. ἐπιπόνως δὲ ηὑρίσκετο, διότι οἱ παρόντες τοῖς ἔργοις ἑκάστοις οὐ ταὐτὰ περὶ τῶν αὐτῶν ἔλεγον, ἀλλ' ὡς ἑκατέρων τις εὐνοίας ἢ μνήμης ἔχοι.
>
> As to the events of the war themselves, however, I resolved not to rely in my writing on what I learned from chance sources or even on my own impressions, but both in the cases where I was present myself and in those where I depended on others I investigated every detail with the utmost concern for accuracy. This was a laborious process of research, be-

---

[52] See Thomas 2006: 103 on 'Thucydides producing his own medical history', although I disagree with the claim about Thucydides' 'poor view of the efficacy of doctors' in general.

cause eyewitnesses at the various events reported the same things differently, depending on which side they favoured and on their powers of memory.[53]

Comparing the statements in *Aphorisms* and *Precepts* to Thucydides' remarks here puts a slightly different spin on the subsequent claim that his work is 'composed to be a possession for all time' (κτῆμα ἐς αἰεί). The life-span that Thucydides envisages for his work, its futurity, is backed up by the labour, the painstaking research and the immense time that has gone into its making. Futurity – the applicability of the work to the future – has been purchased through an immense investment of time in the past. In turn, this time has been turned into an intelligible, historical past that is retrievable by future readers for whom the open-ended future of the work is also their own future. We can see the motif of time-rich historical composition at work elsewhere in the *History*. In the second authorial preface at 5.26 Thucydides reminds us of his opening statement in Book 1, that he started writing down the war at its outbreak (ἀρξάμενος εὐθὺς καθισταμένου), and reinforces this statement with the further claim that he has written everything continually (ἑξῆς), right down to the end of the war. This chapter drives home the point that Thucydides has kept time with the war, following it in real time as it unfolded, but the point is not the marking of time per se, but the fact that Thucydides claims to have spent all of this time in careful observation (see the discussion on p. 93 above).

The same association between time dedicated to research and inquiry (including travel) and the futurity of the work are also evident in Herodotus' *Histories*. The proem to the *Histories* foregrounds the visible, tangible output of Herodotus' research – his ἱστορίης ἀπόδεξις, whether one is reading the text oneself or listening to and watching someone else read from a written copy of the text. Next we are told that this investment of time in *historiē* was undertaken to prevent 'the traces of human events being erased by time (τῷ χρόνῳ)' and to ensure renown for great deeds in the past. Again, the implicit metaphor is one of the historical work as a cache of time: time past preserved for and projected into the future. There can be no doubt about the futurity of Herodotus' *Histories*, in the sense of the author addressing his account of the past to a future that includes and exceeds his lifetime. Over and above the external prolepses that feature in the *Histories*,[54] we have the famous instance of self-historicisation at 1.5.4, where Herodotus informs his readers that,

---

53 Thuc. *Hist.* 1.22.2–3.
54 See Rood 2007a: 117. See also Rood (*ibid.*) on 'the difficulty of marking the end of Herodotus' story'.

> ὁμοίως μικρὰ καὶ μεγάλα ἄστεα ἀνθρώπων ἐπεξιών. Τὰ γὰρ τὸ πάλαι μεγάλα ἦν, τὰ πολλὰ αὐτῶν σμικρὰ γέγονε· τὰ δὲ ἐπ' ἐμέο ἦν μεγάλα, πρότερον ἦν σμικρά. Τὴν ἀνθρωπηίην ὦν ἐπιστάμενος εὐδαιμονίην οὐδαμὰ ἐν τὠυτῷ μένουσαν, ἐπιμνήσομαι ἀμφοτέρων ὁμοίως.
>
> I will cover minor and major human settlements equally, because most of those which were important in the past have diminished in significance by now, and those which were great in my own time were small in times past. I will mention both equally because I know that human happiness never remains long in the same place.

Not only does Herodotus project his own time into the past, but he also gives us an omni-temporal pronouncement that human prosperity fluctuates.

In contrast to the histories of Herodotus and Thucydides, in the *Hellenica* Xenophon generally circumscribes the future with the limits of his work. At 2.4.43, commenting on the amnesty in Athens after the collapse of the Thirty Tyrants, Xenophon remarks that, 'to this day (ἔτι καὶ νῦν) they live as fellow citizens and the people abide by their oaths'. At 4.3.16 the battle of Coronea is described as a battle quite unlike any other in our time (ἐφ' ἡμῶν), and at 6.4.37, he comments that one of the men who joined the wife of Tisiphonus in the plot against her husband, 'became the ruler and has remained so up to the time that this narrative was written' (ἄχρι οὗ ὅδε ὁ λόγος ἐγράφετο). The exceptions are the moral judgments that Xenophon offers on good and bad leadership and conduct in war,[55] which are omni-temporal, and the very end of the work, which constitutes an instance of what we might call indeterminate futurity (*Hellenica* 6.5.27):

> ἀκρισία δὲ καὶ ταραχὴ ἔτι πλείων μετὰ τὴν μάχην ἐγένετο ἢ πρόσθεν ἐν τῇ Ἑλλάδι. ἐμοὶ μὲν δὴ μέχρι τούτου γραφέσθω· τὰ δὲ μετὰ ταῦτα ἴσως ἄλλῳ μελήσει.
>
> In Greece as a whole there was more uncertainty and disturbance after the battle than there had been before. To this point, then, let it be written by me. Perhaps someone else will be concerned with what happened after this.

Marking an exact point where the time of the narrative and the time of the story coincide (μέχρι τούτου γραφέσθω), Xenophon ends this work on the cusp of a future – a potential inter-textual future that will be the *meta tauta* to his account, just as his account was the *meta tauta* to that of Thucydides. The ending also postpones the resolution of the upheaval narrated in Thucydides' text: at the

---

[55] See, e.g., *Hellenica* 3.4.18 (transl. Marincola 2009) on Agesilaus mobilizing the army in Ephesus: 'One would have been encouraged, too, by the sight of Agesilaus in the lead and the rest of the soldiers garlanded as they went from the gymnasia to dedicate their garlands to Artemis. For whenever men honour the gods, prepare themselves vigorously for war, and take care to obey their commanders, it is reasonable for everyone to be full of high hopes.'

point at which Xenophon's account ends, Greece is still in the grip of uncertainty and disturbance, raising implicit questions about whether or not this state of affairs will continue into the future.

Time-rich prose

I have suggested that the historians' careful analysis of the relationship between human temporality and complex patterns of causation contributes to the sense that these texts encapsulate vast stretches of time and the lessons of vast stretches of time: in short, they are time-rich. The self-consciousness about how the genre of historiography intervenes in and contributes to historical time is taken up in other prose genres. By way of comparison, I consider the continuation of this intellectual futurity in the Socratic dialogues of Plato, which oscillate between a professed commitment to educating political leaders of the future and the abandonment of the political sphere in favour of philosophy. The dialogues model a life spent in philosophy and the immense time that philosophical inquiry entails.

The Platonic dialogues have a rich, multi-layered temporality: the relationship between their historical dates and their dates of composition, the development of Platonic philosophy that exists in productive tension with the ethical constancy of Plato's Socrates, and the overarching, intra-diegetic and extra-diegetic prolepsis that structures the entire genre of Socratic literature: the foreshadowing of the death of Socrates.[56] Related to all of these different temporal dimensions, the dialogues also represent a more ambitious futurity, over and above the proleptic knowledge that Socrates will die. The retrospective narration of Socrates' life and practice of philosophy constitutes a considerable cache of time, past time, ensuring that readers in the future can benefit from the insights of a life lived in philosophy. While Socrates' biological life ends, as narrated at the end of the *Phaedo*, the life in philosophy persists and offers readers of the future a compelling return for the time spent reading them: they will acquire an intensive, lifetime's work, lived in philosophy. The sense of philosophical discussion time contained in the dialogues is reinforced by the sense of iteration,

---

[56] Kathryn Morgan expresses this elegantly (2007b, 369): 'The focalisation of the narrative (and indeed the genre) through a Socratic disciple creates, then, a kind of implied prolepsis: a narrative of the past looks to a future event that, while still in the past from the point of view of the narrator, continues to have repercussions in the present.'

with each dialogue representing typical conversations that Socrates engaged with on numerous occasions.[57]

Like Thucydides' scrupulously researched narrative, the Platonic-Socratic dialogues are time-rich. In contrast to his fellow citizens, the Platonic-Socratic[58] philosopher has time, which he can devote to the unhurried inquiry into the truth. This is how Socrates expresses the opposition between philosopher time and citizen time in the *Theaetetus* (172d4-e1):

> Socrates: Because the one man always has what you mentioned just now – plenty of time (σχολή). When he talks, he talks in peace and quiet, and his time is his own (καὶ τοὺς λόγους ἐν εἰρήνῃ ἐπὶ σχολῆς ποιοῦνται). It is so with us now: here we are beginning on our third new discussion; and he can do the same if he is like us, and prefers the newcomer to the question in hand. It does not matter to such men *if their conversations are brief or long* whether they talk for a day or for a year,[59] if only they hit upon that which is (καὶ διὰ μακρῶν ἢ βραχέων μέλει οὐδὲν λέγειν, ἂν μόνον τύχωσι τοῦ ὄντος). But the other – the man of the law courts – is always in a hurry when he is talking (οἱ δὲ ἐν ἀσχολίᾳ τε ἀεὶ λέγουσι); he has to speak with one eye on the clock (κατεπείγει γὰρ ὕδωρ ῥέον) ... .[60]

In fact, the logic of the Platonic-Socratic philosopher's values requires that Socrates will meet his end due to his incompatibility with the chronotope of the lawcourts: he cannot adapt to the time constraints of the lawcourts, nor the particular tropes observed in that space (see *Gorgias* 521c-e; and *Apology* 17c-18a).

At the end of the *Apology*, against the dramatic backdrop of the *klepsydra*, trickling away time, the Platonic Socrates taunts his audience with temporal miscalculation: they have voted to put him to death, making themselves hostage to future critics, when his natural life span might have done the job for them (*Apology* 38c1–7):

> It is for the sake of a short time (οὐ πολλοῦ γ' ἕνεκα χρόνου), gentlemen of the jury, that you will acquire the reputation and the guilt, in the eyes of those who want to denigrate the city, of having killed Socrates, a wise man, for they who want to revile you will say that I am a wise man even if I am not. If you had waited but a little while (εἰ γοῦν περιεμείνατε ὀλίγον χρόνον), this would have happened of its own accord. You see my age, that I am already advanced in years and close to death.[61]

---

57 See Morgan 2007b, 348 'Reading the dialogues makes one aware that Socrates asks the same kind of questions in the same kind of way over and over again'.
58 = Written by Plato, modelled on Socrates.
59 The phrase in italics indicates a substitution for a phrase in Levett / Burnyeat's translation (the latter is marked by strikethrough font).
60 Transl. M. J. Levett (rev. M.F. Burnyeat) in Cooper and Hutchinson (eds.) 1997.
61 Transl. G.M.A. Grube in Cooper and Hutchinson (eds.) 1997.

The emphasis is on the Athenian jury staking a severe judgment on a brief period of time —the short span of time that remains of Socrates' life. The shortness of the time involved is repeated: οὐ πολλοῦ γ' ἕνεκα χρόνου ... εἰ γοῦν περιεμείνατε ὀλίγον χρόνον. Socrates uses his impending death to issue a prophecy, exploiting the mythical convention of the foresight accorded to those about to die (*Apology* 39c1–8):

> Now I want to prophesy (τὸ δὲ δὴ μετὰ τοῦτο ἐπιθυμῶ ὑμῖν χρησμῳδῆσαι) to those who convicted me, for I am at the point when men prophesy most, when they are about to die. I say, gentlemen, to those who voted to kill me, that vengeance will come upon you immediately after my death, a vengeance much harder to bear than that which you took in killing me. You did this in the belief that you would avoid giving an account of your life, but I maintain that quite the opposite will happen to you.

Xenophon gives us some of the details of the judgment / vengeance that fell to Socrates' accusers in his apologetic Socratic works – the *Apology* and the *Memorabilia*. To my mind, what is more striking here is the fact that Socrates' accusations of his jury at the end of the *Apology* are corroborated by the textual frame, by the very fact of Plato's writing, which will redeem Socrates' life and do a pretty thorough job of convicting his jury in the judgment of posterity. Similarly, when Socrates takes leave of the jury at the very end of the speech, the death for which he departs is a Platonic afterlife, which buries the perspective of the jurors such that scholars are still trying to excavate the motives of the Athenians who put him to death. The *Apology* ends with Socrates' anticipation of his death (*Apology* 42a2–3): 'Now the hour to part has come. I go to die, you go to live' (ἀλλὰ γὰρ ἤδη ὥρα ἀπιέναι, ἐμοὶ μὲν ἀποθανουμένῳ, ὑμῖν δὲ βιωσομένοις). In view of the arguments that have preceded this peroration, one can compare Socrates' claim to the concept of the life-span of art versus the brevity of human life expressed in the Hippocratic aphorism quoted on p.69 above (ὁ βίος βραχὺς, ἡ δὲ τέχνη μακρή). In this instance, Plato's philosophical art secures a long life for Socratic (and Platonic) thought.

Conclusion

I have argued that Greek historiography is informed by an implicit futurity that stems from a sense of the practical, prospective relevance of the past in conversation with the other genres of knowledge. The time-rich sense of historical accounts stores up a cache of expertise, predicated on a close study of human temporality, for use in the present and future.

Further work remains to be done on the rich texture of the future in extant Greek historiography. I have presented a broad schema for understanding the role that futurity plays in establishing the authority of Greek historiography vis-à-vis other forms of expertise in the Greek *polis*. The next step would be to analyse and classify the different futures present in the works of Herodotus, Thucydides and Xenophon to better understand the sophistication of their presentation of future temporality. Here a starting point might be to distinguish between micro-futures, understood as short term projections of the future that are fulfilled within the scope of the narrative, and macro-futures that are extra-textual and open-ended. Within the category of micro-futures, one might then begin to consider further distinctions such as the 'strategic future', 'the prophetic future', and 'the incipient future', to cite just three examples. The strategic future would include the tactical forecasts that pervade the battle narratives in Herodotus, Thucydides and Xenophon, as well as the exhortatory rhetoric on the part of generals, which forecasts future outcomes.[62] Take, for instance, Nicias' statement at 6.68.1–2 that, 'We have together here Argives, Mantineans, Athenians and the pick of the islanders. Surely, therefore, with so many allies of such quality every one of us can have the highest hopes of victory … .' Prophetic futures would include the future perspectives introduced by oracles, prophecies and soothsayers, of the kind mentioned by Herodotus (cited at p. 79 above). Incipient or ingressive futures help to pinpoint moments, in the historian's judgment, where lines are crossed that set the course for the denouement of future events and outcomes. These futures typically occur in the context of narratorial interventions, for instance Thucydides 6.1.1 'and they were unaware that they were taking on a war on almost the same scale as that against the Peloponnesians'. Such research will enable us to better understand the complexity of past futures, and to achieve greater self-awareness of how we introduce projections of our own futures into our reading of Greek historiography.

---

[62] See, recently, Hans-Peter Stahl's discussion of decision-making processes that precede military actions in Herodotus and Thucydides (Stahl 2012).

Antonis Tsakmakis
Between Thucydides and the Future: Narrative Prolepsis and Xenophon's Concept of Historiography

I

The ways classical historians become visible in their works (or step aside) is an intriguing issue.[1] Herodotus, Thucydides and Xenophon each follow different practices in their works, beginning with the declaration of their names as authors, the presentation of their role at the narrated events, the passing of judgment on fellow historians (either by naming them or not), and the inclusion of comments on both historical and historiographical issues. The solutions adopted by each historian reveal differences of historical perspective, historiographical theory and literary self-consciousness. Accordingly, their full appreciation requires both content analysis of their statements and a literary and narratological approach to their text.[2]

Following an already established practice, Thucydides and Herodotus identify themselves as authors in the proems of their works;[3] Thucydides' name as the author is also regularly recalled in the closing formulas of the ending of each year's narrative. Having been active in the war he records, he also names himself in the third person whenever he has to report events in which he was involved. He avoids, however, confusion of his two roles: he omits his name in the closing formula of the year he had mentioned himself in the narrative (4.116.3). Thus he discourages identification of Thucydides the author with Thucydides the general, even though this ploy can also be interpreted as indirect avowal of his double function. Xenophon's choice is more sophisticated in this respect: in his *Anabasis*, where he holds a role of protagonist, he avoids altogether revealing his authorship. On the contrary, he evades explicit identification by inventing an author for the work, even if this happens in a later text, at the be-

---
[1] I wish to thank Alexandra Lianeri for very thoughtful comments on an earlier version of this paper.
[2] On the theoretical aspects regarding this dual task of the analysis of historical narrative cf. Ankersmit 2008.
[3] On proems in historiography cf. Lachenaud 2004, 63–98. On Xenophon's exceptional practice regarding his self-presentation Luce 1997, 102–105.

ginning of the second part of his *Hellenica*, when he briefly alludes to the events narrated in his earlier monograph; there, he attributes the *Anabasis* to a "Themistogenes of Syracuse" (3.1.2).[4] The situation in the *Hellenica* is different. Xenophon remains silent about his own participation at certain events, although the contrary would be an option. On the other hand, he rather surprisingly omits his name as an author, a fact that can partly be explained through the lack of a proem, as his narrative continues Thucydides' interrupted work. His practice contrasts with a standard convention of the genre, but is consistent with his own habit as an author. Nevertheless, authorial comments and interventions are not avoided in the *Hellenica*. Thus, Xenophon's views can not only be inferred from the work itself, but they can also be obtained from his authorial comments at various places in the work.[5]

This paper deals with a specific category of authorial comments in the *Hellenica*, statements which pursue the impact of narrated events to the time of writing or assess them by anticipating knowledge of the entire interval till then – hence they imbue the narrative with a future perspective. There are three anticipations of this kind in the work. Their analysis will be preceded by some general remarks on narrative anticipation in historiography and a discussion of the epilogue of the *Hellenica*, where the author also vaguely refers to future events and their possible recording by other historians; besides, we also address the implications of the lacking proem, i.e. the absence of any anticipatory announcements which are regularly expected in the opening.

II

Every narrative moves towards a future till it reaches its end. The reader is aware that the main narrative timeline advances ahead and that the reported events develop with it. Thus, a narrative necessarily directs the reader's gaze towards what is coming next – a property which results from the pragmatics of "narrative" as a distinct type of discourse. This future within a narrative is void, except for the addressees' expectations – predictions and wishes, founded or not – and from explicit anticipations.

---

[4] This, however, seems to be no less playful than Plato's ascription of his dialogues to various narrators. Xenophon, who was familiar with Socratic literature, assumed that his readers had the pragmatic knowledge necessary to identify the author (cf. Pomeroy 1994, 10). This, in turn, was self-consciously used as an opportunity for elaborate plays with the authorial personas – until forgery became a real problem (cf. Tulli 2011 on Plato's *Theaetetus*).
[5] For an overview see Gray 2004.

The temporal mechanics of a historical narrative is more complicated than in fiction. The narrative of historiography not only instigates an internal future (which is gradually disclosed), but also avails of a future external to it; the reader is involved in the latter, as well as the author as soon as s/he embarks on the act of narrating. Both internal and external future are not only qualitatively similar, but also interdependent as they form contiguous segments of historical time. Both the author and his addressees occupy positions in the future, if viewed from any moment within the historical narrative – this is a condition of history, which by definition deals with the past. We can accordingly distinguish three phases of the external future: future to the narrative, future to the author, future to the reader or absolute future (these distinctions fade, of course, when the events and their recording or writing and reading approach each other respectively).

Anticipations are important, especially in historiography: they not only convey historical information, they also influence the reader's response to the narrative. While this may be occasionally unwelcome in fiction, where suspense is desired, anticipations may be helpful for readers of historiography, as they allow the complete presentation of a story (Herodotus' reference to the oracle which instructed the Amathusians' to establish a cult of Onesilus would not make sense at a place after 5.114, and, in such a case, the narrative about the Cypriot revolt and the fortune of Onesilus' head would remain deficient), suggest the correlation of events (Thucydides' assertion that the Peloponnesian War lasted twenty seven years, 5.26.1–2, forces the reader to relate the Sicilian Expedition and the Ionian War to the Archidamian War), or make readers aware of the importance of a topic, etc. (when Polybius introduces Hiero II of Syracuse as "the man who later became king", 1.8.3, the reader cannot help focusing on him; and, his presentation and actions are automatically related to future developments). Anticipations may create a feeling of instant satisfaction, as readers acquire more information than they had expected: in a sense, they emancipate the readers, they make them less dependent on the author; in recompense, what is shared, needs not to be proved – thus Thucydides' remarks on the inferiority and corruption of Pericles' successors in 2.65.10–12 anticipates the reader's evaluation: what readers now expect is not to be persuaded whether this is true, but rather to see how it will be adequately demonstrated. References or allusions to events of the external future are marked even more distinctly: they are assumed to imply the historian's evaluation of events which happened after the end of his narrative. But also the main narrative can influence his addressees' "reading" of the future, as a historical work tends to constitute the background information for understanding it. This idea is manifestly proclaimed by Thucydides in his famous statement 1.22.4: the historian asserts his belief that his work may be useful to those who wish to delve into the future (for which the ambiguous formulation allows for the understanding as both referring to events postdating the end of his narrative as well as the reader's future). On the other hand, the reader's knowledge of these events (the time between writing and every new reading) inevitably influences his/her reception of the historical work.

Hints at the author's own time (or, more specifically, to the time of writing) as well as to the writing activity itself form a distinctive type of narrative anticipation. They suggest a wish to cover historical time as exhaustively as possible. Consequently, they implicitly raise the question of further developments and challenge the reader to investigate into the period not covered by the author's statement. A special sub-category is anticipations suggesting continuity: if something is still happening at the time of writing, it prompts readers to wonder whether this is pertinent to their own time or even future. All passages we examine in the following paper fall under this case.

III

The lack of a formal proem in Xenophon's *Greek History* is in agreement with the fact that the work (a continuation of Thucydides' interrupted work on the Peloponnesian War) begins at a point where there is no organic caesura. Accordingly, there has to be no rupture in the narrative despite switching from one author to another.[6] However, Xenophon's decision to become a continuator of someone else and especially the implementation of his plan, have serious consequences. The historian can neither define his own subject, nor launch his work with remarks that relate it to the past, indicate causality, underpin continuities, introduce themes, foreshadow developments, or suggest necessities as Herodotus and Thucydides had done before him. Much of these missing elements will have to be recuperated later; the narrative itself and the authorial statements which are dispersed at various places of the work will provide the key to understand Xenophon's historiography.

Xenophon's predecessors had organised their works around a subject which they put on view against the background of the past in order to make it accessible and understandable – even useful or useable. Their subject suggested a beginning and entailed an end of the narrative; readers were invited to move across the internal future towards the end[7] – beyond this point everything belonged to an external future. Xenophon's opening lacks such a distinction of temporalities.

---

6 For the problems of the transition cf. Henry 1966, 11–54; Krentz 1989, 86.
7 See Stadter 2012, 61–62.

His work looks forward, as if it imitates the flow of natural time. The lack of a proem does not allow for the definition of an external future. The fact that he is a continuator cannot overshadow this impression. Xenophon is not Thucydides and never suppresses his autonomous authorial persona even if he withdraws his name. His work *is* and, at the same time, *is not* the same *History*. Accordingly, the limits between internal and external future as anticipated by Thucydides are suspended from the beginning of Xenophon's work. Xenophon silently agrees with Thucydides in what a historian ought to make visible, not necessarily in what he leaves out.

Eventually, Xenophon expands his narrative beyond the limit set by Thucydides.[8] An implicit justification of his practice (and concealed criticism of Thucydides' conception of the material of historiography) can be deduced from his summary characterisation of the period which immediately follows the Peloponnesian War: *stasis* in Athens (1.3.1). *Stasis* was a prominent topic in Thucydides, even if it is but a side effect of the war.[9] How could Thucydides' reader (who is aware of the importance of *stasis* and devotes a remarkable analysis to the *stasis* in Corcyra) be content by the exclusion of such a period, which is an immediate consequence of the war? Would Thucydides envisage extending his narrative up to this point? This is unanswerable, and it is irrelevant to our discussion: Xenophon at any rate goes on narrating, and the retrospective characterisation of the post-war period as *stasis* is a first step towards the rejection of the war-monograph and the instigation of continuing narrative.

One thing is sure: the reading of Xenophon affects our reading of Thucydides. Once the younger historian had appropriated his predecessor's project, he is entitled to control the definition of temporalities and to transmute them. After Xenophon, Thucydides appears as a ring in a chain which henceforth constitutes the uninterrupted narrative of Greek history.[10] Whereas Thucydides insisted that his work is unique thanks to the importance of its subject matter, which is adequately elaborated to attain an almost a-chronic exemplarity, his successor is concerned to bridge the gap between the narrated events and his own world. In doing so, he creates a new type of historiography, continuous historiography. Unlike Thucydides who, from the continuous flow of historical events extracts a unique subject matter and seeks to demonstrate its greatness by transforming it into a literary artifact which emulates Homeric monumentality, Xenophon seeks the meaning of history in its proximity, guaranteed through

---

8 For a discussion see Tuplin 2007, 165–167.
9 Cf. Th. 1.23.2 for the opposition war-stasis.
10 Cf. also Canfora 1971.

an uninterrupted temporal sequence of events. This becomes particularly visible in the passages which he relates his own time and experience with events he has narrated, including the epilogue.

IV

We have to wait till the epilogue of the work to find a more expressive manifestation of Xenophon's temporal demarcation of his historiography.

> The result of this battle was just the opposite of what everyone expected it would be. Nearly the whole of Greece had been engaged on one side or the other, and everyone imagined that, if a battle was fought, the winner would become the dominant power and the losers would be their subjects. But God so ordered things ... that both parties put up trophies, as for victory, and neither side tried to prevent the other from doing so; both sides gave back the dead under a truce, as though they had won, and both sides received their dead under a truce, as though they had lost. Both sides claimed the victory, but it cannot be said that with regard to the accession of new territory, or cities, or power either side was any better off after the battle than before it. In fact, there was even more uncertainty and confusion in Greece after the battle than there had been previously. Let this, then, be the end of my narrative. Someone else, perhaps, will deal with what happened later (5.7.26–27).

Xenophon encourages prospective historians to continue his own narrative after the battle of Mantinea (τὰ δὲ μετὰ ταῦτα ἴσως ἄλλῳ μελλήσει), in an analogous manner as he had done himself with Thucydides' unfinished work.[11] The expression μετὰ ταῦτα, which also opens the work (μετὰ δὲ ταῦτα οὐ πολλαῖς ἡμέραις ὕστερον...),[12] underpins the analogy and suggests the need for continuity. It confirms that historiography is not solely interested in selected periods. But how does Xenophon understand continuity? Is he advocating an amorphous accumulation of facts? Is the only principle of selection the relative "importance" of certain deeds" (cf. 4.8.1: καὶ τῶν πράξεων τὰς μὲν ἀξιομνημονεύτους γράψω, τὰς δὲ μὴ ἀξίας λόγου παρήσω)? And where does a historian have to stop? Is the future defined exclusively negatively, as physical constraints (old age, death) that do not allow the historian to recount, as many critics seem to take for granted for Xenophon? Is his work, in a sense, also "unfinished"? The concluding passage of the *Hellenica* is an appropriate starting point for a discussion of these issues.

---

[11] For a completely different understanding of Xenophon's stance cf. Luce 1994, 103: "History seems to be going nowhere, although the author hopes his work will find a continuator".
[12] Cf. Krentz 1989, 86.

In the epilogue of his historical work, Xenophon insinuates his divergence from Thucydides' historiographical outlook. While Thucydides had opened his work with a self-confident statement that he had predicted the outbreak of a great war (1.1.1), Xenophon closes his continuation of Thucydides' work with the challenging assertion of human failure to foresee what was coming next. Unlike Thucydides, Xenophon does not distinguish himself from his contemporaries in order to persuade, to impress, or to study them, he is rather included in "all people" (πάντες ἄνθρωποι) – another notion which is familiar from Thucydides' opening: there Thucydides was the observer of the acts of "most men" (ἐπὶ πλεῖστον ἀνθρώπων, Th. 1.1.2), his all-embracing gaze and his authoritative analysis suggest absolute control; now the younger historian uses people as internal observers of events, and he appeals to their surprise in order to communicate more effectively his own embarrassment. Xenophon's novel stance culminates in the terms he selects to describe what followed Mantinea: ἀκρισία καὶ ταραχή. Ἀκρισία is used *hapax* in Xenophon. It is a privative noun as the opposite of *krisis*, the term used by Thucydides to indicate the termination of the Persian Wars; for Thucydides *krisis* is instrumental for the comparison of his own work to that of Herodotus: rapid *krisis* of this conflict proved, in his opinion, its inferiority to the Peloponnesian War (1.23.1) – an argument to exalt the importance of *his* war (and *his* work). For Xenophon's predecessor the crisis of a war proved a criterion for the periodisation of history and for the determination and evaluation of their subject matter. Xenophon did not stop writing when the Peloponnesian War was decided. Now he terminates his work at a moment of *akrisia*. While Xenophon ironically undermines a category which had a heuristic value for his predecessor's historiography, ταραχή seems to hint at Herodotus. In a key passage of the first book which illustrates Croesus' encounter with Solon (an episode Xenophon has rewritten in his *Cyropaedia*), Solon had asserted that the divine is ταραχῶδες (1.32.1), causing the fall of the mighty. This is an idea to which Xenophon fully subscribes. God is explicitly mentioned in this epilogue as the ultimate force behind the outcome. Xenophon's work ends at the moment when repeated attempts of various Greek cities to impose their hegemony over the Greeks proved vain. Only short-lived hegemonies were to be registered; even this seems improbable in the future – this is Xenophon's conviction and this may explain his choice to conclude his work at this point. Xenophon's occasional references to the period after Mantinea indicate that he is not only informed about the future, but also ready to draw on his knowledge of it, if this improves historical understanding.

V

Xenophon's *Hellenica* includes three explicit references to events pertinent to his own time. Two of them are brief remarks in Books 2 and 4, the third concludes a narrative on the Thessalian rulers who rose to power after the assassination of Jason of Pherae, a figure of great importance in Book 6. These passages (both the digression and the narrative on Jason out of which it grows) are worth a closer examination because the literary and narrative arrangement of the material suggests that the historian is not only concerned with historical content but also engaged in a dialogue with his predecessors, which sheds light upon his own historical theory.

The first "till-now"-formula of the *Hellenica* is found in Xenophon's epilogue of the *stasis*-narrative.[13] The historian describes with the following words the end of the hostilities between the demos and the oligarchs in Athens (after the end of the Peloponnesian War, the establishment of the Thirty, the collapse of their regime following their defeat in battle against the exiled democrats, the settlement of oligarchs in Eleusis in an autonomous community within the Athenian state, and the abolition of it after a new confrontation with Athenian forces one and a half years later): "Oaths were sworn that there should be an amnesty for all that had happened in the past, and to this day both parties live together as fellow-citizens and the people abide by the oaths which they have sworn" (2.4.43). A modern commentator rightly observes that, "Xenophon first mentions the famous amnesty here, after the murder of the Eleusinian generals, though it was certainly part of the original reconciliation in 403. By holding the amnesty until this point, Xenophon can end his story on the upbeat note that follows – otherwise the Athenian assault on Eleusis and murder of the generals would seem to have violated the amnesty as well as the autonomy provision of the reconciliation agreement".[14] By modern standards this is a distortion of historical truth, given that the idea of reconciliation was henceforth a pillar of Athenian official memory. On the contrary, for Xenophon an important idea or topic can dictate the choice and arrangement of the material (which does not exclusively aim at historical accuracy and completeness of information); this seems to be the case here. At first sight he praises the Athenians[15] and provides a didactic exam-

---

[13] Such expressions are very common in the *Cyropaedia*, an indication that Xenophon was concerned to bridge the gap between the two worlds, between the fictional, exotic past and the real world of his readers; cf. Delebeque 1957, 395–405.
[14] Krentz 1989, *ad loc.*
[15] Gray 2004, 134.

ple of political behaviour. But the achievement of stability proves not only worth noting per se, but also appropriate for the periodisation of history. Xenophon's synchronism of the oaths with the end of his narrative about the hostilities highlights a turning point in Athenian history, but also marks the end of the continuation of Thucydides; Xenophon can now free himself from any constraints resulting from his decision to continue another work. It is not without importance that it is exactly here that he reminds us of his physical location in historical time and makes himself perceptible as a distinct individual – he is no more in the shadow of his predecessor. At the same time, the anticipatory remark places the theme of reconciliation within a wide historical framework and suggests to the reader a panoramic historical perspective. More accurately, it raises the implicit question whether Xenophon's assertion also holds for the reader's own time. Xenophon encourages readers to relate the story he tells to their own world. For Xenophon the past lives in the present, not only as memory and experience, but also because it shaped the world as it is in the present; similarly, the future guarantees the importance of the present. Therefore, as time goes on and men travel with it towards the future, they should not lose sight of what they leave behind. The historian's duty is – among others – to select and recount those events which are laden with a forward-moving potential: Xenophon's position in the external future of the narrative allows him to discern which events proved historically important, i.e. could influence subsequent developments. Thucydides is also likely to have written his history from the end; nevertheless he adopts a very different, forward looking stance: he is not writing history for the sake of the past, he is looking to the future, equipped with the knowledge of the past.

The battle of Coronea offers Xenophon the next opportunity to cross the interval up to the moment he is writing. In 4.3.15 he states that this battle has been the greatest of his time: διηγήσομαι δὲ καὶ τὴν μάχην, καὶ πῶς ἐγένετο οἵα οὐκ ἄλλη τῶν γ' ἐφ' ἡμῶν. One wonders why a disclaimer was necessary for the description of a battle, since there is nothing unusual in the reporting of military action in historiography. Evidently, Xenophon means more than he says. It is to be noted that the historian does not reveal that he was present in the battlefield and that his first-hand knowledge makes a detailed narrative possible; rather he implies that he could be able to report every battle in a similar manner, if it was worth doing so; by hiding his first-hand knowledge Xenophon may forfeit part of his credibility, on the other hand he eludes suspicions of bias. In addition, if his presence in Coronea has been a reason for his exile from Athens, his silence helps direct the readers' attention away from this incident.

The exaltation of the subject matter is a typical element of a proem, and Xenophon's assertion is probably a belated compensation for having opened his work without a proem. Although it does not become immediately clear what makes the battle of Coronea so exceptional, the expression is rhetorically effective. The historian is not concerned with proving his assertion on the battle's superiority. Instead, he takes its evaluation for granted (giving it the status of a background belief which is shared with his audience) and introduces it as a premise to validate a further pronouncement, namely to justify his decision to describe the battle. For all its vagueness, Xenophon's declaration serves as a marker which draws the reader's attention to details of the narrative, especially to Agesilaus' bravery which is explicitly singled out (19). As Xenophon uses this theme as an opportunity to stress the superiority of this battle to other battles of his time (even though the criteria of the comparison are not clearly declared), he implicitly justifies his decision to continue his narrative beyond Thucydides' intended end. Besides, he also advances a comparison of this battle to a significant part of the Peloponnesian war, a fact which inevitably modulates the latter's importance. Thus, the reader is advised to avoid uncritical admiration of this war and discard Thucydides' maximalist claims about its importance. And since readers are indirectly summoned to interrogate themselves whether this still holds at the time of every new reading of the work, Xenophon seems to remind us that the value of historical comparison is always relative, subject to permanent revision.[16] This is a consequence of his conception of continuous history.

VI

Xenophon's last synchronisation of a narrative anticipation with the time of writing concerns the rule of Tisiphonus in Thessalian Pherae; Xenophon claims that this tyrant had "up to the time when this was written", been holding power in Thessaly (6.4.37). These words conclude a narrative digression which is attached to the main narrative and anticipates events up to the latest possible moment: not only to the time of writing, but also to the time the composition of the work was accomplished. The digression is motivated by an exceptionally remarkable passage,

---

[16] On Xenophon's care not to over-exaggerate see Gray 2004, 134. Xenophon's comment in 4.4.14 (ἐκ δὲ τούτου στρατιαὶ μὲν μεγάλαι ἑκατέρων διεπέπαυντο) implicitly corroborates his claim about the battle, but the pluperfect suggests that this does not hold for the time he is writing. The pluperfect is used to expresss a statement about a continuous state or situation which was still valid at a moment in the past, but does not hold any more at the moment the utterance is made (cf. Plb. 1.6.1: ἔτος μὲν οὖν ἐνειστήκει μετὰ μὲν τὴν ἐν Αἰγὸς ποταμοῖς ναυμαχίαν ἐννεακαιδέκατον). Xenophon's use of the pluperfect here also implies a point of view in the future.

highly elaborate, which addresses questions of overwhelming importance; further on, it includes many puzzling details that require interpretation.

This digression deals with the successors of Jason of Pherae, who had been murdered in 370, sometime before his arrival in Delphi to administer the Pythian festival. Little is known about Jason.[17] We have no information about his family, early career and education. Isocrates counted him among his friends and addressees of his political proposals. It is possible that he had some relation to Lycophron, the Pheraean tyrant who at the beginning of the fourth century had tried to unite Thessaly under his rule. In 375 he had defended Timotheus in a trial in Athens, and Plutarch testifies that he was a friend of Pelopidas. Hostility to the Aleuadae of Larissa is more than sure. Part of the ancient sources and modern bibliography call Jason a tyrant, but Xenophon meticulously avoids that.[18] This may be significant, since Xenophon's use of the term tyrant is consistent throughout his work.

There are three sections about Jason in the sixth Book of the *Hellenica*. The first is a speech by the Pharsalian Polydamas who visits Sparta to ask for help at the opening of the book (6.1.2). Right away he is given the longest, more complex and more informative speech in the work (6.1.4–16); eventually it is an artful analepsis which introduces Jason, his personality and plans to the reader through the eyes of an external focaliser (Polydamas is warmly praised by Xenophon for his integrity and reliability as a manager of his city's finances, and this adds value to the opinions he expresses). The speech contains a narrative of Polydamas' encounter with Jason, and its main part is occupied by the words addressed to the speaker by Jason himself, partly in direct speech, partly summarised. Together with Polydamas' comments the reported speech helps constructing a complete portrait of Jason as a military commander and political leader.[19] He envisages uniting Thessaly, extending his rule over Greece, and leading a campaign against Persia, an idea advertised by Isocrates and apparently endorsed by Xenophon himself.[20] All this is supported by exact calculations of

---

[17] See Lemmermann 1927, Mandel 1980, Sprawski 1999.
[18] But the term appears in a verbatim quotation attributed to him by Aristotle *Pol.* 1277a24: Jason said "'he was a hungry man except he was tyrant', meaning that he did not know how to live in a private station" (transl. Barker); but *tyrannein* is used for 'ruling, governing'). We owe to Aristotle Jason's second surviving citation: "it is necessary to do some injustice, in order to accomplish many just deeds". Thus, the two memorable dicta reveal less about Jason's political career, but probably more about his personality: straightforward, ambitious, self-confident, a realist, cynical lover of power.
[19] Tsakmakis 2013, 673–676.
[20] Cf. Pédech 1964, 96.

manpower and material resources with exact figures, political estimations, and careful planning. Especially Jason's care to avoid the unnecessary use of violence and his worry to gain the support of people by making them friends (whose interests he guarantees), recalls the doctrines of the *Cyropaedia*, while they are in contrast with the image of the tyrant in *Hieron*. Polydamas confirms that Jason is an exceptional personality and offers more details about the difficult negotiation. Yet, his attempt to mobilise Sparta fails, and we encounter Jason again after the battle of Leuctra.

While Diodorus (15.60) reports that Jason was present at the battlefield but was not involed in the fighting, Xenophon's version insists that he was invited by the Thebans after the battle as they tried to safeguard the advantage of their recent victory in case of a renewal of hostilities. This request gives Xenophon the opportunity to focus on Jason's impressive march from Thessaly to the South. Jason's prestige increases through his wise diplomatic advice, especially through his persuasive suggestions to both sides, which nevertheless serve his own interests, as well. Addressing the Thebans, he concludes, "It seems that heaven [God] takes pleasure in raising up the small and bringing down the great" (6.4.23). For the reader of the *Hellenica* it immediately becomes apparent that Jason here is the mouthpiece of the author, since Xenophon fully subscribes to this principle,[21] which is also emblematic for Herodotus. At the same time, the author prepares us to regard him as a tragic hero, who suffers undeserved misfortune, since this *gnomē* ironically applies to his fate, as will become evident soon.

Jason has become *tagos* of all Thessaly,[22] as he had planned, commander of the allied troops of the four districts of the land and the tribes of the mountain areas surrounding the Thessalian plane, respected by his men, admired and feared in all Greece. He appears (at least here) as the head of the amphictiony to administer the Pythian festival of 370. Xenophon's fascination with Jason's magnitude (we note a climactic use of the adjective μέγας and its comparatives in 6.4.28), the emphasis on unique military preparations and accumulation of power (with a statement that those who were still neutral and considered participation in the alliance: συμμάχους πολλούς τούς μὲν ἤδη εἶναι αὐτῷ, τοὺς δὲ καὶ

---

[21] Dillery 1990, 167–168; Giraud 2001, 49–50 with n. 30. For Jason's diplomatic activity in Xenophon see Toalster 2011, 195.
[22] Xenophon foregrounds the election of Jason as a Thessalian *tagos*. He seems to be fully aware of the importance of the political significance of this system, and he makes Jason a passionate paragon of it. Sources, provisions, the centralised system of administration, and the division of tasks to every level up to the bottom level is similar to the effective Persian administration which Xenophon illustrates in the *Cyropaedia*. On the typically Thessalian institution of *tageia* see Helly (1995), Sprawski (1999) 15–23. Carlier (1984) 414–415.

ἔτι βούλεσθαι γίγνεσθαι), in connection with the repeated hints at a wide-spread expectation of a great turbulence in Greece recall Thucydides' description of the outbreak of the Peloponnesian War (1.1). The conclusion μέγιστος δ' ἦν τῶν καθ' αὑτὸν also alludes to analogous expressions used by Thucydides for Themistocles and Pericles (1.127.3, 1.138.6).

The expectation of striking historical developments will prove futile. What seemed probable and possible, the increasing influence of one gifted, promising commander over Greece, will be impeded by Jason's assassination. The vivid description of Jason's initiatives contrasts with the narrator's explicit reservation concerning their real meaning. Xenophon twice uses the introductory verb ἔφασαν (29, 30) and once λέγεται (30) in order to indicate uncertainty about Jason's plans.[23] The most striking example is 6.4.30: "It is said that when the people of Delphi asked the god what they should do if he tried to take any of his treasure, Apollo answered that he would look after that matter himself". (6.4.30) Herodotus cites a very similar oracle during the second Persian invasion.[24]

Most scholars use the end of the story, the murder of Jason by seven youths – Xenophon notes that those who survived were honoured in Greece as tyrannicides –, as a key to interpret the author's and the god's ultimate verdict on the Thessalian *tagos*.[25] But the narrator's neutrality on any negative aspect of Jason's personality and career is a telling literary strategy. It allows the positive side to prevail:[26] Xenophon's illustration of Jason is exceptional; the historian employs complex narrative techniques and rhetorical devices in order to make him appear as an ideal political and military commander. On the other hand, un-

---

23 According to Lévy (1990) 131, λέγεται is used by Xenophon for the introduction of legendary assertions, while ἔφασαν for an impressive content. Alias Delebeque 1957, 438. Sanchez 2001, 164–166 adopts Xenophon's positive image of Jason.
24 ...πυνθανόμενοι ταῦτα ἐς πᾶσαν ἀρρωδίην ἀπίκατο, ἐν δείματι δὲ μεγάλῳ κατεστεῶτες ἐμαντεύοντο περὶ τῶν ἱρῶν χρημάτων, εἴτε σφέα κατὰ γῆς κατορύξωσι εἴτε ἐκκομίσωσι ἐς ἄλλην χώρην· ὁ δὲ θεός σφεα οὐκ ἔα κινέειν, φὰς αὐτὸς ἱκανὸς εἶναι τῶν ἑωυτοῦ προκατῆσθαι. Δελφοὶ δὲ ταῦτα ἀκούσαντες σφέων αὐτῶν πέρι ἐφρόντιζον. Xenophon knew Herodotus and expected the same from his readers; cf. Riemann 1967, 27; Gray 2011 (see also D.H. ad Pomp. 4). The similarity of the oracles may be due to the Delphic sources of the historians; see Cavalli 2004, 268. On the oracle's ambiguous policy Giuliani 2001, 187–188.
25 For a discussion see Tsakmakis 2013, 669–671.
26 The details of the narrative suggest that Jason did not behave like a tyrant. Like Hippias in Thucydides (6.57.2), who was initially very easy to approach (εὐπρόσοδος) before the murder of his brother Hipparchus, he can be contacted by the conspirators who pretend to ask for arbitration in a dispute they had. This is the opposite of what Xenophon's Hiero describes as typical for a tyrant. (*Hier.* 2.10 ὁ δὲ τύραννος οὐδ' ἐπειδὰν εἴσω τῆς οἰκίας παρέλθῃ ἐν ἀκινδύνῳ ἐστίν, ἀλλ' ἐνταῦθα δὴ καὶ μάλιστα φυλακτέον οἴεται εἶναι). On the contrary, a good monarch like Cyrus educates young people by displaying justice and performing the duties of a judge.

certainty is a challenge to the reader to look more carefully into this story, a further sign that the historian attributes special significance to Jason. The pertinent open questions invite the reader to think intensively about this figure. Besides, sufficient signs indicate that Jason's historical importance has to be appreciated against the background of Xenophon's predecessors. Thucydides and Herodotus are recommended as a necessary intertext for the interpretation of this part of Xenophon's work.

An even more convincing answer to the question whether Jason was a tyrant or not is provided by the digression about his successors. Xenophon does not end his Thessalian section with Jason's death, but attaches a digression about the next rulers up to the moment when he was writing the sixth book of the *Hellenica*. Jason's contrast to his successors, who are unambiguously presented as tyrants, is a further proof of Xenophon's positive judgment on Jason. His immediate successor Polyphron will be castigated for the transformation of the *tageia* into a tyranny-like regime[27] (this remark implies that Jason was *not* a tyrant). But making this clear is not the only reason for the inclusion of the digression, which presents some further meaningful Herodotean and Thucydidean reminiscences.

Jason was first followed by his brothers Polydorus and Polyphron – the latter has been made responsible for the sudden death of the former; although this was a conjecture, the expression ὡς ἐδόκει suggests a higher degree of certainty on the part of the author than the expressions used for the rumors about Jason in the preceding chapters. We also observe that the term which is used to denote the grounds of the murder is πρόφασις. It is only here used by Xenophon for "cause", the "reason" for doing something (in all but one of 15 other instances is has the standard meaning "pretext"). Its association with the adjective φανεράν can be paralleled to Thucydides' ἀληθεστάτη πρόφασις (1.23.6), the truest cause which is ἀφανεστάτη λόγῳ and is contrasted to the causes that were overtly stated (ἐς τὸ φανερὸν λεγόμενται αἰτίαι).

Polyphron is killed by Alexander, who is even crueller. A similar story of an *alleged* tyranny which *eventually* became a tyranny after the murder of the previous ruler, who was accessible to the people, was told by Thucydides to explain the Athenians' groundless fear of tyranny. The adjective χαλεπός, is used by both authors more than once in this context, while the parallelism of a regime to tyranny recalls another characteristically Thucydidean motive.[28]

---

[27] The idea is found in Th. 2.62.2, 3.37.2.
[28] The connection to Thucydides is made stronger through the reference to the last Thessalian ruler of this dynasty: The expression πρεσβύτατος ὤν is a further verbatim quotation from Thucydides 1.20.2 on Hippias.

As the digression moves towards its end, more crimes are to be registered, but now there is no political background to be found behind Alexander's end. He was murdered while he was sleeping, after his wife enabled the access of her brothers to their bedchamber during the night. Xenophon knows of two versions about the reason of this conspiracy, and both have to do with the victim's erotic life. A number of motives and the dramatic quality of the narrative recall the opening story of Herodotus' work, the novella of Gyges and the wife of Candaules, and contribute to the impression that Xenophon is writing this part of his work not only with Thucydides' account of Pisistratus' tyranny, but also with Herodotus in mind.[29]

If Herodotus' novella marked a beginning, the correlation of the two similar bedchamber stories implies that the temporally latest event of Xenophon's narrative defines an end point. Herodotus' narrative was organised according to a historical argument: his aim was to illustrate a continuous process which culminates in the Greek victory over the Persian invaders. The novella was the earliest historical incident illustrated in Herodotus' narrative, and is located in a narrative analepsis concerned with the four predecessors of Croesus. Croesus, the first figure to play a major role in Herodotus' history, was the first who threatened Greek freedom and initiated a historical epoch which is characterised by the opposition of Greece and the East and the acme of the Greek *poleis*. Xenophon's Thessalian novella corresponds to the Herodotean novella in many respects. It belongs to a prolepsis which introduces the four successors of Jason, and presents similar motives. Jason, like Croesus, is given a prominent place in the narrative, which is not only justified by historical facts. Croesus story comprises many historically insignificant episodes (clearly fictional), which disclose important aspects of Herodotus' ideology. Jason is equally important for Xenophon, not for his deeds but for what he stands for in the work. The ideal leader of the sixth book of the *Hellenica* is also closer to fiction than to history. His portraiture focuses on his (alleged) skills, his historical contribution is mainly to be sought in his plans, not in his controversial achievements. The exposition of these skills and plans required the historian to highlight a speech which proved ineffective, to celebrate the activity of a commander who did not take part in a battle (but is supposed to have excelled after it as an advisor), to focus on the route to Delphi of a man who was slaughtered before arriving at the sanctuary. Apparently Xenophon was aware that his hero could be regarded as a literary figure, whose presentation encodes wide-ranging ideas about history and historiography.

---

29 Burliga 2011.

VII

Xenophon has been much blamed as a historian. For one thing he was not blamed: that he didn't stop his narrative at the end of the Peloponnesian War. Xenophon invented not only continuous history, but also its predecessors. He is concerned to suggest that the works of Herodotus, Thucydides and his own *Hellenica* form a set of continuous narrative dealing with what was later to be labelled the history of "classical Greece". For Xenophon Greek history has reached a turning point during his lifetime. The focus on Jason, who is presented as an ideal leader, shows what Xenophon expected the next epoch to look like. If (as we have noted above) the future for Xenophon reveals the importance of particular events, now it is the salience of Jason which prompts the historian to follow his heritage into the future. The proleptic digression about Jason's successors which culminates in a synchronisation of writing time and narrated time inscribes Jason into the continuum of experienced time and relates him to the real world of the author's ultimate present. His plans, explicitly or implicitly amplified by the estimations and emotions of external focalisers (Polydamas, the Thebans after Leuctra, the Panhellenic community which was about to celebrate the Pythia, the oracle, the murderers, and those who honoured them) are still to be taken seriously. The status of these plans is not that of an "ungeschehenes Geschehen" but of a pending project. Xenophon's contemporary readers are no doubt aware of what Diodorus reports about the last ruler of Pherae, Tisiphonus. His claims for Panthessalian supremacy were opposed by the dynastic house of Larissa, the Aleuadae, who invited Philip to intervene. He did this successfully, probably after Xenophon had given the final touch to his *Hellenica*. But Xenophon has already shown in Cleigenes' speech in Book V that Macedonia is an alternative candidate to become a superpower. Tim Rood is probably right in suggesting that both Cleigenes' and Polydamas' speech may reflect the situation after the rise of Philip to the Macedonian throne in 359.[30] By reminding the reader that he is writing in Tisiphonus' time, Xenophon suggests that ending the *Hellenica* at Mantinea is a conscious decision.

The *Hellenica* ends with the remark that after Mantinea the hegemony of a Greek city over the Greeks was no longer probable or desired. The future belonged to gifted personalities. Jason had already shown that he was capable of leading Greece. The heirs of his state might succeed or fail; but if they fail, somebody else could occupy their place. After all, both Philip and Jason's sons were addressed by Isocrates for reasons which are not irrelevant to this dis-

---

[30] Rood 2007c, 154. On Xenophon's assessment of Jason's plans cf. Carlier 1978.

cussion. Hegemony seems to be the central question in Jason's story. It is approached dialectically: while Jason is illustrated as a gifted military and political commander, very close to the ideal shared by those who were disappointed in democracy, the story of his successors focuses on the perils of autocracy.

Emily Baragwanath
Knowing Future Time in Xenophon's *Anabasis*

Introduction

For contemporary readers the *Anabasis* will most closely have resembled historical narrative.[1] Despite the lack of a preface, its very opening signals an account of events in chronological order.[2] It provided Lucian with an example for his work on history writing, and *historia* is the label Plutarch attached to it; while a more recent critic aptly describes it as 'microhistory', in contrast to 'macrohistories' like the *Hellenica*.[3] In its approach to temporality and mutability it stands in the tradition of Herodotus (as I shall suggest below, p. 136–137), though generically it signals a future of new forms of historical narrative, focused on the single individuals whose agency becomes key in shaping the brave new world of the fourth century and beyond.[4] Even with its biographical and autobiographical qualities, it therefore remains distinctly historiographical,[5] but intriguingly a history that focuses as much on the future as on the past. This occurs both for literary reasons – Xenophon's narrative strategy entails drawing attention to the future but also keeping it hidden, so that readers may experience un-

---

[1] I would like to express my warm thanks to the conference participants for helpful remarks on my paper, and especially the editor Alexandra Lianeri for her extremely perceptive comments on a written version. Translations of Anabasis are either based on the Loeb (Brownson revised by Dillery) or my own.
[2] Flower 2012, 50, cp. n. 54 below.
[3] Lucian *How to Write History* 23; Plutarch *Moralia* 345e: 'Xenophon became his own history (ἱστορία)'. 'Microhistory': Flower 2012, 48. On the *Anabasis* as historiography see further Marincola 1999, 316, Nicolai 2006, 698–9, Flower 2012, 47–51.
[4] See Dillery 1995, 72, Flower 2012, 42 on how the increasing focus on a single figure as the work goes on anticipates future developments in historiography (the focus on Philip then Alexander); Ferrario 2014 on the increasing historical recognition of the 'Great Man'.
[5] Bradley 2010 argues that the *Anabasis* transforms during its course from history into autobiography, with the increasing focus on Xenophon. Xenophon however also downplays autobiographical aspects by means of the third-person narration and the pseudonymous authorship given to the work in *Hellenica* ('Themistogenes', *Hellenica* 3.1.2). For insightful discussion of genre in Greco-Roman historiography as flexible and continually evolving see Marincola 1999, Pelling 1999 (emphasising the importance of the reader's 'progressive identification of genre and generic affinities', 335).

folding developments alongside the characters[6] – and for historical/explanatory ones: the ability to foresee future developments is a crucial quality of military and political leaders, who play a key role in Xenophon's conceptual and explanatory scheme; and this ability also holds out the possibility for such individuals to shape historical outcomes. Consequently it is above all through the eyes of leaders and would-be leaders – Cyrus the Younger, Clearchus, and especially Xenophon himself – that the *Anabasis* engages with the question of whether, how far, and how one may know about the future. The treatment of future time in this work also has a personal charge, in the evocation of Xenophon's future exile, and of idyllic times spent at his estate near Olympia in the future now past. The *Anabasis* is seeped in an acute personal awareness of change over time and of disappointed futures: the authorial viewpoint is of one looking back with layered temporal perspectives that offer a glimpse of the character Xenophon before the expedition; as a general on the Long March; and later, looking back from a point after his sojourn at Scillus.

1 Ways of knowing future time

According to Xenophon, the key prerequisite of being a good leader in any realm of human activity is knowledge: knowledge of how to bring material and moral advancement to followers that secures their willing obedience.[7] For political and

---

[6] See further below, n. 43 with text, on the effect of the dearth of authorial *prolepseis*. Grethlein 2010a and 2013 address the potential for narrative to enable readers to re-experience the past. The phenomenon is familiar in Greek historiography, including Herodotus (see Pelling 2013, 13–14, Baragwanath 2013) and Thucydides (see Stahl 2003, Grethlein 2010a, 324–7, Grethlein 2010, 241–54, 2013, 29–52, Brock 2013, 50, Hau 2013, 77–85), but occurs in the *Anabasis* in quite sustained and striking form.

[7] Leadership as based on knowledge: e.g. *Anab.* 2.2.6: automatic acceptance of Clearchus as leader for his superior knowledge (τὸ λοιπὸν ὁ μὲν ἦρχεν, οἱ δὲ ἐπείθοντο, οὐχ ἑλόμενοι, ἀλλὰ ὁρῶντες ὅτι μόνος ἐφρόνει οἷα δεῖ τὸν ἄρχοντα, οἱ δ' ἄλλοι ἄπειροι ἦσαν, 'thenceforth he commanded, and they obeyed, not having elected him, but seeing that he alone possessed the knowledge that a commander should have, whereas the others were without experience'), cp. e.g. *Cyr.* 1.1.3: ruling men is possible 'with knowledge' (ἐπισταμένως). See Gray 2011, esp. 7–44, for ideal leadership in Xenophon as based on knowledge of how to bring material/moral improvement to followers. The interest in leadership stands in the tradition of Herodotus and Thucydides (and ultimately Homer), who analyse the leadership of individuals as well as states and address the questions of the difference an individual can make and how far the character of a state determines the character of its individuals. But Xenophon's leaders have more in common with one another than with their compatriots: Athens explains Themistocles in the *Histories* more than it explains 'Xenophon' in the *Anabasis*.

military leaders a crucial dimension of this knowledge is knowledge about the future, as it was for the famous fifth-century statesmen and generals Themistocles and Pericles as depicted by Herodotus and Thucydides. But the new form of history that the *Anabasis* represents, with its stronger focus on individuals, brings what seems a more focused and comprehensive reflection on and articulation of the processes by which individual leaders may grasp such knowledge.

Leaders' knowledge of the future in the *Anabasis* is closely entwined first with practical knowledge and expertise; secondly, with knowledge of character and psychology and the dynamics of interpersonal relationships; and finally, with knowledge of the divine. Each variety of knowledge (all of them interconnected[8]) presents the possibility to some degree not only to read but also *control* the future, at least when combined with the ability to act and to persuade. Controlling the future is the best way to know it; but Xenophon highlights failures even on the part of very skilled leaders correctly to predict, let alone control, future time.

The first ingredient in the recipe for knowing future time in the *Anabasis*, practical knowledge relating to strategy, topography and realities on the ground, is the most straightforward to secure (through one's own expertise along with military intelligence from external sources); and it plays a clear role in shaping outcomes.[9] An important aspect of it, the problem of ἀπορία in space—the difficulty of negotiating the physical terrain on the arduous march of the 10,000 out of the heartland of the Persian Empire and back to Greece—maps directly on to its intangible counterpart of ἀπορία in regard to future time (ignorance about what paths the future holds and how to negotiate them), and so provides an appropriate and tangible metaphor for the predicament of humans as they face the future. Already here we can see how closely knowledge of the future is entwined with knowledge of the present (as well as the past): accurate understanding of present realities is a crucial precondition for attaining it.

Which brings us to the second crucial ingredient in the *Anabasis* to knowing the future: the understanding of character and psychology in relationship to action, both of individuals and groups. Xenophon's narrative exposes a range of motives that accumulate into a broad typology that one might use to predict (and shape) future behaviour, which include fear (and its reverse-face: confidence), self-interest and honour (those motives Thucydides' Athenians famously

---

8 E.g. to get practical advice one must often rely on relationships.
9 E.g. the choice of the best strategy or route to successfully negotiate a particular enemy and particular terrain; see e.g. Xenophon's advice before battle with the Colchians at 4.8.10.

emphasised: Thuc. 1.76), along with others that Herodotus more often highlighted, such as curiosity, jealousy and awareness of *nomos*.[10] The best leaders are attuned to these, understand their potential relationship to future action, and exploit them so as to exercise some control over future developments.

Morale and perceptions—fear and confidence—are thus key indicators of future outcomes in war: success and confidence breed future success (eg. *Anab.* 7.4.21, cp. *Hell.* 4.5.4), fear issues in defeat, and psychological warfare can be extremely effective. As Xenophon tells the Greek mercenaries in a rousing speech when he steps forward as leader after the seizure and murder of their generals, psychological disposition on the part of those fighting is what usually (ὡς ἐπὶ τὸ πολὺ) wins wars, not πλῆθος (numbers) or ἰσχύς (strength) (3.1.42).[11] Xenophon adeptly exploits this knowledge: his most important personal contribution in bringing the Greek mercenaries through to safety is by appearing at moments of *athumia* and transforming them into moments of *tharsos*: thus he successfully replaces the future of defeat and death that constantly threatened, with one of survival. Again, understanding the drives of self-interest and honour is why the younger Cyrus generously rewards and honours men who perform a service, with the effect of inspiring similar behaviour in future.

Philia and *xenia* (and positive reciprocal relationships more generally) are also crucial explanatory principles that the actors on the stage of history can put to good use. Xenophon highlights Cyrus' relationships of *xenia*, for example, as fundamental to the preparation for his future endeavour: he fosters a new friendship with Clearchus (1.1.9) and relies on existing relationships of *xenia* in the case of the other Greek generals, while his implicit focalisation recording his initial plans to overthrow his brother registers the importance of *philia* as a principle that drives history (1.1.4–5).[12] Elsewhere too the same principles come to the fore.

---

[10] Self-interest: e.g. 5.6.18 (Silanus), 6.2.13–14 (Neon), 7.2.2 (four generals). Honour: e.g. *Anab.* 1.9.14–18 (Cyrus honours and rewards the brave and virtuous), 6.1.20 (Xenophon's desire for honour). Jealousy: e.g. 5.7.10.

[11] Psychological warfare: e.g. *Anab.* 2.3.9 (Clearchus contrives φόβος in the enemy), 3.5.6 (Tissaphernes' men burning their own land in an effort to deprive the Greeks of supplies; Xenophon remarks: 'it seems to me that we should go against those setting the fires, as though on behalf of our own land'; Chirisophus retorts: 'rather, let us also burn, and thus more quickly they will stop').

[12] *Philia* and *xenia*: e.g. Cyrus fostering friendship with Clearchus (1.1.9), relying on existing relationships of *xenia* in the case of the other Greek generals (1.1.10, 1.1.11, 1.2.1) and on considerations of *philia* in making his attempt against Artaxerxes (ὁ δ' ὡς ἀπῆλθε κινδυνεύσας καὶ ἀτιμασθείς, βουλεύεται ὅπως μήποτε ἔτι ἔσται ἐπὶ τῷ ἀδελφῷ, ἀλλά, ἢν δύνηται, βασιλεύσει ἀντ' ἐκείνου. Παρύσατις μὲν δὴ ἡ μήτηρ ὑπῆρχε τῷ Κύρῳ, **φιλοῦσα αὐτὸν μᾶλλον ἢ τὸν**

But even as these human drives surface as important explanatory models whose explanatory power is recognised by individuals in the text and corroborated by the author, they prove limited in their efficacy even in the hands of the very best leaders as tools for predicting the future, since the motives of individuals may test the general principles. Self-interest, for example, is not inevitable: most obviously the self-interested motives of those around him are a foil to Xenophon's own focus on the soldiers, the city of Athens and Greece. It can also be hard to tell where self-interest really lies: Tissaphernes deceives Clearchus and others by painting a picture of personal profit in the form of his safe return to Greece and potential ascent to the Persian throne; in hindsight it becomes evident that his self-interest lay elsewhere.[13] It is a particular mystery and indication of the challenge of the task that the Spartan commander Clearchus—elsewhere so adept at reading and exploiting character—here fails to do so, despite the abundant character evidence that could have pointed to Tissaphernes' treacherous tendencies (e.g. in an episode recounted in *Hellenica* (1.1.9) his earlier seizure of Alcibiades, who was bringing gifts).

Failures to read the future often turn on mistaken readings of relationships. Xenophon thus sets out the precisely reciprocal model of human behaviour that shaped his expectations about the Thracian King Seuthes' future conduct—'I thought that by how much (ὅσῳ) I helped him bear his poverty, by this much (τοσούτῳ) would he more be my friend when he gained power' (7.6.20)—and notes that he and his men have given Seuthes every possible reason to reciprocate their friendship: 'If there is such a thing as precaution toward friends, I know that we took every precaution not to afford this man a just pretext for not paying us what he had promised' (7.6.22, cp. Xenophon to Seuthes: 7.7.43). But Seuthes fails to repay *philia* with *philia*. His behaviour instead exposes

---

βασιλεύοντα Ἀρταξέρξην. ὅστις δ' ἀφικνεῖτο τῶν παρὰ βασιλέως πρὸς αὐτὸν πάντας **οὕτω διατιθείς** ἀπεπέμπετο **ὥστε αὐτῷ μᾶλλον φίλους εἶναι ἢ βασιλεῖ**. καὶ τῶν παρ' ἑαυτῷ δὲ βαρβάρων ἐπεμελεῖτο ὡς πολεμεῖν τε ἱκανοὶ εἴησαν καὶ **εὐνοϊκῶς ἔχοιεν αὐτῷ**), cp. 1.9.10 (Cyrus' obituary) for his practice of never abandoning a friend. The same principles elsewhere: e.g. introduction of Xenophon the character (highlights through negation that the bond of *xenia* with Proxenus alone precipitated his involvement in the expedition: Ἦν δέ τις ἐν τῇ στρατιᾷ Ξενοφῶν Ἀθηναῖος, ὃς **οὔτε** στρατηγὸς **οὔτε** λοχαγὸς **οὔτε** στρατιώτης ὢν συνηκολούθει, **ἀλλὰ Πρόξενος αὐτὸν μετεπέμψατο οἴκοθεν ξένος ὢν ἀρχαῖος** (3.1.4); Proxenus also promised to make him a *philos* of Cyrus: 3.1.4). Socrates' warning about possible negative consequences of his participation invokes the power of *philia* from the perspective of the party excluded, Athens: his becoming a friend of Cyrus may bring trouble *vis-à-vis* Athens (3.1.5). Cp. Azoulay 2004, Rood 2006, 60: 'the language of reciprocity pervades and structures the work'. For Cyrus' army as founded on ties of *xenia*, see Mitchell 2002: 119–20 (with references).

13 Tissaphernes' implying profit for himself to deceive Clearchus 2.5.23, cp. Braun 2004, 107.

how such a model may in reality fall short, since it is contingent on the character of the person involved.[14] The *Anabasis* more generally reveals failures on the part of assumed friends to reciprocate friendship, failures correctly to read ostensible friends, and assumptions of reciprocity that prove misguided.[15]

Failures to read character, which bring in their train failures to read the future, pervade the *Anabasis* and mark key narrative developments, right from the Greeks' failure to read Cyrus' intentions (to attack the King)—the catalyst of the whole story. At the other end of the work—in Sparta's fickle behaviour, for which Xenophon indicates no rhyme or reason—we are reminded that states can be as difficult to map onto patterns as individuals, and the consequences for knowing future history still weightier.

Xenophon thus sets out a picture of human character and motivation that may be grasped by good leaders and contributes to a model of future behaviour, but that deals in probabilities not certainties. And it *is* especially on the human level that Xenophon in this work exposes the manifold challenges involved in reading future time, even as it is also on the human level that most can be known and understood. As Robert Parker expresses it, 'To rely on divine guidance on matters within the scope of human understanding is quite wrong, and unproductive' (2004, 134; Xenophon's Socrates expresses much the same sentiment at *Memorabilia* 1.1.9). It is only after all possibilities on the human level have been exhausted that Xenophon turns to the gods for advice.[16] This brings us to the third means of knowing the future in this work, which entails borrowing from the omniscience of the gods. Again there is not merely an epis-

---

[14] 7.6.20: 'As soon as I see him having success, I recognise his true character (γιγνώσκω δὴ αὐτοῦ τὴν γνώμην).'

[15] Failures to read or reciprocate *philia/xenia:* Cyrus taking Tissaphernes 'as a friend' (ὡς φίλον, 1.1.2) to visit his ailing father, juxtaposed with Tissaphernes' slanderous charge against Cyrus to Artaxerxes (made more persuasive by the apparent friendship: Tissaphernes would be in a position to know about such a plot). Artaxerxes' persuasion by Tissaphernes is another failure to read character: a failure (in believing Tissaphernes) to see the sort of person he is; and after such an action to let Cyrus live is a further failure to envisage how a man like Cyrus is bound to respond. Tissaphernes exploits Clearchus' assumption of reciprocity in *xenia* to concoct his deception and the consequent seizure of the generals (2.5.27–31). The Ten Thousand fail to respond as true friends to Xenophon the φιλοστρατιώτης ('friend of the soldiers'): 7.6.4. Cp. the failure of oaths/ *pistis:* e.g. detail of oaths the Greek officers make with Ariaeus and the *barbaroi* (2.2.8–9), and of pledges the King makes with the Greeks (2.3.26–8), but these lead respectively to increasing mutual suspicion between the Greeks and Ariaeus (2.4.1–2, 2.4.9–12), and to the deceit and killing of the generals.

[16] As Parker continues, 'But in situations impermeable to human intelligence, the only rational thing to do is to seek such guidance. By turning to divination one is not surrendering use of one's intelligence, but merely acknowledging its limits.'

temological, but also an instrumental aspect, since the gods, if kept happy, may be expected to help one shape a certain future; and yet in every case in which the agency of the divine is invoked, the human level retains an important explanatory power.

Xenophon is often regarded as a thinker especially attuned to religious explanation; and in the *Hellenica* the divine is a moral force that shapes the future by punishing human injustice. The narrator of the *Anabasis* is however more secular, and the agency of the divine in this work is circumscribed.[17] Where it does play a role is by providing the character Xenophon with guidance in making decisions that help determine his personal future: but these moments reveal the interdependence of secular and divine insight. The episode that secured Xenophon's involvement in the expedition thus sets closely in parallel divine and human sources of knowledge: Xenophon acts on advice from Socrates, to inquire of Delphi, with the same verb used of each of these inquiries about the future.[18] It is the combined advice (of Delphi, to sacrifice to particular gods, and of Socrates that his problematic formulation of the question meant he would indeed have to go on the expedition: 3.1.7) that prompts Xenophon's participation.

Even in the presence of divine guidance, the other (human) sources of knowledge remain important, including one's understanding of others' psychology. Thus effective reading and shaping of the future occurs in the episode of Xenophon's dream at *Anabasis* 4.3.8, when the army needs to cross the Centrites river:

ἐνταῦθα δὴ πολλὴ ἀθυμία ἦν τοῖς Ἕλλησιν, ὁρῶσι μὲν τοῦ ποταμοῦ τὴν δυσπορίαν, ὁρῶσι δὲ τοὺς διαβαίνειν κωλύσοντας, ὁρῶσι δὲ τοῖς διαβαίνουσιν ἐπικεισομένους τοὺς Καρδούχους ὄπισθεν. ταύτην μὲν οὖν τὴν ἡμέραν καὶ νύκτα ἔμειναν ἐν πολλῇ ἀπορίᾳ ὄντες. Ξενοφῶν δὲ ὄναρ εἶδεν· ἔδοξεν ἐν πέδαις δεδέσθαι, αὗται δὲ αὐτῷ αὐτόμαται περιρρυῆναι, ὥστε

---

17 Divine power as moral force in *Hellenica* 5.4.1 (overthrow of Spartan tyrants and Spartan defeat represents divine punishment for Spartan *hubris*), cp. 7.4.3, 7.5.26. More secular persona of the narrator of *Anabasis*: Tuplin 1993, 215, Gray 2004, 136. Perhaps the closest we get in authorial voice is the picture of *tuche* (luck) as a moral force, planning for the future: 'this plan of campaign meant nothing more than to run away or to flee; but chance commanded better (ἡ δὲ τύχη ἐστρατήγησε κάλλιον)', 2.2.13. See n. 19 below for an example of chance aligned with divine agency (*Anab.* 5.2.25).
18 Xenophon inquiring of Socrates and of Apollo: ἀνακοινοῦται Σωκράτει τῷ Ἀθηναίῳ ~ ἀνακοινῶσαι τῷ θεῷ, 3.1.5, cp. Flower 2012, 123: the use of the same phrase 'suggests that Socrates's advice transcends mere human wisdom, and that in turn implies that Socrates correctly prophesied the reason for Xenophon's eventual exile' (123). Commentators note the contrast here drawn between Socrates' wisdom and Xenophon's ignorance, but an equally strong contrast is produced between the omniscience of gods and the limited wisdom of humans. See further below, pp. 126–128, and n. 20 with text on Socrates' advice.

λυθῆναι καὶ **διαβαίνειν** (cf. διαβαίνειν, διαβαίνουσιν above, also προσέτρεχον below?) ὁπόσον ἐβούλετο. ἐπεὶ δὲ ὄρθρος ἦν, ἔρχεται πρὸς τὸν Χειρίσοφον καὶ λέγει ὅτι ἐλπίδας ἔχει καλῶς ἔσεσθαι, καὶ διηγεῖται αὐτῷ τὸ ὄναρ. ὁ δὲ ἥδετό τε καὶ ὡς τάχιστα ἕως ὑπέφαινεν ἐθύοντο πάντες παρόντες οἱ στρατηγοί· καὶ τὰ ἱερὰ καλὰ ἦν εὐθὺς ἐπὶ τοῦ πρώτου. καὶ ἀπιόντες ἀπὸ τῶν ἱερῶν οἱ στρατηγοὶ καὶ λοχαγοὶ παρήγγελλον τῇ στρατιᾷ ἀριστοποιεῖσθαι. καὶ ἀριστῶντι τῷ Ξενοφῶντι <u>προσέτρεχον</u> δύο νεανίσκω· ᾔδεσαν γὰρ πάντες ὅτι ἐξείη αὐτῷ καὶ ἀριστῶντι καὶ δειπνοῦντι προσελθεῖν καὶ εἰ καθεύδοι ἐπεγείραντα εἰπεῖν, εἴ τίς τι ἔχοι τῶν πρὸς τὸν πόλεμον... (4.3.7–10)

'Then it was that deep despondency fell upon the Greeks, as they saw before them a river difficult to cross, beyond it troops that would prevent them <u>from crossing</u>, and behind them the Carduchians, ready to fall upon their rear <u>as they tried to cross</u>. That day and night, accordingly, they remained there, in great perplexity. But Xenophon had a dream; he thought that he was bound in fetters, but that the fetters fell off from him of their own accord, so that he was released and **could take as long steps** (Brownson tr.) as he pleased. When dawn came, he went to Chirisophus, told him he had hopes that all would be well, and related to him his dream. Chirisophus was pleased, and as soon as day began to break, all the generals were at hand and proceeded to offer sacrifices. And with the very first victim the omens were favourable. Then the generals and captains withdrew from the sacrifice and gave orders to the troops to prepare breakfast. While Xenophon was breakfasting, two young men <u>came running up</u> to him; for all knew that they might go to him whether he was breakfasting or dining, and that if he were asleep, they might awaken him and tell him whatever they might have to tell that concerned the war...' (and they report evidence of a safe crossing place.)

In this instance Xenophon's responsiveness to communication from the divine is combined with excellence as a leader who knows that the best way to count on receiving good advice is by promoting a culture that welcomes it.[19] And *diabainein*—to step, or step across—which suggests crossing the river, perhaps even finds a further referent in the steps of the young men who run up. By contrast, his vision of a future city founded at Cotyora (*Anab.* 5.6.15–16) is not realised, because despite favourable omens from the gods (5.6.29), he fails to anticipate

---

19 Cp. Flower 2012, 134, underlining Xenophon's agency ('It is Xenophon's round-the-clock accessibility to everyone and anyone with something important to say that makes divine intervention efficacious'). Cp. 5.2.24–5: divine help appears to Xenophon and the men in a state of perplexity after an expedition in search of provisions into the territory of the Drilae—but only late in the piece, and in the form only of providing a means of safety: a sudden fire lit by an individual, that *gives Xenophon an idea* for saving the men; and 4.2.2, where the narrative presents a combination of divine and human initiative tending to a successful future outcome: while Xenophon and the rear guard take the visible road, in an effort to distract observation from the party taking the roundabout route, ὕδωρ πολὺ ἦν ἐξ οὐρανοῦ, 'there was a heavy downpour of rain from heaven/the sky'.

his seer's act of sabotage and so loses the possibility of presenting a persuasive case to the troops.

Thus successful readings and shapings of the future tend to combine all available varieties of knowledge. Wise human advisors and informants often play a crucial role. At the same time, human advice is attended by serious limitations: it is limited in range, at times deceptive, and the product of unclear sight of the future. Even Socrates' advice comes in the form of a mere 'suspicion' (not sure knowledge):[20]

> καὶ ὁ Σωκράτης **ὑποπτεύσας** μή τι πρὸς τῆς πόλεως ὑπαίτιον εἴη Κύρῳ φίλον γενέσθαι, ὅτι ἐδόκει ὁ Κῦρος προθύμως τοῖς Λακεδαιμονίοις ἐπὶ τὰς Ἀθήνας συμπολεμῆσαι, συμβουλεύει τῷ Ξενοφῶντι ἐλθόντα εἰς Δελφοὺς ἀνακοινῶσαι τῷ θεῷ περὶ τῆς πορείας (3.1.5).

> 'And Socrates, **suspecting** that his becoming a friend of Cyrus might be a cause for accusation against Xenophon on the part of the Athenian government, for the reason that Cyrus was thought to have given the Lacedaemonians zealous aid in their war against Athens, advised Xenophon to go to Delphi and consult the god in regard to this journey.'

It also appears to arise from Socrates' own subjective experience: the future troubles he envisages for Xenophon parallel his own in relation to the Athenians.[21]

Only gods in the *Anabasis* have a 'clear' vision of the future.[22] The contrast between opacity on the human level and the clarity of divine perspective comes out sharply in a scene where Xenophon ponders whether to accept the troops' offer of sole command:

> ὁ δὲ Ξενοφῶν τῇ μὲν ἐβούλετο ταῦτα, νομίζων καὶ τὴν τιμὴν μείζω οὕτως ἑαυτῷ γίγνεσθαι πρὸς τοὺς φίλους καὶ εἰς τὴν πόλιν τοὔνομα μεῖζον ἀφίξεσθαι αὐτοῦ, τυχὸν δὲ καὶ ἀγαθοῦ τινος ἂν αἴτιος τῇ στρατιᾷ γενέσθαι. τὰ μὲν δὴ τοιαῦτα ἐνθυμήματα ἐπῆρεν αὐτὸν ἐπιθυμεῖν αὐτοκράτορα γενέσθαι ἄρχοντα. ὁπότε δ' αὖ ἐνθυμοῖτο **ὅτι ἄδηλον μὲν παντὶ ἀνθρώπῳ**

---

20 The 'suspicions' that hang over book one (as well as subsequent books) add to this sense of humans' unclear sight of the future, with the *hupo-* stem suggesting something *concealed* and *unclear*.
21 Human advice as deceptive, e.g. 4.1.23–4 (a local conceals the existence of an alternative route for the sake of his daughter), 6.2.14 (Neon gives advice aimed at preventing others from sharing in the opportunity; Xenophon highlights the irony: διὰ ταῦτα συνεβούλευε). On advisors in the *Anabasis* see Rood 2006 (suggesting at pp. 56–60 that Socrates does not accurately predict Xenophon's troubles, which rather concern the *Persians* and being left in the middle of Asia).
22 Cp. Rood 2013, on the use of μελήσει both of Artemis at 5.3.13 (inscription on the temple at Scillus) and of a possible future continuator at the end of the *Hellenica*: 'we can see Xenophon as setting up an opposition between the human contingency of history and the realm of the divine, untouched by uncertainty' (208).

ὅπῃ τὸ μέλλον ἕξει, διὰ τοῦτο δὲ καὶ κίνδυνος εἴη καὶ τὴν προειργασμένην δόξαν ἀποβαλεῖν, ἠπορεῖτο. διαπορουμένῳ δὲ αὐτῷ διακρῖναι ἔδοξε κράτιστον εἶναι τοῖς θεοῖς ἀνακοινῶσαι· .... οὕτω δὴ θυομένῳ αὐτῷ **διαφανῶς ὁ θεὸς σημαίνει** μήτε προσδεῖσθαι τῆς ἀρχῆς μήτε εἰ αἱροῖντο ἀποδέχεσθαι (6.1.20–22, 24).

'From one point of view, Xenophon was inclined to accept, for he thought that if he did so he would enjoy greater honour among his friends and a greater name when he reached his native city, and furthermore he might perhaps be the agent of some good for the army. Such considerations, then, roused in him the desire to become sole commander. On the other hand, when he reflected **that it is unclear to every human being in what way the future will turn out** and that consequently he ran the risk of throwing away even his previously achieved reputation, he was at a loss. Unable to decide the question, it seemed best to him to consult the gods... So it was, then that Xenophon made sacrifice, and **the god signified to him quite clearly** that he should neither strive for the command nor accept it if he should be chosen'.

He is in two minds. On the one hand, thought of future advantages 'roused in him the desire to become sole commander' (6.1.20–21). On the other, when he reflects on the uncertainty of the future, how 'it is unclear (ἄδηλον) to every human being in what way the future will be' and that consequently 'he risked ruining his reputation', he was at a loss.[23] In this moment of *aporia* (cp. ἠπορεῖτο: 6.1.21, ἀπορουμένῳ δὲ αὐτῷ: 6.1.22) Xenophon sacrifices, and 'the god signalled **manifestly/transparently (διαφανῶς)**' that he should neither ask for the command nor accept it if chosen. In retrospect, events confirm his decision as the better one. Chirisophus' command lasts for only six days before the men break into separate divisions, with damaging consequences.

Renouncing the possibility of 'clear' (σαφῶς) knowledge of the future, the character Xenophon thus acknowledges that the future is 'unclear', ἄδηλον (cp. 5.1.10, 6.1.21). Before taking action he works as closely as possible with advisors in realms both human and divine (as at 5.2.9–10) and takes a prudential attitude more generally so far as the future is concerned.[24]

---

[23] Xenophon's expression here perhaps recalls the advice of Herodotus' famous advisor, Solon, and perhaps especially the penultimate sentence of his speech to Croesus: Σκοπέειν δὲ χρὴ παντὸς χρήματος τὴν τελευτὴν κῇ ἀποβήσεται (1.32).

[24] For lack of clarity of human knowledge of the future see also 5.1.10 ff.: Xenophon advises that the army collect ships, since they cannot be sure whether Clearchus will secure an adequate number (**εἰ μὲν ἠπιστάμεθα σαφῶς** ('if we could know clearly') ὅτι ἥξει πλοῖα Χειρίσοφος ἄγων ἱκανά, οὐδὲν ἂν ἔδει ὧν μέλλω λέγειν· **νῦν δ' ἐπεὶ τοῦτο ἄδηλον**, δοκεῖ μοι πειρᾶσθαι πλοῖα συμπαρασκευάζειν καὶ αὐτόθεν. ἢν μὲν γὰρ ἔλθῃ, ὑπαρχόντων ἐνθάδε ἐν ἀφθονωτέροις πλευσόμεθα· ἢν δὲ μὴ ἄγῃ, τοῖς ἐνθάδε χρησόμεθα, 5.1.10). He advises the army to build roads as well, in case they should still fail to have enough ships (5.1.12)—but at their uproar in opposition, 'when he recognised their foolishness', he personally undertook to persuade

2 Probable versus actual futures

Xenophon's narrative, then, underscores the obscurity of future time and exposes problems associated with attaining it. The best one can do is work on the basis of probabilities—*eikos:* but this may be misleading, and on occasion all sources work in tandem to build up a sustained picture of a probable, and yet incorrect future.

This is powerfully conveyed in the clash of probable with actual futures in *Anabasis* book one. On both human and divine levels, Cyrus the Younger is regarded as a man destined to be a future king. His leadership ability has won recognition (from his father and the Ionians, who revolt to join his side), and his clear initiative stands in contrast to his brother Artaxerxes' passivity. Divine portents confirm the trajectory: when Cyrus' army cross the Euphrates and remain dry above chest-level 'it seemed that this was divine intervention, and that clearly (σαφῶς) the river had retired before Cyrus because he was destined to be king' (1.4.18). Intertextual resonances with Herodotus have the same effect.[25]

The depiction of Cyrus' firm resolve for the future after his narrow escape from death strengthens the impression still further. Thus sections 1.1.4–5, focalised through Cyrus' gaze, present the future outcome Cyrus wants to achieve, and how he plans to achieve it:

ὁ δ' ὡς ἀπῆλθε κινδυνεύσας καὶ ἀτιμασθείς, **βουλεύεται ὅπως** μήποτε ἔτι ἔσται ἐπὶ τῷ ἀδελφῷ, ἀλλά, ἢν δύνηται, βασιλεύσει ἀντ' ἐκείνου. Παρύσατις μὲν δὴ ἡ μήτηρ ὑπῆρχε τῷ Κύρῳ, φιλοῦσα αὐτὸν μᾶλλον ἢ τὸν βασιλεύοντα Ἀρταξέρξην. ὅστις δ' ἀφικνεῖτο τῶν παρὰ βασιλέως πρὸς αὐτὸν πάντας **οὕτω διατιθεὶς** ἀπεπέμπετο **ὥστε** αὐτῷ μᾶλλον φίλους εἶναι ἢ βασιλεῖ. καὶ τῶν παρ' ἑαυτῷ δὲ βαρβάρων **ἐπεμελεῖτο ὡς** πολεμεῖν τε ἱκανοὶ εἴησαν καὶ εὐνοϊκῶς ἔχοιεν αὐτῷ. τὴν δὲ Ἑλληνικὴν δύναμιν ἤθροιζεν ὡς μάλιστα ἐδύνατο ἐπικρυπτόμενος, **ὅπως ὅτι** ἀπαρασκευότατον λάβοι βασιλέα (1.1.4–6).

'Now when Cyrus had thus returned, after his danger and disgrace, **he set about planning that** he might never again be in the power of his brother, but, if possible, might be king in his stead. He had, in the first place, the support of Parysatis, his mother, for she loved him

---

local cities to build the roads (5.2.14). The worth of such a prudential attitude is later confirmed: when Chirisophus fails to return and there are not enough ships, the bulk of the army sets off down the road (5.3.1).

25 There is confirmation of Cyrus' worthiness to rule in the obituary: 1.9.1–2. Cp. vocabulary: Cyrus summoned 'from the satrapy/ rule' (ἀπὸ τῆς ἀρχῆς, 1.1.2). Divine signs: cp. the watchword 'Zeus the Saviour and Victory' that Cyrus accepts. Herodotean resonances: narrative pattern of younger son destined to rule (Perdiccas: Hdt. 5.22, Lycophron: 3.50–53), Persian Queen Mother serving as king-maker (Atossa for Xerxes: 7.3; cp. Candaules' wife, king-maker for Gyges: 1.11–13).

better than the son who was king, Artaxerxes. Again, when any of the King's court came to visit him, **he treated them all in such a way that** when he sent them back they were more devoted to him than to the King. **He also took care that** the barbarians of his own province should be capable soldiers and should feel kindly toward him. Lastly, as regards his Greek force, he proceeded to collect it with the utmost secrecy, **so that** he might take the King as completely unprepared as possible.'

The succinct pairing of plans and desired outcomes suggests, from Cyrus' perspective, the direct connection between these things. This is a man of action looking ahead to the future and seeking to control it, and a man aware of some of the text's key explanatory principles.[26]

Strategic calculations contribute to the sense of a possible, even inevitable future. The narrative of book one builds up an impression of the extraordinary speed of Cyrus' progress despite the hard terrain. At 1.5.9 the narrator summarises and then delves into Cyrus' mind to expose the calculation he employs in planning for the future, and finally gives authorial confirmation that a swift attack could meet with success:

τὸ δὲ σύμπαν δῆλος ἦν Κῦρος ὡς σπεύδων πᾶσαν τὴν ὁδὸν καὶ οὐ διατρίβων ὅπου μὴ ἐπισιτισμοῦ ἕνεκα ἢ τινος ἄλλου ἀναγκαίου ἐκαθέζετο, **νομίζων, ὅσῳ θᾶττον ἔλθοι, τοσούτῳ ἀπαρασκευαστοτέρῳ βασιλεῖ μαχεῖσθαι, ὅσῳ δὲ σχολαίτερον, τοσούτῳ πλέον συναγείρεσθαι βασιλεῖ στράτευμα.** καὶ συνιδεῖν δ' ἦν τῷ προσέχοντι τὸν νοῦν τῇ βασιλέως ἀρχῇ πλήθει μὲν χώρας καὶ ἀνθρώπων ἰσχυρᾷ οὖσα, τοῖς δὲ μήκεσι τῶν ὁδῶν καὶ τῷ διεσπάσθαι τὰς δυνάμεις ἀσθενής, εἴ τις διὰ ταχέων τὸν πόλεμον ποιοῖτο (1.5.9).

'In general it was clear that Cyrus was making haste through the entire journey and making no delays unless he stopped for the sake of provisions or some other necessity; **for he was thinking that by how much he went more quickly, by this much the king would be less prepared to fight, but by how much he went more slowly, by this much a larger army would gather for the king.** And **for anyone who turned his attention to it, it was possible to see** that the power of the king was strong in the number of lands and of men, but weak in the length of the roads and in the scattered nature of its forces, if one should make war swiftly'. [27]

Readers are drawn to reflect on this future and its wider implications by the spectre of what this would mean to the Greek mercenaries: in his speech to

---

[26] Cyrus' last noted concern, to gather the Greek force 'with the utmost secrecy', is amplified in the chapters that follow—which highlight further the model of action we already see here: friendship and relationships as key explanatory factors. Cyrus builds a relationship of *xenia* with Clearchus (1.1.9), and that becomes central to Clearchus' contriving that the mercenaries stay; and employing his *xenoi* Aristippus (1.1.10), Proxenus, Sophaenetus and Socrates the Achaean (1.1.11), to build up armies for him; cp. n. 12 above with text.

[27] Cp. Cyrus' speech evoking a splendid future: 1.7.

the Greek generals and captains Cyrus evokes a splendid future of their choosing to stay with him rather than return home (1.7.4), and expresses fear not that he will not have enough to give his friends, but that he will not have enough friends to give it to (1.7.7).

And yet alongside these evocations of the future the text highlights possible misreadings of it, tied to misreadings of individual motivation. We are presented with artful examples of how to mislead others about one's future intentions.[28] And finally Cyrus—himself such a skilled forger of false future intentions—fails to read the intentions of his own brother in the lead-up to Cunaxa. Xenophon points this up by supplying Cyrus' thoughts about the immediate future juxtaposed with implicit corrections,[29] and including a detail that highlights the misreading, the note of a previous bet, when Cyrus had promised his seer ten talents if his prediction that the king would not fight within ten days was correct, and claimed that if he would not fight within that period he would not fight at all (1.7.18).[30] Thus Cyrus' army proceeds more and more carelessly (1.8.20). What we are given in fact is a picture of distinct *un*preparedness, whereas the *King* on the following day is sighted 'approaching with a large army *prepared for battle*' (1.8.1, ὡς εἰς μάχην παρεσκευασμένος) —in ironic tension with Cyrus' earlier desire to so act as to catch the king as unprepared as possible (ἀπαρασκευότατον, 1.1.6). A final act which lacks discipline follows and secures a changed future: for Cyrus 'does not check himself' but rushes into the midst of battle to strike his brother (1.8.26), and is killed.

---

28 Cp. Braun 2004, 110 on Cyrus' expedition as a story of elaborate deception. Cyrus contrives an impression of future plans—*prophaseis* ('pretexts'/ 'explanations') for action—that conceals his real one: Tissaphernes (and the King) are deceived for some time, the Greek mercenaries for far longer. Clearchus (1.3.2 ff.) likewise contrives a misleading impression of his future plans (informing the Greeks that despite bonds of *xenia* with Cyrus, he will desert him to stay with them).
29 Failed predictions: Cyrus holds a midnight review of his troops 'for he thought' (ἐδόκει γὰρ) that the king would do battle at the next dawn (εἰς τὴν ἐπιοῦσαν ἕω) (1.7.1) ~ on the following day at daybreak (ἅμα τῇ ἐπιούσῃ ἡμέρᾳ) (not the king's army but) deserters come bringing reports (1.7.2). From there he marches with the army in battle formation 'for he thought that the king would engage in battle on this day' (ᾤετο γὰρ ταύτῃ τῇ ἡμέρᾳ μαχεῖσθαι βασιλέα, 1.7.14), because they had encountered a deep trench ~ 'Now on this day the king did not engage in battle' (ταύτῃ μὲν οὖν τῇ ἡμέρᾳ οὐκ ἐμαχέσατο βασιλεύς, 1.7.17), but tracks of horses and men in retreat were visible.
30 Note too how Cyrus' explicitly didactic stance in his speech to the Greek generals and captains —'I who know will teach you' (1.7.4)—lends emphasis to his mistaken prediction (which Xenophon later highlights) that the Persian army 'will attack with a great outcry' (1.7.4, cp. 1.8.11: ἐψεύθη τοῦτο).

So, the future does not unfold in accordance with likelihood: by the end of book one, hopes and expectations of Xenophon and the Ten Thousand are dashed and the probable future—Cyrus' defeat of his brother and ascent to the Persian throne—is derailed, after a contingent event (Cyrus' death) sets the future on a different track.

We have addressed readings that relate primarily to the most immediate future: but Xenophon's presentation highlights the interconnections involved in reading and understanding the past, present, immediate future and longer-range future. Cyrus' ambitious hopes for the more distant future depend on the realisation of his shorter-term aims and so likewise remain unfulfilled.

3 Ideal versus actual futures

The obscurity of future time and the difficulty of predicting or influencing it is further spotlighted by the text's systematic exploration of other such tensions as well between desires and expectations or aspirations for the future on the one hand, and future actuality on the other.

Thus desired and actual futures stand in tension in relation to the theme of homecoming deferred. The soldiers', and (especially in book seven) the character Xenophon's, desires for (and in Xenophon's case concrete preparations for, e.g. 7.8.57) a future return home are often referred to and emphasised, but repeatedly frustrated. The same tension is encoded in narrative form: readers are led to expect closure, and closure of a particular sort: Odyssean intertextuality looks forward to a return narrative, at least for Xenophon if not his comrades (Odysseus' of course perished *en route*): but the *nostos* never comes.[31]

In a related opposition, aspirational futures stand in tension with actual ones. The text thus builds up the spectre of Xenophon and the Cyreans as Homeric or perhaps (Rood 2004: 317) Persian-War-like heroes who will return to honour and praise: an aspirational future that is largely a product of the character Xenophon's own conscious shaping of the future 'story' and its future reception. We see this most clearly in his address to surviving officers after the seizure of the

---

[31] Return/ home-coming deferred: Ma 2004 and Azoulay 2004, 333–4 (*Anab.* is about the *impossibility* of returning home), Bradley 2010, 540–43 (*Anab.* builds up impossible expectations), Purves 2010, 159–95 (evocation and deferral of the notion of homeland), Flower 2012: 46: 'the real denouement of the story of the Greeks' return to their homeland does not take place in the *Anabasis*, where one might reasonably have expected to find it, but appears indirectly in the *Hellenica*' (3.4.20; cp. 4.3.20). Return and (lack of) narrative closure, with reference to the *Odyssey*: Purves 2010, 163 ff., Flower 2012, 44–7, 111, Grethlein 2013, 75–83.

generals, and in its aftermath, when he strives to open up a possible future in which the Greeks fight a Homeric-style *agon* that will secure their future fame and memory, and invites the survivors to embrace this future by bold action.[32] Other characters in the *Anabasis* likewise explicitly address the Cyreans' future reception: their remembrance through time and future praise.[33] In the narrative as well, the men are frequently described in terms that recall Homeric and contemporary athletic heroism (they are *agathoi* competing in *agones*).

And yet this *aspirational* future of men fighting valorously, actively shaping the future, being praised on return home, and remembered forever, stands in strong tension with reality: for the men are never greeted as heroes; often they do not act like heroes;[34] this is *not* a Homeric-style war involving hand-to-hand combat between equals, but guerrilla style warfare involving raids and booty grabs; nor does the campaign appear to change anything. But equally

---

[32] Ten Thousand as Homeric-style heroes: e.g. Xenophon at 3.1.17: none of us is planning countermeasures 'in order that we will contend most finely' (ὅπως ὡς κάλλιστα ἀγωνιούμεθα, 3.1.16, cp. 3.1.22: ἀγῶνα); now that the truce has broken, 'all the good things are prizes (ἆθλα) for whichever of us shall prove the better men' (3.1.21), with the gods standing over as ἀγωνοθέται. Let us not wait for others to summon us ἐπὶ τὰ κάλλιστα ἔργα, but rather take the lead ourselves in arousing the rest, too, to virtue (ἐπὶ τὴν ἀρετήν, 3.1.24). Show yourselves to be the best of the captains (τῶν λοχαγῶν ἄριστοι, 3.1.24). Cp. 3.1.37: the officers ought to surpass the soldiers, 'since when there was peace, you exceeded these men in money and in honours; and now that there is war, you must deem it right to be better than the crowd, and to plan on their behalf and labour on their behalf, if there is need' (3.1.37, cp. *Iliad* 12.310). Those who seek in war to live in whatever possible way tend to die badly and shamefully, whereas those who have recognized that death is inevitable for humans and strive to die nobly (καλῶς) more likely reach old age and live happily (3.1.44). The men must be ἄνδρας ἀγαθούς and call others to be so too. Chirisophus praises Xenophon's words and deeds (3.1.45) and urges the soldiers to 'be brave men (ἄνδρας ἀγαθοὺς τελέθειν) and not to yield', but either to be saved καλῶς in victory, or to die καλῶς, and never to fall into the hands of their enemies alive (3.2.3). See Dillery 1995, 69–77 on the representation of the Ten Thousand in the phase after Cunaxa as a 'heroic community' or 'quasi-epic army or 'Warrior-band'' (76). On Homeric touches in the *Anabasis*: Tuplin 2003, 115–42.

[33] Future memory: e.g. Clearchus to Phalinus, envisaging the expedition's future fame: 2.1.17, cp. Rood 2006, 52; Xenophon encouraging his men: 'it will surely be sweet, through some manly and noble thing which one may say or do today, to furnish memory (μνήμην) in those whom he wishes to remember him' (6.5.24), cp. 7.6.32: keeping safe 'any fine thing' (τι καλόν) done against the barbarians of Asia, they have gained 'other glory' (ἄλλην εὔκλειαν) vanquishing Thracians in Europe: thus implying that the process of their future memory has already begun. See Flower 2012, 34–8 on the *Anabasis* as *lieu de memoire* for the Ten Thousand, aware of its ability to seal its characters' reputations for the future; Xenophon 'exercises a tight control both over who and what is remembered and over how they are remembered' (36).

[34] *Not* so heroic: Dillery 1995, 77–91 (dissolution of the ideal community), Tuplin 2003, 142–52.

this aspirational future is not *merely* aspirational: we are shown how a good leader can put it to use. It proves a source of *in*spiration for the men, at times eliciting the heroic behaviour it imagines, and so indeed shaping immediate future outcomes—not only in the scene in the night after the massacre of the generals, but elsewhere as well;[35] and these short-term successes play their part in securing an important longer-term future, that of the safe arrival of many back on the fringes of Greece. Perhaps this hints at an effect beyond the text of aspirational futures more generally: perhaps ideals cannot transform individuals into real heroes or perfect leaders, but have the potential to shape human behaviour and play a role in forging a better future.

Another such clash is that of the desired or aspirational future of a Greek colony founded in Asia, which in actuality fails: it is a possible future viewed first in terms of Xenophon's desire, scuppered by his seer's action (5.6.15–18); and then implied in the description of Port Calpe, which conjures up an environment ideal for such a foundation: so ideal indeed that the soldiers refuse to encamp there, 'but it seemed to them that the fact of their coming to such a place was a plot on the part of certain people who wished to found a city' (6.4.3–8).[36] Does this represent a future-now-passed, a missed opportunity? – for the leader fails to effect this future. Or does it hint at a future possibility that remains real, a settlement of Greeks in the Persian Empire, a project perhaps of Panhellenic character? Or even at a future possible defeat of the Great King and appropriation of his empire, as Alexander would go on to do?[37] The answer must depend on one's wider interpretation of Xenophon's approach to future time; my own would favour the first possibility.

4 Ideals, realities, and mutability across genres

These tensions between ideals and realities are in part a reflection of a broader preoccupation that spans Xenophon's oeuvre. At the same time however—to an-

---

35 Aspirational future a source of inspiration: e.g. in securing the capture of the Taochians' stronghold (4.7.8–14): 'For all these men were rivals in *arete*, and continually contending against one another; and thus in rivalry they captured the stronghold. For once they had run in, no further stone was borne down from above' (4.7.12). Cp. the encounter with the Colchians (Xenophon advises Homerically, 'if we can, we must eat these men raw!': 4.8.14), 6.3.17.
36 Cp. 3.2.24–6 (threat of the Greeks' permanent settlement in Asia). On the motif of colonisation: Grethlein 2013, 70–75.
37 See the nuanced discussion of Rood 2004, who remarks that the *Anabasis* 'can easily be read as stressing the difficulty of such an expedition rather than its feasibility' (320).

ticipate our argument later in this section—in the *Anabasis* their inflection is distinctly historiographical.

Across his entire literary oeuvre Xenophon displays profound awareness of change over time and of the disjunctions that occur between past and present, between present and future, and between ideals and reality.[38] The focus on leadership implies optimism about the leader's ability to shape the future, bringing in its train the assumption that individuals can make a difference in the processes of history.[39] And yet as often as not these individuals fail to make a great difference, either to the immediate future, or ultimately: Cyrus the Younger dies; the order of the Elder Cyrus (in the *Cyropaedia*) fails to outlast his death. Leaders can themselves be aware of the tension.[40] The dissonance between ideals and reality is frequently expressed through the *topos* of temporal rupture: rupture between past (ideals, expectations, aspirations) and present or future (realities). Temporal rupture is expressed in the palinodic structure of several of Xenophon's works, including the romanticising biography *Cyropaedia*, where the idealised depiction of Cyrus the Elder issues in a description of the degenerate condition of Persia nowadays, and the *Constitution of the Spartans*, where the glowing portrayal of Lycurgan Sparta is followed by an account of her debased contemporary character.

In Xenophon's historiographical works, beyond a single moment of rupture, we find the depiction of *incessant* change, which even more powerfully underscores mutability and uncertainty as characteristic of human history and the human condition. In the *Anabasis*, Xenophon's final great speeches stand as a bookend to the leitmotif of failed expectations and broken promises. The speech to the army meditates on the fickle nature of human fortune and human character and presents Xenophon himself as having suffered a stark transformation in fortune: once subject of the highest praise, he is now threatened with being stoned to death. As Xenophon opens his address: 'So then, a human being should expect everything...' (Ἀλλὰ πάντα μὲν ἄρα ἄνθρωπον ὄντα προσδοκᾶν δεῖ..., 7.6.11). The work's two authorial *prolepseis* are strangely uninformative about

---

[38] See e.g. Higgins 1977, 12–14, Ma 2004, and below.
[39] E.g. Xenophon's address to the Cyrean officers: leaders to replace the dead must be appointed 'for without leaders nothing fine or good can occur in any field, so to speak, and especially not in warfare' (3.1.38), cp. 3.2.8, 10. Cp. *Hell.* 3.2.7: the leader of the (former) Cyreans observes that the men campaigning in Asia are the same; the reason for their not being at fault now is the different commander.
[40] Thus in contrast to the optimism of his speech, Xenophon's private thoughts disclose uncertainty: 3.2.7.

the future, and this again underscores the theme of unfulfilled expectations and the unpredictable changeability of human experience in relation to time. Thus use of the imperfect tense within the *prolepsis* forward to Xenophon's future retreat at Scillus (5.3.7–13) intimates perhaps that the settled situation there would be ephemeral and has been replaced in a still more distant future by a different situation, about which readers are given no information.[41] The *prolepsis* revealing Xenophon's future exile from Athens fails to explain its cause (7.7.57). Even at the end of the work there is scarcely a glance to future events. The last sentence provides only the barest possible record of the immediate future in its ingressive imperfect—

Ἐν τούτῳ Θίβρων παραγενόμενος παρέλαβε τὸ στράτευμα καὶ συμμείξας τῷ ἄλλῳ Ἑλληνικῷ **ἐπολέμει** πρὸς Τισσαφέρνην καὶ Φαρνάβαζον ('Meanwhile Thibron arrived and took over the army and after uniting it with the rest of the Greek force **started to make war** against Tissaphernes and Pharnabazus', 7.8.24)

—even as the way we have returned to where we started, back to Asia Minor with a war being waged against Tissaphernes, does give the sense of an on-going story, perhaps even the sense that history may be about to repeat.[42] The dearth of authorial *prolepseis* in the *Anabasis* keeps readers in a position parallel to that of the participants on the march as they experienced the unfolding of time, denied glimpses of the future, and therefore exposed to the full force of chance and contingency.[43] This textual cultivation of uncertainty about the future is part of what makes the tale so gripping: it generates suspense by keeping the (immediate) future unknown and alive to readers. But beyond being merely a narrative device it intimates that the unclarity of future time is part of the human condition, and makes predicting the future a very difficult task.

The emphasis on the obscurity of the future is a distinct feature of Xenophon's historiographical rather than non-historiographical works, and a function not simply of a genre that employs chronological narrative, but also of one that engages self-consciously and critically with problems of epistemology in relation to human events. Xenophon's approach is closely aligned to that of his historiographical predecessor Herodotus, who emphasised the uncertainty and unknow-

---

[41] Cp. Rood 2007c, 161 (use of imperfect tense marking either narrative iteration, or the fact of Xenophon's having left Scillus by the time of writing—which the proleptic inscription might likewise suggest).
[42] Back to the beginning at the end: Lossau 1990, 51, Azoulay 2004, 335, Flower 2012, 49 (including for the sense of an 'ongoing story').
[43] Cp. Grethlein 2013, 54–75, also Bradley 2010, 546.

ability of future time,⁴⁴ and whose work exposed general patterns that expressed only likelihoods, not certainties, and did not equip one to predict the future in particular cases.⁴⁵ We find nothing in Herodotus or in Xenophon's historiography akin to Thucydides' startling expression in his 'methodological chapter' of optimism that his work will last forever, or his aspiration that it be found useful by future readers who would wish to have a view of **τὸ σαφές** ('the clarity', or 'clear truth') not merely of past events, but also of future ones; and his prediction that these would be '(exactly) such as' past events, or 'similar', on the grounds of the constancy of human nature (τὸ ἀνθρώπινον).⁴⁶ So far from offering a 'clear' view of the future, the end of Xenophon's *Hellenica* suggests extreme and increasing *lack* of clarity about future time.⁴⁷ At the same time, Thucydides' own narrative in important ways qualifies and stands in tension with the optimism of his methodological chapter.⁴⁸

When Xenophon turned to writing history, Herodotus' emphasis on uncertainty and opacity well fit the extreme political insecurity in the Greek world in the decades that followed the Peloponnesian war. Building on Herodotus,

---

44 Herodotean uncertainty: e.g. regarding the waxing and waning of cities, the *majority* of those once great are now small (τὰ γὰρ τὸ πάλαι μεγάλα ἦν, **τὰ πολλὰ** σμικρὰ αὐτῶν γέγονε: τὰ δὲ ἐπ' ἐμεῦ ἦν μεγάλα, πρότερον ἦν σμικρά), cp. Solon: σκοπέειν δὲ χρὴ παντὸς χρήματος τὴν τελευτὴν κῇ ἀποβήσεται ('one must look to the end, to know how things will turn out', 1.32), Artabanus: τὸ μὴ ἅμα ἀρχῇ πᾶν τέλος καταφαίνεσθαι ('the end/outcome of events is not always obvious at the beginning', 5.1.3).
45 Solon expresses no *certainty* about Croesus' future fall: he simply observes that until a man is dead, the question of his happiness remains open (cp. esp. 3.32.7–9). Cp. Grethlein 2010: 192 (in relation to Croesus' failure to prevent Cyrus' downfall): 'the only consistency is life's inconsistency'. Xerxes remains in power at the end of Herodotus' narrative.
46 In Thucydides' secular view, the sharp human intellect of a Themistocles or a Pericles is the most effective key to grasping the future—with the important qualification that one's grasp may not be wholly secure, and irrational events may throw a spanner in the works of even the best-laid plans (see esp. Stahl 2003). The warning of Thucydides' Athenians about the unpredictability of war (1.78.1–2) is thus borne out by the narrative of the plague at Athens and events on Pylos (which highlight the role of chance, and humans' responses to it).
47 Instead of the clear outcome with clear winners and losers that everyone expected, the situation after the battle of Mantinea was only more confused and disordered: ἀκρισία δὲ καὶ ταραχὴ ἔτι πλείων μετὰ τὴν μάχην ἐγένετο (7.5.27), cp. Dillery 1995, 20–22. See p. 136 above on 7.8.24.
48 See the works cited in n. 6 above. Grethlein 2010 plays down the tension, observing about the utility of Thucydides' work that 'the *History* provides its readers not so much with patterns as with a manifold, complex foil that allows for a better understanding of any other time' (274); 'the very reading of the *History* constitutes an important exercise in the art of conjecturing and reasoning that forms an important aspect of life in general and politics in particular' (279). See too the enlightening comments of Pelling 1999: 353–5.

he constructed an idea of time and the historical that is centred upon the volatility of human affairs and the notion of change as central to human history. But more so than in Herodotus, in the *Anabasis* the consciousness of mutability is applied with especial force to the relationship of present and future (more than past and present). Intriguingly, the emphasis on the challenge of knowing future time appears to overshadow or even replace the emphasis found in earlier historians on the challenge of knowing the past: the *Anabasis* (like the *Hellenica*) contains remarkably little source criticism in the manner of Herodotus,[49] and no explicit discussion (as in Thucydides) of the difficulty of grasping the truth of past events. Xenophon forged a new sort of historiography that was oriented forward more than backwards.

5 The utility of history

Taking a leaf from Xenophon's future recipients—the ancient critics who came later—moderns often assume that his historiographical works have the same morally transformative agenda as the rest of his oeuvre: that they supply examples of virtuous and base behaviour to follow or avoid in the fashion of his encomiastic *Agesilaus* or biographical *Memorabilia*. In the latter, for example, Xenophon says that Socrates did not profess to be a teacher of virtue, but 'by clearly (φανερός) being such a man [i.e. virtuous], he made his followers hope that by imitating him they would be such' (*Mem.* 1.2.3).[50] But Xenophon does not claim as much for his historiographical works, and most of the leaders depicted therein, far from offering 'clear' examples to imitate, are too complex to supply easily imitable models.[51]

As regards the specific skill of reading the future, Cyrus the Elder in the romanticising biographical *Cyropaedia* can by and large see the future clearly: he can for instance predict that a good relationship *will* follow from the kindness

---

49 Herodotus discovered 'the problem of sources': Fowler 1996.
50 Moral usefulness: e.g. Pownall 2004, Gray 2011, 51–54. Practical guide: e.g. Gray 2011, esp. 53–54. For further discussion of Xenophon's agenda in writing the *Anabasis* see *inter alia* Dillery 1995, 63–64. Agesilaus as a model for imitation: *Ages.* 10.2.
51 Compare *Anabasis*' narrative strategy, which refuses to explain a complex narrative in terms of a too-simple explanatory model, cp. Bradley 2010: it 'uniformly refrains from presenting any comprehensive analyses or judgments about the events ... described' (537), with the effect that 'the reader is compelled to re-evaluate the narrative at each step in light of the preceding narrative, without the guiding hand of the narrator'. See Tamiolaki 2012, 563–89.

shown allies (*Cyr.* 4.2.44⁵²), whereas Xenophon in the *Anabasis* in his dealings with Seuthes could not successfully predict even so much as that (p. 123–124 above). Cyrus the Elder is also far better placed than the leaders of the *Anabasis* directly to *shape* the future of individuals and nations.[53] At his appearance in Xenophon's *Apology* Socrates makes a clear and correct prediction about Anytus' son (30–31), which the narrator immediately corroborates (ταῦτα δ' εἰπὼν οὐκ ἐψεύσατο); whereas in the *Anabasis* the philosopher's knowledge of the future was conspicuously limited (p. 126–127 above). Prediction may be an ability Socrates in the former work possesses by virtue of being close to death, but equally it may be explicable by the fact that the *Apology* is not history.

Presumably Xenophon chose to work in different genres for a reason.[54] His historiographical works, the *Anabasis* among them, underline the elusiveness of knowledge, that relates to future time, and suggest scepticism about the possibility for historical leaders or his readers not only to know the future, but even to learn from the past so as to correct the present. These works instead hold out the promise of making readers better *interpreters* (as well as more successful and morally aware inhabitants) of their future worlds. That knowledge too is of course an important possession of an aspiring leader. But, Xenophon in the *Anabasis* implies, there is no quick and easy recipe for acquiring it.

---

52 The Persians should allow the allies to divide the spoils, and if they themselves get less, should consider it profit (4.2.43): for 'because of the gain, they will remain with us more gladly; whereas profiting now would furnish us wealth that is short-lived…' (4.2.44).
53 Croesus thus asks Cyrus whether Apollo's declaration that through self-knowledge he will be happy (cp. *Cyr.* 7.2.20) still holds true, and explains that he has asked the question 'since it seems to me that you would judge this best in present circumstances: for you are also capable of fulfilling it' (ἄριστ' ἄν μοι δοκεῖς εἰκάσαι τοῦτο ἐν τῷ παρόντι· καὶ γὰρ δύνασαι ποιῆσαι, *Cyr.* 7.2.25). Cyrus shapes the future also e.g. by developing the rationale for and enacting new Persian *nomoi*, which the narrator affirms are 'still now' functioning.
54 Thus in writing historigraphy Xenophon shows himself acutely aware of historiographical predecessors: see Gray 1989, 2003, Tuplin 2004, Nicolai 2006, Tamiolaki 2009, Baragwanath 2012. Cp. Flower 2012: 50: 'an ancient reader would have inferred from the content of the works themselves [in this instance *Anabasis* and *Cyropaedia*] that they were doing different things and had different aims and purposes.'

Nikos Miltsios
Knowledge and Foresight in Polybius

In the introduction to the main part of his work, Polybius expressly states that the main benefit of his history lies in the fact that it will enable future readers to form an assessment of Roman rule and to judge whether this form of government is worthy of imitation or condemnation (3.4.7–9). This passage is perhaps the best known of its kind in the *Histories* but certainly not the only one, since the Polybian narrator very often interrupts his narrative and addresses his narratees in the first person in order to explain how useful his account might be to future readers. In 8.21.10–11, for example, he notes that the story of Achaeus that he has recounted in detail in the previous chapters can teach later generations not to trust others too easily and not to be arrogant when one is at the height of one's power but rather to be aware of one's own human limitations. Similarly, in 30.9.20–21, he explains that he has dwelt at length on Polyaratus and Deinon in order to show their recklessness and to help anyone in a comparable situation to think more wisely.[1]

It is interesting that in these and other similar cases Polybius does not merely address the future readers of his work; he also stresses that the situations he is describing are likely to be repeated.[2] For Polybius, the usefulness of history resides precisely in the fact that those who study it can apply the knowledge they gain to their own particular cases, so that they can deal with situations similar to those they have read about more effectively. Indeed, in 12.25b.3 he observes that knowledge of the past enables those who acquire it not only to prepare themselves better for what they will face in the future but also to foresee it:

> ἐκ γὰρ τῶν ὁμοίων ἐπὶ τοὺς οἰκείους μεταφερομένων καιροὺς ἀφορμαὶ γίνονται καὶ προλήψεις εἰς τὸ προϊδέσθαι τὸ μέλλον, καὶ ποτὲ μὲν εὐλαβηθῆναι, ποτὲ δὲ μιμούμενον τὰ προγεγονότα θαρραλεώτερον ἐγχειρεῖν τοῖς ἐπιφερομένοις.

> For it is the mental transference of similar circumstances to our own times that gives us the means of forming presentiments of what is about to happen, and enables us at certain times to take precautions and at others by reproducing former conditions to face with more confidence the difficulties that menace us.[3]

---
[1] The notion that their works would be able to attract the attention of later generations and meet their needs was particularly widespread among ancient historians. Cf., e.g., Hdt. 1.1; Thuc. 1.22.4; Dio 72.23.4; Hdn. 1.1.3.
[2] Cf. also 9.9.10–11, 10.13; 10.17.5, 33.6–7; 23.14.12; 30.6.4, 9.21.
[3] Translations are from W. R. Paton's text in the Loeb Classical Library.

The same point is made in 6.3.2, where Polybius remarks that it is not difficult to foresee the future on the basis of the past (... τό τε προειπεῖν ὑπὲρ τοῦ μέλλοντος στοχαζόμενον ἐκ τῶν ἤδη γεγονότων εὐμαρές).

In this paper, I will attempt to shed light on Polybius' conception of future time by examining the fundamental role that the theme of foresight plays in his work. I will begin by discussing the contexts in which this theme is introduced (part 1). My findings will be qualified by a look at two examples which show that even the best-laid plans can fail due to external, unforeseeable factors (part 2). I will then try to reconcile Polybius' awareness of this element of uncertainty with his optimism about people's ability to gain insights into future possibilities (part 3). Finally, I will analyse some of Polybius' views on the proper function of history and, in particular, his understanding of the way it may help readers cope with future uncertainty (part 4).

1 Foresight and its contexts

For Polybius, the connection between knowledge and the ability it gives to those who possess it to foresee something of the future or, at least, to prepare themselves better for what they may face in the future appears not to be just a theoretical argument intended to promote the value of history and thereby win readers and convince them to devote time to the study of his work. It is much rather a sincere and deep-rooted conviction which must have played a role in his decision to concern himself with the writing of history and which left its mark on many parts of his work. The most impressive example of the practical application of this view can be found in the sixth book. Here after first expounding the theory on the anacyclosis of systems of government, i.e. the way in which the various forms of government (monarchy, tyranny, aristocracy, oligarchy, democracy and ochlocracy) succeed one another and eventually return to the original form, Polybius states that whoever understands this cyclical pattern may, in speaking of the future, fall wide of the mark in predicting how long it will take for each transformation to occur but will rarely be wrong about what kind of political system will follow (6.9.11).[4]

Examples of this sort are easy to find in the *Histories*. This is because Polybius does not restrict the ability to foresee the future to the sphere of political

---

[4] Valuable discussions of book 6 and the theory of anacyclosis are found in Pédech 1964, 302–30; Trompf 1979, 1–115; Alonso-Nuñez 1986; Podes 1991; Hahm 1995; Walbank 1998; Millar 2002, 23–36; and McGing 2010, 169–202.

theory. Many characters in the *Histories* are presented as having the ability to predict the immediate future. It is characteristic that the verb προορῶμαι occurs in the extant text over forty times, without including its synonyms.[5] In some cases the future is foreseen in a fortuitous and inexplicable way. Thus, in 27.16.5 it is stated that Nestor the Cropian foresaw the future in a mysterious way (δαιμονίως πως ... τὸ μέλλον ὀττευσάμενος) and forced the consul A. Hostilius Mancinus, who was staying at his house, to leave the city during the night in order to escape the ambush that had been set for him. On other occasions the prediction may be of a very general kind and may not presuppose any special ability on the part of the person who makes it but may simply be based on common sense. Something like this occurs when Lyciscus, the ambassador of the Acarnanians, warns the Spartans about the grave dangers that a union between the Aetolians and the Romans poses for Greece (9.37.10) or when Polybius observes that in the past the human race had been imperilled by numerous natural disasters and that it would suffer more in the future (6.5.5–6).

However, when a prediction concerns something more specific, such as the enemy's next moves in a military conflict, Polybius usually explains the way in which it happens and lauds the abilities of the character who makes it. Very often a character's far-sightedness is presented as being the result of his perspicacity. The close attention with which P. Cornelius Scipio observes his opponents' habits before the Battle of Ilipa in Spain (11.22.1–3) enables him to gain a significant strategic advantage in the conflict and to defeat the enemy. Specifically, Scipio manages to deploy his troops in the manner that suits him best precisely because he can predict his opponents' tactics on the basis of their previous activities (6.24.6–7). In other cases, the characters are shown to rest on their knowledge of the motives behind human behaviour in order to predict the moves their opponents will make. A remarkable example is that of Hannibal, who, while in Italy, foresees that C. Flaminius will not be able to endure the scorn of his troops if the countryside is ravaged and will be drawn into battle (3.80.3–5). It is noteworthy that Polybius uses the same verb (προορῶμαι) in order to lay even greater emphasis on the difference between Hannibal, whose calculations and predictions are proved correct (ἃ δὴ καὶ τότε προϊδόμενος καὶ συλλογισάμενος Ἀννίβας περὶ τοῦ τῶν ἐναντίων ἡγεμόνος οὐ διεσφάλη τῆς ἐπιβολῆς, 3.81.12), and Flaminius, who hastens to join battle, without giving any consideration to timing or

---

[5] See, e.g., 1.59.11, 66.9; 2.47.4, 58.1, 67.4; 3.15.1, 16.1, 17.4, 18.9, 112.7; 4.72.2; 6.6.5; 7.17.5; 11.21.2; 18.43.5; 21.26.12; 28.6.4; 31.15.8; and 38.15.9–10 (where the use of προορώμενοι is qualified by ὡσανεί). Synonyms of προορῶμαι include ὀττεύομαι (1.11.15; 27.16.5; 30.2.1), προλέγω (1.54.6), and προνοοῦμαι (5.35.6, 92.7; 18.14.12).

terrain (οὐ καιρόν, οὐ τόπον προορώμενος, 3.82.7).[6] Polybius generally believes that far-sightedness is a priceless virtue both in war and in politics. Thus, he usually applauds all those who possess it and speaks disparagingly of those who lack it. For example, he says of Deinocrates of Messene that, despite his illustrious achievements on the battlefield, he was completely incapable of correctly predicting future developments (προϊδέσθαι τὸ μέλλον ἀσφαλῶς) and of understanding that he was the cause of terrible misfortunes for his homeland (23.5.8–9).

All this shows that for Polybius the future was not a totally inaccessible or inscrutable domain. A careful study of the facts, when indeed combined with the experience that is offered by a knowledge of the past, can help us gain an idea of what is going to happen in the future or – in certain exceptional cases – even to control it. 'It is indeed very easy to conjecture what will happen (λίαν δ' εὐμαρῶς ἔστι συλλογίσασθαι τὸ μέλλον) from the past', the Aetolian envoy Chlaeneas reminds the Spartans (9.30.8–9). This idea may be expressed by a character, yet the fact that it is presented as an argument in an oration indicates its persuasive power and, judging by what Polybius says in 1.35.7–10, we have every reason to believe that he himself embraces it. Indeed, in referring to the educational value of history, Polybius notes:

> δυεῖν γὰρ ὄντων τρόπων πᾶσιν ἀνθρώποις τῆς ἐπὶ τὸ βέλτιον μεταθέσεως, τοῦ τε διὰ τῶν ἰδίων συμπτωμάτων καὶ τοῦ διὰ τῶν ἀλλοτρίων, ἐναργέστερον μὲν εἶναι συμβαίνει τὸν διὰ τῶν οἰκείων περιπετειῶν, ἀβλαβέστερον δὲ τὸν διὰ τῶν ἀλλοτρίων. διὸ τὸν μὲν οὐδέποθ' ἑκουσίως αἱρετέον, ἐπεὶ μετὰ μεγάλων πόνων καὶ κινδύνων ποιεῖ τὴν διόρθωσιν, τὸν δ' ἀεὶ θηρευτέον, ἐπεὶ χωρὶς βλάβης ἔστι συνιδεῖν ἐν αὐτῷ τὸ βέλτιον. ἐξ ὧν συνιδόντι καλλίστην παιδείαν ἡγητέον πρὸς ἀληθινὸν βίον τὴν ἐκ τῆς πραγματικῆς ἱστορίας περιγινομένην ἐμπειρίαν· μόνη γὰρ αὕτη χωρὶς βλάβης ἐπὶ παντὸς καιροῦ καὶ περιστάσεως κριτὰς ἀληθινοὺς ἀποτελεῖ τοῦ βελτίονος.

> For there are two ways by which all men can reform themselves, the one through their own mischances, the other through those of others, and of these the former is the more impressive, but the latter less hurtful. Therefore we should never choose the first method if we can help it, as it corrects by means of great pain and peril, but ever pursue the other, since by it we can discern what is best without suffering hurt. Reflecting on this we should regard as the best discipline for actual life the experience that accrues from serious history; for this alone makes us, without inflicting any harm on us, the most competent judges of what is best at every time and in every circumstance.

---

[6] On Polybius' presentation of the different leadership behaviours of Hannibal and Flaminius see Wiater 2010, 87–91; Miltsios 2013, 102–3.

Here Polybius suggests that history provides knowledge of general patterns, which readers may use as guidelines for their own actions in order to increase their chances of success.[7] In the same vein, in 7.11.2, prompted by the change in the behaviour of Philip V, he observes that all those who engage in politics can benefit from the examples provided by history. The views expressed by Polybius in these cases are based on the notion that history, due to the general principles that govern human nature, can in some sense repeat itself. Therefore, from the moment one accepts that future situations may arise that are similar to situations that have already occurred in the past, one can make use of the lessons one draws from the study of history and apply them to one's own situation.

And yet, despite this optimistic perspective, the *Histories* is teeming with examples of people who fail dismally to foresee the future. Polybius presents numerous characters who entertain hopes that prove illusory and make plans that are never realised. I have argued elsewhere that Polybius' use of this pattern creates an atmosphere of foreboding and suspense, thus being an important part of his narrative strategy.[8] The great frequency with which Polybius mentions his characters' mistaken expectations may also be attributed to his intention to fulfill his didactic purposes, since it helps him to show his readers what they should avoid.[9] Indeed, many characters fail because they make wrong choices. They may place their trust in unsuitable associates or be led astray by their friends and advisors, or they may be so engrossed in achieving their ambitions

---

[7] Sacks 1981 argues that Polybius' desire to promote the usefulness of his work 'leads him … into a logical crux that he never faces' (191). That is, although Polybius repeatedly claims that readers may benefit by learning from the mistakes of others, when it comes to history writing he insists that aspiring writers must draw on their own personal experience in order to produce a really useful work (cf., e.g., 12.25g.1–3, 28a.8–10). This tension, however, can be resolved, if one realises that the two arguments are divided and function at different levels. That Polybius believes that it is possible to learn from the experiences of others can be seen in 15.21.6–7, where he attributes this ability to wild animals, contrasting them with thoughtless people who tend to repeat the same mistakes again and again: '… not only when they [sc. animals] have got into trouble themselves from snares and nets, but if they see another animal in danger will not readily approach such engines again, but are even suspicious of the place and mistrust everything they see'. Cf. L. Aemilius Paullus' argument in 29.20.4: "'The difference … between foolish and wise men lies in this, that the former are schooled by their own misfortunes and the latter by those of others'". On the other hand, Polybius' insistence on the importance of personal experience for the would-be historian is related to his convictions about the proper method of history writing and springs from his resentment against historians who rely more on library research than on travel and actual participation.

[8] Miltsios 2009.

[9] On the process of learning from negative examples see Marincola 1997, 221; Duff 1999, 46–47.

that they do not to grasp the gravity of the dangers that threaten them.[10] Of course, there are also certain characters who, despite making correct assessments of the situation and taking the necessary steps to secure success, still fail in the end. The following section presents relevant examples.

2 Failures of strategic foresight

In 9.6–8 Polybius describes two incidents which show that the outcome of a venture very often depends on fortuitous and imponderable factors. The first story concerns Hannibal's attempt to attack Rome. When he realised that it was impossible to raise Ap. Claudius Pulcher's siege of Capua, Hannibal decided to head for Rome and attempt to capture it. He calculated that by his unexpected appearance he would be able to terrify its inhabitants. Yet even if he did not succeed in doing this he believed that his movement would force Appius either to raise his siege of Capua and hasten to help his native city or to divide his forces. When he set his plan in motion he took all the necessary precautions to increase his chances of success. He informed the inhabitants of Capua of his intentions in order to encourage them in their resistance to the siege, while trying to conceal his movements from the enemy. Thus, when he set off he left the fires in his camp still burning so that his departure might go unnoticed and he also took care to send some of his men ahead to reconnoitre the territory through which he was going to pass. These precautions paid off because his arrival outside Rome surprised and alarmed its inhabitants. Hannibal was in fact very close to achieving his objective but, as Polybius remarks, an unexpected and chance event saved the city (9.6.5–6). The consuls Cn. Fulvius Centumalus and P. Sulpicius Galba were in the process of recruiting soldiers for a legion after having ordered the soldiers of another one to appear at Rome armed on that very day. In an entirely fortuitous manner, then, a large number of troops happened to be gathered together at Rome just at the right moment. As soon as he was informed of the situation, Hannibal abandoned his plan and lost the opportunity to take the city.

Hannibal's failed operation prompts Polybius to relate a similar incident from Greek history (9.8). When Epaminondas observed that the Spartans had gathered all their forces at Mantinea in order to fight the Thebans, he conceived the idea of attacking Sparta itself. Like Hannibal, he too acted with prudence. He set off at night and took care to conceal his real intentions by creating the im-

---

[10] E.g. 3.70.7 (Ti. Sempronius Longus); 5.35.1 (Cleomenes); 8.17.10–11 (Achaeus); 14.2.10 (Syphax).

pression that he was hurrying to occupy certain key positions for the forthcoming battle. When he reached Sparta he found it destitute of defenders. His plan would have come off if a certain deserter had not managed to tell King Agesilaus what was going on, with the result that the Spartan force arrived just as Epaminondas was occupying the city and managed to stop him. Polybius concludes that in this case Epaminondas did all that a good general should have done but, like Hannibal, luck was not on his side (9.8.13). The conclusion that can be drawn from the above is that even the best-laid plans can fail as a result of chance factors. Nevertheless, it is interesting to see how the juxtaposition of these two episodes, in which fortune plays such a crucial role, shows just how history can repeat itself.

3 Foresight in the face of an uncertain future

The influence of fortune in human affairs is a prominent theme in Polybius' work.[11] Although in many of its 129 occurrences in the extant text τύχη is used in a metaphorical or rhetorical sense,[12] there are cases, as we have just seen, where its role is shown to be vital in determining the outcome of the characters' actions.[13] The pervasive presence of fortune in the text alerts readers to the difficulties that beset attempts to think about the future on the basis of general patterns deduced from the past. It expresses the idea of the instability of human life, continually reminding readers that outcomes are often determined by forces outside of one's own control and that things can turn out completely differently than expected.[14]

Time and again, Polybius draws his readers' attention to the existence of this element of uncertainty. Already in the introduction to the first book he states that a basic lesson one can learn from history is the importance of enduring the vicissitudes of fortune with courage (1.1.2). Polybius usually returns to the theme of the fickleness of fortune when he is relating some important success or failure. When, for example, Antiochus III weeps at the strange sight of the once mighty Achaeus humbled before him, we are informed that his reaction is due to the fact that he realises how hard it is for humans to protect themselves from sudden

---

[11] For discussion and bibliography see Hau 2011.
[12] See Roveri 1956, 40–3; Hau 2011, 186–93.
[13] Other examples include 21.39.13–14 (Cn. Manlius Vulso rescued by a force of Roman foragers) and 29.22 (Eumenes' misfortunes).
[14] For a thorough study of Polybius' approach to historical contingency and instability see Maier 2012a.

changes of fortune (8.20.10). Similarly, the sight of Carthage in flames brings tears to the eyes of P. Cornelius Scipio Aemilianus, as it causes him to reflect that the same fate may one day overtake Rome (38.22). In commenting on this incident, Polybius stresses that it is the mark of a great and perfect man (ἀνδρός ἐστι μεγάλου καὶ τελείου) to contemplate, at the moment of his greatest triumph, the fickleness of fortune and the possible reverse of his own situation (38.21.2–3). Awareness of the decisive role that fortune plays in life enables one to face both success and failure with dignity and to be prepared for situations to develop in unexpected ways. Otherwise, without this awareness, it is possible to suffer the same fate as the Aetolians, who, even before fighting the Medionians, were convening in order to decide which general should distribute the booty and whose name should be inscribed on the shields that would be dedicated to the gods (2.2.8–11). Polybius observes that their defeat was a clear illustration of the precariousness of human plans (2.4.5):

> Αἰτωλοὶ δὲ τῇ παραδόξῳ χρησάμενοι συμφορᾷ πάντας ἐδίδαξαν μηδέποτε βουλεύεσθαι περὶ τοῦ μέλλοντος ὡς ἤδη γεγονότος, μηδὲ προκατελπίζειν βεβαιουμένους ὑπὲρ ὧν ἀκμὴν ἐνδεχόμενόν ἐστιν ἄλλως γενέσθαι, νέμειν δὲ μερίδα τῷ παραδόξῳ πανταχῇ μὲν ἀνθρώπους ὄντας, μάλιστα δ' ἐν τοῖς πολεμικοῖς.

> The unlooked-for calamity of the Aetolians was a lesson to mankind never to discuss the future as if it were the present, or to have any confident hope about things that may still turn out quite otherwise. We are but men, and should in every matter assign its share to the unexpected, this being especially true of war.

Nevertheless, the various difficulties that arise in life as a result of the presence of imponderable factors should not lead to a fatalistic attitude towards the future. Polybius very often advises his readers to prefer action to inaction and to dare to undertake even risky ventures, provided of course that they take the necessary precautions.[15] When, for example, in 8.35 he mentions certain cases of men who were betrayed by those they had trusted, he does not apportion an equal share of the blame to everyone. He stresses that trusting nobody gets one nowhere, while if one acts with prudent caution, even if one fails, one can at least defend oneself by arguing that one did everything within one's power (8.36.1–6). Moreover, a careful and well-organised plan of action can improve one's chances of succeeding even in the most demanding endeavours (9.12.1). Consequently, instead of being discouraged by the large number of unforeseeable factors in life, people should rather be prompted to deal more effectively with what they can control (9.16.2–4):

---

[15] On Polybius' belief in personal responsibility see Eckstein 1995, 272–81.

ἱκανὰ γὰρ καὶ τὰ παρὰ δόξαν γινόμενα (μὴ δυνάμενα) τυγχάνειν προνοίας ἀκριβοῦς εἰς τὸ πολλὴν ἀπορίαν παρασκευάζειν καὶ πολλάκις, οἷον ὄμβρων καὶ ποταμῶν ἐπιφοραὶ καὶ πάγων ὑπερβολαὶ καὶ χιόνες, ἔτι δ' ὁ καπνώδης καὶ συννεφὴς ἀὴρ καὶ τἄλλα τὰ παραπλήσια τούτοις. εἰ δὲ καὶ περὶ ὧν δυνατόν ἐστι προϊδέσθαι, καὶ τούτων ὀλιγωρήσομεν, πῶς οὐκ εἰκότως ἐν τοῖς πλείστοις ἀποτευξόμεθα δι' αὑτούς;

For those accidents which take us by surprise and cannot be accurately foreseen are quite sufficiently numerous to expose us to great and frequent difficulties, I mean sudden rains and floods, exceeding great frosts and snowfalls, a foggy and clouded state of the atmosphere and the like, and if we pay no attention even to such things as can be foreseen, we are sure to fail in most enterprises by our own fault.

Dealing carefully with all the things that can be foreseen provides one not only with a justification in the event of failure but also various opportunities to counterbalance the dangers posed by the fickleness of fortune.

Indeed, Polybius describes a number of incidents which show that the imponderable factors that led to the failure of certain ventures could have been neutralised if those who had organised the ventures had had the necessary knowledge and appropriate experience. An indicative example is that of Aratus of Sicyon (9.17). When he was planning to capture Cynaetha, Aratus arranged with his accomplices in the city to attack the officers guarding the gate and to send one of their men to stand at an agreed point to show that everything was ready. At this signal, the Achaeans would rush the gate to force their way into the city. As the time for the attack drew near, Aratus concealed himself somewhere nearby and waited for the signal. Purely by chance, however, the owner of a flock of sheep happened to be in the area looking for his shepherd. As soon as Aratus and his troops saw him, they thought that it was the signal they had been waiting for and began to run towards the gate. However, as their accomplices in the city had not managed to carry out any of the agreed preparations, the operation failed. It is clear that this outcome could reasonably be attributed to fortune. Polybius, however, lays the blame on Aratus himself, who, on account of his youthfulness, did not know that he should have arranged a greater number of signals in order to ensure the success of his operation (9.17.9).

Another noteworthy example is that of the consul M. Claudius Marcellus (10.32). Seeking to gather information about Hannibal's camp, he set out with two troops of cavalry and a few other soldiers to reconnoitre the area. By coincidence, some Numidians, who were accustomed to lie in ambush, had concealed themselves at the foot of the hill that Marcellus was intending to use as his vantage point. When the Numidians realised the Romans were there, they rushed forwards and cut off their route of retreat. In next to no time they managed to kill Marcellus and a few other soldiers, while the Romans back in the camp, although they could see what was going on, had no time to help. Commenting on the event, Polybius lays the blame fully on Marcellus. He believes that Marcellus should have taken account of the danger and should have known that it was not right for the commander to take part in such operations due to his importance to the army as a whole.[16] As he points out, in such cases the following proverb applies: 'Let the risk be for the Carian ... and not for the general. And as for saying "I should never have thought it" or "Who would have expected it to happen?" that in a general is a most manifest sign of incompetence and dullness' (10.32.11–12).

Polybius, therefore, shows that human beings are vulnerable to the unforeseen vicissitudes of the world, but not defenceless. In his view, foresight depends largely on the depth or breadth of the knowledge acquired throughout life. Knowledge allows one to think in advance about many possibilities, even unlikely ones, and thus become better prepared for the challenges that lie ahead. Polybius' belief in the importance of knowledge as a means of coping with uncertainty about the future is particularly observable in 9.12–20.[17] There Polybius provides an extensive description of the qualities and knowledge that military leaders should possess in order to increase their chances of success. First of all, they should move with extreme secrecy and announce their intentions only to those without whose help they would not be able to fulfill them; what is more, they should not announce their intentions sooner than necessary but only at the time they actually require the services of the others (9.13.2–4). In addition, it is important that they should have experience of both night-time and daytime marches and that they should have an accurate knowledge of the distances that they will have to cover on land and at sea (9.13.6). A certain knowledge of astronomy and geometry will also prove valuable to them as it will enable them to calculate correctly the time and space required for military operations (9.13.7–20.3). Polybius admits that he could be accused of placing excessive demands on aspiring generals, yet he justifies his approach by emphasising the importance of their office (9.20.5–9) and its challenges: anything connected with military operations requires great caution (9.12.1). The difficulty of these operations lies in the fact that they depend to a large extent on chance factors; as he notes in 9.12.10, just one unimportant detail is enough to cause failure, while, to achieve success, it is barely enough to observe all the essential requirements that he has described. When someone acts with prudence and care, success is indeed possible (9.12.1–2), though not certain.

---

16 On the general's obligation to avoid unnecessary risks see also 10.24.3, 33.1–7; 11.2.9–11.
17 Cf. Maier 2012b, 161.

4 The role of the historian

The mutability of fortune increases not only the responsibility that military commanders have to bear but also that which the historians who record their deeds must shoulder. Polybius maintains that historians should not place special emphasis on the narration of strange and chance events. As he claims, such topics might have a short-lived appeal but in the long term they are of no benefit to either readers or authors (15.36.4–6):

> ζηλοῦν μὲν γὰρ τίς ἂν βουληθείη τὰς παραλόγους περιπετείας; οὐδὲ μὴν θεώμενος οὐδ' ἀκούων ἥδεται συνεχῶς οὐδεὶς τῶν παρὰ φύσιν γενομένων πραγμάτων καὶ παρὰ τὴν κοινὴν ἔννοιαν τῶν ἀνθρώπων. ἀλλ' εἰσάπαξ μὲν καὶ πρῶτον σπουδάζομεν ἃ μὲν ἰδεῖν, ἃ δ' ἀκοῦσαι, χάριν τοῦ γνῶναι τὸ μὴ δοκοῦν δυνατὸν εἶναι διότι δυνατόν ἐστιν· ὅταν δὲ πιστεύωμεν, οὐδεὶς τοῖς παρὰ φύσιν ἐγχρονίζων εὐδοκεῖ· τῷ δ' αὐτῷ πλεονάκις ἐγκυρεῖν οὐδ' ὅλως ἂν βουληθείη.

> For not only do abnormal reversals of fortune arouse no emulation, but no one has any permanent pleasure in seeing or reading of things which are contrary to nature and contrary to the general sentiment of mankind. It is true we are interested in seeing or hearing of them once for all and at first, just for the sake of observing that what seemed to be impossible is possible, but once we are convinced of this no one takes any pleasure in dwelling on the unnatural, and there is none who would have the least wish to meet with frequent references to the same event of this class.

It is better, therefore, for historians to concern themselves with individuals who deserve to be admired and imitated on account of their abilities, and to mention fortune and its influence on human affairs only occasionally (15.35.7). It is also important for them to distinguish between things which are really caused by fortune and things which are determined by human choices (36.17.2–4):

> ὧν μὲν νὴ Δί' ἀδύνατον ἢ δυσχερὲς τὰς αἰτίας καταλαβεῖν ἄνθρωπον ὄντα, περὶ τούτων ἴσως ἄν τις ἀπορῶν ἐπὶ τὸν θεὸν τὴν ἀναφορὰν ποιοῖτο καὶ τὴν τύχην, οἷον ὄμβρων καὶ νιφετῶν ἐξαισίων ἐπιφορὰ συνεχής, ἢ τἀναντία πάλιν αὐχμῶν καὶ πάγων καὶ διὰ ταῦτα φθορὰ καρπῶν, ὁμοίως λοιμικαὶ διαθέσεις συνεχεῖς, ἄλλα παραπλήσια τούτοις, ὧν οὐκ εὐμαρὲς τὴν αἰτίαν εὑρεῖν ... ὧν δὲ δυνατόν ἐστι τὴν αἰτίαν εὑρεῖν, ἐξ ἧς καὶ δι' ἣν ἐγένετο τὸ συμβαῖνον, οὐχί μοι δοκεῖ τῶν τοιούτων δεῖν ἐπὶ τὸ θεῖον ποιεῖσθαι τὴν ἀναφοράν.

> Now indeed as regards things the causes of which it is impossible or difficult for a mere man to understand, we may perhaps be justified in getting out of the difficulty by setting them down to the action of a god or of chance, I mean such things as exceptionally heavy and continuous rain or snow, or on the other hand the destruction of crops by severe drought or frost, or a persistent outbreak of plague or other similar things of which it is not easy to detect the cause ... But as for matters the efficient and final cause of which it is possible to discover we should not, I think, put them down to divine action.

Indeed, very often Polybius attempts to provide a rational explanation for events which seem to some to be strange or fortuitous.[18] In 15.21.3–5, for example, he points out that the disasters which befell the inhabitants of Cius were not due to fortune or to the malice of their neighbours but to the policy that they themselves had pursued, since in order to make money they had promoted corrupt men and punished all those who disagreed with them.[19] When, again, in 18.28.3–5 he presents a short introduction to his comparison between the Roman legion and the Macedonian phalanx, he states that the differences between them will reveal the real reason why Roman troops are superior to Macedonian ones in battle, and so he will have no need, as thoughtless men have done, to ascribe the victors' success merely to fortune. His reasoning is the same when he comments on the case of P. Cornelius Scipio, who, on account of his great achievements, was renowned as a man favoured by fortune and pleasing to the gods (10.2.5–6). Polybius regards this estimation of him as wrong or at least inadequate (10.5.8):

οἱ γὰρ μὴ δυνάμενοι τοὺς καιροὺς μηδὲ τὰς αἰτίας καὶ διαθέσεις ἑκάστων ἀκριβῶς συνθεωρεῖν, ἢ διὰ φαυλότητα φύσεως ἢ δι' ἀπειρίαν καὶ ῥᾳθυμίαν, εἰς θεοὺς καὶ τύχας ἀναφέρουσι τὰς αἰτίας τῶν δι' ἀγχίνοιαν ἐκ λογισμοῦ (καὶ) προνοίας ἐπιτελουμένων.

For those who are incapable of taking an accurate view of opportunities, causes, and dispositions, either from lack of natural ability or from inexperience and indolence, attribute to the gods and to fortune the causes of what is accomplished by shrewdness and with calculation and foresight.

Polybius, in contrast, analyses in detail the tactics that Scipio pursued when he claimed the office of aedile (10.4–5) and, later, during the siege of New Carthage (10.8–15) in order to show that all his actions were dictated by his good sense and foresight (ἕκαστα μετὰ λογισμοῦ καὶ προνοίας ἔπραττε, 10.2.13).[20]

Although Polybius does not reject τύχη as an explanatory device in serious historiography, it is clear that in his analytical or polemical passages he limits its application.[21] Polybius' attitude to τύχη is determined by his wish to produce a

---

[18] At 2.38.5 he forcefully maintains that 'every event whether probable or improbable must have some cause'.
[19] For other examples of people whose failure was not due to fortune but to their own ignorance see 1.37.3–4 and 2.6–7.
[20] Cf. 10.9.2–3: 'Although authors agree that he made these calculations, yet when they come to the accomplishment of his plan, they attribute for some unknown reason the success not to the man and his foresight (τὴν τούτου πρόνοιαν), but to the gods and to chance'.
[21] See McGing 2010, 195–201; Hau 2011, 193; Longley 2012, 74.

useful work.²² In his view, history is useful because it reveals the causes of past events.²³ As he remarks in 3.31.11–13, writers and readers of history should focus more on the causes of events rather than their presentation:

> διόπερ οὐχ οὕτως ἐστὶ φροντιστέον τῆς αὐτῶν τῶν πράξεων ἐξηγήσεως, οὔτε τοῖς γράφουσιν οὔτε τοῖς ἀναγινώσκουσι τὰς ἱστορίας, ὡς τῶν πρότερον καὶ τῶν ἅμα καὶ τῶν ἐπιγινομένων τοῖς ἔργοις. ἱστορίας γὰρ ἐὰν ἀφέλῃ τις τὸ διὰ τί καὶ πῶς καὶ τίνος χάριν ἐπράχθη τὸ πραχθὲν καὶ πότερον εὔλογον ἔσχε τὸ τέλος, τὸ καταλειπόμενον αὐτῆς ἀγώνισμα μέν, μάθημα δ' οὐ γίνεται, καὶ παραυτίκα μὲν τέρπει, πρὸς δὲ τὸ μέλλον οὐδὲν ὠφελεῖ τὸ παράπαν.

> Therefore both writers and readers of history should not pay so much attention to the actual narrative of events, as to what precedes, what accompanies, and what follows each. For if we take from history the discussion of why, how, and wherefore each thing was done, and whether the result was what we should have reasonably expected, what is left is a clever essay but not a lesson, and while pleasing for the moment of no possible benefit for the future.

In keeping with his own rule, Polybius displays an unremitting interest in the reasons behind actions. He systematically seeks the causes of events, speculates about his characters' mindset,²⁴ and generally shows a concern to sensitise readers to issues of causality.²⁵ Interestingly, Polybius argues that the study of causes not only deepens readers' understanding of events but also trains them to use this knowledge to deal more effectively with the challenges they might face in their own lives (3.31.3–10). This argument is significant in inviting us to recognise that historical analysis prepares us for the future in ways other than through the presentation of situations which may recur. It sharpens our thinking by allowing us to observe the historian identifying patterns, weighing conflicting evidence, and drawing conclusions. This process is similar to what we do when we use our critical thinking to make predictions about the future.²⁶

Polybius does not deny that uncontrollable and unforeseeable factors play a large role in human affairs. Yet it is precisely the incalculable element in life that makes it more imperative to embrace history's lessons. Polybius' work educates readers on how to cope with future uncertainty not only through the examples it mentions but also, and perhaps more importantly, through the method it employs to analyse these examples. Polybius, as we have seen, constantly attempts

---

22 See Walbank 1972, 60.
23 See, e.g., 3.32.6; 6.2.8; 12.25b. On causality in Polybius see Pédech 1964, 75–78; Mohm 1977, 151–58, 183–98; Sacks 1981, 123–32; Derow 1994; McGing 2010, 76–80.
24 For a discussion of Polybius' ascriptions of motives see Miltsios 2013, 92–99.
25 See, e.g., his theory of causes, pretexts, and beginnings at 3.6–7.
26 On the relationship between historical analysis and future thinking see Staley 2007.

to trace the causes of the events he describes, even when these appear at first glance to be strange or inexplicable. To be sure, in many cases the results themselves will have led him to the causes. If M. Minucius Rufus had defeated Hannibal at Lake Trasimene, for instance, it is very likely that he would have been held up as the model of a prudent and capable general. On the other hand, this does not mean that Hannibal won by luck or that in fact he did not make more accurate calculations than his opponent, if not necessarily those we read about. In any event, regardless of its historical accuracy, the exhaustive treatment to which Polybius subjects his material in order to give meaning to the past helps his readers in their efforts to think about the future. It may not guarantee them an ability to foresee the future, such as that possessed by the most successful and far-sighted characters in the *Histories*, but it will provide them with valuable assistance in their attempts to understand it.

Christopher Pelling
Preparing for Posterity: Dionysius and Polybius

I

Dionysius of Halicarnassus ends his history at the point where Polybius begins. On one level, that simply reflects the notion of a serial canon that crops up often enough in Greek and Roman historiography;[1] by the time that Dionysius wrote, Posidonius and Strabo had already crafted the equivalent continuation at the other end of Polybius' narrative, so that Dionysius' first readers would now have a continuous sequence of histories in Greek reaching from Rome's earliest days to the late Republic (Posidonius) and Augustus (Strabo).[2]

Still, there is more to it than this. Dionysius' gesture may certainly be homage to Polybius' history, the original core that invited a writer to supplement rather than rewrite; it is also a generous acknowledgment that in choosing to start at 265 BCE Polybius had identified a vital turning-point.[3] But it also reflects a fundamental disagreement.[4] Polybius' theme, or at least the theme of his initial conception of his history, was how Rome became great:

> For who could be so worthless or lazy as not to want to know how, and by what *politeia*, virtually all the inhabited world was conquered in less than fifty-three years, and fell under the sole rule of the Romans?[5]

A large part of the answer lay in that Roman *politeia* – their constitution, but more than what we would normally understand by that word, for *politeia* embraced all the healthy institutions that their way of political life had embraced. For Dionysius, that is not enough. In his view, to understand Rome and Rome's success one has to go back earlier, much earlier: right back to the beginnings, in fact, and trace their history from its foundations '745 years' ago (*Ant. Rom.* 1.3.4): the precision of that number sounds a bell, contrasting with Polybius' '53'. It has to be done in detail too. It takes him a whole book to reach Romulus, and four

---

1 Marincola 1989, 237–41 and especially the collection of examples at 289–92.
2 Balsdon 1971, 19.
3 Fromentin 1998, xxv.
4 Cf. Delcourt 2005, 50–3; Wiater 2011a, 194–8.
5 Plb. 1.1.5.

books to get as far as Livy, not normally thought of as the snappiest of writers, manages by the end of his Book 1.

Politeiai matter for Dionysius too, but for him it is in the plural:

> I shall also go through all the forms of *politeiai* that they had, both under the kingship and after the end of the monarchy, and explain what was the ordering of each.[6]

So there has been a whole series of *politeiai*, as at several stages the Romans have taken stock of what constitutional direction they wanted to go in next.[7] All of those constitutions have made a difference, contributing something bit by bit; very early in the narrative Dionysius singles out Rome's characteristic ability to 'build up their political system on the basis of many experiences, taking something useful from one critical opportunity after another'.[8] And another leading theme, perhaps *the* leading theme, is how Rome has from those earliest origins been Greek, and has learnt continually from Greek models. It is not only their own experience that can prove so salutary.

So Dionysius' whole history looks both backwards and forwards. It looks backwards to those 'many experiences' from which the Romans continually learn, but it also has the future looming in the background, the future beyond the scope of his own work. In a way he takes for granted that story of Rome's Polybian march to Mediterranean primacy, even as he claims that it demands the different perspective that he offers, the perspective that stretches so many centuries further back. And, if he looks that far into the future, wouldn't it be odd if he failed to look further still, to the Augustan present?

II

Let us look a little more at the way in which the future is hinted in Dionysius' early books. Naturally, the reader is assumed to know that this is the start of something big: the proem has made that clear enough, and the theme soon recurs, with a glance forward, here as already in that proem,[9] to a posterity that will come long after Dionysius himself:

---

[6] Dion. Hal. 1.8.2.
[7] Dion. Hal. 2.3.7–8, 2.57, 3.1, 3.46, 4.72–5, 7.55, 11.60.4–5: more on these below.
[8] Dion. Hal. 1.9.4
[9] Thus at 1.1.2 Dionysius talks of his own desire to leave 'a monument of his soul' for the future: cf. Delcourt 2005, 68, and below, p. 173.

> In time fate was to build this tiny village, just big enough for those who had come in two ships from Greece, to a scale never reached by any state, Greek or barbarian, in the size of its foundation, in the majesty of its dominion, and in every other sort of prosperity: a city that will be remembered above all others as long as the human race survives.[10]

Yet a striking difference from Livy, and even more from the *Aeneid*, is that Romans themselves are given barely a hint of the future that awaits their descendants. Thus it is Livy and Plutarch, not Dionysius, who have Proculus Iulius reporting his vision of Romulus descending from Heaven and announcing that "the gods wish my Rome to become the capital of the world: let them practise the soldierly skills and tell their descendants that no human power can stand up to Roman arms"[11] or that the Romans "will be the greatest power among humans";[12] it is again Livy and Plutarch, not Dionysius, who tell the story of the Sabine cow whose sacrifice will decide where "future *imperium* is to be"[13] or which city "is fated to be the greatest and to rule over all Italy".[14] There are very few passages of that sort in Dionysius. Admittedly, one comes very early: when Aeneas is pondering whether to stay or move on in search of better land, a mysterious voice tells him that this miserable settlement will one day produce a great and enduring empire;[15] a few chapters later he interprets an ambivalent omen in similar, perhaps echoing, language.[16] Then, centuries later, the altars of Terminus and Iuuentas will not move when Tarquinius Priscus wants to found the temple to the Capitoline Triad, and the seers infer that

> no crisis will ever move the boundaries of the Roman city nor change its vigour; and down to my own day both of those insights have remained true, down to what is now its twenty-fourth generation.[17]

So that is a touch of *Roma aeterna*, but not really very much – nothing of a world-power in that last passage, just the durability of physical Rome itself, and even there with that hint of 'so far so good'. Dionysius' omens more typically concern the prospects of figures in the story, such as those surrounding the ar-

---

10 Dion. Hal. 1.31.3.
11 Livy 1.16.6.
12 Plut. *Rom.* 28.3.
13 Livy 1.45.5.
14 Plut. *Roman Questions* 4 264c.
15 Dion. Hal. 1.56.3–4.
16 Dion. Hal. 1.59.5.
17 Dion. Hal. 3.69.6.

rival of Tarquinius Priscus in Rome[18] or the birth of Servius Tullius:[19] ones about individuals, even if it is their future Roman standing that makes those individuals memorable. There is certainly nothing of *imperium sine fine dedi*, and that difference is only partly explicable in terms of the absence of the *Aeneid*'s personal gods.

When Rome's great future does come into play for Dionysius, it tends to be in ways that have only become clear in retrospect. Thus the wisdom of Romulus' marriage legislation was shown by the way that it stood the test of time, all those centuries that passed before the first Roman divorce;[20] just as his wise introduction of patronage and *clientela* created a harmony that lasted so long,

> so that for many generations the links of clients and patrons remained indistinguishable from those of family relationships, passed on to children's children.[21]

That was indeed symptomatic of a broader harmony between people and elite that was owed to Romulus' regulations:

> That, then, was the basis for Roman concord, so firmly established by the customs instituted by Romulus that never, in the course of 630 years, did they move against one another in bloodshed and slaughter despite many great political disputes between the people and those in power, just as always tends to happen in every city great or small. No, they dealt with these by a process of persuasion and instruction, sometimes making concessions and sometimes receiving them, and thus they resolved their complaints in a civic and civil way. That lasted until C. Gracchus gained power as a tribune and destroyed the concord of the state; and since then they have ceaselessly been killing and driving each other into exile and not holding back from anything, however irreparable, when victory was in point (οὐδενὸς τῶν ἀνηκέστων ἀπεχόμενοι παρὰ τὸ νικᾶν).[22]

Those last words incorporate a Thucydidean echo, for in Thucydides' first debate his Corinthians talk solemnly about "the sort of crisis where men are moving

---

18 Dion. Hal. 3.47.3.
19 Dion. Hal. 4.2.
20 Dion. Hal. 2.25.7.
21 Dion. Hal. 2.10.4.
22 Dion. Hal. 2.11.2–3 The force of the παρά is hard to gauge there, and this is the reason for my awkward translation: either, or more likely both, LSJ s.v. C.I.7, 'alongside of'', 'compared with' ('they refrained from nothing when weighing it against victory') or/and LSJ C.I.10, 'precisely at the moment of' that victory. The first has victory not yet won (cf. 5.46.4) and would align Dionysius closely with (e.g.) Sallust's *et sane Gracchis cupidine uictoriae haud satis moderatus animus fuit* and with the Thucydides passage mentioned above in the text (1.41.2); the second is closer to Sallust's following and mirroring *igitur ea uictoria nobilitas ex lubidine sua usa* (*BJ* 42.2–4; cf. also *BC* 38.4).

against their own enemies and care about nothing else except victory" (τῶν ἁπάντων ἀπερίοπτοί εἰσι παρὰ τὸ νικᾶν):[23] that indeed is the sort of crisis, marked by the civic strife that was another Thucydidean hallmark, that has beset Rome for the century before Dionysius' own day. Again, then, that future, so distant from the events that he is describing, is in the thoughts of Dionysius and his audience; but omens, good or bad, are not his favourite way of looking so far ahead.

Romans do think hard about their constitution, but those deliberations too do not take a very long forward view. I have already mentioned the ways that they think about it, and take decisions on the directions they want to go: they do so at the beginning and at the end of Romulus' reign, then again at the deaths of Numa and Ancus and when Tarquinius Superbus is overthrown, then in the middle of the Coriolanus story, then when the consular tribunate is established.[24] But on the whole, it is a matter of little steps: there is no vast utopian view of planning something that is going to go far, preparing them for anything that a glorious future may bring. Romulus' elaborate constitution may seem suitable for a much more developed polity, but there is no explicit emphasis on his planning for future increase and success: less than in the provident wisdom of the *nomothetes* that we sometimes get in Greek forensic speeches;[25] certainly less than that of Livy's Romulus, on whose advice a city is fortified of a scale 'more suited to his hope of a future populousness than to their current numbers' (1.8.4); and vastly less than we see in the almost mantically long-sighted Romulus of Cicero's *De Re Publica*, whose choice of location suggests 'that he had already divined that this city would one day provide the seat and home for the greatest of empires'.[26] In Dionysius there is not much emphasis on foresight at all.[27] The Romans look at what has worked well, and they either decide that it's not broken and doesn't need fixing, or that they need to make a change.

---

23 Thuc. 1.41.2.
24 Dion. Hal. 2.3.7–8, 2.57, 3.1, 3.46, 4.72–5, 7.55, 11.60.4–5.
25 This is a particularly favourite ploy of Aeschines: cf. e.g. 1.6 (where Fisher 2001, 126–7 has a useful note), 11, 17–8, 24–32, 139–40, 183–4; 3.20–22, 31, 33, 44–7, 175–6. Elsewhere cf. Lysias 1.31, Demosth. 18. 6–7, 20.91–4, 21.42–50, 22.6; Plato, *Laws* 625d–6b. I have here benefitted greatly from discussions with Alia Rodrigues and Guy Westwood.
26 'Scipio' in Cic. *de Re P.* 2.10, cf. 2.5, 2.12.
27 This suggests a qualification of the argument of Fox 1996, ch. 3. I agree with Fox about the 'idealised' nature of much of the regal narrative, at least in the sense that it fits 'an already defined conception of what regal history was about, of what Rome's early development was leading to' (63): but insofar as this is 'shown to be the result of the conscious reflection of the historical figures' (ib.), I suggest that the reflection is more backward-looking than forward-looking, and those figures themselves do not have such a conscious insight into Rome's trajectory.

Under the Alban kings it has worked fine, so let's have another king – Romulus is the man for the job, as we have "learned through experience, not just through talk";[28] under Tarquinius Superbus it hasn't, so let's adopt this new idea of a couple of consuls and a sharing of power.[29] Hindsight is the thinking person's foresight; that is what gives you the lessons you can learn, rather as (to take a non-constitutional example) Ancus Marcius looks at the religious mistakes Tullus Hostilius has made and decides to go back to the wiser practices of Numa.[30] It is indeed, in the words of that passage quoted earlier, "building up their political system on the basis of many experiences, taking something useful from one critical opportunity after another."[31]

There is nothing very startling about this; it is really a narrative elaboration of Polybius' claim that the Romans evolved their ideal constitution through experience rather than by the aprioristic, once-for-all theorising of a visionary Lycurgus:

> Lycurgus, then, foresaw through some sort of reasoning the cause and character of events as they naturally happen, and therefore put together this *politeia* without anything harmful; the Romans have achieved the same result in the way their state is set up, but have not done so by reasoning but through many trials and experiences, continually choosing the better course on the basis of what they came to understand in the midst of events. That is how they came to the same conclusion as Lycurgus, and it is the best of the *politeiai* in our time.[32]

And Cicero makes his Scipio say something very similar to launch Book 2 of the *De Re Publica*.[33] But, particularly in Dionysius, this does give quite an impression of muddling through, even though the Romans have got a flair for it: here again we can contrast Cicero's *de Re Publica*, where such gradualism still leaves room

---

[28] Dion. Hal. 2.3–4. That is the way that on later occasions too the Roman people decide who is to be their king, looking thoughtfully at the qualities that a man has shown in his earlier life: Fromentin 2004.
[29] Dion. Hal. 4.72–5.
[30] Dion. Hal. 3.36.
[31] Dion. Hal. 1.9.4, above p. 156.
[32] Plb 6.10.12–14. Plutarch too, perhaps following Polybius' lead, credits Lycurgus with a particularly far-sighted view of the future (*Lycurgus* 7, 29). On Dionysius' own treatment of Lycurgus cf. Delcourt 2005, 174–88.
[33] Cic. *De re pub.* 2.2, quoting Cato. Dillery 2009, 100–1 has some interesting remarks on that reported view of Cato.

for Romulus to possess that extraordinary predictive insight.³⁴ In Dionysius, quite a bit of the hindsight also rests on looking across to Greece and *their* past experience, just as Romulus himself learnt from Athens, Thessaly and Sparta;³⁵ sometimes perhaps there is some feel for chronology, as when Brutus looks across to Spartan and Athenian constitutional arrangements at precisely the time when Cleisthenic democracy is getting underway;³⁶ sometimes it is more anachronistic, as with Romulus or when Tullus Hostilius talks of Athenian generosity with the citizenship some time around 670.³⁷ Learning from experience, their own or others', is what the Romans do.³⁸

III

Let us go back to those moments when Dionysius himself hints at a future that is beyond anything within his characters' own foresight. Sometimes, indeed, these are more than hints, and they often carry a clear statement that things are not what they used to be. We have already seen that in the case of Gaius Gracchus and his wrecking of internal harmony.³⁹ These days magistrates rush to grab magistracies or lead armies into action and ignore the clear signs that heaven disapproves – look at Crassus and the Parthians.⁴⁰ Triumphal processions have lost their splendid simplicity and these days they are just vulgar.⁴¹ The

---

34 Above, p. 159. Thus Cicero's Romulus builds on that initial foresight to develop some further political wisdom gradually during his reign: Fox 1996, 15. That Romulus is far from being a muddler through.
35 Dion. Hal. 2.8.1–2, 9.2–3, 13.4, 14.2.
36 Dion. Hal. 4.72.3, 73.4, 74.2–4. Thus Luraghi 2003, 278.
37 Dion. Hal. 3.11.4. Tullus alludes to Sparta too (3.10.3–6), but there the anachronism is less marked. On the resonance of these allusions see Richard 1993, bringing out how they chime with Dionysius' concerns elsewhere, Poma 1989, 188–92, and Fox 1996, 86–90.
38 On this learning from past history cf. now Schultze 2012, esp. 126–37. It is interesting to compare Schultze's essay with those of the other contributors to that volume, discussing a range of different authors (Grethlein/Krebs 2012). A recurrent theme is how the lessons drawn from the 'plupast' by figures in the texts are often in tension with those that the narratives themselves suggest, but Schultze finds little of that in Dionysius. The lessons may be contestable and contested, and some speakers are clearly much wiser than others (Appii Claudii are notoriously wrongheaded), but the inferences are normally 'germane to the situation, and are positively received' (137). It is fair to say that Dionysius' speakers are better learners than those in many other authors.
39 Dion. Hal. 2.11.3, above, p. 158.
40 Dion. Hal. 2.6.3–4.
41 Dion. Hal. 2.34.3.

greed of the rich has come to know no bounds.⁴² Manumission is now a travesty.⁴³ The dictatorship has been thoroughly abused since Sulla.⁴⁴ Military commanders have lost all respect for the senate too.⁴⁵ It is worth noticing that a lot of those explicit foresnaps are more concerned with the late Republic than with Augustus: of course, one could always argue that these were the failings that Augustus came along to put right.

Still, more often the gesturing to the future is not explicit. It is rather that the narrative seems to be working through future events in anticipation: these, then, are matters of similarity rather than, as with those explicit passages we have just seen, of change and decline. Of course there are the continuities that suggest only a feeling that the same sorts of issues constantly recur (and that feeling may not, after all, be wholly wrong): thus the Struggle of the Orders often focuses on issues that had been as live in the last generations of the Republic as they had four-and-a-half centuries earlier – the failures of the rich to do enough for the poor, the difficulties of getting and distributing enough corn, the pressure for agrarian reform, the rights of tribunes (here Dionysius comments explicitly that this remained an issue in 'the civil war at Rome in my times, the greatest one that had ever happened',⁴⁶ the struggles between people and senate over the right to legislate, the interaction of Italian and urban issues. But some of the foreshadowing is more specific. The scenes of uproar at the end of Book 4 have unmistakable hints of those on the Ides of March, where another Brutus would have a role to play in trying to cope with them;⁴⁷ and those same scenes after Caesar's assassination may well have influenced Dionysius' picture of the outpouring of popular grief after Verginia's death.⁴⁸ Elsewhere Servius Tullius, in a rabble-rousing speech, appropriates Caesar's *satis diu uel naturae uixi uel gloriae*;⁴⁹ Aulus Verginius, in a speech disingenuously alleging a patrician plot against the people, borrows several elements from the Catilinarian conspiracy

---

42 Dion. Hal. 2.74.5.
43 Dion. Hal. 4.24.
44 Dion. Hal. 5.77.
45 Dion. Hal. 5.60.2. Other cases are listed by Luraghi 2003, 273–4, Wiater 2011a, 201–4, and Peirano 2010, 46–7: Peirano argues that seeds of that decline can already be traced in the fragments of Dionysius' final books.
46 Dion. Hal. 8.87.7–8.
47 Note that Tarquin has killed Brutus' father (4.68.2, 77.3) as well as his brother; in Livy it is just his brother (1.56.7). That brings this Brutus closer to the Brutus of 44 BCE, who famously had to reconcile with the killer of *his* father, i.e. Pompey (Plut. *Brut.* 4.1–4, *Pomp.* 16.4–8).
48 Dion. Hal. 11.39.5–7. Thus Burck 1934, 40.
49 Dion. Hal. 4.11.6, Cic. *Marc.* 25.

of 63 BCE.[50] And there is a whole cluster of incidents surrounding the murder of Servius Tullius and the accession of Tarquinius Superbus where the atmosphere of the 50 s and 40 s, especially the Ides of March, is very strong – demonstrations of enthusiasm, dangers of riots, bloodshed looming.[51]

So we again see that a sense of the future pervades the narrative at crucial moments, even though the participants are not allowed to sense much of it themselves. Future greatness and future problems are not just something that requires the historian to go back to the distant past to explain; it is as if the future was already there. It clearly matters.

IV

Why should this be? What is all that foreshadowing of future events *about*? It is not just a Dionysius question, of course.[52] Enough of the first-century colouring is shared by Livy and Dionysius to suggest that it goes back to some common source-material, though each has sufficient distinctive contemporary colouring of his own to suggest that both of them are individually adding some more.

By now we cannot think that this simply came from a shortage of material, that Livy and Dionysius *needed* to fill in gaps by drawing on their own experience. However much or (more likely) however little we may believe in its historical accuracy, there was certainly a lot of material about: that is shown by the number of items shared by Dionysius and Livy that are not so rich in contemporary resonance, and we might recall also Cn. Gellius, who does not reach the Second Punic War till Book 30 or 33, and the 75-plus books of Valerius Antias.[53] So

---

50 Dion. Hal. 10.10. Ogilvie 1965, 423–424 suggests that Livy (3.15–18) was the one who 'introduced Catilinarian overtones' into the story: the parallel with Dionysius suggests differently, and some – probably not all – of the Catilinarian elements will go back to the source-material that the two authors share. That does not affect the point here, which is that both Dionysius and his audience would have sensed the resonance.
51 Dion. Hal. 4.37–40.
52 Oakley 1997, 86–8 lists and discusses similar phenomena in Livy's account of the Struggle of the Orders.
53 On Cn. Gellius and Valerius Antias see now *FRHist* i–iii (Cornell 2013); Gellius (*FRHist* 14) is discussed at i.252–5 (J. Briscoe) and Valerius Antias (*FRHist* 25) at i.293–304 (J.W. Rich); their testimonia and fragments are printed at ii.363–83 and ii.548–99 respectively, with commentary at iii.229–42 and 330–67. For earlier discussions of the 'expansion' or 'construction' of the past see esp. Wiseman 1979, Oakley 1997, 72–99, and on Antias in particular Rich 2005, esp. 147–55.

whatever Livy and Dionysius think they are doing, it is not because they would otherwise have nothing to say.

So what *are* they doing? The question has some similarity with the issues that have been raised recently about intertextuality in historiography,[54] though in those cases the emphasis has fallen more on echoes of the past, not of the future. I have had my say about that elsewhere,[55] and will not go over the same ground again here, except to make two very simple points, one about immediacy and one about plausibility. The two are in fact related. On immediacy, reading about contemporary-style crowd violence in the sixth century BCE would make it seem the sort of story that Dionysius' audience could picture very clearly indeed – not something sunk in a past that was "all so unimaginably different and all so long ago", in MacNeice's wonderfully ironic words, but something all very imaginably similar (which was arguably MacNeice's underlying point in those lines from *Autumn Journal*).[56] And it would be a matter not just of picturability, but also of relevance: it all still mattered, because it could happen like that even in the contemporary world.[57]

Still, that would only work if the immediacy goes with plausibility. Our own suspicious antennae tend to twitch if we find a portrayal of a sixteenth-century lady or gentleman talking like a modern head of state, as we know it was all so different and so long ago. Livy's or Dionysius' audience may not have reacted in the same way; in fact we can be pretty clear that they did not, if one thinks of the way that e.g. buildings or monuments are described in ways that were fairly up-to-date[58] or that battles and their topography tend to be moulded according to stereotypical patterns.[59] Of course Dionysius was aware that history changed, to a degree; that was clear in those nostalgic comments on how things had changed for the worse, and he has plenty of references to ancient customs that have disappeared by the time of the historian's own day. But it is still true enough that the pace of change was not as fast as all that, and that audiences were not accustomed to a casual assumption that everything must have been

---

54 Esp. O'Gorman 2009; Levene 2010, 84–6; Damon 2010; Marincola 2010a; Pelling 2013a; Lushkov 2013.
55 Pelling 2013.
56 The MacNeice quotation is from 'Autumn Journal' (1938), ix.
57 Cf. Fox 1993, 46: 'the function of the early Romans *as moral models and exemplary Greeks* [my italics], and the view of writing which leads Dionysius to represent them as he does, imparts no fixed temporal identity against which modernity, antiquity, or anachronism could be judged'.
58 Cf. Ogilvie 1965, 162–3 on Livy 1.41.4; Wiseman 1979, 43–5; Oakley 1997, 86.
59 Cf. e.g. Horsfall 1985; Oakley 1997, 83–4.

so different – even unimaginably different.⁶⁰ So here too one can make the same move as in those discussions of intertextuality. If you know that a particular pattern of behaviour or activity held in the world of Homer or of Thucydides *or of now*, then you are more likely to believe that it would also hold in the world of – whatever it is that you are talking or reading about. It happened or is happening like that once; nothing precludes one from believing that it happened on another occasion. In the case of intertextuality, one can believe that 'it', whatever it is, happened in the events described because it had already happened in the past; in the case of foreshadowing, you can believe that it happened in the past because it happened recently.

There may even be more fundamental reasons why phenomena should recur in the same or similar ways, perhaps through a Thucydidean view of a human nature which recurrently imposes itself, perhaps in more elaborate Polybian terms of *anakuklosis*, perhaps even because friendly or hostile gods continue to behave in their same old ways. But whatever the explanation, familiar phenomena are easier to believe. And the more one can believe and the more immediate one finds them, the more one can also accept that there are lessons to be learnt for the here-and-now: there is no reason why the same things should not go on to happen yet again, unless one learns from the past how to avoid them, or at least how to manage them well.⁶¹

---

60 Thus Marincola 2009a, 18, arguing that the pace of change was 'glacial': 'So far as we can tell, no event in antiquity matched the world-altering effect of, say, the Industrial Revolution or even of the French Revolution, not to mention the intellectual and moral upheavals brought in their train'. The comments of Wiseman 1979, 41–53 on 'unhistorical thinking' are still stimulating, even if that is an unfriendly way of putting it: cf. Marincola 2009a, 16–18 and 2010a, 265.
61 See Fox 2011, 97–9 on what he sees as Dionysius' 'anti-historicism', grounding analyses in particular cases from the past but diminishing their historical specificity in ways that make clearer their applicability to the present: '[h]istory here follows constant laws of probability, not in accordance with any clear sense of the character of particular historical periods' (99). This approach has something in common with what I have argued for Plutarch, suggesting a 'timelessness' in his historical categories which shies away from features specific to a particular society or age: Pelling 2002, 225–6 and chs. 10–11. Still, I also argued there that Plutarch is 'timeless' in a further sense, showing a reluctance to suggest too close a parallel between past events and his own times. The contemporary resonances are louder in Dionysius.

V

We should not lose hold of those two points of immediacy and plausibility, but we might also wonder if, as again in the case of intertextuality, there may be a point of interpretation as well. Every time we feel a hint of the late Republic, we may also capture a hint of where events are heading, for good and for ill: if our initial premise was right, explaining those later events was the reason why Dionysius needed to go back so much earlier than Polybius. But there is a further point too, for all those hints of late Republican violence draw our attention to the alternative history that did *not* then happen, but could so easily have done if those early events had anticipated the later ones even more closely, with even more bloodshed and violence than happened back then. The anticipation of the distant future can make both a point not just about now, how the worse was going to come one day, but also about then, how easily it could all have been much worse but was not. The here-and-now future of Dionysius' own day also points to those alternative futures that might have happened in the past.

Nor is that the only way in which Dionysius points to alternative futures. Another again involves intertextuality, with many echoes of Thucydides' Corcyra suggesting the devastating consequences of civic strife that Rome managed to avoid.⁶² But he can also look sideways at parallel events in other states, and leave his readers to draw their conclusions. Take for instance an episode that comes just as Rome is about to suffer the buffeting that came with Coriolanus, and Dionysius gives what on the face of it is surprising space to the story of Aristodemus of Cumae.⁶³ He too, like Coriolanus, is a war-hero, glorious from a heroic hand-to-hand encounter in the front-line;⁶⁴ but he is much more of a textbook case, stimulating jealousy among the aristocrats rather than the demos, then emerging as a demagogic leader with popular support.⁶⁵ A bloody coup follows, as he exemplifies the Platonic/Aristotelian stereotype of the demagogue seizing tyrannical power.⁶⁶ The reign itself then has something of a further pat-

---

62 Gabba 1991, 81–5: cf. below, p. 168.
63 Dion. Hal. 7.2–11. This episode is well discussed by Daniel Hogg in an outstanding dissertation (Hogg, 2008, 133–6). On the origins of this material – probably not any independent 'Cumaean chronicle' but a tradition heavily influenced by Roman historians and annalists even if it also draws on some Greek material – see Gallia 2007.
64 Dion. Hal. 7.4.3.
65 Dion. Hal. 7.4.5.
66 'In the old days, when the same person was both demagogue and general, there were revolutions to tyrannies: for generally most of the early tyrants got to that position from being demagogues' (Arist. *Pol.* 5.1305a7–10, cf. 1310b14–16); 'I suppose it is fairly clear that tyranny

tern familiar from Aristotle and Polybius, one where a *basileus* changes into a *turannos*.⁶⁷ Aristodemus begins with fair words, but also with 'the worst of all political measures among mankind, ones that every tyranny uses as its prologue – distribution of land and abolition of debt';⁶⁸ soon, though, matters turn more gruesome, with echoes of some bloody moments in Herodotus as well – so once again intertextuality too comes into play, as we remember other cities that shared the same experience that Rome contrived to miss.⁶⁹ That demagogue-into-tyrant pattern was mentioned a book earlier by the abominable Ap. Claudius,⁷⁰ and it is taken for granted a little later, ironically by Coriolanus himself when he is indignantly defending himself against the charge of tyrannical aspirations: if I was aiming at tyranny, I would hardly be trying to throw out the *demos*, 'by whom tyranny is particularly grown and nurtured'.⁷¹ I know how to do it, and it is not like this. It is as if he too has read his Plato and Aristotle, even if they have not actually written yet.⁷² Once again, then, we have another history that did not happen, this time one with tyranny as the grim alternative future that could so easily have become reality at Rome as well.⁷³

So why did Rome survive so well for so long, and why has it all turned out so much worse in the here-and-now? Part of the answer has been in our mind since early in the *History*: it was the tradition of violence that was instituted by C.

---

comes in a revolution from democracy' (Plato, *Republic* 8.562a). I collect further illustrative passages from Plato, Aristotle and elsewhere in my n. on Plut. *Caes.* 28.5 (Pelling 2011, 278), and then later discuss the Platonic analysis in particular when exploring the subtle ways in which Plutarch's Caesar differs from that stereotype (Pelling 2011, 421).

67 Arist. *Nic. Eth.* 8.1160b7 – 12, *Pol.* 5.1310b16 – 31, 1312b39 – 13a3, 1314a33 – 7; Polybius 2.47.3, 4.77.4, 6.4.8, 6.7.8, 7.13.8; and, for a Roman transposition, Cic. *de Re P.* 2.47 – 8, of Tarquinius Superbus. That is also a pattern which Peirano 2010, 47 – 8 finds in a later Dionysian side-glance at a non-Roman regime, that of Pyrrhus in the closing books.

68 Dion. Hal. 7.8.1.

69 Thus the denouement of 7.9 – 11 recalls in turn the Lemnian children at Hdt. 6.138, Cyrus and the Lydians at 1.155.4 and Zopyrus at 3.154; the last of these has already been recalled at 4.55, but now a tyrant's ploy is being turned against a tyrant.

70 Dion. Hal. 6.60.2.

71 Dion. Hal. 7.62.3.

72 Not that we should be too pernickety about this sort of 'anachronism'. Fox 1993, 42 and 46 (n. 24 above) is good on this: the Greek texts are embodying a sort of timeless wisdom, applicable to further periods and cultures, earlier as well as later, besides the immediate ones they are describing.

73 Gallia 2007, 52, 65 – 6 argued that such a 'comparative perspective' will also have featured in Dionysius' sources for Aristodemus; that may well be right, but should not obscure Dionysius' own development of that approach.

Gracchus.⁷⁴ But much of the answer rests on the 'then' rather than the 'now', points about what was right in the past rather than what has now gone wrong. One aspect is simply the good people that Rome had back then, men of outstanding virtue and wisdom: there is something of that in the preface, and the point recurs often enough.⁷⁵ But Dionysius has a sharper answer too, one that again comes in that passage about C. Gracchus and at other points too, including one in the middle of the great crisis posed by Coriolanus:

> It was like brothers dealing with brothers or children dealing with parents in a well-ordered house: they would talk to one another about fairness and justice, and settle their quarrels through persuasion and talk, and not allow themselves to do anything irreparable or wicked against one another. Contrast what the Corcyreans did during their faction, and the Argives, and the Milesians, and all Sicily, and many other cities.⁷⁶

People would talk to one another. Dionysius' Romans certainly make speech after speech after speech, but that is not because he is just a rhetorician who cannot resist it: they make speeches because they work.⁷⁷ That is why the different sides were more reluctant to come to blows than they have so often been in Dionysius' recent past, and than they were in the various intertextual models of *stasis* that are also in the background, especially that case of Thucydides' Corcyra that 7.66.5 mentions explicitly.

It is, then, a matter of interpretation too, not just of immediacy and plausibility. The distant future is helpful in pointing to the other alternative futures that could have happened along the way: it prompts us, and Dionysius, to explain both what went well for so long, and what has gone badly now.

VI

What about that very distant future, and Augustus? Rome had always been able to learn lessons from experience. What lessons are there to be learned now?

The easy answer is the straightforward Augustan one. We see the wise things Romulus did, and we think of the wise things Augustus is doing similarly. We re-

---

74 Dion. Hal. 2.11.2–3, p. 158.
75 Dion. Hal. 1.5.4, then e.g. 5.60.2, 10.17.6 (below, p. 172), 19.8.8, and 20.6.1. Cf. Hogg 2008, 179: 'the message of decline which Livy and Sallust point, explore, and occasionally complicate will be accompanied in Dionysius by the constant reminder that Rome can produce men capable of preventing it'.
76 Dion. Hal. 7.66.5.
77 Schultze 1986, 131–2.

call the mess that the Republic had got into after the good old days, and we think how Augustus is putting all that right. There is a particular passage that tells that way too, one on a Greek model: they had begun with monarchies, changed to other governments when the going got difficult, but then saw the error of their ways and reverted to monarchical rule.[78] Even some of the constitutional discussion can point in that direction; one thing that comes out in the discussion of the early tribunate – a charged topic in itself for Augustus, with his paraded *tribunicia potestas* – is the insight that the constitutional set-up may matter rather less than what sort of tribunes you end up with.[79] It is not perhaps the most thrillingly insightful remark he ever made, but it is not wrong; he says something very similar about the dictatorship at the end of Book 5.[80] The person, not the system, is what counts; and we know what sort of person Rome has ended up with in Dionysius' own day. If there are few people these days who would refuse monarchic power, if offered, and resemble instead those great and frugal men of old,[81] we can certainly put a name to one of them.

There may be something in that; any picture of Dionysius as a subtle subversive does not convince.[82] But there are also some areas where a contemporary resonance can be found, and Dionysius' treatment is less than delicate. I have pointed elsewhere to one of those, the question of the decemvirate's status once its legal term had expired but no successors had been appointed.[83] That is almost exactly the issue that arose about Octavian himself and his triumviral colleagues in 36 and 32 BCE[84] – not at all a particularly comfortable issue for the *princeps* to see highlighted, especially as Dionysius treats the decemvirs' case with so little sympathy. Better, perhaps, to stick with that earlier emphasis on immediacy and plausibility, and see Dionysius as meshing with contemporary themes without crudely sounding a pro-Augustan or anti-Augustan gong. The way that so much seems so up-to-date can be taken simply as a pointer to the way that the themes still matter, and the way they matter so much now can make us readier to believe that they also mattered so much in the past.

---

[78] Dion. Hal. 5.74.1–3.
[79] Dion. Hal. 7.65.
[80] Dion. Hal. 5.77.6.
[81] Dion. Hal. 10.17.6.
[82] For a measured and insightful discussion of Dionysius and Augustan ideology, see now Wiater 2011a, 206–16.
[83] Dion. Hal. 11.5–6, etc Pelling 2007, 256–7.
[84] Pelling 1996, 26–7, 48, 67–8.

VII

One last question, primed by that initial stress on Dionysius' relationship to Polybius, and one that puts any 'preparing for posterity' in a more searching light. In the light of that importance of Polybius, Dionysius must surely have pondered one of the most startling passages in the earlier text. That is the extended set-piece at 36.9 where Polybius thinks of all the different ways in which people might judge, and did judge, Rome's destruction of Carthage. It sketches the "many things that were said, and of all sorts" (πολλοὶ καὶ παντοῖοι διεφέροντο λόγοι) in Greece about what Rome had done. One view was that the Romans were thoroughly wise and statesmanlike, removing this menace that had hung over them for so long. A second reflected that up to now Romans had been wise enough to stop when their adversaries had admitted defeat; this though was crude 'lust for domination', φιλαρχία, ignoring the way that the Carthaginians were prepared to obey the Roman bidding. The third view contrasted the Roman way of fighting with that of the past: they had tricked Carthage, and that was not traditional. Finally, a fourth view stressed that there had been no deception; the Carthaginians had surrendered unconditionally, and they should have realised what that meant.

> This, then, was what was said about the Romans and the Carthaginians.[85]

Polybius himself is also writing under the shadow of a mammoth earlier figure, and that is Thucydides. It is not hard to extrapolate from that passage a challenge not just to contemporary but also to future readers of a 'possession for ever' (κτῆμα ἐς αἰεί),[86] all those readers whom Polybius so often treats as potentially drawing inferences for their own immediate political experience and circumstances, whatever and whenever those may be: perhaps indeed after Rome's fall, that catastrophe to which Polybius makes Scipio look forward as he looks on the destruction of Carthage and weeps. Scipio quotes Homer:

> ἔσσεται ἦμαρ ὅταν ποτ' ὀλώλῃ Ἴλιος ἱρὴ
> καὶ Πρίαμος καὶ λαὸς ἐυμμελίω Πριάμοιο.
>
> The day will come when sacred Ilion dies, and Priam, and the people of Priam of the ashen spear.[87]

---

85 Dion. Hal. 36.10.1
86 Thuc. 1.22.4
87 Polybius 38.22.2, quoting *Iliad* 6.448–9

As early as the prologue, Dionysius introduces his own version of the familiar 'sequence of empires', placing Rome in the sequence of Assyrians and Medes and Persians and Macedonians,[88] just as Polybius had done a sentence or so before that Homeric quotation, there echoing his own proem.[89] Dionysius' point is admittedly there one of duration – Rome has lasted so much longer – rather than Scipio's transience; but it is not too hard to take Scipio's further step as well, that Rome's empire may pass just as those earlier empires have passed.[90] Dionysius and his Romans may indeed have to 'prepare for posterity' and posterity's judgement: not just explanation, then, of Rome's success, but verdict too. And Dionysius presents posterity with a good deal more material on which that verdict can be based.

Roman imperialism is in its infancy for most of Dionysius' narrative, but it is there, and clearly relevant to this question: at this stage it is largely a matter of the takeover of Italy and the handling of the other Italian tribes. One recurrent theme there is how *nice* Rome has been to the peoples it has conquered, at least once it has won: and not just in sparing them but in welcoming them too, accepting them into citizenship, patronage and *clientela*. One passage under Romulus is particularly relevant here, and it is another where the presence of Polybius is particularly felt.

> But the city of Rome, even while it was engaged in great wars in Spain and Italy and in the recovery of Sicily after its revolt and Sardinia, and when matters in Macedonia and Greece had been brought to a state of war against them, and Carthage was rising again to fight for supremacy, and Italy was not merely almost all in revolt but was joining in to bring the so-called Hannibalic War against them – when it had fallen into dangers of such magnitude all at once at the same time – even so it was not brought low by the fortunes of the time, but gained additional strength from them which even surpassed what they had had before. The numbers of their fighting force made them able to confront all the perils, and it was not simply, as some people suppose, a matter of the goodwill brought by Fortune. If it had all been left to Fortune, the city would have been sunk by the disaster at Cannae, when of 6000 cavalry 370 survived and from a levy of 80,000 men in the common army a little more than 3000 survived.[91]

---

88 Dion. Hal. 1.2.2–4.
89 Dion. Hal. 1.2.2–7.
90 Alonso-Nuñez 1983 brings out that Dionysius' treatment of this sequence is more precise than Polybius'; Martin 1993 explores the ways in which Dionysius elaborates and complicates Polybius' sequence to bring out the Greekness of Rome's empire; Weißenberger 2002 observes that Dionysius adds a mention of Rome's achievements in peace as well as in war (1.2.1). Dionysius accordingly stresses the 'beauty' (τὸ κάλλος) of Rome's achievements, not just their greatness: that goes with the proem's general emphasis on the good behaviour of those early Romans, not just their success ('the greatest and most just of their actions', 1.6.3). The narrative will then fill out the ways in which the goodness promoted the success.
91 Dion. Hal. 2.17.3–4.

Dionysius has just been stressing the enlightened policy of Roman colonisation and extension of citizenship,[92] and here he is *contrasting* Greek practice rather than stressing the Roman debt to it. Their failure to follow a similar path was, so he claims, a principal reason why the Spartan, Theban and Athenian empires proved so easy to overthrow. The period to which he is referring is Polybius' period, that of the great wars in and with Spain, Sicily, Sardinia, Macedonia, Greece and Carthage. The stress on Fortune may again be a gesture at Polybius, who makes so much of *Tyche*; and Cannae, here so stressed, was the point where Polybius inserted his own explanation of Roman success and resilience, and it was a very different one. Once again, too, we see that Dionysius' explanation takes events vastly further back, to a policy of assimilation and generosity that took shape in Rome's earliest days, and it is again one whose wisdom could only be grasped in retrospect.

Is there then a verdict on Rome, of the sort of that Polybius 36.9 invited? There may well be an implication that Rome's beastliness to Carthage was not typical: more than an excusable aberration, doubtless, because of the importance of that critical phase, but an action that was out of keeping with the traditions of the city. Dionysius typically constructs his audience as Greeks[93] – Greeks who are interested in Rome and deserve the chance to read about Rome in their own language. In the prologue he draws out the implications that Greeks might learn as they ponder the greatness of Rome: they should learn, as their wiser predecessors have done, that Rome is a good master to have, and they should accept subjection willingly,[94] "learning from my history that Rome from its very beginning produced myriads of examples of human virtue, men whose piety and justice and prudence and formidable might have never been matched by any city, Greek or barbarian". That justice and prudence evidently include those qualities that we have seen Dionysius' stressing: their openness to foreigners, their capacity to avoid bloodiness by talking things through. So on balance, if there is a verdict, it is a positive one.

---

92 This theme starts as early as 1.9.4; then we have e.g. 2.16.1, 35–6, 2.46, 2.55.6, 3.29 (incorporation of noble Alban families into *patricii* and senate), and 6.55; this is still Roman policy in the early fourth century with the Tusculans, 14.6. Tullus Hostilius can justly pride the city on this policy at 3.11.4, in a speech that reprises several of the themes of the previous book. Tarquinius Priscus is then accordingly attracted to Rome when he hears 'that the city willingly welcomes all strangers, makes them citizens, and honours them according to their worth' (3.47.2). On this as a characteristic Dionysian theme, and a notably good point, cf. Balsdon 1971, 27 and n. 57 and especially Poma 1989.
93 Schultze 1986, 138–9; Gabba 1991, 79–80; Fox 1996, 53–5; Fromentin 1998, xxxv–xxxvii; Delcourt 2005, 65–9; Wiater 2011a, 218–20.
94 Dion. Hal. 1.5.2–3.

Perhaps, though, it is more a response than a verdict; perhaps the posterity passing judgement includes future posterities as well, generations that will pass their verdicts on Dionysius' own present as well as on his past. There are enough hints too of Roman readers reading over the Greeks' shoulder, themselves alert to any lessons there are to be learned;[95] both Greeks and Romans, indeed, may be nudged into a more generous view of one another by that reading performance itself, with an awareness that they are both part of the same 'imagined community' of readers.[96] There are implications for those Roman readers too, not merely in those nudges towards appreciation of Greek culture but also in any further dealings they may have with any non-Romans, perhaps new enemies once they are vanquished, perhaps simply provincials.[97] Hindsight can be the thinking person's foresight for them too, as they dwell on what went well in the past as well as on what was shaming. The proem calls on "the present and future descendants of those godlike men" to do "nothing unworthy of their ancestors",[98] and the inferences are there to draw for any Romans, not just those of ancestral nobility.[99] All of them might well be afraid of posterity's judgement, as Tacitus affects to think his readers might be afraid.[100] The way to nurture a favourable verdict is still open to them, if they can only learn the right lessons from the distant past, and one of those is generosity rather than brutality. Romans have always learned from the Greeks. They can draw a further lesson now from another Greek, the one from Halicarnassus.

---

95 Cf. works cited in previous note and especially Luraghi 2003, 272–3, who goes on to argue (281–285) that Dionysius is tactfully masking his criticism of contemporary Roman realities and competition with earlier Roman writers by presenting himself as writing for a hypothetical Greek audience. This may underplay the importance of real Greek readers and overplay the potential effectiveness of any such 'masking'.
96 Wiater 2011b.
97 On this see now the thoughtful remarks of Fox 2011, comparing the emphasis in Dionysius' critical works on the value of classical models for his readers' own literary production: thus we should 'think of Dionysius' efforts both as an historian and a critic as being focussed not so much in the past, as on the future … his frame of reference is not so much the recreation of the past, as the demonstration of the potential of revival for the forging of a more effective political identity in time to come' (95).
98 1.6.4.
99 Cf. Delcourt 2005, 68.
100 Tac. *Ann.* 3.65.1.

Temporalities of the Future
and the Times of Historical Action

Catherine Darbo-Peschanski
The Future and the Logic of Closure in Greek Historiography

Translated by Anna Barton

In order to understand how the future functions, in and through the *historiai*, it seems to me that two complementary approaches must be intertwined: on the one hand, the external time organisation in which works like these take place as discrete units (I will expand on this point shortly); on the other hand, the internal organisation of temporality within these works, which leads us to two further aspects: first, the mechanisms by which the *historiai* bring to life the sequence of events they recount (which serves as an internal driving force for time within them and, indeed, sketches out a future); secondly, the particular treatment given to the future within this temporality – specifically, their means of achieving closure.

1 The external temporal organisation of the works called *historiai*

1.1 Logos vs. chronos

For our purposes, a fundamental distinction can be found in the contrasting definitions of epic, tragedy and, to a lesser extent, of the *historia*, which Aristotle gives in the *Poetics*: while epic and tragedy draw, albeit differently, on part of a *logos*, that is, on a story passed down by tradition or created by the poet himself, although apparently not without tapping into existing narratives (I am thinking here of Aeschylus' *Persians*), the *historia*, instead, carves out a period in the passage of time (a *chronos*)[1]. The differences run deeper than this, however.

---

1 Aristotle, Poet. 1459a17–30: Περὶ δὲ τῆς διηγηματικῆς καὶ ἐν μέτρῳ μιμητικῆς, ὅτι δεῖ τοὺς μύθους καθάπερ ἐν ταῖς τραγῳδίαις συνιστάναι δραματικοὺς καὶ περὶ μίαν πρᾶξιν ὅλην καὶ τελείαν ἔχουσαν ἀρχὴν καὶ μέσα καὶ τέλος, ἵν' ὥσπερ ζῷον ἐν ὅλον ποιῇ τὴν οἰκείαν ἡδονήν, δῆλον, καὶ μὴ ὁμοίας ἱστορίαις τὰς συνθέσεις εἶναι, ἐν αἷς ἀνάγκη οὐχὶ μιᾶς πράξεως ποιεῖσθαι δήλωσιν ἀλλ' ἑνὸς χρόνου, ὅσα ἐν τούτῳ συνέβη περὶ ἕνα ἢ πλείους, ὧν ἕκαστον ὡς ἔτυχεν ἔχει πρὸς ἄλληλα. ὥσπερ γὰρ κατὰ τοὺς αὐτοὺς χρόνους ἥ τ' ἐν Σαλαμῖνι ἐγένετο ναυμαχία καὶ ἡ ἐν

The first difference concerns epic and tragedy. The former (epic) is, in fact, *"polymythical"*: in other words, it involves various plot lines, and is played out in episodes that give it a rather broad scope²; the latter (tragedy), on the other hand, focuses on just one *muthos*, which has a specific structure in that it is "centred on a particular act (*praxis*) with a beginning, a middle and an end" and, as a result, forms a complete whole. The specificity of the tragic *muthos* sheds greater light on the character of the *historia*: because the *historia* only describes a portion of "calendar" time, as P. Ricœur would say, it carries with it a plurality of acts, like an epic, except in as far as those acts are only contingentally linked (*hôs etuchen*), whereas in epic they are drawn from the same *logos*, for example the Trojan cycle or the Theban cycle. The fundamental distinction here regarding temporality, although it is not discussed in great detail, is that the broader narrative discourse of the *logos* comes with the internal temporality (or temporalities) belonging to its plot line(s), while the portion of time (*chronos*) in a given calendar, as retold by the *historia*³, does not bring with it consistency either in terms of plot line, or in terms of internal temporal connection.

If we were to extend the logic of Aristotle's distinctions further, we could therefore say that genealogies come in between works of the epic or tragic genres (which draw on part of a *logos* that brings with it an intrinsic temporality in its

---

Σικελίᾳ Καρχηδονίων μάχη οὐδὲν πρὸς τὸ αὐτὸ συντείνουσαι τέλος, οὕτω καὶ <u>ἐν τοῖς ἐφεξῆς χρόνοις</u> ἐνίοτε γίνεται θάτερον μετὰ θάτερον, ἐξ ὧν <u>ἓν οὐδὲν γίνεται τέλος</u>.
We come now to the art of representation which is narrative and in metre. Clearly the story (*muthoi*) must be constructed as in tragedy, dramatically, round <u>a single piece of action, whole and complete in itself, with a beginning, middle and end,</u> so that like a single living organism it may produce its own peculiar form of pleasure (*the Aristotelian muthos or plot cf. Veyne and Ricœur*). <u>It must not be such as we normally find in history,</u> where what is required is an exposition <u>not of a single piece of action</u> but of a <u>single period of time</u>, showing all that within the period befell one or more persons, <u>events</u> that have <u>a merely casual relation to each other</u>. For just as the battle of Salamis <u>occurred at the same time</u> as the Carthaginian battle in Sicily, but <u>they do not converge to the same result</u>, so, too, in <u>any sequence of time</u> one event may follow another and yet <u>they may not issue in any one result.</u>

2 Aristotle, *Poet.* 1455b 15–16: Ἐν μὲν οὖν τοῖς δράμασιν τὰ ἐπεισόδια σύντομα, ἡ δ' ἐποποιία τούτοις μηκύνεται. Now in drama the episodes are short, but it is by them that the epic gains its length. Aristotle, *Poet.* 1456a 10–16: χρὴ δὲ ὅπερ εἴρηται πολλάκις μεμνῆσθαι καὶ μὴ ποιεῖν <u>ἐποποιικὸν σύστημα</u> τραγῳδίαν—ἐποποιικὸν δὲ λέγω <u>τὸ πολύμυθον</u>— οἷον εἴ τις τὸν τῆς Ἰλιάδος ὅλον ποιοῖ μῦθον. ἐκεῖ μὲν γὰρ διὰ τὸ μῆκος λαμβάνει τὰ μέρη τὸ πρέπον μέγεθος, ἐν δὲ τοῖς δράμασι πολὺ παρὰ τὴν ὑπόληψιν ἀποβαίνει. One must remember, as we have often said, not to make a tragedy an <u>epic structure</u>: by epic I mean made up of <u>many stories</u> – suppose, for instance, one were to dramatise <u>the *Iliad* as a whole</u>. The length of the *Iliad* allows to the parts their proper size, but in plays the result is full of disappointment.
3 As it happens, the Herodotean *historia* is Aristotle's prime example of a *historia*.

plot line) and those that recount, in what is seen as objective time, a period, devoid of internal logic or chronology. Genealogies like those of Hecataeus, Pherecydes of Leros, Acusilaus of Lesbos, or (in part) Hellanicus, are in fact akin to works built on a *logos*. The *logos* here is a tradition, whose plot line is formed out of the successive and ramified generations of faraway heroes. It is appropriate to distinguish these from simple calendar genealogies, organised by generation, from which a certain period is selected; that is the case at the beginning of Herodotus' *historia*, for example. Such examples rather have the form of the *chronos* Aristotle describes, which records events without plot, contingently.

1.2 The succession of the *historiai* and epic rhapsody

Since Thucydides' *suggraphê*, works that carve out periods of time have been organised in series, or, in the case of *koinai historiai* like Diodorus', have undertaken to cover within themselves the entirety of time up to the *historiographos*' present. The externality of this organisational principle, which does not dictate the method or subject focus of each work, enables them to mutually interlink, while remaining open to the possibility of intensely polemic relationships arising between them. Thucydides, for example, takes issue with the Herodotean *historia*, yet partly picks up his tale at the point where Herodotus left off. Xenophon begins his *Hellenica* where Thucydides ended. According to Photius, Isocrates more or less took hold of time, as reconfigured by Thucydides' narrative, by both ends, giving Ephorus the task of covering the events prior to those included in Thucydides' tale, and allocating to Theopompus the account of events that took place later. Demophilus, son of Ephorus, begins his own story by narrating the events with which his father's finished. Polybius picks up not only where Aratus of Sicyon left off, but also where Timaeus, a historian whom he criticised heavily, had closed his tale; and so on – all this is well known.

Similarly, from the fourth century onwards, and undoubtedly influenced by Aristotle, all these connected works starting with Herodotus and his *apodexis istoriês* were given the name *historiai* – again, on the basis of purely external criteria.

But, you may object, there was also succession in epic.[4] Indeed there was; however, to cut a long story short, a different mechanism was at work there. This was the *hupobolê*, which consisted in breaking off a first aoidos' account

---

4 Scholia to Clement of Alexandria, *Protrepticus*, 2, 30, Stählin, 1, 305–306: The poets we call "cyclic poets" (*kuklikoi poiêtai*) are those who composed their works around the *Iliad* (*ta kuklôi tês Iliadês*), whether shortly before, or shortly after, not including those who wrote the Homeric poems themselves.

mid-way, and looking "beneath" for its underlying *logos*.[5] On the one hand, as Aristotle says, we can see this having some grounding in a *chronos* divided into periods; on the other hand, it focuses on the *logos*.

Since their beginnings, then, the *historiai* have been an open series, rooted in a time that is seen as objective, and itself open onto an unbounded future. This time is measured in terms of the periods chosen for each work, but also, and most frequently, the life of the *historiographos* himself. He writes up until the moment of his death, and it is not unusual for him to entrust the task of continuation to a designated successor. Xenophon does so explicitly, after himself having taken up Thucydides' unfinished work, which perhaps implicitly called out to be continued; so too does Polybius. As for Demophilus, by choosing to narrate the period following on from that re-told by his father, he demonstrates that the succession of generations of writers mirrors the objective progression of time that their narratives are based on. The course of events and succession of generations run side by side into an open future.

2 The temporality of plot lines

Intrinsically, the *Historiai* must themselves create the plot line of their narrative, since it is not given by their structure and, in so doing, must create an internal temporality connected to that plot.

---

[5] Read *Iliad* I.292 (Agamemnon and Achilles' dispute) together with *Iliad*, XIX.78–82 (the speaking protocol at the Assembly, as decreed by Agamemnon) and the definition that Eustathius of Thessalonica, in *Commentarii ad Homeri Iliadem pertinentes*, gives of the verb *hupoballein* –
Iliad I.292: Brilliant Achilles broke in upon him [that is, "interrupting": hupoblêdên] and replied: Τὸν δ' ἄρ' ὑποβλήδην ἠμείβετο δῖος Ἀχιλλεύς· ;
Iliad XIX.78–82: My friends, Danaan warriors, squires of Ares, meet is it to give ear to him that standeth to speak, nor is it seemly to <u>break in upon his words</u>; grievous were that even for one well-skilled. And amid the uproar of many how should a man either hear or speak? – hampered is he then, clear-voiced talker though he be.
ὦ φίλοι ἥρωες Δαναοὶ θεράποντες Ἄρηος
ἑσταότος μὲν καλὸν ἀκούειν, οὐδὲ ἔοικεν
<u>ὑββάλλειν</u>· χαλεπὸν γὰρ ἐπισταμένῳ περ ἐόντι.
ἀνδρῶν δ' ἐν πολλῷ ὁμάδῳ πῶς κέν τις ἀκούσαι
ἢ εἴποι; βλάβεται δὲ λιγύς περ ἐὼν ἀγορητής.
Eustathius ὑποβλήδην *Il.* I.292: not to tolerate that a person currently speaking should come to the end of their point, but to introduce one's own point " underneath ", which is exactly what Achilles does. For, not wanting the king to complete his accusation, he responds to him *hupoblêdên*.

I will be swift on this point and say only that, overall, three main drivers of temporality are found in the various *historiai:* justice, human nature and the dialectic between a force at work organising events and human actions (*praxeis*).

The first of these, justice, is closely linked in Herodotus with the interpretation of the Greco-Persian wars as an accumulation of transgressions, in an understanding of conquest forgetful of all limitations (physical, social or religious) that create order in the inhabited world. Time can therefore be described as an incessant pendulum swinging, at many different levels, between offences and their reparation. Every Herodotean event is indeed either one or the other of these, and time thus progresses from a violation of just order to the reinstatement, or supposed reinstatement, of that order (*dikên didonai, dikên labein*). Here too, time is theoretically open to an unbounded future.

The situation is similar for the second driving force of time: human nature, which replaces justice as the "temporalising" power in Thucydides. The events' protagonists do of course still invoke justice in their speech, but it is no longer the objective force portrayed as governing the world and its history. It has instead become the object of debates, even eristic arguments, in which it is constantly redefined and set at odds with itself. The true driving force of time here is human nature, with its eternal propensity to give in to the passions that continually feed war. Its story is therefore one of wars and of great heroes who are able to curb those passions in the name of reason, for a time, and thus save the world from the otherwise inevitable contingency of *tuchê*. Xenophon can also be seen to follow this model to a certain extent. In his writings too, justice is not the driving force, and instead, in a world left prey to a variety of appetites, the rare islets of order come together around a few charismatic leaders.

For the third type of temporality, I am inclined to draw an example from Polybius. In the game of nature that determines the succession of regimes, in which human events (*praxeis*) are born of a psychology in which instances of clarity and reason confront instances of blindness and error, *tuchê* enters the stage and mixes together, in Roman affairs, matters that were thus far dispersed among events. *Tuchê* and the *atuchêmata* of human actions therefore come into conflict and create the course of history, whose future may appear, once again, indeterminable and open-ended.

3 Principles of closure

Nevertheless, a common feature of all the *historiai* is that they include the future at the expense of imposing closure, in a variety of ways, on its unbounded infinity. As far as I see it, there are four principles of closure.

3.1 The arresting blow of divine punishment: "The dialectic of master and slave"

The first, most clearly manifested in Herodotus' *Histories*, consists of a divine sanction which, by means of a significant punishment, puts an end to a long series of injustices and transgressions whose wrongs have not yet been settled. If we look closely, we could even say that the whole set of events re-told in the *Histories* is encased between two divine blows that fix its boundaries with the past and the future.

In order to end with the Greco-Persian wars, Herodotus' long narrative in fact starts well before the time of Croesus, even though he is known as "the one who first started the series of unjust actions" (I. 5). The buffer in the past is Croesus' ancestor Gyges, who was the collateral victim of an original curse condemning king Candaules, for an offence the text does not explain: "it was necessary for bad to come to Candaules".[6] This curse obliges Gyges to choose whether to usurp the throne or to lose his own life and, by so doing (since he chooses the former) to commit the first injustice. His action forges the first link in an uninterrupted chain of offences and atonement, to which Croesus will later add.

At the other end of the *Histories*, Herodotus defends the truthfulness of the Bakis oracle, who interprets Salamis as a defeat inflicted by Justice (Dikè), flanked by Arès, Zeus and Nikè alongside the Greeks, on Greed and Excess, themselves on the side of the Persians, who had thrown a ship's deck into the sea.[7]

---

[6] Herodotus, *Hist.* 1.8.7: χρῆν γὰρ Κανδαύλῃ γενέσθαι κακῶς.
[7] Herodotus, *Hist.* 8.77
Χρησμοῖσι δὲ οὐκ ἔχω ἀντιλέγειν ὡς οὐκ εἰσὶ ἀληθέες, οὐ βουλόμενος ἐναργέως λέγοντας πειρᾶσθαι καταβάλλειν, ἐς τοιάδε ῥήματα ἐσβλέψας·
"'Ἀλλ' ὅταν Ἀρτέμιδος χρυσαόρου ἱερὸν ἀκτὴν
"νηυσὶ γεφυρώσωσι καὶ εἰναλίην Κυνόσουραν,
"ἐλπίδι μαινομένῃ λιπαρὰς πέρσαντες Ἀθήνας,
"δῖα Δίκη σβέσσει κρατερὸν Κόρον, Ὕβριος υἱόν,
"δεινὸν μαιμώοντα, δοκεῦντ' ἅμα πάντα πίεσθαι.
"Χαλκὸς γὰρ χαλκῷ συμμίξεται, αἵματι δ' Ἄρης
"πόντον φοινίξει. Τότ' ἐλεύθερον Ἑλλάδος ἦμαρ
"εὐρύοπα Κρονίδης ἐπάγει καὶ πότνια Νίκη."
[Ἐς] τοιαῦτα μὲν καὶ οὕτω ἐναργέως λέγοντι Βάκιδι ἀντιλογίας χρησμῶν πέρι οὔτε αὐτὸς λέγειν τολμέω οὔτε παρ' ἄλλων ἐνδέκομαι.
I cannot say against oracles that they are not true, and I do not wish to try to discredit them when they speak plainly. Look at the following matter:
When the sacred headland of golden-sworded Artemis and Cynosura by the sea they bridge with ships,

Yet, one may object, Herodotus' narrative does not stop at VIII.77, after Salamis, and there seems to be, alongside the closure of divine punishment, another principle obstructing the indefinite and unlimited openness of the future.

Indeed, the course of events continues after the invasion of Persia has been halted: thanks to the participation of the Athenians, the Greeks are able to pursue the Persians and take Sestos. It is then, just as Herodotus notes that the Athenians have left and taken with them many valuable objects (IX. 121),[8] that we are reminded (IX. 122)[9] of the master-slave dialectic – first mentioned by Croesus in book I — which is at play: positions are inverted by the gradual weakening of the dominant populations, once austere but later corrupted by all kind of riches taken from the defeated.

It therefore seems reasonable to me that we could see an analogy between the Greco-Persian wars, in which the Greeks end up forming an alliance against the Persians, and the future hegemony of Athens, which in turn results in the coalition of the rest of Greece, sometimes with the help of the Persians, against

---

After sacking shiny Athens in mad hope,
Divine Justice will extinguish mighty Greed the son of Insolence
Lusting terribly, thinking to devour all.
Bronze will come together with bronze, and Ares
Will redden the sea with blood. To Hellas the day of freedom
Far-seeing Zeus and august Victory will bring.
Considering this, I dare to say nothing against Bacis concerning oracles when he speaks so plainly, nor will I consent to it by others.

8 Hist. 9.121: Ταῦτα δὲ ποιήσαντες ἀπέπλεον ἐς τὴν Ἑλλάδα, <u>τά τε ἄλλα χρήματα ἄγοντες</u> καὶ δὴ καὶ τὰ ὅπλα τῶν γεφυρέων ὡς ἀναθήσοντες ἐς τὰ ἱρά. Καὶ κατὰ τὸ ἔτος τοῦτο οὐδὲν ἐπὶ πλέον τούτων ἐγένετο.
This done, they sailed away to Hellas, carrying with them the cables of the bridges to be dedicated in their temples, and <u>all sorts of precious things in addition</u>. This, then, is all that was done in this year.

9 Hist., 9.122. Recall that previously the king reacted to Artembares, who recommended conquest to Cyrus and the Persians as a way to leave their small, rocky territory and go to gain better lands and achieve the respected position of masters, thus: Κῦρος δέ, ταῦτα ἀκούσας καὶ οὐ θωμάσας τὸν λόγον, ἐκέλευε ποιέειν ταῦτα, οὕτω δὲ αὐτοῖσι παραίνεε κελεύων παρασκευάζεσθαι <u>ὡς οὐκέτι ἄρξοντας ἀλλ' ἀξομένους</u>· φιλέειν γὰρ ἐκ τῶν μαλακῶν χώρων μαλακοὺς ἄνδρας γίνεσθαι (...) Ὥστε συγγνόντες Πέρσαι οἴχοντο ἀποστάντες, ἑσσωθέντες τῇ γνώμῃ πρὸς Κύρου, ἄρχειν τε εἵλοντο λυπρὴν οἰκέοντες μᾶλλον ἢ πεδιάδα σπείροντες ἄλλοισι δουλεύειν: Cyrus heard them, and found nothing to marvel at in their design; "Go ahead and do this," he said; "but if you do so, be prepared <u>no longer to be rulers but rather subjects</u>. Soft lands breed soft men; (...) The Persians now realised that Cyrus reasoned better than they, and they departed, choosing rather to be rulers on a barren mountain side <u>than</u> dwelling in tilled valleys <u>to be slaves to others</u>."

Athens and her allies. It can be seen as a symmetrical repetition of the same deadly imperialist impulse, with no regard for other peoples' freedom, even one's own allies, nor, perhaps, for its own consequences.

This thesis is all the more tenable given that in Thucydides, who as we have seen to some extent made his work out to be the sequel to Herodotus' narrative, the principle of analogy is also present, and *explicitly* functions as a means of closure.

3.2 Paradigm and analogy

You will no doubt recall the well-known passage of book I of *The Peloponnesian War*.[10] Because this war is considered exceptionally important, the facts reported in *The Peloponnesian War* form a model (the famous *ktêma eis aiei*) that can be translated equally well into the past as into the future, to enable us to clearly understand what it is that has happened, or will happen, on any occasion (hence *aiei*).

The grounding principle that enables events from such distant periods to be connected in this way is their common human character (*to anthrôpinon*).

As we have already seen, in fact,[11] Thucydides makes human nature, with its fundamental immutability, into the driving force of history. It is thanks to human

---

10 Thucydides 1.22.4: ἐς μὲν ἀκρόασιν ἴσως τὸ μὴ μυθῶδες αὐτῶν ἀτερπέστερον φανεῖται· ὅσοι δὲ βουλήσονται <u>τῶν τε γενομένων τὸ σαφὲς σκοπεῖν</u> καὶ <u>τῶν μελλόντων</u> ποτὲ αὖθις <u>κατὰ τὸ ἀνθρώπινον</u> τοιούτων καὶ παραπλησίων ἔσεσθαι, ὠφέλιμα κρίνειν αὐτὰ ἀρκούντως ἕξει. <u>κτῆμά τε ἐς αἰεὶ</u> μᾶλλον ἢ ἀγώνισμα <u>ἐς τὸ παραχρῆμα</u> ἀκούειν ξύγκειται.
The absence of romance in my history will, I fear, detract somewhat from its interest; but if it be judged useful by those inquirers who desire <u>an exact knowledge of the past</u> as an aid to the interpretation of <u>the future, which in the course of human things must resemble</u> if it does not reflect it, I shall be content. In fine, I have written my work, not as an essay which is to win the applause <u>of the moment</u>, but as <u>a possession for all time</u>.
11 Thucydides, 3.82: καὶ ἐπέπεσε πολλὰ καὶ χαλεπὰ κατὰ στάσιν ταῖς πόλεσι, <u>γιγνόμενα μὲν καὶ αἰεὶ ἐσόμενα, ἕως ἂν ἡ αὐτὴ φύσις ἀνθρώπων ᾖ</u>, μᾶλλον δὲ καὶ ἡσυχαίτερα καὶ τοῖς εἴδεσι διηλλαγμένα, ὡς ἂν <u>ἕκασται αἱ μεταβολαὶ τῶν ξυντυχιῶν</u> ἐφιστῶνται. ἐν μὲν γὰρ εἰρήνῃ καὶ ἀγαθοῖς πράγμασιν αἵ τε πόλεις καὶ οἱ ἰδιῶται ἀμείνους τὰς γνώμας ἔχουσι διὰ τὸ μὴ ἐς ἀκουσίους ἀνάγκας πίπτειν· ὁ δὲ πόλεμος ὑφελὼν τὴν εὐπορίαν τοῦ καθ' ἡμέραν βίαιος διδάσκαλος καὶ <u>πρὸς τὰ παρόντα</u> τὰς ὀργὰς τῶν πολλῶν ὁμοιοῖ.
The sufferings which revolution entailed upon the cities were many and terrible, <u>such as have occurred and always will occur, as long as the nature of mankind remains the same</u>; though in a severer or milder form, and varying in their symptoms, according to <u>the variety of the particular cases</u>. In peace and prosperity states and individuals have better sentiments, because they do not find themselves suddenly confronted with imperious necessities; but war takes

nature that passions (*orgê*, *elpis*, *pleonexia*) are freely unleashed as soon as leaders cease to be able to contain the population. It is human nature, too, that imprisons events' protagonists in the present; in the same present, the listeners are seduced by the myth and poetry, and turn a deaf ear to the statement of stark truth from *suggrapheus* Thucydides (1.22.4), and in the same present, our memory of the past adapts according to the feelings of each moment and is constantly transformed (2.54.3).

It is, furthermore, a result of human nature that wars arise, and it is in war that human nature demonstrates its full potential. Precisely because it is the eternal source of war and finds in war its best expression, human nature renders all wars comparable and as such is itself a principle of continuity that opens up the future. Hence an understanding of what the most important war is about is enough to enable us to understand—and therefore be able to narrate – all wars.

As privileged fora for the expression of human nature, wars enable us, rather as time did in Plato and Aristotle, to be the number of the movement driven by that nature. Yet once we accept that all wars can be reduced to the model of the Peloponnesian War, the future must be confined to the mere repetition of the same pattern.

Polybius follows a similar logic, at least when he envisages the cycle of constitutions. Here, once again, nature (this time physical foremost, then animal, and lastly specifically human) is the driving force behind regime changes, which move away from monarchy at first, only to return to it in the end.

After vast natural cataclysms have destroyed everything (in an alliance of Platonism and Stoicism), humans end up being reborn from the seeds (*spermata*) that survived. They gather together to offset their natural weakness and, just as other animals follow the strongest and most energetic, they respect whoever among them has the greatest physical strength (*sômatikê rhômê*) and bravery, also physical: *tolmê*. This is monarchy. This common life together grants the people an appreciation of goodness, the ability to exercise intelligence, reason (*nous*, *logismos*), justice (*dikaiosunê*), and all other values, abilities and virtues that distinguish them from other animals.

Human nature, thus fully formed, thenceforth has free rein over further regime transformations: royalty is born from the accession of people with the values, capacities and virtues previously mentioned. However, from the second generation of leaders onwards, the excesses of their desires (*epithumiai*) and

---

away the easy supply of daily wants, and so proves a rough master, that brings most men's characters to a level with their fortunes.

imbalances of their behaviour provoke envy (*phthonos*), hatred (*misos*) and anger (*orgê*) among their subjects, who overturn the regime. Royalty then leads to tyranny, which outrages the most respected of the community, on whom the people rely. Aristocracy therefore follows, which, in its second generation, develops into oligarchy through the same development of the leaders' desires and avidity. Anger, hatred and jealousy against this regime push the people into relying on themselves, and so democracy is born. However, a second generation, forgetting equality and, once again, falling prey to desire, will then remodel democracy with the original power of brute strength (*cheirokratia*) in which humans lose their specific distinctions from other animals, and return to their initial state as wild beasts.

The cycle thus described closes time by invariably bringing political events back to the same point, and so enables prediction (*proeipein uper tou mellontos*). The Roman regime, just like any other democracy – since Polybius sees it as a democracy – will necessarily fall into ochlocracy: the savage mob regime.[12]

---

12 Polybius, *Hist.* 4.57.1–2: Ὅτι μὲν οὖν πᾶσι τοῖς οὖσιν ὑπόκειται φθορὰ καὶ μεταβολὴ σχεδὸν οὐ προσδεῖ λόγων· ἱκανὴ γὰρ ἡ τῆς φύσεως ἀνάγκη παραστῆσαι τὴν τοιαύτην πίστιν. δυεῖν δὲ τρόπων ὄντων, καθ' οὓς φθείρεσθαι πέφυκε πᾶν γένος πολιτείας, τοῦ μὲν ἔξωθεν, τοῦ δ' ἐν αὑτοῖς φυομένου, τὸν μὲν ἐκτὸς ἄστατον ἔχειν συμβαίνει τὴν θεωρίαν, τὸν δ' ἐξ αὑτῶν τεταγμένην. τί μὲν δὴ πρῶτον φύεται γένος πολιτείας καὶ τί δεύτερον, καὶ πῶς εἰς ἄλληλα μεταπίπτουσιν, εἴρηται πρόσθεν ἡμῖν, ὥστε τοὺς δυναμένους τὰς ἀρχὰς τῷ τέλει συνάπτειν τῆς ἐνεστώσης ὑποθέσεως κἂν αὐτοὺς ἤδη προειπεῖν ὑπὲρ τοῦ μέλλοντος. ἔστι δ', ὡς ἔγωμαι, δῆλον. ὅταν γὰρ πολλοὺς καὶ μεγάλους κινδύνους διωσαμένη πολιτεία μετὰ ταῦτα εἰς ὑπεροχὴν καὶ δυναστείαν ἀδήριτον ἀφίκηται, φανερὸν ὡς εἰσοικιζομένης εἰς αὐτὴν ἐπὶ πολὺ τῆς εὐδαιμονίας συμβαίνει τοὺς μὲν βίους γίνεσθαι πολυτελεστέρους, τοὺς δ' ἄνδρας φιλονεικοτέρους τοῦ δέοντος περί τε τὰς ἀρχὰς καὶ τὰς ἄλλας ἐπιβολάς. ὧν προβαινόντων ἐπὶ πλέον ἄρξει μὲν τῆς ἐπὶ τὸ χεῖρον μεταβολῆς ἡ φιλαρχία καὶ τὸ τῆς ἀδοξίας ὄνειδος, πρὸς δὲ τούτοις ἡ περὶ τοὺς βίους ἀλαζονεία καὶ πολυτέλεια, λήψεται δὲ τὴν ἐπιγραφὴν τῆς μεταβολῆς ὁ δῆμος, ὅταν ὑφ' ὧν μὲν ἀδικεῖσθαι δόξῃ διὰ τὴν πλεονεξίαν, ὑφ' ὧν δὲ χαυνωθῇ κολακευόμενος διὰ τὴν φιλαρχίαν. τότε γὰρ ἐξοργισθεὶς καὶ θυμῷ πάντα βουλευόμενος οὐκέτι θελήσει πειθαρχεῖν οὐδ' ἴσον ἔχειν τοῖς προεστῶσιν, ἀλλὰ πᾶν καὶ τὸ πλεῖστον αὐτός. οὗ γενομένου τῶν μὲν ὀνομάτων τὸ κάλλιστον ἡ πολιτεία μεταλήψεται, τὴν ἐλευθερίαν καὶ δημοκρατίαν, τῶν δὲ πραγμάτων τὸ χείριστον, τὴν ὀχλοκρατίαν.

That to all things, then, which exist there is ordained decay and change I think requires no further arguments to show: for the inexorable course of nature is sufficient to convince us of it. But in all polities we observe two sources of decay existing from natural causes, the one external, the other internal and self-produced. The external admits of no certain or fixed definition, but the internal follows a definite order. What kind of polity, then, comes naturally first, and what second, I have already stated in such a way, that those who are capable of taking in the whole drift of my argument can henceforth draw their own conclusions as to the future of the Roman polity. For it is quite clear, in my opinion. When a commonwealth, after warding off many great dangers, has arrived at a high pitch of prosperity and undisputed power, it is evident

Yet Polybius does not stop there. In fact he states (VI.57.1)[13] that, if such natural necessity (*tês phuseôs anagkê*) exists, intrinsically setting in motion the transition from one regime to another, this implies that nature (*pephuke*) also acts from the outside, and it is not possible to form a stable notion of that external action (its *theôria* is *astatos*). Nature's double role therefore leaves part of the temporal movement it drives open to an indeterminate, unbounded future.

As a result, Polybius turns to another principle of closure.

This principle, the third in my sequence, is that of the spatialisation of time.

In his theory of the succession of empires,[14] Polybius affirms that Roman domination has extended across "almost the entirety" of the world, in contrast to previous dominations, which had remained confined to only one part of the *oikoumene*.

---

that, by the lengthened continuance of great wealth within it, the manner of life of its citizens will become more extravagant; and that the rivalry for office, and in other spheres of activity, will become fiercer than it ought to be. And as this state of things goes on more and more, the desire of office and the shame of losing reputation, as well as the ostentation and extravagance of living, will prove the beginning of a deterioration. And of this change the people will be credited with being the authors, when they become convinced that they are being cheated by some from avarice, and are puffed up with flattery by others from love of office. For when that comes about, in their passionate resentment and acting under the dictates of anger, they will refuse to obey any longer, or to be content with having equal powers with their leaders, but will demand to have all or far the greatest themselves. And when that comes to pass the constitution will receive a new name, which sounds better than any other in the world, liberty or democracy; but, in fact, it will become that worst of all governments, mob-rule.

13 Cf. *supra*, n. 11.
14 Polybius, *Hist*. 1.2.5: Ἀλλ' ὅμως οὗτοι πλείστων δόξαντες καὶ τόπων καὶ πραγμάτων γενέσθαι κύριοι, τὸ πολὺ μέρος ἀκμὴν ἀπέλιπον τῆς οἰκουμένης ἀλλότριον. Σικελίας μὲν γὰρ καὶ Σαρδοῦς καὶ Λιβύης οὐδ' ἐπεβάλοντο καθάπαξ ἀμφισβητεῖν, τῆς δ' Εὐρώπης τὰ μαχιμώτατα γένη τῶν προσεσπερίων ἐθνῶν ἰσχνῶς εἰπεῖν οὐδ' ἐγίνωσκον. ῥωμαῖοι γε μὴν οὐ τινὰ μέρη, σχεδὸν δὲ πᾶσαν πεποιημένοι τὴν οἰκουμένην ὑπήκοον αὑτοῖς, (ἀνυπόστα)τον μὲν τοῖς (ὑπάρχουσι πᾶσιν, ἀνυπέ(ρ)βλητον δὲ καὶ) τοῖς ἐπιγι(νομένοις ὑπερ)οχὴν κα(τέλιπον τῆς αὑτῶν) δυναστ(είας. Περὶ δὲ τοῦ) μεντο|λαδιατ
And yet, though they (the Macedonians) had the credit of having made themselves masters of a larger number of countries and states than any people had ever done, they still left the greater half of the inhabited world in the hands of others. They never so much as thought of attempting Sicily, Sardinia or Libya: and as to Europe, to speak the plain truth, they never even knew of the most warlike tribes of the West. The Roman conquest, on the other hand, was not partial. Nearly the whole inhabited world was reduced by them to obedience: and they left behind them an empire not to be paralleled in the past or rivalled in the future.

This coincidence, which binds the world to Rome, at the same time binds the world's natural temporalisation to the temporalisation at work in Rome, whether we envisage that as an internal or external process. If internal, then as the Romans become more savage, the entire world will be mobilised, yet within Rome's limits: this disorder is predictable, although it cannot be defined in detail; if external, only easily definable local factors on which Rome can intervene will be at play. From both these points of view, Rome remains coextensive with the world, and thus with the boundaries of becoming whatever it will.

Plutarch's parallelism provides a further illustration of spatialisation as a principle of future limitation.

Parallelism is, in its time, a mathematical notion used in geometry. It is frequently, even extensively, employed by Strabo, even more by Hipparchus and Eratosthenes, and also by Ptolemy in his works on astronomy, geography and mathematics.

And indeed we can see very well, right from the introduction to the *Life of Theseus*, that Plutarch's temporal parallelism summons, so to speak, a spatial parallelism, in particular the geometric spatial parallelism of cartography:

> Just as geographers (*en tais geôgraphiais (...) hoi historikoi*), O Socius Senecio, crowd on to the outer edges of their maps (*tois eschatois meresi tôn pinakôn*) the parts of the earth which elude their knowledge, with explanatory notes (*paragraphousi*) that "What lies beyond is sandy desert without water and full of wild beasts," or "blind marsh," or "Scythian cold," or "frozen sea," so in the writing of my Parallel Lives, now that I have traversed those periods of time (*dielthonti chronon*) which are accessible to probable reasoning and which afford basis for a history dealing with facts (*basimon historiai pragmatôn echomenei*), I might well say of the earlier periods (*peri tôn anôterô*). "What lies beyond is full of marvels and unreality, a land of poets and fabulists, of doubt and obscurity [without proof (*pistin*) or certainty (*saphêneian*)]".[15]

In addition, it is very clear that the notion of parallelism retains, in Plutarch, something of its technical geometric value. As J. Boulogne demonstrates very well in his article on the *synkriseis* of the *Lives*,[16] Plutarch identifies the idiosyncrasies of the two characters chosen in each case, then enters these into exaggerating diacritical formulae, which compare and contrast, in order to pick out what it is that distinguishes them, despite their similarity, and which ultimately makes their lives mirror images of one another. In this way, he builds up an accumulation of facts, in between the two mirrors, which are not reducible to either of

---

15 Plutarch, *Life of Theseus* I.1. Translation used is B. Perrin (http://perseus.mpiwg-berlin.-mpg.de/cgi-bin/ptext?lookup=Plut.+Thes.+1.1) with amendment in last line in brackets.
16 Boulogne, 2000.

them. The result of this synthesis is that a third "man" appears in between the mirrors, who has a real *êthos*. In other words, parallelism always retains the distance separating the lines of the two lives in question, in between which their difference is continuously at work.[17] The concept of parallelism cannot be reduced to similarity; it retains its technical, geometric character as of two lines that never cross in a given plane.

The plane in question is, once again, the reach of the Roman Empire, in whose defined space both past and present are bounded, through the Greeks and Romans, and in which *in the present* "syncretic" forms of new humanity can develop.

However – and here is the fourth principle of closure – there is much more at work here than simple geometric parallelism. There are also the global philosophical systems, expressing physics, logic and ethics, which established themselves, from the Hellenistic period onwards, through Stoicism, Epicureanism and Middle Platonism, and which pervaded, to a varying extent, those works whose aim was to tell of the world and the course of events.

I will focus here on what a Middle Platonic treatise, in particular the *Peri heirmarmene* by Pseudo-Plutarch, has to say about fate and its relationship with the finite and infinite, as well as about the implications of the holistic understanding in which it is written,[18] on time, causality and "evenementiality" (évenémentialité).

The author begins with a paradox that may interest us, which he considers apparent: although fate embraces the infinity of things coming into existence, *cyclically*, from time immemorial and until infinity, it is itself constrained, and not infinite.[19]

---

17 Plutarch, *Comparison of Lycurgus and Numa* 23.3 – 4: τῶν δὲ ἰδίᾳ ἑκατέρου καλῶν πρῶτόν ἐστι Νομᾷ μὲν ἡ παράληψις τῆς βασιλείας, Λυκούργῳ δὲ ἡ παράδοσις. ὁ μὲν γὰρ οὐκ αἰτῶν ἔλαβεν, ὁ δὲ ἔχων ἀπέδωκε. καὶ τὸν μὲν ἕτεροι κύριον αὐτῶν κατέστησαν ἰδιώτην καὶ ξένον ὄντα, ὁ δὲ αὐτὸς αὑτὸν ἰδιώτην ἐκ βασιλέως ἐποίησε.
To begin with, Numa accepted, but Lycurgus resigned, a kingdom. One got it without asking for it, the other had it and gave it up. One was made by others their sovereign, though a private person and a stranger; the other made himself a private person, though he was a king.

18 Pseudo-Plutarch, *Peri heirmarnene* 568 F: Πάλιν γε μὴν τὴν κατ' ἐνέργειαν εἱμαρμένην ἀναλαβόντες λέγωμεν· περὶ γὰρ ταύτην τὰ πολλὰ ζητήματα φυσικά τε καὶ ἠθικὰ καὶ διαλεκτικὰ τυγχάνει ὄντα.
But let us once more turn our attention to active fate, as the greater number of problems – physical, ethical, and dialectical – are concerned with it.

19 *Peri heirmarnene* 568 F-569 A: τίς μὲν οὖν ἐστιν, ἐπιεικῶς ἀφώρισται· ὁποία δ' ἐστίν, ἑξῆς ῥητέον, εἰ καὶ πολλοῖς ἄτοπον φαίνεται. | ἀπείρων γάρ, εἰ καὶ πολλοῖς ἄτοπον φαίνεται. | ἀπείρων γὰρ ἐξ ἀπείρου καὶ εἰς ἄπειρον <ὄντων> τῶν γινομένων τὰ πάντα περιβαλοῦς' ἐν κύκλῳ ἡ

This assertion is based on a cosmological theory inspired by Plato's *Timaeus*, according to which the eight spheres of the universe rotate as one, with an equal and uniform movement measured by time, which is also global. Everything in the heavens and on the earth will necessarily return to its former state. The author states that this is the law of the universe, and that a law cannot be anything but determined and constrained, because it itself determines and constrains. He here introduces a fundamental comparison between divine law of the universe, and civic law (*politikos*): both govern and limit generalities, while particularities are the domain of the infinite (*apeiron*).[20]

As for the understanding of activity (*energeia*) that the author attributes to fate, this too is based on the Timaeus and connected with the tripartite structure given to *pronoia* (providence). The demiurge attributed with the first *pronoia* – which is at once its desire (*boulêsis*: that which determines the end of an action in Aristotle) and its intelligence/intuition (*noêsis*) – imposes a law on the *kosmos* it organises. In so doing, that *pronoia* gives birth to fate (which is, as we have seen, a law): this is where fate comes from. Together with the young gods that it has just created, who are given the task of creating mortal beings and instilling them with what remains of a soul, the demiurge gives birth to a second *pronoia*, which is at once contemporary with fate and subsumed, with it, in the first *pronoia*. Lastly, the author dares to put forward a personal interpretation of the Platonic texts, positing the existence of a third *pronoia*, which is produced *after* the second, and therefore contained within it. This third *pronoia* constitutes a third order of divine entities: "demons" (*daimones*), scattered around the earth (*peri gên*) who supervise (*phulakes kai episkopoi*) human actions (*praxeis*). That is of course why everything is done according to providence and fate, yet some things

---

εἱμαρμένη οὐκ ἄπειρος ἀλλὰ πεπερασμένη ἐστίν· οὔτε γὰρ νόμος οὔτε λόγος οὔτε τι θεῖον ἄπειρον ἂν εἴη. τι θεῖον ἄπειρον ἂν εἴη.

Its (fate's) substance has been adequately defined; we must next tell its quality, strange though it may appear to many. Although events are infinite, extending infinitely into the past and future, fate, which encloses them all in a cycle, is nevertheless not infinite but finite, as neither a law nor a formula nor anything divine can be infinite.

20 Pseudo-Plutarch, *Peri heirmarnene* 569 f-570 A: |τὸ μὲν γὰρ ὡρισμένον οἰκεῖον τῇ θείᾳ φρονήσει ἐν τῷ καθόλου μᾶλλον θεωρεῖται (τοιοῦτος μέντοι γε ὁ θεῖος νόμος καὶ ὁ πολιτικός), τὸ δ' ἄπειρον ἐν τῷ καθ' ἕκαστα.

The determinate, which is appropriate to divine wisdom, is seen rather in the universal – and the divine law and the political are of this description — while the unlimited is seen in the particular.

depend on fate and others on providence or on something else.²¹ This is a first case of pluralisation.

Another fundamental case of pluralisation is introduced by the thesis of the possible: there is no *dunamis* (capacity) without substance (*ousia*) – man is a substance, but so are stars and everything else that exists – the *dunamis* is built on substance which, thereby, is the *dunamenon* that precedes the possible (*dunaton*). Hence, the author says, the possible is that which is naturally produced (*pephuke gignesthai*) by the *dunamis* (grounded on substance), when nothing external (*exôthen*) gets in its way.

With the division of the *dunaton*, the author introduces the contingent, the "depending on us", fortune and chance. For among the possibles, there is the possible that cannot be prevented (the necessary possible, which is most often encountered in astronomical phemomena such as the rising and setting of the sun), and the contingent possible (*to endechomenon dunaton*). The contingent possible can itself be divided into "what happens most often" (*ôs epi to polu*), like heat in summer; "what happens most rarely" and "what happens as often as not". It is in this final category that the "depending on us" (*to eph' êmin*) is found. It in turn can be subdivided, into things that depend on our desire (*epithumia*), on our "capacity to be affected" (*pathos*) or our ardour (*thumos*), and things "that depend on our reasoning (*epilogismos*) and reflection (*dianoia*)". This last category is known as *eph' êmin kata pronoian*: "by choice".

Choice (a significant part of the practical philosophy of Aristotelian obedience, since it marked the beginning of *praxis*) is understandably therefore not only a part of that which depends on us, but thereby also of the contingent.

It only remains for fortune (*tuchê*) and chance (*to automaton*) to intervene. *Tuchê*, according to the author, is a cause (*aition*); however, causes are divisible into causes *per se*, and accidental causes (*kata sumbebêkos*) – for example, that the architect who built the house is also a musician – and it is in these that we encounter fortune. Accidental causes are, in fact, infinitely numerous (*polla kai apeira*) and, within a single person, wholly different from one another (*pantapasin diapheronta allêlôn*). They are to be found not only in those things that hap-

---

21 Pseudo-Plutarch, *Peri heirmarnene* 574 B: τριττῆς γὰρ οὔσης τῆς προνοίας ἡ μὲν ἅτε γεννήσασα τὴν εἱμαρμένην τρόπον τινὰ αὐτὴν περιλαμβάνει, ἡ δὲ συγγεννηθεῖσα τῇ εἱμαρμένῃ πάντως αὐτῇ συμπεριλαμβάνεται, ἡ δ' ὡς ὕστερον τῆς εἱμαρμένης γενομένη κατὰ τὰ αὐτὰ δὴ ἐμπεριέχεται ὑπ' αὐτῆς, καθ' ἃ καὶ τὸ ἐφ' ἡμῖν καὶ ἡ τύχη εἴρηται. As providence is threefold, the first, since it has begotten fate, includes it in a sense; the second, having been begotten together with fate, is most certainly included together with it; and the third, since it is begotten later than fate, is contained in it in the same way as what is in our power and chance were said to be contained in fate.

pen for an end, but also in those things that happen as a result of our choice (*proairesis*); these are the occasions when we can talk about *tuchê*. As for chance, defined as that which happens in place of a natural event that fails to happen, it encompasses fortune, as it has two types: chance that depends on the unspecified contingent and, thereby, is common to all animate and inanimate beings, and chance that depends on the specified contingent in the "things depending on us" and more specifically "things that depend on us by choice".

From all these "trees" and from the introduction of the theory of the possible, it not only follows that fate is something connected with the conditional[22] and can assume the logical form of a proposition with "if", but also that if it is true that fate comprises everything, then everything does not happen according to fate: an apparently anti-Stoic position[23]. Reading into events and human actions, therefore, becomes a demanding task, since it is necessary to discern at each stage the role of *pronoia*, of the possible, of the contingent, of chance, of *tuchê*, of "what depends on the doer", of passions, and of reason, both in the infinity of the particular, and within the limits of the law and cosmic necessities. We have pictured a closed world, but one that harbours within itself the infinity of all that can occur to people and by people.

It seems to me that we can read the very challenging opening passage of the *Vie de Sertorius*,[24] to which an article by P. Desideri[25] first drew my attention, in

---

22 Pseudo-Plutarch, *Peri heirmarnene* 570 A: μετὰ δὴ ταῦτα, οἷον μέν ἐστι <τὸ> ἐξ ὑποθέσεως, ὅτι δὲ τοιοῦτον καὶ ἡ εἱμαρμένη, ὁριζέσθω. ἐξ ὑποθέσεως δὴ ἔφαμεν τὸ μὴ καθ' ἑαυτὸ τιθέμενον, ἀλλά πως ἑτέρῳ τινὶ ὡς ἀληθῶς ὑποτεθέν, ὁπόσα ἀκολουθίαν σημαίνει.
Let us next determine the character of what is "consequent of an hypothesis," and show that fate is of that character.
We meant by "consequent of an hypothesis" that which is not laid down independently, but in some fashion is really "subjoined" to something else.

23 Pseudo-Plutarch, *Peri heirmarnene* 570 E : πάντα μὲν τὰ γινόμεν' ἡ εἱμαρμένη περιλαμβάνει, πολλὰ δὲ τῶν ἐν αὐτῇ καὶ σχεδὸν ὅσα προηγεῖται οὐκ ὀρθὸν λέγειν καθ' εἱμαρμένην (...) ἡ μὲν γὰρ εἱμαρμένη πάντα περιέχει καθάπερ καὶ δοκεῖ· τὰ δ' οὐκ ἐξ ἀνάγκης γενήσεται.
Fate, then, includes everything that occurs, but much of what is thus included, and I might say all antecedents, could not rightly be said to be in conformity with fate (...) For fate contains them all, as indeed it is held to do; yet these things will not occur necessarily, but each will follow its own nature in its manner of occurrence.

24 Plutarch, *Life of Sertorius* 1.1 : Θαυμαστὸν μὲν ἴσως οὐκ ἔστιν, ἐν ἀπείρῳ τῷ χρόνῳ τῆς τύχης ἄλλοτ' ἄλλως ῥεούσης, ἐπὶ ταὐτὰ συμπτώματα πολλάκις καταφέρεσθαι τὸ αὐτό–ματον. εἴτε γὰρ οὐκ ἔστι τῶν ὑποκειμένων ὡρισμένον τὸ πλῆθος, ἄφθονον ἔχει τῆς τῶν ἀποτελουμένων ὁμοιότητος χορηγὸν ἡ τύχη τὴν τῆς ὕλης ἀπειρίαν· εἴτ' ἔκ τινων ὡρισμένων ἀριθμῷ συμπλέκεται τὰ πράγματα, πολλάκις ἀνάγκη ταῦτα γίνεσθαι, διὰ τῶν αὐτῶν περαινόμενα. ἐπεὶ δ' ἀγαπῶντες ἔνιοι τὰ τοιαῦτα συνάγουσιν ἱστορίᾳ καὶ ἀκοῇ τῶν κατὰ τύχην γεγονότων ὅσα λογισμοῦ καὶ προνοίας ἔργοις ἔοικεν.

the light of this. In this passage, P. Desideri sees evidence of Plutarch's subscription to a true physics of events. Likewise, we might also see something of Polybius' Epicurean physics, in the *sumplokê* of events and in the mass of human actions, previously divided into separate units, which now operates under the control of *tuchê*.

In any case, in the light of what I have been trying to say, it also seems to me that Plutarch here subscribes to one of these systems in which physics, logic and ethics enter into synergy, notably by means of a philosophy of action, and which, thereby, sets up another very complex and refined system of temporal closure that strives to be coherent with infinity. In this case, the future is not posited as indeterminable, rather the diversity of the past and present is posited as innumerable and irreducible.

These are the shapes of the future and the strategies for addressing it that I feel can be read in just one part of Greek historiography, though it is a part which I believe to be representative. The closure of time, whether by a divine sanction, or through analogy with situations in the context of the permanence of human nature, or by closure of the geographical space given over to human action seems, in all the cases we have seen, to cause the "makers of *historiai*" to come face to face, in the various ways that they approach time, with the problem of the infinite and indeterminate nature of the particularities of human action.

It is perhaps not to be wondered at, since fortune is ever changing her course and time is infinite, that the same incidents should occur many times, spontaneously. For, if the multitude of elements is unlimited, fortune has in the abundance of her material an ample provider of coincidences; and if, on the other hand, there is a limited number of elements from which events are interwoven, the same things must happen many times, being brought to pass by the same agencies. Now, there are some who delight to collect, from reading and hearsay, such accidental happenings as look like works of calculation and forethought.

Katharina Wesselmann
No Future? Possibilities and Permanence in Herodotus' *Histories*[1]

Every character in Herodotus – every individual, city, or people – has a future, owing to the rather banal fact that every story has an ending which at some point in the narrative has not yet happened and therefore is 'future'. While this is the case in practically all narrative texts, Herodotus is in the special habit of pointing out the endings of his micro-stories long before they actually happen. Apart from these 'actual' futures of the protagonists, which, from the narrator's point, lie in the past, there are less obvious cases of future in the *Histories*, such as the characters' *possible* future that does not happen, and the future outside the narrative, for example Herodotus' Athenian readers' future.

Added to that is another temporality which I will call 'mythical' – in the sense of a traditional pattern of events: in the *Histories*, the same stories, or very similar ones, seem to be happening again and again, only to different people. When this is the case, there can be no concept of future in a progressive sense, no true change or perfectibility. Instead, we have permanence, something like an 'eternal return of the same', a *perpetuum mobile* with variations and changing personnel that nevertheless in its entirety consists of a continuous system of plot rules. While the actors are exchanged, the play stays much the same.

1 Future

1.1 Intradiegetic future

1.1.1 'Past' future

As long as their narrative is not completed, all of Herodotus' characters have futures. Everybody has a story and that story ends, so at some point the ending is still anticipated as 'future'. Of course, from the narrator's point of view, this future is already past, and Herodotus is sometimes eager to point out even at very early stages of a story how things will turn out – have turned out – for his pro-

---

[1] A million thanks to Debby Boedeker for turning my clumsy English into, well, less clumsy English, and to her and Alexandra Lianeri and Magdalene Stoevesandt for their helpful and critical comments.

tagonists. These prolepses can take on different forms, for example Herodotus' famous formula 'It was fated that things would turn out badly for him', ἔδεέ οἱ κακῶς γενέσθαι (or similar) which he uses to prepare the reader for the fate of Candaules (1.8.2), Apries (2.161.3), Polycrates (3.43.1), Scyles (4.79.1), the city of Corinth (5.92.δ.1), Miltiades (6.135.3) and Artaÿnte (9.109.2). This device is a kind of dramatic irony, as it gives the reader privileged knowledge while he watches the character in question meet their fate.

A similar narrative instrument consists of different kinds of divination, which Herodotus also likes to use in an ironic way. When Croesus plans to attack the Persians and hears from the Delphic oracle that he will 'destroy a great kingdom' (μεγάλην ἀρχήν μιν καταλύσειν, 1.53.3), the reader, unlike Croesus, can imagine what to expect. Like the modern-day audience of an action movie who watches the soon-to-be-retired policeman tell his young colleague about the cruise he has already booked for himself and his long-neglected wife, Herodotus' reader can tell from Croesus' euphoric reaction to the oracle[2] (which must, of course, be speaking about the Persian kingdom; it never crosses his mind that it could refer to his own) that no good will come of this. Another example, also from the Lydian logos, is the story of Atys and Adrastos (whose very name is proleptic: 'the one who can't escape'). Young Atys reassures his father about the dream that has predicted to Croesus his son's premature death by an iron spear. Since wild boars do not fight with iron spears, the boy reasons, nothing will happen to him at the boar hunt. Also, Adrastos will take good care of him. Croesus is convinced, unlike Herodotus' audience: few readers then or now would have expected the story to have a happy outcome (3.34–45). Oracles, dreams, warnings by wise advisers, even a name can work as a proleptic device.

1.1.2 'Possible' future

Apart from the 'actual' future of single characters, cities or peoples, the future that is fulfilled and becomes 'past' from the point of view of narrator and audience, there is another type of character-future that never becomes past because it never actually happens. Part of the phenomenon of 'counterfactual' history, this possible future that never takes place can be indicated in the description of a turning point in history, an open situation where various possibilities exist, until finally one path is decided upon, often by a hair's breadth.

---

[2] ὑπερήσθη τε τοῖσι χρηστηρίοισι (1.54.1); cf. Herodotus' use of the adjective περιχαρής which "always foreshadows suffering for the person so described" (Chiasson 2005, 49).

But what about predetermination? There is no denying that in some Herodotean stories, fate is clearly at work, dictating the outcome of things. As in the formula 'It was fated[3] that things would turn out badly for him' (which I mentioned above), predetermined outcomes are often hinted at in the *Histories*, even if 'tragic' double causality is at work. Such is the case with Astyages, whose downfall is caused by his cruelty (1.130.1) – but his cruelty is the consequence of his fear of downfall: convinced by dreams that his grandson would dethrone him, he plans to kill the boy. However, his servant Harpagos does not commit the murder, and when Astyages later finds out, he punishes him cruelly by slaughtering Harpagos' own child and making him eat the meat. It is only this cruelty that gives Harpagos the idea to defect to Cyrus and encourage him to conquer the Medes in the first place (1.107f.). Other cases do not reach this level of moral complexity: fate is explicitly mentioned by the Delphic priestess, who explains to Croesus that even the god Apollo cannot save his devout servant if the Μοῖραι will not be deflected (1.91.2).

The mere fact that oracles and prophetic dreams exist and are often right (that they are easily misunderstood is quite another matter), making the future potentially foreseeable, proves a certain degree of predetermination. The fact that oracles and dreams are not *always* right[4] does not alter this fact. But while this awkward subject, which every modern reader of Greek tragedy – and 'tragic' historiography[5] – struggles with, has much to do with free will and therefore morals, it is of little consequence as regards the subject of future. The only aspect of future that is actually influenced by the existence or lack of

---

[3] Mostly, the verb δεῖν is used ('he *had to* end badly'), apart from the synonymous χρῆν (1.8.2), and μέλλοι (3.43.1: 'he *would* end badly').

[4] Sometimes they will lead their clients astray on purpose, if they have asked a preposterous question and deserve to be destroyed: 1.157–160: the Cymaeans ask the Branchidai oracle if they should hand over the supplicant Paktyes to the Persians and are told to do so – so that they can be justly destroyed for asking such an outrageous thing; 2.139: king Sabakos dreams that a man tells him to cut the Egyptian priests in half; wisely, the king resigns in order to avoid comitting sacrilege; 5.86.2.δ: the Spartan Glaukos asks the Delphic oracle if he can get away with swearing a false oath in order to keep some money entrusted to him by the Milesians; the God tells him: "Swear!", but also, that he and his house will be destroyed for even contemplating the deed; 6.134f.: the Parian priestess (justified by the Delphic oracle) leads Miltiades to his unhappy destiny; 7.12–18: Xerxes is led to invade Greece by pernicious dreams. – All this can still be explained by predetermination: the sinners have to be tricked into their destiny. But every so often, priests are bribed (5.63.1) and seers lie (7.6.3f.), and then sometimes oracles can be plain wrong (2.174; 1.46–49; 8.136.3 [see below]).

[5] Tragic elements in Herodotus have frequently been discussed; for bibliography cf. Chiasson 2003; Griffin 2006; Wesselmann 2011, 39–42 with nn.

'fate' is the aspect of 'possibility'. If everything is predetermined, there should be no reflections of other possible futures. But there are.

Donald Lateiner has found an elegant and persuasive solution for this inconsistency. It is plainly wrong to look for a consistent theological or philosophical system in Herodotus. There are tendencies, no doubt, but no reliable order that works the same way in every case. Lateiner has shown how different "systems of explanation" simultaneously work in Herodotus, for example such mutually exclusive poles as 'Divinities', 'Historical Analysis' and 'Fate' (1989, 196–206).[6] 'Fate' is one of several explanations, sometimes more and sometimes less likely, a flexible, fragile concept. The reflexions on possible futures in the *Histories* add to this flexibility. Even if some sort of fate exists in some cases, it is still valuable to remind oneself that there is a multitude of possibilities.

One of the most famous instances of such an open situation is the so-called 'constitutional debate' of the Persians (3.80–83): After the seven conspirators have overthrown the rule of the Magi, they discuss what sort of constitution Persia should have in the future. An orderly and respectful debate follows, where Otanes campaigns for democracy, Megabyzus for oligarchy and Dareius for monarchy; in the end there is an actual poll where (only) four out of seven men vote for monarchy. This kind of procedure seems congruent with a genuinely democratic culture rather than the slave and master mentality of the violently hierarchical Persian monarchy, at least as Herodotus and other Greek authors depict it both before and after the rule of Dareius. Indeed, Herodotus feels the need to introduce the scene with a justification:

> Ἐπείτε δὲ κατέστη ὁ θόρυβος καὶ ἐκτὸς πέντε ἡμερέων ἐγένετο, ἐβουλεύοντο οἱ ἐπαναστάντες τοῖσι μάγοισι περὶ τῶν πάντων πρηγμάτων, καὶ ἐλέχθησαν λόγοι ἄπιστοι μὲν ἐνίοισι Ἑλλήνων, ἐλέχθησαν δ' ὦν.
>
> Five days later, when the commotion had subsided, the men who had revolted against the Magi consulted with one another about the whole state of affairs. Now there are some Hellenes who do not believe the following speeches took place at all, but they certainly did.[7]

Of course, this is not a turning point in the history of mankind. Persian monarchy prevails and eventually leads to war with Greece; both Herodotus and his

---

6 A striking case of explanatory contradiction that supports Lateiner but is not mentioned by him is 1.32.4, where Herodotus has Solon say that every day in life is different and human life all about chance (συμφορή), and, shortly afterwards, 1.34.1, interprets Croesus' misfortune not as accidental, but as punishment from the gods. Happenstance and logical causality are offered side by side.

7 All translations of Herodotus cited here are by Andrea Purvis (Strassler 2007).

audience know that. For them, the discussion is an assembly of rejected alternative scenarios, but from the point of view of the protagonists, they constitute an at least possible 'future'. This perspective is by no means to be neglected, as the audience's identification with the protagonists seems to be of vital importance especially in those parts of the *Histories* where the process of decision-making is portrayed in detail. Therefore, having the characters analyse the pros and cons of different systems is not just an exercise in political science, it is also a glimpse into what at one point in history could have been the future – an almost unthinkable future though it may be, as Herodotus himself concedes. Nevertheless, at this important moment, the beginning of Achaemenid rule, the author stresses that things could at least theoretically have happened very differently.

A more explicit way of considering possible futures is a device known from Homeric epic, the so-called 'if-not-situation' after the pattern 'and now x would have happened, if y had not happened.'[8] One of these 'would-be turning points' is Herodotus' own reflection on the disastrous possible outcome of the Persian War if the Athenians had defected:

> Ἐνθαῦτα ἀναγκαίῃ ἐξέργομαι γνώμην ἀποδέξασθαι ἐπίφθονον μὲν πρὸς τῶν πλεόνων ἀνθρώπων, ὅμως δέ, τῇ γέ μοι φαίνεται εἶναι ἀληθές, οὐκ ἐπισχήσω. Εἰ Ἀθηναῖοι καταρρωδήσαντες τὸν ἐπιόντα κίνδυνον ἐξέλιπον τὴν σφετέρην, ἢ καὶ μὴ ἐκλιπόντες ἀλλὰ μείναντες ἔδοσαν σφέας αὐτοὺς Ξέρξῃ, κατὰ τὴν θάλασσαν οὐδαμοὶ ἂν ἐπειρῶντο ἀντιούμενοι βασιλέϊ. Εἰ τοίνυν κατὰ τὴν θάλασσαν μηδεὶς ἠντιοῦτο Ξέρξῃ, κατά γε ἂν τὴν ἤπειρον τοιάδε ἐγένετο. Εἰ καὶ πολλοὶ τειχέων κιθῶνες ἦσαν ἐληλαμένοι διὰ τοῦ Ἰσθμοῦ Πελοποννησίοισι, προδοθέντες ἂν Λακεδαιμόνιοι ὑπὸ τῶν συμμάχων, —οὐκ ἑκόντων ἀλλ᾽ ὑπ᾽ ἀναγκαίης, κατὰ πόλις ἁλισκομένων ὑπὸ τοῦ ναυτικοῦ στρατοῦ τοῦ βαρβάρου, – ἐμουνώθησαν· μουνωθέντες δὲ ἂν καὶ ἀποδεξάμενοι ἔργα μεγάλα ἀπέθανον γενναίως· ἢ ταῦτα ἂν ἔπαθον, ἢ πρὸ τοῦ ὁρῶντες ἂν καὶ τοὺς ἄλλους Ἕλληνας μηδίζοντας ὁμολογίῃ ἂν ἐχρήσαντο πρὸς Ξέρξην. Καὶ οὕτω ἂν ἐπ᾽ ἀμφότερα ἡ Ἑλλὰς ἐγίνετο ὑπὸ Πέρσῃσι· τὴν γὰρ ὠφελίην τὴν τῶν τειχέων τῶν διὰ τοῦ Ἰσθμοῦ ἐληλαμένων οὐ δύναμαι πυθέσθαι ἥτις ἂν ἦν βασιλέος ἐπικρατέοντος τῆς θαλάσσης ... (7.139.1–4)

> I have now reached a point at which I am compelled to declare an opinion that will cause offence to many people, but which nevertheless appears to me to be true, so I shall not restrain myself. If the Athenians had evacuated their land in terror of the danger approaching them, or if they had not left their land but remained and surrendered themselves to Xerxes, no one at all would have tried to oppose the King at sea. And if no one had then opposed Xerxes at sea, this is what would have happened on land. The Peloponnesians, even if they had covered over their isthmus with walls, would have been abandoned by their allies, who, seeing their cities conquered one by one by the barbarian fleet, would have been forced to submit against their will. Finally those thus deserted, now all alone, would have performed great feats and died honourably. Of course that might not be their fate if

---

[8] Cf. Brügger/Stoevesandt/Visser 2003 *ad* 2.155–156.

they had earlier seen how the rest of the Hellenes were medising and would have come to an agreement of their own with Xerxes. Thus, either way, Hellas would have been conquered by the Persians. For I cannot discern what advantage could have been derived from walls extended across the isthmus if the King had control of the sea ...

This time, the musings on what might have happened are not presented as secondary focalisation of the characters, but as the *ex post facto* thoughts of the narrator. With no protagonist to imagine or discuss this possible future, the 'counterfactual history' is in this case revealed as such from the start; therefore it feels less like possible 'future' than the earlier example, the proposition of introducing democracy into Persia. Nevertheless, Herodotus and some of his contemporaries would have remembered the time when an Athenian capitulation was still very much an option. The passage thus has the quality of a 'recent future', a possibility still recalled as an actual future scenario – and by pointing out how easily it could have come true and how disastrous the consequences for the whole of Greece would have been, the merits of the Athenians are dramatically stressed. As is the case with the Persian constitutional debate, Herodotus feels the need to justify his musings beforehand: 'I have now reached a point at which I am compelled to declare an opinion that will cause offense to many people, but which nevertheless appears to me to be true, so I shall not restrain myself.'

Again, it is important to point out that the present – the past's future that we now inhabit – is no matter of course. All the possibilities were there at one point. Both these examples are presented not as prognoses such as an oracle would give, but as political planning – they are not inevitable, predetermined futures, but active decisions of human beings. It is interesting that Herodotus puts so much emphasis on the fact that such decisions are actually possible.

This is especially striking in another example, where oracles seem to be regarded as arguments for human reasoning, but by no means as infallible and inevitble predictions: the preliminaries to the mission of the Macedonian prince Alexandros, when the Persian general Mardonius sends him to convince the Athenians to collaborate with the Persian king.

Μαρδόνιος δὲ ἐπιλεξάμενος ὅ τι δὴ λέγοντα ἦν τὰ χρηστήρια, μετὰ ταῦτα ἔπεμψε ἄγγελον ἐς Ἀθήνας Ἀλέξανδρον τὸν Ἀμύντεω ἄνδρα Μακεδόνα ... ὁ Μαρδόνιος πυθόμενος ὅτι πρόξεινός τε εἴη <ἐκεῖ> καὶ εὐεργέτης ὁ Ἀλέξανδρος ἔπεμπε. Τοὺς γὰρ Ἀθηναίους οὕτω ἐδόκεε μάλιστα προσκτήσεσθαι, λεών τε πολλὸν ἄρα ἀκούων εἶναι καὶ ἄλκιμον, τά τε κατὰ τὴν θάλασσαν συντυχόντα σφι παθήματα κατεργασαμένους μάλιστα Ἀθηναίους ἐπίστατο. Τούτων δὲ προσγενομένων κατήλπιζε εὐπετέως τῆς θα-λάσσης κρατήσειν, τά περ ἂν καὶ ἦν, πεζῇ τε ἐδόκεε πολλῷ εἶναι κρέσσων· οὕτω τε ἐλογίζετο κατύπερθέ οἱ τὰ πρήγματα ἔσεσθαι τῶν Ἑλληνικῶν. Τάχα δ' ἂν καὶ τὰ χρηστήρια ταῦτά οἱ προλέγοι, συμβουλεύοντα σύμμαχον τὸν Ἀθηναῖον ποιέεσθαι· τοῖσι δὴ πειθόμενος ἔπεμπε. (8.136)

> After Mardonios had read the oracles, he sent Alexandros of Macedon, the son of Amyntas, as a messenger to Athens … since Mardonios had heard that Alexandros was a *proxenos* and a benefactor of Athens, he thought that by this move he could best succeed in winning the Athenians over to his side. Because he had learned that they were a populous and warlike people, and he knew that the disaster that had befallen the Persians at sea had been accomplished mainly by the Athenians, he fully anticipated that if they were on his side, he would easily gain control over the sea, which was certainly a correct assumption. Thus, he reasoned, he would be able to prevail over the Hellenes. Perhaps the oracles had predicted this outcome to him and advised him to form an alliance with Athens, and it was in obedience to their advice that he now sent off Alexandros.

It is remarkable that Herodotus allows for the possibility that oracles brought Mardonios to the erroneous assumption that he might win over the Athenians. As stated above, oracles can be a formidable authority, if not an infallible one; but this passage suggests that there may actually have been an oracle predicting a future that did not come true, and that it led to an unsuccessful plan of action. Again, we have a situation where the outcome for the protagonists is wide open, especially considering the benevolent, wise and friendly words with which Alexandros urges the Athenians to see reason and accept Mardonios' generous offer of peace, as opposed to their futile resistance against the vastly superior Persian king. The reader half expects them to change their minds.

Herodotus even seems to play with these expectations a little when he eventually has the Athenians react: of course they refuse collaboration with the Persians, they will oppose them 'as long as the sun continues on the same course as it now travels' (8.143.2). This kind of *adynaton* is a common figure of speech in all languages and literatures, but sometimes it is realised, even in Herodotus. Croesus had interpreted the oracle about a mule becoming king of the Persians as an *adynaton*, and yet the oracle meant Cyrus, who like a mule, was the son of an inferior father and a superior mother (1.55). And even the *adynaton* used here by the Athenians can occur, as we know from Greek myth: after the cruel meal that Atreus serves to his brother Thyestes, the horrified sun-god changes his course.[9] Further, in the *Histories* eclipses of the sun are powerful signs for a change of fortune (1.74;[10] 7.37). Maybe even in their harsh rebuke of the Persian offer, the Athenians – or the narrator – leave behind a shadow of a doubt.

---

9 Cf. for example E. *El.* 727–742; *Or.* 996–1011; Apollod. *Ep.* 2.10.61–67 = *Ep.* 2.12. Sen. *Thy.* 776–779.
10 The eclipse occurs in the wider context of one of Herodotus' own 'Thyestean feasts'; I think it is an adaptation of the myth (cf. Wesselmann 2011, 262; 2012, chapter 5).

These are just three examples of a narrative practice that is very common in Herodotus. There are many 'if-not'-scenarios,[11] and similarly, there are turning-points that almost do not happen – sometimes for an excruciatingly long time, for example the battle of Salamis, which is preceded by endless negotiations and hesitations (8.49–84).[12] Herodotus' audience is often shown what could have happened otherwise, and the consideration of such alternatives is important, as Artabanos, one of the wisest advisers in the *Histories*, states in the course of the lengthy discussion about whether Xerxes should attack Greece or not:

Ὦ βασιλεῦ, μὴ λεχθεισέων μὲν γνωμέων ἀντιέων ἀλλήλῃσι οὐκ ἔστι τὴν ἀμείνω αἱρεόμενον ἑλέσθαι, ἀλλὰ δεῖ τῇ εἰρημένῃ χρᾶσθαι· λεχθεισέων δὲ ἔστι, ὥσπερ τὸν χρυσὸν τὸν ἀκήρατον αὐτὸν μὲν ἐπ' ἑωυτοῦ οὐ διαγινώσκομεν, ἐπεὰν δὲ παρατρίψωμεν ἄλλῳ χρυσῷ, διαγινώσκομεν τὸν ἀμείνω. (7.10.1α)

Sire, if no opposing opinions are expressed in the course of a discussion, it becomes impossible to try to choose and to finally select the better one. Instead, one will have to make do with the proposal that has been stated. But when a different opinion is set forth, it is just like comparing two grades of gold: we cannot distinguish gold that is pure in isolation, but when we rub it next to another piece of gold, we can pick out the better of the two.

Things may not always turn out to be pure gold, but the message is clear: more than one option ought to be considered.

1.2 Extradiegetic future: Herodotus and his contemporaries

So much for the intradiegetic future. There is also a kind of future that might seem even more relevant to Herodotus and his contemporaries (although it is less manifest in the text, due to the *Histories*' antiquarian nature), and that is their own future.

On a very basic level, we find anticipations of the future with regard to the text itself; Herodotus frequently tells us what he intends to tell now or later.[13]

---

[11] Cf. for example 1.170, 1.191.5f., 2.120, 3.15, 3.25.5, 3.49.1, 3.55.1, 5.48, 6.30.1.
[12] Another example is the fateful decision to fight at Marathon which is narrowly saved by the vote of the *polemarchos* urged on by Miltiades in a fiery speech full of conditional clauses advertising freedom and power rather than slavery and weakness (6.109).
[13] Obviously in the proem, and very often where ethnographical, geographical and mythical matters are concerned (for example 1.192.1, 1.194.1, 2.14.1, 2.24.1, 2.38.2, 2.51.1, 2.147.1, 2.156.6, 3.6.2, 4.14.1, 4.45.5, 4.82, 4.99.2, 4.145.1, 5.22.1, 5.65.5, 6.55).

(That he does not always keep his promises is a different matter.[14]) On a wider scale, there is the question of the years between the occupation of Sestos in 479, with which the *Histories* end, and the latest possible date of the work's completion around 424, and even of the years after that, literally the future of his contemporary audience, which Herodotus, master of prolepsis, may well have anticipated in some way.

With its crucifixion of the Persian governor Artaÿctes and the brutal stoning of his son before the father's eyes (9.120.4), the end of the *Histories* has always drawn special attention to this extradiegetic future. Since this kind of punishment is so plainly un-Greek and barbaric in nature, the scene has often been interpreted as an implicit external prolepsis: a warning to imperialist Athens that is in danger of falling into barbarism itself.[15] If we read the story this way, it points to or even substitutes the future, not *ex post facto* this time but prophetic, anticipating the disaster that the Peloponnesian War will prove to be, especially for Athens.[16]

There is another, less famous, example that points into the same direction: the original sin of Athenian imperialism is painted in strong colours when the Athenians lay siege to Andros and other islands after the battle of Salamis (8.111f.). More clearly than the Artaÿctes passage, this chapter shows the beginning of Athenian megalomania, starting with greedy Themistocles: 'the Andrians were the first of the islanders from whom Themistocles had demanded money', Herodotus says,[17] continuing with a classical dichotomy between tyrannical brutality, formerly thought of as typically barbarian, and typically Greek witty and intelligent ruse. Themistocles tells the Andrians that 'the Athenians had come with two great gods, Persuasion and Necessity' (Πειθώ τε καὶ Ἀναγκαίην), to which the Andrians reply that they have nothing to give and that the power of the great Athenian gods could not be stronger than the powerlessness of their own great gods, Poverty and Helplessness (Πενίην τε καὶ Ἀμηχανίην). Showing no sense of humour, the Athenians besiege Andros, and the end of the passage clearly points to a future beyond the time covered by the *Histories*:

---

14 Herodotus does not fulfill his promises to relate the Medes' capture of Nineveh (1.106.2), to mention some kings of Babylon (1.184), and to tell the full story of Ephialtes (7.213.3).
15 Cf. Nagy 1990a, 307–313; Georges 1994, 130; Moles 1996, 276f.; Pelling 1997, 60f.; Rood 2007a, 116f. (see 126–128 for more examples of external prolepsis). Cf. 6.98.2 und 8.2–3 for Herodotus' highly pessimistic outlook on Athenian imperialism.
16 Herodotus mentions the Peloponnesian War several times (for example 7.137; 9.73), although it is not part of his actual narrative anymore and he probably did not live to see its outcome.
17 Or 'the first who refuse': the full sentence reads: πρῶτοι γὰρ Ἄνδριοι νησιωτέων αἰτηθέντες πρὸς Θεμιστοκλέος χρήματα οὐκ ἔδοσαν, and πρῶτοι can be taken with αἰτηθέντες or ἔδοσαν; in any case, it is clear Andros is not the only community that Athens presses for tribute money.

Θεμιστοκλέης δέ, οὐ γὰρ ἐπαύετο πλεονεκτέων, ἐσπέμπων ἐς τὰς ἄλλας νήσους ἀπειλητηρίους λόγους αἴτεε χρήματα διὰ τῶν αὐτῶν ἀγγέλων [χρεώμενος] τοῖσι καὶ πρὸς βασιλέα ἐχρήσατο, λέγων ὡς εἰ μὴ δώσουσι τὸ αἰτεόμενον, ἐπάξει <σφι> τὴν στρατιὴν τῶν Ἑλλήνων καὶ πολιορκέων ἐξαιρήσει.

There was no satisfying the greed of Themistokles. He sent threatening requests for money to the other islands through the same messengers that he had sent to the King, warning them that if they did not give what was asked, he would lead the Greek forces against them and destroy them by siege if necessary ...

The examples I have shown so far demonstrate the complexity of 'future' in the *Histories*, be it the 'past future' of Herodotus' protagonists, 'possible' or hypothetical future, or the 'present future' of Herodotus and his readers. However, as I noted before, so far we have dealt only with the future of individuals: single characters like Candaules, or bigger groups like the Persians, the Greeks, the Athenians. If we take a step back and look at 'the bigger concept' I mentioned before, the phenomenon of the traditional story patterns in the *Histories*, Herodotus' concept of future gains a significant additional dimension.

2 No Future

2.1 Mythical temporalities: Repetition of patterns

Different kinds of story patterns exist in Herodotus' text. Some patterns can be found in narratives outside the *Histories*, such as the exposure story of the heroic child that Herodotus tells about the Persian king Cyrus, and which we know as an integral part of heroic biography from many different literatures.[18] Other structures are repeated within the text of the *Histories* itself, such as the desecration of waters by barbaric kings: Herodotus tells us in a repetitive, climactic manner how rivers and the sea are subdued by human rulers, a theme associated with sacrilegious transgression of boundaries, usually followed by ill fortune; there is Croesus' original sin of crossing the river Halys (1.75), Cyrus, parting the river Gyndes into 360 canals (1.189 f.; 5.52) and unnecessarily traversing the Araxes (1.205–208), Dareios, bridging the Bosporus (4.83–89, 118) and finally Xerxes, bridging and insulting the Hellespont (7.33–36).[19] Similarly, Herodotus

---

18 Cf. Binder 1964; 1977; Huys 1995; Wesselmann 2011, 201–226.
19 Cf. Romm 2006, 187 f.; for the detailed parallels of Xerxes' and Dareios' crossings see Hartog 1980, 54–57; Rengakos 2001, 256–261; for the subject of transgression in Herodotus, cf. La-

makes a pattern out of great powers attacking seemingly weaker ones and losing, and even has Artabanos, the wise Persian warner, explicitly express this in the context of Xerxes' plan to march against Greece:

> Ἐγὼ μέν, ὦ βασιλεῦ, οἷα ἄνθρωπος ἰδὼν ἤδη πολλά τε καὶ μεγάλα πεσόντα πρήγματα ὑπὸ ἡσσόνων, οὐκ ἔων σε τὰ πάντα τῇ ἡλικίῃ εἴκειν, ἐπιστάμενος ὡς κακὸν εἴη τὸ πολλῶν ἐπιθυμέειν, μεμνημένος μὲν τὸν ἐπὶ Μασσαγέτας Κύρου στόλον ὡς ἔπρηξε, μεμνημένος δὲ καὶ τὸν ἐπ' Αἰθίοπας τὸν Καμβύσεω, συστρατευόμενος δὲ καὶ Δαρείῳ ἐπὶ Σκύθας. (7.18.2)
>
> Sire, I, being a person who has already seen many great powers fall to lesser ones, was unwilling to permit you to give up everything you have to the impetuosity of your youth, knowing as I do how evil it is to desire too many things. I remembered how Cyrus' attack on the Massagetai turned out, and I remembered also the expedition of Cambyses against the Ethiopians, and when I accompanied Dareios on his campaign against the Scythians.

However, all patterns, be they extra- or intradiegetic, or both, have one effect in common: the impression of history repeating itself. There may be different protagonists, but similar stories happen to them. One might now raise the objection that similar things happen to different people not just in Herodotus' narrative but also in real life, but many of the patterns in question are too detailed and specific to be accidental, as numerous studies of mythical motifs in Herodotus have shown, starting with Pohlmann's 1912 *De arte qua fabellae Herodoteae narratae sint* and Aly's 1921 *Volksmärchen, Sage und Novelle bei Herodot und seinen Zeitgenossen*. Important contemporary studies include Vernant's 1981 comparison of Herodotus' story of Cypselus with the myth of the Labdacids, Boedeker's studies on mythical patterns in Herodotus in general (2002) and in particular (1987 on Demaratus, 1988 on Artaÿctes, 1993 on the bones of Orestes), Hansen's juxtaposition of Herodotus' Lydian logos with the Brothers Grimm's *Marienkind* and other folktales (2002, 316–327), and Stadter's analysis of the story of Adrastos, the traditional 'tale of the exiled killer' (2004, 38–42). In addition to mythical parallels, there have been studies on ritual structures shaping Herodotus' narrative, such as Sourvinou-Inwood on the relationship between Periander and his son Lycophron (1991, 244–284), where she detects many metaphorical references to initiatory rites, Griffiths 1999 on mythical and ritual traditionalisms in Herodotus' story of "Euenius the Negligent Nightwatchman (Herodotus 9.92–6)", and Chiasson 2005 on mythical and ritual elements in the famous story of Cleobis and Biton. The topic has certainly not been exhausted by my own 2011 attempt to accomplish an overview at least of the most important tradi-

---

teiner 1985; 1989, 126–135; for the *Histories*' intra-textual patterns in general cf. e.g. Immerwahr 1966, 148–237; Gray 2002.

tional story-patterns in Herodotus, their origin and traditional connotations; there has since appeared a conference volume on *Myth, Truth, and Narrative in Herodotus* (Baragwanath/De Bakker 2012), assembling a number of single studies on mythical elements in the *Histories*, and also providing the reader with important methodological tools (such as a definition of myth, its relation to history and literature, and its function in Herodotus' text) in an introductory chapter.

Seeing the great number of mythical narratives in the *Histories*, it seems almost as if there is a limited number of stories, a typology of fates that many of Herodotus' protagonists more or less consciously get to choose from: as long as the world exists, dangerous children will be exposed, others will be slaughtered and their meat served to their fathers,[20] conquerors will desecrate sanctuaries and be punished with disease,[21] generals will disguise themselves as traitors to infiltrate the enemy,[22] kings will act according to deceitful dreams,[23] young aristocrats will inadvertently kill a relative and be exiled,[24] wicked stepmothers will plot against their stepdaughters,[25] important men will have both mortal

---

[20] Hdt. 1.73 (Scythians slaughter Cyaxares' son); 1.119 (Astyages slaughters Harpagos' son); cf. the mythical stories of Lycaon, Thyestes, Tantalos, Procne and others. For *loci* and detailed discussion see Wesselmann 2011, 252–269.

[21] Cambyses' death (3.66.1f.) is possibly a punishment for the murder of the Apis bull in 3.27–29 (part of a series of other sacrilegious acts: 3.16; 3.25.3; 3.37; cf. 3.38.1), which Herodotus hints at: 3.64.3; Cleomenes' madness and death are linked to his desecration of temples: 6.75.3; 6.84.1; Miltiades fatally injures his leg while breaking into the Demeter temple at Paros: 6.134–136; Themistocles says that the Persians have lost against the Greeks because the gods do not support the impious: 8.109.3 (cf. the Persian army's desecrations of holy areas in 3.147; 6.19; 6.32; 6.96; 6.101; 8.32f.; 8.53.2; 9.13.2; 9.116). Cf. the mythical stories of Meleager and Atalante desecrating the temple and being turned into lions, or Aias' rape of Cassandra in the temple. For *loci* and a detailed discussion especially of the complexity of causality in Herodotus' accounts of temple desecration and disease or madness, see Wesselmann 2011, 79–143.

[22] Cf. the story of Zopyros (3.153–160); the mythical models are Odysseus (*Od.* 4.234–264) and Sinon (already attested in the Epic Cycle, cf. Arist. *Po.* 1459b for the *Little Ilias*, Procl. *arg. Iliup.* 5 West, then in Verg. *A.* 2.57–198; Quint. Smyrn. 12.243–388); cf. Wesselmann 2011, 161–167.

[23] Xerxes (7.8–19); the mythical model is Agamemnon at the beginning of *Il.* 2; cf. for example Macan 1908 on 7.15; Pohlenz 1937, 118; Immerwahr 1954, 34–37; Huber 1965, 38; Saïd 1981, 22–25; Wesselmann 2011, 167–174.

[24] Adrastos (1.34–45); the mythical models are for example Peleus, Tydeus, Phoinix, Patroclus; cf. Parker 1983, 375–392; Stadter 2004, 38–42; Nünlist 2009.

[25] The stepmother of Phronime (4.154f.); cf. for example the mythical stepmothers Ino and Hera; a close parallel is also the story of the stepmother falsely accusing the step*son* (or younger household member); for *loci* and detailed discussion cf. Wesselmann 2011, 239–252.

and heroic fathers.²⁶ Of course, the stories are not exactly the same. It is often the differences from their intra- or extratextual parallels that are of importance for the interpretation.²⁷ But a tendency to repetitiveness cannot be disputed.

What does this repetition of stories say about Herodotus' concept of future? Can we really speak of the future of, say, an exposed child, when we realise that the story has happened countless times before? After all, it is a mythical story – a timeless narrative. Baby Cyrus' *fated* future – the rescue, the recovery of his birthright – is not really in the future: it has already happened to Oedipus, Paris, Aegisthus and numerous others in the *past*. In these cases, it seems, we are dealing with a quasi-identity of what Reinhart Koselleck calls *Erwartung* and *Erfahrung* – expectation and experience. Normally, these categories are fundamentally different (if not exactly opposites): while you can expect something you have experienced before, you cannot really experience an expectation; a consequence expected is not yet an experience. To put it simply: experience can prove expectation wrong, things can always go differently to what one expected. This friction between expectation and experience provokes new solutions, Koselleck tells us, and thereby creates *historical time*. But this is not always the case in Herodotus. The whole process of adapting historical events to traditional patterns, of recognising the mythical in the historical, goes against historicity, or historical time. In a repetitive system, a mythical temporality, expectation and experience tend to overlap, creating a kind of omnitemporal permanence.²⁸ I would not go so far as to say that nothing new ever happens in the *Histories* – not everything in the *Histories* is a repetition – but rather that repetitiveness is included in the plurality of Herodotean future concepts. But in the cases where events are practically seen as reenactments of former actions, when there is an almost perfect coincidence of expectation and experience, historical time does not exist; and therefore there is no past, no present, no future – objectively, that is, because the protagonists are not usually aware of the timelessness of their fates.

One should think that the characters might eventually learn from history. The repetitiveness of patterns implies a sort of causal continuity, in the sense

---

26 Demaratus (6.63–70); cf. Boedeker 1987; Burkert 1990.
27 Cf. Pelling 2006 for the differences between Herodotus' Homeric allusions and the 'originals', and for Herodotus' critical stance on "one-size-fits-all explanations" (104) despite all continuity. See also Marincola 2006, 23: "Xerxes is very much like Cyrus, Cambyses and Dareios, but he is not *exactly* like any of them, and his own story is unique."
28 Koselleck 1976. Of course, this idea is not only found in Herodotus; cf. for example Thuc. 1.22.4, who speaks about 'the future that will, due to human nature, be alike or similar': τῶν μελλόντων ποτὲ αὖθις κατὰ τὸ ἀνθρώπινον τοιούτων καὶ παραπλησίων ἔσεσθαι.

that action A will (not) lead to result B: exposing a child will not lead to the death of said child, bridging the sea will instigate disaster, etc. But of course the characters do not realise this. The whole idea of a pattern is that it happens after an (almost) identical fashion every time, meaning that when Astyages decides to have baby Cyrus exposed, no one will walk up to him and remind him of the cases of Paris, Aegisthus, Oedipus and so on. If Astyages knew the pattern, he would desist from it – that is, if he cared to listen to the warning, as there is even an instance where someone is made aware of a pattern and still pays no attention to it: Xerxes cannot be dissuaded from his attack on Greece by Artabanos, although he cites Dareios' unsuccessful Scythian campaign with its highly dangerous bridging of the Bosporus (7.10.2–7; cf. also 7.18.2, cited above).[29]

Herodotus' individual characters are clearly rather clueless about their future – anticipating it *as such*, not from the vantage point of the narrator or the reader who knows the pattern and recognises its proleptic function.

2.2 The cycle as a universal pattern

Another aspect of repetitiveness is Herodotus' idea of a κύκλος τῶν ἀνθρωπηίων πρηγμάτων, a 'wheel of fortune' that "does not permit the same person to enjoy good fortune forever" (1.207.2). It seems omnipresent in the *Histories* and is prominently stated almost at the beginning of Book 1:

> προβήσομαι ἐς τὸ πρόσω τοῦ λόγου, ὁμοίως μικρὰ καὶ μεγάλα ἄστεα ἀνθρώπων ἐπεξιών. τὰ γὰρ τὸ πάλαι μεγάλα ἦν, τὰ πολλὰ αὐτῶν σμικρὰ γέγονε, τὰ δὲ ἐπ' ἐμεῦ ἦν μεγάλα, πρότερον ἦν σμικρά. τὴν ἀνθρωπηίην ὦν ἐπιστάμενος εὐδαιμονίην οὐδαμὰ ἐν τὠυτῷ μένουσαν ἐπιμνήσομαι ἀμφοτέρων ὁμοίως. (1.5.3f.)
>
> I shall ... proceed with the rest of my story recounting cities both lesser and greater, since many of those that were great long ago have become inferior, and some that were great in my own time were inferior before. And so, resting on my knowledge that human prosperity never remains constant, I shall make mention of both without discrimination.

It is tempting to include the repetitiveness of plot patterns into the system of cyclicality, in the sense that the cycle of human fortune makes certain events or stories appear again and again, like a number on a roulette wheel that is always there and sometimes becomes relevant: as certain as number 7 will pop up every once in a

---

[29] Admittedly, this is a very special case, as Xerxes, after harshly rebuking Artabanos immediately after his speech (7.11), does take the advice to heart later and changes his mind, only to be persuaded otherwise again by deceitful dreams (7.12–19).

while at the roulette table, the story pattern of the exposed child will turn up in history time and again. Ludwig Huber has brought the concept of repetition and the metaphor of the cycle together: "was auch immer Agamemnon, Achilleus und Priamos erlitten hatten, Kroisos und Kyros wiederholen nur deren Rollen, wie es dem 'Kreislauf der menschlichen Dinge' entspricht" (1965, 36).

This is one way of seeing it, but considering that Herodotus never connects the repetition of story patterns with his idea of cyclicality (which is purely a matter of alternating 'good' and 'bad' fortune), it does more justice to the text to turn the hierarchy around and read Herodotean cyclicality as one type of repetitive pattern, albeit a very broad one.[30] After all, the statement that some are doing well, but will end up badly (or the other way round) is a story pattern, even if it is very simple and consists only of two plot elements: 'doing well' and 'ending up badly', or even, if one is pedantic, of one motif: 'change of fortune'. Pattern or motif, this idea of cyclicality is a repetitive element, just like the exposure of the heroic child or the crossing of rivers. Like other repetitive patterns, it does not happen to everyone. Herodotus speaks about πολλά, many cities, in 1.5.3, not about all of them.[31] Accordingly, a change of fortune can be perceived in many careers of single characters or peoples in the *Histories*, but not in all of them, famous counter-examples being Tellos of Athens, whose happy life is crowned by a heroic death, and Cleobis and Biton, whose life is frozen at its peak, and who themselves are immortalised with statues (1.30f.). Heroisation in general is a means of beating death or downfall, and it is mentioned quite often in the *Histories*.[32] It means more than mere commemoration, for the Heroes are thought of like living men in an eternal, 'heroic' present.[33] Nevertheless, this exit out of the cycle is the exception to the rule: almost everyone is subject to the repetitive motif that is 'change of fortune'.

The fact that Herodotus' protagonists are not aware of the patterns which determine their fates applies to the broad pattern of the cycle as well, although some characters have more insight into it than others. A very obvious example

---

30 Immerwahr 1966, 148–237, has already labelled the cycle of rise, power and fall of Eastern and Western tyrants as a pattern; I think it can easily be extended to cities or peoples.
31 A strict Herodotean (or, indeed, 'Greek') cyclical thinking was already contested by Momigliano 1966 (esp. 11).
32 1.168: Timesios of Klazomenai, 5.47.2: Philippos of Croton, 5.114f.: Onesilos of Salamis (Cyprus), 7.117.2: the Persian Artachaies, builder of the Athos canal, 7.167.2: Amilkas of Carchedon.
33 Their cultic presence is often treated and discussed like the presence of real people, cf. Adrastos and Melanippos (5.67), the Tyndarids (5.75.2), the Aiacids (5.80.2–81.1); cf. also the strange power of the Epidaurian statues (5.82–88) and the Delphic heroes joining battle (8.38f.).

is the story of Polycrates, whose Egyptian friend Amasis deduces from his knowledge of the cycle-pattern that the unbridled success of the Samian king will lead to downfall (3.39–43). The Athenians, too, use the pattern of the cycle as a justification in their dispute with the Tegeans on the eve of the battle of Plataea, when both parties claim the lead of one army wing (9.26 f.). The Tegeans claim their right to the wing by resorting to the heroic deed of their mythical king Echemos, who drove the Heraclids out of the Peloponnese by winning the duel with their leader Hyllos; since then the Tegeans have always been given the right to lead the other Peloponnesians in all campaigns "both ancient and recent", καὶ τὸ παλαιὸν καὶ τὸ νέον. Now, the Tegeans have not read their Herodotus attentively – they do not understand that while history can be generated by repetitions, this does not mean that the state of things remains the same, especially not if the pattern is called 'cycle'. The Athenians, however, have realised that very well. After listing their own great deeds of the past in one elegant *praeteritio*,[34] concluding, "We know that this meeting has been convened to prepare for battle against the barbarians and not for speeches", they remind their antagonists of the mutability of individual fate:

> Ἀλλ' οὐ γάρ τι προέχει τούτων ἐπιμεμνῆσθαι· καὶ γὰρ ἂν χρηστοὶ τότε ἐόντες ὡυτοὶ νῦν ἂν εἶεν φλαυρότεροι καὶ τότε ἐόντες φλαῦροι νῦν ἂν εἶεν ἀμείνονες. (9.27.4)
>
> But there is no profit in recalling all this, for the same men who were valiant back then could now be inferior, and those who were inferior then could be been superior now.

This is a direct echo of 1.5.3 f. and refers to the pattern of the cycle: the valiant Tegeans of the past may have become inferior to the formerly inferior Athenians. In the same way that baby Cyrus shares elements of his future with characters of the past, the Tegeans share their more abstract and general pattern – change of fortune – with many other cities: their past is glorious, their future may not be, just like the future of many great cities of the past was not.

2.3 The 'rape-stories': Programming repetition

That the concept of repetition seems important to Herodotus can be deduced from the very beginning of the *Histories*, where we find the famous 'rape-stories' (1.1–5). Seeing history – at least partly – as an endless repetition of patterns,

---

[34] See for a detailed analysis of this passage Baragwanath 2012a, 40–43; Boedeker 2012, 18–23.

these stories can be interpreted as programmatical.[35] Of course, there is obvious repetition in the list of retribution rapes that Herodotus tells us: Io is abducted from Argos, Europa is abducted from Tyre, Medeia is abducted from Colchis, Helen is abducted from Sparta. History clearly repeats itself here (and indeed, the abduction of women is an incident of some consequence that keeps repeating itself in the *Histories* even outside the stories told in the first chapters[36]).

Especially in the story of Io, there may be more than meets the eye on a metapoetic level. First, we get a version of the Persian *logioi*: Phoenician merchants have come to the coast of Argos. When princess Io wants to take a look at their goods, they throw her into the ship and sail away. The Phoenicians themselves, however, tell a different story: they did not take Io with them using force; the girl, they say, had already slept with the captain of the ship in Argos and fled her homeland when realising she was pregnant. Together, the stories about Io show an uncanny resemblance to the *Odyssey*'s tale of Eumaios' nurse. The swine-herd tells it to Odysseus in 15.415–475: when he was a boy, his wealthy parents had a Phoenician slave-woman who served as a nurse to him on the island of Syria near Sicily. One day, Phoenician merchants had landed on the island. One of them started an affair with the nurse, who told him that she was actually the daughter of a rich Phoenician family, but that pirates have abducted her and sold her to Eumaios' family as a slave. The Phoenician merchant offered to take her with them and she in return promised to rob the house of Eumaios' parents and bring the little boy himself to sell as a slave. While Eumaios' mother and her female servants were taking a good look at the trinkets the Phoenicians have brought along, they seized the moment and escaped. We can recognise the following elements:

1. A Phoenician ship lands in Greece.
2. The women have special interest in the offered goods.[37]
3. One of the customers is a rich and noble woman, Io or Eumaios' nurse, a slave but originally the daughter of rich Sidonians.[38]

---

35 Modern scholarship on Herodotus' unusual introduction has often concentrated on his statement that he does not want to decide between versions but rather report things he is able to 'know' about Croesus (1.5.3). This sounds programmatic already, and the 'rape-stories' themselves have been considered in this way, too: as an announcement of new rationalism (Rose 1940, 79; Asheri 1988, 74), as a parody on traditional reports (Flory 1987, 23–48; Goldhill 2002, 13–15), or as a geographical outline of the *oikumene* (Dewald 2006, 146f.).
36 For example 2.54–57; 6.65.2; 6.138.1; 7.191.2.
37 *Od.* 15.416: μυρί' ἄγοντες ἀθύρματα, Hdt. 1.1.4: τῶν φορτίων τῶν σφι [the women] ἦν θυμὸς μάλιστα.
38 Io is King Inachus' daughter; the Homeric nurse's parents are ἀφνειοί (15.432) and live in a large mansion (ὑψερεφὲς δῶ, 433).

4. She has an affair with one of the Phoenicians.
5. She elopes with the Phoenicians.
6. She takes a child with her (Io has the yet unborn child of the captain with her, the Homeric nurse takes little Eumaios).

A seventh common element is structural: both stories contain some kind of doubling. Homer has a double 'rape-story': the nurse is originally Phoenician; she has been abducted and taken to Greece, now she is abducted again. Herodotus tells two versions of one tale.

The Homeric parallel fits Herodotus' combination of the two versions, the Persian variant containing elements 1 and 2 – which are, of course, implied in the Phoenician version, too, but not explicitly told –, the Phoenician version supplying the rest. The audience merges the versions and makes the association with the *Odyssey*. By adapting the 'rape-story' to the Homeric tale, it is distilled into a kind of typical and canonical 'rape-story'. Tradition is perfected, myth made more mythical, even without the figure of Zeus: whatever the Persians and Phoenicians say, even when contradicting each other – the result will inevitably be the same, eternal story. This impression is confirmed by the element of doubling: Homer's story, too, is a reprise: Eumaios' nurse has been abducted before – repetition is a fundamental component of the narrative.

Seeing that the Homeric allusion only works when the versions of the Phoenicians and the Persians are synthesised, the story appears self-generated, thereby again depicting the constant and inevitable repetition that is part of all history.

3 Conclusion

To sum up: The future exists in Herodotus, in several different forms. Individual protagonists have futures, even hypothetical, possible futures, when they themselves or the narrator open up alternative scenarios. Herodotus and his readers have a future, for which some parts of the *Histories* may constitute advice or warning. But there is also an omnitemporal continuity of repetition. Many stories are fashioned after patterns, therefore creating an eternal return of the same. In these cases, expectation and experience become almost identical, a mythical temporality is established and historical time eliminated – not from the vantage point of the protagonists, who are usually not aware of the patterns, but from the perspective of Herodotus and his audience, who generally are.

In his famous proem, Herodotus explicitly states the *Histories*' purpose which is commemorating the great deeds of the Greeks and barbarians:

> ... ὡς μήτε τὰ γενόμενα ἐξ ἀνθρώπων τῷ χρόνῳ ἐξίτηλα γένηται μήτε ἔργα μεγάλα τε καὶ θωμαστά, τὰ μὲν Ἕλλησι, τὰ δὲ βαρβάροισι ἀποδεχθέντα, ἀκλεᾶ γένηται ...
>
> ... so that human events do not fade with time, and that the great and wonderful deeds – some brought forth by the Hellenes, others by the barbarians – may not go unsung.

What, then, is the use of commemoration? A first reason to remember would be the hope that we, the audience of the *Histories*, might – in contrast to most of the protagonists – actually learn from history by recognition of similar situations – patterns – that allow us to draw from the experiences of people who have taken a right or wrong turn in the same place where we find ourselves now. Their past becomes our present, and, if we act as they did, our future; the boundaries of time are blurred.

A second reason seems to be to make past events durable, permanent, even timeless. This becomes possible via the traditional pattern, which in every single instance – as *parole*, to speak in the terms of Ferdinand de Saussure – transports events of an irretrievable past, but which *as such* – as *langue* – is an abstract language system of timeless value for past, present and future. These are, of course, the thoughts of Claude Lévi-Strauss,[39] who explains the existence of historiography in similar terms:

> L'intérêt que nous croyons prendre au passé n'est donc, en fait, qu'un intérêt pour le présent; en le reliant fermement au passé, nous croyons rendre le présent plus durable, l'arrimer pour l'empêcher de fuir et de devenir lui-même du passé. Comme si, mis au contact du présent, le passé allait par une miraculeuse osmose devenir lui-même présent, et que du même coup le présent fût prémuni contre son propre sort, qui est de devenir du passé. (1971, 542)
>
> The interest we believe we take in the past is really nothing but our interest in the present; while linking it firmly with the past, we think we make the present more durable, fastening it, trying to avoid that it escape us and become past itself. Like that, being in touch with the present, the past will become present itself by some miraculous osmosis, and in one fell swoop the present is fortified against its own fate—against becoming the past. (my translation)

---

39 Cf. Lévi-Strauss 1958, 231, on myth: "On vient de distinguer la *langue* et la *parole* au moyen des systèmes temporels auxquels elles se réfèrent l'une et l'autre. Or, le mythe se définit aussi par un système temporel, qui combine les propriétés des deux autres. Un mythe se rapporte toujours à des événements passés: 'avant la création du monde' ou 'pendant les premiers âges', en tout cas, 'il y a longtemps'. Mais la valeur intrinsèque attribuée au mythe provient de ce que ces événements, censés se dérouler à un moment du temps, forment aussi une structure permanente. Celle-ci se rapporte simultanément au passé, au présent et au futur ... Cette double structure, à la fois *historique* et *anhistorique*, explique que le mythe puisse simultanément relever du domaine de la *parole* (et être analysé en tant que tel) et du celui de la *langue* (dans laquelle il est formulé) tout en offrant, à un troisième niveau, le même caractère d'objet absolu."

If linear time is eliminated in this way, there is no future. As has been shown, Herodotus is by no means consistent in his achievement of this timelessness. But the very process of organising history by recognisable patterns will produce a mythical temporality, a permanence that is the contrary of historical time. In the end, all historiography will do this to a certain extent, since the main function of the genre is 'making the past present' – eliminating the boundaries of time. But the tendency is especially strong in Herodotus, because never again will historiography be so full of tradition.

Karen Bassi
Fading into the Future: Visibility and Legibility in Thucydides' *History*

1 Introduction

In 1975 M.I. Finley stated that Thucydides' archaeological arguments reveal "a gross ignorance and misunderstanding of the past on several points of major significance."[1] His point was not that archaeology could prove the ancient historian wrong but that Thucydides' account of the past is undermined by his own misunderstanding of material or visible remains. This stark indictment of the great historian's understanding of the past seems especially harsh in light of more recent studies that take seriously the proposition that history is not simply a marshaling of past facts.[2] Nonetheless, the question that Finley's remark raises is still pertinent: What is the role of material or visible phenomena as evidence for historical events in Thucydides' *History* and, by extension, of history writing in general?

Finley's remark in fact invites us to start from the opposite premise, namely, that Thucydides' understanding of the past is *revealed* in his so-called archaeological arguments, i.e., in the spatial and temporal disposition of objects and architectural features in his narrative. Regardless of whether the historian's conclusions correspond to what archaeologists may unearth, the material or visual bases of measuring and evaluating historical time in the *History* are not determined by the extent to which they correspond to a prior empirical reality. Rather, they are the means by which the historian negotiates a path between the past and the future. More concretely, material or visible remains – as objects of verbal description and emplotment – position the historian and the reader of history between the past (in the remains' reference to a given historical event) and the future (as objects whose evidentiary value emerges with the passing of time). If the former is tied to the fact of the object's material existence, moreover, the latter is somewhat paradoxically revealed in its succumbing to a process of decay and destruction.

These temporal distinctions are implicit in what the art historian Alois Riegl has called the "historical value" and the "age-value" of artifacts and monu-

---

[1] Finley 1975, 19. See also Connor 1984, 160 with reference to Rawlings 1981, 62–67.
[2] See, for example, Greenwood 2006 on visual perception in the *History*; Grethlein (2010) and (2010a) on the *History* as narrative.

ments. According to Riegl, age-value is measured in how an object changes over time while historical value "singles out one moment in the developmental continuum of the past and places it before our eyes as if it belonged to the present."[3] As I've noted elsewhere, Riegl is interested in these values as they inhere in actual objects or artifacts and not in their narrative descriptions.[4] But it is clear that both values are prefigured in – if not determined by – how visible or material objects are narrativised within a given literary or historical tradition. Insofar as this process takes place in both fictional and historical works, moreover, it complicates the strict empiricism according to which the past is imagined as prior to and independent of linguistic representation. In putting the past "before our eyes," in other words, descriptions of objects and features in narrative expose what Hayden White calls "the gap between historical events and the language used to represent them."[5]

But if this gap denotes the limits of our encounter with the historical past it also determines our encounter with the historical future. Here the phrase "historical future" is not meant to suggest that narrative history is predictive. Rather, it is meant to introduce the idea that the past and the future are mutually productive temporal categories in history writing or, more properly, that they are dialogic. The aim of this chapter is to explore this proposition in the disposition of visible evidence in Thucydides' *History*, beginning with the *Archaeology* and the historian's methodological statements. I then turn to selected examples of a particular linguistic usage, namely, passages in which the adjective *aphanês* ("invisible" or "unseen") is predicated of the future in the *History*. My larger aim is to explore how the inherent premise of narrative history, namely, that the past can be known, is tied to the proposition that the future is, by definition, unknowable. More specifically, I argue that the invisibility of the future in the *History* is, somewhat paradoxically, an expression of the limits of what can be known about the past.

---

3 Riegl 1982b, 38.
4 Bassi 2014a.
5 White, Foreword to Koseleck 2002, xiii. Cf. Greenwood 2006. 11 – 13. Also, Porter 2010, 291 – 292 on the "radical gap between *logos* and its own contents" in the works of Gorgias. Cf. Bakker 2006 on the significance of Thucydides' statements, beginning with the first line of the *History*, that he "wrote the war" (*xunegrapse ton polemon*, 1.1.1). Bakker concludes that in these phrases, writing presents "a transitive link between the author's name and the War" (p. 110). In other words, it works to close the gap between narrative and event.

2 The vanishing of the past

Anton Froeyman summarises the source of these limits in the relationship between three basic concepts in the philosophy of history:"[6]

> These concepts are "subject" (the historian herself), "object" (history itself, whatever this may mean) and "language/text/symbolisation" (which mediates between subject and object). Most if not all essential differences between theories of history are rooted in different conceptions about the interrelation between these three concepts... [Philosophers] need an account which does not presuppose that there is a past independent of us which we can gain access to by means of language, and which still claims that it makes sense to talk of the past itself, independent of our linguistic representation.

Two general points pertain to the present discussion. The first is that while "the past itself" may be a necessary if difficult-to-grasp concept in historical research, the conundrum Froeyman describes is not unique to the discipline of history.[7] The question of a past that precedes its expression in language is raised in the Greek literary tradition, beginning with the Homeric poems.[8] The exemplary passage is the proem to the Catalogue of Ships in the *Iliad* where the narrator famously professes his inability to recite the names of all the Greek leaders who came to Troy without the help of the Muses, even if he had "ten tongues and ten mouths" (*Iliad* 2.488–493). Here the poet acknowledges that speech both enables and limits what can be known about the past. Thus, Froeyman's implicit equation of the "past itself" with "history itself" is somewhat overstated even as he expresses doubt over what the latter may mean ("history itself, whatever this may mean"). In short, the idea of "the past itself" may simply be a symptom of the fact that the past has always been a function of "language/text/symbolisation."

Second and more important, in Greek poetic or literary texts knowledge about the past is often expressed in the temporal dimension of visible phenomena, i.e., in the existence and physical condition of objects and architectural features. Here, Homer's account of the Achaean wall in the *Iliad* is a singular example of how material remains are measures of the passing of time in the epic.

---

[6] Froeyman 2012, 394. See also, Pieters 2000, 28 on the "ontological level of the past itself" as a recurring point of reference in the philosophy of history.
[7] Cf. Barthes 1986, 138: "Hence, we understand why the notion of historical 'fact' has so often given rise to a certain mistrust. Once language intervenes (and when does it not intervene?), a fact can be defined only tautologically..."
[8] See Purves 2010, 36–38 on this passage. Rengakos 2006, 286–292 analyzes Thucydides' debts to Homer and Herodotus, including their shared temporal structures.

Indeed, in the history of scholarship on the *Iliad* the question of the historicity of the poem itself is tied to Homer's account of the wall's disappearance.[9] My point then is that descriptions of visible or material remains complicate what might be called the temporal divide between fiction and history writing, i.e., between an actual past and a hypothetical past. Such descriptions reveal the extent to which language creates and mediates both temporal categories.

Where does this leave the historical future? In Froeyman's analysis, past and future are distinguished first of all by their referential qualities. The past refers (in principle) to a prior reality, while the future (again in principle) is precisely what has no prior referent.[10] This latter definition is obviously reductive since the future is an effect – if not a reflection – of what has happened in the past, whether this effect is implicit or explicit in a given narrative. In Greek narrative history, the anticipation of future events – often accompanied by hope or fear – is an effect of events that are reported to have happened in fact.[11] In the terms introduced by Aristotle in the *Poetics*, "what has happened" (*ta genomena*) is the source of "what could and would happen according to what is probable or necessary" (*hoia an genoito kai ta dunata kata to eikos ê to anagkaion*).[12] As the defining characteristics of *historia* and *poiêsis* respectively, Aristotle's categories exemplify the complex relationship between past and future, reality and potentiality, and fact and fiction, that continues to define and differentiate these genres. The fact that Aristotle – writing in the fourth century – has trouble keeping these temporal and generic categories distinct in the *Poetics* may be the founding moment of Froeyman's conundrum.[13] History and poetry each have a share in "what could and would happen according to what is probable or necessary." In other terms, they each have a share in the future just as they each have a share in the past.

In his influential book *Futures Past: On the Semantics of Historical Time* Reinhardt Koselleck explores the implications of this conclusion for the writing of history. Koselleck begins by asking, "How in a given present, are the temporal dimensions of past and future related?"[14] In responding to this question, Koselleck argues for a history of concepts (*Begriffsgeschichte*) in which the introduc-

---

9 *Iliad* 12.9–18. I discuss this aspect of the Achaean wall in Bassi 2014 with bibliography. See also, Garcia 2013, 109–110 and 148–157.
10 Cf. Rood 1998, 10 with reference to narratology as an approach to history writing.
11 Plato, *Laws* 644c defines hope as "opinion about future events" (δόξας μελλόντων).
12 *Poetics* 1451a36–38.
13 I discuss this aspect of the *Poetics* in Bassi 2014a.
14 Koselleck 2004, 3.

tion, persistence and transformation of certain key terms (for example, *democracy*) are the source of this relationship. As he explains:[15]

> The diachronic principle constitutes *Begriffsgeschichte* as an autonomous domain of research, which methodologically, in its reflection on concepts and their change, must initially disregard their extralinguistic content – the specific sphere of social history. Persistence, change, or novelty in the meaning of words must first be grasped before they can be used as indices of this extralinguistic content, as indicators of social structures or situations of political conflict.

If I understand Koselleck correctly, he is claiming that changes in the meaning of concepts (or lexical items) over time determine – rather than reflect – their extralinguistic content. To extend this idea, the future can be understood – in Koselleck's terms – as the time in which this content has not yet been "grasped." The future, in other words, is only or essentially linguistic representation, independent of both a prior and a present reality construed as such.

According to Koselleck, however, narrative history is the source and limiting factor of the future:[16]

> History indicates the conditions of a possible future that cannot be solely derived from the sum of individual events. But in the events which it investigates there appear structures which condition and limit room for maneuver in the future. History thus shows us the boundaries of the possible otherness of our future.

In his review of Koselleck's book, David Carr concisely captures its sometimes enigmatic thesis:[17]

> Thus the subject-matter of history is in an important sense not fact but possibility, not past but future; or, more precisely past possibilities and prospects, past conceptions of the future: futures past.

In this formulation, the past does not simply precede the future in lockstep with a linear chronology, either as a relation of cause and effect or in the march of progress. Rather, within any work of narrative history and – I would add, within any narrative form – past and future are mutually productive. This mutuality can be stated in a loose analogy: the historical past is to what Koselleck calls "the fictional nature of narrated events" as the historical future is to the reality of

---

15 Koselleck 2004, 83.
16 Koselleck 2004, 114.
17 Carr 1987, 198.

the past.[18] The point of the analogy is not to deny the existence of "the past itself." Rather, it is meant to suggest that the historical future is a measure of the extent to which the historical past is dependent on linguistic representation.

In a chapter titled "*Res Factae* and *Res Fictae*," Koselleck briefly engages with Aristotle's distinction between poetry and history in presenting the intellectual milieu out of which post-Enlightenment historiography emerged.[19] He argues that "The Enlightenment ... forced *res fictae* and *res factae* out of their pure relation of opposition" and he sums up his conclusions in the following paragraph:[20]

> The remarks made up to this point should suffice to make two things plain: first, that our classic couplet of *res factae* and *res fictae* continues to present an epistemological challenge to the contemporary historian, practiced in theory and conscious of hypothesis; second, that it is in particular the modern discovery of a specific historical time which impels the historian toward the perspectivistic fiction of the factual if he wishes to restore a once vanished past [wenn er die einmal entschwundene Vergangenheit wiedergeben will]. No sworn or cited source is sufficient to eliminate the risk involved in the statement of historical reality.

As suggested above, the "pure relation of opposition" between fact and fiction (or history and poetry) is somewhat overstated as it applies to Aristotle in particular and to Greek narrative forms more generally.[21] Nor do *res factae* and *res fictae* neatly correspond to the temporal categories in Aristotle's formulation, i.e., *ta genomena* and *hoia an genoito*. Nonetheless, Koselleck's insistence on the risks and limits presented by historical sources is key to approaching the historian's "epistemological challenge:"[22]

> The facticity of events established ex post is never identical with a totality of past circumstances thought of as formerly real. Every event historically established and presented lives on the *fiction of actuality*; reality itself is past and gone. This does not mean, however, that a historical event can be arbitrarily set up in this or that manner. The sources provide control over what might not be stated. They do not, however, prescribe what may be said. Historians have a negative obligation to the witnesses of past reality. (emphasis added)

---

18 Koselleck 2004, 80.
19 Koselleck 2004, 205–209.
20 Koselleck 2004, 208–209, with reference to Thucydides' "fictitious speeches."
21 That this "pure" opposition is compromised in terms of Greek genres is demonstrated by Bowie (2001) in his discussion of Simonides' Plataea elegy.
22 Koselleck 2004, 111–112.

If, as Koselleck suggests above, history "shows us the boundaries of the possible otherness of our future," those boundaries are not set by the actuality of the past. Rather they are set by "the fiction of [a past] actuality." As an expression of the fact that "reality itself is past and gone," moreover, this notion has its analogue in the fact that the future (by definition) will never arrive; both are determined by a temporal impasse that compromises any claim to "reality itself."

The insights of Koselleck's book – too briefly presented here – may seem far afield from the concerns of ancient history; the fact that they are focused on *modernity's* future is decisive.[23] And Koselleck has little to say about how visible phenomena may be a limiting factor in what can or cannot be stated about the historical past and the historical future. But his remarks provide a basis for approaching the question of how such phenomena place particular limits on "the past conception of the future" in Greek historiography. His remarks also imply that the effect of the future in historical narrative – as suggested in the Introduction to this chapter – is to reveal the limits placed on knowing the past. In invoking the image of a "once vanished past," moreover, Koselleck demonstrates that the relationship between what can be *seen* in the present and what can be known about the past – and by extension what can be said about the future – constitutes a historiographic trope.[24]

3 The future is behind us

Before turning to Thucydides, a brief detour into the emergence of this trope in Greek literary history will help to contextualize the argument. In an article published in the early 80's, G.E. Dunkel explores phrases that refer to the past as "in front" and the future as "behind" in archaic Greek poetry. Signified by the adverbs ὀπίσσω, πρόσσω and similar terms, this spatio-temporal relationship is explained by a visual metaphor as exemplified by the T scholion on *Iliad* 18.250. In

---

23 Put in very schematic terms, Koselleck argues that the future of modernity is "open" as opposed to the kinds of "closed" futures produced in antiquity and pre-modernity. The former is constrained by the precept of *historia magistra vitae*, the latter by apocalyptic or "endtime" narratives. On Koselleck's book and its relationship to aspects of contingency in the Greek historians, see Grethlein 2010, 7–8.
24 Cf. Koselleck 2004, 208: "The historian rather is fundamentally impelled to make use of the linguistic means of a fiction to render available a reality whose actuality has vanished." See also the visual metaphors in Ricoeur's remarks on Ranke 1984–1988, Vol. 3, p. 185, and Walter Benjamin's well-known description of the "angel of history" whose "face is turned toward the past" (2003, 392–393).

this passage, Polydamas is described as someone "who alone saw before and after" (ὃ γὰρ οἶος ὅρα πρόσσω καὶ ὀπίσσω). The scholiast explains:²⁵

> πρόσσω τὸ παρελθόν, ἐπειδὴ τὸ ἔμπροσθεν βλέπεται· καλεῖται δὲ πρόνοια. ὀπίσσω δὲ τὸ μέλλον, ὅτι ἀφανές ἐστι· καλεῖται δὲ ἀγχίνοια.
>
> *prossô* refers to the past, since what is in front is seen; and this is called *pronoia*. *opissô* refers to the future, because [what is behind] is invisible (*aphanes*); and this is called *anchinoia*.

As Dunkel summarises, "The future is envisioned as lying behind us, and thus invisible or unknown. Conversely, the past lies in front of us, and is visible or known."²⁶ Based on earlier and contemporaneous examples from Vedic Sanskrit and Anatolian, Dunkel debunks the *communis opinio* that limits these expressions to archaic Greek texts. In the process of doing so, he also calls into question what has become the "orthodox" interpretation offered by the scholiast. In contrast, he concludes that:²⁷

> The 'behindness' of the future refers not to us, but to the fact that the future follows the present. Correspondingly, the past stands 'in front' of the present. The subject or speaker's position (*ego*) is, on the contrary, objective or achronic – completely outside the frame of

---

25 Erbse 1969–1988, ad loc. with reference also to *Iliad* 1.343. For the future as "behind," see *Iliad* 6.358 and *Theogony* 210 and 500. At *Theogony* 182 Cronos throws Ouranos' genitals "behind" him (ἐξοπίσω). Does this mean that he throws them metaphorically into the future, where the blood will give rise to various beings "as the years succeed one another" (περιπλομένων δ' ἐνιαυτῶν, 184)?

26 Dunkel 1982–1983, 67. In quoting the scholion, Dunkel leaves out both phrases with *kaleitai*. Erbse's notes refer to Eustathius 1141, 61: "to see what lies in front is called πρόνοια, and to see things that are behind and invisible [ἀφανῆ] is called ἀγχίνοια." Not discussed by Dunkel 1982–1983 but also relevant to the current discussion is Herodotus' use of the adjective *husteros*, often together with *chronos* in the dative, to mean "later" or "in the future" relative to a given event. In spatial terms, *husteros*, like *opisô* and *opisthe*, refers to what "comes after" or is "behind." So, for example, at *Histories* 7.87.1 Herodotus reports that the Arabian camel-riding contingent was placed behind the rest of Xerxes' army so that the cavalry would not be frightened (ὕστεροι ἐτετάχατο, ἵνα μὴ φοβέοιτο τὸ ἱππικόν). The inference here is that this arrangement prevented the horses from seeing (smelling?) the camels (cf. 1.80). Interestingly, Herodotus also uses *husteros* –again like *opisô* and *opisthe* – to refer to what he will show later in his work, i.e., at 2.101.2 where he says that he "will make clear later" (ὕστερον δηλώσω) certain details relating to the works of King Moeris. Other examples of *husteron* with *chronos* in the dative in the *Histories* include 1.171.5; 3.123.1; 3.126.1; 3.129.1; 4.78.2; 5.21.2; 6.73.1; 7.33.1; 7.170.3; 7.213.2; 9.64.2; 9.75.1; 9.101.2. Herodotus also uses *loipos* in the genitive (τοῦ λοιποῦ) to refer to the future, i.e., at 1.11.2. Cf. Thucydides, *History* 8.29.1 and 8.69.4. See Maul 2008 for a similar spatio-temporal orientation in Near Eastern texts.

27 Dunkel 1982–1983, 80–81. See also his discussion of *apo* on p. 80, note 69.

time...Disengaged from the present, the subject looks down *along* the path of time ... to see events in their order relative to each other. (emphasis in the original)

This conclusion is persuasive even if it invokes one visual metaphor ("the subject looks down the path of time...") in the process of dismissing another. According to Dunkel, the temporal dimensions of "behind" (*opissô*) and "in front" (*prossô*) do not depend upon the visual orientation of a viewing subject. Rather, the past is "in front" and the future is "behind" relative to the present. But while the Homeric scholiast may be "confused," as Dunkel charges, his "confusion" may reveal more than it obscures.[28]

With the exception of a passage from Herodotus (to which I will return), Dunkel does not discuss the spatio-temporal orientation of adverbs in the historians. But a selective overview, including but not limited to those discussed by Dunkel, suggests that they function in similar ways. In the *Histories*, Herodotus commonly uses *opisô* – and, less frequently, *opisthe* – in phrases meaning to sail back, to return to a place, to follow behind, etc. In other words, the adverbs are principally spatial and refer to what is behind relative to a subject's present position. In three noteworthy instances, he also uses these adverbs to refer to a later part of his own work (1.75.1; 5.22.1; 7.213.3). In each case, *opisô* or *opisthe* is paired with *logoi* and the first-person future of *apodeiknumi* or *sêmainô* to refer to explanations that he will give later in his narrative. Thus, for example, Herodotus says that he "will clarify in the books that lie behind" (*en toisi opisô logoisi sêmaneô*) why Cyrus was holding Astyages captive, even though Astyages was his own mother's father (1.75.1). Dunkel concludes that "the Herodotean ὀπίσω λόγοι refers not to the books we as readers have behind *us* (= the preceding books), but to the books which are behind *the present book* (= the following books)".[29] This seems clear

---

28 Dunkel 1982–1983, 82. On the T scholion, see Dickey 2006, 19–20 and, on the complex history of the Homeric scholia in general, Nagy 1996. No earlier source is named for the scholion in question.
29 Dunkel 1982–1983, 81, Cf. 1.5.3 where, in a famous passage, Herodotus says that after he has identified the man who first undertook unjust deeds against the Greeks he will then proceed with his account (τοῦτον σημήνας προβήσομαι ἐς τὸ πρόσω τοῦ λόγου). Here *prosô tou logou* seems to be the paradoxical equivalent of *opisô logoi*. Both refer to what is to come in the work but with adverbs that point in opposite directions. But there may be a qualitative difference between *prosô* and *opisô* in these phrases. The former seems to refer to the content of Herodotus' work as a whole (the past) while the latter refers to specific explanations that he will give later (in the future). This difference is also suggested by the use of the singular *logos* at 1.5.3 as opposed to the plural *logoi* at 1.75.1, 5.22.1, and 7.213.3. The use of *es* in the former and *en* in the latter may also contribute to this conclusion, along with the difference between "proceeding" (*prosbêsomai*) and "signifying" (*sêmaneô* and *apodexô*). All this is highly speculative, of course.

even while these passages compromise Dunkel's conclusion that the *ego* is "achronic." In these cases, the verbs in the first-person future together with the redundant personal pronoun testify to the fact that the *egô* is not "outside the frame of time" but is the present coordinate from which the past is distinguished from the future.

While there are no explicit visual metaphors in these passages, the verbs *apodeiknumi* and *sêmainô* commonly refer to making things visible in the *Histories*.[30] In the three passages under discussion here, the implication is that the work itself, as a succession of *logoi*, is a process of making visible what is presently invisible. This process may not be exactly what the scholiast on the *Iliad* had in mind when he said that "*opissô* refers to the future, because [what is behind] is invisible (*aphanes*)." But Herodotus' use of *apodeiknumi* at 5.22.1 to talk about what he will show "in the books that lie behind" (ἐν τοῖσι ὄπισθε λόγοισι ἀποδέξω) resonates with the programmatic beginning of his work (*Histories* 1. proem):

Ἡροδότου Ἁλικαρνησσέος ἱστορίης ἀπόδεξις ἥδε, ὡς μήτε τὰ γενόμενα ἐξ ἀνθρώπων τῷ χρόνῳ ἐξίτηλα γένηται, μήτε ἔργα μεγάλα τε καὶ θωμαστά, τὰ μὲν Ἕλλησι τὰ δὲ βαρβάροισι ἀποδεχθέντα, ἀκλεᾶ γένηται, τά τε ἄλλα καὶ δι' ἣν αἰτίην ἐπολέμησαν ἀλλήλοισι.

This is the setting forth (ἀπόδεξις) of the inquiry of Herodotus of Halicarnassus, to ensure that the past actions of humans do not fade with time (τῷ χρόνῳ ἐξίτηλα) and that the great and marvellous deeds, some manifested (ἀποδεχθέντα) by the Greeks, others by the barbarians, may not be without fame, and especially the cause for which they went to war with each other.

As I've argued elsewhere, the historiographical trope referred to at the end of the previous section is inaugurated here in the *Histories* where the metaphor of fading with time – to adopt Koselleck's phrasing – implies that the future is constituted in the vanishing of the past.[31] In accentuating this metaphor, the polyptoton with *apodeiknumi* (noun and participle) extends the idea that the historical past is equated with what can be seen (where seeing may also refer to the practice of reading the *Histories*) and serves to credit Herodotus' *historiês apodexis*

---

[30] In Herodotus, *sêmainô* can mean "to give a [visual] sign," for example, at 2.38.3; cf. 1.116.4. *Sêmainô* is also used to refer to future events, for example, when Croesus tells Adrastus that responsibility for his son's death lies with the god who "indicated long ago what would happen in the future" (ὅς μοι καὶ πάλαι προεσήμαινε τὰ μέλλοντα ἔσεσθαι, 1.45.2). For similar examples that suggest that the future is what needs to be made visible, see 1.108.2 and 6.27.1. The visual aspect of *apodeiknumi* is explicit at 2.101.5 where it refers to the structures built by Moeris. See also, 1.125.6; 1.171.25; 4.92.1; 5.45.1; 5.45.2; 6.86b.1.
[31] Bassi 2014.

with preventing its disappearance in the future.³² It may be going too far to suggest that the idea that the past "fades with time" is predicated on the belief that the future is invisible. But even if the evidence for this conclusion from adverbial usage is spotty, Herodotus' unique metaphor plots the historical past and the historical future on a continuum from visibility to invisibility.

4 Visible evidence in the *History*

Turning now to Thucydides' *History*, the relationship between temporal categories and visible phenomena is first encountered in the *Archaeology* where the historian argues that the farther back in time events are located, the less reliable is the present account of them (*History* 1.10.1–2).³³ He illustrates this point by the remains of cities that, due to their great distance in time (*pollou chronou*), are not reliable proof of their military and political power (*dunamis*) in their prime. Here, visible evidence in the present can lead to unsupportable claims about the past.³⁴ More specifically, Thucydides suggests that there is an inverse relationship between the size and opulence of a city's built environment and its power. The exemplary case is Mycenae (1.10.1):

> καὶ ὅτι μὲν Μυκῆναι μικρὸν ἦν, ἢ εἴ τι τῶν τότε πόλισμα νῦν μὴ ἀξιόχρεων δοκεῖ εἶναι, οὐκ ἀκριβεῖ ἄν τις σημείῳ χρώμενος ἀπιστοίη μὴ γενέσθαι τὸν στόλον τοσοῦτον ὅσον οἵ τε ποιηταὶ εἰρήκασι καὶ ὁ λόγος κατέχει.
>
> Because Mycenae was small, or if the buildings of the town then seems not to be worthy of note now, someone not using an accurate proof would doubt that [Agamemnon's] armament was such as the poets say and reason supports.

Thucydides makes this claim from the point of view of a hypothetical "someone" who bases his wrong conclusion about the power of Mycenae during the Trojan War (when the city was at its height) on the inaccurate proof provided by the size and quality of its present ruins (οὐκ ἀκριβεῖ ἄν τις σημείῳ χρώμενος). This then becomes the standard of proof against which the future ruins of Sparta and Athens are to be evaluated. In the case of the former, Thucydides conjectures that her power would be thought to be less than it now is; in the case of the latter,

---

32 Cf. the use of *apodeixis* at Thucydides, *History* 2.13.9, discussed by Greenwood 2006, 34.
33 On the visual sense in Thucydides, see Connor 1985, 10; Immerwahr 1960, 281; Greenwood 2006, 25.
34 Cf. Grethlein 2010, 213 and Reynolds 2009, 336.

it is likely that her power would be thought to be twice as great as it is, based on "clear visible evidence" (*apo tês phaneras opseôs*, 1.10.2):

φαίνοιτ' ἂν ὑποδεεστέρα, Ἀθηναίων δὲ τὸ αὐτὸ τοῦτο παθόντων διπλασίαν ἂν τὴν δύναμιν εἰκάζεσθαι ἀπὸ τῆς φανερᾶς ὄψεως τῆς πόλεως ἢ ἔστιν.

[Lacedaemon] would appear to be less [powerful than it is], but if Athens were to suffer the same thing [I think that] the power of the city would appear to be twice as great as it is on the basis of clear visible evidence.

The bibliography on these passages is extensive.[35] My limited focus is on the effect of projecting the counterintuitive evaluation of visible evidence in the present (the ruins of Mycenae) onto the future ruins of Sparta and Athens. To begin with, those ruins exist simultaneously in the future (in relation to Thucydides' present) and in a hypothetical past (in relation to a future viewer). Here, in other words, the future is the basis for making judgments about a past that has not yet happened, where those judgments are based on the limits of empirical observation in the present.[36] Thucydides tells us that at the time he began writing the *History*, Athens and Sparta were both "at the height of their preparation" for the war (ἀκμάζοντές τε ἦσαν ἐς αὐτὸν ἀμφότεροι παρασκευῇ τῇ πάσῃ 1.1.1). This period, in which the cities were at the apex of their powers, is the actual past to which their future ruins will be inaccurate or counterfactual guides.[37]

The possibility that Sparta will seem less powerful than in her prime while Athens will seem twice as powerful is clearly an ironic comment on the outcome of the war.[38] But this is not a simple case of prolepsis.[39] As a time for evaluating

---

35 Rood 2006a, 233–240 provides a good overview. See also, Ober 1998, 59–60. Hornblower 1991–2008.1, ad loc., citing Cook 1955) notes that while Mycenae, with its Lion Gate, may seem impressive today, it "would have looked to Th. like an inferior vision of what he was used to already." Gomme / Andrewes / Dover 1945–1981, ad loc. are more helpful on this point, with reference to Mycenae's role in the Peloponnesian War and to Pausanias' description of the site at ii.16.5–6.
36 Cf. Williams 2001, 13; Bakker 2006, 118.
37 On debates over when this passage may have been written, i.e., before or after 404, see Gomme / Andrewes / Dover 1945–1981, ad loc. When Thucydides has Pericles say in the Funeral Oration that Athens has everywhere set up "imperishable monuments of evil and good" (πανταχοῦ δὲ μνημεῖα κακῶν τε κἀγαθῶν ἀίδια ξυγκατοικίσαντες, 2.41.4), the statesman's words can be contrasted with the conclusion reached in 1.10. Cf. Ober 1998, 85–86: "Once again we are being implicitly reminded that only Thucydides' accurate account of the historical facts, his 'imperishable possession,' will allow readers to know about either the real past or the probable future" (p. 86).
38 Thucydides explicitly refers to the outcome of the war in the so-called second preface where he says that he "wrote up to the point when the Lacedaemonians and their allies put an end to

what the past has "left behind" (*leiphtheiê*, 1.10.2), the future is expressed in terms of what can and cannot be seen. The irony in the appeal to future *ruins* as clear visible evidence (*phaneros*) of the past, moreover, cannot be missed; the counterfactual conclusion to which these ruins lead is based on a past that can no longer be seen, i.e., the cities in all their prior glory. In making this claim, Thucydides exposes the limits of the inherent connection between the actuality of the past and its priority, expressed in a counterfactual example of cause and effect.

The role of visible perception in accounting for the historical past has a different but related effect in Thucydides' well-known methodological statement, in which his own presence at events is a measure of the accuracy of his written account of what happened in the war (*History* 1.22.2–3):[40]

> τὰ δ' ἔργα τῶν πραχθέντων ἐν τῷ πολέμῳ οὐκ ἐκ τοῦ παρατυχόντος πυνθανόμενος ἠξίωσα γράφειν, οὐδ' ὡς ἐμοὶ ἐδόκει, ἀλλ' οἷς τε αὐτὸς παρῆν καὶ παρὰ τῶν ἄλλων ὅσον δυνατὸν ἀκριβείᾳ περὶ ἑκάστου ἐπεξελθών. ἐπιπόνως δὲ ηὑρίσκετο, διότι οἱ παρόντες τοῖς ἔργοις ἑκάστοις οὐ ταὐτὰ περὶ τῶν αὐτῶν ἔλεγον, ἀλλ' ὡς ἑκατέρων τις εὐνοίας ἢ μνήμης ἔχοι.

> I have deemed it worthy to write the deeds that resulted from the things that were done in the war, not as I learned them from just anybody, nor as seemed best to me, but relying on events at which I myself was present (*autos parên*) and from others [who were present] after I had gone through each detail as accurately as possible. I have found this task to be extremely difficult since those who were present (*hoi parontes*) at these various events were not saying the same things about the same events, but each person [spoke] singly in accordance with his partiality or his memory.

Here the phrase *hois te autos parên* ("events at which I myself was present") operates within a hierarchy of evidentiary positions in which first-person empirical observation holds pride of place.[41] The historian's own presence at events promises the

---

the Athenian empire and took the Long Walls and Piraeus" (5.26.1). According to Rood 2006a, 230, "Thucydides stresses that his act of writing is itself something that is now past." See also, Bakker 2006, 114–115.

39 See Greenwood 2006, 24 on other proleptic references to Athens' defeat.
40 The translation is adapted from that of Blanco 1998. Gomme / Andrewes / Dover 1945–1981, vol. i. ad loc. have a useful discussion of the debates over translation and interpretation of the passage. See also, Hornblower 1991–2008.1, ad loc.; and Kallet 2006, 339–340. Tsakmakis 1998, 251–253 analyzes Thucydides' methodological debts to forensic rhetoric. Meyer 2008, 28–29 discusses Thucydides' preference for visual (including inscriptional) as opposed to oral proofs. See also, Rood 2006a, 236–238.
41 Hornblower 1991–2008.1, ad loc. translates the phrase αὐτὸς παρῆν as "I...myself saw." Schepens 1980, 89–90 discusses the reliability of autopsy vs. oral inquiry in Thucydides. See also, Marincola 1997, 63–9 on the primacy of visual proof in Thucydides. This passage

greatest degree of accuracy (*akribeia*), followed by the presence of others – inferred by *hoi parontes* in the final sentence above – which can succumb to partiality (*eunoia*) or to what is implicitly equated with partiality, memory (*mnêmê*).[42]

In this account, direct empirical observation does not ensure consensus about past events. The passage thus refers to a general category of evidence to which the specific examples in the *Archaeology* apply. But the implication is also clear that the historian's account of events at which he was present is less distorted by personal bias or faulty memory (although these negative connotations of *eunoia* and *mnêmê* are left unsaid).[43] The historian's claim to a greater degree of accuracy and neutrality may seem to be a necessary – even natural – defence against the doubts of future readers.[44] But it also raises the question of why Thucydides acknowledges the sources of that doubt in the first place. In doing so, he both recognises and resists the gap between empirical observation and linguistic representation in accounting for the past.[45] In Koselleck's terms, the admission that evidence based on the physical presence of historical actors

---

can be compared with Odysseus' remarks to the blind Demodocus in the *Odyssey* (8.487–491), where a similar hierarchy based on physical presence is invoked, with some irony.

42 Cf. Gomme / Andrewes / Dover 1945–1981, vol. 1.143: "To say that Thucydides is here proudly asserting his own complete knowledge and trustworthiness when he was present at an action in contrast to the bias and faulty memories of others, is, to me at least, singularly perverse." See also, Hedrick 1993, 31, who argues that Thucydides' trustworthiness is subject to the same criticism he levels against his informants at 1.22.2–3: "[H]e criticises his sources and admits complicity in their flaws." I take a position somewhere between these two views. The historian privileges the account of what he himself has heard and seen, attested to by the emphatic use of the pronoun *autos* (= *myself*) at 1.22.1 and 2 (*autos êkousa* and *autos parên*). While he may be complicit in the flaws of his sources, he minimises his own flaws by privileging his degree of proximity to the events in question.

43 On memory in Thucydides, see Meyer 2008, 30.

44 On Thucydides' neutrality as a source of his authority, see the remarks of Rood 2006a, 229–230.

45 Several scholars argue that the *History* is isomorphic with the war. Bakker 2006, 116, for example, concludes that "*The War of the Peloponnesians and Athenians* is the War of the Peloponnesians and Athenians." This equation, founded on grammatical constructions that interpellate future readers, is persuasive. But appeals to the "presence" of the past in the future seem overly optimistic. Rather, Thucydides recognises – even if he works to deny – the gap between his subject and his writing. Cf. Plutarch, *Moralia* 347 A, where he describes the style of Thucydides: "[Thucydides] certainly always strives after this vividness in his account, eagerly trying to transform his reader into a spectator and to let the sufferings that were so striking and upsetting to those who beheld them have a similar effect on those who read about them." This passage is discussed by Debnar 2001, 21. See also, the remarks of Rood 2006a, 228; Rood 1998, 1–5; Greenwood 2006, 66–67; Ober 1998, 53–63. Tsakmakis 1998, 244 refers to "die Auffassung der Realität als Interaktion zwischen λόγος und ἔργον."

is contested and unreliable – even (or especially) in light of the historian's somewhat ambivalent denial of that unreliability in his own case – has the effect of exposing the "fiction of actuality" in historical narrative.⁴⁶

Based on the historical actor's physical presence at events – which includes an implicit censure of memory – this hierarchy is also what distinguishes Thucydides' work from the fictional or poetic genres (*to muthôdes*, 1.22.4). His method necessarily excludes from the proper sphere of history events that occurred in a distant and highly embellished past, i.e., the sorts of events that are proper to the work of poets and logographers (*History* 1.21.1; cf. 1.20.1).⁴⁷ In this respect, the fact that Thucydides nowhere makes use of the Homeric redundancy of seeing characters and events with one's "own eyes," on the one hand, or of Herodotus' appeals to an eyewitness or *autoptês*, on the other, are signs of his method in practice.⁴⁸ Somewhat ironically, these particular expressions would bring with them the generic traces of what is fictional or incredible.

The criterion of physical presence at historical events is immediately followed by an explicit visual metaphor in Thucydides' well-known statement about the intended effect of what he has written (1.22.4):

ὅσοι δὲ βουλήσονται τῶν τε γενομένων τὸ σαφὲς σκοπεῖν καὶ τῶν μελλόντων ποτὲ αὖθις κατὰ τὸ ἀνθρώπινον τοιούτων καὶ παραπλησίων ἔσεσθαι, ὠφέλιμα κρίνειν αὐτὰ ἀρκούντως ἕξει.

As many as will wish to have a clear view (*to saphes skopein*) of the things that have happened and of similar things that will happen again in the future (*tôn mellôntôn pote authis*)

---

46 Kallet 2006, 339, note 16 comments that Parry 1981, 103 "rightly notes that when speaking about the lack of agreement among sources for an event, Thucydides refers to 'accounts that agree with each other', not with a reality, and continues, 'The implication is that whatever is known about an event is largely a creation of language.'"
47 Grethlein 2010, 208–209 argues that *logographos* refers not only to prose authors, among whom Herodotus is representative, but also and principally to the orators whose works are the primary examples of "media of memory." See also, Tsakmakis 1998; Ober 1998, 55; Rood 2006a, 235–236. Dunn 2007, 114 discusses the relationship between Thucydides' claims to accuracy and his interest in "current affairs" and claims that "The narrator anticipates the future in order to motivate judgment of the episode at hand, rather than to demonstrate a connection between earlier and later events" (116).
48 On this Homeric redundancy, see Bassi 2014. Gomme / Andrewes / Dover 1945–1981, ad loc. translate ἑώρων ὄψει at 6.31.1 (in the description of the fleet leaving for Sicily) as "which they saw with their own eyes," with comparable examples. But these do not include words for "eyes." *Ophthalmos* is found only twice in Thucydides and in both instances it refers to symptoms of the plague and not to seeing objects or people (2.49.2 and 2.49.8). *Ommasi* occurs at 2.11.7, where Archidamus argues that the Athenians will be urged to fight in the field when they see the Spartans laying waste to their land.

in accordance with human affairs (*kata to anthrôpinon*), it will be enough that they judge these things [my work] to be useful (*ôphelima*).

In what may be an implicit criticism of the naiveté of Herodotus' aim in writing the *Histories*, namely, so that the deeds of humans will not "fade with time," Thucydides offers a more cautious – even tentative – assessment of the purpose of his work. But like Herodotus, he also uses a visual metaphor to express this purpose. In the first reference in the *History* to the future as a conceptual category (as opposed to a specific eventuality, as at 1.10.2), moreover, he extends the metaphor to encompass the future.[49] More precisely, the ability to clearly see the past is the implied prior basis for the ability to clearly see the future.[50]

As Egbert Bakker has argued with reference to this passage, *skopein* "denotes a critical looking into matters that do not provide ready or obvious evidence."[51] This is also the verb used in the *Archaeology* to sum up the effect of seeing the visual aspects of cities (1.10.3):

---

[49] Hornblower 1991–2008.1, ad loc. translates "and similar events which may be expected to happen in the future." See also, Kallet 2006, 337 who argues that the utility to which Thucydides refers has to do with "understanding events outside his text." Gomme / Andrewes / Dover 1945–1981, ad loc. argue that: "It should not be necessary, but it is, to explain that τῶν μελλόντων ... ἔσεσθαι is future to Thucydides, not to his readers: the latter will not find his work useful in order to divine what will happen in the future, as though it were a sort of horoscope, but for the understanding of other events besides the Peloponnesian war, future to Thucydides, but past or contemporary to the reader." Ober 1998, 60, note 19 comments – and I agree – that this conclusion "strains the sense of the passage." On Thucydides' future audiences, see also Greenwood 2006, 8–11.

[50] Loraux 1986, 154 refers to *skopein* as an intellectual and intransitive activity in Thucydides: "[D]ans ses emplois les plus marqués, *skopein* chez Thucydide n' a pas d' objet." 1.10.3 and 1.22.4 seem to complicate this conclusion. Walker 1993, 375 links *skopein* with the trope of *enargeia* in providing a "realistic representation" in Thucydides. Kallet 2001, 38–39; 56–58; and 98–100, notes the parallels between 1.10.3 and the description of the fleet as it sets out for Sicily at 6.31.4; these parallels are based on a shared scepticism about visual displays of power. See also Ober 1998, 114, note 14 on *History* 6.31.1: "This example of the masses' false confidence resulting from *seeing* demonstrates that ...visual perception can be just as misleading as verbal persuasion" (emphasis in the original). The variable I would add to these analyses is time, i.e., that both passages (1.10.3 and 6.31.4) look to the future for validating the discrepancy between Athens' actual power and its apparent power. The former passage presents a hypothetical past when Athens is in ruins; the latter passage presents (implicitly) an actual future when the Athenians (as the informed reader of Thucydides knows) will be defeated in Sicily. In a sense, this past and future are the same time. Cf. Rengakos 2006, 287 who notes that "all the flash-forwards in the *History* concern Athens' defeat in 404."

[51] Bakker 2006, 117. Cf. Meyer 2008, 32.

> οὔκουν ἀπιστεῖν εἰκός, οὐδὲ τὰς ὄψεις τῶν πόλεων μᾶλλον σκοπεῖν ἢ τὰς δυνάμεις.
>
> It is therefore not reasonable to distrust [the power of Mycenae], nor to look into (*skopein*) the visual aspects of cities more than their powers.

Here *skopein* shifts between a literal and a figural meaning; it refers both to looking at the visible evidence (*tas opseis*) and, by catachresis, to considering the powers that somehow exceed that evidence.[52] Commenting on its use in 1.22.4, Bakker concludes that "Thucydides' work … presents *itself* as the object of its future readers' σκοπεῖν (emphasis added).[53] This self-referential quality, in which Thucydides reveals what he expects of future readers, is a common way of understanding the passage. But if the metaphor of seeing things clearly (*to saphes skopein*) mediates between the past and the future, it also crosses the fine line between reality and potentiality. In implicitly equating the historical past with the historical future, the visual metaphor emphasises their shared contingencies, based on the limits of what can be known about either. These shared limits are also implied in the address to a subset of readers who will wish to see the past and future clearly (ὅσοι δὲ βουλήσονται). Followed by the hesitancy expressed in the phrase "it will be enough" (ἀρκούντως ἕξει), this address undermines the possibility of knowing what has happened by, in effect, contaminating it with the impossibility of knowing what will happen. Wishing to know the future, in other words, exposes the limits of wishing to know the past.

---

52 Rood 2006a, 239 notes that the phrase "Those who want to have a clear picture of things that have happened," is similar to a phrase found on Athenian public inscriptions: τῷ βουλομένῳ σκοπεῖν. Refuting claims that Thucydides is "undemocratic," Rood continues: "[Thucydides'] own text, he implies, is like an inscription available for public consultation – and the voluntary nature of this participation is a key aspect of democratic ideology." Cf. Bakker 2006, 121 with note 32 (with examples of inscriptions), and with reference to Moles 1999. See also, Ober 1998, 60–63.
53 Bakker 2006, 118. See also, Kallet 2006, 354: "In the case of the plague, the 'looking carefully' applies also implicitly to the hermeneutic acts that others in the future must perform." Greenwood 2006, 14–16 discusses the significance of writing which, as the principal medium of the *History*, allows readers to "'look again' at what they have read, and to re-examine it countless times."

5 The invisibility of the future

The first instance of *aphanês* ("invisible") in the *History* occurs, somewhat surprisingly, in Thucydides' summary statement about the "truest" cause of the outbreak of the war (1.23.5–6):[54]

> διότι δ' ἔλυσαν, τὰς αἰτίας προύγραψα πρῶτον καὶ τὰς διαφοράς, τοῦ μή τινα ζητῆσαί ποτε ἐξ ὅτου τοσοῦτος πόλεμος τοῖς Ἕλλησι κατέστη. τὴν μὲν γὰρ ἀληθεστάτην πρόφασιν, ἀφανεστάτην δὲ λόγῳ, τοὺς Ἀθηναίους ἡγοῦμαι μεγάλους γιγνομένους καὶ φόβον παρέχοντας τοῖς Λακεδαιμονίοις ἀναγκάσαι ἐς τὸ πολεμεῖν· αἱ δ' ἐς τὸ φανερὸν λεγόμεναι αἰτίαι αἵδ' ἦσαν ἑκατέρων, ἀφ' ὧν λύσαντες τὰς σπονδὰς ἐς τὸν πόλεμον κατέστησαν.

> With respect to why they broke the treaty, I have written the causes first and the grounds of disagreement, so that no one need search for the immediate reason why the Hellenes became involved in such a war. For I think that the truest explanation (*alêthestatên prophasin*), but the one most hidden from view (*aphanestatên*), is that war was necessary because the growth of Athenian greatness was making the Lacedaemonians afraid. But the causes spoken about in the open (*es to phaneron*) on either side, on account of which they broke the peace and then went to war, are as follows.

What is striking about this passage is the coordinated use of the superlatives to express an equation between what is most true and what is most hidden from view, with the further implication that what is clearly visible (*phaneron*) is, in this case, false.[55] In this aetiological context, the counterfactual evidence provided by the visible ruins of cities in 1.10 is brought to a higher level of discourse.[56]

---

[54] Tsakmakis 1995, 22 suggests that in using the phrase *alethestatê prophasis*, "Thucydides stresses his effort to emancipate himself from Herodotean tradition and announces indirectly a historical account which is conceived in a manner different from his predecessor's." Cf. Porter 2010, 282–284 and 298–307 on *aphanês* as a feature of materialist discourses in the fifth century.

[55] Cf. Hornblower 1991–2008.1, ad loc.: "The word πρόφασις could be derived either from πρόφημι, from a root meaning 'say' or 'speak'; or from προφαίνω from a root meaning 'show'." Hornblower provides a useful summary of the debate over which root is the most compelling.

[56] Greenwood 2006, 37 argues that this passage "draws on a well-established tradition in Greek thought that speech often conceals the truth [with reference to *Iliad* 9.312–313]. Thucydides' written account, which is ideologically opposed to the spoken word, holds out visible words to its readers so as to give them a clear view of what happened in a way that was not visible to audiences listening to speeches at the time." This is a compelling conclusion. But as I will argue below, Thucydides' description of the inscriptions pertaining to the tyranny in Athens poses a challenge to the clarity of "visible words." I would also say that reading is a different order of seeing than the kinds of "theatrical culture" Greenwood is analyzing. On the

In the earlier passage, the ability to know what happened in the hypothetical past from the vantage point of the future was limited by the counterintuitive nature of what had been left behind (*leiphtheiê*, 1.10.2) and could still be seen.

Here the analogue is expressed in the notion that the truth about the cause of the war is what is most hidden from view.[57] It is the historian's task to uncover or reveal this hidden cause, as he does here and again at 1.88. In this passage, Thucydides brings together the principal elements of his methodology: the ability to see the counterfactual truth when confronted with "clear visible evidence" (*apo tês phaneras opseôs*, 1.10.2); the ability to adjudicate between conflicting accounts of those who were present (*hoi parontes*, 1.22.2–3); and the ability to facilitate a clear view of the future based on a clear view of the past (*to saphes skopein*, 1.22.4). In all three cases, the historian navigates a metaphorical path between what is hidden from sight and what is available to view, beginning with the very cause of the war itself.[58] In short, visual perception is the dominant figural means of referring to the relationship between temporal distance and evidentiary value in the *History*.

To return to the broader focus of this chapter, the metaphors of visibility and invisibility are Thucydides' way of expressing – in Hayden White's words again – "the gap between historical events and the language used to represent them." This gap, perceived in the historian's ambivalence about the evidentiary value of visual or empirical observation, is manifested here in the dialogic relationship between the past as a prior reality and the future as pure possibility. In this respect – and although it would stretch the syntax of the sentence – the meaning of *kata to anthrôpinon* at 1.22.4 may differ from the usual translation "in accordance with human affairs." In this evidentiary context, what Rosalind Thomas has called "a statement about human nature as a universal constant" may refer more specifically to the epistemological contingencies inherent in history writing it-

---

"most hidden cause" of the war in relation to the speeches of the Corcyreans and Corinthians in Athens in Book 1, see Ober 1998, 77.

57 Cf. Dunn 2007, 111–150 on narrative uncertainty as an effect of Thucydides' presentation of events "as they unfold" (p. 139).

58 In Herodotus, forms of *aphanês* and *aphanizô* are used almost exclusively to refer to the physical disappearance of things, people or natural phenomena, i.e., the Lycus river at 7.30.1. The closest correlation of the future with what is *aphanes* in the *Histories* is found at 4.150.15 where Herodotus says that the Therans did not know where Libya was and would therefore not dare to send off a colony "into an uncertain situation" (*es aphanes chrema*). Here *aphanes* refers to a future eventuality, although *chrema* may specify a physical location.

self.⁵⁹ What is "human," in other words, is the wish to have a clear view of what has happened in the past and what will happen in the future. Thucydides' work is useful (*ôphelima*) because it both produces this wish and acknowledges the contingencies that resist its fulfillment.

This interplay between wish and fulfilment is embedded in the narrative proper in Nicias' first speech prior to the Sicilian Expedition, in which he invokes the invisibility of the future in attempting to persuade the Athenians to reconsider their resolve (6.9.3):⁶⁰

καὶ πρὸς μὲν τοὺς τρόπους τοὺς ὑμετέρους ἀσθενὴς ἄν μου ὁ λόγος εἴη, εἰ τά τε ὑπάρχοντα σῴζειν παραινοίην καὶ μὴ τοῖς ἑτοίμοις περὶ τῶν ἀφανῶν καὶ μελλόντων κινδυνεύειν· ὡς δὲ οὔτε ἐν καιρῷ σπεύδετε οὔτε ῥᾴδιά ἐστι κατασχεῖν ἐφ' ἃ ὥρμησθε, ταῦτα διδάξω.

Against your character my speech would be weak, if I should advise you to preserve what you have already and not to put your present possessions at risk for things that are unseen and in the future (*peri tôn aphanôn kai mellontôn*); that, however, your zeal is ill-timed and that it is not easy to attain the things that you are striving for, these things I will show/teach [you].

In this speech, Nicias equates the future with what is unseen or invisible as part of a cautionary tale.⁶¹ The Athenians, he says, are inclined to sacrifice what they have in

---

59 Thomas 2006, 87. Cf. the phrase *phusis anthrôpôn* at 3.82.2: "The sufferings which *stasis* inflicted on the cities were many and difficult, such as have been and always will be, as long as the nature of humans remains the same" (ἕως ἂν ἡ αὐτὴ φύσις ἀνθρώπων ᾖ). The fact that *to anthrôpinon* is part of a conditional sentence at 1.22.4 and that *phusis anthrôpôn* is part of an indefinite temporal clause at 3.82.2 put pressure on the idea of "human nature as a universal constant:" In his speech in defense of upholding the decision to kill the men of Mytilene and enslave the women and children, Cleon argues that they not be spared on the grounds that their mistake was *anthrôpinôs* (ὡς ξύγγνωμον ἁμαρτεῖν ἀνθρωπίνως λήψονται 3.40.1). Coming from "the most violent man from among the citizens" (βιαιότατος τῶν πολιτῶν, 3.36.6), this suspicion of the explanatory value of "human nature" shows that its "constant" quality can be manipulated. Ober 1998, 67 remarks that "Thucydides assumes throughout that humans will, by nature, act according to perceived self-interest." But as Ober goes on to demonstrate, this self-interest is not the defining characteristic of individuals but is expressed in the democratic "myth" of a collective political unity. See also, Young-Bruehl 1986, 4; Reynolds 2009, 360–363, with additional bibliography.
60 Thucydides' programmatic statements about his method of composing the speeches in the *History* (1.22.1) are the object of extensive scholarship. He aims for accuracy (*tên akribeian*), but necessarily settles for something less than verbatim quotation. Here too, a hierarchy of spatio-temporal positions is established in which what the historian himself has heard (*autos êkousa*) is implicitly favoured as evidence over what others report to have heard. But in both cases, the principle of physical (and temporal) proximity to what was originally said applies.
61 On the character and career of Nicias, see Tsakmakis 2006, 168–169. Gribble 2006, 459–462 notes the extent to which Nicias' avoidance of risk is "un-Athenian" and how this avoidance differs from the "mind-set required by the Periclean statesman" in the *History* (p. 459). Speaking

hand for future gain; this is part of their character (*tropos*).⁶² Speaking of the three speeches at the beginning of Book 6, Simon Hornblower suggests that "The most important structural point to note about these three speeches is the way they anticipate the subsequent narrative; this is especially true of Nikias' speeches."⁶³ What is "unseen and in the future" is of course the disastrous outcome of the Sicilian Expedition, an outcome that the reader of Thucydides' *History* will know but whose narrative she is yet to read.⁶⁴ As James V. Morrison remarks:⁶⁵

> In his speeches regarding the proposed Sicilian Expedition (6.9–14, 6.20–23), Nicias makes various predictions and warnings that the narrative of the following two years confirms. He anticipates the danger of dividing Athenian power, the difficulty of rule in Sicily (6.10–11), the risk that Sicilian cities may join together, the likely need for reinforcements, and the precarious isolation of an Athenian force in a distant, hostile locale (6.20–21).

At the point when Nicias delivers this speech, in other words, what is "unseen and in the future" is Thucydides' narrative of the Expedition. From the point of view of a future reader, of course, these events have already happened. But since knowledge of what happened to the Athenians in Sicily is in part a result of having read the *History*, Nicias' "unseen" future is coincident with the past (*ta genomena*) as the topic of Thucydides' narrative.⁶⁶ Here, in other words, the gap between a past reality and its linguistic representation is paradoxically bridged by Nicias' speech about what will happen in the future.⁶⁷

The fact that *aphanês* is predicated both of the truest explanation of the beginning of the war (1.23.6) and, if less explicitly, of what might be called the truest – if not the only – explanation of its end (the Athenian defeat in Sicily) also

---

of 6.9, Tompkins 1972, 185 notes that "the potential optative construction is typical of Nicias." See also the remarks of Greenwood 2006, 76–81.
62 Cf. Thucydides' characterisation of Themistocles as someone who "was especially able to see in advance the good and evil in what was unseen" (τό τε ἄμεινον ἢ χεῖρον ἐν τῷ ἀφανεῖ ἔτι προεώρα μάλιστα, 1.138.3). This passage is briefly discussed by Tsakmakis 2006, 174. Gomme / Andrewes / Dover 1945–1981, ad loc. note that "Dionysius disapproved of its eccentricity of expression: *Ep. ad Amm.* ii. 4, p. 794 and 6, p. 807.
63 Hornblower 1991–2008.3, 321–322, with bibliography.
64 On Nicias' contributions to that outcome, see Gribble 2006, 460–461.
65 Morrison 2006a, 266.
66 I am not suggesting that there are no other sources for the Peloponnesian War, only that Thucydides' *History* is the principal source.
67 Cf. Barthes 1986, 130–131 on the effect of temporal "shifters" in historical narrative: "In effect, the shifters of organization attest ... to the historian's predictive function: it is insofar as he knows what has not yet been recounted that the historian, like the agent of myth, needs to double the chronic splitting of events by references to the actual time of his speech." He also calls this "paper time."

creates a figural link between them. More to the point, the Spartans' fear (*phobos*, 1.23.6) of the growing power of Athens is implicitly contrasted with the Athenians' daring (*kinduneuein*, 6.9.3) in going to Sicily. This may simply be another instance of the distinct national character traits (as they have been called) of the combatants, as summarised in the speech of the Corinthians in Sparta in Book 1 (1.70.4).[68] But it also suggests the counterintuitive proposition that fear leads to victory while daring leads to defeat.[69] In both cases, *aphanês* specifies an unpredictable relationship between the "truth" about the historical past and its consequences for the historical future.[70]

Nicias' characterisation of the Athenians in 6.9.3 is also anticipated with no little irony in the Athenian commanders' characterisation of the Melians in the Melian dialogue. In their summation, the Athenians warn the Melians against looking to the future (5.113):

ἀλλ' οὖν μόνοι γε ἀπὸ τούτων τῶν βουλευμάτων, ὡς ἡμῖν δοκεῖτε, τὰ μὲν μέλλοντα τῶν ὁρωμένων σαφέστερα κρίνετε, τὰ δὲ ἀφανῆ τῷ βούλεσθαι ὡς γιγνόμενα ἤδη θεᾶσθε, καὶ Λακεδαιμονίοις καὶ τύχῃ καὶ ἐλπίσι πλεῖστον δὴ παραβεβλημένοι καὶ πιστεύσαντες πλεῖστον καὶ σφαλήσεσθε.

Well, you alone, as you seem to us, based on these resolutions, judge (*krinete*) what is future (*ta mellonta*) as more clear than what is before your eyes (*tôn horômenôn saphestera*), and – wishing it to be so – you look at what is invisible (*ta aphanê*) as happening (*gignomena theasthe*), and as you have staked your fortune and your hopes most on the Lacedaemonians and trusted most in them, so will you be most completely undone.

---

68 On these "national character traits," see Bassi 2005, 185, with the bibliography in note 45. Reynolds 2009, 347–354 shows how the Athenians and Spartans differ in their approaches to evaluating and acting upon signs and indirect evidence. Rengakos 2006, 291 notes that the "accelerated tempo of the narrative in the second part of the *Pentekontaetia* (98–118) ... serves to suggest that the *polypragmosunê* of Athens, the cause of Sparta's fear of increasing Athenian power (the ἀληθεστάτη πρόφασις of the Peloponnesian War), is turning into a growing threat."
69 At 6.6.1 Thucydides asserts that "the truest explanation" for the Sicilian Expedition was that the Athenians' were "aiming to rule the entire island" (ἐφιέμενοι μὲν τῇ ἀληθεστάτῃ προφάσει τῆς πάσης ἄρξαι) and that the Athenians hid this design under the pretence (*euprepôs*) of wishing to give aid to their kin and allies. Here again the "truest explanation" of the war (Spartan fear) can be contrasted with the "truest explanation" of the Sicilian Expedition (Athenian daring). Young-Bruehl 1986, 9–10 analyzes *prophasis* as a "form of proximate cause" in both passages.
70 Cf. Tsakmakis 2006, 168: "[Nicias] misjudges the possible effect of his second speech and provokes the opposite reaction to the one he intended (6.24)." This "opposite reaction" can be attributed to the fact that Nicias failed to heed his own cautionary remarks about what is *aphanês* in his first speech. Cf. Stahl 1973, 68, quoted by Morrison 2006a, 266: "What a sad triumph for Nicias to find the analysis he gave at Athens so thoroughly justified by the later course of events..." If there is a "sad triumph," it belongs to Thucydides.

As has long been noted, the narrative contiguity between the end of Book 5 (in which Thucydides' briefly describes the fate of the Melians, 5.116.4) and the beginning of Book 6 (when he turns the reader's attention to Sicily, 6.1.1) links the Athenians' killing and enslavement of the inhabitants of this small island with the defeat and captivity of their own forces on the larger island of Sicily.[71] The Melians are therefore not alone (*monoi*) since the speech says as much if not more about the Athenians' own lack of clarity about the future as it does about the Melians'.

Together with Nicias' speech to the Athenians, the Athenians' speech to the Melians creates a Janus-like effect in which the relationship of past to future is less a matter of linear chronology or cause and effect than of figuration and narrative structure.[72] Thus, while it may be true – as Gomme remarks – that putting faith in an unknown future is "by Thucydides' own judgement a fault to which all mankind is liable," the visual metaphor used to express this liability indicates that it is less a fault than a motivating principle of the *History*.[73] For if Nicias' words in Athens echo those of the Athenian commanders on Melos, both speeches also adopt the language of Thucydides' methodological statement at 1.22.4 (quoted above). More specifically, the wish (τῷ βούλεσθαι) to see what will happen recalls the historian's address to his future readers as those who "will wish to see the past and future clearly" (ὅσοι δὲ βουλήσονται 1.22.4). Outside the work's methodological framework and attributed to historical actors, this wish is embedded in a narrative about the limits of clarity or, to extend the metaphor, about the Athenians' blindness.

Finally, by way of a conclusion, I would like to turn briefly to Thucydides' account of the tyrannicide in Athens in Book 6. Inserted into the narrative following the departure of the fleet for Sicily in 415, the complexities of this narrative have been carefully analyzed by scholars.[74] My interest is in the two inscribed altars that, according to Thucydides, were dedicated by Hippias' son

---

71 See Liebeschuetz 1968, 76–77; Debnar 2001, 19; Rengakos 2006, 297. Gomme / Andrewes / Dover 1945–1981, vol. iv, pp. 180–187, review the scholarship and the debates to date, including comparisons with the speeches regarding Mytilene in Book 3.
72 Cf. Greenwood 2006, 9: "[T]he addition of the phrase 'possession for all time' ... suggests that the use of the future tense is deliberately open-ended." On Thucydides' contemporary audience, see Luraghi 2000.
73 Gomme / Andrewes / Dover 1945–1981 on 5.113 (p. 181). As Gomme notes, Pericles makes a virtue of this "fault" in the Funeral Oration (2.42.4).
74 Gomme / Andrewes / Dover 1945–1981, 317–329 summarise the points of the argument and its problems. Meyer 2008 provides a compelling account of the excursus on the tyannicide and its placement in the narrative, including its relationship to Thucydides' methodological statements in 1.22.

Peisistratus and serve as additional proof that Hippias and not his brother Hipparchus was tyrant at the time of the tyrannicide in 514 BCE (*History* 6.54.7):[75]

> καὶ τῷ μὲν ἐν τῇ ἀγορᾷ προσοικοδομήσας ὕστερον ὁ δῆμος Ἀθηναίων μεῖζον μῆκος τοῦ βωμοῦ ἠφάνισε τοὐπίγραμμα· τοῦ δ' ἐν Πυθίου ἔτι καὶ νῦν δῆλόν ἐστιν ἀμυδροῖς γράμμασι λέγον τάδε· μνῆμα τόδ' ἧς ἀρχῆς Πεισίστρατος Ἱππίου υἱὸς θῆκεν Ἀπόλλωνος Πυθίου ἐν τεμένει.

> Later the *dêmos* of the Athenians extended the length of the altar [to the twelve gods] in the agora, and in doing so it made the inscription disappear (*êphanise*). But [the inscription on the altar-stone] in the Pythian precinct is even now still (*eti kai nun*) visible (*dêlon*), although in indistinct letters (*amudrois grammasi*), and says the following:

> Peisistratus, the son of Hippias, set up this memorial
> to his office in the precinct of Pythian Apollo.

As evidence for the Athenians' ignorance of their own distant past, the effect of these inscriptions in the narrative seems unambiguous. According to Jonas Grethlein:[76]

> Thucydides only rarely refers to or even quotes inscriptions. I suggest that there is a simple explanation for the striking accumulation of inscriptions in the discussion of the tyrannicide. Thucydides wants to drive home the point that the truth about the tyrannicide is not that difficult to establish: 'One might also understand it simply from the following' (6.55.1). Seen from this angle, the references to the inscriptions are neither owed to a scientific attitude nor are they supposed to give readers insight into the historian's workshop, but they demonstrate the Athenians' sloppiness – they do not bother to take into account even what is open to everybody (to say nothing about serious research).

In other words, the inscriptions exemplify the extent to which "clear visible evidence" can be ignored. But the physical condition of the inscriptions, beginning with the statement that the *dêmos* made the inscription on the altar to the twelve

---

[75] Thucydides introduces this corrective at 1.20 as an example of the sorts of things that have been "forgotten because of time" (χρόνῳ ἀμνηστούμενα, 1.20.3). On this episode, see Bakker 2006, 116; Kallet 2006, 340–344; Meyer 2008, 29. On the significance of dedicatory inscriptions, exemplified by this passage in Thucydides, see Keesling 2005, 47. Immerwahr 1960, 280 refers to this passage as evidence for "the transitory nature of monuments" in Thucydides. Gomme / Andrewes / Dover 1945–1981, 317–329 summarise the points of the argument and its problems. Porter 2010, 515 briefly mentions Peisistratus' dedicatory inscription in the context of an illuminating discussion of the fragility of monuments.
[76] Grethlein 2010, 218. Cf. Meyer 2008, 29. Smarczyk 2006 provides an overview of the use of inscriptions in the *History* and in the context of Athens' "epigraphical culture" (the phrase is found on p. 501). He discusses the two inscriptions dedicated by Peisistratus, the son of Hippias, on pp. 507–509.

gods disappear (*êphanise*), both deepens and complicates this conclusion. Explained as the consequence of a building project, this inscription was visible in the past but is invisible in the present. As such, it concretises or literalises the metaphors of visibility and invisibility in the *History*. Together with the "indistinct" but still visible letters of the second inscription, moreover, it brings together the criteria of visibility and legibility (seeing and reading) as mediating factors between the historical past and the historical future where that future coincides with the historian's present (*eti kai nun*).

When the editor of a modern English translation of Thucydides' text remarks in a footnote that the altar stone "exists today and its inscription is still legible. See Illustration 6.54," that future also coincides with our own.[77] The intended effect of this datum and the accompanying photograph is clear; visible remains validate the historian's account of the past. But it also creates the effect of a *mise en abyme* in which the photograph stands in for the verbatim quotation of the inscription in the text.[78] And the fact that the inscription is barely visible in the photograph only ironically confirms – in our own eyes – Thucydides' description of its letters as "indistinct" (*amudrois grammasi*).[79] The combined fates of these two inscriptions thus constitute a material analogue to what Herodotus had presented as a general programmatic statement at the beginning of the *His-*

---

[77] The quotation is from Strassler 1996, 391. See Gomme / Andrewes / Dover 1945–1981, vol. iv. ad loc.: "The inscription survives (*IG* i².761 = ML 11 = Kirchner, *Imagines Inscriptionum Atticarum*, no. 11), and its letters are by no means 'faint' to us, as Greek inscriptions go; but no doubt the letters of any inscription a hundred years old were faint to Thucydides by contrast with the great number of much more recent inscriptions to be seen in Athens." See also, Meiggs and Lewis 1988, 19–20, who suggest that "The epithet ἀμυδροῖς... almost certainly refers to the disappearance of the paint with which the letters had been filled (20)." So also, Smarczyk 2006, 507–508. On the dating and archaeological evidence for the altars, including the debate over letter forms, see Gomme / Andrewes / Dover 1945–1981, ad loc. (specifically on *amudrois grammasi*).

[78] Walker 1993, 362 defines *mise en abyme* as a reference "to the character in the text whose activity somehow resembles ('replicates' or 'reflects') the activity of the reader." The "activity" that receives most attention in Walker's essay is the reader as spectator, figured by the description of the spectators who watch the Athenian fleet leaving for Sicily and those that watch the battle in Syracuse. He cites as exemplary Winkler's ground-breaking discussion of the opening scene of the *Aethiopica* (1982). As Walker rightly suggests, the *mise en abyme* "can call attention to the artificialities (and shortcomings) of representation, creating as a consequence a text concerned with discourse over and *against* representation" (p. 363, emphasis in the original). On photography's relationship to the "real," see Barthes 1986, 139. Gribble 1998 discusses the effects of focalisation in Thucydides. See also, Fowler 1996, 69–71 on what he calls the historian's "voiceprint."

[79] The adjective *amudros* ("indistinct") occurs only here in Thucydides.

tories, namely, the possibility that the past actions of human beings may fade with time. In invoking a future that comprehends both the present time of writing the *History* and the subsequent time of reading it, the fate of the inscriptions also illustrates, in Koselleck's suggestive phrase, "the boundaries of the possible otherness of our future."

This "possible otherness" is perhaps most vividly expressed in the cautionary speech of the Athenian envoys in Sparta before the war is declared (1.78.1–3):[80]

> τοῦ δὲ πολέμου τὸν παράλογον, ὅσος ἐστί, πρὶν ἐν αὐτῷ γενέσθαι προδιάγνωτε· μηκυνόμενος γὰρ φιλεῖ ἐς τύχας τὰ πολλὰ περιίστασθαι, ὧν ἴσον τε ἀπέχομεν καὶ ὁποτέρως ἔσται ἐν ἀδήλῳ κινδυνεύεται. ἰόντες τε οἱ ἄνθρωποι ἐς τοὺς πολέμους τῶν ἔργων πρότερον ἔχονται, ἃ χρῆν ὕστερον δρᾶν, κακοπαθοῦντες δὲ ἤδη τῶν λόγων ἅπτονται.
>
> Consider the unexpectedness (*paralogon*) of war, how great it is, before you become involved in it. As war is protracted it loves to leave many things to chance, of which we each have an equal share, and whichever way it will turn out is a risk taken in what cannot be seen (*en adêlôi*). For when men go to war they concern themselves with deeds first and the things that must be done later, but then when they are suffering ills they take hold of deliberation.

The observation that the unexpectedness of war (τοῦ δὲ πολέμου τὸν παράλογον) is a "commonplace in Thucydides" may support the assumption that this speech (or at least this part of it) is not based on documentary evidence but constitutes an opportunity for the historian to state a general principle.[81] But whether it is "authentic" or whether Thucydides added it "later," it anticipates his comment about the unexpected quality of the Athenians' "power and daring" in fighting two wars at once. Spoken by unnamed Athenian envoys who happen to be present in the Spartan Assembly (1.72.1), the principle is explained in terms similar to those invoked by Thucydides at 7.28: the length of the war, what the combatants think before and after it begins, and what they do as a consequence of the sufferings it inflicts (ἐκάκωσε, 7.27.3; cf. κακοπαθοῦντες, 1.78.3).

In spite of its cautious and generic qualities, however, the envoys' speech has the effect of inducing Sparta to enter a war that – by inference – the city is not expected to win (1.87–88). This inference is developed in the envoys' ref-

---

[80] Cf. 1.42.2 where the Corinthians admonish the Athenians not to enter into an alliance with the Corcyreans since "the coming of the war with which the Corcyreans frighten you and order you to act unjustly still lies in what is invisible" (καὶ τὸ μέλλον τοῦ πολέμου ᾧ φοβοῦντες ὑμᾶς Κερκυραῖοι κελεύουσιν ἀδικεῖν ἐν ἀφανεῖ ἔτι κεῖται). On this passage and the utility of predicting the war to come in the speeches of the Corcyreans and the Corinthians, see Ober 1998, 76–79.
[81] The quote is from Gomme / Andrewes / Dover 1959–1981, ad loc.

erences to the Battle of Salamis (1.73.4–74.2; cf. 1.144.3–4) and in the hesitant character of Archidamus' speech that follows (1.81.4–6). In short, what is implicitly *paralogon* before the war begins is the possibility that Athens will lose. From the vantage point of Thucydides' contemporaries, i.e., those Athenians who – like himself – had acted and suffered in the war, this possibility will have an immediate and singular impact.

But the historian has a different reading audience in mind, one for whom his work will be "a possession for all time" (*ktêma es aiei*, 1.22.4).[82] As a means of contrasting his own work with the sort of *muthôdes* that pleases for the moment (*parachrêma*) Thucydides extends the concept of the historical future (*ta mellonta*) into a future that never ends (*es aiei*). This may be nothing more than a straightforward expression of the historian's faith in the durability of his work. But if irony is inherent in hyperbole, the image of the *History* as an object that lasts forever has a contradictory effect. On the one hand, it resists the invisibility of the future by proclaiming the eternal legibility of the text. But in doing so, it also contributes to the conclusion that the future is the limiting factor of what can be known about the past, exemplified in the historian's account of the future ruins of Sparta and Athens.

---

[82] I discuss the ephemeral quality of *ktêmata* in the context of Thucydides' claim in Bassi 2005, 26–27. See also, Greenwood 2006, 6.

Nicolas Wiater
Shifting Endings, Ambiguity and Deferred Closure in Polybius' *Histories*

Finem lauda – the end matters: few things are more irritating than missing the end of a story, fictional or historical, and it is probably commonly agreed upon that the *denouement* is an essential, maybe the most important, part of a narrative. It is the point where the threads come together, where it all makes sense. In this chapter I will argue that Polybius deliberately denies his readers this 'sense of an ending', to adopt Frank Kermode's famous phrase, and the closure that would go hand-in-hand with it. Polybius, we might say, conceives his work as part of a *historia perpetua* not only with regard to the past, as a continuation of Timaeus' account (1.5.1), but also towards the future, by leaving his own narrative open-ended and to be continued by the narratives to come.

My argument is organised in two sections. The first section examines the role of the end in Polybius' authorial explanations about the new design of his work in the second preface, at the beginning of the third book. Polybius deliberately destroys the narrative and explanatory unity of the original design of his work by adding ten books that continue the narrative so as to include the events down to 146. Moreover, he specifically calls the last part of his work, the account of the period of ταραχὴ καὶ κίνησις, 'a new beginning' (3.4.13). This should be read, I argue, as a deliberate refusal to provide closure and a direct reflection of Polybius' assessment of the state of events after 146: the stability of the *oikumene* achieved by the rise of Roman power (συμπλοκή) and, with it, the future of the political structure of the Mediterranean had become an open question again, and it fell to future generations to create and record the results of this process. Through the openness of his narrative, Polybius encourages his readers to do exactly this and take an active stance in the flux of events to determine the future of Roman power and of the world in which they live. This fits with Polybius' conception of his readers as active statesmen and politicians whose decisions and actions the *Histories* seeks to shape: Polybius prepares his readers to take over where he leaves off.

This also provides a new angle on the question of whether Polybius believed that Roman power was about to fall or would endure. So far, any attempt to pin down Polybius' narrative on a definitive answer has failed and, I will argue, is bound to fail. The ambiguity inherent in Polybius' work can be read more profitably as part of the *Histories*' openness: at the time of the ταραχὴ καὶ κίνησις, neither Polybius nor his readers nor, indeed, the Romans were capable of anticipating the future development of Roman power. This is why Polybius prompts his readers actively to evaluate the quality of Roman power and then make a decision whether to support or oppose it (3.4.7–9), but he does not anticipate the results of this assessment and he does not seek to influence it. This is up to future generations of ἄνδρες πραγματικοί alone.

The second section underpins the interpretation of Polybius' authorial statements with an analysis of one of the ending points of the *Histories*, the destruction of Carthage. The discussion will show that this scene conveys the same sense of openness, uncertainty and lack of closure that informs the overall design of Polybius' narrative. Scipio pondering the possibility of the downfall of Roman power while triumphing over Rome's last big adversary encapsulates the ambiguous state of Roman power in 146, thus ending the *Histories* with a question to which only the readers can provide the answer.

1 Between teleology and contingency: Shifting endings, reader response and 'futurity' in the *Histories*

A discussion of the role of the future in the *Histories* needs to start with an exploration of the role of the beginning of Polybius' narrative. As will become clear in the course of the argument, in Polybius' concept of narrative and historical explanation one cannot be thought of without the other. At 1.1.5 Polybius describes the topic of the *Histories* as 'how and under what system of polity the Romans in less than fifty-three years', i.e., between 220 and 168/7 bce, 'succeeded in subjecting nearly the whole inhabited world to their sole government – a thing unique in history'.[1] He thus defines his work as a narrative distinguished by a clearly defined beginning and a clearly defined end and the explanatory power of this narrative as depending precisely on these two clearly defined temporal markers: understanding the rise of Roman power depends on understanding when this process began and when it ended.

It quickly emerges, however, that things are far more complicated. For, Polybius explains at 1.5.5, there lies a beginning before the beginning, and readers will need to understand the former in order to be able to understand the latter:

---

[1] Translations are taken, and often adapted, from Paton's Loeb, revised by F.W. Walbank and C. Habicht (6 vols. Cambridge, MA and London 2010–2012).

'For if there is any ignorance or indeed any dispute regarding the beginning, it is impossible that what follows should meet with acceptance [παραδοχῆς] or credence [πίστεως]'. He therefore separates the actual beginning of his *narrative* with the events of 220–217 in the third book[2] from the beginning of his *work*, i.e., the first and second books, which describe the events from the Romans' first military operation outside Italy, the crossing to Sicily in 264, down to the year 221.[3]

At the same time, Polybius is aware that the definition of such a fixed starting-point is an artificial act and conscious intervention of the narrator. Narratives of causes have a habit of spawning narratives seeking to explore the causes behind the causes,[4] thus resulting in a narrative as well as analytical *regressus in infinitum* away from the topic in question, into the depths of the past (1.5.3):[5]

> The actual cause of their crossing [to Sicily] must be stated without comment [ψιλῶς];[6] for if I were to seek the cause of the cause and so on, the beginning of my entire project and its examination [θεωρία] would lose their foundation [ἀνυπόστατος].

Even though these passages address problems of the beginning of Polybius' narrative, they contain aspects crucial for an exploration of the role of the future in the *Histories*. In particular, this concerns the importance Polybius attributes to continuity for historical understanding: only if a narrative starts from an agreed-upon beginning can readers be expected to accept (ἀποδοχῆς) 'all the subsequent narrative' (πᾶς ὁ συνεχὴς λόγος); this beginning, however, is not inherent in the historical events themselves but created by the narrative order that is imposed on these events artificially by the narrator. History does not begin, historical narratives do. The question of 'continuity' is thus placed prominently at the heart of Polybius' entire project.[7] It links the key factors truth and credibility with historical continuity, and historical continuity with the order given

---

[2] Specifically, Polybius identifies the 'Social War' (220–217), the 'Fourth Syrian War' (219–217), and the Romans' war against Hannibal (218–201) as the events marking the beginning of the rise of Roman power.
[3] The so-called *prokataskeue* (1.3.10); see Miltsios 2013, 30–57.
[4] Miltsios 2013, 16, speaks of 'repeated analepses'. He points out (ibid.) that even the *prokataskeue* contains several *analepses*, which he sees as 'the most direct proof of Polybius' concern with beginnings'.
[5] See Hoffmann 2002, 210, who detects an influence of Arist. *Metaph.* 1.994a1–2, 8–11.
[6] But see 1.12.5 with Rood 2007, 172–3.
[7] On the crucial importance in Polybian thought of the idea that the beginning determines the end see the illuminating, if somewhat simplifying, study by Hoffmann 2002.

to the events in and through the narrative.[8] The question of the role of the future is implied in the very concept of continuity as the key to historical understanding. Moreover, the kind of continuity Polybius has in mind here is the continuation of the narrative from the starting point into the future, that is, from 264 to 220 and beyond. This kind of future continuity can be achieved only through the deliberate rejection of its alternative, the infinite continuity of the narrative into the past in search of the causes behind the causes. Thus the beginning of Polybius' historical narrative already turns out to be all about future time: the *Histories* as Polybius defines it here is not simply a work about the past; it is deliberately and programmatically a work about the 'future past', the future, that is, as seen from the perspective of one specific point in the past.[9]

Consequently, the *Histories* in its original design, describing the development of Roman power from 220 to 168/7 in 28 books (excluding the *prokataskeue*), would have formed a carefully organised explanatory-cum-narrative unity with a well-defined beginning, middle and end (3.1.4–5):

> It is one event [ἑνὸς ἔργου] and one object of inquiry [θεάματος ἑνός] that the unity/ the whole [τοῦ σύμπαντος] consists of, about which I have undertaken to write, namely the how, when and, wherefore of the subjection of the known parts of the world to the dominion of Rome, and this unity has a recognized beginning [τὴν ἀρχὴν γνωριζομένην], a fixed duration [τὸν χρόνον ὡρισμένον], and a generally acknowlegded end [τὴν συντέλειαν ὁμολογουμένην]; I therefore think it will be advantageous to give a brief prefatory survey of the chief parts of this whole from the beginning to the end. For I believe this will be the best means of giving students an adequate idea of my whole plan [ἱκανὴν ἔννοιαν τῆς ὅλης ἐπιβολῆς].

---

8 Polybius identifies *res gestae* and *historia rerum gestarum*; see Zangara 2007, 42–43, and already Vattuone 1994, 9; see further Wiater (forthcoming); Grethlein 2013, 230–234. Narrative techniques are thus also ways of controlling the past (cf. n.40 below): Polybius prevents the period 'before the beginning' from becoming a narrative in its own right by de facto reducing its significance to an *analepsis* (ἀναδραμόντες τοῖς χρόνοις, 1.12.6) (Miltsios 2013, 13 and 74–79 on *analepses* in the *Histories*; cf. Rood 2007, 178), a period, that is, which becomes meaningless without the period to which it forms the precursor. This is borne out in the narrative by Polybius using the *prokataskeue* to 'promote the coherence of the narrative by highlighting links and firm connections between its different segments' and 'convey the work's key ideas' (Miltsios 2013, 16). It is important not to forget, however, that this 'stabilising' effect of the definition of beginnings comes at the price of the awareness of the artificiality of beginnings and, hence, of narrative, and thus historical, continuity. It is this latter aspect which I am interested in. Cf. Rood 2007, 173; Grethlein 2013, 235 and in this volume.
9 On the concept of 'futures past' see Grethlein 2013 and in this volume; on 'the assumption that […] the end is contained in the beginning' in Polybian thought Grethlein 2013, 226; cf. Hoffmann 2002.

Wholeness, completeness and unity are a dominant theme in this short passage. As at the beginning of the first book, to which this passage harks back, the key idea is that the power of Polybius' work to explain (ἱκανὴν ἔννοιαν) the 'how, when and wherefore' of the rise of Roman power is inextricably interwoven with two crucial assumptions: first, that the development of Roman power constitutes a unified structure within the past events; Polybius calls this the *symploke*,[10] the process brought about by *tyche* (1.4.1),[11] by which the individual states in the Mediterranean and their local histories become interdependent and integrated parts of the new, larger whole of Roman power. Second, that this unified structure of events is described, or rather represented, in an equally unified narrative structure, the design of Polybius' historical narrative: ἓν ἔργον and ἓν θέαμα.[12] The noticeable echoes of Aristotle, *Poetics* 23, in this passage need not concern us in detail here; it is important to note, however, that they indicate that Polybius invests the original design of his work with considerable aesthetic value alongside its explanatory function.[13] Historical understanding, narrative design and aesthetics form a tightly-knit complex.

This makes it all the more significant that shortly after the above passage Polybius deliberately unravels this unity, substituting the clearly-defined ending of both the historical development described in his work and his narrative with a horizon of uncertainty (3.4.1–8). The importance of this passage justifies citing it in full:

> Now if from their success or failure alone we could form an adequate judgment how far states and individuals are worthy of praise or blame, I could here lay down my pen, bringing my narrative and this whole work to a close with the last-mentioned events,[14] as was my original intention [κατὰ τὴν ἐξ ἀρχῆς πρόθεσιν]. For the period of fifty-three years finished here, and the growth and advance of Roman power had reached its completion [ἐτετελείωτο]. Besides which it now seemed universally accepted that henceforth all must submit to the Romans and obey their orders. But since judgments regarding either the conquerors or the conquered based purely on the actual struggle are by no means complete in themselves

---

10 Cf. Walbank 1975; Wiater (forthcoming).
11 On *tyche* see Hoffmann 2002, 202–6; Hau 2011; Maier 2012a, 224–245.
12 See n. 8 above.
13 On the Aristotelian echoes see Walbank 1957, 297; Hoffmann 2002, 211; Wiater (in preparation). Polybius probably knew Aristotle only 'über mehrere Mittelglieder' (Ziegler 1952, col. 1468; Hoffmann 2002, 211); Marincola (2010) and (2013). On the implications of this passage for the relationship between truth and narrative aesthetics in Polybian thought see Wiater (forthcoming).
14 The events mentioned at 3.3.8–9, including the Third Macedonian War (171–168) and the Sixth Syrian War, which the Romans brought to a close by forcing Antiochus IV Epiphanes to retreat from Egypt in 168.

[αὐτοτελεῖς] – what is thought to be the greatest success having brought the greatest calamities on many, if they do not make proper [δεόντως] use of it, and the most dreadful catastrophes [περιπετείας] often having turned into [περιπεπτωκέναι] the advantage of those who faced them bravely – I must append [προσθετέον] to the history of the above period an account of the subsequent attitude of those in power – what it was like after their success and how it caused them to exert their universal rule – as well as of the judgments and opinions about the rulers entertained by their subjects – how many there were and what kinds –, and finally I must describe what were the prevailing and dominant tendencies and ambitions of the various peoples in their private and public life. For it is evident that contemporaries will thus be able to see clearly whether the Roman rule is to be shunned or, on the contrary, be embraced, and future generations whether their government should be considered to have been worthy of praise and emulation or rather of blame. And indeed it is just in this that the chief usefulness [τὸ ὠφέλιμον (...) πλεῖστον] of this work for the present and the future [πρός τε τὸ παρὸν καὶ πρὸς τὸ μέλλον] will lie.

The radical nature of this modification to the original design of the *Histories* is not always properly appreciated.[15] The most fundamental change concerns the ending of the *Histories:* instead of a self-enclosed unity defined by beginning, middle and end, Polybius now describes the narrative as he had originally conceived it as 'not complete in itself' (αὐτοτελής). Together with ἐτετελείωτο, the term raises the question of the 'end' (τέλος) of the historical processes and their narrative representation alike. The passage thus provides a complement to Polybius' discussion of beginnings in the first book (see above): the problem there was the elusive nature of beginnings, which could only be overcome (if imperfectly) by the narrator artificially imposing such a beginning on the events. After this had been done, however, it seemed that the end of the process and the narrative describing it would be stable: the issue was not where to end the narrative, but where to begin it. At the beginning of the third book, this stability of the end has become as questionable and untenable as that of the beginning: the year 168 has lost its significance as an end to the historical process and its narrative alike.[16]

---

[15] Some scholars, most notably Erbse 1951, 175–6, and, more recently, Hoffmann ('eine einheitliche Konzeption', 2002, 214), even believe that Polybius always planned to add the last ten books. But if this were the case, why introduce them only in the third book and specifically define them as an addition, as Polybius manifestly does at 3.4.1–8 (esp. κατὰ τὴν ἐξ ἀρχῆς πρόθεσιν, 3.4.1; προσθετέον, 3.4.6)? A rare exception is Millar 1987, 3 ('crucial to his whole historical perspective').

[16] In developing my approach to the *Histories* as an open-ended narrative I have learnt a lot from David Levene's insightful discussion of Sallust's *Jugurtha* as a 'historical fragment' (Levene 1992).

But Polybius even goes one step further: he also defines the *Histories* in their revised design as open-ended, engaging in a sophisticated play with beginnings and endings (3.4.12–13):

> So the final end [τελεσιούργημα] achieved by this work will be, to gain knowledge of what was the condition of each people after all had been crushed and had come under the dominion of Rome, until (and including)¹⁷ the disturbed and troubled time that afterwards ensued.¹⁸ About this latter, owing to the importance of the actions and the unexpected character of the events, and chiefly because I not only witnessed most but took part and even directed some, I was induced to write as if making a new beginning [ἀρχὴν ποιησάμενος ἄλλην].

Playing with the double meaning of 'end' as 'ending point' and 'end' as 'purpose', the term τελεσιούργημα nicely encapsulates the shift away from the possibility of a meaningful concrete ending point of historical development and historical narrative alike towards a metaphorical ending of the *Histories*: their 'end' is not so much any longer the description of a specific event in the last book but the 'ethical' purpose of his narrative, the way in which it shapes the readers' attitudes and behaviour outside and beyond itself.¹⁹

It is against this background that we have to read Polybius' definition of the final portion of his work, the account of the 'disturbed and troubled time' (ταραχὴ καὶ κίνησις) between 158 and the traumatic destruction of both Carthage and Corinth in 146,²⁰ as 'a new beginning'. The interpretation that Polybius orig-

---

[17] I agree with Grethlein 2013, 238–239, that ἕως is inclusive, readers are expected to include the period of ταραχὴ καὶ κίνησις in their assessment of the quality of Roman power.

[18] Polybius is distinguishing *three* distinct periods: the period of the rise of Roman power is followed by a period of stability (μετὰ τὸ καταγωνισθῆναι τὰ ὅλα καὶ πεσεῖν εἰς τὴν τῶν Ῥωμαίων ἐξουσίαν) which reaches up to the third period of ταραχὴ καὶ κίνησις. Μετὰ ταῦτα (3.4.12), referring to the events preceding the ταραχὴ καὶ κίνησις, cannot therefore 'hark back to τὸ καταγωνισθῆναι τὰ ὅλα καὶ πεσεῖν εἰς τὴν τῶν Ῥωμαίων ἐξουσίαν and signify the time of Rome's ascension' (Grethlein 2013, 238), as this would make the period of ταραχὴ καὶ κίνησις the second and final period.

[19] With Wayne C. Booth (1988, 8) I use the term 'ethical' as referring to 'the entire range of effects on the "character" or "person" or "self"'.

[20] The beginning of the period of ταραχὴ καὶ κίνησις is debated in scholarship. Walbank's (1957, 303) suggestion of 151, which is accepted by Baronowski (2011, 160), is based solely on the unfounded assumption that the geographical excursus of book 34 must have marked the beginning of this new part of the narrative. This is flatly contradicted by the fact that the earliest events of this period listed by Polybius at 3.5.1–3 occurred in 158, namely the expulsion of the Cappadocian king Ariarathes IV (3.5.2). More importantly, this discussion misses the point that ἀρχὴν ἄλλην does not refer to the beginning of the ταραχὴ καὶ κίνησις at all but de-

inally intended to write a 'separate monograph' about this period (Grethlein 2013, 239) is excluded by οἷον: Polybius is speaking figuratively, describing the ambiguous character of what is supposed to conclude ('bring to an end') his narrative,[21] an ambiguity further emphasised by Polybius calling the ending point of his narrative, the fall of Corinth and Carthage and the demise of the Achaean League, 'the beginning and end of the general calamity of Greece' (ἅμα τὴν ἀρχὴν καὶ τὸ τέλος ἔσχε τὸ κοινὸν ἀτύχημα πάσης τῆς Ἑλλάδος, 3.5.6). Beginning and end are conflated in the final part of the *Histories*, and just as beginnings spawn ever new narratives into the past, about their beginnings, unless the narrator puts a halt to them, endings merely defer the end further into the future and, as such, constitute new beginnings: choosing 168/7 as the original ending point merely deferred the end of the narrative to 146, and 146 opens it up into the future. The *Histories* stop, but they never end.

Understandably, Polybius' statement about the ταραχὴ καὶ κίνησις has caused considerable debate about its implications for his view of Roman power. Especially when read against Polybius' earlier statement, that after 168 it 'seemed universally accepted that henceforth all must submit to the Romans and obey their orders' (3.4.3), ending the *Histories* with a renewed (πάλιν, 3.4.12) period of disturbance and unrest inevitably raises the question of the stability of Roman power after 158 at the latest. πάλιν refers to a renewal of the state of affairs during the time when the Romans were still establishing their universal rule through a series of wars and struggles (note καταγωνισθῆναι τὰ ὅλα, 3.4.12).[22] The passage therefore suggests an unravelling of the συμπλοκή,[23] much rather than that Rome 'managed to cope' with these turmoils, let alone that she emerged from them 'stronger than before'.[24] And while Walbank is right that

---

fines this *entire period*, that is, all events cumulatively, as constituting a new phase both in history and in Polybius' historical narrative. Full discussion in Wiater (in preparation).
21 Also note the tenses of ποιησάμενος and γράφειν: it is through the continuous narrative (present) of the events of the ταραχὴ καὶ κίνησις that Pol. 'makes' (aorist) the 'new beginning'.
22 Thus, rightly, Grethlein 2013, 238.
23 Cf. Dreyer 2011, 63.
24 Grethlein 2013, 239; but see his chapter in this volume for a more nuanced approach that is close to my own reading; Hoffmann 2002, 220–221. Cf. Baronowski 2011, 90, who sees the period between 168 and 145 as 'a phase characterized by preservation', and ibid. 161: 'the extension of the *Histories* was intended to show that Roman power would endure in the foreseeable future. Contemporaries must accept Roman rule, not only because Rome was stronger but also because her dominion was moderate and beneficent'. Baronowski's struggle to reconcile the passages pointing to the possibility of a demise of the Roman empire with his own interpretation of a continuing and uninterrupted 'moderate and beneficent' (ibid. 161) character of Roman

'it nowhere implies that the verdict will be unfavourable to Roman rule',[25] it should be stressed that there is no implication of a favourable verdict, either.[26]

I argue that the attempt to identify a pro- or anti-Roman slant in this passage misses the point: the purpose of chapter 3.4 is precisely to inscribe the future of Roman power (and its narrative) into an horizon of uncertainty. The *Histories* in its revised design poses the question of the future development, rather than answer it.[27] Moreover, through its deliberate open-endedness,[28] Polybius' narrative passes the ball to the readers, creating, quite literally, a blank space for them to fill.

This fits well with Polybius' envisaged readership. Polybius conceives of the relationship between author and reader, text and extra-textual reality, as cyclical. At the heart of this conception is the idea of both author and reader as ἀνὴρ πραγματικός:[29] the purpose of historiography is to provide guidance for present and future generations of political and military leaders, but it can do so only if historical authors, like Polybius, have themselves had a successful career in politics and warfare.[30] Based (partly) on the experience gained from such reliable ('pragmatic') historical accounts, readers can assess concrete situations in war and politics more competently and have a better chance of choosing a successful course of action.[31] Afterwards, they will ideally write down their own experiences, just as Polybius did, thus converting their own achievements into knowledge and experience for the next generation(s) of statesmen.[32]

---

power only demonstrates that Polybius' text is too complex to be forced into such a straightforward and one-sided reading.

25 Walbank 1957, 302.
26 *Pace* Ferrary 1988, 341–343.
27 Cf. Grethlein (this volume).
28 See above and the discussion of 38.21 in section 2 below.
29 See, e.g., 7.11.1–2; 9.1.4, 9.9–10; 15.36; cf. 18.15; cf. Meissner 1986, esp. 346–348.
30 See Wiater 2010, 99–104; Maier 2012a, 273–340; 2012c.
31 The key passage is 12.25b.2–3: 'The mere statement of a fact may intrigue us but is of no benefit to us: but when we add the cause of it, study of history becomes fruitful. It is the mental transference of similar circumstances to our own times [ἐκ (...) τῶν ὁμοίων ἐπὶ τοὺς οἰκείους μεταφερομένων καιρούς] that gives us the means of forming presentiments of what is about to happen, and enables us at certain times to take precautions and at others by modelling our own actions on past actions to face with more confidence the difficulties that menace us'. This statement must not be misinterpreted as implying a simplistic deterministic worldview on Polybius' part. The comparative θαρραλεώτερον is instrumental: choosing a course of action based on knowledge of the past merely has a greater chance of success than simply picking one at random: there is no alternative to rational analysis of the present on the basis of experience, but success is never guaranteed. See Maier 2012a, 91–98, 280–284, esp. 281.
32 See esp. 12.28.3–5: 'it will be well with history either when men of action undertake to write history, not as now happens in a perfunctory manner, but when in the belief that this is

It is to such an active reader-cum-statesman that the openness of the *Histories* is addressed. Polybius sends a clear signal that his own evaluation of the quality of Roman power is no longer decisive. It is now up to his readers, in leading positions in politics and the military all over the *oikumene*, to assess the quality of Roman power and their own situation within it and, on this basis, devise a course of action (φευκτὴν ἢ τοὐναντίον αἱρετήν, ἐπαινετὴν καὶ ζηλωτὴν ἢ ψεκτήν, 3.4.7). Polybius is thus integrating the responses of his readers to his account into the scope of his work by prompting them to determine (and write) the contents of the next chapters of the story of Roman power begun by Polybius. By re-defining his narrative as merely a large chapter of a narrative that remains as yet to be enacted *and* written, he takes away one vantage point, from which the past makes sense, and substitutes it with a plethora of vantage points and, consequently, a plethora of continuously shifting senses of the past:[33] his readers are prompted to supply an ever-renewed end to the 'new beginning' constituted by the last part his work. Whether the plethora of historical works resulting from this process will tell the story of Rome's recovery from the ταραχὴ καὶ κίνησις or the continuing demise of Roman power is in his readers' hands.

The openness of the *Histories* can be productively brought into dialogue with Amir Eshel's concept of 'futurity'.[34] Drawing on Richard Rorty's notion of 're-description', that is, the way in which 'writers and readers of literature reconstitute themselves [...] by telling and retelling stories about where they came from and where they are going',[35] Eshel examines the ways in which narratives prompt and help readers to deal actively and constructively with collective traumas such as the Holocaust in their own lives. He explores how literature produces 'narrative sequences' and a specific vocabulary 'we use to describe ourselves and our realities and thus the very language we draw on as we reshape ourselves' and the ways in which it confronts readers with 'ethically and politically ambivalent situations', thereby helping 'to open possibilities for the future by inviting us to debate what may have caused' a particular traumatic situation (Eshel

---

a most necessary and most noble thing they apply themselves all through their life to it with undivided attention, or again when would-be authors regard a training in actual affairs as necessary for writing history'.

[33] Grethlein (this volume) speaks of a potential *regressus ad infinitum* with regard to the reader's future stance towards Rome's past military successes.

[34] Eshel 2013.

[35] Eshel 2013, 9, citing R. Rorty, *Contingency, Irony, and Solidarity*, Cambridge 1989, 40–41, and 'Persuasion is a Good Thing', in *Take Care of Freedom and Truth Will Take Care of Itself*, Stanford 2006, 70–72.

speaks of 'catastrophe') and 'what might make its recurrence unlikely'.[36] Literature, he continues, 'creates the "open, future, possible" by expanding our vocabularies, by probing the human ability to act, and by prompting reflection and debate'.[37] Instead of an object of inquiry, the past thus becomes the basis for present and future action, it becomes a 'domain of the practical'.[38]

Even though Eshel's discussion focuses on contemporary fictional literature, 'futurity' provides us with a useful theoretical tool to conceptualise the interrelation of past narrative and future action in the *Histories*. In particular, I argue, the change in the design of the *Histories* reflects exactly a change in emphasis from the past as an object of historical inquiry to the 'practical past', a change which goes hand-in-hand with a shift from a predominantly author- to a predominantly reader-centred narrative.

In the original conception of the *Histories*, the reader was, quite literally, a spectator,[39] watching the narrator unfold the interrelations of the individual events, thus revealing the new *symploke* structure of the *oikumene* under Roman rule. The narrator, in this setup, was the reader's guide through a complex and variegated landscape of the past, selecting, arranging and showing them only the relevant bits in order to make the hidden processes visible that were underlying the development of Roman hegemony.[40]

---

[36] Eshel 2013, 4.
[37] Ibid.
[38] Eshel 2013, 10, adopting Oakshott's concept of the 'practical past'.
[39] Visual metaphors are an important element of Polybius' conceptual vocabulary, e.g. 1.1.6 (θεαμάτων) about the topic of his work, the rise of Roman power; 1.2.7 (θεώρημα); 1.4.3 (ὁρῶν); 1.4.11 (κατοπτεύσας), and generally the idea of history as a body developed in 1.4, as well as Polybius' emphasis on σύνοψις as distinctive of his universal historical approach (e.g., 1.4.1; 14.1a.1). See Zangara 2007, 40–54; Wiater (forthcoming); cf. Davidson 1991; Vattuone 1994.
[40] This is another important aspect of the close interrelation of narrative structure and historical interpretation in Polybius' thought (see n.8 above). Selection is crucial to Polybius' concept of the superior truth provided by his universal history as opposed to local historians' accounts which focus on events of only local importance and compromise historical truth by elaborating on them in order to make them seem more important than they really are, see esp. 29.12.3–9. It is by granting each event the narrative treatment 'it deserves' (τὸν καθήκοντα λόγον, 29.12.6), which includes not mentioning many events at all, that the account of universal histories is 'true and unvarnished' (τὸν ἀληθῆ καὶ κύριον [...] λόγον, 29.12.8). I will discuss this aspect of Polybius' work in a chapter on 'Dealing with Diversity: (Re-)Defining the (Greek) World in Polybius, Dionysius and Chariton', in preparation for J. König/ N. Wiater (eds.), *Rethinking Late Hellenistic Greek Literature and the Second Sophistic*. Proceedings of a Conference held at St Andrews, 5. and 6. September 2013; cf. Grethlein 2013, 247–248.

To be sure, the 'practical' benefits of history, the *Histories*' usefulness for a political career and for dealing with the vicissitudes of fortune, were already important in this design, but they were taken for granted and secondary to 'the very unexpectedness [παράδοξον] of the events I have chosen as my theme' (1.1.4) and the *Histories*' main purpose, to understand (γνῶναι) 'by what means and under what system of polity the Romans in less than fifty-three years have succeeded in subjecting nearly the whole inhabited world to their sole government – a thing unique in history' (1.1.5).[41] Contrast this with 3.4.1–8 and the shift described there of the focus of the narrative to what happens outside and beyond it: the usefulness of Polybius' work, its influence on the readers' actions, has now become an aspect at least as crucial and prominent (ὠφέλιμον […] πλεῖστον) as acquiring knowledge about Roman power and its development. The *Histories* is, quite literally, 'probing' the readers 'to act' and prompt 'reflection and debate', namely about the nature, quality and response to Roman power.

Vocabulary, concepts and narrative structures play a crucial role in this process. In their original design, the *Histories* provided the readers with a powerful metaphor to conceptualise the subjugation of the entire *oikumene* under Roman power – an event which might not quite qualify as a 'catastrophe' in Eshel's sense but is clearly and frequently marked as an unprecedented, maybe even shocking, occurrence by Polybius from the very beginning of his work.[42] Polybius offers his readers the metaphor of the συμπλοκή and the image of the individual parts of the world as having now finally become the parts of a complete, beautiful body (1.4.3–11, esp. καλοῦ σώματος, ἐνεργείας […] καὶ καλλονῆς, 1.4.7) to come to terms with this event. The concept of Roman power as the uniting force of a beautiful body, the limbs of which were previously 'dissevered' (διερριμμένα, 1.4.8), invests the rise of Roman power with a strongly positive aesthetic note, thus inviting a generally favourable response from the reader.[43]

Matters are much less clear, as mentioned above, for the second, this time truly traumatic, event on which the *Histories* prompts reflection and towards which it invites the readers to take a stance: the destruction of Corinth (and Carthage) and the demise of the Achaean League in the same year 146, the 'beginning and end of the general calamity of Greece' (3.5.6, cited above). While the *Histories* in its original design invited readers to view themselves as part of a

---

[41] Note that Polybius introduces the 'practical benefits' of his work in the form of a *praeteritio* (1.1.1).

[42] 1.1.4: τὸ παράδοξον τῶν πράξεων; 1.1.5: ὃ πρότερον οὐχ εὑρίσκεται γεγονός; 1.2.1: παράδοξον καὶ μέγα; 1.4.1: τὸ […] θαυμάσιον τῶν καθ' ἡμᾶς καιρῶν.

[43] I will discuss this in detail in 'Dealing with Diversity' (n. 40 above).

transformation from the 'particular' (κατὰ μέρος) to the 'universal' (καθόλου) (1.4.3),⁴⁴ from the limbs to the complete body, the new, open-ended structure of the narrative invites readers critically to assess whether the original metaphor of the συμπλοκή still offers a useful and profitable way of conceptualising Roman power and its effects and to take steps accordingly.

As pointed out above, Polybius does not anticipate the results of this intellectual process. This notwithstanding, the new focus on the individual readers' judgment and actions, in their respective parts of the *oikumene*, as the determining factors of the future development of Roman power clearly does lead to a shift of emphasis back from the καθόλου to the κατὰ μέρος, from the body to its limbs, and from the centre of Roman power to the periphery. As Polybius puts it programmatically at 3.4.12 (cited above): the purpose of his work is now τὸ γνῶναι τὴν κατάστασιν *παρ' ἑκάστοις*, ποία τις ἦν μετὰ τὸ καταγωνισθῆναι *τὰ ὅλα* καὶ πεσεῖν εἰς τὴν τῶν Ῥωμαίων ἐξουσίαν. The dense, crowded and packed list of the events occurring in the period of ταραχὴ καὶ κίνησις in the individual theatres of action all over the *oikumene* (3.5.1–6) clearly reflects this shift in the narrative from the universal back to the particular and from order to disorder. As does the very addition of ten books which deliberately mars the perfect, analytical, narrative and aesthetic unity of the original design (ἓν ἔργον and ἓν θέαμα),⁴⁵ as well as the diminishing distance between Polybius as a narrator and Polybius as an active participant in the events in the last phase of his narrative, which eventually collapses the two sides of the ἀνὴρ πραγματικός:⁴⁶ Polybius' passage from historical inquirer to 'eye-witness' (αὐτόπτης), 'participant' (συνεργός) and 'actor' (χειριστής) (3.4.13, cited above) mirrors the passage expected of the reader from 'spectator' of the rise of Roman power to active participant in the shaping of its future.⁴⁷ It is up to them to decide whether it is still worthwhile to conceive of themselves and their peoples as integrated parts of a larger whole and to record their actions and the outcome of these actions for future generations.

These observations should warn us not to overemphasise the teleological aspect of Polybius' thought.⁴⁸ Teleology certainly played an important part in the

---

44 See esp. τὴν καθόλου καὶ συλλήβδην οἰκονομίαν (ibid.).
45 See p. 246–247 above.
46 Cf. p. 251 above.
47 Polybius repeatedly stresses that even the actions of one man can effect the entire *oikumene*; see, e.g., 1.35.4–5 (Xanthippus); 8.3.3, 7.7 (Archimedes); 9.22 (Hannibal).
48 Hoffmann 2002, though he makes many important observations, is too extreme; Grethlein 2013 still sees Polybius as a champion of teleology but offers a more nuanced discussion, taking into account the narrative elements (the 'mimetic' narrative) that allow readers to experience the

first design of the *Histories* but is deliberately undercut through the revised design. And by announcing the revision to the structure of his work at the beginning of the third book, the beginning of the historical narrative proper, Polybius makes this tension between teleology and openness, between, in Bernstein's terms, backshadowing and sideshadowing,[49] a constitutive element of his narrative from the start.[50] This tension between teleology and contingency, between the *Histories* in their original and the *Histories* in their revised versions, can itself be seen as Polybius enacting his experience of the nature of events through his historical narrative. The idea that events can take sudden turns and thus unexpectedly change the course of history (for the better and for the worse) is prominent throughout the *Histories*;[51] in fact, Polybius defines fostering the ability to deal with such sudden reversals of fortune as one of the key purposes of historiography.[52] The realisation that constellations of events and, with them, their evaluation, can change quickly and unexpectedly also lies behind his decision to undercut the previous concept and design of his work by adding the last ten books (3.4.5–6, cited above):

> since judgments regarding either the conquerors or the conquered based purely on the actual struggle are by no means complete in themselves [αὐτοτελεῖς] – what is thought to be the greatest success having brought the greatest calamities [συμφοράς] on many, if they do not make proper [δεόντως] use of it, and the most dreadful catastrophes [περιπετείας] often having turned into [περιπεπτωκέναι] the advantage of those who faced them bravely – I

---

openness of the past as it happens, as well as the analytical passages, which strongly draw on the benefit of hindsight. The best and most comprehensive study of this important topic is Maier 2012a, who shows conclusively that contingency is a much more prominent element of Polybius' historical thought than has previously been acknowledged.

49 Bernstein 1994. Sideshadowing should be added to the narrative features that prompt readers to reflect and act in Eshel's sense (see above): it rejects an analytical concept of truth as preordained (and, hence, detectable from within the flux of events), locating it instead 'in the ordinary and quotidian actions of our communal existence', and by creating awareness of temporality and 'a recognition of the differences it entails' it is 'an indispensable foundation of moral judgment' (Bernstein 1994, 92–93). For an application of the concept to ancient texts see Grethlein 2010; 2013, esp. 15; Maier 2012a, 118–137.

50 It is true that Polybius asks readers to evaluate Roman power only on the basis of the last ten books. But it is difficult to believe that Polybius' very statement at 3.4.6–8, that Roman power is in need of evaluation, is not meant to shape the reader's attitude towards the Roman empire from the third book onwards.

51 See, e.g., 1.13.11, 37.3; 3.97.8; 9.8.6; 9.3; 20.5.6. For complete references see *Polybios-Lexikon* s.v. περιπέτεια 1, 2 and 3a, listing 6 counts of περιπέτεια favourable (s.v. 2), and 48 counts of περιπέτεια unfavourable to the historical actors (s.v. 3).

52 1.1.2: the τῶν ἀλλοτρίων περιπετειῶν ὑπόμνησις as ἐναργεστάτη [...] καὶ μόνη διδάσκαλος τοῦ δύνασθαι τὰς τύχης μεταβολὰς γενναίως ὑποφέρειν.

must append [προσθετέον] to the history of the above period an account of the subsequent attitude of those in power [...].

The historical writer Polybius thus puts into practice the experiences of the historical actor Polybius, presumably especially those during the period of ταραχὴ καὶ κίνησις,[53] which, as demonstrated above, raised the possibility of an unravelling of the συμπλοκή and prominently posed the question of the future of Roman power and the sequel to Polybius' *Histories*. The change in design thus not only shows us Polybius learning from history and acting upon it. The 40, instead of 30, books are also a physical representation of the force of contingency (περιπέτεια) in history and an effective demonstration of how ideas and concepts taken for granted can suddenly be in danger of becoming meaningless through unexpected turns of events.

2 Lack of closure enacted: Multiple perspectives in Polybius' account of the fall of Carthage

A discussion of the role of endings in the *Histories* would not be complete without at least a glimpse of the actual end of Polybius' narrative. The lacunose state of this part of the *Histories* makes a comprehensive discussion impossible. Fortunately, however, we do have parts of Polybius' account of one of the catastrophic events in which the period of ταραχὴ καὶ κίνησις culminates, the destruction of Carthage in book 38. The remains of this episode allow us to offer some remarks on how the horizon of insecurity into which Polybius inscribes his work in the third book translated into the narrative parts of the *Histories*.

Since, as shown in the previous section, Polybius describes the ending point of his account in terms of a new beginning, it is significant that his description of the destruction of Carthage contains a prediction of the future (38.21):

> [...] so it is said by <the poet> [sc. Homer, *Iliad* 6.448–9: 'A day will come when sacred Troy shall perish, And Priam and his people shall be slain']⁵⁴. Turning round to me at once and

---

53 Cf. Walbank 1972, 18.
54 This information has to be supplied from Appian's account of the event, *Pun.* 132 (= Pol. 38.22); cf. DS 32.24. Where exactly reference was made to Homer in the original text (and whether the lines from the *Iliad* were quoted *verbatim*) is difficult to determine. There is little room before the beginning of this fragment, but maybe just enough to fit in the reference to the *Iliad*. However, since this fragment is itself only an excerpt, the text might have been altered by the excerptor and the quotation cut out as unnecessary. From the fact that the quotation occurs in both Appian and Diodorus,

grasping my hand Scipio said, 'A glorious moment, Polybius; but I dread and foresee that some day the same doom will be pronounced on my own country'. It would be difficult to mention an utterance more statesmanlike and more profound. For at the moment of our greatest triumph and of disaster to our enemies to reflect on our own situation and on the possible reversal of circumstances, and generally to bear in mind at the season of success the mutability of Fortune, is like a great and perfect man, a man in short worthy to be remembered.

As Tim Rood has pointed out, Scipio's tears (which we have to supply from Appian's and Diodorus' accounts) introduce several layers of meaning into this episode. They evoke 'Antiochus' tears towards the end of Hieronymus' history, while the general stress on mutability also looks back to Herodotus' reflection that cities once great were now small and that cities now great were once small (1.5.4) and to Thucydides' anticipation of Athens and Sparta as ruins (1.10.2)'.[55] Moreover, there is an important intra-textual reference to which Hornblower has drawn attention, namely Demetrius of Phalerum's prediction of the fall of the Macedonian empire as an example of the mutability of fortune in his treatise *On Fortune*, which would have concluded the *Histories* in its original design (29.21.1–7):[56]

> It is therefore appropriate to call to mind, often and in earnest, the words of Demetrius of Phalerum [...]: 'For if you consider not countless years or many generations, but merely these last fifty years, you will read in them the cruelty of Fortune. I ask you, do you think that fifty years ago either the Persians and the Persian king or the Macedonians and the king of Macedon, if some god had foretold the future to them, would ever have believed that at the time when we live, the very name of the Persians would have perished utterly – the Persians who were masters of almost the whole world – and that the Macedonians, whose name was formerly almost unknown, would now be the lords of it all? But nevertheless this Fortune, who never compacts with life, who always defeats our reckoning by some novel stroke; she who ever demonstrates her power by foiling our expectations, now also, as it seems to me, makes it clear to all men, by endowing the Macedonians

---

Walbank (1979, 723) convincingly concludes that it was in Polybius' text; we simply do not know where exactly. Diodorus has Scipio quote the couplet as an explanation for his tears when watching Carthage burn, while in Appian Scipio weeps, cites Homer and is then asked by Polybius to explain the quotation (ὁ λόγος, 38.22.3). Since it seems more likely that Polybius would enquire about Scipio's tears rather than the meaning of the quotation, Diodorus' version might be closer to Polybius' original account (Walbank ibid.), but we cannot know.

55 Rood 2007, 181; Baronowski 2011, 153, compares the tears of Antigonus when seeing the head of Pyrrhus and the tears of Xerxes at Abydus (Hdt. 7.45–6); cf. Grethlein 2013, 261–262. The latter parallel extends to Xerxes being asked about his tears by Artabanus, just as Polybius asks Scipio to explain his tears. On the motif of the 'victor weeping over the vanquished' see already Hornblower 1981, 104–106, citing these and other passages.

56 Hornblower 1981, 105.

with the whole wealth of Persia, that she has but lent them these blessings until she decides to deal differently with them.' And this now happened in the time of Perseus.

Baronowski, quite rightly, sees both passages as an expression of 'the transience of imperial power as a leading motif in Polybius' work'.[57] However, the power and reliability of both Demetrius' prediction and Scipio's foreboding are much more complex and ambiguous than Baronowski acknowledges. In fact, neither passage should be taken to imply any reliable conclusions about the future of the Roman empire, positive or negative.

To begin with, while Polybius recalls Demetrius' prediction *after* Perseus' empire has actually fallen (and the Romans have taken over, just as the Macedonians once took over from the Persians), when Scipio is speaking the future of Roman power is still completely open. This fits the result of the discussion in the preceding section, that the last ten books reduce the distance between historical narrator and historical actor, thus prompting the readers' transition from 'spectators' of the rise of Roman power to active and determining factors in its future.[58] At the end of book 38, Scipio and the readers face the same uncertainty about Rome's future: 'The "future past" that creates a gap between historical agents and historians is transformed into a pure future, the distinction between the former and the latter being erased'.[59]

Moreover, it often goes unnoticed that Demetrius of Phalerum's prediction is inherently contradictory, as it combines the idea of the unpredictability of the reversals of *tyche* with an attempt to anticipate the future on the basis of regularities identified in past historical processes. As much as Demetrius emphasises the unpredictability of *tyche*, his view of the future of the Macedonian empire is ultimately based on the pattern of the succession of empires. This, in turn, evokes Polybius' own enumeration of the different empires preceding that of the Romans at 1.2.1–7. Polybius even invites the reader to bring Demetrius' prediction into dialogue with his enumeration and to inscribe the Romans into the historical pattern identified by Demetrius: since the fall of the Macedonian empire, in the context of which Polybius relates the prediction, constitutes the final step of the Romans' rise to universal power (the completion of the συμπλοκή), the parallel between the formerly unknown Macedonians who took over from the Persians, and the Italian community from the margins of the Greek world now taking the place of the Macedonians, almost seems inevitable.[60] Polybius

---

57 Baronowski 2011, 154.
58 See above, p. 253–255.
59 Grethlein 2013, 262.
60 Cf. Baronowski 2011, 154.

thus undoubtedly conjures up the notion that the Roman empire, too, will eventually fall, just like the empires preceding it. At the same time, however, he calls the applicability of the pattern of the rise and fall of empires to Roman power into question by emphasizing that Rome is, in fact, very *un*-like her predecessors, something entirely new and unexpected (παράδοξον, 1.1.4; ὃ πρότερον οὐχ εὑρίσκεται γεγονός, 1.1.5; τὸ [...] τῆς ἡμετέρας πραγματείας ἴδιον καὶ τὸ θαυμάσιον τῶν καθ' ἡμᾶς καιρῶν, 1.4.1).[61]

As in Demetrius' prediction, regularity and contingency undercut each other and leave the reader with a profound sense of uncertainty and an awareness of the ambiguity of historical processes. Polybius' text does not allow for definitive statements about the future nor does it reveal methods of how to anticipate it. It does invite readers to ponder possible developments of the future on the basis of similar events in the past,[62] but it also balances the idea of the reliability of such anticipations with the awareness of the power of the unpredictable (*tyche*).[63] By evoking Demetrius' prediction and the former end of the *Histories*, 38.21 prompts readers to reflect on the possibilities of and limits to anticipating future development on the basis of an analysis of past events. The passage thus reflects the same tension between backshadowing and sideshadowing that I argued above is constitutive of the revised design of the *Histories* as a whole.

These considerations have important consequences for our approach to the prediction at the new 'end' of the *Histories*, Scipio's reaction to the fall of Carthage. In particular, as Walbank (1979, 724) has already pointed out, the scene should not be taken to imply a simple pessimistic outlook on the future of Roman power and an allusion to the fall of the city and its empire.[64] However, the purely psychological reading that 'the flames [...] impressed Scipio as a melancholy illustration of the mutability of human fortune', suggested by Walbank (ibid.), is not satisfactory either: Scipio's words 'I have a dread foreboding that

---

61 Cf. Marincola 1997, 38.
62 See above, p. 251.
63 See above, p. 255–258. Álvarez de Miranda (1956, 54–56) senses the similarity between Demetrius and Polybius but wrongly concludes that Polybius intends to invest his pragmatic historiography with a sort of oracular power allowing readers to make predictions about the future on a 'scientific and rational' basis (56); Walbank (1979, 394) rightly criticises this conclusion by pointing out that 'Demetrius' foresight [...] was merely a deduction from the behaviour of *Tyche*'. It should be noted that this criticism does not concern the existence of the similarities, merely the conclusions Álvarez de Miranda draws from them.
64 Thus, most recently, Grethlein 2013, 262: 'the capture of Troy [...] serves as a mirror to the fall of Carthage, present for Scipio and past for the narrator. At the same time, Scipio makes it adumbrate something that is future not only for him, but also for the narrator: the downfall of Rome'; Eckstein 1995, 232.

some day the same doom will be pronounced upon my own country' explicitly raise the question of the implications of the fall of Carthage for the future of Roman power, especially when read alongside Demetrius' prophecy and the pattern of the succession of empires introduced by Polybius himself at 1.2.1–7. The narrative thus leaves the reader with the same question that was implied in Polybius' description of the new design of his work in the third book, and, as at the beginning of the third book, there is no clear-cut answer.

This uncertainty, I will argue now, is borne out in the episode itself. Moreover, it is born out through that very element, the Homeric quotation, which appears to invite a 'pessimistic' interpretation of Scipio's forebodings because it draws a parallel between Carthage and Troy and thus evokes the cycle of the rise and fall of empires to which Rome, too, might be subjected one day.[65]

A closer reading of the quotation shows, I suggest, that the narrative does not allow for such a clear trajectory. Scipio's reasoning is not that Carthage has fallen and that therefore it is likely that Rome might fall as well. He introduces a third element, the fall of Troy, that mediates between the fall of Carthage and the prospect of the possible fall of Rome. A direct comparison of Rome and Carthage is thus avoided and, with it, any straightforward reading of the fall of Carthage as a foreboding of the fall of Rome. For the reference to the prolepsis of the fall of Troy in the *Iliad* is itself not unambiguous but invites two coexisting, opposite readings. Previous discussions of this episode have exclusively focused on *Iliad* 6.448–9 as the 'literary ancestor' of this episode.[66] It is important to remember, though, that the same lines pronounced as a dreaded foreboding by Hector in the sixth book are spoken as an anticipation of the Greek victory by Agamemnon in the fourth book (ll. 164–165).[67] Scipio thus appears to be standing in the tradition of both Iliadic heroes: he is enacting the victory anticipated by Agamemnon while remembering that the same victory also constitutes the defeat of the Trojans and might, as such, prefigure the defeat of Rome.

This ambiguity of the quotation is further reinforced by Polybius' moralising interpretation of the scene which equally stresses the *coexistence* of 'our greatest triumph' and the 'disaster to our enemies'; moreover, by prompting Scipio to reflect 'on our own situation and the possible reversal of circumstances, and gen-

---

[65] Cf. Grethlein 2013, 262: 'Through the intertexts, Polybius inserts Scipio and Rome into a long series of men and empires, most of which underwent a downfall after their great successes'.
[66] Thus, e.g., Hornblower 1981, 105 (the quote ibid.); Baronowski 2011, 153; Grethlein 2013, 261. Walbank (1979, 722–723) more carefully only speaks of 'Homeric lines'.
[67] Such 'multiple identifications' with characters in intertextual references to the Homeric poems go back to the very beginnings of Homeric reception. See John Winkler's brilliant analysis of Sappho 1 in Winkler 1990, esp. 169–170.

erally [...] the mutability of Fortune' (38.21.3) the same pessimistic potential, as it were, of the situation emphatically reaffirms Scipio's competence and greatness as a leader (πραγματικωτέραν καὶ νουνεχεστέραν, 38.21.2; ἀνδρὸς [...] μεγάλου καὶ τελείου, 38.21.3). Both the scene itself and the quotation are ambiguous and lay equal stress on the triumph of the winner *and* the possible implications of the situation of the vanquished. It is important not to gloss over this ambiguity by seeing the Homeric quotation simply as a reference to the possible fall of Rome while ignoring the echoes of the Greek triumph. They are two sides of the same coin.

Scipio's words 'I dread and foresee that some day the same doom will be pronounced on my own country', while raising the possibility of the fall of Roman power, thus also prompt the question 'pronounced by whom'? After all, the Carthaginians were the last big and powerful adversary of the Romans, and Scipio's tears can only do so much to obliterate the fact that this gloomy episode is, in fact, a Roman success and a clear demonstration of Roman power. If we further take into account that the fall of Carthage is part of a period of general upheaval and chaos throughout the *oikumene*, with the Greeks being affected particularly badly, the rise of the next Achilles among the Greeks to take on the Romans seems rather unlikely.[68] Scipio's seemingly unequivocal 'prediction' undermines the possibility of a fall of Rome as much as it evokes it.

This interpretation can be further underpinned by reading it alongside the crucial passage 3.4.1–8, where Polybius justifies the extension of his work. This passage provides the philosophical basis, as it were, for the reader's assessment of the implications of the destruction of Carthage for the future of Roman power. In fact, the ambiguous nature of the episode of Scipio at Carthage can be seen as a concrete example of the general rule formulated there (3.4.5), that

> what is thought to be the greatest success has brought the greatest calamities on many, if they do not make proper [δεόντως] use of it, and the most dreadful catastrophes [περιπετείας] often have turned into [περιπεπτωκέναι] the advantage of those who faced them bravely [εὐγενῶς (...) ἀναδέξωνται].

Success and failure are not final states of events, even though they might look like it. They are cross-roads from which events can develop either way, depending, and this is the essential point, on the attitude and behaviour of the people involved (δεόντως; εὐγενῶς [...] ἀναδέξωνται): the boundaries between success and failure are much less stable than they seem, and one can turn quickly into the other.

---

68 Cf. Millar 1987, 5.

The episode of Scipio at burning Carthage is informed by the same ambiguity: for the Romans it is a triumph that might foreshadow future catastrophe, for the Carthaginians (and, after Corinth, the Greeks) it is a catastrophe that can potentially be turned into triumph, depending, once more, on how it is handled by either party.

If this interpretation is acceptable, it is essential not to limit the intertext evoked by this passage to *Iliad* 6 nor to impose a definitive answer to the question of the future of Roman power onto this episode. And it is equally important that Polybius does not give one, either.[69] Instead, he refers the reader to the trans-temporal lesson they can learn from Scipio's behaviour.[70]

Seeing his own possible future in the downfall of Carthage, at the moment of greatest triumph, Scipio displayed an attitude that could hardly be 'more statesmanlike and more sensible' (πραγματικωτέραν καὶ νουνεχεστέραν, 38.21.2).[71] Πραγματικωτέραν evokes the concept of the ἀνὴρ πραγματικός, both as historical actor and as recipient of Polybius' work. Polybius introduces Scipio as an example of a kind of attitude that his readers should adopt during their own actions. As mentioned above, the ability to deal with contingency, with the sudden reversals of fortune, is one of the main qualities of character that the *Histories* is designed to instil.[72] The lessons from the past cannot protect from the effects of those sudden changes, just as the ability to identify similarities between past and present situations is not a guarantee that a course of action that was successful in the past will be successful in the present as well.[73] But implementing this kind of attitude in everyday decisions and actions offers the best chance of success in the face of contingency because it prevents arrogance and the negligence associated with it in success and, in case catastrophe strikes,

---

[69] Closest to my position is Millar 1987, 4: 'There is no simple or unambiguous way of stating Polybius' conclusion', even though I do not subscribe to his further conclusion that 'Polybius, though he expresses himself obliquely, took an increasingly distant and hostile view of Roman domination'.

[70] Cf. the discussion above, p. 249, of the shift from 'end' in the sense of concrete 'ending point' to 'end' in the sense of '(educational/ethical) purpose' implied in τελεσιούργημα (3.4.12).

[71] The main noun on which the two adjectives in the comparative depend is lost. Büttner-Wobst supplies δύναμιν, but it is unclear what exactly the word is supposed to mean in this context. Paton/ Walbank/ Habicht only print ταύτης, but that only pushes the problem one step further back, as the question now arises what the feminine demonstrative pronoun is supposed to refer to. One would expect a word like προαίρεσιν; a reconstruction along the lines of Heyse's <Ἧς μὲν ἀποφάσεως ἄλλην καὶ> is also a possibility.

[72] 1.1.2, discussed above, p. 256.

[73] See above, p. 251 with n. 31.

facilitates recovery because it helps retain composure and make rational decisions (note νουνεχεστέραν).⁷⁴

Scipio as a successful ἀνὴρ πραγματικός thus becomes a model for Polybius' readers and exemplifies an attitude they should themselves adopt when stepping away from Polybius' narrative: for his non-Roman readers, when they take their stance in the turmoil of the ταραχὴ καὶ κίνησις – for, with, or, indeed, against Rome; for his Roman readers when they must now ponder their future actions in order to maintain their recently gained, but precarious position of superiority. From this point of view it is certainly significant that Polybius, as Eckstein noted,⁷⁵ portrays the attitude and conduct of Scipio as increasingly old-fashioned, thus warning his Roman readers in particular that a further deviation from the values and principles exemplified by this 'great and perfect man' (38.21.3, note τελείου) might have negative effects on the stability of Roman power.⁷⁶

For the reader, Greek or not, the cycle between the two poles of the ἀνὴρ πραγματικός has closed, and the transition from spectator to actor is complete, just as Polybius had made the step from the active participant who stood next to Scipio in front of burning Carthage in 146 to recording these events in order to prepare others for action. It is now the task of the reader-turned-actor to give

---

74 I therefore agree with Baronowski 2011, 89–99, that this educational aspect, as it were, is a key element of this episode. But he does not go far enough when considering its only purpose to be 'to avoid disgrace' in case of failure (ibid. 99). 'Modesty' should rather be regarded as an important quality that helps the πραγματικὸς ἀνήρ succeed. 1.35 illustrates the 'pragmatic' importance of modesty. Polybius here comments on the sudden reversal of Regulus' fate who imposed humiliating and merciless terms of a peace treaty on the Carthaginians (1.31.5–8) and shortly afterwards found himself a Carthaginian prisoner, at the mercy of his enemy. Walbank (1957, 93) is right that Polybius does not construe a causal link between Regulus' arrogance in success and his downfall. However, Polybius does clearly state that learning from such situations as Regulus' 'makes us [...] the most competent judges of what is best at every time and in every circumstance' (1.35.10). Hence even though Polybius leaves the exact relationship between 'modesty' and successful political and military decisions open, he does suggest that such moral qualities have some positive influence on the way in which people assess and deal with concrete situations; it might simply make them more careful and weigh their different options more thoroughly. Cf. 3.118.9: it is because the Senate 'deliberated about their options with manly coolness' (ἐβουλεύετο [...] περὶ τῶν ἐνδεχομένων ἀνδρωδῶς, 3.118.7; cf. κριτὰς ἀληθινοὺς [...] τοῦ βελτίονος, 1.35.10) after the unexpected catastrophe at Cannae that the Romans 'not only recovered their supremacy in Italy [...] but in a few years made themselves masters of the whole world'.
75 Eckstein 1995, 230–233, esp 232.
76 I agree with Baronowski 2011, 161, on this point. I disagree, though, that the passage signals 'the continuation of Roman rule in the immediate future': Polybius leaves it entirely open when the potential demise of Roman power might begin; cf. Rood 2007, 181.

the answer to the question raised by Scipio, one way or the other, by way of their own actions on the basis of the lessons learned from Polybius' narrative: with the end of the *Histories*, history has just begun.

Paolo Desideri
Plutarch on the Future of an Ancient World

General introduction

There can be no doubt that historical research and writing were one of Plutarch's strongest intellectual interests – his biographies, above all the *Parallel Lives*, bear clear witness to this – but it is much more difficult to define the true nature of that interest.[1] One cannot content oneself with just saying that Plutarch wrote biographies, and not out-and-out histories.[2] This would be merely a partial answer: indeed, far from dealing with the substance of the problem, such an overstatement of the differences between the two historiographical forms overlooks the fact that Plutarch adopted biography in order to better meet the requirements posed by his very way of understanding history – which is what we really ought to clarify. In my opinion, to put it roughly, studying and writing history were Plutarch's answer to the general decline which was the most evident feature of the Greek world of his time, as revealed not only in its politics, but also in its economy, demographic characteristics and even culture. Plutarch was well aware of this decline, which he denounced overtly, as we shall see, in more than one of his essays – for instance in *De defectu oraculorum*, in *Praecepta rei publicae gerendae*, in *De aere alieno* – while at the same time seeking a way to resist it, or at least to keep hoping for a different arrangement in the future, a light after the darkness as it were. I would say, therefore, that in Plutarch's mind studying and writing the lives of the great men of the past was the best way, from a cultural point of view, to approach this decline: certainly it involved a withdrawal from an unsatisfactory present, but one which was aimed not at a nostalgic contemplation of a great and unrecoverable past, but rather at the shaping of a new possible future.

To Plutarch it was not true, as the Augustan and post-Augustan ideology maintained, that human history must be interpreted in terms of a linear evolution which had already led to an ultimate result: the Roman Empire. Without doubt, in

---

[1] It is impossible to give here an adequate bibliographical list even of the main titles related to this subject: I limit myself to indicating just those which I found most useful: Jones 1971, 72–109 and 1982, 967–981; Humble 2010; Nikolaidis 2005; Pelling 2002 and 2010; Stadter 2010. Moreover, I have written myself a concise profile of Plutarch's historiographical production (Desideri forthcoming): to this essay I refer for further bibliography.
[2] On the relationship between 'history' and 'biography' in antiquity (and especially in Plutarch) see Desideri 2015.

his view the empire was, as we shall see, a positive result in comparison to the previous state of political disorder in which the world had fallen after the death of Alexander the Great; although it was due only to the whims of τύχη, which had prevented Alexander from achieving the empire himself, it could in a certain sense be considered a matter of divine design: but it certainly was not the ultimate accomplishment of history. Thus the past could not be reconstructed as a series of events that unavoidably led to the present state of affairs. Rather, one should rethink that past as a whole of biographical experiences of men who had succeeded in affecting the lives of entire cities and peoples: in this way, there would be an opportunity to give a new and different meaning to the knowledge of history. In retracing the variety and creativity shown in the lives of great Greek and Roman figures – the most significant examples of the human race, for better or for worse – a path could be opened up before us, leading towards a future to be built on the basis of an in-depth knowledge of human sentiment and behaviour. Those lives would form a kaleidoscope of experiences capable of indicating new routes upon which the great souls yet to come should channel their energies.

With these premises as a starting point, Plutarch progressively honed his tools for digging into the past, ever keeping to the biographical "formula": he thus progressed from his initial experiments with individual biographies to the more complex plan of the *Lives* of emperors in a diachronic sequence, finally arriving with the *Parallel Lives* at a historical discourse in which diachronic order has been almost completely dismissed. In fact, as we have mentioned, here diachronic order makes way for an enormous range of experiences which, as a whole, sketch out something of a system of models for ethical, political and even military behaviour. Among these models, readers are expressly urged to identify the examples to be followed (or avoided) – bearing in mind the specific situations in which each of them finds himself – so that he may plan the construction of a future not only for himself, but also for the world in which he lives. The choice to set Greek and Roman figures side by side clearly serves to give the collection variety and richness, while the final *Comparisons* of the individual pairs (and even the introductions of some of them) aim to direct the reader's reflection towards certain points for which Plutarch felt that the formula of parallels might better clarify particular behavioural traits worthy of meditation. However, behind this complex construction there hides an educational intention, the final goal of which is to provide the tools for building one or more possible futures for the Greek people and for humanity in general.

The decline of Greece and Rome's success as consequences of Alexander's death

The idea that the present is not absolutely the best place to live in, at least for a Greek, emerges, with a decidedly political connotation, in a celebrated passage of *Praecepta rei publicae gerendae*, the one in which Plutarch complains about "the weak condition of Greek affairs, in which it is best for wise men to accept one advantage – a life of harmony and quiet – since fortune has left us no prize open for competition".[3] Apparently, this is not a criticism of the Roman Empire, which – as Plutarch has just said a few lines before – ensures an overall undisputed peace: "all war, both Greek and foreign, has been banished from among us and has disappeared"; but the consequence of Roman supremacy, in any case, is the failure of Greek political liberty (even though – as Plutarch adds – "of liberty the peoples have as great a share as our rulers grant them, and perhaps more would not be better for them"[4]). In addition, we have an even more general complaint about the decline of Greece in Ammonius' famous statement (in *De defectu oraculorum*) that "Greece has far more than its share in the general depopulation which the earlier discords and wars have wrought throughout practically the whole inhabited world, and (that) to-day the whole of Greece would hardly muster three thousand men-at-arms, which is the number that the one city of the Megarians sent forth to Plataea."[5] It is evident that in Plutarch, mixed feelings live side by side: he believes that the Roman government is the best possible solution for the problems of the human race at the moment; and in particular, as regards Greece, he is highly grateful (in *De Pythiae oraculis*) "to the man who has been the leader in our administration and has planned and carried out practically all that has been done" – a reference to the emperor Hadrian, perhaps;[6] but he is also convinced that things could have evolved in a different way, more favourable to the Greek people: for instance, if Alexander the Great had managed to survive for a convenient number of years, instead of dying suddenly in his prime, immediately after conquering the Persian Empire.

---

[3] *Mor.* 824 e (see Desideri 2012 [2011], 125 f.); this English translation, like all translations of Plutarch's texts used in this essay, are from the LCL edition.
[4] *Mor.* 824 c.
[5] *Mor.* 413 f–414a (see Desideri 1996, 91–94).
[6] *Mor.* 409 c (the identity of the person alluded is highly controversial, indeed: see Jones 1966, 63–65; Stadter 2002, 12).

As is well known, Plutarch dealt with this problem, which could be defined as a problem of counterfactual or virtual, history, in his incomplete essay *De fortuna Romanorum* (not just a rhetorical exercise, indeed) which breaks off precisely with his mention of Alexander, at the end of the enumeration of episodes proving that the rise of Rome had been strongly aided by Fortune's benevolence: "and to Fortune I ascribe also", says Plutarch", the death of Alexander, a man who, by great good luck and brilliant successes, the result of his invincible daring and lofty aspirations, was sweeping swiftly through the world like a shooting star from East to West, and was already allowing the lustre of his arms to gleam upon Italy, since the destruction of Alexander the Molossian at the hands of the Bruttians and Lucanians served him as pretext for the campaign"[7]. Plutarch's firm belief, in any case, was that Rome's success – "this most beautiful of human works", as he says at the beginning – was due to a unique co-operation of Fortune and Virtue; but it is important that in his opinion Alexander's untimely death was also a gift from Fortune to Rome. And I would suggest that the terrible state of confusion and disorder of the Greek world – described vividly in that very beginning – in other words the political chaos which made it possible for the Romans to establish their domination everywhere, was in Plutarch's opinion likewise a consequence of Alexander's death. This event was, in fact, the necessary condition for the foundation, at Time's hands and with the help of God (χρόνος μετὰ θεοῦ), of the Roman State, which was to become "for all mankind a Hearth, in truth both holy and beneficent, a steadfast cable, a principle abiding for ever ... amid the shifting conditions of human affairs":[8] a passage in which Plutarch demonstrates, again, great appreciation for the accomplishments of that empire.

However, even in this work Plutarch does not consider the Roman Empire to be the final accomplishment of history. Although he uses the Democritean image of cosmic order emerging from the primeval chaos – thus seeming to characterise it in terms of cosmological necessity – to define the historical phenomenon of Rome's imposition on the world's stage, this is nothing more than a brilliant metaphor, while the basic idea remains that a crucial role in the occurrence of this phenomenon was played by luck, or chance: and in fact all that remains of the pamphlet is, as we have already mentioned, a long dissertation on the theme of the Romans' luck.

---

7 *Mor.* 326a–b; on this Plutarchan essay see Desideri 2012 [2005], 142–144; on the problems of its dating see Pelling 2002, 30, n.5; 84; on the general problem of fortune in Plutarch's way of conceiving Greek and Roman history see Swain 1989.
8 *Mor.* 316f–317a.

History and cosmology: A plurality of worlds

A series of reflections that we find scattered among the three pamphlets – *De E apud Delphos, De Pythiae oraculis, De defectu oraculorum* – which fall under the title of *Delphic Dialogues*, enables us to attain a more developed idea of what might have been the true cosmological context in which human history is situated according to Plutarch – and therefore, of how one must construct a historical discourse in order to be able to achieve its primary educational objectives. The core aim of these dialogues, far beyond the multiple themes and episodes which are proposed therein, is – as we shall see – to establish the idea of a close relationship between divination and memory: which in itself strongly supports the idea that the gods have a stable presence on Earth and a direct involvement in the life of men.[9] However it is precisely in *De defectu oraculorum* that Plutarch proposes, through the words of Cleombrotus – one of the main figures of the dialogue – a theory on the plurality of the (human) worlds (κόσμοι), whose number and arrangement he even believes he can accurately determine (here, Cleombrotus is recounting what he heard from 'the barbarian of the Red Sea', a sage he has met at the Eastern borders of the world). "These worlds – he declares – are not infinite in number, nor one, nor five, but one hundred and eighty-three, arranged in the form of a triangle, each side of the triangle having sixty worlds; of the three left over each is placed at an angle, and those that are next to one another are in contact and revolve gently as in a dance".[10] What we must observe here is, first of all, that the very idea of a plurality of the worlds is not only clearly oriented towards relativising the value of the world in which each of us happens to live – first and foremost Plutarch's own world, of course; more specifically, the idea rejects any hypothesis of necessity (in the philosophical sense of the term), let alone progress, which one could be induced to discover in the sequence of the historical events of his own world.

Not less interesting is the geometrical structure of the cosmic compound. It seems to imply the idea of a spatial contiguity among the different worlds, that is the different cultures which have flourished in the past and/or flourish, at one and the same time, throughout the Earth: this is, first of all, the basis for an anthropological, or more aptly a comparative, approach to human societies, removing any kind of superiority complex towards 'the other'. But even more important, from our point of view, are Cleombrotus' next words. "The inner area of

---

9 For an interpretation of these *Dialogues* as regards their cosmological background see Desideri 2012, 355–366.
10 *Mor.* 422b.

the triangle" he says, still speaking in the words of the foreigner from the Red Sea "is the common hearth of all, and is called the Plain of Truth (πεδίον ἀληθείας), in which the accounts, the forms, and the patterns of all things that have come to pass and of all that shall come to pass rest undisturbed; and round about them lies Eternity, whence Time, like an ever-flowing stream, is conveyed to the worlds".[11] In this very striking passage – which has a Platonic as well as a Pythagorean sound – I would like to underline, first, the image of Time which, at the right moment, gives life to the individual worlds: the fact that this same image is to be found, as we have seen above, in *De fortuna Romanorum*, with respect to the foundation of the Roman Empire, confirms, to my mind, the coherence of Plutarch's theoretical grounds, as regards the idea of history. Moreover, the image of the Plain of Truth, the inner area of the triangle of the worlds, is particularly significant. Here we encounter an attempt to represent in a visible form the idea that the various human cultures, though differing from one another from either a spatial or chronological point of view, are, when all is said and done, bound together by common elements, which ensure the likelihood of reciprocal exchange and mutual communication.

As we are now interested above all in the way in which the future can be envisioned, that is in diachronic communication, it is worthwhile to stress Plutarch's idea of a general storehouse, so to speak, containing a limited number of embryos, which Time uses at different moments to produce all the various historical realities, each of which represents the context of every man's life. In other words, I believe that with this image Plutarch seeks to set up the essential requirement for establishing a dialogue, not only between the different cultures that coexist at any given time all over the world, but also between the historical worlds that follow one after the other over time, that is between past, present and future.

No future without the past:
Diachronic connections between the worlds

In the *De defectu oraculorum* Plutarch actually presents another idea, different from the one just considered, but not alien to it, concerning the relationships among the various historical worlds: an idea which is strictly connected with a definition of the present that can be found in a passage of *De E apud Delphos*, in which Ammonius says that it is "crowded out into the future and the past, like

---

[11] *Mor.* 422a–c; on this passage see the commentary by Rescigno 1995, 346 ff.

a flash to those who try to look at it";[12] in fact, its very short life consists of remembrance of the past and expectation of the future. And the following is the passage in *De defectu oraculorum*, where Plutarch explains the reasons why, in his opinion, there is a close relationship between memory and divination (the core aim of the complex of these *Dialogues*, as we have said):

> We ought not feel surprised or incredulous at this [relationship], when we see in the soul... that faculty which is the complement of prophecy (τὴν ἀντίστροφον τῇ μαντικῇ δύναμιν), and which we call memory, and how great an achievement is displayed in preserving and guarding the past, or rather what has been the present, since nothing of all that has come to pass has any existence or substantiality, because the very instant when anything comes to pass, that is the end of it – of actions, words, experiences alike; for time like an everflowing stream bears all things onward... Hence, as I said, it is no wonder that, if it [i.e. the soul] has command over things that no longer are, it anticipates many of those which have not yet come to pass, since these are more closely related to it, and with these it has much in common; for its attachments and associations are with the future, and it is quit of all that is past and ended, save only to remember it.[13]

In other words, nothing really exists except for the future, but it will never come unless you remember the past: "since all present events follow in close conjunction with past events, in accordance with a regular procedure which brings them to fulfilment from beginning to end, only the man who understands, in consonance with Nature, how to fathom the connexions and interrelation of the causes one with another can also declare 'what now is, and in future shall be, and has been aforetime'"[14] – which is, as we all remember, the Homeric definition of Calchas (*Il.* 1.70).

Even though this passage clearly presents us with an idea of the relationships between the different historical worlds which tends to underline their causal concatenation, rather than the intimate kinship resulting from their being the products of the same original embryos, the important thing, from our point of view at least, is that not only does it reaffirm the connection between the times of history, but it also establishes the essentially "forward-looking", "futuristic" – as we could perhaps say – dimension of the life of men, and consequently of Plutarch's historical interest as well.

---

12 *Mor.* 392f ἐκθλίβεται γὰρ [i.e. τό 'νῦν'] εἰς τὸ μέλλον καὶ τὸ παρῳχημένον ὥσπερ αὐγὴ [Eusebius] βουλομένοις ἰδεῖν ἐξ ἀνάγκης διιστάμενον.
13 *Mor.* 432a–b.
14 *Mor.* 387b.

Away from the present: Analysing and emulating the behaviour of the great men of the past

At this point we can go back and look at the historiographical project of the *Parallel Lives* again. Our starting point will be the results we have obtained thus far. Plutarch is convinced that contemporary Greece is in serious decline, even though the situation may improve; but the solution cannot be found in an impossible disavowal of the Roman domination, which, after all, has produced some good results, nor in a sterile regret of Alexander the Great's untimely death. Greece – and not only Greece, actually – will have to draw energy from recovering and re-evaluating the past; not just its own past, again, but also the Roman past, as the Romans have proved in many cases over the centuries to be even ἑλληνικώτεροι than the Greeks themselves. A better future will only arise from relativising the present, which will reveal all its meagreness when compared with the great actions of yesteryear; as Plutarch says at the beginning of his *Life of Aemilius Paulus*, he continues to call to mind the great men of the past, in order to obtain appropriate models of behaviour, as opposed to "the viciousness and abjection and baseness which are proposed by the environment where we are compelled to live".[15] Historical investigation and writing are in fact the equivalent, at the social level, of making an effort to remember something at a private level; and both can and must achieve the aim of creating new and better prospects for the future.

Plutarch's research centres on great individuals because his main aim is to improve the men of the present, and above all to prepare the men of the future – that's why he wrote biographies. A passage in *De profectibus in virtute* gives us what could be considered an example of the psychological effects of recalling the great men of old. Starting with the remark of Themistocles "that the trophy of Miltiades would not suffer him to sleep", Plutarch says that it is not just the philosopher's words that stimulate improvement of oneself. "More than that, the man who is truly making progress, comparing himself with the deeds and conduct of a good and perfect man, and being pricked by the consciousness of his own shortcomings, yet at the same time rejoicing because of his hope and yearning, and being filled with an urging that is never still, is ready in the words of Simonides 'to run like weanling colt beside its dam' ... With men of this sort", Plutarch continues, "it has already become a constant practice, on proceeding

---

15 *Aem.* 1.5 εἴ τι φαῦλον ἢ κακόηθες ἢ ἀγεννὲς αἱ τῶν συνόντων ἐξ ἀνάγκης ὁμιλίαι προσβάλλουσιν.

to any business, or on taking office, or on encountering any dispensation of Fortune, to set before their eyes good men of the present or of the past, and to reflect: 'What would Plato have done in this case? What would Epaminondas have said? How would Lycurgus have conducted himself, or Agesilaus'? And before such mirrors as these, figuratively speaking, they array themselves or readjust their habit, and either repress some of their more ignoble utterances, or resist the onset of some emotions".[16] The historical reconstruction must therefore be aimed at highlighting the moral, but also the political and even the military qualities of the great men of old, in the belief that "the Good creates a stir of activity towards itself, and implants at once in the spectator an active impulse; it does not form his character by ideal representation alone, but through the investigation of its work it furnishes him with a dominant purpose", as Plutarch says in the introduction to *Pericles*.[17]

Great men struggling with their times

It is not possible, of course, to provide even a quick survey of the Plutarchan passages from the *Parallel Lives* which could be cited as proof of the above. I would however like to draw the reader's attention to one of the most distinctive elements of Plutarch's way of recalling historical figures: that of the relationship between each figure and the general spirit of his own times; actually, according to Plutarch, great men can never operate outside the historical context in which they live, even though, of course, they must try to do their best to improve the current situation. This theme is present in many of Plutarch's *Lives*, but one can say that it is at the very heart of the *Lives* of Phocion and Cato the Younger. As regards the Athenian Phocion, Plutarch says, just at the beginning of his *Life*, that "his virtue, which may be said to have found an antagonist in a grievous and violent time, the fortunes of Greece rendered obscure"; Plutarch compares him with his contemporary Demades, who proposed and favoured "many measures which were at variance with the dignity and character of the city", and claimed to be justified "because he was in command of a shipwrecked state"; indeed, Plutarch exclaims, he "was himself but wreckage of the state", whereas Phocion never searched for a justification for his failures in the ruin of the Athenian state at that moment.[18] And as for Cato the Younger, about whom Cicero said that "he

---

[16] *Mor.* 84d–85b (see Desideri 2012 [1992], 232).
[17] *Per.* 2.3 (see Desideri 2012 [1989], 202–203).
[18] *Phoc.* 1.1–3 (see Desideri 2012 [1992], 235 f.).

acted as he lived in Plato's commonwealth, and not among the dregs of Romulus", Plutarch himself thought that "he fared just as fruits do, which make their appearance out of season", which are not really appreciated, even though consumers look upon them with delight and admiration. But the greatness of that man is demonstrated by the fact that, even though "he was repulsed from ruddersweeps and pilotage, he nevertheless gave Fortune a great contest. She did, indeed, seize and overthrow the commonwealth ... but with difficulty, slowly, after a long time, and when it had almost won the day[19] through Cato and the virtue of Cato".[20]

Plutarch's biographies as seen by Nietzsche

These considerations lead us to the idea that according to Plutarch the death of Cato and the end of the Roman Republic had brought about the end of a historic cycle – in the terms of Plutarch's Cleombrotus perhaps we should say "a world" – in which the rise and fall of the free Greek city has been followed, after a few generations, by another one, akin in principle: that of the free Roman state.[21] This is certainly the reason why the *Parallel Lives* stop at Caesar. What had followed, and yet remained in Plutarch's time, was a world in which the Roman Empire, as we have seen, ensured stability, peace and order, but at the price of a drastic restriction of liberties and, as far as the Greek world in particular is concerned, a considerable demographic decline and the disappearance of any really important political life; to Plutarch, the last true Greek – let us not forget it – had been Philopoemen[22]. This tangible sense of dissatisfaction with his own times that pervades Plutarch's biographical works along with his equally evident determination to avoid a sense of "epigonism", leading him to advocate rather for passions and impulses towards creative action in the future, aroused particular attention in modern times, and an attitude which we might well define as one of spiritual kinship, in one of the greatest philosophers of the late 19th century: Friederich Nietzsche. Nietzsche makes explicit reference to the Greek author

---

19 καὶ βραδέως καὶ χρόνῳ πολλῷ καὶ παρὰ μικρὸν ἐλθοῦσαν περιγενέσθαι [πολιτείαν] διὰ Κάτωνα καὶ τὴν Κάτωνος ἀρετήν.
20 *Phoc.* 3.5.
21 On the "parallel rise-and-fall pattern" of Greece and Rome in Plutarch's *Parallel Lives* see Desideri forthcoming.
22 *Phil.* 1.4.

in, among other contexts,[23] a highly significant passage of his *Vom Nutzen und Nachteil der Historie*, the second of his *Unzeitgemässe Betrachtungen* (*Untimely Meditations*), published in February 1874. As is well known, this work is fiercely critical of an idea of history such as that of Hegelian historicism, which to Nietzsche's mind, causes the suffocation of any impulse to action, inducing a dangerous sense of indulgent, lifeless acceptance of what exists.[24]

In that passage the German philosopher encourages his readers to read biographies: but – as he points out – not those in which the protagonists are fully immersed in, and satisfied with, the context of their time, but those, like the Plutarchan biographies, whose title could be "ein Kämpfer gegen seine Zeit". After stating that it is precisely the ability to foresee a great future that gives us the ability and the right to understand the past – "wer nicht einiges größer und höher erlebt hat als alle, wird auch nichts Großes und Hohes aus der Vergangenheit zu deuten wissen" – Nietzsche goes on to proclaim that "der Spruch der Vergangenheit ist immer ein Orakelspruch", and makes an enigmatic reference to the Delphic priests, whose extraordinarily wide influence was due, in his opinion, to the fact that they had a thorough knowledge of the past – "man erklärt jetzt die außerordentlich tiefe und weite Wirkung Delphis besonders daraus, daß die delphischen Priester genaue Kenner des Vergangnen waren." Therefore, he concluded, "zieht um euch den Zaun einer großen und umfänglichen Hoffnung, eines hoffenden Strebens. Formt in euch ein Bild, dem die Zu-

---

23 As may be seen in his notebooks of the period, in those years Nietzsche makes the following references to Plutarchan passages (apart from that to *De defectu oraculorum*, on which see n. 26): 1) Nietzsche 1978a, 352: the lengthy reflection on the introduction of *Pericles* (fr. 10 [1], dating to the early weeks of 1871); and 2) Nietzsche 1978a, 432: the implied reference to *Them.* 3. 4 (and perhaps also to *De profectibus in virtute*, *Mor.* 84d ff., the passage considered above in the text), on the glory of Miltiades which kept Themistocles from sleeping (fr. 16 [35]), written just a few months later). Directly connected to Plutarch in the second *Untimely Meditation* is, moreover, fr. 19 [33] (Nietzsche 1978b, 14), written between the summer of 1872 and early 1873, in which Nietzsche deplores the lack of books that emanate heroic strength in his time, and concludes: "We don't even read Plutarch anymore" (see also fr. 30 [31], of late 1873 (Nietzsche 1978b, 352), in which Plutarch is associated with Montaigne, as in fr. 29 [230]: Nietzsche 1978b, 331). These passages are clearly at the basis of what would later be the praise of Plutarch (from Montaigne) in the third *Untimely Meditation* (*Schopenhauer als Erzieher*), published at the end of 1874: Nietzsche 1972, 344. The best study available on what Plutarch meant to Nietzsche is Ingenkamp 1988.

24 For an approach to this work as a starting point for a more general discussion of the theme of history as monumentality, see the recent Morley 2011 (which also see for the latest bibliography on Nietzsche's concept of historiography), 210–214. For a particularly critical view of Nietzsche's anti-historicism, and especially of his bias towards biography (and Plutarch) see Cancik 1995, 88–90.

kunft entsprechen soll, und vergeßt den Aberglauben, Epigonen zu sein. Ihr habt genug zu ersinnen und zu erfinden, indem ihr auf jenes zukünftige Leben sinnt; aber fragt nicht bei der Geschichte an, daß sie euch das Wie? das Womit? zeige. Wenn ihr euch dagegen in die Geschichte großer Männer hineinlebt, so werdet ihr aus ihr ein oberstes Gebot lernen, reif zu werden und jenem lähmenden Erziehungsbanne der Zeit zu entfliehen, die ihren Nutzen darin sieht, euch nicht reif werden zu lassen, um euch, die Unreifen, zu beherrschen und auszubeuten". And, in conclusion, "sättigt eure Seelen an Plutarch und wagt es, an euch selbst zu glauben, indem ihr an seine Helden glaubt. Mit einem Hundert solcher unmodern erzogener, das heißt reif gewordener und an das Heroische gewöhnter Menschen ist jetzt die ganze lärmende Afterbildung dieser Zeit zum ewigen Schweigen zu bringen".[25]

Here, Nietzsche, making explicit reference to Plutarch's *Lives*, but implicitly to Plutarch's *Delphic Dialogues* as well,[26] gives a good explanation of how historical writings can be useful – especially when proposed in biographical form. In fact, Plutarch is fittingly appreciated for both the "heroic" component present in such an evident manner in the *Lives* – though it does not always take form as the "man fighting against his times" – and his attribution of an educational purpose to history, as an encouragement to overcome the conditioning that the historical context in which we live tends to impose. What Nietzsche found convincing, and shared with Plutarch, was precisely this way of conceiving of history as an urge to action and the creation of a future: the exact opposite of what he considered the characteristically negative element of the Hegelian concept of history. The future is the result of a creative act; it does not automatically descend from a past that has hardened into the present: and the biographical structure of Plutarch's

---

[25] Nietzsche 1972, 290–291.
[26] This issue is not noted in Ingenkamp 1988. The fact that Nietzsche knew in particular of the *De defectu oraculorum* is proven by the reference he had previously made in *Die Geburt der Tragödie* (1872) to the story, narrated by Philip (another of the speakers in the dialogue), of the death of the "great Pan" (*Mor.*, 419b-d: Nietzsche 1972, 71); furthermore, from some even earlier notes we have ascertained that Nietzsche intended to write a tragedy, *Empedocles*, which would include, among other things, the scene of Pan's dethroning (Nietzsche 1978a, 129, fr. 5 [116], written between September 1870 and January 1871; see the formulation of the motto "der große Pan ist tot" in fr. 7 [8], and a kind of outline of the script in frr. 8 [30–37], written between the winter of 1870–71 and the autumn of 1872). A recollection of the Plutarchan story would later return in a more complex form in *Also sprach Zarathustra* (1885), where the reference to that motto (in the modified form of "Gott todt ist") seems to be elevated to an emblematic announcement of the end of the Christian era (Nietzsche 1968, chap. 2). I should like to thank Augusto Guida for having brought some of these passages to my attention (see also Guida 1998, 411).

historiography is in itself the proper way of raising the issue of the future. His biographies attribute to individual creativity the ability to project oneself into the world of tomorrow: indeed, one's own actions set the conditions for the transformations to come. And Plutarch himself maintained – through the cosmological context sketched out in *De defectu oraculorum* – that whatever may be the characters of worlds yet to come, in each world the dialogue with the previous worlds and with those located elsewhere in space would remain open; in fact, all these worlds are born from the same embryos, though they always develop in different ways. Perhaps Plutarch would also have shared with Nietzsche, considering it a legitimate inference from his premises, the idea that only those capable of planning the future are also capable of truly knowing the past.

To conclude, it is in this desire to work towards building the future, beyond the troubles of everyday life, that we find the most profound meaning behind Plutarch's decision to devote himself to the history of the past. In a very different way from Nietzsche, and apparently without knowledge of the philosopher/philologist's reflections, this intention of Plutarch's was later grasped by Adelmo Barigazzi, a distinguished twentieth-century Italian scholar of Plutarch's *Moralia*. In fact, in one of his last essays, entitled *Plutarco e il corso futuro della storia*,[27] Barigazzi wrote that in the future envisioned by Plutarch the Greek *paideia* would become the heart of Roman imperial culture, and would deploy Roman power so as to expand throughout the world. This may not have been the precise hope cherished by Plutarch, who lived in an age in which this universalisation of Greek culture was already part of the present: when thinking about the future, Plutarch probably had something else in mind, something which reached far beyond the Roman Empire. But it is true that he was convinced that the memory of the great past of both Greece and Rome ought to be preserved, so that it could be revived in some future world.

---

[27] Barigazzi 1994 [1984].

Luke Pitcher
Future's Bright? Looking Forward in Appian

Introduction

Appian of Alexandria, the second-century CE historian whose imperfectly-preserved *Rhomaika* constitutes one of the modern world's principal sources for the last century of the Roman Republic, is an interesting test-case for the student of futurity in the history-writing of antiquity. His text is closely related to several of those which we have already seen elsewhere in this collection. Sometimes they are amongst the ultimate sources of his narrative (like Polybius);[1] sometimes their influence on his style and structure is profound (like Thucydides).[2]

Appian's treatment of the future in the *Rhomaika* shows elements of continuity with these texts, but also differences. Unlike some of the other historians who feature in this volume, he shows little overt interest in the future from his own perspective, in what will happen to the world after the *Rhomaika* itself is disseminated. Thucydides offers comments about how some phenomena (or phenomena very similar to them) will recur in future time, as long as human nature remains the same.[3] Polybius predicts the eventual silting-up of the Pontus.[4] Sallust claims to anticipate that there will be those who will criticise the historian's decisions about his lifestyle.[5] Tacitus trails the idea that he may write about the reigns of Nerva and Trajan in his old age, "si vita suppeditet".[6] Appian, at least in the extant portions of the *Rhomaika*, displays little of such forward focus. He does, as we shall see, anticipate some possible responses from his audience to what they will have learned from his work, but, even here, his focus is less on their actual response in the future, and more on his own, present interest in bringing these reactions about.

---

1 For the general importance of Polybius as an ultimate source for some stretches of the *Rhomaika*, see now Rich 2015, 64.
2 Strebel 1935, while rather perfunctory, notes the extent of the debt that Appian owes stylistically to Thucydides.
3 Thuc. 1.22.4, 3.82.2. The bibliography on the question of what Thucydides thinks that such predictions can achieve is vast: Raaflaub 2013, especially 6–7, and Stahl 2013, especially 314, are the latest contributions.
4 Polyb. 4.40.4.
5 Sall. *BJ*.4.
6 Tac. *H.* 1.2.

The future from the historian's own perspective is not, however, the only sort of future that appears in classical historiography. Other contributions to this collection have delivered abundant proof of that. These different senses of the future have much more of a purchase upon the *Rhomaika*. In particular, the issues which Jonas Grethlein has identified in his study of what he calls the historiographical *telos* are very pertinent to the architecture of Appian's enterprise. Like Polybius' history, Appian's *Rhomaika* has features which it is tempting to interpret in terms of a changing conception on the part of the historian as to the ultimate disposition of material within his oeuvre, although the character of this change is rather different. While Polybius explicitly notes the expansion in the chronological scope of his work,[7] Appian seems to change his mind as he is going along about exactly where in his narrative he will treat of particular key moments in Roman History.[8]

Interesting as this is, there is more mileage, for our present purposes, in a different aspect of Grethlein's examination of the so-called *telos*. This is the perception that the ultimate state of affairs which a given work of historiography seems to presuppose can have an important impact on the effect that it generates. Grethlein notes that this ultimate state of affairs need not coincide with the chronological point at which the history's narrative terminates. Sallust's *Bellum Catilinae* is his excellent example of this; a case can equally be made for the "rara temporum felicitate ubi sentire quae velis et quae sentias dicere licet"[9] which Tacitus evokes at the beginning of his *Histories* before presenting the "principes ferro interempti: trina bella civilia, plura externa ac plerumque permixta"[10] that will be his subject-matter.

In this respect, the fragmentary nature of Appian's *Rhomaika* lends the extant text (which effectively ends with the killing of Sextus Pompeius after the Battle of Naulochus at the conclusion to Book Five of the *Civil Wars*) a rather different complexion from that which the author seems to have intended. The full *Rhomaika*, to judge from what Appian claims about its projected scope in his *Proem*,[11] would have generated its effects not so much by disjunction between the end-point of its narrative and the state of affairs which it presupposes, as by studied concinnity between the two. The *Proem* observes that, "from the ad-

---

[7] Polyb. 3.4.6.
[8] For a summary and interpretation of the ways in which Appian seems to contradict himself about the structure of the *Rhomaika*, see Bucher 2000, 418–29.
[9] Tac. *H.* 1.1.
[10] Tac. *H.* 1.2.
[11] However, see note 8 above on the problems involved in using the evidence of the *Proem* to extrapolate the content of the *Rhomaika*'s lost books.

vent of the emperors to the present time is nearly two hundred years more, in the course of which the city has been greatly embellished, its revenue much increased, and in the long reign of peace and security everything has moved towards a lasting prosperity";[12] later, while running through the subject-matter of the books to come, it says that, "the last book will show the present military force of the Romans, the revenues they collect from each province, what they spend for the naval service, and other things of that kind." Unlike the *Bellum Catilinae* or similar texts, the *Rhomaika* announces an intention to bring its narrative right down to the time of the political and social dispensation that it presupposes.

It is not uncommon for works of classical historiography to bring their narratives thus down to what they describe as the present day, or something close to it. Jacoby's notion of *Zeitgeschichte* largely encompasses works in this category.[13] Velleius Paterculus (to give another, extant example) is prone to dating things in relation to the consulship of his dedicatee, Vinicius, in 30 CE,[14] and closes his narrative with the death of Livia in the year before that. Velleius' use of "*hoc* triennium" to refer to the period encompassing Livia's demise also suggests that Vinicius' consulship is being presented as the "now" at which his narrative concludes.[15]

Appian's narrative is rather more committed than most to highlighting the present good order to which the earlier history he describes was heading. Even in the extant books, Appian's distinctive structure (telling the discrete stories of particular areas one by one) means that an explicit narrative movement towards the current state of affairs is advertised on several occasions. "The viewpoint from which Appian's audience is invited to look back at the turbulent events of the *Roman History* is explicitly one where the wild spaces he delineates in the course of his narrative have been brought around to calm and profitable stability, 'to the present well-ordered condition': the final note on an area in Appian is, on several occasions, a reference to the fact that it now receives officials and/or pays regular tribute to Rome."[16] The Roman Civil Wars extort from the narrator at several points significant emphasis on the order that would ultimately arise from their chaos, and the role of the divine in ensuring this process. Thus, the description of the triumviral proscriptions draws forth the comment that, ".... the deity thus shook the most powerful mistress of so many nations

---

[12] App. *Proem* 7.24. Cf. also Hidber 2004, 178.
[13] Jacoby 1956, 34.
[14] Vell. Pat. 1.8.1; 1.12.6; 2.7.5; 2.49.1; 2.65.2.
[15] Vell. Pat. 2.130.4–5.
[16] Pitcher 2012, 232, with the passages collected in note 30. See also Bucher 2000, 430–1.

and of land and sea, and so brought after a long period of time the present well-ordered condition",[17] whereas the Battle of Pharsalus, perhaps *the* pivotal moment for Appian in light of the special importance that he allots to Julius Caesar in securing Roman *hegemonia* and orchestrating the shift to monarchy, receives the gloss "this was the ordering of divine Providence to bring in the imperial power which now embraces everything"[18] when the narrator is explaining the unruliness of Pompeius Magnus's troops.

Explicit narrative prolepsis of this sort – where Appian explicitly breaks narrative sequence to talk for a moment about what will happen later – is not particularly common in the *Rhomaika*, effective though it is when it does occur. The ghosts of what will subsequently happen in the same locality are occasionally permitted to shadow Appian's account of goings-on in a particular place, especially where it has some impact on contemporary practices. We can see this happening in his account of how Pompeius Magnus treated Jerusalem in 63 BCE: "It was afterwards rebuilt, and Vespasian destroyed it again, and Hadrian did the same in our time. On account of these rebellions the poll tax imposed upon all Jews is heavier than that imposed upon the surrounding peoples."[19] Present misfortune (from the perspective of the first-century Jerusalemites) is overlaid with the earnest of future fiscal arrangements. Appian, like Benjamin Franklin, expounds the inevitability of death and taxes. But he does not do so continuously, or even often.

Appian as the main narrator, then, does not freely indulge in use of the future. This is true whether we are speaking about allusions to historical events that happened before Appian's own time but after the events he is currently narrating, or whether we mean speculations on the future world after the dissemination of the *Rhomaika* itself. As has been discussed elsewhere in this volume, however, there are many other sorts of future. Emily Greenwood's happy coinage of "micro-futures" is very pertinent here. Appian's narrator is chary of talking about the future; the characters inside the narrative observe no such embargo. The *Rhomaika* is full of attempts by agents within its text to anticipate, elucidate or prepare for their own immediate futures.

---

[17] App. *BC* 4.16.61. See also Hidber 2004, 182.
[18] App. *BC* 2.71.299.
[19] App. *Syr.* 50.252–3. For other examples of anachrony in Appian's account of particular places, see Pitcher 2012, 231.

1 Plans and prophecies

Appian's treatment of this behaviour needs to be viewed in relationship to the ways in which his historiographical predecessors had done so. Against this backdrop, some aspects of Appian's response to planning for the future on the part of his characters are unsurprising. In particular, Appian occasionally shares with prior historians a sceptical treatment of the ready assumption that a course of action will be "easy". Herodotus, as so often, gets the ball rolling here, with the breezy assurances of his Aristagoras that action against the Persians can be completed εὐπετέως.[20] In Thucydides, the notion that an enterprise can be accomplished ῥᾳδίως is likewise usually followed by a demonstration, shortly afterwards, that it is not.[21] Roman historiography continues this trend, with the appearance of the word "facile" in the works of Caesar a reliable indication that the plan to which it attaches itself will go sideways: the pattern begins with the reported assertion of Orgetorix at the beginning of the *Bellum Gallicum* that the Helvetii will be able to acquire ascendancy over the whole of Gaul "easily", and continues in a similar fashion from there.[22]

With this pattern so thoroughly ingrained in the historiographical tradition, it is not surprising that characters who make assumptions about the prospects for their future plans in the *Rhomaika* tend to be in for disappointment. The archetypal case here is that of Tiberius Gracchus, who fails to take account of the potential difficulties in the passing of his agrarian legislation: τοῦ περὶ αὐτὸ δυσχεροῦς οὐδὲν ἐνεθυμεῖτο.[23] Sure enough, his plan starts the chain of events that include his own death and, ultimately, the downfall of the Roman Republic. Appian, we may note, is more explicit from the outset than his predecessors are in the cases mentioned above that difficulties (τοῦ περὶ αὐτὸ δυσχεροῦς) do actually exist and that Gracchus is ignoring them; Appian is less interested here in generating the narrative *frisson* that is created by delaying the inevitable confirmation of the unavowed difficulty than Herodotus, Thucydides or Caesar.[24] It remains the case that the con-

---

[20] 5.31 (urging Artaphrenes to attack the Cyclades), 5.49.3–4 (on how easy it would be for the Spartans to beat the Persians) and 5.97.1 (on the ease of defeating the Persians again – this time, at Athens). See further Pelling 2007a, 179–80.
[21] Rood 1998, 34 with note 30.
[22] Caes. *BG* 1.2.2. For further analysis of this pattern in the works of Caesar, see Pitcher (forthcoming).
[23] App. *BC*. 1.11.43.
[24] Also, Tiberius Gracchus in Appian is not entirely devoid of the ability to anticipate future problems; note his careful provision that the land is to be inalienable: ὁ γάρ τοι Γράκχος καὶ

viction that courses of action will not pose difficulty is as hazardous for characters in Appian as it was in the works of his predecessors.

The tendency for human expectation to be disappointed or frustrated in the *Rhomaika* goes beyond simple failure to realise difficulties. Some manifestations of this are, again, familiar from other historians. Appian's misinterpreted oracles are less famous than those of Herodotus, whose account of Croesus is one to which Appian alludes.[25] But his account of Antiochus the Great in the *Syriake* includes a number of prophecies – appropriately so, in a book so concerned with advice and a ruler's success or failure in heeding it. Thus, the prophecy regarding Antiochus' advisor Hannibal that, "Libyssan earth shall cover Hannibal's remains", turns out to refer not to a death in Libya, as Hannibal himself believed, but rather to one in Bithynia.[26] In similar vein, the prophetic advice that Seleucus Nicator should avoid Argos ("If you keep away from Argos you will reach your allotted year, but if you approach that place you will die before your time") shows itself to refer not to any of the cities of Argos in the Peloponnese, Amphilochia or Oresteia, all of which the king managed to avoid, but to an altar called Argos on the way to Lysimachia, which he did not.[27]

In some other cases, the putative "prophecies" of the *Rhomaika* are simply wrong. Appian's presentation of Cornelius Lentulus' role in the Catilinarian Conspiracy, at the beginning of Book Two of the *Civil Wars*, may profitably be compared and contrasted with the prophecies that we have already seen. Appian is aware of the claim that Lentulus was motivated in his aspirations by a prophecy that three Cornelii would rule at Rome.[28] The claim appears at the same point in his narrative as it does in that of Sallust, when the Allobroges are turning informant against the individuals who attempted to suborn them.[29] Like Sallust, he

---

τόδε προϊδόμενος [i.e., attempts by the rich to buy up the allotments of others] ἀπηγόρευε μὴ πωλεῖν (App. *BC* 1.10.38).
25 Not for the disastrous river-crossing that stems from misunderstanding an oracle from Delphi, however, but rather for his subsequent relationship with Cyrus: "But Scipio called Syphax to the council, as he had shown himself sagacious and was acquainted with the country and took counsel with him as Cyrus did with Croesus, king of Lydia" (App. *Lib.* 28.116).
26 App. *Syr.* 11.44.
27 App. *Syr.* 63.331–2 with Pitcher 2012, 227 and note 21.
28 App. *BC* 2.4.15: οἱ δ' ὡμολόγουν [sc. "the Allobroges"], ὅσα τοῖς ἀμφὶ τὸν Λέντλον συνῄδεσαν, ἀχθέντας τε ἤλεγχον, ὡς ὁ Κορνήλιος Λέντλος εἴποι πολλάκις εἱμάρθαι τρεῖς Κορνηλίους γενέσθαι Ῥωμαίων μονάρχους, ὧν ἤδη Κίνναν καὶ Σύλλαν γεγονέναι.
29 Sall. *BC* 47: "Eadem Galli fatentur ac Lentulum dissimulantem coarguunt praeter litteras sermonibus, quos ille habere solitus erat: Ex libris Sibyllinis regnum Romae tribus Corneliis portendi; Cinnam atque Sullam antea, se tertium esse, cui fatum foret urbis potiri; praeterea ab incenso

glosses the prediction with the explanation that the other two Cornelii in question had been Cinna and Sulla. Unlike Sallust, however, he does not include the detail that this prophecy allegedly originated in the Sibylline oracles, or the claim that *prodigia* suggested civil war for the twentieth year after the burning of the Capitol. It can be perilous to draw too many conclusions from Appian's omissions. His account of the Catilinarian Conspiracy is perforce much more abbreviated than that of Sallust, who had the luxury of dedicating a whole monograph to the subject rather than a few paragraphs of a longer Roman history. Still, one might note that he deprives Lentulus of the potentially prestigious vatic source for the praetor's assertion, and so effaces even the possibility that the Sibylline books might have been wrong by presenting Lentulus' claim straightforwardly as the unsubstantiated gasconade of a delusional braggart.[30]

Prophecy, then, like other modes of predicting the future, turns out to have a rather limited amount of practical utility in Appian, at least as far as its mortal interpreters are concerned. As we have seen, prophecies that are actually presented as such usually do turn out to be true, albeit frequently susceptible to misinterpretation. We have noted that Appian seems to have trimmed away the genuine vatic elements from Lentulus's "prophecy" of rule at Rome, which was simply wrong.[31] Moreover, there are certainly prophecies in Appian which are easily understood and straightforward; the one from the *Syriake* that Lysimachus would be a king, "only to reign with toil and trouble" is a case in point.[32] There are likewise accurate and reasonably lucid prophetic moments on which people fail to act, or act without effect: Calpurnia's dream on the eve of the Ides of March, which leads her to try to keep Julius Caesar at home, would be a good example here.[33] Indeed, Appian notes as a defining characteristic of

---

Capitolio illum esse vigesumum annum, quem saepe ex prodigiis haruspices respondissent bello civili cruentum fore."

30 In fairness to the praetor, however, neither Sallust nor Appian confirms as narrator that Lentulus actually made these claims, merely that the Allobroges (who at this point had obvious motivation for such vilification) said that he had done so.

31 A more unusual case of a prophecy (of a kind) that was unfulfilled (or, at least, remained unfulfilled at the time of the production of the *Rhomaika*) would be Scipio Aemilianus' quasi-prophetic utterance of Hom. *Il.* 6.448–449 at the fall of Carthage, with an eye towards a possible future of Rome (App. *Lib.* 132.629; cf. also Grethlein 2013, 261), unless one sees this as presaging the speaker's own demise during a period of civil strife in *BC* 1.

32 App. *Syr.* 64.338.

33 App. *BC*. 2.115.480. At a lower level than full-blown prophecy, Appian also presents some cases of justified foreboding about a given course of action on the part of his characters which nevertheless fails to dissuade them from attempting it. Pompeius Magnus quoting Sophocles on

both Caesar and Alexander the Great that they tended to ignore signs and portents, even the ones that presaged their own demises; he devotes the (substantial) penultimate portion of his lengthy *synkrisis* between the two leaders to this topic, and illustrates it with copious examples,[34] commenting explicitly at the end that ἑάλωσαν ὅμως ὑπὸ τῷ λόγῳ τῶν μαντευμάτων.[35] Clear signs of oncoming trouble also gather around the last days of Cassius and Brutus;[36] in this case, the narrator is less interested in what the congregation of omens has to say about the personalities of the two Liberators than in the idea that the barrage of signs shows clear and unambiguous divine displeasure concerning their assassination of Caesar.[37] No one in Appian successfully uses an oracle to *avoid* a future, and the inevitability of Caesar's end (which does not, however, exonerate the Liberators from culpability in murdering their benefactor) draws explicit authorial comment: χρῆν γὰρ ἃ ἐχρῆν Καίσαρι γενέσθαι.[38]

The repeated defiance of expectation by events as they actually pan out in the *Rhomaika* is not very surprising, in light of the often equivocal attitude towards what foresight can reasonably hope to achieve in the works of earlier historians. On the other hand, Appian's *response* to the difficulty that humans have in predicting the future is a little more unusual. Like many classical historians, Appian acknowledges the large part played by the unexpected in human affairs.[39] Unlike many historians, the lesson that he draws from this is (within careful limits) a hopeful one.

---

how one surrenders one's freedom in approaching despotic rulers before disembarking to his death at Pelusium is a case in point (App. *BC*. 2.85.358).

34 App. *BC*. 2.152.636–153.646.
35 App. *BC*. 2.153.646.
36 App. *BC*. 4.134.563–566.
37 App. *BC*. 4.134.563: ἃ καὶ τὸ δαιμόνιον αὐτοῖς ἄρα ἐνεμέσησε καὶ προεσήμηνε πολλάκις. In the case of Brutus and Cassius, as in the case of Julius Caesar before them, Appian delays his coverage of most of the prophetic moments that point towards their demises until the individuals on whom he is focused are dead; he is not, for the most part, recapitulating signs and omens which he has already mentioned in the main narrative. This seems to be aimed at avoiding too much displeasing repetition: the dream of Calpurnia (note 33 above), which *does* appear in the main narrative, is not mentioned in the *synkrisis*, whereas the deformed sacrifice just before the end, which allows a more precise comparison to Alexander, appears in both (App. *BC*. 2.116.488–489 = 153.641).
38 App. *BC*. 2.116.489.
39 On contingency and how to theorise it in relation to thinking about Greek literature, see also Grethlein 2010, especially 6–9.

2 Nectar in a sieve

It is well known that hope, in classical literature, is not always treated as necessarily the good thing which Christian theology has made of it.[40] "Hope lies to mortals, and most believe her, but Man's deceiver was never mine."[41] Appian's stance, however, is rather different from the norm. He not only records instances of unanticipated *good* befalling people (which other historians do), but also draws from them an explicit moral as to the consequences of such a possibility for correct conduct (which is much rarer) and the prudence of maintaining hope in trying circumstances.

Two examples may be helpful here. The first is Viriathus' resistance to Roman mishandling of the Iberian peninsula at the beginning of the 140 s BCE:

> Excited by the new hopes with which he inspired them, they chose him as their leader... As soon as he conjectured that the others had made good their escape, he hastened away in the night by devious paths and arrived at Tribola with his nimble steeds, the Romans not being able to follow him at an equal pace by reason of the weight of their armour, their ignorance of the roads, and the inferiority of their horses. Thus did Viriathus, in an unexpected way, rescue his army from a desperate situation.[42]

This story, of course, illustrates Viriathus' superior tactical sense rather than brute contingency; Viriathus, like many others before and after him, recognises the power of speed, superior acquaintance with one's terrain and guerrilla tactics.[43] It is only really about the unexpected from the perspective of Viriathus' audiences: the Romans whom he foils, and the Iberian survivors whom he emboldens. It is interesting, however, that this is the perspective that Appian's narrator chooses to adopt. Unexpected success rescues an army from despair. Viriathus will fall, later, but not before he has caused the perfidious Romans a great deal of trouble and wrested concessions from them with a treaty. Hope does, in fact, lead the Iberians from a parlous situation.

Alongside this we can set the deliverance, from dire straits, of Cornificius and his men in Sicily:

---

[40] Hesiod *WD* 498–9 is perhaps the *locus classicus* here.
[41] A. E. Housman, *More Poems* VI, 5–8.
[42] App. *Iber.* 62.260–4.
[43] Classical historiography from Herodotus downwards acknowledges the efficacy of such tactics and how disconcerting they can be to their victims. Cf. Hdt. 4.46.7 (the Scythians fighting Cyrus the Great), Thuc. 4.33.2 (Pylos), Caes. *BG* 1.54.1, 4.16.5, 4.19.1–4, 6.29.1, with Krebs 2006, 130–2, and Pitcher (forthcoming).

> While they were in this state Laronius, who had been sent by Agrippa with three legions, made his appearance a long way off. Although it was not yet plain that he was a friend, still, as hope all the time led them to expect a friend, they once more recovered their spirits. When they saw the enemy abandon the water in order not to be exposed to attack on both sides, they shouted for joy with all their strength; and when the troops of Laronius shouted in return, they ran and seized the fountain. The leaders forbade the men to drink to excess; those who neglected this advice died while drinking. In this unexpected manner did Cornificius, and those of his army who managed to get away, escape to Agrippa at Mylae.⁴⁴

Once again, we note the focalisation of this episode through Cornificius and his men. Appian does note that Cornificius and his men do form a correct short-range expectation once Laronius is actually in view ("... hope all the time led them to expect a friend...") and failure to observe due moderation by drinking in excess does kill several of them even at the moment of deliverance. Nonetheless, the narrator's final focus is, again, very much on the *unexpectedness* of the delivery: note the similarity between the closural summations at the end of the two passages ("Thus did Viriathus, in an unexpected way...", "In this unexpected manner did..."). And, once again, the maintenance of hope is an important element in their final success ("hope all the time led them to expect a friend").

The narrator's emphasis here makes sense in light of one of Appian's own rare statements about what he hopes to achieve with the *Rhomaika*. This comes in Book Four of the *Civil Wars*, as Appian explains his reasons for including tales of miraculous escape during the dark times of the triumviral proscriptions: "As for stories of how some people unexpectedly found salvation and prosperity afterward, it is more pleasant for me to tell and it is more profitable to my audience to hope that if they never give up, they will survive."⁴⁵ Again, we note the significant collocation of unexpectedness, salvation, and hope. The tales of escape from the proscriptions illustrate the virtues of maintaining rational optimism, in light of the incalculable turns that the future can take. Appian sees them as having an exemplary force.⁴⁶

For Appian, then, *elpis* is potentially a more positive force than it sometimes appears to be elsewhere in Greek literature. It would be misleading, however, to characterise this attitude as straightforwardly "optimistic" – an adjective which, in conjunction with its antonym, has notoriously produced more heat than light in the consideration of other classical authors, particularly Vergil.⁴⁷ Appian is far

---

44 App. *BC.* 5.115.479–81.
45 App. *BC.* 4.36.149. It is fair to add that Appian's expression here is not straightforward.
46 Exemplary narratives in Appian still require a lot of work, although, *mutatis mutandis*, the insights of Chaplin 2000 on Livy might be applied with profit.
47 Hardie 1998, 94, with note 171.

from suggesting that events will always (or even often) turn out unexpectedly to one's advantage. Even a cursory reading of the *Rhomaika* would dispel such a notion; for one thing, the catalogue of unexpected escapes at the time of the Proscriptions balances a collection of grisly demises during the same period immediately before it.[48] Rather, Appian's attitude is that the *possibility*, however slight, of unexpected advantage should not be ruled out. One has to be, to borrow a contemporary idiom, in it to win it.

Appian's view of contingency in relation to the exercise of human planning emerges as something rather more complex and plausible than the simple assumption that the unexpected will always, almost malevolently, thwart any positive expectation. The unexpected is not, for Appian, a Lucy, who (the audience knows) will invariably snatch away the ball that Charlie Brown hopes to kick at the very last moment. Appian is aware that, *in extremis*, looking for an unexpected deliverance, as unlikely as it may be, is a more rational plan than simple despair – a secular version, if you will, of Pascal's Wager.

In this, he is not, in fact, alone amongst the ancient historians. Polybius, perhaps the most dedicated student amongst the classical historiographers of planning, its importance, and its limitations in the face of *Tyche*,[49] makes this explicit in his treatment of the Medionians, unexpectedly delivered from the Aetolians near the beginning of Book Two. Polybius has already, in the summary of Book One which opens this book, reminded his readers of how important the unexpected has been so far in his narrative: "I described all the terrible atrocities committed in this war, all its dramatic surprises and their issues, until it ended in the final triumph of Carthage".[50] Book Two opens with a description of the Aetolians besieging Medion, in the confident assumption of swift success, an assumption which the narrative soon shows to be unwarranted when the Medionians receive aid from the Illyrians. "The Medionians, thus unexpectedly saved, met in assembly... It seemed as if what had befallen this people was designed by Fortune to display her might to men in general. For in so brief a space of time she put it in their power to do to the enemy the very thing which they thought the enemy was just on the point of doing to themselves. The unlooked-for calamity of the Aetolians was a lesson to mankind never to discuss the future as if it were the present..."[51]

---

48 App. *BC.* 4.13–35.49–148 (though stories of deliverance interlace the grimmer narratives even in this earlier section).
49 On this, see now Maier 2012a.
50 Polyb. 2.1.3.
51 Polyb. 2.4.1–5.

The effect here, it is true, is rather more ambiguous than in Appian. Polybius see-saws between the perspectives of the exultant Medionians and the dejected Aetolians, whereas the passages we have examined from the *Rhomaika* stay more consistently with the point of view of those who have experienced the unexpected success (the men of Viriathus and Cornificius respectively); one might well say that the final impact, centring on what happened to the Aetolians, instantiates the more expected line that a too-confident expectation of success is likely to be thwarted, especially as the narrator claims that the story demonstrates how one should "never have any confident hope about things that may still turn out quite otherwise". On the other hand, Polybius has already engineered his narrative so that his audience's sympathy is more likely to be with the Medionians, since the Aetolians usually receive a bad press in his *Histories*.[52] While less insistent about it than Appian would later be, Polybius is, nevertheless, reminding us that the potency of the unexpected in human affairs – particularly in war-time – can have good consequences as well as bad.

Appian's futures, then, make an interesting topic of study. Unlike some other historians, he shows a very limited interest in the future that looms beyond the publication of the *Rhomaika* itself. His use of narrative prolepsis, while limited, makes a great deal of sense in terms of the larger architecture of the work, and its movement towards a mid-Second Century CE present. But, as with many other classical historians, his most truly compelling "futures" are to be found in the visions of what is to come entertained by the characters within his text – often falsified by experience, but not always to the detriment of the visionary.

---

[52] Cf., e.g., Polyb. 4.3, 18.4, 18.34, and 30.11. Their collective personality is depicted as changing somewhat, however, at Polyb. 32.4.2.

Melina Tamiolaki
Writing for Posterity in Ancient Historiography: Lucian's Perspective

Reflecting upon temporal categories is a challenging but nonetheless complex task.* On the one hand, history has been traditionally viewed as the study of the past. On the other hand, concerns about the future have always pervaded historical thinking: systematic investigation about the future is rather a modern concern which starts in the sixteenth century with T. More's *Utopia*[1] and leads up to sophisticated futurist historical theory,[2] but the history of utopias can be traced back to Plato and Aristophanes.[3] Another aspect of the concern about the future is prophecy: ancient texts are replete with oracles and seers; prophecy was also an essential element in Christian thought, but it would not be very radical to maintain that prophetic thinking is inherent in non-religious works, as well, ranging from Marx to Fukuyama.[4]

That said, the interconnection of *all* categories of time is present in all these discussions:[5] is it not true that reflection upon the future is based on present assumptions and also takes the past into consideration? Then why ask questions about categories of time at all? These questions are certainly legitimate; yet

---

* I am grateful to Alexandra Lianeri for useful suggestions which contributed to the refinement of my thesis. I also thank Jonas Grethlein, Antonis Liakos and Antonis Tsakmakis for further help concerning specific issues treated in this paper. I use the Loeb translation of Lucian (Kilburn 1959), sometimes adapted. Given that the topics treated in this paper are vast, the bibliography cited cannot be exhaustive.
1 See Liakos 2011, 25–45, for the background of the connection between utopian and historical thinking and the studies collected in Lisi 2012, for ancient and modern utopias. Cf. Staley 2007, 29.
2 Staley 2007 highlights the similarities between writing for the past and writing for the future and suggests that it is useful to make futurist scenarios based on present evidence. Cf. also, from a literary perspective, Eshel 2013, who shows how literary texts which deal with the past can help us shape the future.
3 See Bodonich 2002, for the Platonic utopia, and Starnes 1990, for More's relation to Plato. Concerning utopia in Aristophanes, see Konstan 1997, Hubbard 1997, Dobrov 1997a, Zeitlin 1999.
4 See for instance Flower 2008, for the importance of the seer in ancient Greece. Cf. Liakos 2011, 49–144, for modern apocalyptic thinking. See also Koselleck 2004, 9–25, for the shift from Christian thought to modernity. For important observations on Christian historiography, see van Nuffelen 2004 and 2012.
5 Gadamer 1993, 306, comments on the dialogic character of history (concerning past, present and future) and talks about a "fusion of horizons".

they should not aim at privileging one category of time over another,[6] but rather at *redefining* their inter-relation which is often complex and multi-layered: for instance, when Pericles takes pride in the present glory of Athens, he implicitly makes a comparison with its past achievements, but also makes projections about the future;[7] conversely, Isocrates' idealisation of the Athenian past derives from a disillusionment about the present and also involves plans about the future (in this case, the Panhellenic dream and the conquest of the barbarian Asia).[8] Having these broader preliminaries in mind, we can now proceed more specifically to the examination of future time in Greek historiography.

Future time can take two main forms in Greek historiography: firstly, it brings to surface *the narrative* of the historians: episodes which highlight the uncertainty of the future, which contain oracles and divination or attempts to foresee the future before an important political decision are indicative of the function of the future in Greek historiography;[9] besides, one could also mention proleptic passages, that is passages in which the historians, while describing events of the "past", show retrospective awareness of future events,[10] as well

---

[6] E.g. Hartog 2003 and 2011 establishes rather rigid distinctions concerning temporal categories, by claiming that our era is dominated by an obsessive concern with the present (what he calls presentism), in contrast with Antiquity, which valued the past. This assertion is over-simplified. See, for instance, Dunn 2007, who analyses the obsession with the present in late fifth-century Athens. Cf. also Hannoum 2008, for a review of Hartog 2003, who further comments on the methodological issues raised by Hartog's approach.

[7] See Thuc. 2.41.3: τοῖς νῦν καὶ τοῖς ἔπειτα θαυμασθησόμεθα. For the importance of the present in Thucydides, see Dunn 2007, 111–150.

[8] For Isocrates' political ideas, see Bringmann 1965. Cf. Nouhaud 1982, for the use of the past by Attic orators.

[9] See, for instance, for the uncertainty of the future Hdt. 3.65, 5.24.2, Thuc. 5.30.1, 4.64.2, Xen. *Anab.* 6.1.21. Cf. also the articles by Darbo-Peschanski, Tsakmakis, Baragwanath, Wiater and Miltsios in this volume.

[10] Famous proleptic passages are 2.65 and 6.15 in Thucydides, both of which are written from the vantage point of the fall of Athens in 404 BC. This is what Grethlein calls "futures past", Grethlein 2013, 8: "Capitalizing on retrospect, on the other hand, and choosing vantage points remote from the agents leads to strong teleologies. I suggest calling the underlying temporal dynamics 'futures past'. Besides entwining retrospect with prospect, the term captures the asymmetry between characters and historians – what is still future for the former, is already past for the latter – and signifies the point that regulates the balance between experience and teleology: the stronger the future in a given narrative's 'futures past', the stronger its focus on experience; the more the 'futures past' is treated as past, on the other hand, the more prominent becomes its teleology".

as counterfactual statements, that is passages which explicitly or implicitly invite the reader to think about alternatives concerning a given situation.[11]

Secondly, the statements of the historians themselves about the fortune of their work, the famous *topos* of posterity, constitutes another usual reference to future time. Herodotus in his proem states that he narrates important deeds of Greeks and barbarians, so that they do not fade with time,[12] whereas Thucydides intends his work to remain an ever-lasting possession.[13] Xenophon, for his part, inaugurates continuous history and gives an open ending to his *Hellenica*, urging other historians to continue his history in the future.[14] Although all three classical historians display an interest in posterity, on closer inspection we observe some differentiation in their emphases. For Herodotus memory seems to be an end in itself; he does not suggest, at least explicitly, that his work will have a practical utility. Thucydides, on the other hand, views past and future events as symmetrical, but he seems to limit the future impact of his work to those who will want to profit from it (ὅσοι δὲ βουλήσονται...). Finally, Xenophon inherits from both Herodotus and Thucydides, but his innovation lies rather in the fact that, contrary to his predecessors, he places himself more consciously in a tradition of continuity and consequently imagines a future continuator of his history.[15]

These two forms of future time are invariably present in the texts of all ancient historians. However, an attempt to combine these two perspectives raises some disturbing questions: if, as ancient texts continuously emphasise, the future is something unknown and even frightening, does this assertion have an impact on the posterity of the historians' work? Ancient historical texts focus rather

---

11 Famous counterfactual statements are Hdt. 7.139 (*what would have happened if* the Athenians had not saved Greece from the Persians) and Thuc. 2.65 (*what would have happened if* Pericles' successors were more prudent).
12 Hdt 1.1.1: Ἡροδότου Ἁλικαρνησσέος ἱστορίης ἀπόδεξις ἥδε, ὡς μήτε τὰ γενόμενα ἐξ ἀνθρώπων τῷ χρόνῳ ἐξίτηλα γένηται, μήτε ἔργα μεγάλα τε καὶ θωμαστά, τὰ μὲν Ἕλλησι, τὰ δὲ βαρβάροισι ἀποδεχθέντα, ἀκλεᾶ γένηται, τά τε ἄλλα καὶ δι' ἣν αἰτίην ἐπολέμησαν ἀλλήλοισι. See Bakker 2002, who comments on the proem.
13 Thuc. 1.22.4: καὶ ἐς μὲν ἀκρόασιν ἴσως τὸ μὴ μυθῶδες αὐτῶν ἀτερπέστερον φανεῖται· ὅσοι δὲ βουλήσονται τῶν τε γενομένων τὸ σαφὲς σκοπεῖν καὶ τῶν μελλόντων ποτὲ αὖθις κατὰ τὸ ἀνθρώπινον τοιούτων καὶ παραπλησίων ἔσεσθαι, ὠφέλιμα κρίνειν αὐτὰ ἀρκούντως ἕξει. κτῆμά τε ἐς αἰεὶ μᾶλλον ἢ ἀγώνισμα ἐς τὸ παραχρῆμα ἀκούειν ξύγκειται. For analyses of this phrase, see Marincola 1989a, Tsakmakis 1998. Cf. also, below.
14 Xen. *Hell.* 7.5.27: ἐμοὶ μὲν δὴ μέχρι τούτου γραφέσθω· τὰ δὲ μετὰ ταῦτα ἴσως ἄλλῳ μελήσει. See Tuplin 2007, for continuous history in the *Hellenica*.
15 It would be tempting to view these divergent approaches to the future as competing perceptions about time in Greek antiquity; but to dwell on this topic would be beyond the scope of this paper.

on the failure than on the success of predicting, capturing the future;[16] should this acknowledgment qualify the optimism of the historian about the future fortune and utility of his own work? These questions bring us to an examination of the topic of posterity under a new light. In my opinion, this is not simply a *topos* which is repeated from one historian to the other. I have argued elsewhere that there is an underlying tension in the texts of classical historians between their wish and proclamation to teach future audiences and their awareness that this teaching may have a limited scale.[17] The Hellenistic period marks a shift regarding this perception of utility. Polybius shows a greater optimism about it; contrary to the classical historians, he makes concrete statements and suggestions about it.[18] This optimism is inherited in Roman historiography as well. Cicero's famous statement about *historia magistra vitae*[19] certainly reflects this new conceptualisation, which is probably due to the fact that history, in the course of time, acquired a greater independence, became more standardised as a genre and, as a result, gradually had more serious claims to teaching and instructing.

One would thus expect that by the second century AD, when Lucian wrote his work *De Historia Conscribenda*, talking about posterity in historiography would indeed be a *topos* which Lucian could borrow from a long previous tradition. Yet Lucian's exploitation of this idea is rather idiosyncratic and in the course of my analysis I hope to show that he makes his own contribution to the topic of posterity in historiography. Before proceeding to Lucian's text, two preliminary observations are necessary. The first one is related to the way we (should) deal with satire. Lucian's *De Historia Conscribenda* is written in the form of a letter, addressed to Lucian's friend, Philo, but the epistolary status fades in the course of the treatise and the work ends up being a cynical *diatribe*, which combines the serious with the satirical tone.[20] Some scholars exclusively focus on satire and stress Lucian's "comedy of nihilism", to use Tim Whitmarsh's apt characterisation of the Lucianic corpus.[21] Others do not hesitate to take Lucian's statements at face value and examine them from the perspective of the

---

[16] See, for example, Romilly 1965 and 1966, for optimistic approaches concerning Thucydides. Cf., however, the illuminating discussion by Grethlein 2011, who stresses the limitations and intricacies of the role of instructing in ancient historiography.
[17] Tamiolaki 2013b.
[18] Plb. 12.25b.3: ἐκ γὰρ τῶν ὁμοίων ἐπὶ τοὺς οἰκείους μεταφερομένων καιροὺς ἀφορμαὶ γίνονται καὶ προλήψεις εἰς τὸ προϊδέσθαι τὸ μέλλον, καὶ ποτὲ μὲν εὐλαβηθῆναι, ποτὲ δὲ μιμούμενον τὰ προγεγονότα θαρραλεώτερον ἐγχειρεῖν τοῖς ἐπιφερομένοις. See also Plb. 3.4.8, 3.31.13, 12.25e6; cf. Miltsios (in this volume).
[19] Cic. *De or.* 2.36.
[20] See Homeyer 1965, 16–29.
[21] Whitmarsh 2001, 251.

theory of history.²² Not surprisingly, Lucian figures in the works of theoreticians of history, such as R. Koselleck.²³ My work on Lucian so far has been based on a combination of these two perspectives: far from considering Lucian as a forerunner of Koselleck, my aim is to examine closely the connotations of his views about history, taking into consideration the context of the second sophistic and the satirical dimension of his work.

The second preliminary observation concerns Lucian's originality or lack thereof. Lucian exhibits a fascinating familiarisation with classical sources, but this has proved a mixed blessing for him, if not a curse: either his work has been characterised as a pastiche²⁴ or meticulous attempts have been made to trace all of his references to classical sources, with the aim of showing that he is not original.²⁵ Nevertheless, a closer study of the passages which mention (or allude to) classical authors, shows that Lucian can indeed be original: he adapts classical tradition and uses it in a creative manner. I have tried to show this in a number of studies.²⁶ I would like to follow this line of argument in the examination of the topic of posterity in history.

References to posterity in Lucian's *De Historia Conscribenda* can be divided into three categories: a) comments about the historian's task to aspire to the future and descriptions of future audiences; b) references which link the idea of the posterity of historiography with the posterity of Lucian's own work; c) ironical and satirical remarks about historians who narrate future events. Interestingly, the idea of posterity is not spread in several chapters throughout the treatise: it is analysed at the beginning and then appears again with a new and expanded restatement at the end. This ring composition obviously serves to alert the reader to the importance of this idea.

We can now look more closely at these references. Already at the beginning of his work, Lucian, alluding to Thucydides, states that if history is intended to be an ever-lasting possession, this will not be an easy task for the writer of it.²⁷ Then he goes on to develop a central idea of the *De Historia Conscribenda*, ac-

---

22 See, for example, Fox 2001, for a penetrating analysis of Lucian's theoretical statements about truth in history.
23 Koselleck 2004, 131.
24 Bompaire 1958.
25 Avenarius' *Quellenforschung* about the *De Historia Conscribenda* is a characteristic example of this tendency (Avenarius 1956), which is, however, abandoned in recent scholarship on Lucian.
26 Tamiolaki 2013a, forthcoming a, forthcoming b.
27 Luc. *Hist. Conscr.* 5: τὸ δὲ οἶσθά που καὶ αὐτός, ὦ ἑταῖρε, ὡς <u>οὐ τῶν εὐμεταχειρίστων οὐδὲ ῥᾳθύμως συντεθῆναι</u> δυναμένων τοῦτ' ἐστίν, ἀλλ', εἴ τι ἐν λόγοις καὶ ἄλλο, πολλῆς τῆς φροντίδος δεόμενον, ἤν τις, ὡς ὁ Θουκυδίδης φησίν, ἐς ἀεὶ κτῆμα συντιθείη...

cording to which praise, myth and flattery should not have a place in history, since they run counter to the search for the truth; he concludes this section as follows:

> Τοιοῦτοι τῶν συγγραφόντων οἱ πολλοί εἰσι <u>τήμερον</u> καὶ τὸ ἴδιον καὶ τὸ χρειῶδες ὅ τι ἂν ἐκ τῆς ἱστορίας ἐλπίσωσι θεραπεύοντες, οὓς μισεῖσθαι καλῶς εἶχεν, <u>ἐς μὲν τὸ παρὸν</u> <u>κόλακας</u> προδήλους καὶ ἀτέχνους ὄντας, <u>ἐς τοὔπιὸν</u> δὲ ὕποπτον ταῖς ὑπερβολαῖς τὴν ὅλην πραγματείαν ἀποφαίνοντας.

> Most of our historians <u>today</u> are like that, courting private whim and the profit they expect from their history. One might well loathe them as blatant <u>flatterers</u> of no ability <u>in their own time</u>, while <u>to posterity</u> they make the whole business of writing history suspect by their exaggerations.[28]

Although Lucian seems to merge in his treatise praise, myth and flattery, it becomes evident from the subsequent analysis that his focus is mainly on flattery. In chapter 40, which is devoted to the traits of the ideal pupil of history, Lucian states again emphatically:

> ...καὶ ὅλως πῆχυς εἷς καὶ μέτρον ἀκριβές, ἀποβλέπειν <u>μὴ εἰς τοὺς νῦν ἀκούοντας</u> ἀλλ' εἰς τοὺς <u>μετὰ ταῦτα συνεσομένους τοῖς συγγράμμασιν.</u> εἰ δὲ <u>τὸ παραυτίκα</u> τις θεραπεύοι, τῆς τῶν <u>κολακευόντων μερίδος</u> εἰκότως ἂν νομισθείη..

> In short, the one standard, the one yardstick is to keep in view <u>not your present audience</u> but those <u>who will meet your work hereafter</u>. Whoever serves <u>the present</u> will rightly be counted a <u>flatterer</u> – a person on whom history long ago right from the beginning has turned its back...[29]

Finally, at the end of the treatise, in his recapitulation, Lucian again comments upon the distinction between writing for the present (which he views as equivalent to flattery) and writing for the future (which is equivalent to proper history):

> Τὸ δ' ὅλον ἐκείνου μοι μέμνησο – πολλάκις γὰρ τοῦτο ἐρῶ – καὶ <u>μὴ πρὸς τὸ παρὸν</u> μόνον ὁρῶν γράφε ὡς <u>οἱ νῦν</u> ἐπαινέσονταί σε καὶ τιμήσουσιν, ἀλλὰ <u>τοῦ σύμπαντος αἰῶνος</u> ἐστοχασμένος <u>πρὸς τοὺς ἔπειτα</u> μᾶλλον σύγγραφε...Χρὴ τοίνυν καὶ τὴν ἱστορίαν οὕτω γράφεσθαι <u>σὺν τῷ ἀληθεῖ</u> μᾶλλον πρὸς τὴν <u>μέλλουσαν ἐλπίδα</u> ἤπερ <u>σὺν κολακείᾳ</u> πρὸς <u>τὸ ἡδὺ τοῖς νῦν ἐπαινουμένοις.</u> οὗτός σοι κανὼν καὶ στάθμη ἱστορίας δικαίας.

> In general, please remember this – I shall repeat it time and again -: do not write <u>with your eye just on the present</u>, to win praise and honour from your <u>contemporaries</u>; aim <u>at eternity</u> and prefer to write <u>for posterity</u>...History then should be written in that spirit, with <u>truthful-</u>

---

28 Luc. *Hist. Conscr.* 13.
29 Luc. *Hist. Conscr.* 40.

ness and an eye to future expectations rather than with adulation and a view to the pleasure of present praise. There is your rule and standard for impartial history.³⁰

These passages permit several observations. It is evident that Lucian distances himself from the conventional view that teaching and instructing is the main purpose of aspiring to posterity. Lucian's idea of posterity is more concrete: he establishes a clear distinction between writing for the present and writing for the future (although at the final chapter he qualifies this idea), identifying the former with flattery and lies and the latter with truth and posterity. In this way, the *topos* of posterity is transformed into a methodological statement about the qualities of history writing. Furthermore, the idea of posterity is defined negatively: since the essential element in Lucian's argument is flattery, it follows that writing for posterity means *not writing in order to flatter*. There is no clear and positive indication as to how posterity can be achieved. Lucian seems to imply that the recipe for this is not to think at all about the present.

In order to explain Lucian's emphasis on praise in historiography, we should take into account the evolution of Greek historiography from the classical period till his own time. Praise was certainly an element of classical historiography and it developed increasingly from the fourth century onwards.³¹ But it was during the Hellenistic period, especially after the victories of Alexander the Great, that this trait became more predominant. Lucian reports an anecdote, according to which Alexander expresses his contempt for those who exhibit exaggerated tendencies to glorify him.³² Roman historiography also contained praise, this time for emperors³³ and Lucian certainly had experience of this excessive praise. In fact, the event which triggered his interest in writing a treatise about historiography was the Roman victory over the Parthians in AD 166 and the feverish trend of everyone to write history in order to praise the Romans.³⁴ However, Lucian's presentation contains two distinctive traits which deserve further exploration: the privileging of the future over the present and the insistence on flattery.

---

30 Luc. *Hist. Conscr.* 61, 63.
31 Herodotus was aware of the dangers of excessive praise (see, for example, Hdt. 1.95.1, his warning against excessive glorifications of Cyrus the Great). Thucydides also praises important generals such as Pericles and Brasidas, but praise of ideal leaders is a prominent trait of the fourth century BC (e.g. by authors, such as Xenophon and Isocrates). For praise in Greco-Roman Antiquity, see the seminal study of Pernot 1994.
32 Luc. *Hist. Conscr.* 12.
33 See Vout 2009 for representations of the emperor in Roman historiography.
34 Cf. Billault 2010 and Trédé 2010 for the contemporary taint in Lucian's *De Historia Conscribenda*. They both stress the fact that Lucian himself had the Roman emperor in mind when writing his treatise.

The idea that historians should aspire mainly to the future has broader and somewhat ambivalent connotations. The most important implication is the challenging (if not denial) of contemporary history: on the one hand, Lucian admires and extensively quotes Thucydides, who is the champion of contemporary history. On the other hand, he denigrates the present and prioritises the future as source of inspiration and aspiration. Adam Kemezis has recently argued that the lack of interest in contemporary historiography is a general trend of the Antonine period, which reflects the fact that during that period peace and stability prevailed.[35] Lucian does not state explicitly that writers should refrain from writing contemporary history, but he does not allow either for the possibility that someone who writes about a living person could adhere to the principle of truthfulness and objectivity. More provocatively, in a humorous passage, he writes about Homer:

Ὁμήρῳ γοῦν, καίτοι πρὸς τὸ μυθῶδες τὰ πλεῖστα συγγεγραφότι ὑπὲρ τοῦ Ἀχιλλέως, ἤδη καὶ πιστεύειν τινὲς ὑπάγονται, μόνον τοῦτο εἰς ἀπόδειξιν τῆς ἀληθείας μέγα τεκμήριον τιθέμενοι <u>ὅτι μὴ περὶ ζῶντος ἔγραφεν·</u> οὐ γὰρ εὑρίσκουσιν οὗτινος ἕνεκα ἐψεύδετ' ἄν.

Homer indeed in general tended towards the mythical in his account of Achilles, yet some nowadays are inclined to believe him; they cite as important evidence of his truthfulness the single fact that he <u>did not write about him during his lifetime</u>: they cannot find any motive for lying.[36]

That Homeric poetry can have claims to truth is obviously a comic distortion. Yet Lucian makes a point here: he touches upon the topic of historical distance as a prerequisite for impartial history writing. This idea is radical for antiquity, during which contemporary history was practised. Lucian does not raise specific issues which haunt modern historians (such as, for example, how much time should elapse for the writing of an impartial history, how we could have access to events which are very remote in time, the value of written versus oral evidence etc.[37]), although his example about Homer and Achilles might suggest that only a great temporal distance can guarantee impartiality. But his insistence on the future contributes to an alternative theorisation of the concept of historical distance: contrary to modern historical theories, which define historical distance as the

---

35 Kemezis 2010.
36 Luc. *Hist. Conscr.* 40.
37 For the topic of historical distance, see the theme issue of *History and Theory* 50 (2011), especially the studies of Hollander 2011, Hollander/Herman/Peters 2011, Bevir 2011, Philips 2011.

vantage point from which the historian observes the past and which can guarantee his impartiality, the future for Lucian is the ultimate scope to which the historian should aspire.[38] While in modern historical theories the historian looks (or should look) *backwards from* his "future", for Lucian the historian should look only *onwards, to the future*. Lucian thus does not limit historical distance to the temporal gap between the historian's time and the time of the events narrated; rather he amplifies its content, by stressing the open and indefinite character of the future which the historian should always have in mind. The ultimate implication of this emphasis on the historian's aspiration to the future is that the historian *should not be attached to his own time*.

The corollary of this radical view is that *he should not be attached to any place, either*. Lucian describes the ideal historian as follows:

> Τοιοῦτος οὖν μοι ὁ συγγραφεὺς ἔστω – ἄφοβος, ἀδέκαστος, ἐλεύθερος, παρρησίας καὶ ἀληθείας φίλος, ὡς ὁ κωμικός φησι, τὰ σῦκα σῦκα, τὴν σκάφην δὲ σκάφην ὀνομάσων, οὐ μίσει οὐδὲ φιλίᾳ τι νέμων οὐδὲ φειδόμενος ἢ ἐλεῶν ἢ αἰσχυνόμενος ἢ δυσωπούμενος, <u>ἴσος δικαστής</u>, εὔνους ἅπασιν ἄχρι τοῦ μὴ θατέρῳ τι ἀπονεῖμαι πλεῖον τοῦ δέοντος, <u>ξένος ἐν τοῖς βιβλίοις καὶ ἄπολις, αὐτόνομος, ἀβασίλευτος</u>, οὐ τί τῷδε ἢ τῷδε δόξει λογιζόμενος, ἀλλὰ τί πέπρακται λέγων.

> That, then, is the sort of man the historian should be: fearless, incorruptible, free, a friend of free expression and the truth, intent, as the comic poet says, on calling a fig a fig and a trough a trough, giving nothing to hatred or to friendship, sparing no one, showing neither pity nor shame nor obsequiousness, <u>an impartial judge</u>, well disposed to all men up to the point of not giving one side more than its due, <u>in his books a stranger and a man without a country, independent, subject to no sovereign</u>, not reckoning what this or that man would think, but stating the facts.[39]

Koselleck remarks that Lucian is the first to introduce the term *apolis* for the ideal historian.[40] Indeed, this is another surprising idea which runs counter to the whole experience of Greek historiography: historians of all times were embedded in their *poleis* and were active citizens, even if some of them were compelled to write their history in exile. Lucian is here influenced by Cynic values which exhibit disdain for political conventions,[41] but the adaptation of Cynic philosophy to the description of the ideal historian is significant: the statement

---

38 There is an allusion to the topic of distance as a measure of objectivity in the comparison of the historian with Zeus (Luc. *Hist. Conscr.* 49), but interestingly, the implication is about *spatial* distance: ἀφ'ὑψηλοῦ ὁρῶντι.
39 Luc. *Hist. Conscr.* 41.
40 Koselleck 2004, 131.
41 See Nesselrath 1990, Porod 2009, for the influence of Cynic philosophy on Lucian.

that the ideal historian should not be attached to any city (the repetition of terms denoting political independence is telling in this passage: ἄπολις, αὐτόνομος, ἀβασίλευτος) complements Lucian's previous advice, that he should not be attached to his own time. Consequently, for Lucian the ideal historian should be detached from space and time – a most incredible creature!

I would like to suggest that Lucian is aware of the radicalness of his view about the distinction between writing for the present and writing for the future, but he pushes this idea to its extreme, in order to make his satire more powerful and effective: writing for posterity means essentially to deny a category of time, in this case the present. For this reason he proceeds to an adaptation of the Thucydidean methodological chapter:

> καὶ ἐς μὲν ἀκρόασιν ἴσως τὸ μὴ μυθῶδες αὐτῶν ἀτερπέστερον φανεῖται· ὅσοι δὲ βουλήσονται τῶν τε γενομένων <u>τὸ σαφὲς</u> σκοπεῖν καὶ τῶν μελλόντων ποτὲ αὖθις κατὰ τὸ ἀνθρώπινον τοιούτων καὶ παραπλησίων ἔσεσθαι, ὠφέλιμα κρίνειν αὐτὰ ἀρκούντως ἕξει. κτῆμά τε ἐς αἰεὶ μᾶλλον ἢ ἀγώνισμα ἐς τὸ παραχρῆμα ἀκούειν ξύγκειται.

And the results, by avoiding patriotic storytelling, will perhaps seem the less enjoyable for listening. Yet if they are judged useful by any who wish to see <u>the clarity</u> about both past events and those that at some future time, in accordance with human nature, will recur in similar or comparable ways, this will suffice. It is a possession for all time, not a competition piece to be heard at the moment for which it has been composed.[42]

Lucian paraphrases as follows:

> Ὁ δ' οὖν Θουκυδίδης εὖ μάλα τοῦτ' ἐνομοθέτησεν...κτῆμά τε γάρ φησι μᾶλλον ἐς ἀεὶ συγγράφειν ᾖπερ ἐς τὸ παρὸν ἀγώνισμα, καὶ μὴ τὸ μυθῶδες ἀσπάζεσθαι ἀλλὰ <u>τὴν ἀλήθειαν τῶν γεγενημένων ἀπολείπειν τοῖς ὑστέρον</u>. καὶ ἐπάγει τὸ <u>χρήσιμον</u> καὶ ὃ τέλος ἄν τις εὖ φρονῶν ὑπόθοιτο ἱστορίας, ὡς εἴ ποτε καὶ αὖθις τὰ ὅμοια καταλάβοι, ἔχοιεν, φησί, <u>πρὸς τὰ προγεγραμμένα ἀποβλέποντες εὖ χρῆσθαι τοῖς ἐν ποσί</u>.

Thucydides laid down this law very well... For Thucydides says that he is writing a possession for ever, rather than a prize-essay for the present occasion, that he does not welcome fiction but is leaving <u>to posterity the true account of what happened.</u> He brings, in, too, the question of <u>usefulness</u> and what is, surely, the purpose of sound history: that if ever again men find themselves in a like situation they may be able, he says, <u>from a consideration of the records of the past to handle rightly what now confronts them.</u>[43]

Lucian introduces the loaded term ἀλήθεια, which is absent from Thucydides, and replaces the word ὠφέλιμα with the more practical term χρήσιμον. Furthermore, Lucian's description is much more concrete than Thucydides'. Thucydides

---

[42] Thuc. 1.22.4. Translation Lattimore 1998 (adapted).
[43] Luc. *Hist. Conscr.* 42.

talks about τὸ σαφὲς of both past and future events,⁴⁴ whereas Lucian, more pragmatically, comments on the practical utility of studying past events for the present (τοῖς ἐν ποσί: the only allusion to the didactic function of history). More importantly, Thucydides does not establish a clear dichotomy between writing for the present and writing for the future and does not raise the issue of flattery, which pervades Lucian's treatise. In brief, Lucian adapts the Thucydidean chapter to fit his idea that historians *should aspire only to the future*.

The adaptation of Thucydides has further connotations which are linked with Lucian's general modelling upon the historian's *persona*. In another paper I have argued that Lucian in the *De Historia Conscribenda* systematically models his *persona* upon the historian's *persona*. By using expressions, images, methodological phrases which allude to classical historians, he displays his acquaintance with this genre and subsequently justifies his task, to write the rules for it.⁴⁵ Lucian has again recourse to Thucydides when he describes the posterity of his own work: he models it upon Thucydides' statement about the plague.⁴⁶ In my opinion, the imitation of Thucydides at this point is significant. Lucian seems to suggest that his treatise will be as useful as Thucydides' history: future historians will benefit from his treatise, in order to write better history, such as future audiences will benefit from Thucydides' history, in order to understand plagues and handle them more successfully.

We can now turn to the description of the future audience of the historian. Lucian describes the (future) audience to which the historian should aspire as follows:

Ἔτι κἀκεῖνο εἰπεῖν ἄξιον ὅτι οὐδὲ τερπνὸν ἐν αὐτῇ <u>τὸ κομιδῇ μυθῶδες καὶ τὸ τῶν ἐπαίνων μάλιστα πρόσαντες</u> παρ' ἑκάτερον τοῖς ἀκούουσιν, ἢν μὴ <u>τὸν συρφετὸν</u> καὶ τὸν <u>πολὺν δῆμον</u> ἐπινοῇς, ἀλλὰ τοὺς <u>δικαστικῶς</u> καὶ νὴ Δία συκοφαντικῶς προσέτι γε ἀκροασομένους, οὓς οὐκ ἄν τι λάθοι παραδραμόν, ὀξύτερον μὲν τοῦ Ἄργου ὁρῶντας καὶ πανταχόθεν τοῦ

---

44 This claim is quite controversial. See Hornblower 1991, *ad loc.*; see also Woodman 1988, 23–28, who links τὸ σαφές with ἐνάργεια.
45 Tamiolaki (forthcoming a).
46 Luc. *Hist. Conscr.* 5: οἶδα μὲν οὖν οὐ πάνυ πολλοὺς αὐτῶν ἐπιστρέψων, ἐνίοις δὲ καὶ πάνυ ἐπαχθὴς δόξων, καὶ μάλιστα ὁπόσοις ἀποτετέλεσται ἤδη καὶ ἐν τῷ κοινῷ δέδεικται ἡ ἱστορία. εἰ δὲ καὶ ἐπῄνηται ὑπὸ τῶν τότε ἀκροασαμένων, μανία ἂν εἴη ἡ ἐλπίς, ὡς οἱ τοιοῦτοι μεταποιήσουσιν ἢ μεταγγράψουσί τι τῶν ἅπαξ κεκυρωμένων καὶ ὥσπερ ἐς τὰς βασιλείους αὐλὰς ἀποκειμένων. ὅμως δὲ οὐ χεῖρον καὶ πρὸς αὐτοὺς ἐκείνους εἰρῆσθαι, ἵν', <u>εἴ ποτε πόλεμος ἄλλος συσταίη</u>, ἢ Κελτοῖς πρὸς Γέτας ἢ Ἰνδοῖς πρὸς Βακτρίους (οὐ γὰρ πρὸς ἡμᾶς γε τολμήσειεν ἄν τις, ἁπάντων ἤδη κεχειρωμένων) ἔχωσιν ἄμεινον συντιθέναι τὸν κανόνα τοῦτον προσάγοντες, ἤνπερ γε δόξῃ αὐτοῖς ὀρθὸς εἶναι· Cf. Thuc. 2.48.3: ἐγὼ δὲ οἷόν τε ἐγίγνετο λέξω, καὶ ἀφ' ὧν ἄν τις σκοπῶν, <u>εἴ ποτε καὶ αὖθις ἐπιπέσοι</u>, μάλιστ' ἂν ἔχοι τι προειδὼς μὴ ἀγνοεῖν, ταῦτα δηλώσω αὐτός τε νοσήσας καὶ αὐτὸς ἰδὼν ἄλλους πάσχοντας.

> σώματος, ἀργυραμοιβικῶς δὲ τῶν λεγομένων ἕκαστα ἐξετάζοντας, ὡς τὰ μὲν παρακεκομ-
> μένα εὐθὺς ἀπορρίπτειν, παραδέχεσθαι δὲ τὰ δόκιμα καὶ ἔννομα καὶ ἀκριβῆ τὸν τύπον,
> πρὸς οὓς ἀποβλέποντα χρὴ συγγράφειν, <u>τῶν δὲ ἄλλων ὀλίγον φροντίζειν, κἂν διαρραγῶσιν
> ἐπαινοῦντες.</u>
>
> In history <u>complete fiction and praise that is heavily biased</u> on one side does not even give pleasure to an audience, if you leave out <u>the common rabble</u> and take note of those who will listen <u>in the spirit of judges</u> and indeed of fault-finders as well. Nothing will get past their scrutiny: their eyes are keener than Argus' like a money-changer, rejecting at once what is false but accepting current coin that is legal tender and correctly minted. These are the people to keep in mind when you write history; <u>do not give the slightest thought to the rest even if they burst themselves with applauding.</u>[47]

The detailed description of the historian's future audience deserves close attention. Classical historians were vague as to the public to which they aspired and we can only infer from their work whether they addressed the masses or the elite or a specific political party or social group.[48] It was only later, in the Hellenistic period and onwards, that historians started giving more sophisticated depictions of their public. Polybius, for example, goes so far as to divide prospective readers of history into three categories.[49] Lucian may borrow from this tradition, but the adaptation he makes is again important: first of all, he explicitly mentions that the ideal historian should aspire to the few; secondly, he raises again the topic of excessive praise, this time of the audience; thirdly, and perhaps more tellingly, he provides a characterisation of the ideal future audience of the historian, which he imagines as very demanding, meticulous and severe. This characterisation fits with the description of the ideal historian that he gave before (note the parallel δικαστικῶς ἀκουσομένους and ἴσος δικαστής). Lucian thus suggests a correspondence between the ideal historian and its public, admittedly a very elitist approach.

Furthermore, again modelling upon the historian, Lucian gives a description of his own future audience:

> οἶδα μὲν οὖν <u>οὐ πάνυ πολλοὺς</u> αὐτῶν ἐπιστρέψων, <u>ἐνίοις δὲ</u> καὶ πάνυ ἐπαχθὴς δόξων.
> Now I know that I shall <u>not</u> convert <u>many</u>: on the contrary, I will seem annoying <u>to some</u>.[50]

It is not by chance that this audience is again an elitist audience, as suggested by the distinction between the few and the many. We should also note the parallel

---

47 Luc. *Hist. Conscr.* 10.
48 See Tamiolaki 2013b (with previous bibliography).
49 Plb. 9.1.2–6.
50 Luc. *Hist. Conscr.* 5.

between ἐπαχθὴς δόξων (seeming annoying), which Lucian uses for the mass of his audience who will be annoyed by his frankness, and ἔπαινοι ἐπαχθεῖς (annoying praise), which he employs in chapter 11, for the mass of the historian's audience who will not like hearing excessive praises for somebody else:

> ἐῶ λέγειν ὅτι οἱ <u>ἔπαινοι ἑνὶ μὲν ἴσως τερπνοί, τῷ ἐπαινουμένῳ, τοῖς δὲ ἄλλοις ἐπαχθεῖς</u>, καὶ μάλιστα ἢν ὑπερφυεῖς τὰς ὑπερβολὰς ἔχωσιν, οἵους αὐτοὺς οἱ πολλοὶ ἀπεργάζονται, τὴν εὔνοιαν τὴν παρὰ τῶν ἐπαινουμένων θηρώμενοι καὶ ἐνδιατρίβοντες ἄχρι τοῦ πᾶσι προφανῆ τὴν κολακείαν ἐξεργάσασθαι.

> I need not say that <u>eulogies may be pleasing to one man, him who is praised, and annoying to others</u>, especially if they contain monstrous overstatements, the kind that most people make when they seek favour from those who are praised, persisting until they have made their flattery obvious to everyone.[51]

Overall, Lucian's presentation of the idea of posterity comprises three distinctive elements: an underestimation of the present, an obsession with the topic of flattery (flattery – or excessive praise – emerges in almost every discussion of posterity as the crucial element historian should avoid) and a concern about the posterity of his own work. In order to interpret Lucian's presentation, we should inscribe it into the broader context of the second sophistic and the concerns of Lucian's time. First of all, flattery is a topic which preoccupied ancient rhetoric: it is abundantly attested and denigrated throughout the Lucianic corpus[52] and is also extensively treated by Lucian's contemporaries, such as Athenaeus and Plutarch.[53] It is thus no wonder that Lucian projects onto historiography a contemporary concern. Secondly, the idea of posterity of Lucian's own work has broader connotations, since it creates a certain merging between rhetoric and history. In an illuminating article, Peter von Moellendorf has argued that Lucian's aim in the *De Historia Conscribenda* is to inscribe historiography to the rhetoric of his time.[54] I find this suggestion compelling and hope that my previous analysis can reinforce it: the good rhetorician (in this case Lucian) can invest his discourse with historiographical elements, in the same way as the good historian is (or should be) equipped with the qualities of the good rhetorician. From this perspective, Lucian suggests that a cardinal quality of the orator, that is the avoidance of flattery, should also characterise the historian.

---

51 Luc. *Hist. Conscr.* 11.
52 Luc. *Nigr.* 23, *Tim.* 48, *De merc. cond.* 28, *Men.* 11, *Pro Imag.* 5, 21, *Apol.* 9.
53 Athen. *Deipn.* 6.66, 6.69, 6.76, Plu. *Mor.* 51 A8, 57D7, 61 A3, 64E1, 66D9, 778D8, 864D7, 868D7.
54 Von Moellendorf 2001.

Another means by which Lucian might serve as a guide for historians is the way he deals with the categories of time (present, past and future) in the *De Historia Conscribenda*. We observed above that he minimises the importance of caring about the present. But does this make him an advocate of "futurism'? Not necessarily: the ideal historian should only *aspire to the future*, but not attempt to describe future events. Lucian is contemptuous of historians who try to imitate seers.[55] What about dealing with the past? And which past? In the course of the treatise, we can discern two different attitudes concerning the Hellenistic and the classical past respectively (we could say a less distant and a more distant past): the former is a constant and lively point of reference for Lucian. All the anecdotes he mentions (about Diogenes and the cloak, about Alexander the Great, about the Cnidian architect) come from this period. Even the feverish trend of historians to write history cannot but recall the sensational historiography of the Hellenistic period. On the other hand, the classical past is viewed as more static, something worthy of admiration and imitation, but with which there is no active interaction. If my hypothesis about Lucian modelling on the historian's *persona* is correct, then Lucian may want to suggest that his way of dealing with the past could also serve as a model for future historians: that a creative use of the distant past and an active engagement with the recent one could be another way to guarantee posterity.

A possible objection to my analysis could be the following: flattery is a form of bias and historians of all times (from Thucydides to Ranke) have commented on the need and difficulty of unbiased historical writing;[56] so there is no originality in Lucian's thesis. However, the originality lies precisely in the fact that Lucian *singles out* flattery among *many forms* of bias. For instance, he could have also elaborated on blame and stated that excessive blame is equally bad. Yet he makes only one passing reference to this issue, at the end of his treatise, in order to criticise Theopompus.[57] Why would he make this choice? In the light of my previous analysis about the merging of the rhetorician and the historian in Lucian's treatise, it would be tempting to interpret this silence as not accidental: Lucian does not insist on blame, because he has himself recourse to blame throughout a great part of his treatise. More broadly, blame is an important element of satire, so dwelling on it would be self-deconstructing. Consequently, the emphasis on flattery and excessive praise is compatible with the concerns of Lucian as both rhetorician and satirist.

---

55 Luc. *Hist. Conscr.* 31.
56 See Luce 1989.
57 Luc. *Hist. Conscr.* 59.

In conclusion, my analysis has shown that Lucian's approach concerning the *topos* of posterity in historiography is manifold. On the one hand, his emphasis on flattery as a trait of writing history for the present reflects the interests of his own time, but also his thematic priorities. On the other hand, Lucian's treatment goes beyond these concerns. His idea of posterity contains original characteristics which render it radical both for Antiquity and for modern times: for Lucian "writing for the future" is transformed into a methodological statement, the implications of which challenge ancient historical practice and can also contribute to the redefinition of modern concepts, such as that of historical distance. Finally, and perhaps more intriguingly, Lucian's treatment has a self-referential aspect: Lucian seems to be interested in the posterity of his own work as well. The idea of posterity thus acquires even broader connotations: it is related to the desire of ancient theoreticians to render their treatises useful. In this way, I would like to suggest, the idea of posterity ultimately contributes to the legitimisation of the genre of the theory of history.

Toward the Modern Futures of Greek Times

Dennis Pausch
On the Shoulders of Greeks?
Future Time in Livy's *Ab urbe condita*

I Introduction: Livy on (his) future

Livy begins book 31, approaching the year 201 BC, with the following words:[1]

> me quoque iuvat, velut ipse in parte laboris ac periculi fuerim, ad finem belli Punici pervenisse. nam etsi profiteri ausum perscripturum res omnes Romanas in partibus singulis tanti operis fatigari minime conveniat, tamen, cum in mentem venit tres et sexaginta annos – tot enim sunt a primo Punico ad secundum bellum finitum – aeque multa volumina occupasse mihi quam occuparint quadringenti duodenonaginta anni a condita urbe ad Ap. Claudium consulem, qui primum bellum Carthaginiensibus intulit, iam provideo animo, velut qui proximis litori vadis inducti mare pedibus ingrediuntur, quidquid progredior, in vastiorem me altitudinem ac velut profundum invehi et crescere paene opus, quod prima quaeque perficiendo minui videbatur.

> I too am happy to have reached the end of the Punic War – I somehow feel I have personally taken part in its hardships and dangers! I realize that it is most inappropriate for one who has made the rash promise to cover all Roman history to flag in specific sections of such a great work; and yet it does occur to me that the sixty-three years between the beginning of the First Punic War and the end of the Second have taken up as many rolls as did the four hundred and eighty-four years between the foundation of the city and the consulship of Appius Claudius, the man who began the first war with Carthage. I feel like someone who wades out into the sea after being initially attracted to the water by the shallows next to the shore; and I foresee any advance only taking me into even more enormous, indeed bottomless, depths, and that this undertaking of mine, which seemed to be diminishing as I was completing the earliest sections, is now almost increasing in size.

What Livy offers here, is a rather exceptional outlook into the future, namely into his own as an historian 'on the job', the one he accepted with the enthusiasm of a young man and will take him his whole lifetime to finish. If one is prepared to take his picture of the coast literally, shoulders would have been quite useful, not least Greek ones, but I am afraid this is a thoroughly Roman passage, talking about one large empire in the real world and another one in terms of historiography, and there can be little doubt that it is placed with some intent at the start of that part of Livy's narrative in the course of which Greece will turn Roman.[2]

---

1 Liv. 31.1.1–5 (Latin text following Briscoe 1991, translation by Yardley 2000).
2 For the well-planned structure of Livy's narrative in the books 31–45 see e.g. Luce 1977.

But apart from this very special scene at the shore, can other kinds of seeing into the future can be observed in Livy's *ab urbe condita* and is it possible to find models for these techniques – or for some of them and not for others – in the works of the Greek historians, especially in the *Histories* of Polybius highly influential in the development of historiography in Rome? To answer this question at least partially and thereby to make a contribution to the general concept of this volume by looking at Greek historiography from a Roman point of view is the aim of the following remarks. After briefly discussing the possible objection that there is no place for future time within the annalistic framework in the strict sense of the word, I would like to sketch the different and quite numerous forms of presenting previews which Livy nonetheless employs in his narrative. In doing so, I will neither follow the chronological order of their appearance in the text nor use an arrangement as suggested by the categorisations of narratology. Instead, I will try to move from techniques well established already by Greek historians (by which within the limits of this paper I mean Polybius more or less) to strategies that seem to be more specific either to Livy in particular or to Roman historiography in general.

II Objection: Annalistic layout and the linearity of time

Not too long ago, most scholars of Latin literature would have subscribed to a view like this: the easiest way to arrange an historical account is to stick to the model of primitive chronicles, writing it year by year, especially in Rome where everything old is considered sacred anyway. Livy being a talented storyteller, but a very limited historian, has opted for this way of writing against more adequate forms like, for instance, the monographs of Sallust without further reflections. The resulting annalistic layout added something to the solemn tone of his work, but was bound up with a number of other disadvantages mainly due to its inflexibility.

One of the problems I have with this view is that it excludes Livy from the intense discussion on how history should be written that is taking place in the middle of the first century BC and in which he surely is deeply involved, even if he is reluctant to make explicit theoretical statements.[3] This debate, of course, is not confined to Roman historians alone. At this time, Dionysius of Halicarnassus, to cite a well-

---

[3] For further argument see e.g. Pausch 2011, 53–65.

known example, is criticising Thucydides for the disorientating effect that his chronological arrangement has on his reader.⁴ Some time before, Polybius spent quite a few words about the right way of structuring historical events in general and about the risks involved in a strictly chronological (and geographical) arrangement.⁵ His methodological statements had been very influential for the development of Roman historiography during the late second and early first century BC, giving rise to the establishment of the monograph as a new subgenre, but also to a modernisation of the annalistic way of writing history.⁶

That is, so to speak, the state of the art, as Livy takes up his pen. And against the backdrop of this ongoing discussion, he will have made his decision only after pondering the assets and drawbacks of the form chosen by him. This does, of course, not necessarily mean that for him the same reasons had been as crucial as for Polybius, who for his part wants to emphasise the intertwining of the events from book 7 onwards (his famous συμπλοκή).⁷ On the contrary, the decisive point for Livy will have been the chronological and geographical orientation of all events towards Rome as the centre of his narrative almost from the outset as well as the centre of the Mediterranean world in future. By presenting the history of the whole *oikoumene* within a firmly Roman time frame almost *ab initio* he not only makes the past commensurable with the present and furthermore to the future, but he highlights the teleological outlook towards Rome's domination in his own times as the vanishing point of his work. Even without the proem and his proud comments on the future of the city to be founded in book 1,⁸ an attentive reader could have guessed the terminus of his work from the way the story is told. We have here, thus, a kind of implicit foreseeing by narrative structure.⁹

Despite his fundamental decision not only to maintain the annalist framework in principle, but also to employ a recurrent pattern within the account of many, but by no means all, individual years, Livy's narration is much more flexible than was often assumed.¹⁰ This is the case even in the sections of his work which looks more or less uniform at first sight, as has been shown in a seminal

---

4 Cf. esp. Dion. Hal. de Thuc. 9,8 and Dion. Hal. Pomp. 3,13–14; for the intellectual context see Wiater 2011a, 130–164.
5 Cf. e.g. Pol. 1.3.3–6; 4.28; 15.24 and 38.5–6.
6 For a relevant summary of Polybius' influence on Roman historians see Davidson 2009.
7 On this concept see e.g. Walbank 1975; Sacks 1981, 116–120; and Rood 2007, 173f.
8 Cf. Liv. praef. esp. 6f.
9 For further argument see e.g. Pausch 2011, 77–102.
10 See e.g. McDonald 1957, 155–159.

paper by John Rich.[11] Especially in books 21 to 45, the structure of the narrative seems to be strictly linear using clear caesurae to highlight the periodic progress through time: at the end of every old year, elections are held, whereas the next year starts with the new consuls entering their office (according to Roman tradition on the 15th of March), assigning their provinces, expiating prodigies and finally leaving Rome together with the narrator who often does not come back to the capital before the end of the year, but switches from one scene of action to the other (usually from one theatre of war to the next).

But even within this fixed pattern Livy employs elements which work against a too strict linearity of time. These techniques are the result of an ongoing process of refurbishment taking place in order to make Roman historiography more readable and better adapted to convey its specific conception of history. This development is influenced by Polybius and other Greek writers, but also by the interests of the Roman authors and their readers. We will now take a closer look at the literary strategies employed by Livy to present future time.

III Variation: Presenting future time by learning from his predecessors

1 Knowing the future: Previews by the primary narrator

The most straightforward way to talk about the future in an historiographic work is, of course, to make use of the fact the author himself knows more about the further course of the events not only than the historical figures (as is natural) but even than his own primary narrator who as a rule maintains the temporal point of view of his characters. Exceptions are usually confined to *praefationes* and similar passages, for which Polybius' summary of Rome's second war against Carthage at the start of his third book offers a good example[12] – and one that is explained at length by the author as well.[13] The narrative option of explicit previews by the primary narrator within an otherwise annalistic framework, however, has not arrested Polybius' theoretical interest in the same way as other methodological problems surely have, although there are quite a number of instances for formal prolepsis in his histories, as has been pointed out by Tim Rood.[14]

---

[11] See Rich 2009 (an earlier version was published in the electronic journal Histos 1997).
[12] Cf. Pol. 3.1.9–3.9.
[13] Cf. Pol. 3.1.4–1.8.
[14] See Rood 2007, 176–181.

Most of them are directed towards Rome's sway over the Mediterranean world as the terminal point of his work[15] or – in the form of external prolepsis – to a decline afterwards.[16] Passages of the first type can be found in Livy, too, whereas external prolepsis is certainly less common in a work getting rather close to the time of its origin. Yet Livy does something similar in giving explicit previews to some of the greatest disasters of Rome's military history, for example, by opening up his ninth book with the remark that this year (321 BC) will lead to the famous defeat of the Caudine forks.[17] The same applies to the even worse result of the battle of Cannae which is previewed several times explicitly as well as implicitly before it actually takes places on 2nd of August 216 BC.[18]

Apart from this, Polybius likes to point out the later penalisation of what – in his view – is unjust behaviour of historical figures (as, for example, the treaty concluded by Antiochus III and Philip V to the detriment of Ptolemy V in 203 BC).[19] In a similar way, Livy alludes to the imminent downfall of Capua in book 26, one of the few cities that changed sides to Hannibal after the battle at Cannae and thus deserves punishment from a Roman point of view (though Livy's following account is more nuanced than one might suppose).[20] In this context, he makes use of a supernatural device, too, as we will find again in one of the next sections, but the decisive point for us here is the confirmation of the interpretation allegedly given by an historical figure in the year 211 BC by the narrator himself as well:[21]

> hoc ultimum, utcumque initum finitumque est, ante deditionem Capuae proelium fuit. medix tuticus, qui summus magistratus apud Campanos est, eo anno Seppius Loesius erat, loco obscuro tenuique fortuna ortus. matrem eius quondam pro pupillo eo procurantem familiare ostentum cum respondisset haruspex summum quod esset imperium Capuae peruenturum ad eum puerum, nihil ad eam spem adgnoscentem dixisse ferunt: 'ne tu perditas res Campanorum narras, ubi summus honos ad filium meum perueniet.' ea ludificatio ueri et ipsa in uerum uertit; nam cum fame ferroque urgerentur nec spes ulla superesset sisti <posse iis qui nati> in spem honorum erant honores detractantibus, Loesius querendo desertam ac proditam a primoribus Capuam, summum magistratum ultimus omnium Campanorum cepit.

---

15 Cf. e.g. Pol. 1.1.15 and 3.118.7–9; see Rood 2007, 177.
16 Cf. esp. Pol. 38.22.1; see Rood 2007, 180f.
17 Cf. Liv. 9.1.1: *sequitur hunc annum nobilis clade Romana Caudina pax T. Veturio Caluino Sp. Postumio consulibus.*
18 Cf. esp. Liv. 22.42.10; see Fuhrmann 1983, 25–28.
19 Cf. Pol. 15.20.5; see Rood 2007, 176.
20 For a more nuanced approach to Livy's narration about Capua see now Levene 2010, 354–375.
21 Cf. Liv. 26.6.13–16 (Latin text following Walsh 1989, translation by Yardley 2006).

Whatever the details of its beginning and end, this was the final battle before the capitulation of Capua. That year the *medix tuticus*, the supreme magistrate amongst the Capuans, was Seppius Loesius, a man of low birth and slender means. The story goes that his mother was once performing expiatory sacrifice on his behalf, Loesius being a minor, in connection with an omen affecting the family. The priest, in delievering his response, stated that the highest power in Capua would come to a boy. At this, the mother, who saw no reason to entertain such hopes, remarked: 'You must be saying that the people of Capua will be in a sorry state at the time when their top office comes to my son!' This snide interpretation of a prophecy that came true turned out to be true itself. When the Capuans were hard pressed by starvation and the sword, and no hope of resistance remained, all those born to the expectation of public offices were turning them down. Complaining that Capua had been abandoned and betrayed by its dignitaries, Loesius became the very last citizen of Capua to gain the city's highest office.

Yet Livy only rarely makes use of this method to look into the future in the narrative proper and outside his proems. This holds true, even if one takes into account previews given in a more implicit way, like king Philip of Macedon's famous ascent of Mt. Haemus in book 40,[22] from where he wants to plan his invasion of Italy, but gets inhibited by fog (a scene that is most likely modelled on a lost passage in Polybius).[23] And if Livy chooses to use this technique nevertheless, it obviously is a way for him to express a high degree of emotional commitment, especially in connection with the defeats and triumphs of the Romans, but also of other people within his narrative.

2 Evoking the future: Previews in the speeches of historical figures

Much more common, in Livy's *ab urbe condita*, is another literary strategy to refer to future events, namely the speeches put into the mouths of historical figures. Unlike the narrator – needless to say – they cannot know what will happen next. Still, they quite often look into what is the future to them, as they make their plans, explain their motives, warn or encourage their audiences. That implies that speeches are a very useful tool for the historian (in the same way as for writers in other genres as, for instance, drama or epic) to give information not only to the internal listeners but also the external reader, information, however, that will inevitably be partial and biased by the perspective of the speaker.[24] Yet exactly this unreliable character of

---

[22] Cf. Liv. 40.21.1–22.14; on this passage see now esp. Jaeger 2007.
[23] Cf. Pol. 24.3 (= Strabo 7.5.1) with Briscoe 2008, 464–468.
[24] On speeches in ancient historiography in general see e.g. Marincola 2007a; Pitcher 2009, 103–111, and the contributions in Pausch 2010.

the data will make the reader start to think and to hypothesise about the further course of the events (thus creating a kind of suspense) as well as to compare the actual outcome with his conjectures later on (thus adding to his historiographical understanding and reflection).[25]

Out of the rather large number of possible examples,[26] I want to focus on two from book 21, which, being the first of the third decade, is extremely rich in hints given towards the further course of the war against Hannibal up to the end of this compositional unit in book 30.[27] They are presented in various ways, but after the proem and a short digression about Hannibal at the start of the book,[28] Livy's narrator restrains himself much more than that of Polybius and lets the historical figures talk instead.[29]

The anticipation on the part of the reader can be enhanced by the repeated allusion to forthcoming events, especially if they are getting more and more precise each time. This is the case with the three addresses of Hannibal in which he gradually reveals the destination of the campaign to his soldiers – along with the readers. Whereas in his first speech he only talks about leaving Spain,[30] in the second one, at the Rhône River, Italy is already named as destination.[31] And in his third oration, in the midst of Alps and facing severe difficulties due to terrain and weather, in order to encourage his men, he goes even further:[32]

> praegressus signa Hannibal in promunturio quodam, unde longe et late prospectus erat, consistere iussis militibus Italiam ostentat subiectosque Alpinis montibus Circumpadanos campos, moeniaque eos tum transcendere non Italiae modo, sed etiam urbis Romanae; cetera

---

25 For an interpretation of the speeches in Livy along these lines see Pausch 2011, esp. 157–189, 237–242.
26 Cf. e.g. Liv. 5.32.6–32.7; Liv. 24.13.1–13.5; Liv. 41.23.5–23.18 and Liv. 42.11.1–14.1.
27 See esp. Burck 1962 and Fuhrmann 1983.
28 Cf. Liv. 21.1.1–1.4; for the historical reliability see e.g. Händl-Sagawe 1995, 15–46.
29 Of course, there are some exceptions, like the presentation of the encounter at the Rhône river 218 BC: whereas Polybius gives an factual account without any outlook into the future (Pol. 3.45), Livy uses the result of this equestrian skirmish – a Roman victory, but only at great costs – as an *omen* for the further course of the war as a whole (Liv. 21.29.1–4, esp. § 4: *hoc principium simul omenque belli ut summae rerum prosperum euentum, ita haud sane incruentam ancipitisque certaminis uictoriam Romanis portendit*).
30 Cf. Liv. 21.21.3–7. Polybius, on the contrary, mentions already here Rome as final destination: Pol. 3.34.7–9.
31 Cf. Liv. 21.30.1–11, esp. § 11; for the impact of this speech on evoking an alternative course of history on the part of the reader see Feldherr 2009, 314f.319f.
32 Cf. Liv. 21.35.8–9 (Latin text following Dorey 1971, translation by Yardley 2006); for the manifold historical problems attached to this passage see Händl-Sagawe 1995, 235f.

plana, proclivia fore; uno aut summum altero proelio arcem et caput Italiae in manu ac potestate habituros.

Hannibal rode ahead of the standards and ordered his men to halt on a spur that offered a deep and broad panorama. Here he pointed out to them Italy, and the plains that surrounded the Po, at the foot of the Alps. At that moment, he told them, they were crossing the defenses not merely of Italy but of the city of Rome. The rest of the way would be flat or downhill; one or at most two battles and they would have that chief bastion of Italy in their hands and at their mercy.

Polybius' version of the same occurrence in the year 281 BC is rather similar in terms of the events described, but much more implicit according to the outlook into the future:[33]

τῆς δὲ χιόνος ἤδη περὶ τοὺς ἄκρους ἀθροιζομένης διὰ τὸ συνάπτειν (τὴν) τῆς Πλειάδος δύσιν, θεωρῶν τὰ πλήθη δυσθύμως διακείμενα καὶ διὰ τὴν προγεγενημένην ταλαιπωρίαν καὶ διὰ τὴν ἔτι προσδοκωμένην, ἐπειρᾶτο συναθροίσας παρακαλεῖν, μίαν ἔχων ἀφορμὴν εἰς τοῦτο τὴν τῆς Ἰταλίας ἐνάργειαν· οὕτως γὰρ ὑποπεπτώκει τοῖς προειρημένοις ὄρεσιν ὥστε συνθεωρουμένων ἀμφοῖν ἀκροπόλεως φαίνεσθαι διάθεσιν ἔχειν τὰς Ἄλπεις τῆς ὅλης Ἰταλίας. διόπερ ἐνδεικνύμενος αὐτοῖς τὰ περὶ τὸν Πάδον πεδία καὶ καθόλου τῆς εὐνοίας ὑπομιμνήσκων τῆς τῶν κατοικούντων αὐτὰ Γαλατῶν, ἅμα δὲ καὶ τὸν τῆς Ῥώμης αὐτῆς τόπον ὑποδεικνύων ἐπὶ ποσὸν εὐθαρσεῖς ἐποίησε τοὺς ἀνθρώπους.

But by this time, it being nearly the period of the setting of the Pleiads, the snow was beginning to be thick on the heights; and seeing his men in low spirits, owing both to the fatigue they had gone through, and that which still lay before them, Hannibal called them together and tried to cheer them by dwelling on the one possible topic of consolation in his power, namely the view of Italy: which lay stretched out in both directions below those mountains, giving the Alps the appearance of a citadel to the whole of Italy. By pointing therefore to the plains of the Padus, and reminding them of the friendly welcome which awaited them from the Gauls who lived there, and at the same time indicating the direction of Rome itself, he did somewhat to raise the drooping spirits of his men.

This fits well into his general reluctance to turn Hannibal's crossing of the Alps into a kind of literary show piece, since he criticises his historiographical predecessors for doing exactly this.[34] The explanation usually adduced, as to why Livy lays more stress on Hannibal's forecast of his forthcoming victory,[35] is

---

[33] Cf. Pol. 3.54.1–3 (Greek text following Büttner-Wobst 1905, translation by Paton 1922).
[34] Cf. Pol. 3.47.5–48.12; see further on this passage e.g. Marincola 2003, 293–302.
[35] This series of previewing speeches can even be expanded, if one takes into account the harangues made by Hannibal and his opponent P. Scipio before the battle at the river Ticinus at the end of 218 BC. Especially in his shorter second address (without counterpart in Polybius), the Carthaginian general already looks ahead beyond the end of the war and holds out to his soldiers not only booty, but estates in Italy (Liv. 21.45.4–5).

that it simply proves to be wrong in the end and that Livy and his Roman readers can thus enjoy an instance of tragic irony[36] at the cost of the Carthaginian general who really believes that he could triumph over Rome.

We will never know, of course, how any individual Roman reader will have reacted to these words, but I think that it can be made plausible that Livy's agenda is a bit more complex than that. This becomes especially apparent by the fact that he employs the same technique also on the other side: a good example is offered by his rendering of the debate taking place in the Roman senate after the capture of Saguntum by Hannibal in 219 BC, finally leading to the declaration of the war against Carthage:[37]

> tantusque simul maeror patres misericordiaque sociorum peremptorum indigne et pudor non lati auxilii et ira in Carthaginienses metusque de summa rerum cepit, velut si iam ad portas hostis esset, ut tot uno tempore motibus animi turbati trepidarent magis quam consulerent: nam neque hostem acriorem bellicosioremque secum congressum nec rem Romanam tam desidem umquam fuisse atque imbellem. Sardos Corsosque et Histros atque Illyrios lacessisse magis quam exercuisse Romana arma, et cum Gallis tumultuatum uerius quam belligeratum: Poenum hostem ueteranum trium et uiginti annorum militia durissima inter Hispanas gentes, semper uictorem, duci acerrimo adsuetum, recentem ab excidio opulentissimae urbis Hiberum transire, trahere secum tot excitos Hispanorum populos; conciturum auidas semper armorum Gallicas gentes: orbe terrarum bellum gerendum in Italia ac pro moenibus Romanis esse.

Various emotions gripped the senators at the same moment: sorrow and pity for the heinous massacre of their allies, shame at their own failure to bring assistance, fury with the Carthaginians, and fear for the security of the state – it was as if the enemy were already at the gates. So many emotions arising together threw them off balance, making them dither rather than deliberate. They realized that they had never come to grips with a more ruthless or combative foe, and Rome had never been in such a shiftless and enervated condition. The Sardinians, the Corsicans, the Istrians, and the Illyrians had teased Roman military power but not really put it to the test, and with the Gauls there had been desultory rather than regular warfare. But the Carthaginians were their enemy of old and they had spent twenty-three years in the hardest kind of campaigning amidst the Spanish tribes, campaigns from which they had always emerged the victors. They were used to the harshest leadership, and they were crossing the Ebro fresh from the destruction of a prosperous city. They had roused to arms, and were dragging along with them, large numbers of Spanish peoples, and they would now stir into action the ever-bel-

---

36 For the concept of 'tragische Ironie' see Pfister 2001, 87–90, esp. 88: "Sie tritt immer dann auf, wenn die sprachliche Äußerung oder das außersprachliche Verhalten einer Figur für den Rezipienten aufgrund seiner überlegenen Informiertheit eine der Intention der Figur widersprechende Zusatzbedeutung erhält."
37 Cf. Liv. 21.16.2–6 (Latin text following Dorey 1971, translation by Yardley 2006); for the historical events recapitulated in this passage see Händl-Sagawe 1995, 98–101, for the literary impact Clauss 1987, esp. 66f.

ligerent Gallic tribes. The Romans would have to fight the whole world, and do so in Italy and before their city walls.

Admittedly, this depiction aims at an (at least partial) exculpation of Rome's abandonment of their ally Saguntum. Yet at the same time, the debate rendered as an unusual kind of 'free indirect discourse' offers an extremely pessimistic outlook into the future from a clearly Roman point of view – and in doing so is playing the first time what during the next books will become a kind of *Hannibal ad portas*-theme.[38] By these and similar passages, Livy creates a truly polyphonic outlook into the narrative future, which forms an important part of his general intent to get his readers involved in his version of the Roman history.[39] Polybius, although he uses the same technique in principle,[40] is less interested in this effect of his narration on the whole, as can be illustrated, for example, by his brusque refusal to render any speeches on this very occasion:[41]

> Οἱ δὲ Ῥωμαῖοι, προσπεπτωκυίας αὐτοῖς ἤδη τῆς τῶν Ζακανθαίων ἁλώσεως, οὐ μὰ Δία περὶ τοῦ πολέμου τότε διαβούλιον ἦγον, καθάπερ ἔνιοι τῶν συγγραφέων φασί, προσκατατάττοντες ἔτι καὶ τοὺς εἰς ἑκάτερα ῥηθέντας λόγους, πάντων ἀτοπώτατον πρᾶγμα ποιοῦντες.
>
> The Romans, when the news of the fall of Saguntum reached them, did not assuredly hold a debate on the question of war, as some authors allege, even setting down the speeches made on both sides – a most absurd proceeding.

Given the fact that Livy will have known this harsh verdict, it is quite fascinating to see that he decided to display speeches nevertheless, even though he strikingly avoided using direct discourse in this instance. But the authority of Polybius' judgment was not sufficient to prevent him from using this literary technique after all. Apparently he did not want to miss this opportunity to give an insight into the thoughts and fears of the contemporary Romans and thereby to enhance the emotional impact of his narrative as well as the multi-perspectivity of his historical account.

---

[38] Cf. e.g. Liv. 21.57.1–3; see further e.g. Fuhrmann 1983, 23.
[39] Another good example for the multiperspectivity of Livy's narration is offered same chapters later by Hanno's speech against the war with Rome in the Carthaginian senate (cf. Liv. 21.10.1–13; see e.g. Chaplin 2000, 78f.: "When he urges the Carthaginians to recollect the defeats of the Aegates Islands and at Mount Eryx, as well as the twenty-four years of suffering in the previous war, the reading audience, unlike those listening to Hanno, knows that he is correct to do so.").
[40] For examples and an excellent interpretation see now Maier 2012a, 119–129.
[41] Cf. Pol. 3.20.1 (Greek text following Büttner-Wobst 1905, translation by Paton 1922).

3 Fearing the future: Previews given through portents

But whereas the rendering of speeches is as common among the Greek as among the Roman historians, we now move on to two other techniques of foreshadowing upcoming events that seem to be a bit more specific to the Roman side. I will start with the highly emotional way of looking into the future by means of supernatural occurrences reported by the historian. This is not unfamiliar to Greek historiography too, of course, at least in principle.[42] But Livy uses this strategy not only more often than Polybius does (narrating, for instance, Hannibal's dream about a dragon, devastating Italy without being able to conquer it, which offers a summary of the war before it even started),[43] but also in a more prominent way, since he, as it was laid out in the Roman annalistic tradition, usually assembles all *omina* that had occurred within a year at the occasion of their expiation at the start of the new year.[44]

Yet, as it was shown especially by David Levene, Livy handles not only the annalistic layout in general, but also this rubric with more flexibility than is often assumed.[45] Thereby, he gets another narrative option to preview further events, above all, of course, the ones threatening to his contemporary Roman readers. The third decade again offers a range of examples. Hinting at the defeat at Lake Trasimene in 217 BC, Livy gives an additional and rather long list of prodigies already at the end of year 218 BC, followed by the regular one at the start of the new year.[46] Both get duly expiated, but the second set only by one of the two consuls, since Gaius Flaminius has decided against taking his office at Rome, as was expected of him not least exactly because of his part in the atonement of the *omina*. It is true, this double emphasis helps Livy to explain Roman defeat (by not giving proper attention to the gods), but it contributes also to the creation of anticipation and of suspense and thus to the involvement of the reader.[47]

Another relevant passage can be found at the start of the year 208 BC, in the further course of which both consuls will be killed in ambush, T. Quinctius Crispinus as well as M. Claudius Marcellus, being the conqueror of Syracuse and one

---

[42] Cf. e.g. Pol. 3.112.6–9.
[43] Cf. Liv. 21.22.6–9; see further e.g. Cic. div. 1.49.
[44] For the general importance of *prodigia* in *ab urbe condita* see Davies 2004, 21–85, and Engels 2007, 188–221.
[45] See Levene 1993, esp. 36f., but now also Satterfield 2012, who argues for the historical correctness of the dates given by Livy for the expiation of the *omina* at the start of each year.
[46] Cf. Liv. 21.62.1–11 and 22.1.8–20; see Fuhrmann 1983, 25–28.
[47] See Levene 1993, 38–43, and Engels 2007, 189.

of the outstanding figures of this period.[48] Livy presages this exceptional event not only by rendering a relatively long list of prodigies,[49] but also by adding two comments of his primary narrator:[50]

> praetores in provincias profecti; consules religio tenebat quod prodigiis aliquot nuntiatis non facile litabant. et ex Campania nuntiata erant Capuae duas aedes, Fortunae et Martis, et sepulcra aliquot de caelo tacta, Cumis – adeo minimis etiam rebus prava religio inserit deos – mures in aede Iovis aurum rosisse, Casini examen apium ingens in foro consedisse; et Ostiae murum portamque de caelo tactam, Caere volturium volasse in aedem Iovis, Volsiniis sanguine lacum manasse. horum prodigiorum causa diem unum supplicatio fuit. per dies aliquot hostiae maiores sine litatione caesae, diuque non impetrata pax deum. in capita consulum re publica incolumi exitiabilis prodigiorum eventus vertit.

> The praetors now left to take up their assignments, but religious concerns detained the consuls: after a number of prodigies had been reported, they were having difficulty obtaining favorable omens. From Campania had come reports of lightning striking two temples in Capua – those of Fortuna and Mars – as well as a number of tombs. At Cumae it had been announced that mice had been gnawing at some gold in the temple of Jupiter – such are the trivialities in which misguided superstition sees divine intervention! – and at Casinum that a huge swarm of bees had settled at the forum. At Ostia, it was said that the city wall and a gate had been struck by lightning; at Caere, that a vulture flew into the temple of Jupiter; and, at Volsinii, that the lake was suffused with blood. A day of public prayer was held because of these prodigies, and over a number of days full-grown victims were sacrificed without favorable omens being attained – it was a long time before the favor of the gods was regained. In fact, the deadly events thus prophesied actually came down on the consuls' heads, and the state remained out of harm's way.

Such explicit comments by the narrator in addition to the effects of the enumerations of *omina* themselves are rare, but not completely without parallel.[51] In a similar situation, on the brink of the war against Perseus of Macedon in book 42,[52] Livy comments on the mood of the people in Rome affected by the prodigies

---

[48] Cf. Liv. 27.26.7–27.14 (death of Marcellus) and 27.33.6–7 (death of Crispinus).
[49] Cf. Liv. 27.23.1–4; see Levene 1993, 63 f. Marcellus' death gets predicted also in the context of the assignment of duties for this year (Liv. 26.29.1–10 – on this see below).
[50] Cf. Livy 27.23.1–4 (Latin text following Walsh 1989, translation by Yardley 2006).
[51] For Livy's occasionally rather sceptical attitude towards the *omina* see Levene 1993, 16–30, and Engels 2007, 204–219, but also Davies 2004, 21–85, who denies any incredulity towards religious phenomena in Livy.
[52] Already in book 41, the war against Perseus is presented as a looming threat by a large number of prodigies (cf. e.g. Liv. 41.9.4–7 and 41.13.1–3; see Levene 1993, 105–107 and Kern 1960, esp. 160); for Livy's creation of suspense in run-up to this war see also below in the context of the assignement of duties.

saying that the whole city was *suspensa ad exspectationem novi belli*,⁵³ which is a phrase that – probably not by chance – resembles one of the key words of the contemporary discussion on the impact that historiography should have on its readers, namely *expectatio*. ⁵⁴ Such comments, acting as amplification without changing the function of the strategy itself, thus can provide insight into the literary intentions behind this technique.

4 Planning the future: Previews from a Roman point of view

The last strategy of narrative forecast that I want to discuss briefly now is perhaps the most Roman feature we have seen so far: like the rendering of prodigies, the assignment of duties to the newly elected magistrates is a consequence of the specific way in which the historical events are presented according to the annalistic framework as it had been developed by Livy's predecessors. In the books 21 to 45 we find this rubric regularly at the start of the new year, offering a good opportunity to preview imminent military conflicts and domestic problems. This narrative strategy is, of course, not unknown to Polybius, but he makes only sporadic use of it, in order to highlight especially important upcoming events in his *histories*.⁵⁵

In Livy's *ab urbe condita*, these outlooks are much more frequent and usually given formally by the narrator, but at once they are often internally focaliced since the decisions are made by the historical figures themselves. This becomes especially apparent whenever the political quarrels over the assignment of the duties to particular persons are reported. The rendering of the debates about the relevance of a certain command or campaign – although they are made up by the historian for the most part – are a useful device to illustrate the variant and often conflicting evaluations of the historical situation by the contempora-

---

[53] Cf. Liv. 42.20.1–6, esp. § 1: *in suspensa ciuitate ad expectationem noui belli, nocturna tempestate columna rostrata in Capitolio bello Punico <priore ... M. Aemili> consulis, cui collega Ser. Fuluius fuit, tota ad imum fulmine discussa est. ea res prodigii loco habita ad senatum relata est.* "On a stormy night, while the city was taut with suspense because of the impending war, a bolt of lightning struck and destroyed the *columna rostrata*; it had been set up on the Capitoline during the First Punic War to commemorate the victory of the consul Marcus Aemilius (the one whose colleague was Servius Fulvius)." (Latin text following Briscoe 1986; translation by Chaplin 2007).
[54] Cf. e.g. Vitr. praef. 5.1 and Cic. fam 5.12.5; on the concept of *exspectatio* in Late Republican and Early Augustan Rome see further Pausch 2011, 58–64, 193–195.
[55] Cf. e.g. Pol. 3.106.1–9 (preparations at Rome for the military actions of the year 216 BC, leading to the defeat at Cannae).

ries.⁵⁶ In this way, the reader is invited to decide for his part which point of view will be right in the end and thus, again, gets more involved in the story.

The beginning of book 37 provides a pertinent passage: both consuls compete for the decisive command in the war against Antiochus III in the year 190 BC.⁵⁷ Due to the relevance attached to the military actions of this year, the senate opts against the assignment by lot, a method used frequently in less important instances, in order to avoid further quarrels. A decision is reached in favour of L. Cornelius Scipio as his brother Africanus signals his readiness to join him and to act as his advisor – in the same way as Hannibal already does on the side of the Seleucid king. The fact that by this means both generals repeat the constellation of Zama stirs the imagination of the senators – and with this focalised view into the future put at the end of the discussion, the narrator moves on to another topic:⁵⁸

> haec vox magno adsensu audita sustulit certamen; experiri libebat, utrum plus regi Antiocho in Hannibale victo an in victore Africano consuli legionibusque Romanis auxilii foret; ac prope omnes Scipioni Graeciam, Laelio Italiam decreverunt.

> This statement was received with great approval, and brought the contest to an end. The senate wished to put to the test which of the two had the more reliable support – Antiochus in the defeated Hannibal, or the consul and the Roman legions in the victorious Africanus. The decision to assign Greece to Scipio and Italy to Laelius was practically unanimous.

In this case, the hopes of the senators will be fulfilled by the victory in battle at Magnesia (190 BC). But again, this strategy is not limited to the announcement of Roman success. The death of the consul M. Claudius Marcellus, mentioned above in conjunction with prodigies, is likewise predicted in the context of the assignment of provinces, emphasised this time by the subsequent change of the result as it was drawn by lot and described as an intervention of fate by the narrator.⁵⁹

---

56 For a reading of the (quite numerous) triumphal debates in Livy along these lines see now Pittenger 2008.
57 Cf. Liv. 37.1.7–10; for the historical background see Briscoe 1981, 291–293. This military conflict, also known as the Roman-Syrian War (192–188 BC), constitutes the central topic of the books 36 to 40 of Livy's history (on the structure of this narrative unit see e.g. Kern 1960, 142–145; Luce 1977, 75–113; and Tsitsiou-Chelidoni 2007).
58 Cf. Liv. 37.1.10 (Latin text following Walsh 1999; translation by Yardley 2000).
59 Cf. Liv. 26.29.1–10, esp. § 9f.: *ita senatus, cum quid placeret magis ostendisset quam decreuisset, dimittitur. inter ipsos consules permutatio prouinciarum, rapiente fato Marcellum ad Hannibalem, facta est, ut ex quo primus post <aduersa omnia haud> aduersae pugnae gloriam ceperat, in eius laudem postremus Romanorum imperatorum prosperis tum maxime bellicis rebus caderet.* "And so the Senate was adjourned after making its wishes known, but without

Likewise, it is not the rule that the anticipatory character of this section is made explicit, but the instances where such comments are added are, of course, especially suited to observe how this literary technique works. This applies also to the use of a narrative strategy that is closely related to the regular assignment of duties, but offers an even stronger focalised view into the future. This is the case in a passage that serves as a kind of 'finale furioso' to the extremely widespread arc of suspense Livy uses to prepare the outbreak of the war against Perseus of Macedon (171–168 BC) during the books 39 to 42 (mentioned briefly already above).[60] By now, Perseus is officially announced enemy of the Roman people by the senate, the war is ceremonially declared, and after all these retarding elements have been mastered, the narrator takes his time to describe the departure of the Roman army at some length (usually a matter of routine barely mentioned):[61]

> per hos forte dies P. Licinius consul votis in Capitolio nuncupatis, paludatus ab urbe profectus est. semper quidem ea res cum magna dignitate ac maiestate †quaeritur†; praecipue convertit oculos animosque, cum ad magnum nobilemque aut virtute aut fortuna hostem euntem consulem prosequuntur. contrahit enim non officii modo cura, sed etiam studium spectaculi, ut videant ducem suum, cuius imperio consilioque summam rem publicam tuendam permiserunt. subit deinde cogitatio animos, qui belli casus, quam incertus fortunae eventus communisque Mars belli sit; adversa secundaque, quae inscitia et temeritate ducum clades saepe acciderint, quae contra bona prudentia et virtus attulerit. quem scire mortalium, utrius mentis, utrius fortunae consulem ad bellum mittant? triumphantemne mox cum exercitu victore scandentem in Capitolium ad eosdem deos, a quibus proficiscatur, visuri, an hostibus eam praebituri laetitiam sint?

> In that same period, as it happened, the consul Publius Licinius pronounced vows on the Capitol, adopted military attire, and set out from the city. Such a departure is always conducted with great solemnity and majesty; it especially attracts people's gaze and thoughts when they escort a consul setting out against an enemy who is endowed with consequence and renown, either for his innate character or for his good fortune. Not just respect for the office draws people, but also a passion for the spectacle itself, so that they can see the leader to whose authority and judgment they have entrusted the supreme defense of the state. Then their minds dwell on the hazards of war, the uncertainty of fortune, and the danger of

---

a formal decree. A private arrangement was then made between the consuls to exchange their provinces, as destiny swept Marcellus on to confront Hannibal. Marcellus would be the first man to have won from him the glory of a battle which, after all the failures, was not a defeat, and the last of the Roman generals to enhance the Carthaginian's reputation by falling in battle, and that just when the Romans were achieving military success." (Latin text following Walsh 1989, translation by Yardley 2006).

[60] For further interpretation see e.g. Kern 1960, esp. 258–261, Luce 1977, esp. 114, and Pausch 2011, 225–237.

[61] Cf. Liv. 42.49.1–6 (Latin text following Briscoe 1986, translation by Chaplin 2007).

combat for both sides: they think of defeats and victories, the disasters too often caused by imprudence and rashness on the part of the leaders, but also the successes brought about by the virtues of foresight and courage. What mortal can know the character and luck of the consul they are sending to war? Will they soon see him holding a triumph and climbing the capitol with his victorious army, on his way back to the same gods who attended his departure? Or will they be offering that joy to their enemies?

Although no exact prototype has survived in the remainders of his *Histories*, it has often been assumed that this account is modelled on a passage by Polybius[62] (pointing, among others, to the famous description of a *pompa funebris* in book 6 as a similar example).[63] As long as the larger part of Polybius' work remains lost, it is, of course, hard to establish the opposite. Nevertheless, I would like to understand such passages rather as a proof of Livy's ability to refine the techniques of previewing developed by his Greek and Roman predecessors.

One reason for this is that what is achieved by literary strategies like these fits very well with a general tendency of Livy's way to narrate history:[64] even if most of his readers will have been aware of the final result of this war in terms of the Roman victory at Pydna 168 BC, Livy's narration quite often aims at the anticipation of a positive and a negative outcome as well. The resulting impression of an open end of the further events can, of course, easily be cut short by the recollection of the historical facts on the part of the reader. But such passages nonetheless have the power to change the perception of otherwise well-known events by creating a kind of anomalous suspense[65] – especially if they are presented in an effective way like in our example, using the focalisation through the eyes of the people in Rome as an amplification.

IV Recapitulation: Seeing a little further?

After presenting – in a rather cursory fashion – four of Livy's strategies to look into the future, I want to end with a few concluding remarks, mainly consisting

---

[62] See most recently Briscoe 2008, 322: "This digression on the departure of consuls on campaign is clearly taken from Polybius, though doubtless there is elaboration by L. The former was addressing his Greek readers, who had never witnessed the spectacle."
[63] Cf. Pol. 6.53–54.
[64] See e.g. Luce 1977, 131: "… scenes describing crowd psychology are more characteristic of Livy (…) than of Polybius."; for a reading focusing further on the 'spectacular' elements of this scene see Feldherr 1998, 9–12.
[65] For a psychological description of this phenomenon see Gerrig 1989; for an adaption of this concept on Livy's way of narrating history see Pausch 2011, esp. 195–200.

of a working hypothesis along the lines of the title of this paper: Livy's undeniable debt to Polybius is usually imagined in such a way as though he has more or less rewritten the *Histories* in Latin – except in those parts of his work where he has decided to follow the Roman tradition instead (supposedly much to his disadvantage). I would like to argue for a more self-conscious approach, according to which Livy has not only reflected about which parts of the content of the *Histories* he would like to adopt for his work, but also which elements of Polybius' literary technique might be useful for his conception of history – and which might perhaps be improved.

It is not only the political change that happened during the decades that passed since Polybius wrote his history on the Roman Empire, it is the art of writing historiography, too, that saw considerable progress and refinement in Late Republican Rome. In terms of giving previews to further events, innovative elements include the highly polyphonic presentation and the creation of a kind of anomalous suspense. Livy's preferences thus seem to be on the side of more indirect, more literary devices and those aiming at enhancement of the emotional involvement of the reader and at an open-ended anticipation, whereas Polybius favours direct and unmistakable interventions of his primary narrator. Part of the explanation for this difference may be sought in the circumstance that for Polybius the question, how 'Roman' the Mediterranean world would be in the future, was of particular importance and that he wanted to persuade his readers that he was the one who could explain the future course of events to them. In Livy's time, this 'Polybian' future has already become reality, which enabled him to take the narrative strategies one step further and to use them in a more general and at the same time emphatic manner. Understood in this way, to sit on the shoulders of Greeks does not only mean to see a little further, but also to do it in a slightly different way.

Antonis Liakos
Constituting the Modern World as the Future of Greek Antiquity

Rubens on the changing structure of historical time

In 1632 the great Dutch painter Peter Paul Rubens engraved the title-page of the book *Romanae et Graecae antiquitatis monumenta*, a numismatic collection by Hubert Goltzius, published in Antwerp in 1645. The gravure depicts the decline of the old and the rise of the new configuration of historical time. This transformation of historical time was part of a more general change in the cognitive and cultural landscape of seventeenth century. Central to the new image of the past was the concept of Antiquity.

The title of the book was written in a square at the centre, surrounded by an allegorical scene representing the re-emergence of antiquity. Antiquity was depicted as a woman in the centre, decorated with a numismatic chain, with an open book in front of her, and a phoenix (a symbol of revival) on her head. The figures around her tell a story. Time and Death, in the top-right corner, hurl four figures down, towards the abyss. The first figure is an allegory of Rome, the second an allegory of Macedonia, the third of Persia and the fourth of Media.[1]

At the centre bottom of the page there is a dark cave, an allegory of oblivion. While the dark cave is the destination of the four falling figures, Mercury, on the left, can be seen pulling out of the same cave three broken Greek and Roman statues. From here, the activity on the page moves from the bottom to the top of the page. The statues are the result of excavation, and this is represented through the depiction of archaeological tools. Above Mercury stands Hercules, handing a pot containing coins to a slave; and in the top left-hand corner of the page is Athena who, with a torch, illuminates the whole venture to recover the knowledge of antiquity.

This title-page seems to narrate a strange story. We understand that the offering of a treasury of coins to the goddess of learning is a metaphor for the contribution of the book to our knowledge of antiquity. But why are Time and Death pushing into oblivion four figures which, after all, belong to antiquity?

---
[1] Burchard 1977, v. 2, 275–278.

275. C. Galle, *Title-page* for H. Goltzius, *Romanae et Graecae Antiquitatis Monumenta*, engraving (No. 82)

Why are four figures of antiquity being substituted in order to recover an invented and abstract figure, antiquity and its material relics?

This is now a forgotten story, but the four symbols, representing Median, Persian, Macedonian and Roman empires comes from an interpretation of a dream by the prophet Daniel. According to this story, the Persian king Nebuchadnezzar had a dream about a statue whose head was made of gold, its chest and arms of silver, its belly and thighs of bronze, its legs of iron, its feet partly of iron and partly of baked clay. Suddenly a rock was cut out from the mountain, struck the statue on its feet of iron and clay and smashed them. Then, all the materials that constituted the statue were pulverised and the rock that struck the statue became a huge mountain and filled the whole earth.[2]

This vision, which in another way was narrated by Daniel with the story of the four beasts emerging from the sea, became not only the matrix of Apocalypse but also the backbone of a periodisation of world history in the Christian era. The story of the succession of the major empires of antiquity was told by the Greek and Roman historians Herodotus, Ctesias, Demetrius of Phalerum, Dionysius of Halicarnassus, Polybious, Aemilius Sura and Velleius Paterculus. Joseph Ward Swain and Arnaldo Momigliano have documented Daniel's links to Greek and Roman sources.[3] But, besides the Greek impact, the story acquired a central place in imagining the history of the past because the interpretation of Daniel was canonised by the Christian fathers. The story was the object of controversy and polemics between the pagan philosopher Porphyry and Jerome in the fourth century.[4] It was also open to speculation on what constituted the future. For Christian writers of the fourth and fifth century, the Roman Empire and the church were the last phase of the story. For Eusebius, the church and the Roman Empire, since its Christianisation, would constitute an eternal present.[5] But there was also another interpretation which prevailed in subsequent centuries: the Roman Empire was and would be the last empire, and its end would coincide with the Last Judgment and the End of the world.[6] The story of the succession of the four empires (or "world monarchies") connected history and eschatology. It was also powerful not only in linking the experienced history with the itinerary of the world, but imposing also a sense of the imminent End of the world. The capture of Constantinople, the wars of the Reformation and the English civil war were such events in which history, theology and action

---

2 Collins/Flint 2002.
3 Swain 1940; Momigliano 1994.
4 Young 1949; Georgiadis 1891.
5 Eusebius, *Church History* 1.2, 15–27.
6 Vasiliev 1943–1944; Guran 2007; 2006.

World History at a glance. The image of the Colossus, engraved by Tobias Conrad Lotter in 1744

were mixed. The strongest point of this story was the implied theory of *Translatio imperii*, a political theory legitimising the rise and fall of these empires as a transference of power from one people to the other, from the Babylonians to the Persians, from the Persians to the Greeks and from the Greeks to the Romans. In medieval times, this theory was used to present the German emperor with the title of Holy Roman Emperor (Otto von Freising [twelveth century] and Alexander von Roes [thirteenth century]).⁷

In this periodisation of history, the present was incorporated into a succession of pasts of long duration. Johannes Sleidanus or Sleidan, who lived from 1506 to 1556, was one of the principal historians of Reformation, earning him the title of the Thucydides of the Reformation. He wrote a history in four volumes.⁸ Each book comprised the history of one of the four empires, and the last book, much bigger, was dedicated to the Roman Empire, encompassing the period from the first to the sixteenth centuries. Sleidanus concluded his series by writing that Daniel's vision was verified by the course of world history! He wasn't an obscure writer, but one of the first to go to the archives, and was familiar with the writings of the Greek and Roman historians. In his book there is a rational explanation of historical deeds, but these are framed in a prophetic history. This sense of the past wasn't totally arbitrary in his era. The name of the emperors was still Roman, an echo of the Roman Imperial title Caesar/es (in Germany and Austria: "Kaiser", in Russia: "Tsar", in the Ottoman Empire: *Kayser-i-Rûm*). The official language in most courts and state bureaucracies was still Latin, Roman law and the Justinian code were still taught in the universities. According Reinhart Koselleck, we should understand this sense of non-differentiation from the past as a plain space which endured until the massive transformations of European society in seventeenth and eighteenth centuries.⁹ This means that expectations were linked to experience, and this is obvious in the writings of historians and political thinkers from the fifteenth to the seventeenth centuries, such as Niccolo Machiavelli, James Harrington (*Oceana),* and others who used the experience of Roman antiquity to illuminate their contemporary political situation and to advice the prince.¹⁰

This story of the four empires was also read as a synopsis of world history, long before 1774, when Tobias Conrad Lotter (1717–1777) engraved one of the most diffused images of the legendary Colossus, upon whose figure he wrote a chronicle of the main events from the times of king Nimrod of Mesopotamia to his contemporary Joseph II, emperor of the Habsburg Empire. This was a common use of the story. Martin Luther had such an image in his mind and used to read its details, even those written in the fingers of the imaginary statue. He read in the one foot the five nations emerged from the western part of the Roman Empire (Spain, France, Italy, England and Germany) and on the other,

---

7 Kelley 1991.
8 Sleidan 1563.
9 Koselleck 1985.
10 Pocock 2003, 339–341.

those emerging from the Eastern Empire (Greece, Egypt, Syria, Asia and Africa). The same names were written also in the fingers of Lotter's gravure. Not all of them referred to nations or kingdoms with the same status or size. But this was of less importance. This was an inherited mental geography of the world. The image of the present through the past. This story of the four empires was also taught in German universities. For Philipp Melanchthon, it offered a bird's eye view on the whole of human history.[11] It was history at a glance, and a real grand narrative for understanding each one place in the flow of time and the world events. Indeed, the story of the four empires served to place historical time within the cosmological time.

Details of the Colossus depicting the image of the contemporary world

As a consequence, the Rubens' engraving picturing the pushing of the four figures back into the cave of oblivion was a sign of a bigger change in the understanding of history and time. Here it is possible to observe a certain historical irony: the abandonment of the temporal frame that was handed down by the Greek tradition through its biblical transcription (the scheme of succession), was presupposed to the reconstitution of this tradition as the key source for ancient history.

What was the context of this change? How did a conception of temporality based on the succession of the four world empires turn into another conception, based on the succession of three eras – antiquity, medieval times and the modern era?

Jean Bodin was a sixteenth-century historian who belonged to the French Nobles of the Robe. He was also jurist and high state official. In 1566, he published a book entitled *Methodus ad facilem historiarum cognitionem* (Method for the easy comprehension of history). He wrote an entire chapter against the theory of the four empires. His argumentation is another sign of the change in historical

---

[11] Miegge 1995, 41–52.

consciousness. He saw world history as richer than the biblical narrative, which didn't comprise the Hispanic and the Ottoman empires. His main argument was that the biblical narrative was pessimist, as the succession of metals from the gold to clay suggested. Our golden era was not in the past but in front of us. His advice was to ignore the dark writer of the apocalypse.[12]

Yet, the decisive event for the abandonment of the old structure of history was the awareness that China was much older than the old empires of the Bible. According to the Jesuits who had penetrated the forbidden centre of Chinese culture, China escaped Noah's flood and had a history different from that of the biblical peoples. In 1615, the manuscript of Matteo Ricci, the first Jesuit who penetrated and lived for many years in Beijing, was published.[13] In 1665, Isaac La Peyrère, a Jewish Marrano, published a book in Amsterdam on the existence of the "pre-Adamites", people from the era before Adam, based on anthropological observations in Greenland. These ideas were considered as equivalent to the second death of Adam.[14] The discovery also of gigantic fossils led to the hypothesis that they were remnants of a previous world. Indeed the Christian narrative about the creation and the end of the world was incorporated into a bigger narrative of many successive worlds, and Apocalypse was interpreted by Thomas Barnet, in his book *Telluris Theoria Sacra* (London 1681), as the natural destruction of the world and the passage from the one to the other world.[15] All these theories shook the faith in the stories narrated in the Old Testament.

The world experience required a new structure of time. Nevertheless, the new structure of time was also Eurocentric. The idea of the three eras emerged in Reformation attitudes towards the history of the church: the first Christian era was succeeded by a long period of decline under the papacy, and authentic belief re-emerged with the Reformation. The end of the wars of religion, with the treaty of Westphalia (1648), created also a sense of a new beginning in Europe.

Terms related to antiquity, medium-aevum (moyen age, Mittelalter) and modernity were employed until the seventeenth century without any consistency. But at the end of this century, these terms were used for canonising a new division of historical time. Christoph Cellarius (Keller) wrote and published in Jena three textbooks, each one dedicated to an historical epoch: *Historia nova* in 1669, *Historia antiqua* in 1685, and *Historia medii aevi* in 1696. Cellarius also defined the beginning and the end of the middle ages with Constantine, the first Christian Roman emperor in the fourth century, and the Reformation

---

[12] Bodin 1969, 291; Garosci 1934, 174.
[13] Van Kley 1971.
[14] Livingstone 2008.
[15] Rossi 1984, 123–187.

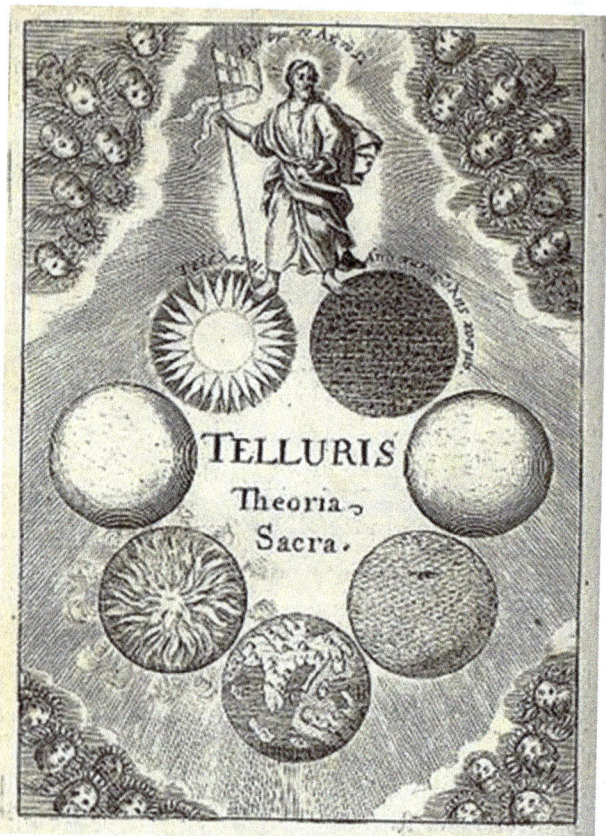

The theory of many worlds: Figure in the book of Thomas Barnet, *Telluris Theoria Sacra*, London, 1681

of the church in the sixteenth century.¹⁶ The invention of the middle ages was more important for the study of antiquity than for the middle ages themselves. In the humanist era, the key for the opening of the thesaurus of knowledge was antiquity and not medieval times.¹⁷ But for antiquity to become a key to knowledge, historical knowledge had to escape from the conception of the succession of empires. This structure had no space for the classical past. According to Dionysius of Halicarnassus, it was senseless to compare Greek and Roman history given the incomparability of their dimension and duration:

---

16 Ferguson 1948; Grafton 1988; 2003.
17 Schaeffer 1976, 21–30.

τὴν Ῥωμαίων ἡγεμονίαν ἁπάσας ὑπερβεβλημένην ὄψεται τὰς πρὸ αὐτῆς μνημονευομένας, οὐ μόνον κατὰ τὸ μέγεθος τῆς ἀρχῆς ... ἀλλὰ καὶ κατὰ τὸ μῆκος τοῦ περιειληφότος αὐτὴν χρόνου ... τὰς γὰρ Ἑλληνικὰς δυνάμεις οὐκ ἄξιον αὐταῖς ἀντιπαρεξετάζειν, οὔτε μέγεθος ἀρχῆς οὔτε χρόνον ἐπιφανείας τοσοῦτον ὅσον ἐκεῖναι [empires] λαβούσας[18]

Greek antiquity didn't even appear in Eusebius, the founder of Church history. In his "Chronical Canon" (Χρονικός Κανών), there is little room for the history of the Greek cities. Historians and thinkers of history were for centuries imprisoned in a structure of history grounded on the concept of the four world empires.

It is impressive how rapidly the new historical structure of time was created in a relatively short time span, despite the fact that old and new structures lived side by side during the sixteenth and seventeenth centuries. In 1559 the concept of the 'century' emerged, which, ever since, has been used to ascribe particular features for hundred-year blocks of time. In 1627 Domenicus Petavius established the distinct enumeration of the years before and after the birth of Christ. Ten years later, in 1637, René Descartes' work *Le Discours de la method: Pour bien conduire sa raison, et chercher la vérité dans les sciences* appeared. This is the historical context of the making and publication of Ruben's gravure. During this period not only did the historical time change but also the presuppositions of knowledge.[19] The new structure of time provided new narrative devices for understanding past realities. Terms like antiquity, the middle ages, the Renaissance and modernity are not only periods in which we place the historical facts. They are "general ideas", according Siegfried Kracauer.[20] Frank Ankersmit has named such concepts "narrative substances" without which historical narratives can't be constructed. Indeed, the change in the configuration of time created the space for new historical representations of the past.[21]

The transition from the old to the new historical time had to do with different forms of historical consciousness. In the old mental framework of time, history was indeed the unfolding of a deeper text defined by God, in which the last human empire would be replaced by the kingdom of God. The new framework was different also from another point of view: in 1543 Copernicus used the experience of the traveller to depict the experience of time as a change of images.[22] The same image was used by Bodin, in the same epoch, for describing historical experience over the passage of time. Time was no longer structured as a bipolar

---

18 DionHal 1.2–3.
19 Wilcox 1987, 8–9.
20 Kracauer 1995.
21 Ankersmit 1983; 2001.
22 Grafton 2007.

system of promise and fulfilment and a dialogue between the divine and the human, but as a flow of distinct moments. The new *Ars Historica* was connected with the Copernician revolution in the understanding of time.

Conclusion

This essay refers to the shift in European thought from one temporal order to another, from conceiving the history of the world as the succession of four empires, to a new order, positing Antiquity, the Middle Ages and Renaissance as a genealogical succession of periods leading to modernity. Greek antiquity, being in the margins of these world empires, was effaced. This reading of the past entailed a temporality that indicated the divine intervention as the future and the inevitable end of the world. From this perspective, the present was an extended sequel of the past. With the shift to the new temporality, depicted with the emergence of Antiquity, it was introduced a succession of heterogeneous historical frameworks. This sequence posited Renaissance and the modern world as a new kind of future which presupposed antiquity as its past. In the new temporality the present was part of the future of the past. The great dividing line which bordered the present was no longer drawn between the present and the future, but between the present and the past. The new predicament was not to stick with and to hold on to the tradition, but to anticipate the future. This is the line which demarcated history as the other bank of the time river. The image engraved by Rubens is evidence of this crucial moment of transition which has constituted Renaissance and the modern world as the future of Greek antiquity. It was a description of what was happening during his era, and an imperative of what should happen. For this reason the two figures pushing to oblivion the four symbols of the past Empires were Time and Death.[23]

---

[23] I'd like to thank Alexandra Lianeri, not only for her invitation to take part to the conference *Knowing Future Time in and through Greek Historiography*, but also for giving me the chance to re-think on this case, which was originally part of my book *Apocalypse, Utopia and History. The Transformation of Historical Consciousness*, (in Greek, Athens, Polis, 2011) through her reading. Her insightful suggestions re-framed the initial idea, putting this moment of the changing structures of temporality to the process of remaking the concept of future in the beginnings of the modern European era.

Tim Rood
Horoscopes of Empires:
Future Ruins from Thucydides to Macaulay

> Now we have ... gossiped looking towards Wren's grand dome, shaping Macaulay's dream of the far future, with the tourist New Zealander upon the broken parapets, contemplating something matching – 'The glory that was Greece – The grandeur that was Rome.'
> G. Doré and B. Jerrold, *London: A Pilgrimage*[1]

Thucydides' *History* for the most part maintains a firm focus on the present of the Peloponnesian War while anchoring its claim to universal significance in the future in the expectation that it will be 'judged useful by those who want to have a clear view of what happened in the past and what – the human condition being what it is – can be expected to happen again some time in the future in similar or much same ways' (1.22.4[2]). At the same time, Thucydides' account contains a small number of more specific anticipations of likely or possible futures.[3] Some of these – the return of plague (2.48.3), or of a 'Dorian war' accompanied by famine (2.54.3), or of the acute sufferings of civil war (3.82.2) – offer proleptic glimpses of human suffering. Another passage expresses the strong expectation that silting at the mouth of the River Achelous will continue until the Echinades islands become part of the mainland (2.102.3). My focus here, however, will be the first of Thucydides' futures, located at a central point in the *Archaeology* – his opening account of Greek history designed to justify the claim that the Peloponnesian War was the greatest war ever. In this section, Thucydides is particularly concerned to promote the claims of his war over two earlier encounters, the Trojan and Persian Wars, both of which he characterises as significant, but inferior,

---

[1] 1872, 190 (with Nead 2000, 212–214).
[2] References are to Thucydides unless otherwise stated; all translations from Thucydides are from Mynott.
[3] As Immerwahr 1960, 283 n. notes, there are also many allusions to future fame in characters' thoughts (5.16.1, 7.56.2) and speeches (2.11.9, 2.41.4, 2.43.2, 2.64.3–5, 4.18.5, 6.16.5, 6.33.5, 6.80.4); I disregard here the even more numerous projections of more immediate futures focalised through characters that lie in the narrator's past. The narrator also applies the vocabulary of memorialising to physical monuments (μνῆμα at 1.132.2, 6.54.7; μνημεῖον at 1.138.5, 5.11.1; contrast σῆμα at 2.34.5, 6.59.3), while bringing out that memorials can be destroyed (1.132.2, 5.11.1, 6.54.7).

wars. The glimpse of the future appears as he pauses to consider a possible objection to the claim that the Trojan War was a major encounter:

> Now, just because Mycenae was a small place – or because some other township of that period does not now seem to amount to much, that is not a valid reason to doubt the size of the joint force as reported by the poets and as traditionally accepted. For just suppose the city of Sparta were wiped out and all that was left were its shrines and the foundations of its buildings, I think that years later future generations would find it hard to believe that its power matched up to its reputation. Yet in fact the Spartans occupy two-fifths of the Peloponnese and are leaders of the whole of it as well as of many allies beyond it. Nevertheless, because they are not united in one city and have no lavish shrines or public buildings but instead live in village settlements in the traditional Greek manner, they would be underestimated. On the other hand, if the Athenians were to suffer the same fate they would be thought twice as powerful as they actually are just on the evidence of what one can see. (1.10.1–2)

Thucydides' 'thought experiment'[4] about the potential future ruins of Sparta and Athens dismisses the argument that the small size of major power centres at the time of the Trojan War proves that Agamemnon's army could not have been as great as recorded by Homer.

Modern scholars have approached this passage in a variety of ways. In recent years, the potentially unsettling methodological implications of Thucydides' analysis of the physical appearance of Mycenae, Sparta and Athens have been of particular interest,[5] with his suggestion that the visual evidence of buildings is not always a reliable guide to power often read as a critique of Herodotean methodology.[6] Many scholars of older generations were more concerned with the compositional implications of the anticipation of Athens' ruin: given that Athens' power was not as great at the end as at the start of the Peloponnesian War, at what stage did Thucydides think it appropriate to argue that the Athenians would be thought twice as powerful 'as they actually are'?[7] Adam Parry, by contrast, found it more compelling to see Thucydides' vision of ruin as emblematic of a historical perspective that pervades his work as a whole: for Thucydides, the Peloponnesian War was 'the end of the world, after the world had reached its high point'.[8]

---

4 Dillery 1995, 124.
5 E.g. Bassi 2005, 18–20.
6 For 1.10 as critique of Herodotus, see e.g. Hornblower 1987, 31; Boedeker and Raaflaub 1998a, 2–3; Morley 2011, 223; see further n. 52. Immerwahr 1960, 281 concludes from 1.10 that 'on the whole, Thucydides thinks little of the visible as a criterion for knowledge'; the point rather is that the visual ruins of Athens and Sparta would be exceptional in being misleading.
7 See e.g. Harrison 1912.
8 Parry 1989 [1972], 288.

Horoscopes of Empires: Future Ruins from Thucydides to Macaulay — 341

In this chapter, I propose to explore from a comparative perspective what Thucydides' glimpse at the hypothetical ruins of Athens and Sparta can reveal about his ideas of the future. My main focus will be on authors in Thucydides' own future. From the second half of the eighteenth century, anticipations of future ruins became a major theme in European (and especially British and French) art and literature. Found in a variety of literary genres, including poetry, periodical articles and travel narratives, and in the work of artists such as Hubert Robert and John Gandy, the theme is most famously expressed in the figure of Macaulay's New Zealander, who achieved a long afterlife, notably in an engraving by Doré, after being unveiled in 1840 in a review of Ranke's *History of the Popes:* 'some traveller from New Zealand shall, in the midst of a vast solitude, take his stand on a broken arch of London Bridge to sketch the ruins of St. Paul's.'[9] My aim in this chapter is to highlight what is distinctive about Thucydides' glimpse of future ruins by reading it against a number of eighteenth- and nineteenth-century manifestations of the motif. Owing to the constraints of space, I will focus on two aspects in particular: the way future ruins are used as a means of reflecting on imperial power and glory, and the way in which different writers construct the future figures which view or contemplate ruins.

This chapter will also be concerned with two authors in Thucydides' past. I will end with some comparisons between Thucydides and Herodotus, but it will be helpful to note from the outset that Thucydides' anticipation of future ruins has precedents of sorts in Homer. The *Iliad* shows an awareness of the changing signification of material remains, notably in Nestor's suggestion that the stone chosen as a turning-point for the chariot race in Patroclus' funeral games may mark the grave of an unknown man from the past (23.326–32).[10] The *Iliad* also contains repeated reflections on the future destruction of the city of Troy and of the Achaean wall – two events that lie beyond the poem's end but in the narrator's past. Closest to Thucydides' anticipation of ruin is the perspective

---

9 Macaulay 1866 [1840], vi.455; the argument is that the Catholic Church 'may still exist in undiminished vigour' at this point. A precedent in a travel journal Macaulay wrote in Italy in 1838 is noted by Edwards (1999), 80. See e.g. Macaulay 1953, Junod 1984, Harries 1994, 87–94, Chandler 1998, 110–11, Woodward 2001, Skilton 2007 for general reflections on the motif; Dubin 2010 on Robert and Lukacher 2006 on Gandy; also e.g. Carnall 1960, 11–13; Burrow 1981, 68; and on ruins more broadly, e.g. Mortier 1974, Ousby 2002 [1990], 72–99, Fritzsche 2004, 92–130, and 2013 (distinguishing four categories: 'admonitory', 'confiscatory', 'adversarial', 'the ruin of the ruin'). I have drawn on these works for examples of the 'future ruins' motif while also including some examples that I have not seen in the literature. For the reception of Macaulay's figure, see Dingley 2000 and Skilton 2004; Harrison 1912, 248 sensed the link with Thucydides ('Macaulay contemplated the ruin of London before ever Germany had Dreadnoughts. Thucydides may have contemplated the ruin of Athens at any time of his life').
10 Cf. Grethlein 2008, 31–2.

of two characters, Agamemnon and Hector, who reflect that 'the day will come when sacred Ilios shall be destroyed, and Priam, and the people of Priam of the fine ash spear' (4.164–5, 6.448–9, transl. Hammond). This prophecy of Troy's doom was cited, as we shall see, as a reflection on the mutability of fortune later in antiquity as well as in the modern era, but it lacks two key features that are found in Thucydides and in most of the other passages we will be looking at – a focus on actual ruins and the evocation of a hypothetical future viewer.

Through a comparative analysis with both earlier and later authors, I aim not just to illuminate Thucydides' ideas of the future but also to make some (necessarily tentative) comparisons between ancient and modern temporalities. The popularity of the motif of future ruins from the middle of the eighteenth century is particularly striking because it coincides with what philosophers of history such as Reinhart Kosselleck have seen as a shift in conceptions of history.[11] The old Ciceronian doctrine of 'historia magistra vitae' (grounded in a view of universal human nature) gave way to a new focus on historical difference: the past began to seem more of a foreign country. This increasing attention to historical difference in the past seems to chime with a greater sensitivity to the sort of historical difference in the future exemplified by the idea of future ruins. And yet any explanation that ties a fascination with future ruins to a sense of rupture embodied in a new regime of historicity seems to leave Thucydides' glimpse of the ruins of Sparta and Athens in a limbo – given that Thucydides' *History* itself is often seen as an exemplary expression of the idea of a universal, transhistorical human nature. To resolve this apparent contradiction, we must explore in more detail some of the uses of future ruins in both ancient and modern writers.

We start with two men who visited Greece in the early years of the nineteenth century – a French aristocrat, François-René de Chateaubriand, and an Anglo-Irish painter, Edward Dodwell. Chateaubriand's *Travels to Jerusalem and the Holy Land* is a romanticised portrait of a journey undertaken in 1806. Throughout, he responds strongly to the presence of ruins in Greece. In his preface he speaks of 'indulging my reveries among the ruins of Greece' as among 'the most serious reflections' offered by his work. At Athens, he quotes reflections on the mutability of fortune from a sixteenth-century geographical work on Greece: 'Proficiscere Athenas, et pro magnificentissimis operibus videto ru-

---

[11] See Koselleck 2002 (note the summary at pp. 165–9, and also pp. 84–93 on the new temporalisation of utopia in Mercier's 1770 novel *The Year 2440*) and 2004 [1979], esp. Ch. 1; also e.g. Hartog 2003 on changing 'regimes of historicity' (with the important methodological qualifications of Hannoum 2008). Schiffman 2011 places the 'discovery of the past' somewhat earlier in the eighteenth century, with Montesquieu. For further discussion see e.g. the essays in Lorenz and Bevernage 2013.

dera et lamentabiles ruinas. Noli, noli nimium fidere viribus tuis ...' ('Go to Athens, and, instead of the most magnificent works, behold heaps of rubbish, and lamentable ruins. Beware, beware of confiding too much in thine own strength ...'). At Sparta, he utters an impassioned cry of 'Leonidas! Leonidas!', but 'no ruin repeated this great name, and Sparta herself seemed to have forgotten her hero'. It is only as he describes an (alleged) climb up a mountain near the Isthmus of Corinth that he casts himself imaginatively into his future. He surveys the Peloponnese and the Isthmus, with the sea stretching eastwards and westwards, seeming 'to tempt me with the recollection of France', before reflecting: 'What a desert! what silence! ... Shall France one day be stripped in like manner of her glory? Shall she, in the course of ages, be thus laid waste and trampled under foot?'[12] His anxiety for France provokes an affected desire to return home at once rather than continue his travels further east.

Edward Dodwell offers a much less passionate account of his travels in Greece. His account is full of references to Strabo and Pausanias as well as to the mythical associations of the places he visits. He rises to more emotional heights at Mycenae, where he applies to the remote past a phrase from a famous Shakespearian evocation of the future:

> I approached the Cyclopian city of Perseus with a greater degree of veneration than any other place in Greece had inspired. Its remote antiquity, enveloped in the deepest recesses of recorded time, and its present extraordinary remains, combined to fill my mind with a sentiment in which awe was mingled with admiration.[13]

Following this echo of Macbeth's soliloquy ('... to the last syllable of recorded time'), Dodwell again strikes a scholarly note: he adds a long discussion of the size of the ancient city (though without referencing Thucydides), and compares Strabo's claim that no trace of the ancient city remained with Livy's notices of the destruction 'without traces' of Italian cities whose ruins can in fact still be seen. It is the great Panhellenic sanctuary of Olympia that inspires a future perspective. Here the vision of the future is mediated explicitly through a future traveller:

> we approach the venerable, though humbled, ruins of the Olympian Jove with those feelings of regret, and those sentiments of veneration, which will, at some far distant day, be

---

[12] Chateaubriand 1835 [1811], i.p. iv, 18 (from Nikolaus Gerbel's preface to Sophianus' *Descriptio Graeciae*), 118, 146–7 (allusion in Macaulay 1953, 118). On Chateaubriand and ruins, cf. Mortier 1974, 170–92; also Hartog 2003, Ch. 3, for Chateaubriand as transitional figure.
[13] Dodwell 1819, ii.229, echoing *Macbeth* v.5.21.

> experienced by the traveller, who, when Grecian ruins shall have entirely vanished from the site, will wander over the deserted locality of London or of Rome! [14]

Through his invocation of a hypothetical traveller, Dodwell conveys a stronger sense than Chateaubriand of the materiality of the ruined city in the future. At the same time, the idea of impermanence is intensified by the idea that even the ruins of Olympia will perish – a replay of sorts of a neat epigram in Lucan's account of Caesar's visit to the ruins of Troy (9.969: 'etiam periere ruinae').[15]

For both Chateaubriand and Dodwell, the spectre of future ruins is a vehicle for some fairly conventional reflections on the transience of power and, in Dodwell's case, on the further idea of a temporal and geographical progression from Greece to Rome. The familiarity of that further idea is shown by the reflections on the remains of Syracuse offered by a Fellow of a Cambridge college, Thomas Smart Hughes, in his *Travels in Sicily, Greece and Albania* (1820):

> Athens, Rome, and Syracuse, have been. The time too may come, when father Thames shall roll his waves amidst the ruins of that splendid capital which rises now so proudly on his banks. If that period should arrive, we have at least the satisfaction to know, that its name will be inserted among those that have been most glorious in their day: that the future traveller, should he wander over its deserted site, will feel his heart glow, as he treads upon the soil where freedom flourished.[16]

Hughes himself flags the conventionality by mentioning an ancient precedent – the tears of the Roman general Marcellus after his conquest of Syracuse in the Second Punic War. As Marcellus sees 'what was probably at the time the world's most beautiful city stretched out before his eye', he recalls the city's ancient glories, and 'it occurred to him that in the space of an hour it would all be ablaze and reduced to ashes' (Livy 25.24.11–13, transl. Yardley). 'After a lapse of 2000 years,' Hughes now reflects, 'we looked down from the same spot, and saw the scene of desolation quite complete.' As if conscious of indulging in an excess of sentiment, Hughes then describes how his meditations were interrupted by a snake slithering from the undergrowth.

Another famous ancient passage prompted similar reflections in the preface to the Rev. John Eustace's *Tour through Italy* (1813). Eustace quoted the Iliadic

---

14 Dodwell 1819, ii.235, 242–3, 332.
15 Lucan's account of Caesar at Troy is often read intertextually against Virgil's account of Aeneas' visit to the future site of Rome in *Aeneid* 8, suggesting that the ruins Caesar sees anticipate the eventual fate of Rome (e.g. Hardie 1993, 106–7); for possible hints of future ruin in Virgil's own account, cf. Currie 2006, 353 with n. 99.
16 Hughes 1820, i.84–5.

lines on the future destruction of Troy – as later quoted by the Roman general Scipio at the end of the Third Punic War, as he looked upon the present destruction of Carthage and anticipated the future destruction of Rome (Plb. 38.22 = App. *Pun.* 132).[17] Eustace then complicated the dense temporal layering provided by this citation of a citation with a prophecy of his own:

> Empire, like the sun, has hitherto rolled westward: when we contemplate the dominions of Great Britain, and its wide extended power, we may without presumption imagine that it now hovers over Great Britain; but it is still on the wing; ... the days of England's glory have their number, and the period of her decline will at length arrive. The inhabitants of these islands may, like the sons of Greece and Italy, lie prostrate at the feet of a victorious enemy ...[18]

As in Hughes, the prospect of comparison with the ruins of antiquity offers compensation for the impermanence of mortal power. In both authors, moreover, transience is figured through an aspect of nature: in Eustace, the movement of empire follows the course of the sun, while in Hughes it is a river that does the rolling – like ruins themselves, an image of both change and continuity.

Greek ruins could introduce a note of disquiet about the future even for travellers from the United States, beneficiaries of the next westward migration of empire. In his private journal and letters Nicholas Biddle, a Philadelphia banker who visited Greece in 1806, offered many gung-ho celebrations of American superiority that might seem to militate against any anxieties over the future. Indeed, for American writers in the first half of the nineteenth century the ruins of antiquity were more likely not to be associated with future loss, but to be seen as symbols of a past civilisation that would be replaced and transcended by the new republic. It was only with the Civil War that the picturesque aesthetic of ancient ruins was applied to the destruction wrought by the likes of Sherman.[19] A different vision of ancient ruins appears, however, as Biddle describes his visit to Sparta: 'Over the ruins of Sparta a republican has a melancholy pleasure. My own country offers an interesting analogy of which I have thought much.'[20] What is this 'interesting analogy' that the United States offers? Biddle does not seem to be thinking of any actual ruins in the United States. The architectural historian Christopher Woodward suggests, then, that Biddle was 'uplifted by the sight of a completely empty plain' owing to 'the disappearance of the monuments of a military tyranny', and contrasts his interpretation of the survival of Athens' monuments as 'a demonstration of the ultimate triumph of

---

[17] The Appian passage is discussed in relation to later 'imperial ruin gazers' by Hell 2010.
[18] Eustace 1813, i.p. xxxii (Koselleck 2004, 192).
[19] Rood 2010, index s.v. 'ruins'.
[20] Biddle 1993, 186.

democracy'. Woodward then cites Thucydides to show that Biddle had 'misread the language of ruins': the ruins of Sparta were not a proper indication of its ancient power.[21]

Woodward makes Biddle's pleasure in Sparta's ruined state conform to the patriotic sentiments he expresses elsewhere. The problem with this reading, however, is that Biddle's pleasure does not spring from the fact that Sparta was a military tyranny. In keeping with many French and American readings at the time, Biddle regards both the current and the ancient inhabitants of Sparta as 'surly republicans'.[22] And far from ignoring Thucydides, he picks up – with a twist – Thucydides' invitation to compare the ruins of Sparta and Athens:

> Sparta is no more. Its freedom has fled; the monuments of its glory have all returned to the earth which covers its children; the very spot which it occupied is deserted by an unworthy posterity. Athens still boasts of some sad monuments of its greatness & its arts, but the ruins of Sparta offer nothing to arrest the emotions of melancholy & despair.[23]

The twist is that Biddle is thinking not of the military power of Sparta and Athens but of the two cities as models of republican virtue and cultural greatness respectively. It is for this reason that the United States provides an 'interesting analogy' to Sparta. Biddle is thinking of how his country would look if it were reduced to the same state as Sparta. His concern is for the lack of grand classical architecture in the United States; on his return, he played a prominent role in the Greek Revival architectural movement in the United States, constructing a notable private residence, a university building and numerous bank branches in the

---

[21] Woodward 2001, 201–2 (to which I owe knowledge of Biddle); cf. Woodward 2007, 13: 'Biddle had not read his Thucydides. ... Biddle was deceived.'
[22] Biddle 1993, 184, contrasting the 'social Athenians'.
[23] Biddle 1993, 182. Biddle does not explicitly invoke Thucydides at this point, though he does go on to comment admiringly on Sparta's lack of walls, which is one of Thucydides' key points (Biddle 1993, 182: 'Sparta, in its infant freedom, had no defense but its institutions & its arms ...'). A neat parallel to Biddle's opposition of Athens and Sparta occurs in Rousseau's *First Discourse* (1750), an essay submitted to a prize competition on the theme of whether moral virtue is corrupted by progress in science and the arts. Rousseau writes of Athens that 'the elegance of its Buildings matched that of the language', and the city produced 'those astounding works that will stand as models in every corrupt age'; while as for Sparta, 'all that is left us of its Inhabitants is the memory of their heroic deeds. Are such monuments worth less to us than the quaint marbles left us by Athens?' (1997, 12). Like Biddle, Rousseau makes the same point as Thucydides about the physical appearance of the ruins of the cities, while discarding Thucydides' concern with power in favour of moral or political virtue.

Grecian style.²⁴ He wanted his country to be more like Athens in its current glory (and future ruin?).

The idea of future ruins was used by many British writers to express a similar anxiety about the architectural state of their country – and particularly about London in the aftermath of the glorious victory in the Napoleonic Wars. This theme extended well beyond travel writing. The Tory historian Sir Archibald Alison was following a well-trodden path when he claimed in his mammoth account of the Napoleonic Wars that the ruins of London 'will convey to future ages no adequate conception either of its present magnificence or beauty'.²⁵ In 1819, a writer in the *Literary Gazette* had written that 'if London was to become another Herculaneum, it would not be worth while to disclose its ruins, except for St Paul's',²⁶ while four years after that the architect James Elmes had more generously included the bridges of London and Sir John Soane's Bank of England building in the 'ruins left to indicate its present greatness' when London is fallen.²⁷ The contexts in which these various utterances were made suggest that the anxiety about London's lack of distinguished monumental architecture was stoked above all by contrast with the grandeur of Paris. The importance of the London-Paris comparison is shown particularly well in an 1836 periodical article on the 'British School of Architecture':

> We often speak of the French as a gay and volatile race, incapable of steadily pursuing any object for any length of time together; fickle in their passions, fickler still in their attachments, and totally unworthy to enter the list with the sober steadfast march of the English people. Will France, however, or England, stand highest two hundred years hence, from the monuments of the age of Napoleon and Wellington which they have left? Future generations will then as now look with undiminished interest on the splendid monuments of Paris ... what will London have to show, to stand in comparison? What will the conquering nation have to exhibit to rival the trophies of the vanquished?²⁸

Here the contrast between the victorious side that is paradoxically defeated by the monuments of the defeated reprises Thucydides' comparison of Sparta and

---

24 McNeal 1993, 11–12.
25 Alison 1848, xx.69.
26 Anon. 1819, 345 (Lukacher 2006, 105).
27 Elmes 1823, 401–2 (Lukacher 2006, 162).
28 Anon. 1836, 234 (partly cited by Lukacher 2006, 156). This passage does not explicitly state that the monuments will be in ruins when viewed two hundred years hence, but the argument of the whole article – which focuses (like Alison later) on the use of solid stone as opposed to brick with decorative cladding and which mentions the continuing impression made by the ruins of castles in the English countryside – presupposes deterioration of each capital's buildings from their current state.

Athens – and even the temperaments attributed to the two nations bear some resemblance to Thucydides' characterisation of his protagonists.[29]

The fear that the ruins of London may seem underwhelming to future generations springs from the notion that monumental architecture in lasting materials is the proper way for a nation to leave its mark in the pages of history. And yet a different perspective on the process of decay was also possible. In his reflections on the ruins of Syracuse, Thomas Smart Hughes noted that 'every production of art or nature comes to a close, and motion seems necessary to the state of human affairs; for the high tide of prosperity soon ebbs, and the very excess of civilisation seems to hasten the period of dissolution'.[30] Hughes here combines two distinct notions. On the one hand, growth and decline are natural processes: it is almost as if the very necessity of decline is an impetus to motion. On the other hand, his closing comment about the 'excess of civilisation' seems to echo a familiar theme in both ancient and early modern political thought: luxury corrupts virtue. Hughes' suggestion that greatness and ruin are mutually implicated is given an architectural twist by the Scottish journalist Robert Mudie in his *Second Judgment of Babylon the Great* (1829) – a polemical description of London. For Mudie, indulging in large-scale and expensive building projects is itself a symptom of a self-defeating spirit of luxury: 'how can we avoid dreading that the infection may be caught, that we too may become corrupt and perish; and that the monument of England's mighty genius may one day be as desolate as those of the Athenian Minerva and the Roman Jupiter?'[31]

The writers we have explored so far have all in their different ways been using the future as a way of celebrating, commemorating or criticising the present. The dominant concern with the present is suggested by the vagueness with which the future is conjured up: ruins have been imagined at some unspecified point in the future, perceived if at all simply by an anonymous traveller. At times, however, writers have been concerned to define the future more precisely in terms of both time and perspective. The more distant the future, evidently, the more time for decay – though just how far writers look into the future can often seem a matter of whimsy.[32] Of greater importance, as we shall see, is the question of who sees the ruins.

A small degree of characterisation emerges when travellers who have seen ruins in classic lands cast their imagined future travellers in the same mould

---

[29] See 1.70 and 8.96.5 for the contrast between the swift Athenians and slow Spartans.
[30] Hughes 1820, i.84.
[31] Mudie 1829, ii.143.
[32] A precise year is sometimes given: e.g. Lyttelton 1780, 1–16 ('a Letter from an American Traveller, Dated from the Ruinous Portico of St. Paul's, in the Year 2199').

as themselves. This is the image projected by Constantin-François de Volney at the start of *The Ruins* – perhaps the most famous work in the literature of ruins, though largely an essay on ancient history designed to explain the transience of empire. Volney here describes how he ponders on a vision he supposedly had at Palmyra of the city in its bustling heyday:

> Reflecting that if the places before me had once exhibited this animated picture: who, said I to myself, can assure me that their present desolation will not one day be the lot of our own country? who knows but that hereafter some traveller like myself will sit down upon the banks of the Seine, the Thames, or the Zuyder sea, where now, in the tumult of enjoyment, the heart and the eyes are too slow to take in the multitude of sensations; who knows but he will sit down solitary amid silent ruins, and weep a people inurned, and their greatness changed into an empty name?[33]

Looking ahead to an undefined future, Volney anticipates a traveller in other respects similar to himself visiting one of the great cities of the modern world – Paris, London or Amsterdam. And just as that future traveller would weep, Volney goes on to say that the idea 'brought tears' into his own eyes. This future, open to the same aesthetic engagement that Volney enjoys in his present, is both defamiliarised and familiarised.

A greater challenge is posed to readers when the identity of the future traveller is markedly different from that of the present traveller. A good example of this technique is found in an account written by an Anglo-Irish aristocrat, Lord Charlemont, of his visit to Athens in 1749:

> Is this the renowned Athens? How melancholy would be the reflection should we suppose, what certainly must come to pass, that in a few ages hence, London, the Carthage, the Memphis, the Athens of the present world, shall be reduced to a state like this, and travellers shall come, *perhaps from America*, to view its ruins.[34]

The identity of Charlemont's traveller strengthens the historicising gesture of the 'future ruins' trope: London, Charlemont implies, will feature on the grand tour of travellers from the next great imperial power. This historicising perspective is reinforced by the analogy between London and three great ancient commercial cities and also by the context in which these musings appear in the journal. Charlemont worked up and modified a narrative of his travels over the course of many years, and these reflections appear after an account of Athens' history right up to the early eighteenth

---

[33] Volney 1796, 12 (cf. Hartog 2003, 127). For Volney's engagement with Thuc. 1.10 in his travel book on America, cf. Rood 2015, 486–487.
[34] Charlemont 1984, 135.

century. He then broke off to reflect on mutability – and to illustrate the theme by the fate of Britain, 'the Greece, the Italy of latter Times!', whose liberty had declined into tyranny since the days of Pitt. He then continued: 'I find in my note book the following fantastical flight on my first contemplating the ruins of Athens, which, with the assistance of a little superstition, might be exalted into *something prophetic*.' His anticipation of a future traveller is framed, then, in a later context in which the decline of Britain is already under way.[35]

The most famous evocation of a future traveller specifically from America appears in a letter written in 1774 by the English writer Horace Walpole to Horace Mann, a long-standing British diplomat in Florence. Expressing a weary dissatisfaction with the state of literature in Europe, Walpole looks ahead to its resurgence in America:

> The next Augustan age will dawn on the other side of the Atlantic. There will, perhaps, be a Thucydides at Boston, a Xenophon at New York, and, in time, a Virgil in Mexico, and a Newton at Peru. At last, some curious traveller from Lima will visit England and give a description of the ruins of St Paul's, like the editions of Balbec and Palmyra.[36]

Walpole was writing as the political situation in North America was getting more heated, but his prediction owes more to literary conceit than to a deep engagement with the patterns of history: a fortnight earlier, he had told Mann that 'every day may bring us critical news from America', but that he was himself 'in perfect ignorance of the situation there', preferring a life of quiet retirement in old age.[37] The conceit of his remark lies in the neatness with which a north-south trajectory is imposed on the westward move of empire: the chronological shift in the figures mentioned (from Thucydides to Newton) chimes with a spatial shift from north to south (from Boston to Peru). Walpole also shows an arch awareness of the literariness of the trope: his traveller from Lima will not just see the ruins of St Paul's but write an account of them, probably with drawings (Horace Mann would have easily picked up his allusion to the works of Robert Wood, author of *The Ruins of Balbec* (1753) and *The Ruins of Palmyra* (1757)). He then breaks off by deflating his own preten-

---

[35] Charlemont 1984, 134–5. Woodward 2001, 190 speculates that 'Charlemont inserted these prescient remarks on American tourists after the War of Independence', but does not note how the passage is set out as a quotation from an original diary. Elsewhere Charlemont glossed the remark that 'Britons are now Athenians!' (1984, 179) by explaining that it was written in the reign of George II (i.e. before 1760).
[36] Walpole 1843–1844, i.370 (Gerbi 1973, 173–4; Dingley 2000, 20).
[37] Walpole 1843–1844, i.367.

sions: 'but am I not prophesying, contrary to my consummate prudence, and casting horoscopes of empires like Rousseau?'[38]

The American travellers to London imagined by Charlemont and Walpole are obvious forerunners of Macaulay's New Zealander, who made his debut, as we have seen, in 1840, in a review of Ranke. Macaulay was not in fact the first writer to adopt New Zealand as a centre of future civilisation: earlier writers had suggested that New Zealand might produce 'the Hume of the southern hemisphere' (Gibbon) or 'her Lockes, her Newtons, and her Montesquieus' (the translator of a French account of the South Seas).[39] Nor was Macaulay's Ranke review his first stab at the trope. The future ruins of St Paul's already stood as London's supreme relic sixteen years earlier, in a review of Mitford's *History of Greece*:

> when civilisation and knowledge shall have fixed their abode in distant continents; when the sceptre shall have passed away from England; when, perhaps, travellers from distant regions shall in vain labour to decipher on some mouldering pedestal the name of our proudest chief; shall hear savage hymns chaunted to some misshapen idol over the ruined dome of our proudest temple; and shall see a single naked fisherman wash his nets in the river of the ten thousand masts ... [40]

It was the Ranke review, however, that established the New Zealander as the classic figure for imagining how the present might seem in the future.[41] Its popularity sprang from one point in particular: at the time he was writing, Macaulay's New Zealander would have been understood not as a descendant of British settlers of the islands, but as a Maori – a more exotic figure than Charlemont's American, but also one who (unlike Walpole's Peruvian) might be assumed to have benefited from the civilising influence of the British.

Macaulay's review of Mitford points to another respect in which the perspective of a future traveller could be defamiliarising. By the time his future travellers visit England, the evidential basis for recovering the history of England seems to lie in its ruins. Hence they 'labour to decipher on some mouldering pedestal the name of our proudest chief' – perhaps, at the time of the review, a reference to the Achilles statue recently set up in Hyde Park with a dedication to Wellington. A precedent for Macaulay's usage appears in Horace Smith's sonnet 'Ozymandias', written in 1818 in competition with his friend Shelley. Smith imagines a

---

38 Walpole 1843–1844, i.370.
39 Gibbon 1994 [1776], i.1001; La Billardière 1800, p. vii (Smith 1985, 150).
40 Macaulay 1866 [1824], vii.703 (Burrow 1981, 68).
41 E.g. a periodical reviewer objected to analytical approaches to Homer by using the analogy of a New Zealander 2000 years hence arguing that Spencer was not the sole poet of *The Faerie Queen* (Anon. 1858, 413). For the reception of Macaulay's figure, see n. 9.

modern traveller astonished at the sight of a gigantic leg in a sandy desert whose inscription is the only surviving memorial of a once great city:

> We wonder, and some hunter may express
> Wonder like ours, when through the wilderness
> Where London stood, holding the wolf in chace,
> He meets some fragment huge, and stoops to guess
> What wonderful, but unrecorded race
> Once dwelt in that annihilated place.⁴²

Smith envisages a more desolate future, where civilisation has regressed, and it is a hunter, not a traveller from a great new metropolis, who stumbles on the ruin. Yet (like Volney's future traveller) this hunter is still bound with the poet and his contemporaries by his sensitivity for ruins – here a Herodotean sense of wonder rather than the tears of a Marcellus or a Scipio. A temporal perspective equally complex as that found in Smith's poem lies behind Macaulay's reference to St Paul's as 'our proudest temple'. It seems that the future travellers no longer understand that St Paul's is a Christian cathedral and assimilate it instead to the temples of Greece and Rome. And yet in one sense they are right to do so, for St Paul's was at the same time, as we have seen, frequently hailed in support of Britain's claim to the same status as Greece and Rome.

The intellectual challenge posed to future travellers by surviving monuments was increased by the British habit of importing antiquities from the Mediterranean and the Near East. In a 1753 letter thanking Horace Mann for sending an altar-tomb from Italy, Walpole claimed it was just the thing he wanted for the garden he was developing at his new Gothic villa, Strawberry Hill – and expressed the hope that 'it will remain till some future virtuoso shall dig it up, and publish it in a *collection of Roman antiquities in Britain*'.⁴³ The irony here is the stronger for the plausibility of the false attribution. At the same time, the iconic setting of Walpole's Italian import serves as a reminder that pleasure in the form of ancient relics was central to the cult of the picturesque, an aesthetic marked by a preference for a diversified and natural look rather than a French formality. Stranger conclusions still about the inhabitants of the British Isles are suggested when Sir John Soane imagines future visitors to his house trying to make inferences about the inhabitants of London from

---

42 Smith 1821, 213 (Dingley 2000, 26). For the earlier tradition of such confusions about excavated material, cf. Prettejohn 2012, 149: 'A recurring anecdote in art writing since the Renaissance revolves around a fantasy in which the archaeologists of some distant future come upon a long-buried work of modern art, and mistake it for an antique.'
43 Walpole 1833, ii.216 (Skilton 2007, 98).

his miscellaneous archaeological collection;[44] or again in Dante Gabriel Rossetti's 1856 poem 'The Burden of Nineveh', in which he imagines 'some tribe of the Australian plough' excavating the ruins of the British Museum and carrying off one of the Nineveh bulls, 'a relic now / Of London, not of Nineveh!'.[45] The cognitive difficulty of interpreting monuments is in these cases caused not just by time, but by the British imperial appropriation of the past. Present and future time is viewed as itself layered with different temporalities.

We have seen, then, that the 'future ruins' trope was open to a number of uses during the eighteenth and nineteenth centuries. At its simplest, it could express the idea of the transience of worldly power. At a time when Greco-Roman civilisation was central to the self-fashioning of modern imperial powers, this idea was congenial to the increasing number of aristocrats and artists indulging in travel to the classic lands of Italy and Greece, where the sight of ancient ruins could foster historical reflection on the transfer of power from southern to northern Europe. But the idea could also be developed in a number of more complex, dialectical ways, to suggest a variety of historical trajectories – in particular, the notion that the shift of empire from southern to northern Europe would itself be followed by a further shift of power to new and distant worlds. These trajectories of the future also speak to a sense that the pace of historical change was quickening – a sense that has sometimes been thought linked with the increased feeling of risk-taking and the at times acute economic worries caused by the spread of credit.[46] They speak, too, to the idea of the past as remote, in some sense a foreign country,[47] undermining any simple notion of historical continuity, even as the feelings attributed to the figure of the future traveller transcend any notion of an unbridgeable temporal gap.

It is time now to return to Thucydides – a figure who has been an absent presence in the preceding pages. One or two passages can be read as possible reminiscences of his work, but we have not come across any authors who use Thucydides' glimpse of the future as a vehicle for reflecting on their own future. It was historians of ancient Greece and travellers to modern Greece who responded most to Thucydides' anticipation of the future ruins of Athens and Sparta.

The lack of interaction between the Thucydidean and modern articulation of the 'future ruins' motif stems from one key difference between Thucydides and the writers discussed above. Thucydides is concerned more with the inferences

---

[44] Soane 1999 (Woodward 2001, 169–72).
[45] Rossetti 1881, 178 (Skilton 2004).
[46] Cf. Dubin 2010, drawing on Pocock 1985, 91–102.
[47] See n. 11.

about power that can be drawn from physical remains than with the impermanence of power itself.[48] Even when modern writers are concerned with buildings as a monumental display of power, their concern is not whether architectural display equates with actual strength but whether it ensures future reputation. It is telling that three nineteenth-century travellers who visited Athens and Sparta with Thucydides' analysis in mind applied it when describing the unimpressive remains of Sparta rather than the impressive remains of Athens. The same two travellers also misrepresented Thucydides as saying that the impression of power given by Athens' ruins would match (rather than exceed) their actual power.[49] Thucydides' reasoning that the impression of Athenian power would exceed reality was replaced by a tendency to make Athens an imperishable source of cultural and spiritual values.[50]

The idea of transience can nonetheless be felt beneath the surface of Thucydides' text. The impermanence of power is a theme in some of the speeches, most memorably expressed by Pericles: 'even if we do now have to accept some eventual loss (everything being subject to natural decline)' (2.64.3). That same theme is hinted at by the opening of our passage: 'Now, just because Mycenae was a small place ...' (ὅτι μὲν Μυκῆναι μικρὸν ἦν ...). It is not that Thucydides is presenting himself as a traveller reflecting on the sight of the ruins of Mycenae – though that is how he has often been portrayed by modern scholars:

---

48 We should, then, add 'testimonial' to the four categories of ruins posited by Fritzsche (n. 9 above).
49 Douglas 1813, 23 speaks of the ruins of Sparta 'accomplishing the prophecy of Thucydides, that while Athens would retain the semblance of its grandeur to its last day, the little that would soon exist of Sparta might induce future ages to disbelieve its former consequence'; Wordsworth notes that Thucydides' 'prophecy' has been 'fully verified', while earlier in describing Thebes he writes that the vestiges of Athens 'are such as to leave no doubt in the mind of the spectator with regard to the truth of the tradition he has received of its pristine glory' (1839, 335, 27); also Giffard 1837, 300 ('No prophecy can be more true'). These passages suggest that Millett 2009, 74 is correct when he claims that more attention has been paid to the prophecy about Sparta. An exception to the neglect of Thucydides' argument about Athens is Grote 1904–6, v.508–9, who (in line with his own pro-Athenian attitude) gives Thucydides an anti-Spartan twist (Athens' buildings 'gave to her an appearance of power even greater than the reality, and especially *put to shame* the old-fashioned simplicity of Sparta' (my emphasis)) and attributes to Pericles himself the perception that 'the visual splendor of the city, so new to all his contemporaries, would cause her great power to appear greater still'.
50 E.g. Macaulay 1866 [1824], vii.703 (from the review of Mitford cited earlier) on 'the gift of Athens to man': 'her intellectual empire is imperishable. And when those who have rivalled her greatness shall have shared her fate ... her influence and her glory will still survive,—fresh in eternal youth, exempt from mutability and decay, immortal as the intellectual principle from which they derived their origin, and over which they exercise their control.'

there is in fact nothing in Thucydides' words to suggest either that he had visited Mycenae or that Mycenae was in ruins.⁵¹ Rather, the bare formulation rewrites a well-known passage towards the start of Herodotus' work – his explanation of why his work will encompass cities both great and small: 'many of those that were great long ago have become inferior, and some that were great in my own time were inferior before' (Τὰ γὰρ τὸ πάλαι μεγάλα ἦν, τὰ πολλὰ αὐτῶν σμικρὰ γέγονε· τὰ δὲ ἐπ' ἐμέο ἦν μεγάλα, πρότερον ἦν σμικρά, 1.5.4, translation adapted from Purvis).⁵² Here the idea of transience is reinforced by the use of an imperfect tense for Herodotus' present – presupposing a future perspective (though not the sight of ruins as such).⁵³ While Thucydides is overtly concerned not with the alternation in Mycenae's fortunes but with the fact that its small size does not necessarily indicate a lack of greatness, he nonetheless conveys a sense

---

51 The gloss 'ruins' is used by e.g. Finley 1975, 19, who strongly criticises Thucydides for having no notion of the collapse of Mycenaean civilisation, and by Foster 2010, 28, who reformulates Thucydides' argument as being based on the fact that 'the ruins of Mycenae are unimpressive' (note the present tense and reference to ruins). Thucydides' imperfect could refer either to the state of Mycenae at the time of the Trojan War or to the destruction of Mycenae by Argos in 468 BC (Jowett 1881, ii.16–17); the following clause 'or because some other township of that period ...' then refers to the current reputation of the leading towns at the time of the Trojan War. Modern constructions of the collapse of Mycenaean civilisation are not relevant to Thucydides' argument.
52 Thomas 2000, 114 suggests that 'Thucydides' comparison of Mycenae, once great, Sparta and Athens' takes up the theme of mutability from Hdt. 1.5.4 (so too Foster 2010, 34 n. 49): my suggestion is that the phrasing at Thuc. 1.10.1 evokes Hdt. 1.5.4 even though it makes a different point – viz. Mycenae was once great even though small, not first great and then small (cf. Dillery 1995, 124, Saïd 2011, 72). Hedrick 1993, 27 suggests Thuc. 1.10 is critiquing Hdt. 1.5.4, but while Thucydides certainly departs from Herodotean method in paying little attention to buildings (cf. n. 6 above), 1.10 need not in itself be read as a critique. Herodotus in general sees great building works as worthy of commemoration, not as an index of power: an exception is 7.24.1 (the Athos canal), but here he expresses Xerxes' thoughts. At 1.192.1, when Herodotus is concerned with the power of the Babylonians, he selects the exceptional fertility of their land as an indication, not their physical structures, which he has described earlier.
53 Cf. Moles 1996, 278; Naiden 1999; Rösler 2000, 219 (I have altered Purvis' translation, which uses a present tense instead). Naiden 1999, 136 suggests that the prospective imperfect is applied by Herodotus particularly to 'objects or places that are vulnerable to the passage of time'. Herodotus does twice use the noun ἐρείπια for 'ruins', in both cases of remains left in foreign lands (2.154.5: houses of Greek settlers in Egypt who were relocated to Memphis; 4.124.1: Darius' half-finished fortifications in Scythia), but at 1.5.4 he does not specify in what ways cities' alternations between smallness and greatness are reflected in physical changes.

of transience by viewing it wholly as a city whose time is past, not as a city that enjoys a cycle of weakness and strength.

From what perspective does Thucydides imagine future ruins? When he hypothesises about the future appearance of Sparta, he invokes future generations (τοῖς ἔπειτα) who lie in an indefinite but distant future (προελθόντος πολλοῦ χρόνου).[54] This vague conception of people in the future is matched in the projections of future fame made by characters (cf. τῶν/τοῖς ἔπειτα: 2.41.4, 6.16.5, 7.56.2; τοῖς ἐπιγιγνομένοις: 2.64.3).[55] It is typical of the language of epideictic oratory, grounded in the fictive continuity of an imagined interpretative community. This continuity is further shown by the fact that Thucydides presents his future viewer as having the same critical faculties as a contemporary observer (rather as the *Archaeology* as a whole projects a unified model of power back to the time of the Trojan War). When Mycenae was at its most powerful, there were no other models of urban settlement in the Greek world that could have made Mycenae seem disproportionately weak. It is above all the presence of (modern, exceptional) Athens that makes the physical buildings of old-fashioned Sparta a deceptive indicator of the city's strength. Thucydides does not allow for the possibility that Athens might seem as old-fashioned to observers in his future as Sparta did in his present.

The continuity between Thucydides' present and his future viewer is further shown by the fact that Thucydides does not conjure up any equivalent of Macaulay's New Zealander. The absence of a foreign perspective is in one sense unsurprising: unlike the French or British in modern times, ancient Greeks did not themselves indulge in visits to the ruins of former imperial powers, and so did not imagine non-Greeks visiting Greek ruins in the future. Nonetheless, the fixity of Thucydides' (implicitly Greek) future perspective demands to be read against his earlier temporalisation of the Greek/barbarian antithesis. In the course of his opening sketch of the development of Greek history, Thucydides broadens an analysis of the prevalence of piracy in early Greece into a more general analysis of historical differentiation: at the time of the Trojan War Greeks had the same way of life as non-Greeks, but now that way of life is found in only a few remote areas of the Greek mainland and among non-Greeks. 'One might point,' Thucydides concludes, 'to many other respects in which the customs of Greece long ago resemble those of the barbarians today' (1.6.6).[56] But while Thucydides shows an awareness of past changes in the

---

[54] Strictly Thucydides does not speak of anyone actually visiting Sparta in the future, though his argument depends on the ruins of Sparta having been seen by at least one person whose report would be accepted as reliable, and visual language becomes stronger when he turns to Athens.
[55] Other terms are ἐς τὸ ἔπειτα: 2.64.5, 4.18.5; τῷ μέλλοντι χρόνῳ: 5.16.1.
[56] Cf. Koselleck 2004, 164.

configuration of Greek-barbarian relations, he does not carry the process of change and development over into the future.[57]

Modern exponents of progress are more likely to project different futures for contemporary 'primitive' peoples. Thucydides' own comments on piracy were used to show the prospect of improvement in a discussion in a Victorian periodical of Malay piracy:

> If the Malay be addicted to piracy we presume the taint may be eradicated from his blood, because he belongs to a state of society such as that described by Thucydides, when he tells us of the origin of the Grecian States. The buccaneers of Hellas lived in an antiquity so remote that Pericles might have been pardoned had he been ignorant of its appropriate legends. Their descendants were heroes. It is no doubt necessary to put down the system of Indian piracy with an uncompromising hand.[58]

That is, harsh treatment of Malay piracy now was justified because this piracy was part of a historical process. Often, it was accounts of the primitive state of Britain and Germany in ancient Roman authors that inspired this faith in progress. Thus it was Gibbon's reading of Ammianus Marcellinus' account of the Scots that inspired 'the pleasing hope' already mentioned, that 'New Zealand may produce, in some future age, the Hume of the southern hemisphere' – for 'if, in the neighbourhood of the commercial and literary town of Glasgow, a race of cannibals had really existed, we may contemplate, in the period of the Scottish history, the opposite extremes of savage and civilised life.'[59]

Even if the developmental model of Thucydides' *Archaeology* is not continued into the future, it may still help us to understand his anticipation of the future ruins of Sparta and Athens. Despite the strong elements of continuity between past and present in the human motivations underlying Thucydides' analysis in the *Archaeology*, the developmental model does repeatedly gesture towards a sense of a temporal gap between past and present. This gap is particularly prominent when Thucydides discusses the mode of life in Homeric Greece – a time when arms-wearing and piracy were customary. It is here that he points to

---

57 De Romilly 1966, 179 notes that the *Archaeology* as a whole pays no attention to progress in the future. In the main war narrative, Thucydides rules out the possibility of the Scythians ever developing unified power (2.97.6), echoing the similar future-oriented comment on the Thracians at Hdt. 5.3.1. It is not that ancient historians were averse to using foreign perspectives to comment on Greek or Roman affairs, but these tend to be synchronic rather than diachronic comments – criticisms of imperialism by noble savages rather than visions of transience by heirs to empire.
58 Anon. 1852, 75.
59 Gibbon 1994 [1776], i.1001. Like Macaulay (who may have been inspired by this passage), he evidently had the indigenous inhabitants rather than British settlers in mind.

a strong separation of past and present in mainland Greece, with these customs that were at one time universal confined to remote areas in the North-West of the Greek mainland and to the non-Greek world (1.5–6). Perhaps, then, it is no accident that it is precisely where the idea of a temporal gap in the past is strongest that Thucydides looks ahead to a temporal gap in the future. In the same way Herodotus makes his most extraordinary prophecy about the future in his account of Egypt – the section of his work most deeply pervaded by the past.[60] That Thucydides' historical analysis of the Trojan War helped him to historicise his own present is confirmed by the way he speaks of the future reputation of Sparta and by the way he makes Pericles speak of the future reputation of Athens. Thucydides' hypothetical enquirer in the future will match the ruins of Sparta against the Spartans' κλέος – the lingering reputation to which Homeric heroes aspire and which Herodotus saw it as his task to preserve.[61] Homer is again to the fore in Pericles' celebration of Athens: 'The proof of our power is supported by the strongest evidence and by every possible witness. … We need no Homer to sing our praises … we have established everywhere lasting memorials of our power for good and ill' (2.41.4). Here the historical perspective is more complex: the mention of Homer opens up a metahistoriographical reading, with Thucydides as the new Homer, author of a work more reliable not just than the poets but also than the monuments to which Pericles appeals.[62]

---

60 See 2.11.4, where Herodotus looks ahead to the silting caused by the Nile 20,000 years in the future if it were diverted to flow into the Arabian gulf; also 2.13 on the amount of silting within a smaller time-period, where the link between inferences about the future and historical knowledge of the past is particularly clear.

61 Cf. Thuc. 1.25.4 on the Corcyraeans' pride in the naval renown of the Phaeacians, earlier inhabitants of their island. The word is elsewhere used in Thucydides only in Pericles' funeral oration (2.45.2), where contemporary women are said to achieve good repute through having no κλέος for either good or ill. There is no sense at this point that Thucydides' own *History* will play any part in the future reputation of Sparta, *pace* Foster 2010, 35 n. 42, who claims that 'Thucydides rescues Spartan *kleos* from our errors'.

62 For metahistoriographical readings of the mention of Homer, see Gomme, Andrewes and Dover 1945–1981, ii.130; Rood 1998, 201; Hunter 2004, 240; Grethlein 2010, 222, 224; Rutherford 2012, 14. Ober 1988, 85–6 reads 2.41.4 against 1.10, suggesting that Thucydides points to the greater accuracy of his own account as opposed to monuments (cf. Grethlein 2010, 227 n. 82; Taylor 2010, 71; also the hyperbolical claim of Greenwood 2006, 117 that 1.10 implies that 'Thucydides' *History* will be the only true remnant of his era'). Ober's claim that Pericles is shown by 1.10 to make 'a painfully empty boast' (86) is, however, strained: even if the future viewers of 1.10 form an exaggerated notion of Athenian power, Athens' buildings will still be an index of power, and Ober in any case acknowledges that Pericles also has in mind monuments established by Athens abroad (85 n. 64).

I have argued, then, that Thucydides' exploration of the future ruins of Athens and Sparta differs in important ways from uses of the motif in the eighteenth and nineteenth centuries. Thucydides is concerned above all with monuments as a potentially deceptive index of power: his anticipation of a future viewer ensures that ruins are endowed with a historicity of their own rather than being an ahistorical emblem of either the decay or the endurance of the past. To be interpreted correctly as historical evidence, Thucydides implies, ruins require a historicising gaze that transcends the cultural parameters of any particular period. Modern writers, by contrast, have been more concerned with memorialisation and historical stature. They have also built into the sight of ruins more complex historical patterns than Thucydides' implied parallel between the future collapse of Athens and Sparta and the decline of Mycenae. Despite these differences, I have nonetheless suggested that for Thucydides too future ruins reflect an idea of historical rupture.[63] Indeed, it is precisely that sense of rupture that explains why he looks into the future at all at this point: his basic argument that Mycenae's small size is no proof of its inability to orchestrate a large war could equally have been supported by invoking a contemporary traveller to Sparta. Thucydides also resembles his modern counterparts in being primarily interested in the future as a way of thinking about the present. And in their different ways the various writers discussed above have all been using the future as a vehicle for literary or intellectual display.

How does Thucydides' vision of future ruins fit his other anticipations of the future? The recurrence of plague, the shifts in historical memory that will accompany the return of a 'Dorian war', the disasters that accompany civil war, varying in type and intensity according to circumstances – these are all events that shake social foundations and disrupt conventional values. This openness to historical rupture may seem at odds with the vision of the regular silting of the River Achelous – but that reflects the difference between regular natural and irregular human temporalities. It may seem more seriously at odds, however, with the view of a universal human nature that underlies his claim that his own work

---

63 This idea can be supported by the broader fifth-century trends analysed by Dunn 2007 ('present shock', with 111–50 on Thucydides) and D'Angour 2011. Koselleck himself noted that Thucydides 'explicitly constructed a far-reaching structural change in Hellenic history' in his *Archaeology* (2002, 55) and spoke of the 'accelerated change of experience' in the fifth century BC (2002, 77; cf. 165 for acceleration as a criterion of modernity). Koselleck was here drawing on Meier (1990), who himself analysed changes in fifth-century BC Greece in the light of Koselleck's analysis of changes in the second half of the eighteenth century (see esp. pp. 157–9, with the rather unsatisfactory proviso on p. 176 that '"politicisation" was to the conceptual world of the fifth century what "temporalisation" was to the period 1750–1850').

will be a 'possession for all time' (1.22.4). As noted earlier, that view of human nature is generally thought typical of the type of exemplary historiography that gave way in the eighteenth century to a greater focus on historical difference in the past – a focus that also seems in line with the sensitivity to historical difference in the future suggested by the thought of future ruins. Yet to see Thucydides' work as conforming to a simple model of exemplary historiography that is eclipsed in the eighteenth century by a new openness to historical difference may be to succumb to a self-fulfilling perception that Thucydides' conception of the past must necessarily differ profoundly from modern conceptions. The continuing homage paid in many quarters to the 'modernity' of Thucydides shows, after all, that the greater sense of the past as a foreign country has not put paid to the idea that history offers lessons. And the 'modernity' of Thucydides is itself in part reflected in the way his few overt glimpses of the future maintain a tight dialectic between historical difference and similarity while being sensitive at the same time to the threat of rupture.[64]

---

[64] I am grateful to the editor, Thomas Phillips, and Alison Rosenblitt for comments, as well as to the participants in the Thessaloniki conference.

Aviezer Tucker
Historiographic Ancients and Moderns: The Difference between Thucydides and Ranke

This paper identifies the theoretical and methodological turning point that distinguishes modern from ancient historiography. Since Thucydides is considered rightly to be the greatest ancient historian and Ranke is the founder of modern scientific historiography, the question about the difference between ancient and modern historiography can be personalised as asking what Ranke revised or added methodologically to Thucydides' achievements?

Krieger puzzled at the consideration of Ranke as the "Copernicus" or "Kant" of historiography: The critical attitude to sources dates back to Thucydides.[1] The crucial significance of original documents for historiographic reasoning had already been recognised in humanist scholarship since the fifteenth century and was defended systematically by Jean Mabillon and the Maurists in the seventeenth century. The theories and methods of philology developed in seminars in the early nineteenth century and were applied 'spectacularly' to Roman historiography by Barthold Georg Niebuhr, whom Ranke acknowledged as his mentor. I argue that modern "Rankean" historiography is distinguishable from its ancient predecessors by a special relation with the evidence. Around the turn of the nineteenth century, scholars from apparently different fields all began to use a form of probabilistic inference from multiple units of evidence like testimonies, languages and texts that allowed them to obtain new knowledge of the past. Ranke's attempt was the first successful application of this probabilistic method to historiography. Thucydides, though critical of his sources, did not infer from multiple testimonies as Ranke and his successors did; therefore he did not mention his sources.[2]

Historians, like other professionals such as scientists, lawyers or politicians have only a limited abstract systematic understanding of their methods and practices. People often rationalise and excuse their own practices; they attempt to present them as exemplifying the values they imagine their target audience shares. Experts are no different. Experts often possess tacit knowledge. Historiographic institutional practices display the hallmarks of what Collins called "col-

---

[1] Krieger 1977, 3.
[2] Kosso 1993, 9.

lective tacit knowledge."[3] Training transmits tacit knowledge through an apprenticeship that cannot be formalised and written down in a textbook. Tacit knowledge must be acquired directly, by "hanging around" people who possess it, such as teachers and peers. Collective tacit knowledge is acquired through social embedding. Still, tacit knowledge may have theoretical foundations that can be elucidated systematically and abstractly.

I attempt to understand here the tacit knowledge that Ranke possessed. I pay little attention to what Ranke may have thought about his own methodology and theoretical assumption, and even less to decontextualised and anachronistic misinterpretations of Ranke's own possible misrepresentations of the innovations of Rankean historiography: Some contemporary commentators focus on one phrase, *wie es eigentlich gewesen*, which they misinterpret as "positivism" or "empiricism," and a historiographic emphasis on political history at the expense of other historiographic subfields such as social or cultural historiography.[4] *Wie es eigentlich gewesen* has often been misinterpreted by people who have not only saved themselves the trouble of reading anything else by Ranke, but did not even bother to read the whole paragraph in which this phrase is embedded. The decontextualised reading of this phrase misinterpreted it as bordering on empiricist megalomania, pretending to be able to know exactly how things were, as if the historian could observe events that are not observable and can only be inferred from the evidence. In fact, as Koselleck noted,[5] Ranke's intention was not to broaden the epistemic claims of historiography to knowledge beyond their natural limitations, but quite the opposite, to limit the epistemic claims of historiography to what happened in the past, excluding judgments and lessons for the future in the tradition of *historia magistra vitae*, let alone make claims about the meaning of history.

The Rankean *method* does not require an exclusive emphasis on political historiography. Ranke's non-exclusive focus on political historiography resulted from contingent evidential circumstances rather than from intrinsic substantial methodological reasons. The lowest fruits on the tree of historiographic knowledge, given Ranke's new method and the archival evidential material at his dis-

---

[3] Collins 2010.
[4] Harloe / Morley 2012a, 9. Ironically, Harloe and Morley's criticism of the misuse of Thucydides in political theory is just as applicable *mutandis mutatis* to contemporary misuses of Ranke: "The authority of Thucydides' work – and it should be emphasised that this frequently means the *idea* of Thucydides' work, based on a few key passages and a set of received notions, which at times seems to have only limited connection to the text itself – seems to be a given, but is refigured according to the prevailing discourse of knowledge." (Harloe/Morley 2012a, 19)
[5] Koselleck 2004, 36, 131.

posal, happened to be of political history. "[T]he Neo-Rankeans largely misinterpreted Ranke by claiming that Ranke had considered the development of states and the system of states as a sort of superior reality, which was elevated beyond the subjectivity of party opinion and party strife."[6] The critical theories and methods that Ranke used do not imply a political theory about the causal efficacy of the state in relation to other social institutions; their content is the transmission of information from events to evidence. Butterfield suggested that the school of "Neo-Rankeans" emerged out of "educational routine that had taken the line of least resistance."[7] But with other sources of evidence or ingenious use of theories to extract more information from existing evidence, the Rankean method can and did produce economic, social and cultural historiographies.

Rhetorically, to convince, Ranke attempted to present or misrepresent his innovative work in terms that fitted contemporary values. Two different and even inconsistent systems of values were dominant. One was empiricist, following the success of Newtonian physics and other branches of the natural sciences. The other was traditional and classical; it admired Thucydides as the ultimate master historian. Thucydides "naturalised" historiography in comparison with Herodotus in rejecting supernatural causes. But he cannot be accused of empirical values in their seventeenth-century European sense... Historiography cannot be empiricist in an observational seventeenth-century sense. Historians cannot observe history. They observe its information preserving effects, remnants. All references to historiography as empirical science, unless referring to present evidence that can be observed in the archives, are poor metaphors at best.[8]

---

[6] Mommsen 1990, 132.
[7] Butterfield 1955, 118.
[8] I do not think there are many more "teleological" historiographies (as distinct from philosophies of history à la Hegel) than ones based on "experience." I dispute Grethlein's (2013) binary classification of teleology vs. experience in the writing of historiography. Historiographic "hindsight" is the outcome of having more information preserving evidence about the events than the agents who experienced them, not teleology. For example, if I write that Thucydides died in 400 BCE and that he was the most celebrated ancient historian, I write things that Thucydides could not have been conscious of. He did not know when he would die, and he could not have known that he would become the most celebrated ancient historian. The periodisation of the "ancient" world and the counting of years in relation to the birth of Jesus would have made no sense to him. Yet, the above sentence does not assume that Thucydides' destiny was to die in 400 BCE or that some sort of causal power was pulling his historiographic writing from the future in the direction of becoming the most celebrated historian. Modern historians rarely resort to teleology to explain history as Plato in his *Timaeus* and *Philebus* thought that teleology was necessary for explaining how brute causality generates meaningful ordered outcomes. (Tucker 2009) The above sentence merely relies on readily available evidence that Thucydides and his contemporaries did not have. The historian's "vantage point" from an epistemic perspective depends on

There is insufficient evidence to distinguish Ranke's own (possibly false) consciousness of what he was doing from the rhetorical appeals he had to make to prevailing values. To borrow decontextualised, but otherwise appropriate, phrases from Koselleck relating to the concept of *historia magistra vitae:* "It was not unusual for historiographers to reduce the topos to an empty rubric, only used in prefaces. It is therefore more difficult to identify the difference that always prevailed between the mere use of a commonplace and its practical effectiveness."[9] It is not surprising that Ranke interpreted Thucydides as an earlier version of himself. "The greatest historian of antiquity inspired the greatest historian of the present: that was the comparison which Ranke drew between Thucydides and himself."[10] Pires showed how generations of modern historians likewise projected their own perspectives on their interpretations of Thucydides.[11]

Though Ranke strived to legitimise his innovative historiographic methodology by presenting it in terms of the received model for great historiography, Thucydides', "that could not be surpassed," he surpassed Thucydides' methodology. Like other radical modernisers, Ranke presented his innovations as fitting a traditional model of knowledge to be accepted by "the old school." Thucydides and Herodotus became respectively encoded symbols for historiography as science and art. The endorsement of "Thucydides" meant a "scientific", rather than "artistic", view of historiography. What "science" meant, however, for different au-

---

the information available at the time of writing. This vantage point is not commensurable with distance in time from the events. Information signals gradually decay after the events that generate them as memories fade and witnesses die. But other evidence surfaces only years after the events. Evidence for processes in which events formed a part emerges usually only after the process ends.

Phenomenological historiography that attempts to understand the consciousness of historical agents, including their "future past," their horizons of expectations and meaning, is teleological in the sense that the world appears in consciousness imbued with meaning. However, phenomenological historiography can offer only limited understanding of history since historical agents were rarely conscious of the slow changes that make history: the people who made the Renaissance or the Industrial Revolution were not conscious of them. It is also more difficult to find evidence that preserves information about mental states than about actions. For example, Thucydides is criticised often for attributing motivations and other mental states to participants in the Peloponnesian War for which he could not have had evidence. (Hornblower 1987, 81) "In Thucydides,... speeches and introspection are crucial in restoring presentness to the past, though in most cases they are arguably fictional." (Grethlein 2013, 15) But if it is fiction, it is not historiography, not evidence-based probable knowledge of the past.

9 Koselleck 2004, 27.
10 Muhlack 2011, 208.
11 Pires 2006.

thors and their audiences could be quite different.¹² It took a non-academic historian like Schlegel to be able to finally make the distinction between Thucydides' artistic historiography and modern scientific historiography.¹³

My methodology for understanding the science of Ranke and his paradigm, how he surpassed the classical model of historiography, is to look at what he *did* rather than what he *said* about what he was doing.

Tim Rood concluded that Thucydides "was writing for an audience used to weighing up competing oral testimonies, and not as a modern historian weighing up a wide variety of different sorts of sources. He was seeking to produce an account that transcended the partial narratives typical of the courtroom. Thucydides says little about how he went about the task of analysing conflicting claims from eyewitnesses."¹⁴ Rood was deeply insightful in connecting historiographic methodological practices with jurisprudence and in noting that Thucydides and his successors merely sought to find the reliabilities of witnesses, especially when they disagreed. They practised source criticism, partly by considering biases as in court, but did not seek to infer new historiographic knowledge from multiple testimonies of varying reliabilities, as Ranke and following him modern historians would.¹⁵ When facing inconsistent testimonies, for example reports by the ambassadors of different countries, Ranke did not consider their respective reliabilities nor side with one or the other, but inferred new knowledge that was based on them.¹⁶ This is the essence of the Rankean revolution and paradigm in historiography that I attempt to explicate next.

Eighteenth-century discussion of probabilities and testimonies

As Rood noted, the methodologies of historiography and jurisprudence are quite similar. Both attempt to infer representations of what happened, to a large extent from the testimonies of witnesses who can be unreliable. Though both fields paid attention to the reliabilities of witnesses, jurisprudence received more formal probabilistic analysis. Jurisprudence and the calculus of probabilities were indistinguishable during the late seventeenth and eighteenth centuries.

---

[12] Muhlack 2011.
[13] Süßmann 2012.
[14] Rood 2006a, 237.
[15] Grafton 1997, 73–78.
[16] Grafton 1997, 52.

In medieval Roman law, the strength of legal proofs was described in terms of fractions. "[T]he corroborative testimony of two unimpeachable eyewitnesses constituted a complete proof."[17] If only witnesses of inferior quality, whose reliability was represented by low fractions, were available, their testimonies could add up to a "full proof," if there were enough of them. This was also Thucydides' and the best of pre-Rankean historiography's approach to generating knowledge of the past from multiple testimonies. It was necessary to first inquire about the reliability of witnesses and then find two reliable ones with similar testimonies or more testimonies of lower reliability.

The article about *probabilité* in the *Encyclopédie* in 1765, written probably by Diderot, represents an intermediary phase between ancient and modern approaches to inferring probabilistically from multiple testimonies. The article formulated the advantage of two witnesses in generating knowledge as $1-(1-\text{reliability rate})^2$, for example, the reliability of what two witnesses with a 0.9 reliability agree on in their testimonies is 0.99: $1-(1-0.9)^2$.[2] The article recognised the decreasing reliability of hearsay evidence, oral transmission and the greater overall reliability of written records, all principles that Ranke would endorse. The article avoided historiographic scepticism by relying on multiple information transmission chains that transmit information from past to present and the vanishing probability of their accidental coincidence. Still, this article did not consider the effect of the prior probabilities of what the witnesses testify to, why surprising testimonies that agree generate more reliable knowledge than predictable testimonies. Most significantly, this article omitted mentioning the independence of the witnesses as a necessary condition.[18]

The distinctly modern epistemology of inference from multiple units of evidence, including testimonies, was formalised by Ranke's older contemporary, Laplace, in his treatise on probabilities from 1796. In the groundbreaking last couple of pages of the chapter on testimonies, Laplace[19] formalised the generation of knowledge from multiple testimonies by applying what would be known as Bayes' theorem. He demonstrated that in a draw of one from one hundred numbers (i.e. the prior probability of each number is 1:100), when two witnesses report that the same number was drawn and their reliabilities are respectively 0.9 and 0.7, the posterior probability that their testimonies are true leaps to 2079/2080, considerably higher than that of each of the individual testimonies. Prior probabilities matter very much because low priors increase the posterior

---

[17] Daston 1988, 42.
[18] Daston 1988, 318–320.
[19] Laplace 1840, 136–156.

probability of what independent testimonies agree on. This is how knowledge is habitually *generated* by inferring from testimonies, even of *unreliable* but *multiple independent* witnesses. Ranke and his philologist older contemporaries practised extensively this new method of inference from testimonies (whether or not they were aware of the jurists' and Laplace's formal explication of their methodology). This kind of probabilistic inference had been unknown and had not been practised prior to the late eighteenth century.

Elaborating the inference of knowledge from multiple evidence

The method that Ranke and a generation of older philologists used for generating knowledge of the past from multiple information-preserving units of evidence like testimonies, documents and languages requires the assistance of theories about the preservation of information in time. The method traces information signals from the past and separates information signals generated by a common source, an origin, from "noise," information signals that did not originate in a source common to all the units of evidence. If it is possible to trace the information signals back to their source, it may be possible to infer the properties of the source from the signals it generated in the present. This process of generation of knowledge is modular; it proceeded in three consecutive stages, each conditionally dependent on its predecessor:

Stage I

The properties of multiple testimonies that are relevant for the generation of knowledge are those that tend to *preserve information that was generated by a common source*. Information theories about kinds of evidence that tend to preserve information reliably that may appear today commonsensical or trivial were crucial. The emphasis on primary sources in historiography and the requirement that witnesses testify exclusively to firsthand knowledge and the exclusion of most hearsay in Common Law were introduced to exclude testimonies that were more likely to be mixed with much noise. Simple theories about the evolution of language, specifying which parts are likely to change more slowly and preserve more ancient information like words referring to body parts, immediate family members, fauna and flora, places, names of God, and the first few numbers were as useful as the simple theory that verse preserves oral information better than prose.

The first stage in the process of generation of knowledge from multiple units of evidence should ascertain that the evidence preserves information about *some common information source whose properties are not specified*. For example, detailed multiple testimonies to a historical event probably share *some* common source; it could be the event they describe or a conspiracy to forge the historical record. At this *first stage* it does not matter. Whatever is the common source, it is unlikely that these detailed testimonies have no common information source and that all the witnesses generated the same story spontaneously. By contrast, generic testimonies may reflect various interests of different witnesses without a common source. For example, in a society where the worst insults to a man were to say that he married a prostitute or committed incest with his children, one may expect that different enemies of the same person would allege the same generic insults.

The likelihood of multiple testimonies given separate sources of information is assessed by considering the various advantages that the testimonies may have conferred on the witnesses, given background knowledge about their social context. Testimonies that convey coherent information but had no value for the testifiers or were even disadvantageous for them are highly *unlikely* given separate sources of information. The likelihood of testimony that conflicts with the interests or biases of witnesses is low; the likelihood of a set of such testimonies, given separate sources of information, is vanishing.

Multiple testimonies that transmit coherent information *do not increase the posterior probability of a common information source; rather they decrease exponentially the posterior probability of the only alternative, separate sources*. Therefore, Rankean historians exert themselves to discover multiple testimonies (or other independent sources of evidence like material archaeological remains). Since a small number of detailed testimonies that convey coherent information is usually sufficient to decrease the likelihood of the testimonies given separate sources to close to zero, additional testimonies are redundant. The first stage of generation of knowledge from multiple testimonies consists of the comparison of the likelihoods of multiple testimonies given some common information source multiplied by its prior probability, and given separate sources multiplied by their prior probabilities. Precision is unnecessary if it is possible to prove the vanishing likelihood of the testimonies given one hypothesis, since the common and separate information source hypotheses are exhaustive and mutually exclusive.

Since elaborate and detailed coherent sets of testimonies are unlikely in most cases given separate sources of information, their likelihood given some common information source, as low as it may be, is still significantly higher. The *psycholog-*

ical association between testimonial reliability and detail that originates in the first stage of generation of knowledge from multiple testimonies is exploited by con-artists, pathological liars and forgers, to create the false impression of reliability of *single* detailed and elaborate testimonies.[20] However, this is an epistemic fallacy; degree of detail does not affect the reliability of any *single* testimony.

Stage II: Alternative information flow nets

If some common source of information increases the likelihood of the testimonies considerably more than separate sources, several alternative types of information flow nets are possible:

1. *A single* information source. For two testimonies, the information flow chart will look like the letter V.

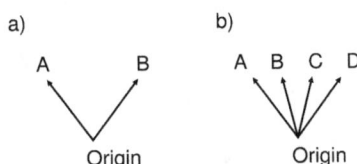

2. *Multiple common information sources:* Testimonies may transmit information from the same multiple sources. In the simple case of three testimonies preserving information from the same two sources, the information flow chart looks like the letter W:

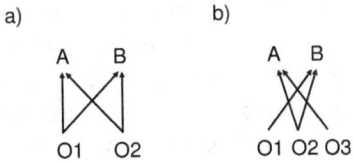

3. *The information source may be a member of the set of multiple testimonies.* The testimonies may duplicate one of them. The information transmission chart will look like:

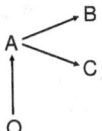

---

20 Grafton 1990.

4. *All the testimonies may result from mutual exchange of information.* For example, a group of witnesses may discuss and deliberate to produce a consensus account of an event (or to frame a victim):

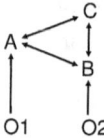

5. *Combinations of information flows of types 1 or 2, with types 3 or 4.* For example, the witnesses observed an event independently but then discussed it among themselves prior to testifying. In the simple case of two testimonies, the information flow chart may have then the shape of an inverted A:

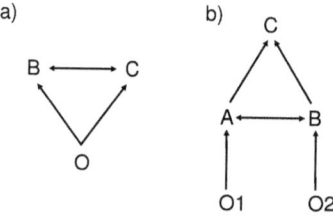

Testimonies in information nets of types 1 and 2, unlike types 3 and 4 are *independent* of each other in the sense of absence of intersection between the information signal transmission flows that connect them with their originating common source or sources. Type 5 mixes independent with dependent information flows and so inferring knowledge from such a net requires the separation of the independent from the dependent information flows. This is the art of textual critics who detect information signals that indicate the temporal and local origins of the elements of composite testimonial documents and their likely origins. Some testimonies may mention explicitly their multiple sources. Others may preserve linguistic, terminological or conceptual differences that signal different origins. Historians and textual critics look for discontinuities in style, conceptual framework and implicit values; internal contradictions, gaps in narratives, and parts that are inconsistent with the alleged identity of the author.[21] Ranke's initial impressive achievement was in tracing and proving information flows that proved that Guicciardini was not an independent source despite being a contemporary who even participated in some of the events he wrote about. "Ranke divided the pages of his folio notebook into two columns, one devoted to Guicciar-

---

21 Grafton 1990; Tucker 2004, 46–91.

dini, the other to complementary or divergent accounts. Systematic comparison revealed the Florentine historian's dependencies and defects. As Ranke set out to explain his conclusions, the notebooks metamorphosed almost spontaneously into a radical critique."[22]

Stage III: Knowledge from multiple testimonies

The final stage in the generation of knowledge from multiple testimonies attempts to determine the properties of the original information sources, the events in historiography, ur-languages in philology, and original documents in textual criticism, give content to the information net. It consists of comparing the likelihoods of the independent testimonies or languages or documents given competing hypotheses about the properties of their common information sources-origins. This requires first the evaluation of the prior probabilities of these hypotheses by considering their coherence with everything else we know. The prior probability of a common source hypothesis is then multiplied by the likelihoods of the testimonies. The art of historians, journalists, intelligence analysts and detectives is to know where to find relevant evidence and which theories to use to assess such likelihoods. With sufficient evidence, it is possible to follow the genealogies of testimonies to determine their sources, as Jardine[23] proposed.

The historiographic revolution

The Judeo-Christian scriptures were not the easiest evidence to infer probabilistically from because of the complex and partly underdetermined net of information transmission that led to them, especially during the eighteenth century prior to the archaeological discoveries of other documents from the biblical period and material evidence in biblical sites.

As a paradigm, biblical criticism started circa 1780.[24] The main theology centres at the universities of Halle, Jena and Göttingen trained their students in critical methods. From the founding of the University of Berlin in 1810 to 1819, de Wette, who institutionalised the paradigm in biblical criticism, taught at the uni-

---

[22] Grafton 1997, 45.
[23] Jardine 2008.
[24] Rogerson 1985, 18.

versity of the Prussian capital, where Ranke, the paradigm founder of historiography, would be based from 1825.

Eichhorn's *Einleitung ins alte Testament*, Introduction to the Old Testament, (1780–83),[25] substantiated the documentary hypothesis that the Bible is a composite of many different documents that were written by different people at different times in different places and were edited together after the return of the exiles from Babylon. Eichhorn assumed a theory of the historical development of language as constantly mutating. Consequently, texts that share a similar vocabulary and grammar were written at the same time and place. The best explanation of textual linguistic similarity and difference is the historical period and space of composition. Languages absorb foreign words when their speakers interact with speakers of source languages. The presence of borrowed foreign words in a text dates it to no earlier than the historical period when speakers of the two languages came into contact. The method that follows from this simple theory of language is the comparative philological analysis of texts. Since the language of the Pentateuch is not significantly different from that of Samuel and Kings, it must have been given its current form at the same time as Samuel and Kings. Eichhorn followed Astruc in dividing *Genesis* according to the different names of God used into *Jehovah* (Judaic) and *Elohim* (Israelite) sources. Since Psalms is linguistically heterogeneous, it must be composed of documents from various times and places. The later texts in the Bible can be dated according to their use of Aramaic words, borrowed after the Babylonian exile.

Eichhorn concluded that Chronicles was written after the Babylonian exile also on the basis of a comparison of its religious conceptual framework with that of Samuel and Kings and the concepts of the Zoroastrian religion of ancient Persia. Chronicles mentions Satan often and has a developed angelology. By contrast, Samuel and Kings make no reference to Satan or a developed angelology. In Chronicles, Satan induces king David to conduct the prohibited census, whereas in Samuel it is God's wrath. Eichhorn proposed that Persian influence is the best explanation of the similarity between the dualistic conceptual framework of Chronicles and the religion of ancient Persia that is not shared by Samuel and Kings. This explanation makes the evidence more likely than, for example, a spontaneous evolution of Judaism or a faction of it that invented Satan independently of Zoroastrianism and wrote Chronicles at the same time as Kings was written by another faction that denied Satan. Eichhorn must have assumed a theory that evaluates the probability that Judaism mutated spontaneously to become dualistic as far lower than the probability that it incorporated elements of the Zoroastrian religion as a result of coming

---

[25] Wolf 1985, 227–231.

into contact with it during the Babylonian exile. Consequently, it is possible to date Chronicles to the period that followed the contact between Jews and Persians. Further discrepancies between 2 Samuel, 1 Kings and Chronicles led Eichhorn to believe that the earlier books could not have been direct sources for the later book. The best explanation for the overwhelming similarities was in Eichhorn's hypothesis a lost common source that reached the author of Chronicles in a short and mutated version.[26]

W. M. L. de Wette in *Beiträge zur Einleitung in das Alte Testament* (2 vols, 1806–7 *Contributions to Introduction to the Old Testament*)[27] agreed with Eichhorn that Chronicles was composed long after Samuel and Kings, as well as on the reasons for believing so. Yet, de Wette argued against Eichhorn that there is insufficient evidence for claiming that Chronicles shared a lost common source with Samuel and Kings. A more parsimonious hypothesis is that Samuel and Kings were some of the sources for Chronicles.[28] The similarities between Chronicles, Samuel and Kings cannot be coincidental. So, either they had a common source, or the earlier books affected the later book. Wette appealed first to the cognitive value of parsimony to prefer the later hypothesis. Had the Pentateuch been written 500 years before the monarchic period, it would have been written in an archaic form of Hebrew, not in the same language as the monarchic books of the Bible. The Pentateuch ascribes to Moses religious practices and institutionalised structures that could have been introduced only in an organised temple with a specialised priesthood during the monarchy. De Wette suggested that the discovery of the Book of Law in the temple during the reign of king Josiah, as described in 2 Kings, refers to a part of Deuteronomy. Much of the Pentateuch could have been written to legitimise king Josiah's late seventh century BCE reforms and the attempt to centralise and monopolise religious worship in the Jerusalem temple. The Pentateuch is not mentioned in Samuel and Kings, quite possibly because it had not been written yet.

C.P.W. Gramberg attempted in *Kritische Geschichte de Religionsideen des Alten Testaments* (*Critical History of the Religious Ideas of the Old Testament*, posthumous 1830) to date the Old Testament, assuming the theory that the function of historiography in traditionalist cultures is to legitimise new practices by inventing their ancient history. The Pentateuch and Joshua were composed in connection with king Josiah's centralist political and religious revolution because these books are replete with projections onto earlier periods of post-revo-

---

26 Rogerson 1985, 22.
27 de Wette 1806–7.
28 Rogerson 1985, 28.

lutionary practices. Gramberg suggested that these precedents were invented as part of the religious and political struggle of the Jerusalem religious centre and priesthood against existing decentralised polytheistic practices. Gramberg suggested that the best explanation of the biblical "prophecies" is that they were written after they had been "fulfilled." It is possible then to infer the earliest possible date for their composition. For example, Abraham is presented in Genesis as a precursor of king David, therefore it could not have been written before the establishment of the Davidian dynasty in Jerusalem. The book of Joshua presents retroactive explanations of later monarchic realities, but does not explain the reality that the book of Judges reflects. Therefore Joshua must have been written after the materials that compose Judges.[29]

The founders of biblical criticism were comparing parts of the Bible as units of evidence, concluding that the best explanation of the similarities and differences between the various linguistic levels, religious conceptual schemes and descriptions of social, political and ritualistic practices is that most of the Bible was written in conjunction with king Josiah's revolution, while the later books were written during and after the Babylonian exile. The Bible is not a reliable source for history prior to the seventh century BCE, but can serve as evidence for later history.

Classical philology

Theories and methods that were developed in biblical criticism were applied next to the analysis of ancient Greek and Latin texts. Friedrich August Wolf applied in his *Prolegomena ad Homerum*[30] the new critical theories to analyse the *Iliad* and the *Odyssey*. "Wolf's main achievement ... was the annexation for classical studies of a sophisticated set of methods formed by a contemporary [Eichhorn] in another field of work [biblical criticism]."[31] The *Prolegomena* initiated a paradigm shift in classical studies. The young scholars who filled the new Humboldtian Classical Philology departments accepted Wolf's paradigm against the older generation of philologists. For example, F. K. Heinrich followed Wolf's model in 1802 to analyse the origins of Hesiod's *Shield of Hercules*. "Why did contemporaries – and even Wolf himself – come to see the *Prolegomena* as the source rather than the tributary of theological research, the fountainhead of Tü-

---

29 Rogerson 1985, 57–63.
30 Wolf 1985 [1795].
31 Grafton et al. 1985, 26.

bingen rather than an offshoot of Göttingen?"[32] The answers for this question are just as relevant for a parallel question about Ranke's status as the paradigm founder in historiography: I think that the informed reading public in what would become Germany had already accepted Wolf's theories and methods before he applied them to classical philology. As Grafton et al. note,[33] Wolf's *Prolegomena* (1795) was directly modelled after J. G. Eichhorn's *Einleitung ins Alte Testament* (1780-). Eichhorn studied in Göttingen under Heyne, who was also Wolf's teacher. Heyne affirmed that Wolf appropriated the methods of biblical criticism. Wolf approached the *Iliad* as Eichhorn approached the Bible. The text of the Bible went through many changes and a change of alphabet, word divisions, and the introduction of vowels. Accents and marginal notes of variant readings were introduced by the *masoretes*, Hebrew grammarians of the first millennium CE. The Venice *scholia* resembled the *Masorah* in producing the 'authorised' version of Homer. Neither preserved individual recensions or attempted to distinguish earlier from later sources.[34]

Wolf theorised that long text such as the *Iliad* cannot be written before some necessary conditions are satisfied. Material conditions include the presence of appropriate writing materials: stones, woods, pieces of metal, and waxed tablets are not useful for the preservation of long texts. The first appropriate material in Greece was parchment. Papyrus was adopted only in the sixth century BCE. A system of writing, appropriate for the spoken language of the text is also necessary. It must have taken time to adapt the Phoenician system to the Greek language, more time for it to be used for composing long texts in a crude fifteen-letter alphabet, and even more time for that knowledge to be disseminated widely. The twenty four-letter Greek alphabet in which the Homeric sagas are written dates only to 403 BCE.

Laws are shorter and their fixed form is more important for society than the codification of heroic sagas. Therefore the Homeric poems could not have been written before the first laws in Greece. The first Athenian written laws are Solon's from 594 BCE. Since prose unlike poetry cannot be memorised, nobody would compose it without a method for preserving it. The emergence of prose must follow the wide spread use of writing.[35] Therefore, the presence of prose is an indicator of wide spread literacy. In the case of Greece, this indicates again an era no earlier than that of Solon. Book length texts could and did appear only during the reign of the Athenian tyrant Pisistratus (560 – 527 BCE).

---

32 Grafton et al. 1985, 29.
33 Grafton et al, 1985, 19 – 26.
34 Grafton et al, 1985, 19 – 26.
35 Grafton et al, 1985, 91.

These considerations led Wolf to defend the historiographic hypothesis that the Homeric poems were composed and transmitted by illiterate rhapsodists. There is no intrinsic evidence to the contrary because the Homeric poems do not mention writing. The rhapsodists spent their lives reciting, memorising and inventing poems. This led to corruptions as memory failed, poets 'improved' on what they received with their own verses and stringed together poems of diverse sources. They were not interested in preserving originality, but in satisfying an audience. Wolf conjectured that the poems are too long and reflect too much knowledge for any single man to have invented or memorised, or even performed all at once. The documentary hypothesis is further supported by inconsistencies in the narrative of the *Iliad*, for example, in its depiction of Achilles as heroic and unheroic. Wolf cited as examples several places where the poetic flow is broken or the style changes radically. Unusual words and phrases are also evidence for late imitations that were inserted into the text.

The task of the classical philologist is to infer the histories of texts, the information transmission nets, from their present versions and historiographic evidence about its editing. This task should be easier than that of biblical critics: "The orientalists would rejoice, I believe, if it were certain in even three places what Gamaliel or another Jewish teacher of the early period read in Moses and the Prophets; in Homer we know what Zenodotus read in some four hundred passages, what Aristophanes read in two hundred, and what Aristarchus read in over a thousand."[36]

Comparative linguistics

Scientific comparative linguistics is associated usually with the books of Rasmus Rask (1814), Bopp (1816), and Grimm (1814–1822). Rask developed simple theories about the transmission of linguistic information in time. The rate of change of grammatical structures is slower than that of vocabularies, even basic ones, partly because they are more resistant to foreign influences. Grammatical agreement in inflection and structure is a more reliable indicator of a genetic relationship than vocabulary. Languages tend to mutate in the direction of losing their grammatical inflections and endings. This theory is confirmed by the greater simplicity of Danish in relation to Icelandic, English in relation to Anglo-Saxon, Italian in relation to Latin, modern in relation to ancient Greek, and contemporary in relation to old German. Therefore, newer languages have simpler

---

36 Wolf 1985, 173.

grammar than their progenitors and related languages whose grammar was codified earlier.³⁷ Languages with common origins display similarity in lexical stock and grammatical structure, the most stable parts of language. When Rask found that two languages such as Icelandic and Welsh do not share a grammatical structure, he assumed that lexical similarity must be the result of borrowing rather than common origins.

Rask's "Indo-European" thesis was actually only a European thesis. He did not consider the Indian languages. Rask compared exclusively the grammatical structures of Greek, Latin, the Germanic languages, most notably Icelandic, and the Slavic languages and discovered that their inflections are similar; they have three noun forms (feminine, masculine, and neuter) and five cases, unlike other languages. Rask deduced from this similarity that they are all descendants of a single language that he called Thracian, after the possible homeland of the ancient speakers of that original European language. Since Icelandic inflections are simpler than Greek and Latin ones, Rask inferred that it was derived from "Thracian" later than Greek and Latin.

Franz Bopp is the paradigm founder of comparative linguistics, Ranke's equal and colleague. Bopp was appointed professor at the University of Berlin in 1821. He confirmed the Indo-European hypothesis through a systematic comparison of verb structures and inflections in Sanskrit, Greek, Latin and Persian.³⁸

> Bopp brought to linguistics... a *paradigm* of historical explanation, in the sense in which Kuhn has introduced this term. A historical explanation of an inflectional form was to him a demonstration that the form was derived from a proto-form in which each of the primitive concepts into which its meaning was analyzable was expressed by a separate morpheme. This paradigm was based on the belief that the methods of comparative reconstruction, applied to what Bopp considered the greatly decayed and disorganised morphological debris of the attested Indo-European languages, would yield a proto-morphology.³⁹

Bopp was able to formulate criteria for genetically relevant similarity according to laws of morphological correspondence between languages. The Indo-European hypothesis hypothesised that an extinct language from which all the Indo-European languages descended was the best explanation of these similarities. Bopp could not infer the properties of the hypothetical proto-Indo-European language and the stages of linguistic development that could mediate between it and known languages. Bopp introduced several hypothetical intermediary

---

37 Rask 1967, 31–37.
38 Bopp 1974 [1816].
39 Kiparsky 1974, 333.

links, for which there is no direct evidence. Later linguistics rejected these speculative hypotheses. Kiparsky concluded that Bopp was not interested in the history of the Indo-European languages, only in their common origin, corresponding exclusively with the first stage of the three stages of inference outlines above.

Jacob Grimm, who discovered rules of consonant shift in his Germanic Grammar, completed the work of Rask and Bopp. He introduced nine rules of correspondence between German, Greek, Latin, Sanskrit and other Indo-European languages. Grimm's laws had a wide scope that allowed individual linguists to work on puzzle solving within their framework for the next half century. When Ranke founded scientific historiography, it was against the background of established, successful and fruitful paradigmatic, theoretically founded biblical criticism, classical philology and comparative linguistics. The theoretical foundations and methods of all these reconstructions of the past are quite similar.

Scientific historiography

"…The German historians who applied a critical method to the sources of medieval and early modern history imitated what German classical scholars had already done for the sources of ancient literary and political history."[40] Butterfield[41] argued that a new historiography was born around 1760 by historians with background in biblical criticism, especially in Göttingen, where a philological approach to the Bible espoused by Mosheim, Semler and Michaelis, and to classic Greek sources developed by Gesner and Heyne, had already been established. In Butterfield's opinion, modern historiography began with the nomination of Johann Christoph Gatterer to the chair of history in Göttingen in 1759. Gatterer established a historical institute that Butterfield considered a precursor to the seminar, as well as promoted auxiliary sciences such as geography, genealogy, heraldry, numismatics etc. and founded scholarly journals of historiography. By 1768 Gatterer proposed to produce a critical edition of the evidential sources for historiography of Germany. The Göttingen historians mastered the critical approach to historical evidence and began to apply it to the historiographies of other nations by collecting all the relevant sources-evidence and subjecting them to criticism.

Niebuhr attempted to distinguish mythical from historical events in Roman legal history by speculating whether the evidence for them is connected to the

---

[40] Grafton 1997, 83–84.
[41] Butterfield 1955.

events it reports by one of the above three types of information chains. Niebuhr clearly attempted to copy the theories and methods of biblical critics and classical philologists, most notably Wolf. Niebuhr described Wolf's *Prolegomena* in 1827 as an investigation "in which the higher branch of criticism reached its perfection."[42] Niebuhr was the first to examine critically the evidence for early Roman history. Niebuhr accepted Perizonius' testimony that information from the early period of Roman history reached historians who wrote hundreds of years later though three institutional information transmission chains, banquet songs (*carmina*), funeral panegyrics, and annals kept by the high priest, *pontifex maximus*. No direct evidence for these alleged media of transmission existed. Niebuhr's evidence for the three information delivery chains consisted of two sentences in Cicero allegedly based on Cato and an incomplete sentence by Varro that can be found in Nonius. His hypotheses were that Plebeian poetry was composed of banquet songs, *carmina*, while the Patricians' poetry was in the form of the annals of the pontiffs. Nitzsch criticised Niebuhr's hypothesis, noting that had the source for the Roman legends been Plebeian poetry, it would not be likely that all the heroes of those legends would be Patricians.[43] Though Niebuhr's Italian disciple, De Sanctis, "felt that Niebuhr's theory provided the best explanation for the legendary character of early Roman tradition",[44] Niebuhr's contemporaries thought they had better explanations of the evidence. A. W. Schlegel and Mommsen considered the similarities between Greek and Roman legends and inferred that Greek legends, rather than ancient Roman oral poetry, are the best explanation for late Roman accounts of ancient Roman history. Momigliano[45] summed up the reasons for rejecting Niebuhr's hypotheses. The similarities between known Greek sources and the Roman legends could not be coincidental. Since the Greek sources were earlier, it is probable that they influenced the later Roman sources during the Hellenic period or even earlier. The "poems hypothesis" does not make the content of Roman legends likely because heroic poetry usually did not "allow" its heroes to die in bed of old age or blur the line between "friends" and "enemies" as Roman legends did; nor did the legends keep a strict class distinction between patricians and plebeians, unlikely in fourth-fifth century BCE literature because that was the period of class strife in Rome. The legends seem to reflect in that respect a third century BCE social reality. Women figure prominently in the legends, an unlikely feature of poetry that should have originated in male banquets. The subject of

---

42 Grafton et al. 1985, 28.
43 Momigliano 1977, 235–236.
44 Momigliano 1977, 236.
45 Momigliano 1977, 239–241.

many of the legends is local: Traditions, monuments and cult places. This feature is better explained by local traditions that attached legends to visible objects in their environment than by Niebuhr's lost poems. Momigliano concluded that the extant traditions on ancient Rome most likely originated in the third century BC. The annalists who wrote them down may have been influenced by more ancient, possibly poetic, traditions. But their highly selective editing of these sources prevents us today from knowing anything about those possible poetic sources.

Unsurprisingly, Ranke's upbringing brought him under the influence of three disciplines, protestant theology, classical philology, and comparative linguistics: Ranke studied at the university of Leipzig theology and classical philology. Ranke's favourite authors were Niebuhr and Thucydides. Despite his denials, Ranke clearly learned much of his critical methods from Gottfried Hermann who introduced him to the methods of classical philology, which he then exported to historiography.[46] Ranke's first book, the *Histories of the Latin and Germanic Nations* (1824), already contained the main principles of the Rankean paradigm. Historiographic consensus can be built on the basis of public evidence, documents. "Any one who steeps himself in these dry studies, and has access to all the historical documents, especially the electoral rolls of the ecclesiastical princes, will be able to discover, from Frederick II's time, a new history...."[47] Ranke ordered known sources according to their temporal proximity to the hypothesised events. When an author was not an eyewitness, Ranke inquired for the source of the information. Ranke preferred primary sources written by contemporaries of the events that were not intended to record history, such as diaries, "the truth of which it is impossible to doubt,"[48] and letters to narrative interpreted historiography that was designed to create an impression of the past. Ranke examined the identity of the authors of narrative historiography to identify possible biases. Crucially, in comparison with ancient historiography, when considering different sources, Ranke considered whether they were independent of each other. For example, he traced a mistake common to several English historians (Hume, Rapin and Bacon) to their common source, Polydore Virgil.[49] Ranke concluded that Guicciardini, who appeared to emulate Thucydides' classical model of historiography, copied other books, much of what he copied was false in the first place, much was doubtful, speeches were invented, treaties altered, and important facts were misrepresented.[50]

---

46 Grafton 1997, 86–93.
47 Ranke 1909, 103.
48 Ranke 1909, 170.
49 Ranke 1909, 130, note 7.
50 Gooch 1959, 72–97; Grafton 1997, 40–44.

The theoretical core of critical historiography coincides with that of biblical criticism, classical philology and comparative linguistics. These sciences attempt to infer information about an origin from relevant similarities among its putative present effects, the evidence, by inferring the information-causal chains that connected the cause, the alleged source of the information, with its effects, the alleged receptors of the information. In the case of Ranke's historiography, the similar effects are documentary evidence. The likelihood that independent texts would describe details of similar events without a common cause that is the source of the information is usually negligible. One obvious hypothesis is that the common cause that best explains the similarity is the event that the similar evidence describe. Alternative hypotheses would suggest other common causes such as late forgeries. Critical historians find which hypothesis explains better the evidence by discovering the history of the evidence, examine the links on the information-causal chain that may connect the similar evidence with a common cause. Historians assume a theory of the gradual involuntary mutation of information, as do biblical critics, classical philologists and comparative linguists about languages, oral poems and copied documents. To minimise possible corruption of the information, Ranke introduced a methodology that usually admits as evidence only the testimony of eyewitnesses, and excludes memoirs and later narrative accounts that must be at best copies of copies. Even when evidence for many of the links on the information-causal chain is missing, it is possible to infer with high probability the properties of some of the missing links and the cause.

A second group of historiographic theories are of common sense psychology. These theories explain why evidence may misrepresent what took place. Historians must ask themselves why do people in general misrepresent what they know to be true and whether such circumstances were present when the evidence was generated: People have interests and may wish to spread false information to gain an advantage, other people may be in a position where they are forced to lie, personal sympathies and antipathies cause people to misrepresent themselves and groups they identify with or resent, vanity causes people to misrepresent their own actions as more important than they actually were, some writers misrepresent what took place to fit the values and fashions of their intended readership, aesthetic, literary and rhetorical norms may cause writers to embellish their accounts to fit mythical or heroic narrative models.[51] In traditionalist societies, fabrications of the past were designed to establish a historiographic precedence for a desired social or international state of affairs or to ma-

---

51 Langlois / Seignobos 1926, 166–172.

nipulate the behaviour of readers by generating consciousness of alleged historical grievances that need to be redressed or avenged; or to instil suspicion or mistrust in certain groups; or to excuse by denial historical personal or group behaviour that the author has an interest in concealing; or any of many other reasons that motivate people to misrepresent the past. The simplest method for avoiding misrepresentations of the past is to avoid when possible relying on intentionally written historiographic interpretations, or if there is insufficient non-intentional evidence, rely on evidence that goes counter to the interests and vanity of its authors.[52]

Ranke became the founder of a new paradigm not just because of the theories and methods he borrowed from biblical criticism and philology, but because these theories and methods have been fruitful in directing him and his followers to the discovery of new evidence and consequently to the confirmation of many new and surprising historiographic hypotheses. Ranke's first discovery of evidence was of the Venetian *Relazioni*, three centuries of reports by Venetian ambassadors from European courts. Ranke was the first historian to examine them as well as archives in Rome and Florence. Though the archives of the Vatican remained closed to him, he was able to use the archives he had access to, to write the *History of the Popes*. His *German History in the Reformation Era* used the 96 volumes of reports of the Frankfurt deputies at the Imperial Diet 1414–1613. Ranke supplanted them with discoveries in archives in Weimar, Dresden and Dessau. Ranke found in Brussels the correspondence of Charles V that he compared with the Paris archives and some of the Italian materials he collected earlier. *The history of Prussia* was based on letters of the French ambassador and on opening the Prussian archives to the state historiographer. Ranke researched the archives of France, Italy, Belgium, Germany, England and Spain for his 1853 *History of France*. Ranke dismissed on the basis of his superior theory and successful results the established authorities in French historiography: Davila's *History of the Civil Wars* was derived from De Thou;

> Richelieu's Memoirs were almost wholly spurious, those of De Retz genuine but grossly misleading. On reaching Saint-Simon he emphasized the late date of composition and the violence of his prejudices, and confronts him with the contemporary authority of Dangeau and the correspondence of Charlotte of Orleans with her German relatives. The 'French History,' with its mass of new material was welcomed in France."[53]

---

52 Langlois / Seignobos 1926, 186–187.
53 Gooch 1959, 87–8.

The research programme of Ranke's historiography has led to the discovery of new evidence that is the hallmark of scientific theories as well as necessary for deciding among competing theories. Ranke was able then to revise his historiographies as he discovered new evidence.[54] The new scientific historiography became a progressive science.[55]

Thucydides as evidence

From a modern, Rankean, perspective, Thucydides' *History of the Peloponnesian War* is an evidential source. Historians attempt with difficulty to trace its sources from the few clues in the text.[56] Historians assess the reliability of Thucydides as a historian and compare his testimony with independent evidence. Kosso[57] distinguished several types of independent evidence: Material remains, both in the form of inscriptions and archaeological findings; descriptions of medical symptoms and astronomical events can be compared with contemporary scientific data, general background information about Greek culture and history can be compared with numerous other sources. Though Thucydides has been the main source for our knowledge of the Peloponnesian War, Herodotus' *Histories* covered the era immediately preceding it and Xenophon covered the period immediately after it. These works are in general coherence. Though Diodorus Siculus and Plutarch wrote centuries after Thucydides, it is plausible that their historiographies were based also on other contemporary sources, now lost, such as Ephorus of Cyme, because they include some information (e. g. about aspects of the Megarian decree and the Athenian siege of Syracuse) that is not in Thucydides. Ephorus seems to have a more pro-Athenian bias; he presents some of their military adventures as more successful than Thucydides.[58] Hose[59] concluded that the existing alternative sources are consistent with Thucydides' account and the lost sources did not constitute an alternative tradition, an indication that none of Thucydides' contemporaries was interested and able to produce an alternative historiography of the war.

Historical distance, the comparison of multiple evidential sources that were not available to contemporaries and the ability to colligate events in the context

---

54 Grafton 1997, 52.
55 Lakatos 1978.
56 Hornblower 1987, 77–109.
57 Kosso 1993.
58 Hose 2006, 679–680.
59 Hose 2006.

of longer processes, allow historians in the Rankean paradigm to generate knowledge that was unavailable to contemporary participants or observers.[60]

---

[60] Süßmann 2012, 86.

Oswyn Murray
The Western Futures of Ancient History[1]

Time present and time past
Are both perhaps present in time future,
And time future contained in time past.
If all time is eternally present
All time is unredeemable.

T.S. Eliot, Four Quartets: Burnt Norton (1944)

The study of historiography is not part of the 'classical tradition': the purpose of the study of the past of ancient history is to influence its future, and to clarify the methods and principles that may determine the activity of writing history. All history is and has always been written in and for the present, and is valid only as a myth for the present or as a step towards the future. Unless we are aware of the constraints of tradition on this picture, future histories will continue to be determined by the past: in order to liberate ourselves from tradition and prevent the preoccupations of the present and its past from distorting the future of history, we must investigate the roots of our current concerns.

The study of 'ancient history' in western Europe has always been connected with the influence of Greece and Rome on the formation of European culture. The critical and comparative study of this tradition with other ancient civilisations such as Israel, Egypt, the Near East, India, China and Japan to create an 'ancient world history', arrived late and has remained peripheral to the study of the origins of western culture. My purpose in this brief paper is to explore the consequences of this fact.

The western outlook on 'Ancient History' is therefore limited, and has since the eighteenth century centred around two distinct concepts; these are imperialism and liberty. The first interest, imperialism, explains the fundamental importance of Roman history with its exemplification of the fate of empires, to rise,

---

[1] These reflections were first formulated as a keynote speech for the 2012 International Symposium on Ancient World History in China, June 16–18, Nankai University, Tianjin. They were subsequently developed for a meeting of the European Network for the Study of Ancient Greek History at Tel Aviv University in October 2012, and delivered to seminars at Duke and Northwestern Universities during a visit to the USA. In 2013 they were presented to the Hong Kong Academy of Sciences, to Tokyo University, at a conference at Thessalonica University on 'Knowing Future Time', and at seminars on the Josephus tradition in Oxford and on nineteenth-century nationalism in Durham. I am very grateful to all the participants for their comments, often in opposition.

decline and fall. It began with the discussion provoked by the famous French author Montesquieu in his work *Considérations sur la grandeur et décadence des Romains*, published in Holland in 1734. In this short essay Montesquieu traced the growth of the Roman empire in the second century BC and attributed it to the *vertu* of the Romans, their moral and political character. He showed how moral and political corruption followed, until the traditional liberty of the Romans was extinguished in a monarchic form of government, and their moral character was corrupted by the luxury consequent on empire. This analysis was part of a general movement in the early eighteenth century to contrast the declining power of the French monarchy under its greatest ruler, Louis XIV, in the face of the rise of the English version of constitutional monarchy, in a country essentially governed by the merchant classes after the Glorious Revolution of 1688. The success in war of the English armies under the Duke of Marlborough and the creation of an English naval empire around the world were making it clear that absolute monarchy and territorial conquest were incompatible with the modern expansion of overseas trade based on government by the landed aristocracy and the merchants of the city of London. The message of Montesquieu was accepted by all the thinkers of the Enlightenment, and became the basis of the new critical historiography which reached its zenith in the famous work of Edward Gibbon, in which the whole history of Europe from antiquity to the Renaissance was incorporated into a *History of the Decline and Fall of the Roman Empire* (1776–88).

This perception has dictated the shape of Roman history ever since. The fundamental questions remain the same today as they were formulated in the eighteenth century: how did Rome become an imperial power, on the basis of what political structures was her success achieved, how was her political, social and economic development affected by the consequent advent of luxury and wealth, and why did the system end by only finding stability under a form of absolute monarchy that was incompatible with political liberty? It was only the advent of a new religion, Christianity, and the impact of nomadic barbarian invasions that introduced a new dynamic to history; but that required a break with the past that was only partially resolved in the Renaissance. From this perspective of ancient history as Roman history, it is empire, its rise and fall, that provides the questions to which we still seek answers. And much of the justification of western imperialism in the modern age has been based on the model of the Roman example, from Edmund Burke's eighteenth-century analysis of the faults and virtues of English imperialism in Ireland, north America and India, to the systematic education of administrators for the British Indian Empire on principles that were directly derived from Roman provincial administration. The French and German empires were no different: throughout Europe the virtues and vices and indeed the methods of imperialism have always been conceived in terms of the ancient Roman example.

The second interest, the history of liberty, includes the history of political liberty and democratic forms of government, together with personal liberty and the rise of the concept of the individual: this is seen in terms of a continuing process of development from antiquity to the present, and as especially exemplified in the history of ancient Greece. It explains the obsession of historians of ancient Greece with Athens and the principles of democratic government. We still idealise Athenian democracy as the best form of government, and discuss modern governmental systems in relation to this ancient example. We are still obsessed with the idea of liberty, both political and personal; and as a consequence we judge all forms of government, whatever their historical traditions, in relation to standards that are seen as absolute. This strand in the history of the ancient world is often seen as consequent on the Hegelian view of history as the history of liberty, and on the concern of the Romantic period with the idea of the creativity of the original artistic genius, standing outside tradition. And it is believed that the nineteenth century philosophical movement known as Utilitarianism established the apotheosis of democracy and liberty in the *History of Greece* (1846–56) composed by the Utilitarian radical politician George Grote.

But in fact this concern with liberty and democracy is too a product of the eighteenth century, and of much the same impulse that inspired Montesquieu. The catalyst was the presentation by the Frenchman Nicolas Boileau in 1674 of an obscure ancient work of literary criticism known as *Longinus On the Sublime*. In the last chapter of this work the author mentions an ancient theory that relates artistic creativity to political liberty. This work with its emphasis on the importance of the sublime was fundamental to literary theory in the eighteenth century, and its conclusion was interpreted as an explanation and a vindication for the renewed literary activity in contemporary Britain after the Glorious Revolution. The literature of ancient Greece and especially Athens was interpreted as being a consequence not of aristocratic patronage but of political liberty and Athenian democracy. This view of the benefits of democracy became widespread in the eighteenth century, and lies behind the change from an almost universal dismissal of democratic forms of government as dangerous, unjust and anarchic to an increasing idealisation of democratic institutions. This in turn led to a close identification of ancient Athens with modern Britain and subsequently modern America. The difference between ancient and modern democracy was rightly seen as a difference between direct and representative democracy: the most important innovation in eighteenth-century political theory, due largely to Montesquieu again, was the realisation that representation could be harnessed to the idea of democracy. Despite this obvious difference it was believed that ancient and modern democracy shared common characteristics. The consequent rise of the principle of democratic representative government justified the historical movement from aristocratic forms of government to a new 'democratic', capitalist, oligarchic control of government by the bourgeoisie.

These two strands, imperialism and democracy, have in our generation come together in the new democratic imperialism of the United States of America, which seeks to promote the principles of democracy and capitalism under an American imperial hegemony held to be self-evidently the teaching of human history, for in Hegelian terms the triumph of the individual and of liberty is the lesson of history.

Yet each of these theoretical approaches is problematical in a number of respects, and concentration on them to the exclusion of all others represents an impoverishment of the varieties of human experience. Let us consider each concept in turn.

Imperialism is not synonymous with exploitation and expropriation; it requires an ideology to persuade the master race to conquer and even more to maintain control over other societies: you must believe in your mission or the rulers will lose the will to rule. The Romans came to believe that their version of Greco-Roman civilisation was a gift that would benefit all who came under their domination; in this they were helped by a conception of citizenship that (with certain conditions) was perhaps the most inclusive that the world has experienced. The result was that in the end all subjects of the empire became Roman citizens, and were eligible for the benefits of empire; these benefits of course changed over time, but always remained real enough, and could and did include the possibility of even becoming the emperor himself. The later western model built on this conception of the benefits of civilisation, and added to it the principle of conversion to Christianity as the true faith. But it was always recognised that in principle, if in the distant future the subject peoples should embrace these western principles of government and western religion, such empires would dissolve themselves into some unspecified relationship, whether of universal citizenship or of independence. Moreover whereas the Roman conception of empire had been of an eternal empire (*Roma aeterna*), there was built into its successor, the eighteenth-century conception of empire, the notion of decline and fall; there was therefore always a 'dying fall', a sense of a future ending embodied in western imperialism: the end of empire is envisaged in its beginning. Of course history falsified or usurped these dreams in a variety of ways. But the pure conception of imperialism as exploitation never existed in the west (with the possible exception of the Belgian Congo); and while the analysis of imperialism in terms of its economic benefit to the ruler may help, it is not sufficient to explain all human motivation involved.

The ideas of democracy and freedom are equally problematic. Direct and representative democracy have been recognised to be wholly different forms of government since the eighteenth century. Direct democracy is only suitable for small scale institutions in which the members of the group can meet and make decisions in a form of assembly which contains only those who will execute those decisions. It is today seldom practised even in groups small enough to qualify, and the right to decide or even influence decisions has become simply a residual right confined to occasional almost ritual events. No-one believes in direct ancient democracy as practised by the ancient Athenians, and few people would wish to see its return as a viable form of government. In the nineteenth century it was agreed to be dependent on a form of political education which was essentially unattainable, and the twentieth century added the even less democratic idea of the need for expertise. These criticisms of democracy go back at least to Plato's *Protagoras*.

They have been incorporated into the theory of representative government, which allows an elite to rule with the consent of the majority. The problem that results is that of all forms of government in all periods, the creation of a divide between the rulers and the ruled. In ancient Greek terms all modern forms of government are not democracies, but either tyrannies or oligarchies, depending on whether they obey the rule of law or not.

At least since the time of Benjamin Constant's famous essay "On the liberty of the ancients compared to the liberty of the moderns" (1819) it has been recognised that this difference between ancient and modern democracy is the determining factor behind the difference between ancient and modern conceptions of liberty:

> [Ancient] liberty consisted in exercising collectively but directly most aspects of ancient sovereignty, deliberating in the public square about war and peace, concluding with foreigners treaties of alliance, voting on laws, pronouncing legal judgments, examining the accounts and the decrees and the decisions of magistrates, making them appear before the assembled people, putting them on trial, condemning or acquitting them. But at the same time that this was what the ancients called liberty, they admitted as compatible with their collective liberty the total subjection of the individual to the authority of the community.[2]

Modern ideas of liberty in contrast privilege the freedom of the individual from interference by a system controlled by the ruling classes. Far from deriving from ancient world conceptions of liberty it is a consequence of centuries of conflict between the various sects of the Christian religion, which resulted in the assertion of the freedom of the individual conscience in religious matters. In the mod-

---

2 Constant 1988, 310–11.

ern age this has become extended beyond the sphere of religion to all aspects of the private life of the individual.

Modern writers have wrestled with these differences between ancient and modern democracy and ancient and modern liberty; Isaiah Berlin for instance tried to distinguish between a positive *'freedom to'* (act), which was more akin to ancient political freedom, and a negative *'freedom from'* (interference) which seemed to him to be exemplified in the modern concept of the freedom of the individual. The most recent attempts to relate ancient and modern ideas of freedom and democracy tend to emphasise the importance of duties or responsibilities in the ancient ideas of community life leading to a constraining of the freedom of the individual, in contrast to the absolute selfishness and the anarchic consequences of modern liberty. In that sense the modern western conceptions of democracy and liberty might well indeed learn the limitations of these ideas from studying the ancient world view.

My reflection is however intended to contrast these two conceptions of history derived from ancient western ideas, with the traditions of history that are found elsewhere. It is clearly not true that these two sets of problems exhaust all the historical possibilities that the long history of human society exemplifies. If we reflect on other historical traditions, we can see that this western conception has many faults. It does not consider the necessity of order or decorum in the construction of civilisations, or the significance of continuity and tradition, as exemplified for instance in the Chinese tradition.

Even within western culture this dual tradition also almost completely ignores one of the most powerful forces in historical formation, the importance of religion and the way that beliefs about the divine world structure and permeate almost all social systems: after the collapse of the grand nineteenth-century theories of universal religion, it was not until J.-P. Vernant offered a social and psychological interpretation of ancient religion that it escaped from the sterile grip of myth and ritual antiquarianism. Ancient western history has indeed been inclined until very recently to regard ancient religion as unimportant and irrelevant, no doubt partly due to the bias against all forms of polytheism as primitive and faulty representations of a divine world that was only revealed by God through the true religion of Christianity: so, while apparently ignoring religion, ancient western history has also been profoundly conditioned by a negative reaction to the advent of Christianity.

But it is not of course only Christianity that appears to be marginalised by the dominant western conception of ancient history. Another religion has claims to be far older than Christianity, and possesses a complex historical tradition at least as old as the Chinese – Judaism. The question of how Jewish history might be incorporated into ancient history also began as early as the eighteenth century, as a part of the enlightenment revival of the study of history. This built in turn upon a much neglected aspect of the work of the sole surviving Jewish historian in the ancient classical tradition, Josephus. For it was really Josephus who, in his *Jewish Antiquities*, even more than in his account of the Jewish War, set out to normalise the Jewish historical tradition in terms of classical historiography: he was indeed himself an ancient historian, and shared with them many of the political and rational attitudes that made his account compatible with the canons of ancient history. Independently of the holy texts of Judaism and Christianity it was he who made it possible for later generations to compare and contrast the Jewish historical tradition with that of Greece and Rome. In terms of later generations he therefore bridged the gap between sacred and secular history, and may be regarded as perhaps the most important of all ancient historians for the future of historical writing.

Already in antiquity Josephus was performing this function for the early Christian Church. This explains their interest in copying his works, and even in improving them at a very early date, by interpolating the notorious references to Jesus Christ, his brother James and John the Baptist; by this means Josephus could be made to offer historical support not just to the Old Testament, but also to the Gospel narrative. Josephus has indeed always been more highly regarded in the Christian tradition than in Judaism itself, which tends to regard him as a renegade and a traitor.

Translations of Josephus into the modern European languages were very popular, and especially in Protestant England. At first they were simple translations. The earliest was by Thomas Lodge, the contemporary of Shakespeare in 1602, 'faithfully translated out of the Latin and French'.[3] This was arranged as a continuous historical narrative, from the *Antiquities to the Life, the Jewish Wars, Against Apion, and the martyrdom of the Maccabees*. Exactly a century later in 1702 Sir Roger L'Estrange offered a new translation, following almost the same order, but with the Life coming after the Jewish Wars and Philo's Legation added to extend the historical account. He added two 'discourses' and several 'remarks', on the veracity and chronology of Josephus.[4] This edition was reprinted in Dundee in 1766.[5] But in the meantime the most popular of all the translations of Josephus, that by William Whiston had been published in 1737.

---

3 Lodge 1609.
4 Estrange 1702.
5 Published by Henry Galbraith, Dundee.

This became the most widely read and most widely owned book after the Bible in the English speaking world for the next two centuries.[6]

Whiston had been the successor of Isaac Newton as Professor of Mathematics at Cambridge, and like Newton he combined an interest in ancient chronology with scriptural scholarship[7] To him Josephus appeared to present a narrative of Jewish history exactly comparable to that found in classical ancient historians, and like his predecessors he arranged his translation of the various works to provide a chronological narrative. But in many later editions of his translation an interesting transformation occurred: the narrative of Josephus was combined with a section usually entitled something like 'Sequel to the history of the Jews; continued to the present time.'

The first person to realise the possibility of recording a continuous history of Judaism in this manner was the Huguenot antiquary and friend of Pierre Bayle, Jacques Basnage, Sieur de Beauval (1653–1723), who published in 1706–7 in the Netherlands a work that was immediately translated into English with the author's approval.[8] The English title-page reads:

> The History of the Jews from Jesus Christ to the Present Time: Containing their Antiquities, their Religion, their Rites. The Dispersion of the Ten Tribes in the East, and the Persecutions this Nation has suffered in the West. Being a Supplement and Continuation of the History of Josephus. Written in French by Mr Basnage. Translated into English by Tho. Taylor, A.M. London 1708.[9]

Despite its claim to be a supplement to Josephus, Basnage's work did not include the text of Josephus itself. The earliest edition of Josephus to have combined the two elements in a single volume appears to have been the lavishly illustrated folio of George Henry Maynard, which claims to be a new translation prepared under the royal licence of George III and contains, after the usual works of Josephus and Philo and an appendix defending the authenticity of his references to Christianity, 'a Continuation of the History of the Jews from Josephus down to the present Time Including a Period of more than One thousand seven hundred Years.'[10] The 'Translator's Address to the Reader' ends with the statement:

---

6 Whiston 1737. The standard bibliography of Josephus by L.H. Feldman claims, but does not list some 217 editions of this translation.
7 Force 2002; Whiston 1753.
8 Basnage 1706–7; Subsequent editions: 1711, 1716.
9 Basnage 1708. There is a copy of this relatively rare work in Balliol College Library. For Basnage see Sutcliffe 2003, 79–89.
10 Maynard 1785 (Date according to the Harvard University catalogue).

> To compleat the work, we have annexed a Supplement, collected from authentic Manuscripts, bringing down the Jewish History to the present times, which, being an attempt entirely new, we flatter ourselves, will stamp an additional value upon our undertaking, and make it in every respect worthy of the patronage of a judicious and candid public.[11]

I say that it appears to be the earliest because there is also a second similarly undated but contemporary illustrated edition by 'Thomas Bradshaw D.D. Late of Emmanuel College Cambridge, Lecturer of Painswick, near Gloucester; Master of the Grammar School of Painswick; Chaplain of Pentonville-Chapel and Afternoon-Preacher of Allhallows-Barking, published by Royal Authority and Act of Parliament.' This similarly claims, 'The whole Newly Translated from the Original in the Greek and Hebrew Languages, and Diligently Revised, Corrected, and Compared with other Translations ... to which is added a Continuation of the History of the Jews from the Death of Josephus to the Present Time, including a period of more than 1700 Years.'[12] I have not yet investigated the relationship between these two competing editions, but they cannot be independent of each other.

The tradition of updating Josephus to provide a complete history of Judaism continued. In the (again undated) nineteenth-century family edition of Whiston's Josephus that I inherited from my grandfather I find that this long sequel of 222 pages terminates with a full account of the debate inside and outside the British Parliament on the Jewish Emancipation Bill of 1847, which was provoked by the election of Lionel de Rothschild as MP for the City of London, and his inability to take up his seat because he would not swear the normal religious oath required of Members of Parliament. The debate was indeed the highpoint for the articulation of English philosemitism; speakers included Lord John Russell the Prime Minister, Gladstone, Disraeli, Sir Robert Peel and Lord Ashley the evangelical Zionist (who surprisingly spoke against the Bill). The Bill passed in the Commons by a majority of 73 (277 votes to 204) but was rejected by the House of Lords, and Rothschild did not take up his post until another election success in 1858.[13] It was however the debate in 1847–8 that saw the most memorable and thoughtful speeches. Since it does not mention the final triumph of Rothschild I deduce (perhaps wrongly) that my family edition was published between 1848 and 1858. It would indeed be an interesting study to follow the successive

---

11 Maynard 1785.
12 Bradshaw 1792 (The date of this work is given as [1792?] in the Harvard catalogue).
13 There is an excellent account of the Jewish Question from 1833 to 1858 in Himmelfarb 2011, see chapter 3.

stages of this conception of the continuity of Jewish history under the protection of Josephus.

The first modern Jewish history was not therefore as revolutionary as it might have seemed, for it built on this tradition. H.H. Milman's three volume work *The History of the Jews* of 1830 begins, like Josephus, with Moses, and in its earlier stages is essentially a rationalistic account of his narrative and the Old Testament.[14] For the later period, Milman disparages Basnage and prefers the German Jewish historian Isaak Jost.[15] Milman's work was published contemporaneously with the earliest English translations of the new German scientific histories of the ancient classical world by August Boeckh (1828), B.G. Niebuhr (1828–32) and C.O. Müller (1830).[16] Milman was a close friend of many of the translators who were responsible for these works, and his book is (as his first reviewers saw) an early product of the new interest in German critical history and theology that came to be known as the Higher Criticism. Although his History was generally welcomed in orthodox Jewish circles, it caused an immense scandal in the English Protestant community because it applied rational historical principles to the narrative of a sacred text: the ideas that Abraham was a simple Arab sheikh and that the Jews were a Palestinian tribe fighting for their existence among hostile neighbours were simply too much to accept. The publisher was forced to abandon the series that Milman's book was intended to inaugurate, and Milman himself remained theologically suspect for the rest of his distinguished career: a liberal churchman, who compounded doubts about his orthodoxy when he edited the standard nineteenth century edition of Gibbon, he never rose beyond the status of Dean of Canterbury. Ultimately of course Milman's *History*, revised to take account of later German scholarship, became the standard narrative history of the Jews in English, and remained in print for most of the twentieth century.[17]

Milman defends his approach in the introduction to the third volume of the first edition, and again towards the end of his life in the preface to the edition of 1863:

---

[14] Milman 1830. I have used primarily the second edition, also of 1830, which seems to differ in only minor details from the first. Milman revised his text for the 1863 edition, shortly before his death in 1868; this is most easily available in the Everyman's Library.

[15] Milman 1830, v.3, 158f: 'We differ from Jost, who is a pupil of Eichhorn, on many points, particularly the composition of the older Scriptures, but we gladly bear testimony to the high value of his work, which, both in depth of research and arrangement, is far superior to the desultory, and by no means trustworthy, volumes of Basnage.' For Isaak Jost see Jost 1847.

[16] On these see Murray 2000.

[17] The preface to the 1863 edition lists a number of more recent writers that Milman has used.

> What should be the treatment by a Christian writer, a writer to whom truth is the one paramount object, of the only documents on which rests the earlier history of the Jews, the Scriptures of the Old Testament? Are they, like other historical documents, to be submitted to calm but searching criticism as to their age, their authenticity, their authorship; above all, their historical sense and historical interpretation?[18]
>
> Lawgivers, prophets, apostles, were in all other respects men of like passions (take the word in its vulgar sense) with their fellow-men; they were men of their age and country, who, as they spoke the language, so they thought the thoughts of their nation and their time, clothed those thoughts in the imagery, and illustrated them from the circumstances of their daily life. They had no special knowledge on any subject but moral and religious truth to distinguish them from other men; were as fallible as others on all questions of science, and even of history, extraneous to their religious teaching….
>
> This seems throughout to have been the course of providential government: lawgivers, prophets, apostles, were advanced in religious knowledge alone. In all other respects society, civilisation, developed itself according to its usual laws. The Hebrew in the wilderness, excepting as far as the Law modified his manners and habits, was an Arab of the Desert. Abraham, excepting in his worship and intercourse with the One True God, was a nomad Sheik. The simple and natural tenor of these lives is one of the most impressive guarantees of the truth of the record.[19]

But problems always remained. While allowing for the insertion of Jewish history into the prevailing conceptions of the progress of civilisation, and for the possibility of comparisons such as Moses with Solon, it was not entirely possible to reconcile the principles of Jewish history with those adopted in the new scientific history of ancient Greece and Rome. Even discarding miracles and the direct intervention of God in history in favour of a rational approach, there remained two fundamental problems. Throughout the long tradition of Sacred History the Jews had been regarded as the Chosen People, and their history was the history of the fulfilment of God's covenant to grant them the Promised Land. These were in turn justified in Christian terms by their divine role in producing the Messiah. Christian writers could of course escape from these aspects of the Jewish tradition by claiming that the failure of the Jews to recognise the Messiah had caused them to pass on their special status as chosen people to the Christian community, and they had thereby forfeited their right to a promised land. But it nevertheless made it extremely difficult to produce a historical account that would enable Judaism to be directly compared with Greece and Rome. And Milman himself believed in the divine dispensation of human history; he ends with the declaration:

---

18 Milman 1866, v.1, 10.
19 Milman 1866, v. 1, 15–17.

> History, which is the record of the Past has now discharged its office: it presumes not to raise the mysterious veil which the Almighty has spread over the Future. The destinies of this wonderful people, as of all mankind, are in the hands of the All-Wise Ruler of the Universe; his decrees will be accomplished, his truth, his goodness, and his wisdom vindicated.[20]

Milman did his best to create a modern scientific version of history from the biblical tradition, explaining the interventions of God on rationalistic principles and even playing down the historical significance of the Crucifixion to the same extent as the (interpolated) narrative of Josephus:

> We leave to the Christian historian the description of this event, and all its consequences – inestimable in their importance to mankind, but which produced hardly any *immediate* effect on the affairs of the Jewish nation. Yet our history will have shown that the state of the public mind in Judaea, as well as the character of Pilate, the chief agent in the transaction, harmonize in the most remarkable manner with the narrative of the Evangelists.[21]

The crucifixion, despite the earthquake and unnatural solar darkness that accompanied it according to the gospel narratives, created no more perturbation than the fall of Icarus in Brueghel's famous painting.

Milman had of course many fewer problems to contend with than either his predecessors or his twentieth century successors. He could leave behind the notion that the sufferings of the Jews in the Diaspora were a consequence of their refusal to recognise Christ, and admire the Jewish community for its tenacity and its ability to overcome persecution; he could welcome the new era of mutual tolerance and even assimilation of nineteenth-century western Europe. The future, fortunately for him, as he says was 'in the hands of the All-Wise Ruler of the Universe'. To him classical history and Jewish history were indeed flowing together, and comparison was simply a question of selection from tradition. But how does Milman's problem seem now? What sort of Jewish history do we want to write today, and how far will it be compatible with the dominant conception of a secular Greco-Roman history? These are the problems with which my teacher Arnaldo Momigliano wrestled throughout his life.

Before we consider this question we need also to recall a quite different tradition of the writing of Jewish history, that which arose out of the needs of the Jewish community to understand its own past. In his early editions Milman had already recognised the importance, if only as a source, of the work of Isaac Jost, and he refers in the preface to the edition of 1863 to other recent works of Jewish scholars.[22]

---

[20] Milman 1866, v. 3, 424.
[21] Milman 1866, v. 2, 122.
[22] See note 17.

But he was scarcely aware of the profound reinterpretation of Jewish history that emerged in the age of Romanticism amid the struggles between the various traditions of German Judaism. In 1846 the young Heinrich Graetz published his famous manifesto 'Die Construction der jüdischen Geschichte'[23] and in 1853 began his multi-volume *Geschichte der Juden* with volume 4 on the period 70–500 C.E.[24] 'Another history of the Jews' said Leopold Zunz, the eminent rabbinic scholar – 'But this time a Jewish history,' Graetz replied.

In starting his enterprise from the destruction of the Temple by the Roman authorities, Graetz indicated a new interpretation of Jewish history based on the concept of the Diaspora, which made it fundamentally different from the standard histories of other peoples. His narrative was to combine the political story of the persecutions of the Jews with the history of their inner life, which in the spirit of Maimonides revolved around their moral or divine mission to uphold the true principle of monotheism against their Christian persecutors.

> The Christian conception of history, as is well known, fully denies to Judaism any history, in the higher sense of the word, since the loss of its national independence, an event which coincided with another of great importance to the Christian world structure.[25]

In contrast, Graetz proclaims the idea of history as the story of a cultural or spiritual mission:

> There is scarcely a science, an art, an intellectual province in which Jews have not taken a part, for which Jews have not manifested an equal aptitude. To think was as much a characteristic feature of the Jews as to suffer.[26]
>
> History still has not produced another case of a nation which has laid aside its weapons of war to devote itself entirely to the peaceful pursuits of study and poetry, which has freed itself from the bonds of narrow self-interest and let its thoughts soar to fathom its own nature and its mysterious relationship to the universe and God.[27]

And on the completion of his *History* in 1874 he reflected on the twin legacy of western history in Hellenism and Hebraism:

> The classical Greeks are dead, and toward the deceased posterity behaves properly. Envy and hatred are silent at the grave of the dead; their contributions are, in fact, usually ex-

---

[23] Translated with an important preface and other material in Graetz / Schorsch 1975, from which I take the following translations.
[24] Graetz 1853–75.
[25] Graetz 1975, 93.
[26] Graetz 1975, 126.
[27] Graetz 1975, 136.

aggerated. It is quite different with that other creative nation, the Hebrews. Precisely because they're still alive their contributions to culture are not generally acknowledged; they are criticised, or given another name to partially conceal their authorship or to dislodge them entirely. Even if the fair-minded concede that they introduced the monotheistic idea and a higher morality into the life of nations, very few appreciate the great significance of these admissions. They fail to consider why one creative nation with its rich talents perished, whereas the other, so often on the brink of death, still wanders over the earth having rejuvenated itself several times.[28]

Graetz concludes by characterising the Jewish tradition:

The history of the Israelite nation manifests, therefore, at the beginning a thoroughly irregular pattern. Two factors determine its rise and fall, a physical and spiritual one, or a political and a religious-ethical one.[29]

Thus Graetz's History has a dual structure, as a celebration of Jewish philosophy and learning, but also a history of a religious culture surviving persecution. Despite the romantic language of its formulation and the somewhat unsatisfactory nature of his essentially biographical narrative, this alternative vision of the meaning of ancient history surely deserves more attention than it is given today as a future direction for the study of world ancient history. At the start of the fateful age of the creation of national histories as national myths, Jewish history liberated itself; in this respect it stands alongside the earlier Enlightenment traditions of Greek and Roman ancient history, but it transcends them in offering a new sort of history based on the cultural life of the spirit. No wonder this escape from the political history so dominant in second half of the nineteenth century earned in 1879 the wrath of the most extreme of the German nationalist historians, Heinrich Treitschke.[30]

What is revealed by reflecting on the presuppositions of the western traditions of ancient history is the extent to which the modern western world has continually developed a myth of the past in order to justify contemporary preoccupations. That is of course true of all history that is not pure antiquarianism, but it is important to know why we think in this particular way in order to understand that it is not the

---

[28] Graetz, 1975, 175.
[29] Graetz, 1975, 187.
[30] Graetz's emphasis on the centrality of the Diaspora is perhaps no longer in fashion. In the modern post-holocaust world, Jewish history may be turning back from this cultural interpretation of the Jewish tradition to a form of nationalist historiography based on that evolved by its persecutors in the second half of the nineteenth century, in a search for a political myth based on the Promised Land.

only way that world history can be structured. And when we westerners criticise other historical political traditions for their inability to translate, or understand or even to see as important, concepts like liberty and democracy, we should remember that these are not transcendental human values. The western tradition of ancient world history rests on the eighteenth-century foundations established by the Enlightenment, which combined imperialism with democracy and the free market economy of Adam Smith to create a western interpretation of history; to this it married a Judeo-Christian tradition of a religion capable of being translated into rational history because it was ultimately based on historical narrative rather than myth. But the example of Graetz suggests that this dominant western view is not the only way to structure ancient history. Perhaps the twentieth first century will enable us to construct a new vision of ancient world history that is inclusive of other cultures like China, India and the Near East, and is not based solely on traditional western European values.[31]

---

[31] These reflections are based on a number of previous studies: Murray 1997; 2000; 2008; 2010; 2010a; 2010b; 2010c; 2011.

Bibliography

Abbott, P.H. (2005), "The Future of all Narrative Futures", in: J. Phelan / P.J. Rabinowitz (eds.), *A Companion to Narrative Theory*, Malden, 529–541.
Acton, P. (2014), *Poiesis: Manufacturing in Classical Athens*, Oxford.
Alison, A. (1848), *History of Europe: From the Commencement of the French Revolution in MDCCLXXXIX to the Restoration of the Bourbons in MDCCCXV*, 20 vols, Edinburgh / London.
Alonso-Nuñez, J.M. (1983), "Die Abfolge der Weltreiche bei Polybios und Dionysios von Halikarnassos", in: *Historia* 32, 411–426.
Alonso-Nuñez, J. M. (1986), "The *anacyclosis* in Polybius", in: *Eranos* 84, 17–22.
Álvarez de Miranda, A. (1956), "La irreligiosidad di Polibio", in: *Emerita* 24, 27–65.
Aly, W. (1921), *Volksmärchen, Sage und Novelle bei Herodot und seinen Zeitgenossen*, Göttingen [1969^2;1921^1].
Ankersmit, F. (1983), *Narrative Logic: A Semantic Analysis of the Historian's Language*, The Hague.
Ankersmit, F. (2001), *Historical Representation*, Stanford.
Ankersmit, F. (2008), "Narrative and Interpretation", in: A. Tucker (ed.), *A Companion to the Philosophy of History and Historiography*, Malden, 199–208.
Anon. (1819), "Royal Academy", in: *London Literary Gazette and Journal of Belles Lettres, Science, and Art*, 123, 345–346.
Anon. (1836), "The British School of Architecture", in: *Blackwood's Magazine* 40, 227–238.
Anon. (1852), Review of *Sir Stamford Raffles' Memoirs, et al.*, in: *Edinburgh Review* 96, 54–95.
Anon. (1858), Review of W.E. Gladstone, *Studies on Homer and the Homeric Age*, in: *London Literary Gazette and Journal of Belles Lettres, Science, and Art*, 215 (1 May), 413–415.
Asheri, D. (1988), *Erodoto. Le Storie*, I: *La Lidia e la Persia*, in: D. Asheri (ed.) / V. Antelami (trans.), Milan.
Asheri, D. / Lloyd, A. / Corcella, A. (2007), *A Commentary on Herodotus' Books I–IV*, Oxford.
Avenarius, G. (1956), *Lukians Schrift zur Geschichtsschreibung*, Meisenheim / Glan.
Azoulay, V. (2004), "Exchange as Entrapment: Mercenary Xenophon?", in: Fox (2004), 289–304.
Bakhtin, M. (1981), *The Dialogic Imagination: Four Essays*, M. J. Holquist (trans.), Austin.
Bakhtin, M. (1993), *Problems of Dostoyevsky's Poetics*, C. Emerson (ed. / trans.), Minneapolis.
Bakker, E. (2002), "The Making of History: Herodotus' *Historiês Apodexis*", in: Bakker /de Jong / van Wees (2002), 3–32.
Bakker, E. (2002), "Khrónos, Kléos, and Ideology from Herodotus to Homer" in: M. Reichel / A. Rengakos (eds.), *Epea Pteroenta: Beiträge zur Homerforschung*, Stuttgart, 11–30.
Bakker, E. (2006), "Contract and Design", in: Rengakos / Tsakmakis (2006), 109–129.
Bakker, E./ de Jong, I.J.F. / van Wees, H. (eds.) (2002), *Brill's Companion to Herodotus*, Leiden.
Balsdon, J.P.V.D. (1971), "Dionysius on Romulus: A Political Pamphlet?", in: *JRS* 61, 18–27.
Baragwanath, E. (2012), "A Noble Alliance: Herodotus, Thucydides, and Xenophon's Procles", in: Foster / Lateiner (2012), 316–344.

Baragwanath, E. (2012a), "The Mythic Plupast in Herodotus", in: Grethlein / Krebs (2012), 35–56.
Baragwanath, E. (2013), "Herodotos and the Avoidance of Hindsight", in: Powell (2013), 25–48.
Baragwanath, E. / de Bakker, M. (eds.) (2012), *Myth, Truth, and Narrative in Herodotus*, Oxford.
Barigazzi, A. (1994), *Plutarco e il corso futuro della storia* [1984], in: *Studi su Plutarco*, Firenze, 303–330.
Baronowski, D.W. (2011), *Polybius and Roman Imperialism*, Bristol.
Barthes, R. (1986), *The Rustle of Language*, Berkeley / Los Angeles.
Basnage, J. (1706–7), *L'histoire et la religion des Juifs depuis Jesus-Christ jusqu' à present: Pour servir de supplément et de continuation à l'Histoire de Josèphe*, 5 vols., Rotterdam.
Basnage, J. (1708), *The History of the Jews from Jesus Christ to the Present Time*, T. Taylor (trans.), London.
Bassi, K. (2005), "Things of the Past: Objects and Time in Greek Narrative", in: *Arethusa* 38, 1–32.
Bassi, K. (2014), "Croesus' Offerings and the Value of the Past in Herodotus' *Histories*", in: J. Ker / C. Pieper (eds.), *Valuing the Past in the Greco-Roman World*, Leiden / Boston, 172–195.
Bassi, K. (2014a), "Homer's Achaean Wall and the Hypothetical Past", in V. Wohl (ed.), *Probabilities, Hypotheticals, and Counterfactuals in Ancient Greek Thought*, Cambridge.
Batstone, W. (1988), "The Antithesis of Virtue: Sallust's *Synkrisis* and the Crisis of the Late Republic", in: *ClAnt* 7, 1–29.
Benjamin, W. (2003) [1938–1940], *Selected Writings*, vol. 4, H. Zohn (trans.), *Illuminations*, Cambridge.
Bennington, G. / Derrida J. (1993), *Jacques Derrida*, Chicago.
Bergren, A. (1983), "Odyssean Temporality: Many (Re)turns", in: C. Rubino / C. Shelmerdine (eds.), *Approaches to Homer*, Austin, 38–71.
Bernstein, M.A. (1994), *Foregone Conclusions: Against Apocalyptic History*, Berkeley.
Bevir, M. (2011), "Why Historical Distance is not a Problem", in: *History and Theory* 50, 24–37.
Biddle, N. (1993), *Nicholas Biddle in Greece: The Journals and Letters of 1806*, ed. R.A. McNeal, University Park, PA.
Billault, A. (2010), "Lucien et Thucydide", in: Fromentin / Gotteland / Payen (2010), 199–207.
Binder, G. (1964), *Die Aussetzung des Königskindes: Kyros und Romulus*, Meisenheim.
Binder, G. (1977), "Aussetzung", in: *Enzyklopädie des Märchens* 1, 1048–1065.
Bodin, J. (1969), *Method for the Easy Comprehension of History*, B. Reynolds (trans.), New York.
Bodonich, C. (2002), *Plato's Utopia Recast: his Later Ethics and Politics*, Oxford.
Boedeker, D. (1987), "The Two Faces of Demaratus", in: D. Boedeker / J. Peradotto (eds.), *Herodotus and the Invention of History. Arethusa* 20, 175–184.
Boedeker, D. (1988), "Protesilaos and the End of Herodotus' *Histories*", in: *ClAnt* 7, 30–48.
Boedeker, D. (1993), "Hero Cult and Politics in Herodotus: The Bones of Orestes", in: C. Dougherty / L. Kurke (eds.), *Cultural Poetics in Archaic Greece: Cult, Performance, Politics*, Cambridge, 164–177.

Boedeker, D. (1998), "Presenting the Past in Fifth-Century Athens", in: Boedeker / Raaflaub (1998), 185–202.
Boedeker, D. (2002), "Epic Heritage and Mythical Patterns in Herodotus", in: Bakker / de Jong / van Wees (2002), 97–116.
Boedeker, D. (2012), "The Speaker's Past: Herodotus in the Light of Elegy and Lyric", in: Grethlein / Krebs (2012), 17–34.
Boedeker, D. / Raaflaub, K. (1998) (eds.), *Democracy, Empire and the Arts in Fifth-Century Athens*, Cambridge MA.
Boedeker, D. / Raaflaub, K.A. (1998a), "Introduction", in: Boedeker / Raaflaub (1998), 1–13.
Bompaire, J. (1958), *Lucien écrivain: Imitation et création*, Paris.
Bonneuil, N. (2009), "Do Historians Make the Best Futurists?", in: *History and Theory* 48(1), 98–104.
Booth, W.C. (1988), *The Company We Keep: An Ethics of Fiction*, Berkeley.
Bopp, F. (1974), *Analytical Comparison of the Sanskrit, Greek, Latin and Teutonic Languages*, Amsterdam.
Boulogne, J. (2000), "Les ΣΥΓΚΡΙΣΕΙΣ de Plutarque: Une rhétorique de la ΣΥΝΚΡΑΣΙΣ", in: L. van der Stockt (ed.), *Rhetorical Theory and Praxis in Plutarch*, Louvain / Namur, 33–44.
Bowie, E.L. (2001), "Ancestors of Historiography in Early Greek Elegiac and Iambic Poetry?", in: Nino Luraghi (ed.), *The Historian's Craft in the Age of Herodotus*, Oxford, 45–66.
Bradley, P.J. (2010), "Irony and the Narrator in Xenophon's *Anabasis*", in: V.J. Gray (ed.), *Xenophon*, Oxford / New York 520–552. [Originally published 2001 in: E.I. Tylawsky / C.G. Weiss (eds.), (2001) *Essays in Honor of Gordon Williams*, New Haven, 59–84.]
Bradshaw, T. (1792), *The Whole Genuine and Complete Works of Flavius Josephus*, London.
Branham, R.B. (ed.) (2002), *Bakhtin and the Classics*, Evanston Ill.
Braun, T. (2004), "Xenophon's Dangerous Liaisons", in: Fox (2004), 97–130.
Bringmann, K. (1965), *Studien zu den politischen Ideen des Isokrates*, Göttingen.
Briscoe, J. (1981), *A Commentary on Livy, Books XXXIV–XXXVII*, Oxford.
Briscoe, J. (1986), *Titi Livi: ab urbe condita libri XLI–XLV*, Stuttgart.
Briscoe, J. (1991), *Titi Livi: ab urbe condita libri XXXI–XXXV*, Stuttgart.
Briscoe, J. (2008), *A Commentary on Livy, Books XXXVIII–XL*, Oxford.
Brittain, V. (2000) [1981], *Chronicle of Youth: Great War Diary 1913–17*, ed. A. Bishop, London.
Brittain, V. (2005) [1933], *Testament of Youth: An Autobiographical Study of the War Years 1900–1925*, London.
Brock, R. (2013), "Athens' Sicilian Expedition: Contemporary Scenarios of Its Outcome", in: Powell (2013), 49–70.
Brügger, C. / Stoevesandt, M. / Visser, E. (2003), *Homers Ilias: Gesamtkommentar*, J. Latacz (ed.), II.2: Kommentar, München / Leipzig.
Bucher, G. (2000), "The Origins, Program and Composition of Appian's Roman History", in: *TAPA* 130, 411–458.
Burchard, L. (1977), *Corpus Rubenianum*, part xxi, 2 vols., book Illustrations and title-pages: J.R.Judson / C. Van de Velde, Brussels.
Burck, E. (1934), *Die Erzählungskunst des T. Livius*, Berlin.
Burck, E. (1962), *Einführung in die dritte Dekade des Livius*, Heidelberg.
Burke, P. (1969), *The Renaissance Sense of the Past*, London.

Burke, P. (2001), "The Sense of Anachronism from Petrarch to Poussin", in: C. Humphrey / W.M. Ormrod (eds.), *Time in the Medieval World*, York, 157–73.
Burke, P. (2004), "Reflections on the Cultural History of Time", in: *Viator* xxxv, 617–626.
Burkert, W. (1990), "Demaratos, Astrabakos und Herakles: Königsmythos und Politik zur Zeit der Perserkriege", in: W. Burkert, *Wilder Ursprung: Opferritual und Mythos bei den Griechen*, Berlin, 86–95.
Burliga, B. (2011), "Did Xenophon Read Herodotus? The Tyrant's Bloody End, or the 'Herodotean' Character of Xenophon's Hell. 6. 4. 35–37", in: B. Burliga, *Xenophon: Greece, Persia, and Beyond*, Gdansk, 159–172.
Burnyeat, M. (1990), *The Theaetetus of Plato*, M. J. Levett (trans.), Indianapolis.
Burrow, J.W. (1981), *A Liberal Descent: Victorian Historians and the English Past*, Cambridge.
Butterfield, H. (1955), *Man on His Past: The Study of the History of Historical Scholarship*, Cambridge.
Büttner-Wobst, Th. (1905), *Polybii historiae libri I–III*, Leipzig.
Cancik-Lindemaier, H. / Cancik, H. (1986), "Zensur und Gedächtnis: Zu Tacitus, *Annales* IV 32–36", in: *AU* 29(4), 16–35.
Cancik, H. (1995), *Nietzsches Antike: Vorlesung*, Stuttgart, Weimar.
Canfora, L. (1971), "Il ciclo storico", in: *Belfagor* 26, 653–670.
Carlier, P. (1978) "The Idea of Imperial Monarchy in Xenophon's Cyropaedia", in: *Ktèma* 3, 133–163 (= V. Gray, ed. Xenophon, Oxford 2010, 327–366).
Carlier, P. (1984), *La royauté en Grèce avant Alexandre*, Strasbourg.
Carnall, G. (1960), *Robert Southey and his Age: The Development of a Conservative Mind*, Oxford.
Carr, D. (1987), "*Futures Past: On the Semantics of Historical Time* by Reinhart Koselleck", in: *History and Theory* 26, 197–204.
Cavalli, M. (2004), "Esempi di tecnica digressiva nelle *Elleniche*", in: G. Daverio Rocchi / M. Cavalli (eds.), *Il Peloponneso di Senofonte*, Milan, 257–271.
Ceserani, G. (2011), "Modern Histories of Ancient Greece: Genealogies, Contexts and Eighteenth-Century Narrative Historiography", in: Lianeri (2011), 138–155.
Chandler, J. (1998), *England in 1819: The Politics of Literary Culture and the Case of Romantic Historicism*, Chicago / London.
Chaplin, J. (2000), *Livy's Exemplary History*, Oxford.
Chaplin, J.D. (2007), *Livy: Rome's Mediterranean Empire: Books 41–45*, Oxford.
Charlemont, Lord (1984), *The Travels of Lord Charlemont in Greece and Turkey, 1749*, W. B. Stanford / E.J. Finopoulos (eds.), London.
Chateaubriand, F.-R. de (1835), *Travels to Jerusalem and the Holy Land*, F. Shoberl (trans.), London. [Fr. orig. 1811].
Chiasson, C. (2003), "Herodotus' Use of Attic Tragedy in the Lydian *Logos*", in: *ClAnt* 22.1, 5–36.
Chiasson, C. (2005), "Myth, Ritual, and Authorial Control in Herodotus' Story of Cleobis and Biton", in: *AJPh* 126, 41–64.
Clarke, K. (1999), "Universal Perspectives in Historiography", in: Kraus (1999), 249–279.
Clarke, K. (2008), *Making Time for the Past: Local History and the Polis*, Oxford.
Clauss, J. J. (1987), "Ironic ἔκπληξις in Livy 21,16", in: *Ancient History Bulletin* 1, 65–67.
Collins, H. M. (2010), *Tacit and Explicit Knowledge*, Chicago.

Collins, J. / Flint, P. (eds.) (2002), *The Book of Daniel: Composition and Reception*, 2 vols., Boston / Leiden.
Connor, W.R. (1984), *Thucydides*, Princeton.
Constant, B. (1988), *Political Writings*, F. Biancamaria (ed.), Cambridge.
Cook, R.M. (1955), "Thucydides as Archaeologist", in: *BSA* 50, 266-270.
Cooper, J.M. / Hutchinson, D.S. (eds.) (1997), *Plato: Complete Works*, Indianapolis.
Cornell, T.J. (ed.) (2013), *The Fragments of the Roman Historians* i–iii, Oxford.
Cornford, F.M. (1907), *Thucydides Mythistoricus*, London.
Crane, G. (1996), *The Blinded Eye: Thucydides and the New Written Word*, Lanham / London.
Croke, B. (1983), "A. D. 476. The Manufacture of a Turning Point", in: *Chiron* 13, 81–119.
Csapo E. / Miller E. (1998), "Democracy, Empire, and Art: Toward a Politics of Time and Narrative", in: Boedeker / Raaflaub (1998), 87–126.
Currie, B.G.F. (2006), "Epilogue", in: M.J. Clarke / B.G.F. Currie / R.O.A.M. Lyne (eds.), *Epic Interactions: Perspectives on Homer, Virgil, and the Epic Tradition Presented to Jasper Griffin by Former Pupils*, Oxford, 331–374.
D' Angour, A. (2011), *The Greeks and the New: Novelty in Ancient Greek Imagination and Experience*, Cambridge.
Damon, D. (2010), "Déjà vu or déjà lu? History as Intertext", in: *PLLS* 14, 375–388.
Danto, A. (1985), *Narration and Knowledge: Including the Integral Text of Analytical Philosophy of History*, New York.
Darbo-Peschanski, C. (1988), "Thucydide: historien, juge", in: *Mètis*, 2.1, 109–140.
Daston, L. (1988), *Classical Probability in the Enlightenment*, Princeton.
Davidson, J. (1991), "The Gaze in Polybius' *Histories*", in: *JRS* 81, 10–24.
Davidson, J. (2009), "Polybius", in: A. Feldherr (ed.), *The Cambridge Companion to The Roman Historians*, Cambridge, 123–136.
Davies, J. P. (2004), *Rome's Religious History: Livy, Tacitus, and Ammianus on their Gods*, Cambridge.
Davis, K. (2008), *Periodization and Sovereignty: How Ideas of Feudalism and Secularization Govern the Politics of Time*, Philadelphia.
Davis, K. (2010), "The Sense of an Epoch: Periodization, Sovereignty and the Limits of Secularization", in: A. Cole / D. Vance Smith (eds.), *The Legitimacy of the Middle Ages: On the Unwritten History of Theory*, Durham NC, 39–69.
De Certeau, M. (1986), *Heterologies: Discourse on the Other*, B. Massumi (trans)., Minneapolis.
De Certeau, M. (1988), *The Writing of History*, T. Conley (trans.), New York.
De Jong, I.J.F. (2001), "The Anachronical Structure of Herodotus' *Histories*," in: S.J. Harrison (ed.), *Texts, Ideas, and the Classics. Scholarship, Theory, and Classical Literature*, Oxford, 93–116.
De Jong, I.J.F. (2007), "Introduction: Narratological Theory on Time," in: De Jong / Nünlist (2007), 1–14.
De Jong, I.J.F. (2014), *Narratology and Classics: A Practical Guide*, Oxford.
De Jong, I.J.F. / Nünlist R. (eds.) (2007), *Time in Ancient Greek Literature: Studies in Ancient Greek Narrative*, vol. 2. Mnemosyne Supplement 291, Leiden.
De Jong, I.J.F. / Nünlist R. / Bowie A. (eds.) (2011), *Narrators, Narratees, and Narratives in Ancient Greek Literature*, Leiden.

De Romilly, J. (1965), "L'optimisme de Thucydide et le jugement de l'historien sur Périclès (Thuc. II 65)", in: *REG* 78, 557–575.
De Romilly, J. (1966), "Thucydide et l'idée du progrès", in: *ASNSP* 35, 143–191.
De Romilly, J. (1968), *Time in Greek Tragedy*, Ithaca, NY.
De Romilly, J. (2012) [1967], *The Mind of Thucydides*, E. Rawlings (trans.), Ithaca.
De Ste Croix, G.E.M. (1992), "Aristotle on History and Poetry", in: Rorty (1992), 23–32.
De Wette, W.M.L. (1806–7), *Beiträge zur Einleitung in das Alte Testament*, 2 vols., Halle. (Repr., Hildesheim: Georg Olms, 1971).
Debnar, P. (2001), *Speaking the Same Language, Speech and Audience in Thucydides' Spartan Debates*, Ann Arbor.
Delcourt, A. (2005), *Lecture des Antiquités romaines de Denys d'Halicarnasse: un historien entre deux mondes*, Bruxelles.
Delebeque, E. (1957), *Essai sur la vie de Xenophon*, Paris.
Demandt, A. (1984), *Der Fall Roms: Die Auflösung des römischen Reiches im Urteil der Nachwelt*, Munich.
Derow, P.S. (1994), "Historical Explanation: Polybius and his predecessors", in: Hornblower (1994), 73–90.
Derrida, J. (1985), *The Ear of the Other: Otobiography, Transference, Translation*, C. V. McDonald (ed.), P. Kamuf (trans.), New York.
Derrida, J. (2005), "Preface. A Time for Farewells: Heidegger (read by) Hegel (read by) Malabou", in: C. Malabou, *The Future of Hegel: Plasticity, Temporality and Dialectic*, L. During (trans.), London / New York, vii-xlvii.
Desideri, P. (1992), "Scienze nelle vite di Plutarco", in: I. Gallo (ed.), *Plutarco e le Scienze*, Geneva, 99–120.
Desideri, P. (1996), "Il De defectu oraculorum e la crisi della religione antica in Plutarco", in: E. Gabba / P. Desideri / S. Roda (eds.), *L'Italia sul Baetis: studi di storia romana in memoria di Fernando Gascó*, Torino, 91–102.
Desideri, P. (2012), *Saggi su Plutarco e la sua fortuna*, Firenze.
Desideri, P. (2015), "βίος", in: *Lexicon Historiographicum Graecum et Latinum*, fasc. 3, 9–20.
Desideri, P. (forthcoming), "Plutarch's Lives", in: *The Oxford Handbook to the Second Sophistic* (forthcoming).
Detienne, M. (2007), *The Greeks and Us: A Comparative Anthropology of Ancient Greece*, J. Lloyd (trans.), Cambridge.
Dewald, C. (1997), "Wanton kings, pickled heroes, and gnomic founding fathers: strategies of meaning at the end of Herodotus' *Histories*", in: D.H. Roberts / F. M. Dunn / D. P. Fowler (eds.), *Classical Closure: Reading the End in Greek and Latin Literature*, Princeton, 62–82.
Dewald, C. (2005), *Thucydides' War Narrative. A Structural Study*, Berkeley / LA, California.
Dewald, C. (2006), "Humour and Danger in Herodotus", in: Dewald / Marincola (2006), 145-164.
Dewald, C. (2007), "The Construction of Meaning in the First Three Historians", in: Marincola (2007), 89–101.
Dewald, C. / Marincola, J. (eds.) (2006), *The Cambridge Companion to Herodotus*, Cambridge.
Dickey, E. (2006), *Ancient Greek Scholarship: A Guide to Finding, Reading, and Understanding Scholia, Commentaries, Lexica, and Grammatical Treatises, from their Beginnings to the Byzantine Period*, Oxford.

Dillery, J. (1990), *Xenophon's Historical Perspectives*, PhD thesis, Michigan, Ann Arbor.
Dillery, J. (1995), *Xenophon and the History of His Times*, London.
Dillery, J. (2009), "Roman Historians and the Greeks: Audiences and Models", in: Feldherr (2009), 77–107.
Dingley, R. (2000), "The Ruins of the Future: Macaulay's New Zealander and the Spirit of the Age", in: A. Sandison / R. Dingley (eds.), *Histories of the Future: Studies in Fact, Fantasy and Science Fiction*, Basingstoke, 15–33.
Dobrov, G.W. (1997) (ed.), *The City as Comedy: Society and Representation in Athenian Drama*, Chapel Hill.
Dobrov, G.W. (1997a), "Language, Fiction and Utopia", in: Dobrov (1997), 95–132.
Dodwell, E. (1819), *A Classical and Topographical Tour through Greece during the years 1801, 1805, and 1806*, 2 vols., London.
Doré, G. / Jerrold, B. (1872), *London: A Pilgrimage*, London.
Dorey, T.A. (1971), *Titi Livi: ab urbe condita libri XXI–XXV*, Leipzig.
Douglas, F.S.N. (1813), *An Essay on Certain Points of Resemblance between the Ancient and Modern Greeks*, London.
Dreyer, B. (2011), *Polybios: Leben und Werk im Banne Roms*, Hildesheim.
Droysen, J.G. (1893), *Outline of the Principles of History*, B. Andrews (trans.), Boston.
Drummond, A. (1995), *Law, Politics and Power: Sallust and the Execution of the Catilinarian Conspirators*, Stuttgart.
Dubin, N.L. (2010), *Futures and Ruins: Eighteenth-Century Paris and the Art of Hubert Robert*, Los Angeles.
Duff, T. (1999), *Plutarch's Lives: Exploring Virtue and Vice*, Oxford.
Dunkel, G.E. (1982–83), "πρόσσω καὶ ὀπίσσω", in: *Zeitschrift für vergleichende Sprachforschung* 96, 66–87.
Dunn, F. (2007), *Present Shock in Late Fifth-Century Greece*, Ann Arbor.
Eckstein, A.M. (1995), *Moral Vision in the Histories of Polybius*, Berkeley.
Edelstein, L. (1967), *The Idea of Progress in Classical Antiquity*, Baltimore MD.
Edwards, C. (1999), "Translating Empire? Macaulay's Rome", in: C. Edwards (ed.), *Roman Presences: Receptions of Rome in European Culture, 1789–1945*, Cambridge, 70–87.
Eidinow, E. (2007), *Oracles, Curses, and Risk among the Ancient Greeks*, Oxford.
Eliade, M. (1971), *The Myth of the Eternal Return: Cosmos and History*, W.R. Trask (trans.), Princeton.
Elmes, J. (1823), *Lectures on Architecture*, London.
Engels, D. (2007), *Das römische Vorzeichenwesen (753–27 v. Chr.): Quellen, Terminologie, Kommentar, historische Entwicklung*, Stuttgart.
Erbse, H. (1951), "Zur Entstehung des polybianischen Geschichtswerkes", in: *RhM* 94, 157–179.
Erbse, H. (1969–1988), *Scholia Graeca in Homeri Iliadem*, 7 vols. Berlin.
Eshel, A. (2013), *Futurity: Contemporary Literature and the Quest for the Past*, Chicago.
Estrange, R. (trans.) (1702), *The Works of Flavius Josephus*, London.
Eustace, J.C. (1813), *A Tour through Italy: Exhibiting a View of its Scenery, Antiquities, and Monuments; Particularly as they are Objects of Classical Interest*, 2 vols, London.
Fabian, J. (1983), *Time and the Other: How Anthropology Makes its Object*, New York.
Fasolt, C. (2004), *The Limits of History*, Chicago.
Feldherr, A. (1998), *Spectacle and Society in Livy's History*, Berkeley.

Feldherr, A. (2009), "Delusions of Grandeur: Lucretian 'Passages' in Livy", in: P. Hardie (ed.), *Paradox and the Marvellous in Augustan Literature and Culture*, Oxford, 310–329.
Feldherr, A. (2012), "Magna mihi copia est memorandi", in: Grethlein / Krebs (2012), 95–112.
Feldherr, A. (ed.) (2009), *The Cambridge Companion to the Roman Historians*, Cambridge.
Ferguson, W. (1948), *The Renaissance in Historical Thought: Five Centuries of Interpretation*, Cambridge MA.
Ferrario, S.B. (2014), *Historical Agency and the 'Great Man' in Classical Greece*, Cambridge.
Ferrary, J.-L. (1988), *Philhellénisme et impérialisme: Aspects idéologiques de la conquête romaine du monde héllenistique, de la seconde guerre de Macédoine à la guerre contre Mithridate*, Rome.
Finley, M. (1975), *The Use and Abuse of History*, London.
Fisher, N. (2001), *Aeschines: Against Timarchos*, Oxford.
Flory, S. (1987), *The Archaic Smile of Herodotus*, Detroit, MI.
Flower, M. (2008), *The Seer in Ancient Greece*, Berkeley.
Flower, M. (2012), *Xenophon's* Anabasis, *or, the Expedition of Cyrus*, Oxford.
Force, J. (2002), *William Whiston, Honest Newtonian*, Cambridge.
Fornara, C.W. (1971), *Herodotus: An Interpretative Essay*, Oxford.
Fornara, C. W. (1971a), "Evidence for the Date of Herodotus' Publication", in: *Journal of Hellenic Studies* 91, 25–34.
Foster, E. (2010), *Thucydides, Pericles, and Periclean Imperialism*, Cambridge.
Foster, E. / Lateiner D. (eds.) (2012), *Thucydides and Herodotus*, Oxford.
Fowler, R. (2013), *Early Greek Mythography, Vol. 2: Commentary*, Oxford.
Fowler, R.L. (1996), "Herodotos and His Contemporaries", in: *Journal of Hellenic Studies* 116, 62–87.
Fox, L.R. (ed.) (2004), *The Long March: Xenophon and the Ten Thousand*, New Haven.
Fox, M. (1993), "History and Rhetoric in Dionysius of Halicarnassus", in: *JRS* 83, 31–47.
Fox, M. (1996), *Roman Historical Myths: the Regal Period in Augustan Literature*, Oxford.
Fox, M. (2001), "Dionysius, Lucian and the Prejudice against Rhetoric in History", in: *JRS* 91, 76–93.
Fox, M. (2011), "The Style of the Past: Dionysius of Halicarnassus in Context", in: Schmitz / Wiater (2011), 93–114.
Foxhall, L. / Gehrke H.-J. / Luraghi N. (eds.) (2010), *Intentional History: Spinning Time in Ancient Greece*, Stuttgart.
Frede, D. (1992), "Necessity, Chance, and 'What Happens for the Most Part' in Aristotle's *Poetics*", in: Rorty (1992), 197–220.
Fritzsche, P. (2004), *Stranded in the Present: Modern Time and the Melancholy of History*, Cambridge MA / London.
Fritzsche, P. (2013), "The Ruins of Modernity", in: Lorenz / Bevernage (2013), 57–68.
Froeyman, A. (2012), "Frank Ankersmit and Eelco Runia: The Presence and the Otherness of the Past", in: *Rethinking History: The Journal of Theory and Practice* 16, 393–415.
Fromentin, V. (1998), *Denys d'Halicarnasse, Antiquités Romaines* i, Paris.
Fromentin, V. (2004), "Choisir le meilleur: la royauté élective à Rome selon Denys d'Halicarnasse", in: *Ktèma* 29, 311–323.
Fromentin, V. (2008), "Ordre du temps et ordre des causes: ἀρχή et αἰτία chez Thucydide, Polybe et Denys d' Halicarnasse", in: B. Bureau / C. Nicolas (eds.), *Commencer et finir: débuts et fins dans les littératures grecque, latine et néolatine*, Paris, 59–70.

Fromentin, V. / Gotteland, S. / Payen, P. (eds.) (2010), *Ombres de Thucydide: La réception de l'historien depuis l'antiquité jusqu'au début du XXe siècle*, Bordeaux.

Fuhrmann, M. (1983), "Narrative Techniken im Dienste der Geschichtsschreibung (Livius, Buch 21–22): Eine Skizze", in: E. Lefèvre / E. Olshausen (eds.), *Livius: Werk und Rezeption. Festschrift für Erich Burck*, München, 19–29.

Gabba, E. (1991), *Dionysius and The History of Archaic Rome*, Berkeley / Los Angeles.

Gadamer, H.G. (1993) [1975], *Truth and Method*, J. Weinsheimer / D. Marshall (trans.), New York.

Gallia, A.B. (2007), "Reassessing the 'Cumaean Chronicle': Greek Chronology and Roman History in Dionysius of Halicarnassus", in: *JRS* 97, 50–57.

Gallie, W.B. (1968), *Philosophy and Historical Understanding*, New York.

Garcia, L.F. (2013), *Homeric Durability: Telling Time in the Iliad*, Washington, D.C.

Garosci, A. (1934), *Jean Bodin: Politica e Diritto nel Rinascimento Francese*, Milan.

Gelley, A. (1995), "Introduction", in: *Unruly Examples: On the Rhetoric of Exemplarity*, Stanford, California, 1–24.

Genette, G. (1969), "Vraisemblance et motivation", in: *Figures II*, Paris, 71–99.

Genette, G. (1980), *Narrative Discourse: An Essay in Method*, J. Lewin (trans.), Ithaca, New York.

Genette, G. (1991), *Fiction et diction*, Paris.

Georges, P. (1994), *Barbarian Asia and the Greek Experience*, Baltimore MD / London.

Georgiadis, A. [Γεωργιάδης, Α.] (1891), Περί των κατά Χριστιανών αποσπασμάτων του Πορφυρίου, PhD thesis, University of Erlangen, Leipzig.

Gerbi, A. (1973), *The Dispute of the New World: The History of a Polemic, 1750–1900*, J. Moyle (trans.), Pittsburgh.

Gerrig, R.J. (1989), "Suspense in the Absence of Uncertainty", in: *Journal of Memory and Language* 28, 633–648.

Gibbon, E. (1994), *The History of the Decline and Fall of the Roman Empire*, 3 vols., Harmondsworth. [Orig. pub. 1776–88].

Gibson, B. / Harrison T. (eds.) (2013), *Polybius and His World: Essays in Memory of F.W. Walbank*, Oxford.

Giffard, E. (1837), *A Short Visit to the Ionian Islands, Athens, and the Morea*, London.

Giraud, J.-M. (2001), "Lysandre et le chef ideal de Xénophon", in: *QS* 27, 39–68.

Giuliani, A. (2001), *I rapporti tra Atene e Delfi in età arcaica e classica*, Milan.

Goldhill, S. (2002), *The Invention of Prose*, Oxford.

Gomme, A.W. (1956), *A Historical Commentary on Thucydides*, vol. 1, Oxford.

Gomme, A.W. / Andrewes, A. / Dover, K.J. (1945–1981), *A Historical Commentary on Thucydides*, 5 vols., Oxford.

Gooch, G.P. (1959), *History and Historians in the Nineteenth Century*, Boston.

Goold, G.P. (1959) (ed.), *Lucian VI*, K. Kilburn (trans.), Cambridge / Mass.

Graetz, H. (1853–1975), *Geschichte der Juden*, 11 vols., Leipzig.

Graetz, H. / Schorsch I. (ed. / trans.) (1975), *Heinrich Graetz: The Structure of Jewish History and Other Essays*, New York.

Grafton, A. (1988), "A Vision of the Past and Future", in: *TLS* 12, 151–152.

Grafton, A. (1990), *Forgers and Critics: Creativity and Duplicity in Western Scholarship*, Princeton.

Grafton, A. (1997), *The Footnote: A Curious History*, Cambridge MA.

Grafton, A. (2003), "Dating History: The Renaissance and the Reformation of Chronology", in: *Daedalus* Spring 2003, 74–85.
Grafton, A. (2007), *What Was History? The Art of History in Early Modern Europe*, Cambridge.
Grafton, A. / Most, G. W. / Zetzel, J. E. G. (1985), "Introduction", in: Wolf (1985), 3–35.
Gray, V. (1989), *The Character of Xenophon's Hellenica*, London.
Gray, V. (2002), "Short Stories in Herodotus' *Histories*", in: Bakker / de Jong / van Wees (2002), 291–317.
Gray, V. (2003), "Interventions and Citations in Xenophon, *Hellenica* and *Anabasis*", in: *Classical Quarterly* 53, 111–123.
Gray, V. (2004), "Xenophon", in: De Jong / Nünlist / Bowie (2004), 129–146.
Gray, V. (2011), *Xenophon's Mirror of Princes: Reading the Reflections*, Oxford.
Greenwood, E. (2006), *Thucydides and the Shaping of History*, London.
Greenwood, E. (2012), "The Greek Thucydides: Venizelos' Translation of Thucydides", in: Harloe / Morley (2012), 157–177.
Grethlein, J. (2008), "Memory and Material Objects in the *Iliad* and the *Odyssey*", in: *Journal of Hellenic Studies* 128, 27–51.
Grethlein, J. (2010), *The Greeks and Their Past: Poetry, Oratory and History in the Fifth Century BCE*, Cambridge.
Grethlein, J. (2010a), "Experientiality and 'Narrative Reference,' with Thanks to Thucydides", in: *History and Theory* 49, 315–335.
Grethlein, J. (2011), "*Historia magistra vitae* in Herodotus and Thucydides? The exemplary use of the past and ancient and modern temporalities", in: Lianeri (2011), 247–263.
Grethlein, J. (2013), *Experience and Teleology in Ancient Historiography: 'Futures Past' from Herodotus to Augustine*, Cambridge.
Grethlein, J. (2013a), "The Presence of the Past in Thucydides", in Tsakmakis / Tamiolaki 91–118.
Grethlein, J. (2014a), "'Future Past': Time and Teleology in (Ancient) Historiography", in: *History and Theory* 53(3), 309–330.
Grethlein, J. (2014b) "Time, Tense and Temporality in Ancient Greek Historiography", in: *Oxford Handbooks Online: Classical Studies*. http://www.oxfordhandbooks.com/view/10.1093/oxfordhb/9780199935390.001.0001/oxfordhb-9780199935390-e-43.
Grethlein, J. / Rengakos A. (eds.) (2009), *Narratology and Interpretation*, Berlin.
Grethlein, J. / Krebs C. (eds.) (2012), *Time and Narrative in Ancient Historiography: The 'Plupast' from Herodotus to Appian*, Cambridge.
Grethlein, J. / Krebs C. (2012a), "The Historian's Plupast: Introductory Remarks on its Forms and Functions", in: Grethlein / Krebs (2012), 1–16.
Gribble, D. (2006), "Individuals in Thucydides", in: Rengakos / Tsakmakis (2006), 439–468.
Griffin, J. (2006), "Herodotus and Tragedy", in: Dewald / Marincola (2006), 46–59.
Griffiths, A. (1999), "Euenius the Negligent Nightwatchman (Herodotus 9.92–6)", in: R. Buxton (ed.), *From Myth to Reason? Studies in the Development of Greek Thought*, Oxford, 169–182.
Guida, A. (1998), "L' ultimo oracolo di Delfi per Giuliano", in: *Giuliano imperatore: le sue idee, i suoi amici, i suoi avversari. Atti del Convegno internazionale di studi, Lecce 10–12 dicembre 1988*, Lecce, 389–413.
Gunderson, E. (2000), "The history of the mind and philosophy of history in Sallust's *Bellum Catilinae*", in: *Ramus* 29, 85–126.

Guran, P. (2006), "Genesis and Function of the Last Emperor-Myth in Byzantium", *Bizantinistica: Rivista di Studi Bizantini e Slavi* 8, 273–303.

Guran, P. (2007), "Eschatology and Political Theology in the Last Centuries of Byzantium", *Revue des Études Sud-Est Européennes* 45, 73–85.

Hahm, D.E. (1995), "Polybius' Applied Political Theory", in: A. Laks / M. Schofield (eds.), *Justice and Generosity: Studies in Hellenistic Social and Political Philosophy*, Cambridge, 7–47.

Hammer, E. (2011), *Philosophy and Temporality from Kant to Critical Theory*, Cambridge.

Hammond, M. (2009), *Thucydides. The Peloponnesian War*, M. Hammond (trans.), Oxford.

Händl-Sagawe, U. (1995), *Der Beginn des 2. Punischen Krieges: Ein historisch-kritischer Kommentar zu Livius Buch 21*, München.

Hannoum, A. (2008), "What is an Order of Time? Review of F. Hartog, *Régimes d'historicité. Présentisme et expérience du temps*, Paris, Seuil 2003", in: *History and Theory* 47, 458–471.

Hansen, W. (2002), *Ariadne's Thread: A Guide to International Tales Found in Classical Literature*, Ithaca, NY / London.

Hardie, P.R. (1993), *The Epic Successors of Virgil: A Study in the Dynamics of a Tradition*, Cambridge.

Hardie, P.R. (1998), *Virgil*, Oxford.

Harloe, K. / Morley N. (eds.) (2012), *Thucydides and the Modern World: Reception, Reinterpretation and Influence from the Renaissance to the Present*, Cambridge.

Harloe, K. / N. Morley (2012a), "Introduction: The Modern Reception of Thucydides", in: Harloe / Morley (2012), 1–24.

Harries, E.W. (1994), *The Unfinished Manner: Essays on the Fragment in the Later Eighteenth Century*, Charlottesville / London.

Harrison, E. (1912), "To Save the Athenian Walls from Ruin Bare", in: *CR* 26, 247–249.

Hartog, F. (1980), *Le miroir d'Hérodote: Essai sur la représentation de l'autre*, Paris.

Hartog, F. (2003), *Régimes d'historicité: Présentisme et expériences du temps*, Paris.

Hartog, F. (2011), "Time's Authority", in: Lianeri (2011), 33–47.

Hau, L. (2011), "Tychê in Polybius: Narrative Answers to a Philosophical Question", in: *Histos* 5, 183–207.

Hau, L. I. (2013), "The Shadow of What Might Have Been: Sideshadowing in Thucydides and Xenophon", in: Powell (2013), 71–90.

Havas, L. (1990), "Schemata und Wahrheit in der Darstellung der spätrepublikanischen politischen Ereignisse", in: *Klio* 72, 216–224.

Hawthorn, G. (2012), "Receiving Thucydides Politically", in: Harloe / Morley (2012), 212–228.

Hawthorn, G. (2014), *Thucydides on Politics: Back to the Present*, Cambridge.

Hedrick, C.W. (1993), "The Meaning of Material Culture: Herodotus, Thucydides, and Their Sources", in: R.M. Rosen / J. Farrell (eds.), *Nomodeiktes: Greek Studies in Honor of Martin Ostwald*, Ann Arbor, 17–38.

Hell, J. (2010), "Imperial Ruin Gazers, or Why Did Scipio Weep?", in: Hell, J. / A. Schönle (eds.), *Ruins of Modernity*, Duke NC / London, 169–192.

Helly, B. (1995), *L'état Thessalien: Aleuas le Roux, les tetrades et les tagoi*, Lyon.

Henry, W.P. (1966), *Greek Historical Writing*, Chicago.

Heuß, A. (1956), "Der Untergang der römischen Republik und das Problem der Revolution", in: *HZ* 182, 1–28.

Hidber, T. (2004), "Appian", in: De Jong / Nünlist / Bowie (2004), 175–185.
Higgins, W. E. (1977), *Xenophon the Athenian: The Problem of the Individual and the Society of the Polis*, Albany.
Himmelfarb, G. (2011), *The People of the Book: Philosemitism in England from Cromwell to Churchill*, New York.
Hobsbawm, E. (1993), "Un historien et son temps présent", in: *Écrire l'histoire du temps présent*, Paris.
Hoffmann, U. (2002), "'Der Anfang reicht bis zum Ende': Drei Bemerkungen zu Polybios' teleologischer Denkweise", in: *Saeculum* 53, 193–225.
Hoffmann, W. (1959), "Catilina und die römische Revolution", in: *Gymnasium* 66, 459–477.
Hogg, D.A.W. (2008), *Speech and Action in the Antiquitates Romanae of Dionysius of Halicarnassus: The Question of Historical Change*, D.Phil. thesis, Oxford University.
Hollander, J. den (2011), "Contemporary History and the Art of Self-Distancing", in: *History and Theory* 50, 51–67.
Hollander, J. den / Herman, P. / Peters, R. (2011), "Introduction: The Metaphor of Historical Distance", in: *History and Theory* 50, 1–11.
Hollmann, A. (2011), *The Master of Signs: Signs and the Interpretation of Signs in Herodotus' Histories*, Washington, DC.
Hölscher, L. (1999), *Die Entdeckung der Zukunft*, Frankfurt.
Homeyer, H. (1965), *Lukian: Wie man Geschichte schreiben soll*, Munich.
Hornblower, J. (1981), *Hieronymus of Cardia*, Oxford.
Hornblower, S. (1987), *Thucydides*, London.
Hornblower, S. (1991–2008), *A Commentary on Thucydides*, 3 vols., Oxford.
Hornblower, S. (ed.) (1994), *Greek Historiography*, Oxford.
Hornblower, S. (1994a), "Narratology and Narrative Techniques in Thucydides", in: Hornblower (1994), 131–166.
Horsfall, N. (1985), "Illusion and Reality in Latin Topographical Writing", in: *G&R* 33, 197–208.
Hose, M. (2006), "The Peloponnesian War: Sources Other Than Thucydides", in: Rengakos / Tsakmakis (2006), 669–690.
How, W.W. / Wells J. (1968), *A Commentary on Herodotus*, 2 vols., Oxford.
Hubbard, T.K. (1997), "Utopianism and the Sophistic City in Aristophanes", in: Dobrov (1997), 23–50.
Huber, L. (1965), "Herodots Homerverständnis", in: *Synusia. Festgabe für W. Schadewaldt*, Pfullingen, 29–52.
Hughes, T.S. (1820), *Travels in Sicily, Greece and Albania*, 2 vols., London.
Humble, N. (ed.) (2010), *Plutarch's Lives: Parallelism and Purpose*, Swansea.
Hunter, R. (2004), "Homer and Greek Literature", in: R.L. Fowler (ed.), *The Cambridge Companion to Homer*, Cambridge, 235–253.
Hunter, V. (1982), *Past and Process in Herodotus and Thucydides*, Princeton, N.J.
Huys, M. (1995), *The Tale of the Hero Who Was Exposed at Birth in Euripidean Tragedy: A Study of Motifs*, Leuven.
Ianziti, G. (2012), *Writing History in Renaissance Italy: Leonardo Bruni and the Uses of the Past*, Cambridge MA.
Immerwahr, H.R. (1954), "Historical Action in Herodotus", in: *TAPhA* 85, 16–45.

Immerwahr, H.R. (1960), "*Ergon:* History as a Monument in Herodotus and Thucydides", in: *American Journal of Philology* 81, 261–290.
Immerwahr, H.R. (1966), *Form and Thought in Herodotus*, Cleveland, OH.
Ingenkamp, H.G. (1988), "Der Höhepunkt der deutschen Plutarchrezeption", in: *ICS* 13.2, 505–529.
Jacoby, F. (1956), *Abhandlungen zur griechischen Geschichtsschreibung*, Leiden.
Jaeger, M. (2007), "Fog on the Mountain: Philip and Mt. Haemus in Livy 40.21–22", in: Marincola (2007), 397–403.
Jardine, N. (2008), "Explanatory Genealogies and Historical Testimony", in: *Episteme* 5, 160–179.
Jones, C.P. (1966), "Towards a Chronology of Plutarch's Works", in: *JRS* 56, 61–74. [rpt. in: Scardigli (1995), 95–123].
Jones, C.P. (1971), *Plutarch and Rome*, Oxford.
Jones, C.P. (1982), "Plutarch", in: J.T. Luce (ed.), *Ancient Writers: Greece and Rome*, vol 2., New York, 961–983.
Jost, I. (1847), *Geschichte der Isräeliten seit der Zeit der Maccabäer*, Berlin.
Jouanna, J. (1999), *Hippocrates*, M.B. DeBevoise (trans.), Baltimore / London. [First published in French in 1992].
Jowett, B. (1881), *Thucydides translated into English*, 2 vols., Oxford.
Junod, P. (1984), "Future in the Past", *Oppositions* 26, 43–63.
Kallet, L. (2001), *Money and the Corrosion of Power in Thucydides: The Sicilian Expedition and Its Aftermath*, Berkeley / Los Angeles / London.
Kallett, L. (2006), "Thucydides' Workshop of History and Utility Outside the Text", in Rengakos / Taskmakis (2006), 335–368.
Kelley, D. (1991), *Versions of History from Antiquity to the Enlightenment*, New Haven.
Kemezis, A.M. (2010), "Lucian, Fronto and the Absence of Contemporary Historiography under the Antonines", in: *AJP* 131/2, 285–325.
Kennedy, D. (2013), *Antiquity and the Meanings of Time: A Philosophy of Ancient and Modern Literature*, New York.
Kennedy, G.A. (1991), *Aristotle: On Rhetoric. A Theory of Civil Discourse*, G.A. Kennedy (trans.), Oxford.
Kern, F. (1960), *Aufbau und Gedankengang der Bücher 36–45 des Titus Livius*, (Diss.), Kiel.
Keesling, C.M. (2005), "Misunderstood Gestures: Iconatrophy and the Reception of Greek Sculpture in the Roman Imperial Period", in: *Classical Antiquity* 24, 41-80.
Kilburn, K. (1959), *Lucian VI*, Cambridge MA.
Kiparsky, P. (1974), "From Paleogrammarians to Neogrammarians", in: D. Hymes (ed.), *Studies in the History of Linguistics Traditions and Paradigms*, Bloomington, 331–345.
Kirchner, J. (1935), *Imagines Inscriptionum Atticarum*, Berlin.
Kirkland, S.D. (2014), "Tragic Time", in: T. Chanter / S.D. Kirkland (eds.), *The Returns of Antigone: Interdisciplinary Essays*, Albany NY, 51–68.
Konstan, D. (1997), "The Greek Polis and its Negations: Versions of Utopia in Aristophanes' Birds", in: Dobrov (1997), 3–22.
Konstan, D. / Raaflaub K.A. (2010) (eds.), *Epic and History*, Malden MA / Oxford.
Kontler, L. (2008), "Time and Progress-Time as Progress: An Enlightened Sermon by William Robertson", in: Miller (2008), 195–220.

Koselleck, R. (1975), "Geschichte, Historie", in: *Geschichtliche Grundbegriffe: Historisches Lexikon zur politisch-sozialen Sprache in Deutschland*, O. Brunner / W. Conze / R. Koselleck (eds.), vol. 2, Stuttgart, 593–717.
Koselleck, R. (1976), "'Erfahrungsraum' und 'Erwartungshorizont' – zwei historische Kategorien", in: U. Engelhardt / V. Sellin / H. Stuke, *Soziale Bewegung und politische Verfassung*, Stuttgart, 13–33 (reprint in: Koselleck [1979], 349–375).
Koselleck, R. (1979), *Vergangene Zukunft: Zur Semantik geschichtlicher Zeiten*, Frankfurt am Main.
Koselleck, R. (1985), *Futures Past: On the Semantics of Historical Time*, K. Tribe (trans.), Cambridge MA. [Translation of Koselleck (1979)]
Koselleck, R. (2000), *Zeitgeschichten: Studien zur Historik*, Frankfurt.
Koselleck, R. (2002), *The Practice of Conceptual History: Timing History, Spacing Concepts*, T.S. Presner and others (trans.), Stanford.
Koselleck, R. (2004), *Futures Past: On the Semantics of Historical Time*, K. Tribe (trans.), New York. [Translation of Koselleck (1979)]
Kosso, P. (1993), "Historical Evidence and Epistemic Justification: Thucydides as a Case Study," in: *History and Theory* 32, 1–13.
Kracauer, K. (1995), *History: The Last Things Before the Last*, Princeton.
Kraus, C.S. (ed.) (1999), *The Limits of Historiography: Genre and Narrative in Ancient Historical Texts*, Leiden / Boston.
Krebs, C. (2006), "'Imaginary Geography' in Caesar's 'Bellum Gallicum'", in: *AJP* 127, 111–136.
Krentz, P. (1989), *Xenophon*, Hellenica *I-II.3.10*, Warminster.
Krieger, L. (1977), *Ranke: The Meaning of History*, Chicago.
La Billardière, J.J.H. de (1800), *Voyage in Search of La Pérouse: Performed by Order of the Constituent-Assembly during the Years 1791, 1792, 1793 and 1794*, 2 vols., London. [Fr. orig. 1799]
Lachenaud, G. (2004), *Promettre et écrire: Essais sur l'historiographie des Anciens*, Rennes.
Lakatos, I. (1978), *The Methodology of Scientific Research Programmes*, J. Worrall / G. Currie (ed.), Cambridge.
Langlois, Ch.V / Seignobos, Ch. (1926), *Introduction to the Study of History*, G.G. Berry (trans.), New York.
Laplace, P.-S. (1840), *Essai philosophique sur les probabilités*, 6th Edition, Paris.
Lateiner, D. (1985), "Limit, Propriety, and Transgression in the *Histories* of Herodotus", in: *The Greek Historians. Literature and History.* Papers Presented to A. E. Raubitschek, Saratoga CA, 87–100.
Lateiner, D. (1989), *The Historical Method of Herodotus*, Toronto / Buffalo NY / London.
Lattimore, S. (1998), *Thucydides. The Peloponnesian War*, Indianapolis / Cambridge.
Lebow, R.N. (2003), *The Tragic Vision of Politics: Ethics, Interests and Others*, Cambridge.
Lemmermann, K. (1927), *Jason von Pherai*, Jena.
Levene, D.S. (1992), "Sallust's *Jugurtha*: an 'Historical Fragment'", in: *JRS* 82, 51–70.
Levene, D.S. (1993), *Religion in Livy*, Leiden.
Levene, D.S. (2000), "Sallust's Catiline and Cato the censor", in: *CQ* 50, 170–191.
Levene, D.S. (2010), *Livy on the Hannibalic War*, Oxford.
Lévi-Strauss, C. (1958), *Anthropologie Structurale*, Paris.
Lévi-Strauss, C. (1971), *Mythologiques*, IV: *L'homme nu*, Paris.

Lévy, E. (1990), "L'art de la deformation historique dans les *Helléniques* de Xénophon", in: H. Verdin / G. Schepens / E. de Keyser (eds.), *Purposes of History: Studies in Greek Historiography from the 4th to the 2nd Centuries B.C.*, Leuven.
Lewis, D. et. al (1992), *The Cambridge Ancient History: The Fifth Century B.C.*, vol. 5, Cambridge.
Liakos, A. (2011), Αποκάλυψη, ουτοπία και ιστορία. Οι μεταμορφώσεις της ιστορικής συνείδησης, Athens.
Lianeri, A. (ed.) (2011), *The Western Time of Ancient History: Historiographical Encounters with the Greek and Roman Past*, Cambridge.
Lianeri, A. (2011a), "Introduction: *Un*founding Times: The Idea and Ideal of Ancient History in Western Historical Thought", in: Lianeri (2011), 3–32.
Lianeri, A. (2015), "On Historical Time and Method", in: C. Lee / N. Morley (eds.), *A Handbook to the Reception of Thucydides*, Oxford, 176–196.
Liddell, H.G. / R. Scott / H.S. Jones (1968), *A Greek-English Lexicon*. Compiled by Henry George Liddell and Robert Scott, revised and augmented by Henry Stuart Jones, Oxford.
Liebeschuetz, W. (1968), "The Structure and Function of the Melian Dialogue", in: *The Journal of Hellenic Studies* 88, 73–77.
Lisi, F.L. (ed.) (2012), *Utopia, Ancient and Modern*, Sankt Augustin.
Littré, É. (1839–1861), *Oeuvres complètes d'Hippocrate*, vols. 1–9, Paris. [Reprinted by Hakkert, 1961–1973].
Livingstone, D. (2008), *Adam's Ancestors: Race, Religion and the Politics of Human Origins*, Baltimore.
Lloyd, G.E.R. (1993), *Methods and Problems in Greek Science*, Cambridge.
Lloyd, G.E.R. (2004), *Ancient Worlds, Modern Reflections: Philosophical Perspectives on Greek and Chinese Science and Culture*, Oxford.
Lodge, T. (trans.) (1609), *The Famous and Memorable Workes of Josephus*, London. [First edition 1602]
Longley, G. (2012), "Thucydides, Polybius, and Human Nature", in: C. Smith / L. M. Yarrow (eds.), *Imperialism, Cultural Politics, and Polybius*, Oxford, 68–84.
Loraux, N. (1986), "Thucydides a écrit la guerre du Péloponnèse", in: *Metis* 1, 139–161.
Loraux, N. (1986a), *The Invention of Athens: The Funeral Oration in the Classical City*, A. Sheridan (trans.), Cambridge.
Loraux, N. (1993), *The Children of Athena: Athenian Ideas about Citizenship and the Division between the Sexes*, C. Levine (trans.), Chichester.
Loraux, N. (2002), *The Divided City: On Memory and Forgetting in Ancient Athens*, C. Pache / J. Fort (trans.), New York.
Lorenz, C. / Bevernage B., (2013) (eds.), *Breaking up Time: Negotiating the Borders between Present, Past and Future*, Göttingen.
Lossau, M. (1990), "Xenophons Odyssee", in: *Antike und Abendland* 36, 47–52.
Luce, T.J. (1977), *Livy: The Composition of his History*, Princeton.
Luce, T.J. (1989), "Ancient Views on the Causes of Bias in Historical Writing", in: *CP* 84, 16–31.
Luce, T. J. (1991) "Tacitus on 'History's Highest Function': praecipuum munus annalium (Ann. 3.65)" ANRW II 33.4: 2904-2927.
Luce, T.J., (1997), *The Greek Historians*, London / New York.
Lukacher, B. (2006), *Joseph Gandy: An Architectural Visionary in Georgian London*, London.

Luraghi, N. (2000), "Author and Audience in Thucydides' Archaeology: Some Reflections", in: *Harvard Studies in Classical Philology* 100, 227–239.
Luraghi, N. (2003), "Dionysios von Halicarnassos zwischen Griechen und Römern", in: U. Eigler / U. Gotter / N. Luraghi / U. Walter (eds.), *Formen römischer Geschichtsschreibung von den Anfängen bis Livius*, Darmstadt, 268–286.
Lushkov, A.H. (2013), "Citation and the Dynamics of Tradition in Livy's *AUC*", in: *Histos* 7, at research.ncl.ac.uk/histos/.
Lyttelton, T. (1780), *Poems, by a Young Nobleman, of Distinguished Abilities, lately Deceased; particularly, the State of England, and the once Flourishing City of London. In a letter from an American Traveller, dated from the Ruinous Portico of St. Paul's, in the Year 2199, to a Friend settled in Boston*, London.
Ma, J. (2004), "You Can't Go Home Again: Displacement and Identity in Xenophon's *Anabasis*", in: Fox (2004), 330–345.
Macan, R.W. (1908), *Herodotus. The Seventh, Eighth & Ninth Books. With Introduction, Text, Apparatus, Commentary, Appendices, Indices, Maps*, London.
Macaulay, R. (1953), *The Pleasure of Ruins*, London.
Macaulay, T.B. (1866), *The Works of Lord Macaulay*, 8 vols., London.
Macleod, C.W. (1983), "Thucydides and Tragedy", in: *Collected Essays*, Oxford, 140–158.
Maier, F.K. (2012a), *"Überall mit dem Unerwarteten rechnen." Die Kontingenz historischer Prozesse bei Polybios* (*Vestigia*, Bd. 65), Munich.
Maier, F.K. (2012b), "Learning from History παρὰ δόξαν: A New Approach to Polybius' Manifold View of the Past", in: *Histos* 6, 144–168.
Maier, F.K. (2012c), "Der Feldherr als Geschichtsschreiber: Polybios' Forderung nach Interdisziplinarität", in: *RFIC* 140, 295–330.
Marcone, A. (2008), "A long late antiquity? Considerations on a controversial periodization", in: *Journal of Late Antiquity* 1, 4–19.
Marincola, J. (1989), *Authority and Tradition in Ancient Historiography*, Cambridge.
Marincola, J. (1989a), "Thucydides 1.22.2", in: *CP* 84, 216–223.
Marincola, J. (1997), *Authority and Tradition in Ancient Historiography*, Cambridge.
Marincola, J. (1999), "Genre, Convention and Innovation in Greco-Roman Historiography", in: Kraus (1999), 281–324.
Marincola, J. (2001), *Greek Historians*, Cambridge.
Marincola, J. (2003), "Beyond Pity and Fear: The Emotions of History", in: *Ancient Society* 33, 285–315.
Marincola, J. (2005), "Concluding Narratives: Looking to the End in Classical Historiography", in: F. Cairns (ed.), *Papers of the Langford Latin Seminar 12: Greek and Roman Poetry, Greek and Roman Historiography*, Leeds, 285–320.
Marincola, J. (2006), "Herodotus and the Poetry of the Past", in: Dewald / Marincola (2006), 13–28.
Marincola, J. (ed.) (2007), *A Companion to Greek and Roman Historiography*, Malden.
Marincola, J. (2007a), "Speeches in Classical Historiography", in: Marincola (2007), 118–144.
Marincola, J. (2009), *The Landmark Xenophon's* Hellenika, R.B. Strassler (ed.), J. Marincola (trans.), New York.
Marincola, J. (2009a), "Historiography", in: A. Erskine (ed.), *A Companion to Ancient History*, Malden / Oxford / Victoria, 13–22.

Marincola, J. (2010), "Aristotle's Poetics and 'Tragic History'", in: S. Tsitsirides (ed.), *Parachoregema: Studies on Ancient Theatre in Honour of Professor Gregory M. Sifakis*, Hêrakleio, 445–459.
Marincola, J. (2010a), "The Rhetoric of History: Allusion, Intertextuality, and Exemplarity in Historiographical Speeches", in: Pausch (2010), 259–289.
Marincola, J. (ed.) (2012), *Greek Notions of the Past in the Archaic and Classical Eras: History without Historians*, Edinburgh.
Marincola, J. (2013), "Polybius, Phylarchus, and 'Tragic History': A Reconsideration", in: Gibson / Harrison (2013), 73–90.
Martin, P.M. (1993), "De l'universal à l'éternel: la liste des hégémonies dans la préface des A.R.", in: *Pallas* 39, 193–214.
Maruyama, M. / Harkins, A. (1978) (eds.), *Cultures of the Future*, The Hague.
Maul, S.M. (2008), "Walking Backwards into the Future: The Conception of Time in the Ancient Near East", in: Miller (2008), 15–24.
Maynard, G.H. (trans.) (1785), *The Whole Genuine and Complete Works of Flavius Josephus*, London.
McCullough, H.Y. (1991), "The Historical Process and Theories of History in the *Annales* and *Histories* of Tacitus", in: *ANRW* II.33.4, 2928–2948.
McDonald, A.H. (1957), "The Style of Livy", in: *Journal of Roman Studies* 47, 155–172.
McGing, B.C. (2010), *Polybius' Histories*, Oxford.
McGing, B.C. (2013), "Youthfulness in Polybius: The case of Philip V of Macedon", in: Gibson / Harrison (2013), 181–200.
McNeal, R.A. (1993), "Introduction", in: Biddle (1993), 1–46.
Meier, C. (1990), *The Greek Discovery of Politics*, D. McLintock (trans.), Cambridge MA / London. [Germ. orig. 1980].
Meiggs, R. / Lewis D. (eds.) (1969; rev. 1988), *A Selection of Greek Historical Inscriptions to the End of the Fifth Century B.C.*, Oxford.
Meissner, B. (1986), "ΠΡΑΓΜΑΤΙΚΗ ΙΣΤΟΡΙΑ: Polybius über den Zweck pragmatischer Geschichtsschreibung", in: *Saeculum* 37, 313–351.
Meyer, E.A. (2008), "Thucydides on Harmodius and Aristogeiton, Tyranny and History", in: *Classical Quarterly* 58, 13–34.
Miegge, M. (1995), *Il sogno del re di Babilonia: Profezia e storia da Thomas Muntzer a Isaac Newton*, Milan.
Millar, F. (1987), "Polybius between Greece and Rome", in: J.T.A. Koumoulides (ed.), *Greek Connections: Essays in Culture and Diplomacy*, Notre Dame IN, 1–18.
Millar, F. (2002), *The Roman Republic in Political Thought*, Hanover / London.
Miller, T. (2008) (ed.), *Given World and Time: Temporalities in Context*, Budapest.
Millett, P. (2009), "Finance and Resources: Public, Private, and Personal", in: A. Erskine (ed.), *A Companion to Ancient History*, Oxford / Malden MA, 474–485.
Milman, H.H. (1830), *The History of the Jews: From the Earliest Period to the Present Time*, 3 vols., London.
Milman, H.H. (1866), *The History of the Jews: From the Earliest Period to the Present Time*, revised edition, 3 vols., London.
Miltsios, N. (2009), "The Perils of Expectations: Perceptions, Suspense and Surprise in Polybius *Histories*", in: Grethlein / Rengakos (2009), 481–506.
Miltsios, N. (2013), *The Shaping of Narrative in Polybius*, Berlin.

Mitchell, L.G. (2002), *Greeks Bearing Gifts: The Public Use of Private Relationships in the Greek World, 435–323 BC*, Cambridge.
Mohm, S. (1977), *Untersuchungen zu den historiographischen Anschauungen des Polybios*, Saarbrücken.
Moles, J. (1993), "Truth and Untruth in Herodotus and Thucydides", in: C. Gill / T.P. Wiseman (eds.), *Lies and Fiction in the Ancient World*, Exeter, 88–121.
Moles, J. (1996), "Herodotus Warns the Athenians", in: *PLILS* 9, 259–284.
Moles, J. (1999), "*Anathema Kai Ktema:* The Inscriptional Inheritance of Ancient Historiography", in: *Histos* 3, 27–69.
Moles, J. (2002), "Herodotus and Athens", in: Bakker / De Jong / Van Wees (2002), 33–52.
Möllendorf, von P. (2001), "Frigid Enthusiasts: Lucian on Writing History", in: *PCPS* 47, 117–140.
Momigliano, A. (1966), "Time in Ancient Historiography", in: *History and Theory*, 6(6), 1–23.
Momigliano, A. (1977), *Essays in Ancient and Modern Historiography*, Middletown CT.
Momigliano, A. (1990), *The Classical Foundations of Modern Historiography*, R. di Donato (ed.), Berkeley CA / Oxford.
Momigliano, A. (1994), "Daniel and the Greek Theory of Imperial Succession", in: S. Berti (ed.), *Essays on Ancient and Modern Judaism*, M. Masella-Gayley (trans.), Chicago / London, 29–35.
Mommsen, W.J. (1990), "Ranke and the Neo-Rankean School in Imperial Germany: State-oriented Historiography as a Stabilizing Force", in: G.G. Iggers / J.M. Powell (eds.), *Leopold von Ranke and the Shaping of the Historical Discipline*, Syracuse, 124–149.
Morgan, K.A. (2007a), "Plato", in: de Jong / Nünlist (2007), 345–368.
Morgan, K.A. (2007b), "Xenophon", in: de Jong / Nünlist (2007), 369–382.
Morley, N. (2011), "Monumentality and the Meaning of the Past in ancient and modern historiography", in: Lianeri (2011), 210–226.
Morrison, J.V. (2004), "Memory, Time, and Writing: Oral and Literary Aspects of Thucydides' *History*", in: J.C. Mackie (ed.), *Oral Performance and its Context*, Leiden, 95–116.
Morrison, J.V. (2006), *Reading Thucydides*, Columbus.
Morrison, J.V. (2006a), "Interaction of Speech and Narrative in Thucydides", in: Rengakos / Tsakmakis (2006), 251–278.
Morson, G.S. (1990), *Mikhail Bakhtin: Creation of a Prosaics*, Stanford, California.
Morstein-Marx, R. (2009), "*Dignitas* and *res publica*: Caesar and Republican Legitimacy", in: K.-J. Hölkeskamp (ed.), *Eine politische Kultur (in) der Krise?*, Munich, 115–140.
Mortier, R. (1974), *La poétique des ruines en France: ses origines, ses variations, de la Renaissance à Victor Hugo*, Geneva.
Mudie, R. (1829), *Babylon the Great: A Second Judgment of Babylon the Great: or, More Men and Things in the British Capital*, 2 vols., London.
Muhlack, U. (2011), "Herodotus and Thucydides in the view of nineteenth-century German historians", in: Lianeri (2011), 179–209.
Murray, O. (1997), "The Beginnings of Greats, 1800–1872. II. Ancient History", in: M.G. Brock / M.C. Curthoys (eds.), *The History of the University of Oxford, vol.VI. Nineteenth Century Oxford, Part I*, Oxford, 520–542.
Murray, O. (2000), "Ancient History, 1872–1914", in: M.G. Brock / M.C. Curthoys (eds.), *The History of the University of Oxford, vol.VI. Nineteenth Century Oxford, Part 2*, Oxford, 333–360.

Murray, O. (2008, pub. 2011), "Ireland Invents Greek History: The Lost Historian John Gast", in: *Hermathena* 185, 23–106.

Murray, O. (2010), "In Search of the Key to All Mythologies", S. Rebenich / B. von Reibnitz / T. Späth (eds.), *Translating Antiquity*, Basel, 119–129.

Murray, O. (2010a), "Modern Perceptions of Ancient Realities, from Montesquieu to Mill" and "Conclusion", in: M. Hansen (ed.), *Démocratie athéniennes – Démocratie moderne: Tradition et Influences*, Entretiens Fondation Hardt LVI Vandoeuvres / Genève, 137–66 and 395–401.

Murray, O. (2010b), "Niebuhr in Britain", in: C. Avlami / J. Alvar (eds.), *Historiographie de l'antiquité et transferts culturels: Les histoires anciennes dans l'Europe des XVIIIe et XIXe siècles*, Amsterdam / New York, 239–254.

Murray, O. (2010c, pub. 2011), "Momigliano on Peace and Liberty (1940)", in: *Acta Universitatis Carolinae – Philologica I Graecolatina Pragensia XXIII*, 81–96. [Reprinted in: *The Annual of Texts by Foreign Guest Professors* (University of Prague) 4 (2010), 95–114.]

Murray, O. (2011), "Ancient History in the Eighteenth Century", in: Lianeri (2011), 301–306.

Mynott, J. (2013), Thucydides. *The War of the Peloponnesians and the Athenians*, J. Mynott (ed. / trans.), Cambridge.

Nagy, G. (1990), "Ancient Greek Poetry, Prophecy and Concepts of Theory", in: J.L. Kugel, (ed.) (1990), *Poetry and Prophesy: The Beginnings of a Literary Tradition*, 1990, Ithaca, NY 56–64.

Nagy, G. (1990a), *Pindar's Homer: The Lyric Possession of an Epic Past*, Baltimore MD / London.

Nagy, G. (1996), "Homeric Scholia", in: *A New Companion to Homer*, I. Morris / B.B. Powell (eds.), Leiden / New York / Koln, 101–122.

Naiden, F.S. (1999), "The Prospective Imperfect in Herodotus", in: *HSCP* 99, 135–149.

Nead, L. (2000), *Victorian Babylon: People, Streets and Images in Nineteenth-Century London*, New Haven / London.

Nesselrath, H.-G. (1998), "Lucien et le cynisme", in: *AC* 67, 121–135.

Nicolai, R. (2006), "Thucydides Continued", in: Rengakos / Tsakmakis (2006), 693–719.

Nicolai, R. (2009), "*Ktēma es aiei*: Aspects of the Reception of Thucydides in the Ancient World", in: J. Rusten (ed.), *Thucydides: Oxford Readings in Classical Studies*, Oxford.

Nietzsche, F. (1967-), *Werke: Kritische Gesamtausgabe*, G. Colli / M. Montinari (eds.), Berlin.

Nietzsche, F. (1968), *Also sprach Zarathustra: Ein Buch für Alle und Keinen*, in: Nietzsche (1967-), VI, 1.

Nietzsche, F. (1972), *Die Geburt de Tragödie aus dem Geiste der Musik; Unzeitgemässe Betrachtungen*, in: Nietzsche (1967-), III, 1.

Nietzsche, F. (1978a), *Nachgelassene Fragmente (Herbst 1869 bis Herbst 1872)*, in: Nietzsche (1967-), III, 3.

Nietzsche, F. (1978b), *Nachgelassene Fragmente (Sommer 1872 bis Ende 1874)*, in: Nietzsche (1967-), III, 4.

Nietzsche, F. (1999), *The Birth of Tragedy and Other Writings*, R. Geuss / R. Speirs (eds.), R. Speirs (trans.), Cambridge.

Nightingale, A.W. (1995), *Genres in Dialogue: Plato and the Construct of Philosophy*, Cambridge.

Nikolaidis, A.G. (2005), "Plutarch's Methods: His Cross-References and the Sequence of the *Parallel Lives*", in: A. Pérez Jiménez / F. Titchener (eds.), *Historical and Biographical Values of Plutarch's Works. Studies Devoted to Professor Philip A. Stadter by The International Plutarch Society*, Málaga / Utah, 283–324.

Nouhaud, M. (1982), *L'utilisation de l'histoire par les orateurs attiques*, Paris.

Nünlist, R. (2009), "The Motif of The Exiled Killer", in: U. Dill / C. Walde (eds.), *Antike Mythen: Medien, Transformationen und Konstruktionen*. FS F. Graf, Berlin / New York, 628–644.

O' Gorman, E. (2009), "Intertextuality and Historiography", in: Feldherr (2009), 231–242.

Oakeshott, M. (1983), *On History and Other Essays*, Oxford.

Oakley, S.P. (1997), *A Commentary on Livy Books VI–X, vol. i: Introduction and Book VI*, Oxford.

Ober, J. (1998), *Political Dissent in Democratic Athens: Intellectual Critics of Popular Rule*, Princeton.

Odahl, C.M. (2010), *Cicero and the Catilinarian Conspiracy*, New York.

Ogilvie, R.M. (1965), *A Commentary on Livy Books 1–5*, Oxford.

Ousby, I. (2002), *The Englishman's England: Taste, Travel and the Rise of Tourism*, London.

Parker, R. (1983), *Miasma: Pollution and Purification in Early Greek Religion*, Oxford.

Parker, R.C.T. (2004), "One Man's Piety: The Religious Dimension of the Anabasis", in: Fox (2004), 131–153.

Parry, A. (1981), *Logos and Ergon in Thucydides*, W.R. Connor (ed.), Salem.

Parry, A. (1989), *The Language of Achilles and Other Papers*, Oxford.

Paton, W.R. (1922), *Polybius: The Histories II*, Cambridge MA.

Pausch, D. (ed.) (2010), *Stimmen der Geschichte: Funktionen von Reden in der antiken Historiographie*, Berlin / New York.

Pausch, D. (2011), *Livius und der Leser: Narrative Strukturen in ab urbe condita*, Munich.

Pédech, P. (1964), *La méthode historique de Polybe*, Paris.

Peirano, I. (2010), "Hellenized Romans and Barbarized Greeks: Reading the End of Dionysius of Halicarnassus, *Antiquitates Romanae*", in: *JRS* 100, 32–53.

Pelling, C. (1996), "The Triumviral Period", in: A.K. Bowman / E. Champlin / A. Lintott (eds.), *The Cambridge Ancient History vol. x: The Augustan Empire, 43 B.C. – A.D. 69*, Cambridge, 1–69.

Pelling, C. (1997), "East is East and West is West – Or Are They? National Stereotypes in Herodotus", in: *Histos* 1, 51–66.
http://research.ncl.ac.uk/histos/documents/1997.04PellingEastIsEast5166.pdf (30.09.2013).

Pelling, C. (1999), "Epilogue", in: Kraus (1999), 325–360.

Pelling, C. (2002), *Plutarch and History: Eighteen Studies*, London / Swansea.

Pelling, C. (2006), "Herodotus and Homer", in: M.J. Clarke / B.G.F. Currie / R.O.A.M. Lyne (eds.), *Epic Interactions: Perspectives on Homer, Virgil, and the Epic Tradition. Presented to Jasper Griffin by former pupils*, Oxford, 75–104.

Pelling, C. (2007), "The Greek Historians of Rome", in: Marincola (2007), 244–258.

Pelling, C. (2007a), "Aristagoras: 5.49–55, 97", in: E. Irwin / E. Greenwood (eds.), *Reading Herodotus: a Study of the* Logoi *in Book 5 of Herodotus' Histories*, Cambridge, 179–201.

Pelling, C. (2010), "Plutarch's 'Tale of Two Cities': Do the Parallel Lives Combine as Global Histories?", in: Humble (2010), 217–235.

Pelling, C. (2011), *Plutarch: Caesar*, Oxford.
Pelling, C. (2012), "Aristotle's *Rhetoric*, the *Rhetorica ad Alexandrum*, and the Speeches in Herodotus and Thucydides", in: Foster / Lateiner (2012), 281–315.
Pelling, C. (2013), "Historical Explanation and What Didn't Happen: The Virtues of Virtual History", in: Powell (2013), 1–24.
Pelling, C. (2013a), "Intertextuality, Plausibility and Interpretation", in: *Histos* 7, at research.ncl.ac.uk/histos/.
Perl, G. (1969), "Sallust und die Krise der römischen Republik", in: *Philologus* 113, 201–216.
Pernot, L. (1994), *La rhétorique de l' éloge dans le monde gréco-romain*, Paris.
Pfister, M. ([11]2001), *Das Drama: Theorie und Analyse*, Munich.
Philips, M.S. (2011), "Rethinking Historical Distance: From Doctrine to Heuristic", in: *History and Theory* 50, 11–23.
Pieters, J. (2000), "New Historicism: Postmodern Historiography between Narrative and Heterology", in: *History and Theory* 39, 21–38.
Pires, F.M. (2006), "Thucydidean Modernities: History Between Science and Art", in: Rengakos / Tsakmakis (2006), 811–837.
Pitcher, L. (2009), *Writing Ancient History: An Introduction to Classical Historiography*, London.
Pitcher, L. (2012), "Appian", in: I.J.F. de Jong (ed.), *Space in Ancient Greek Literature*, Leiden, 219–233.
Pitcher, L. (forthcoming), "Caesar and Greek Historians", in: C. Krebs / L. Grillo (eds.), *Companion to Caesar*, Cambridge.
Pittenger, M.R.P. (2008), *Contested Triumphs: Politics, Pageantry, and Performance in Livy's Republican Rome*, Berkeley.
Pocock, J.G.A. (1985), *Virtue, Commerce, and History*, Cambridge.
Pocock, J.G.A. (2003) [1975], *The Machiavellian Moment: Florentine Political Thought and the Atlantic Republican Tradition*, Princeton.
Pocock, J.G.A. (2003a), *Barbarism and Religion*, vol. 3 *The First Decline and Fall*, Cambridge.
Podes, S. (1991), "Polybios' Anakyklosis-Lehre, diskrete Zustandssysteme und das Problem der Mischverfassung", in: *Klio* 73, 382–390.
Pohlenz, M. (1937), *Herodot: Der erste Geschichtsschreiber des Abendlandes*, Leipzig.
Pohlmann, W. (1912), *De arte qua fabellae Herodoteae narratae sint*, Diss. Göttingen.
Poma, G. (1989), "Dionigi d'Alicarnasso e la cittadinanza romana", in: *MEFRA* 101, 187–205.
Pomeroy, S. (1994), *Xenophon's Oeconomicus*, Oxford.
Porod, R. (2009), "Lucian and the Limits of Fiction in Ancient Historiography", in: A. Bartley (ed.), *A Lucian for our Times*, Cambridge, 29–46.
Porter, J.I. (2010), *The Origins of Aesthetic Thought in Ancient Greece: Matter, Sensation, and Experience*, Cambridge.
Pöschl, V. (1981), "Die Reden Caesars und Catos in Sallusts *Catilina*", in: V. Pöschl (ed.), *Sallust*, Darmstadt, 368–397.
Powell, A. (2013) (ed.), *Hindsight in Greek and Roman History*, Swansea.
Pownall, F. (2004), *Lessons from the Past: The Moral Use of History in Fourth-century Prose*, Ann Arbor.
Prettejohn, E. (2012), *The Modernity of Ancient Sculpture: Greek Sculpture and Modern Art from Winckelmann to Picasso*, London.
Purves, A.C. (2010), *Space and Time in Ancient Greek Narrative*, Cambridge.

Raaflaub, K.A. (1987), "Herodotus, political thought, and the meaning of history", in: *Arethusa* 20, 221–248.
Raaflaub, K.A. (2010), "Ulterior Motives in Ancient Historiography: What Exactly, and Why?", in: Foxhall / Gehrke / Luraghi (2010), 189–210.
Raaflaub, K.A. (2013), "*Ktēma es aiei*: Thucydides' Concept of 'Learning Through History' and Its Realization in His Work", in: Tsakmakis / Tamiolaki (2013), 3–21.
Raaflaub, K.A. (2014) (ed.), *Thinking, Recording and Writing History in the Ancient World*, Oxford.
Rancière, J. (1994), *The Names of History: On the Poetics of Knowledge*, H. Melehy (trans.), with a foreword by H. White, Minneapolis.
Rancière, J. (1994a), "Histoire des mots, mots de l' histoire", in: *Communications* 58, 87–101.
Ranke, L. von (1909), *History of the Latin and Teutonic Nations (1494 to 1514)*, G.R. Dennis (trans.), London.
Rask, R. (1967 [1818]), "An Investigation Concerning the Source of the Old Northern or Icelandic Language", in: W.P. Lehmann (ed. / trans.), *A Reader in Nineteenth Century Historical Indo-European Linguistics*, Bloomington, 31–37.
Rawlings, H.R. (1981), *The Structure of Thucydides' History*, Princeton.
Redfield, J. (2000), "Thucydides' Argument with the Facts", in: P. Schine Gold / B.C. Sax (eds.), *Cultural Visions: Essays in the History of Culture*, Amsterdam / Atlanta GA, 91–110.
Rengakos, A. (2001), "Epic Narrative Technique in Herodotus' *Histories*", in: *SemRom* 4.2, 253–270.
Rengakos, A. (2006), "Thucydides' Narrative: The Epic and Herodotean Heritage", in: Rengakos / Tsakmakis (2006), 279–300.
Rengakos, A. / Tsakmakis A. (eds.) (2006), *Brill's Companion to Thucydides*, Leiden.
Rescigno, A. (1995), *Plutarco: L'eclissi degli oracoli*, Napoli.
Reynolds, J.J. (2009), "Proving Power: Signs and Sign-Inference in Thucydides' Archaeology", in: *TAPA* 139, 325–368.
Rich, J.W. (2005), "Valerius Antias and the Construction of the Roman Past", in: *BICS* 48, 137–161.
Rich, J.W. (2009), "Structuring Roman History: The Consular Year and the Roman Historical Tradition", in: J.D. Chaplin / C.S. Kraus (eds.), *Oxford Readings in Classical Studies: Livy*, Oxford, 118–147.
Rich, J.W. (2015), "Appian, Polybius and the Romans' War with Antiochus the Great", in: K. Welch (ed.), *Appian's Rhomaika: Empire and Civil War*, Swansea, 51–105.
Richard, J.-C. (1993), "Sur deux discours-programmes: à propos d'*A.R.* 3.10.3–11.1", in: *Pallas* 39, 125–141.
Ricoeur, P. (1980), in: "Narrative Time", in: *Critical Inquiry* 7, 169–190
Ricoeur, P. (1981), *Hermeneutics and the Human Sciences*, J. B. Thompson (ed. / trans.), Cambridge.
Ricoeur, P. (1984), *The Reality of the Historical Past*, Milwaukee.
Ricoeur, P. (1984–1988), *Time and Narrative*, K. Blamey / D. Pellauer (trans.), 3 vols., Chicago.
Ricoeur, P. (1985), "The History of Religion and the Phenomenology of Time Consciousness", in: *History of Religions*, J.K. Kitagawa (ed.), 13–30.

Ricoeur, P. (1987), "Myth and History", in: M. Eliade (ed.), *Encyclopedia of Religion*, New York, 273–282.
Ricoeur, P. (1995), *Figuring the Sacred: Religion, Narrative, and Imagination*, D. Pellauer (trans.), M.I. Wallace (ed.), Minneapolis.
Ricoeur, P. (2004), *Memory, History and Forgetting*, K. Blamey / D. Pellauer (trans.), Chicago.
Riegl, A. (1982a), "Der Moderne Denkmalskultus, Sein Wesen und Seine Entstehung", in: *Gesammelte Aufsätze*, Ausberg / Vienna, 144–193.
Riegl, A. (1982b), "The Modern Cult of Monuments: Its Character and Its Origin", K.W. Forster / D. Ghirardo (eds. / trans.), in: *Oppositions* 25, 21–51.
Riemann, K.-A. (1927), *Das herodoteische Geschichtswerk in der Antike*, PhD thesis, Munich.
Roark, T. (2011), *Aristotle on Time: A Study of the Physics*, Cambridge.
Rogerson, J. (1985), *Old Testament Criticism in the Nineteenth Century*, Philadelphia.
Romm, J. (2006), "Herodotus and the Natural World", in: Dewald / Marincola (2006), 178–191.
Rood, T. (1998), *Thucydides: Narrative and Explanation*, Oxford.
Rood, T. (2004), "Panhellenism and Self-Presentation: Xenophon's Speeches", in: Fox (2004), 305–329.
Rood, T. (2006), "Advice and Advisers in Xenophon's *Anabasis*", in: D. Spencer / E. Theodorakopoulos (eds.), *Advice and Its Rhetoric in Greece and Rome*, Bari, 47–61.
Rood, T. (2006a), "Objectivity and Authority: Thucydides' Historical Method", in: Rengakos / Tsakmakis (2006), 225–250.
Rood, T. (2007), "Polybius", in: de Jong / Nünlist (2007), 165–181.
Rood, T. (2007a), "Herodotus", in: de Jong / Nünlist (2007), 115–130.
Rood, T. (2007b), "Thucydides", in: de Jong / Nünlist (2007), 131–146.
Rood, T. (2007c), "Xenophon", in: De Jong / Nünlist (2007), 147–163.
Rood, T. (2010), *American Anabasis: Xenophon and the Idea of America from the Mexican War to Iraq*, London.
Rood, T. (2013), "Redeeming Xenophon: Historiographical Reception and the Transhistorical", in: *Classical Receptions Journal* 5, 199–211.
Rood, T. (2015), "The Reception of Thucydides' *Archaeology*", in: N. Morley / C.M.-W. Lee (eds.), *A Handbook to the Reception of Thucydides*, Malden, MA.
Rorty, A.O. (1992) (ed.), *Essays on Aristotle's Poetics*, Princeton.
Rose, H. J. (1940), "Some Herodotean Rationalisms", *CQ* 34: 78-84.
Rosen, R.M. (2004), *Time and Temporality in the Ancient World*, Philadelphia, PA.
Rösler, W. (2000), "Die 'Selbsthistorisierung' des Autors: Zur Stellung Herodots zwischen Mündlichkeit und Schriftlichkeit", in: *Philologus* 135, 215–220.
Rossetti, D.G. (1881), *Poems*, London.
Rossi, P. (1984), *The Dark Abyss of Time: The History of the Earth and the History of Nations from Hooke to Vico*, Chicago.
Rousseau, J.-J. (1997), *The Discourses and Other Early Political Writings*, V. Gourevitch (ed. / trans.), Cambridge.
Roveri, A. (1956), "*Tyche* in Polibio", in: *Convivium* 24, 275–293.
Rüsen, J. (2005), *History: Narration, Interpretation, Orientation*, New York / Oxford.
Rüsen, J. (2006) (ed.), *Meaning and Representation in History*, New York.
Rüsen, J. (2006a), "Sense of History: What Does it Mean? With an Outlook onto Reason and Senselessness", in: Rüsen (2006), 40–64.

Rutherford, R.B. (1994), "Learning from History: Categories and Case Histories", R. Osborne / S. Hornblower (eds.), in: *Ritual, Finance, Politics: Athenian Democratic Accounts Presented to David Lewis*, Oxford, 53–68.
Rutherford, R.B. (2012), "Structure and Meaning in Epic and Historiography", in: Foster / Lateiner (2012), 13–38.
Sacks, K.S. (1981), *Polybius on the Writing of History*, Berkeley.
Sahlins, M. (2004), *Apologies to Thucydides: Understanding History as Culture and Vice Versa*, Chicago.
Saïd, S. (1981), "Dareios et Xerxès dans les *Perses* d' Eschyle", in: *Ktèma* 6, 17–38.
Saïd, S. (2011), "Reading Thucydides' *Archaeology* against the background of Herodotus' preface", in: G. Rechenauer / V. Pothou (eds.), *Thucydides – a Violent Teacher?: History and its Representations*, Göttingen, 61–77.
Sailor, D. (2008), *Writing and Empire in Tacitus*, Cambridge.
Sanchez, P. (2001), *L' Amphictionie des Pyles et de Delphes*, Stuttgart.
Satterfield, S. (2012), "Livy and the Timing of Expiation in the Roman Year", in: *Histos* 6, 67–90.
Scardigli B. (1995) (ed.), *Essays on Plutarch's Lives*, Oxford.
Schaeffer, P. (1976), "The Emergence of the Concept 'Medieval' in Central European Humanism", in: *Sixteenth Century Journal* 7. 2, 21–30.
Schepens, G. (1980), *L' 'Autopsie' dans la méthode des historiens grecs du cinquième siècle avant J.-C.*, Brussels.
Schiffman, Z.S. (2011), *The Birth of the Past*, Baltimore.
Schmal, S. (2001), *Sallust*, Hildesheim.
Schmitz, T. / Wiater, N. (eds.) (2011), *The Struggle for Identity: Greeks and their Past in the First Century BCE*, Stuttgart.
Schultze, C.E. (1986), "Dionysius of Halicarnassus and his Audience", in: I.S. Moxon / J.D. Smart / A.J. Woodman (eds.), *Past Perspectives: Studies in Greek and Roman Historical Writing*, Cambridge, 121–141.
Schultze, C.E. (2012), "Negotiating the Plupast: Dionysius of Halicarnassus and Roman Self-definition", in Grethlein / Krebs (2012), 113–138.
Shankman, S., / Durrant S. (2000), "Before and after Philosophy: Thucydides and Sima Qian", in: Shankman / Durrant, *The Siren and the Sage: Knowledge and Wisdom in Ancient Greece and China*, London / New York, 79–156.
Shimron, B. (1979/80), "Polybius on Rome: A Reexamination of the Evidence", in: *SCI* 5, 94–117.
Skilton, D. (2004), "Contemplating the Ruins of London: Macaulay's New Zealander and Others", in: *Literary London Journal* 2. (http://www.literarylondon.org/london-journal/march2004/skilton.html).
Skilton, D. (2007), "Tourists At The Ruins Of London: The Metropolis and the Struggle for Empire", in: *Cercles* 17, 93–119.
Sklenář, R. (1998), "*La République des Signes*: Caesar, Cato, and the language of Sallustian morality", in: *TAPA* 128, 205–220.
Sleidan, J. (1563), *A Brief Chronicle of the Four Principal Empires*, London.
Smarczyk, B. (2006), "Thucydides and Epigraphy", in: Rengakos / Tsakmakis (2006), 495–522.
Smith, B. (1985), *European Vision and the South Pacific*, New Haven / London.

Smith, H. (1821), *Amarynthus, the Nympolept, with Other Poems*, London.
Smith, J. (1991), "A Slip in Time Saves Nine: Prestigious Origins Again", in: J. Bender / D.E. Wellbery, *Chronotypes: The Construction of Time*, Stanford, 67–76.
Soane, J. (1999), "Crude Hints towards an History of my House in L[incoln's] I[nn] fields", H. Dorey (ed.), in: *Visions of Ruin: Architectural Fantasies & Designs for Garden Follies*, London, 61–78.
Sorabji, R. (1983), *Time Creation and the Continuum: Theories in Antiquity and the Early Middle Ages*, London.
Sourvinou-Inwood, C. (1991), "'Myth' and History. On Herodotus 3.48 and 3.50–53", in: C. Sourvinou-Inwood, *'Reading' Greek Culture*, Oxford, 244–284.
Sprawski, S. (1999), *Jason of Pherae*, Cracow.
Stadter, P.A. (1992), "Herodotus and the Athenian arche", in: *ASNP* III 22, 781–809.
Stadter, P.A. (2002), "Introduction: Setting Plutarch in his Context", in P.A. Stadter / L. Van der Stockt (eds.), *Sage and Emperor: Plutarch, Greek Intellectuals, and Roman Power in the Time of Trajan (98–117 A.D.)*, Leuven, 1–26.
Stadter, P.A. (2004), "From the Mythical to the Historical Paradigm: the Transformation of Myth in Herodotus", in: J.M. Candau Morón / F.J.González Ponce / G. Cruz Andreotti (eds.), *Historia y mito: El pasado legendario como fuente de autoridad*, Actas del Simposio Internacional celebrado en Sevilla, Valverde del Camino y Huelva entre el 22–25 Abril 2003, Málaga, 31–46.
Stadter, P.A. (2010), "Parallels in three dimensions", in: Humble (2010), 197–216.
Stadter, P.A. (2012), "Thucydides as 'Reader' of Herodotus", in: Foster / Lateiner (2012), 39–66.
Stahl, H.-P. (1973), "Speeches and Course of Events in Books Six and Seven of Thucydides", in: P.A. Stadter (ed.), *The Speeches in Thucydides: A Collection of Original Studies with a Bibliography*, Chapel Hill, 60–77.
Stahl, H.-P. (2003), *Thucydides: Man's Place in History*, Swansea.
Stahl, H.-P. (2012), "Herodotus and Thucydides on Blind Decisions Preceding Military Actions," in: Foster / Lateiner (2012), 125–153.
Stahl, H.-P. (2013), "The Dot on the 'I': Thucydidean Epilogues", in: Tsakmakis / Tamiolaki (2013), 309–328.
Staley, D.J. (2002), "A history of the future", in: *History and Theory* 41, 72–89.
Staley, D.J. (2007), *History and Future: Using Historical Thinking to Imagine the Future*, Lanham MD.
Starnes, C. (1990), *The New Republic: A Commentary on Book I of More's Utopia Showing its Relation to Plato's Republic*, Waterloo.
Steinbock, B. (2013), *Social Memory in Athenian Public Discourse: Uses and Meanings of the Past*, Michigan.
Sternberg, M. (2004), "Telling in Time (I): Chronology and Narrative Theory", in: M. Ball, *Narrative Theory: Special Topics*, 93–137.
Strasburger, H. (1955), "Herodot und das perikleische Athen", in: *Historia* 4, 1–25.
Strassler, R.B. (ed.) (1996), *The Landmark Thucydides: A Comprehensive Guide to the Peloponnesian War*, New York.
Strassler, R.B. (ed.) (2007), *The Landmark Herodotus: the Histories*, A.L. Purvis (trans.), New York.

Strebel, H. (1935), *Wertung und Wirkung des Thukydideischen Geschichtswerkes in der griechisch-römischen Literatur: (Eine literargeschichtliche Studie nebst einem Exkurs über Appian als Nachahmer des Thukydides)*, Speyer a. Rh.

Süßmann, J. (2012), "Historicising the Classics: How Nineteenth-Century German Historiography Changed the Perspective on Historical tradition", in: Harloe / Morley (2012), 77–92.

Sutcliffe, A. (2003), *Judaism and Enlightenment*, Cambridge.

Swain, J.W. (1940), "The Theory of the Four Monarchies: Opposition History Under the Romans", in: *Classical Philology* 35, 1–21.

Swain, S. (1989), "Plutarch: Chance, Providence, and History", in: *AJPh* 110, 272–302.

Syme, R. (1964), *Sallust*, Berkeley.

Tamiolaki, M. (2009), "Les *Helléniques* entre tradition et innovation: Aspects de la relation intertextuelle de Xénophon avec Hérodote et Thucydide", in: V. Azoulay (ed.), *Xénophon*, Québec / Ottawa, 15–52.

Tamiolaki, M. (2012), "Virtue and Leadership in Xenophon: Ideal Leaders or Ideal Losers?", in: F. Hobden / C. Tuplin (eds.), *Xenophon: Ethical Principles and Historical Enquiry*, Leiden / Boston, 563–589.

Tamiolaki, M. (2013a), "Lucien précurseur de la *Liar School of Herodotus*: Aspects de la réception d'Hérodote dans l'*Histoire Vraie* de Lucien", in: J. Alaux (ed.), *Hérodote: formes de pensée, figures du récit*, Rennes, 145–158.

Tamiolaki, M. (2013b), "L' historien comme figure du savoir et son dialogue avec le public: Formes et modalités d'une interaction dynamique chez Hérodote, Thucydide et Xénophon", in : A. Macé (ed.), *Le savoir public: La vocation politique du savoir en Grèce ancienne*, Besançon, 241–269.

Tamiolaki, M. (forthcoming a), "Satire and Historiography: The Reception of Classical Models and the Construction of the Author's Persona in Lucian's *De Historia Conscribenda*", *Mnemosyne*.

Tamiolaki, M. (forthcoming b), "Lucian on Truth and Lies in ancient historiography. The Theory and its Limits", in: L. Hau / I. Ruffel (eds.), *Pluralising the Past*, London.

Taylor, M. (2010), *Thucydides, Pericles, and the Idea of Athens*, Cambridge.

Thomas, R. (2000), *Herodotus in Context: Ethnography, Science and the Art of Persuasion*, Cambridge.

Thomas, R. (2006), "Thucydides' Intellectual Milieu and the Plague", in: Rengakos / Tsakmakis (2006), 87–108.

Thomson, A. (2011), "On the Shores of History", in: P. Bowman / R. Stamp (eds.), *Reading Rancière: Critical Dissensus*, London / New York, 200–216.

Tiemersma, D. / Oosterling, H.A.F. (1994) (eds.), *Time and Temporality in Intercultural Perspective*, Atlanta GA.

Toalster, D. (2011), *Unzeitgemäße Feldherren: Der Hipparch als Prototyp des erfolgreichen Feldherrn in Xenophons Hellenika*, Gutenberg.

Tompkins, D.P. (1972), "Stylistic Characterization in Thucydides: Nicias and Alcibiades", in: *Yale Classical Studies* 22, 181–214.

Trédé, M. (2010), "Thucydide et Lucien ou comment lire le traité de Lucien *Sur la manière d'écrire l'histoire?*", in: Fromentin / Gotteland / Payen (eds.) (2010), 191–198.

Trevett, J. (1996), "Did Demosthenes Publish His Deliberative Speeches?", in: *Hermes* 124, 425–441.

Trompf, G.W. (1979), *The Idea of Historical Recurrence in Western Thought*, Berkeley.
Tsakmakis, A. (1995), "Thucydides and Herodotus: Remarks on the Attitude of the Historian Regarding Literature", in: *Scripta Classica Israelica*, 17–32.
Tsakmakis, A. (1998), "Von der Rhetorik zur Geschichtsschreibung: Das 'Methodenkapitel' des Thukydides (1.22.1–3)", in: *RhM* 141, 239–255.
Tsakmakis, A. (2006), "Leaders, Crowds, and the Power of the Image: Political Communication in Thucydides", in: A. Rengakos / A. Tsakmakis (eds.), *Brill's Companion to Thucydides*, Leiden / Boston, 161–188.
Tsakmakis, A. (2013), "Απόλλων Τυραννοκτόνος; Η μοιραία δελφική πανήγυρις του Ιάσονα του Φεραίου στα *Ελληνικά* του Ξενοφώντα", in: N. Birgalias / K. Buraselis / P. Cartledge / A. Gartziou-Tatti (eds.), *War, Peace, and Panhellenic Games*, Athens, 669–685.
Tsakmakis, A. / Tamiolaki M. (2013) (eds.), *Thucydides Between History and Literature*, Berlin / Boston.
Tsitsiou-Chelidoni, C. (2007), "Kleinasien zwischen Osten und Westen: Titus Livius' Bericht über den Kampf zwischen Antiochos III. und den Römern (192–188 v. Chr.)", in: G. Urso (ed.), *Tra Oriente e Occidente: Indigeni, Greci e Romani in Asia Minore*, Pisa, 23–44.
Tucker, A. (2004), *Our Knowledge of the Past: A Philosophy of Historiography*, New York.
Tucker, A. (2009), "Contingency, Necessity, Teleology, and Progress", in: D.A. Yerxa (ed.), *Recent Themes in the History of Science and Religion: Historians in Conversation*, Columbia SC, 124–128.
Tulli, M. (2011), "Platone, il proemio del Teeteto e la poetica del dialogo", in: M. Tulli (ed.), *L'autore pensoso: un seminario per Graziano Arrighetti sulla coscienza letteraria dei Greci. Ricerche di filologia classica, 6. Biblioteca di Studi antichi 95*, Pisa / Rome, 121–133.
Tuplin, C. (2003), "Heroes in Xenophon's *Anabasis*", in: A. Barzanò / C. Bearzot / F. Landucci / L. Prandi / G. Zecchini (eds.), *Modelli Eroici dall' antichità alla cultura europea*, Roma, 115–156.
Tuplin, C. (2004), "Herodotus and Xenophon's *Anabasis*", in: V. Karageorghis / I.G. Taiphakos (eds.), *The World of Herodotus: Proceedings of an International Conference Held at the Foundation Anastasios G. Leventis, Nicosia, September 18–21, 2003*, Nicosia, 351–364.
Tuplin, C. (2007), "Continuous Histories (Hellenica)", in: Marincola (2007), 159–170.
Van Kley, E. (1971), "Europe's 'Discovery' of China and the Writing of World History", in: *American Historical Review* 76.2, 358–385.
Van Nuffelen, P. (2004), *Héritage de paix et de piété: étude sur les histoires ecclésiastiques de Socrate et de Sozomène*, Leuven.
Van Nuffelen, P. (2012), *Orosius and the Rhetoric of History*, Oxford.
Vansina, J. (1985), *Oral Tradition as History*, London.
Vasiliev, A. (1943–44), "Medieval Ideas of the End of the World: West and East", in: *Byzantion* 16.2, 462–502.
Vasunia, P. (2001), *The Gift of the Nile: Hellenizing Egypt from Aeschylus to Alexander*, California LA.
Vattuone, R. (1994), "*Oran ta legomena*: Retorica e storia nella storiografia greca del IV sec. a.C.", in: *Storia della Storiografia* 25, 3–21.
Vernant, J.-P. (1981), "Le Tyran boiteux: d' Oedipe à Périandre", in: *Le Temps de la réflexion* 2, 235–255; reprint in J.-P. Vernant / P. Vidal-Naquet, *Mythe et tragédie en Grèce ancienne*, II, Paris, 45–77.

Vernant, J.-P. (1988), "Intimations of the Will in Greek Tragedy", in: J.-P. Vernant / P. Vidal-Naquet (eds.), *Myth and Tragedy in Ancient Greece*, New York, 49–84.
Veyne, P. (1984), *Writing History: Essay on Epistemology*, Middletown Conn.
Vidal-Naquet, P. (1986), "Divine Time and Human Time", in: *The Black Hunter: Forms of Thought and Forms of Society in the Greek World*, Baltimore / London, 39–60.
Vlassopoulos, K. (2010), "Imperial Encounters: Discourses on Empire and the Uses of Ancient History During the Eighteenth Century", in: M. Bradley (ed.), *Classics and Imperialism in the British Empire*, Oxford, 29–53.
Vlassopoulos, K. (2011), "Acquiring (a) Historicity: Greek History, Temporalities and Eurocentrism in the *Sattelzeit* (1750–1850), in: Lianeri (2011), 156–178.
Volney, C.-F. de (1796), *The Ruins, or, A Survey of the Revolutions of Empires*, London. [Fr. orig. 1791].
Volpi, F. (1999), "The Rehabilitation of Practical Philosophy", E. Buzzetti (trans.), in: R.C. Bartlett / S.D. Collins (eds.), *Action and Contemplation: Studies in the Moral and Political Thought of Aristotle*, Albany, 3–25.
Vout, C. (2009), "Representing the Emperor", in: A. Feldherr (ed.), *The Cambridge Companion to the Roman Historians*, Cambridge, 261–275.
Vretska, K. (1976), *Sallust: De Catilinae coniuratione I-II*, Heidelberg.
Walbank, F.W. (1957), *A Historical Commentary on Polybius*, vol. 1, Oxford.
Walbank, F.W. (1972), *Polybius*, Sather Classical Lectures 42, Berkeley.
Walbank, F.W. (1974), "Polybius between Greece and Rome", in: E. Gabba (ed.), *Polybe*, Geneva, 1–31.
Walbank, F.W. (1975), "Symploke: Its Role in Polybius' *Histories*", in: *YCS* 24, 197–212.
Walbank, F.W. (1977), "Polybius' Last Ten Books", in: T. Reekmans (ed.), *Historiographica Antiqua*, Leuven, 139–162.
Walbank, F.W. (1979), *A Historical Commentary on Polybius*, vol. 3, Oxford.
Walbank, F.W. (1998), "A Greek Looks At Rome: Polybius VI Revisited", in: *Scripta Classica Israelica* 17, 45–59. [reprinted in Walbank 2002, 277–92.]
Walbank, F.W. (2002), *Polybius, Rome, and the Hellenistic World*, Cambridge.
Walker, A.D. (1993), "*Enargeia* and the Spectator in Greek Historiography", in: *Transactions of the American Philological Association* 123, 353–377.
Walpole, H. (1833), *Letters to Sir Horace Mann*, L. Dover (ed.), 3 vols., London.
Walpole, H. (1843–1844), *Letters to Sir Horace Mann: Concluding Series*, L. Dover (ed.), 4 vols., London.
Walsh, P.G. (1989), *Titi Livi: ab urbe condita libri XXVI–XXVII*, Leipzig.
Walsh, P.G. (1999), *Titi Livi: ab urbe condita libri XXXVI–XL*, Oxford.
Warner, R. (1966) (trans.) *A History of My Times*, London.
Waterfield, R. (1998), *Herodotus: The Histories*, R. Waterfield (trans.), With an Introduction and Notes by C. Dewald, Oxford.
Waters, K.H. (1970), "Cicero, Sallust and Catiline", in: *Historia* 19, 195–215.
Weißenberger, M. (2002), "Das imperium Romanum in den Proömien dreier griechischer Historiker: Polybios, Dionysios von Halikarnassos und Appian", in: *RhM* 145, 262–281.
Welser, C. (2009), "Two didactic strategies at the end of Herodotus' *Histories* (9.108–122)", in: *ClAnt* 28, 359–385.
Wesselmann, K. (2011), *Mythische Strukturen in Herodots Historien*, Berlin / Boston.

Wesselmann, K. (2012), *Mythical Structures in Herodotus' Histories*, Online Publications of the Center of Hellenic Studies, Harvard University: http://chs.harvard.edu/wa/pageR?tn=ArticleWrapper&bdc=12&mn=4146.
Whiston, W. (1737) (trans.), *The Genuine Works of Flavius Josephus the Jewish Historian*, London.
Whiston, W. (1753), *Memoirs of the Life and Writings of William Whiston*, London.
White, H. (1999), *Figural Realism: Studies in the Mimesis Effect*, Baltimore.
Whitmarsh, T. (2001), *Greek Literature and the Roman Empire: The Politics of Imitation*, Oxford.
Wiater, N. (2010), "Speeches and Historical Narrative in Polybius' *Histories*: Approaching Speeches in Polybius", in: Pausch (2010), 67–108.
Wiater, N. (2011a), *The Ideology of Classicism: Language, History, and Identity in Dionysius of Halicarnassus*, Berlin / New York.
Wiater, N. (2011b), "Writing Roman History – Shaping Greek Identity: The ideology of Historiography in Dionysius of Halicarnassus", in Schmitz / Wiater (2011), 61–91.
Wiater, N. (forthcoming), "The Aesthetics of Truth: Narrative and Historical Hermeneutics in Polybius' *Histories*", in: L. Hau / I. Ruffell (eds.), *Truth, Belief and Fictionality in Tragedy and Historiography*. Proceedings of Panel VII of the Celtic Classics Conference, Bordeaux, 5–8 September 2012, London.
Wiater, N. (in preparation), *A Commentary on Polybius III*, Oxford.
Wilcox, D. (1987), *The Measures of Times Past*, Chicago.
Williams, B. (2001), "What Was Wrong with Minos? Thucydides and Historical Time", in: *Representations* 74, 1–18.
Williams, B. (2006), *The Sense of the Past: Essays on the History of Philosophy*, M. Burnyeat (ed.), Princeton NJ.
Winkler, J.J. (1982), "The Mendacity of Kalasiris and the Narrative Strategy of Heliodoros' Aithiopika", in: *Yale Classical Studies* 27, 93-158.
Winkler, J.J. (1990), *The Constraints of Desire: The Anthropology of Sex and Gender in Ancient Greece*, New York.
Wiseman, T.P. (1979), *Clio's Cosmetics: Three Studies in Greco-Roman Literature*, Leicester.
Wohl, V. (2014), "Play of the Improbable: Euripides unlikely *Helen*", in: V. Wohl (ed.), *Probabilities, Hypotheticals and Counterfactuals in Ancient Greek Thought*, Cambridge, 142–159.
Wolf, F.A. (1985) [1795], *Prolegomena to Homer*, A. Grafton / G.W. Most / J.E.G. Zetzel (trans.), Princeton.
Woodman, A.J. (1988), *Rhetoric in Classical Historiography*, London.
Woodman, A.J. (1998), *Tacitus Reviewed*, Oxford.
Woodward, C. (2001), *In Ruins*, New York.
Woodward, C. (2007), *American Ruins*, London.
Wordsworth, C. (1839), *Greece: Pictorial, Descriptive, Historical*, London.
Yardley, J.C. (2000), *Livy: The Dawn of the Roman Empire, Books 31–40*, Oxford.
Yardley, J.C. (2006), *Livy: Hannibal's War, Books 21–30*, Oxford.
Young-Bruehl, E. (1986), "What Thucydides Saw", in: *History and Theory* 25, 1–16.
Young, E. (1949), *The Prophecy of Daniel: A Commentary*, Michigan.
Zangara, A. (2007), *Voir l'histoire: Théories anciennes du récit historique, IIe siècle avant J.-C. – IIe siècle après J.-C.*, Paris.

Zeitlin, F. (1999), "Aristophanes: the Performance of Utopia in the *Ecclesiazousae*", in: S. Goldhill / R. Osborne (eds.), *Performance-culture and Athenian Democracy*, Cambridge, 167–200.

Ziegler, K. (1952), "Polybios", in: *RE* 21.2, 1440–1578.

Notes on Contributors

Emily Baragwanath is Associate Professor of Classics at the University of North Carolina at Chapel Hill. She has research interests in Greek literature and culture, and especially historiography. She is the author of *Motivation and Narrative in Herodotus* (Oxford, 2008), co-author of the Herodotus *Oxford Bibliography Online* and co-editor of *Myth, Truth, and Narrative in Herodotus* (Oxford, 2012) (both with Mathieu de Bakker). Currently she is working on a monograph on Xenophon's representation of women.

Karen Bassi is Professor of Classics and Literature at UC Santa Cruz. Her most recent book, *Traces of the Past: Classics between History and Archaeology*, is forthcoming from the University of Michigan Press. She is currently working on a book titled *Imitating the Dead*, an interdisciplinary study of facing death in Greek tragedy.

Catherine Darbo-Peschanski is Research Director at the CNRS (National Center for Scientific Research) in Paris. She is member of the LAS (Laboratory of Social Anthropology) as a researcher in Historical Anthropology of Ancient Greece. Her research fields are: Greek empirical knowledge (*Historia*); Greek ways of structuring time; Greek politics through the study of relationships between the human body physiology and socio-political groups. Currently she is in charge of the ancient studies programme at the MFO (Maison française d'Oxford)

Paolo Desideri is Professor of Roman History at the University of Florence. Retired since 2011, he continues to research widely in the fields of Greek and Roman historiography, Greek literature in Roman imperial times, and the tradition of the Classics in modern European political thought.

Emily Greenwood is Professor of Classics at Yale University. She is the author of *Thucydides and the Shaping of History* (2006) and *Afro-Greeks: Dialogues Between Anglophone Caribbean Literature and Classics in the Twentieth Century* (2010). She has published widely on ancient Greek historiography and Classical Reception Studies.

Jonas Grethlein holds the Chair in Greek literature at Heidelberg University and currently directs the research group 'Experience and Teleology in Ancient Narrative' funded by the ERC. His recent publications include *The Greeks and their*

Past (CUP 2010) and *Experience and Teleology in Ancient Historiography* (CUP 2013).

Antonis Liakos is historian, Professor Emeritus at the University of Athens. He is managing editor of the historical review *Historein*, and chair of the Board of the International Commission for History and Theory of Historiography (2010 – 2015). His recent work *Apokalypse, Historia, Utopia* (2012) examines transformations of historical consciousness in Western historiography.

Alexandra Lianeri is Assistant Professor in Greek literature at the Aristotle University of Thessaloniki. She is working on a monograph on the conceptual history of *dēmokratia* and is the editor of *The Western Time of Ancient History: Historiographical Encounters with the Greek and Roman Pasts* (Cambridge, 2011) and coeditor of *Translation and the Classic* (Oxford, 2008). She has published on the history of political thought, ancient Greek historiography and classical reception studies.

Nikos Miltsios earned his PhD in Classics at the Aristotle University of Thessaloniki in 2010. His research concentrates on Greek historiography, with a special focus on its narrative components. He has published *The Shaping of Narrative in Polybius* (2013) and a series of articles on Herodotus, Thucydides and Polybius.

Oswyn Murray is emeritus Fellow of Balliol College, Oxford. His most recent book is a volume edited with Tim Cornell, *The Legacy of Arnaldo Momigliano* (Warburg Institute Colloquia 25, 2015). He is currently finishing a work on the Greek symposion.

Dennis Pausch is Professor of Latin at Dresden University of Technology. He wrote his PhD (*Biographie und Bildungskultur: Personendarstellungen bei Plinius dem Jüngeren, Gellius und Sueton*, 2004) and his second book (*Livius und der Leser: Narrative Strukturen in Ab Urbe Condita*, 2011), which was awarded the Bruno Snell Prize of the Mommsen-Gesellschaft in 2011, at Gießen University and during his research stay in Edinburgh as Feodor Lynen Fellow of the Alexander von Humboldt Foundation. After that, he taught Latin at Regensburg University, before taking over the chair of Latin Literature at Dresden in 2014.

Christopher Pelling is Regius Professor Emeritus of Greek at Oxford University. He has published extensively on Greek historiography and biography; his most recent books are a commentary on Plutarch's *Life of Caesar* (Oxford, 2011) and, with Maria Wyke, *Twelve Voices from Greece and Rome: Ancient Ideas for*

Modern Times (Oxford, 2014). He is now working with Simon Hornblower on a commentary on Herodotus 6 in the Cambridge Green-and-Yellow series.

Luke Pitcher is Fellow and Tutor in Classics at Somerville College, Oxford. He is the author of *Writing Ancient History: An Introduction to Classical Historiography* (London, 2009) and has edited several entries for *Brill's New Jacoby*. He is working on a monograph about Appian.

Tim Rood is Professor of Greek Literature at the University of Oxford, where he is the Dorothea Gray Fellow and Tutor in Classics at St Hugh's College. His research focuses on Greek historiography and its reception. He is the author of *Thucydides: Narrative and Explanation* (1998) and of two books on the reception of Xenophon's *Anabasis: The Sea! The Sea! The Shout of the Ten Thousand in the Modern Imagination* (2004) and *American Anabasis: Xenophon and the Idea of America from the Mexican War to Iraq* (2010).

Melina Tamiolaki is Assistant Professor in Classics at the University of Crete. She has research interests in Greek historiography, Greek political thought and the theory of history. She is the author of *Liberté et esclavage chez les historiens grecs classiques*, Paris, PUPS 2010 (awarded with the Prix Zappas of the Association des Etudes grecques de Paris, 2011), co-editor (with Antonis Tsakmakis) of *Thucydides Between History and Literature*, Berlin, Walter de Gruyter 2013 and editor of *Comic Wreath. New Trends in the Study of Ancient Greek Comedy*, Rethymnon, Editions of the Facuty of Philosophy of the University of Crete, 2014 (in modern Greek).

Antonis Tsakmakis is Associate Professor of Greek in the Department of Classical Studies and Philosophy (Head since 2013), University of Cyprus. His research interests are Greek historiography, Old comedy, the sophistic movement (Protagoras), Archaic poetry, Greek stylistics, Greek particles, The reception of antiquity in modern times, The teaching of Greek in Secondary Education. He is the author of *Thukydides über die Vergangenheit*, Tübingen 1995 and co-editor of *Brill's Companion to Thucydides, Mnemosyne Suppements*, Leyden: Brill 2006, and *Thucydides between History and Literature*, Berlin – New York 2013. Recently he has completed a new series of textbooks for teaching Greek in High School. His current research projects include Aristophanes' *Thesmophoriazusae*, Euripides' *Suppliant Women* and Herodotus.

Aviezer Tucker is a philosopher of historiography. He authored *Our Knowledge of the Past: A Philosophy of Historiography* (Cambridge University Press 2004) and edited *The Blackwell Companion to the Philosophy of History and Historiography* (Wiley-Blackwell 2009). He is working now on a book project about the metaphysics and epistemology of origins. He lives in Cambridge MA and Prague Czech Republic.

Nicolas Wiater (Dr. phil. Bonn 2008) is lecturer in Classics at the University of St Andrews. His major publications include a monograph on Dionysius of Halicarnassus' classicism (*The Ideology of Classicism. Language, History, and Identity in Dionysius of Halicarnassus*, Berlin 2011), a new German translation with commentary of Dionysius' Roman Antiquities (vol. 1: Stuttgart 2014) and the volume *The Struggle for Identity. Greeks and their Past in the First Century BCE*, which he co-edited with Thomas A. Schmitz (Stuttgart 2011). He is currently working on a new commentary on the third book of Polybius' Histories for Oxford University Press, the second volume of his commented translation of the Roman Antiquities and a narratological and historical study of the Roman-Carthaginian Treaties in the context of Polybius' explanation of the causes of the Hannibalic War (*Histories* 3.6–33).

Katharina Wesselmann gained her doctorate from Basel Unversity in 2010 and continued to work there as a postdoctoral fellow. Her PhD thesis was published in 2011 as *Mythische Erzählstrukturen in Herodots Historien*. Currently, she is working on a commentary on *Iliad* 7. Her research interests include historiography, early Greek epic, myth, narratology, and didactics of Ancient Languages.

Index

accuracy (historical) / ἀκρίβεια   94, 108, 154, 163, 227–229, 234, 358
ambiguity   243, 250, 260–263
Ammianus Marcellinus   357
anacyclosis   142ff, 186
analogy   75, 87, 90, 92, 106, 183f., 193, 219f., 345f., 349, 351
annals, annalistic   30, 61, 74f., 379
anticipation   3f., 10, 21, 26, 28, 32, 41, 46f., 49, 73, 99, 102–104, 110, 162, 166, 202, 218, 258, 260f., 317, 321, 326f., 339–341, 350, 353, 357, 359
Antiochus III   147, 315, 324
antiquity (concept of)   3f., 7, 11–13, 29, 39, 44, 46–53, 73, 164f., 221, 267, 281, 294f., 299f., 307, 329f., 331, 333–338, 342f., 345, 357, 364, 386f., 391
Appian   3, 38f., 257f., 281–292, 345
Aratus   149, 179
Aristotle   15–17, 32, 64, 89f., 111, 167, 177–180, 185, 190, 218, 220, 247
– A. on history   15–17, 64, 177f., 185, 190, 218, 220
– A., *Poetics*   15, 32ff.,177, 218, 247
– A., *Rhetoric*   89–90
asymmetry   24, 60, 75, 294
– temporal a.   24, 60, 75
Athens   7, 9, 11, 22, 24, 36, 49, 62, 67, 71f., 76, 87–89, 96, 105, 108f., 111, 120, 123, 127, 136f., 161, 183f., 201, 203, 209, 225f., 230, 232f., 236f., 239, 241, 258, 285, 294, 338, 340–350, 353–359, 387
– democracy of A.   63, 161, 345–6, 387, 389f.
author   2, 14, 18, 26, 38, 52, 61, 68, 80f., 83, 91f., 94f., 101–104, 106, 112–114, 116, 123, 151f., 161, 163, 187, 189–191, 198f., 229, 251–253, 276, 282, 290, 297, 299, 314, 320, 341f., 345, 350, 353, 357f., 365, 370, 373, 380, 382, 386f., 392
authorial   13f., 29, 42, 70, 79, 94f., 102, 104f., 120, 125, 130, 135f., 243f., 288

authorisation   12, 30–31, 44, 375
autotelēs / αὐτοτελής   248

Bakhtin, M.   3, 13–14
Bank of England   347
Basnage, J.   392, 394
beginning   9, 37, 63f., 67f., 70f., 85, 89, 92f., 98, 101f., 104f., 111, 115, 136f., 153, 155, 159, 172, 178–180, 187, 191, 199, 203, 206, 208, 210, 216f., 224, 233, 235, 237–239, 243–250, 252, 254, 256f., 261, 270, 273–275, 282, 285f., 289, 291, 297f., 311, 316, 318, 324, 335, 338, 388, 398
Berlin, I.   188, 371, 377, 390
Bevernage, B.   7, 11, 342
Bible   335, 372–375, 378, 392
biblical criticism   50, 371, 374f., 378, 381f.
Biddle, N.   345f.
body metaphor   21, 253–255, 367
Boeckh, A.   394
Boileau, N.   387
Bopp, F.   376–378
British Museum   353
Brittain, V.   83–85
Bruni, L.   42–44
Burke, E.   12, 51, 386
Burke, P.   12, 51

Canfora, L.   105
Capua   146, 315f., 322
Carr, D.   219
Carthage / Carthaginians   29, 37, 64, 68–73, 148, 152, 170–172, 244, 249–264, 287, 291, 311, 314, 319, 345, 349
character   3, 6, 24, 40, 59, 61, 76, 120f., 123–125, 128, 132–135, 143–147, 153f., 160f., 165, 178, 184f., 188f., 192, 195f., 199f., 204, 207–210, 229, 234–236, 239, 241, 249f., 261, 263, 275, 279, 282, 284–287, 292–294, 301,

314, 316, 325 f., 339, 342, 356, 379, 386, 396
– c. and psychology   121
Chateaubriand, F.-R. de   49, 342–344
Christianity   386, 388, 390–392
chronos / χρόνος   32, 177–180, 222 (cf. time)
– c. and probabilities   26, 124, 129, 365 ff.
Cicero   51, 68 f., 72 f., 159–161, 275, 296, 379
– C., *De re publica*   159 f.
classical philology   50, 374 f., 378, 380 f.
Claudius Marcellus, M.   149, 321, 324
Cleon   88, 234
closure   17, 20, 32 f., 36 f., 47, 60, 66 f., 132, 177, 181, 183 f., 187, 189, 193, 243 f., 257
– deferred c.   37, 63, 132, 243, 250
– logic of c.   177 f.
Comparative Linguistics   50, 376–378, 380 f.
Constant, B.   18, 22, 165, 168, 208, 212, 233 f., 274, 306, 389
contingency   16, 24, 34 f., 39, 43, 76, 91, 127, 136, 147, 181, 221, 244, 252, 256 f., 260, 263, 288 f., 291
continuity   3, 26, 32 f., 38, 104, 106, 185, 207, 212, 245 f., 281, 295, 345, 353, 356 f., 390, 394
continuous history   26, 110, 116, 295, 392
– vs. war monograph   105
Cornelius Scipio, P.   143, 148, 152, 324
cosmology   271
counterfactual history   29, 200
– c. h. and 'if not' scenarios   202 f.
Crassus, M.L.   161
Croesus   79, 107, 115, 128, 137, 139, 182 f., 196–198, 201, 204, 211, 224, 286
cycle   67, 178, 185 f., 190, 206, 208–210, 261, 264, 276, 356
– c. as a universal pattern   208
cyclicality   208 f.
Cyrus   79, 113, 120, 122–124, 127, 129–132, 135, 137–139, 167, 183, 197, 201, 204 f., 207 f., 210, 223, 286, 289, 299

Davis, K.   51
de Certeau, M.   5, 31
de Jong, I.J.F.   5, 79
Delphi   111, 113, 115, 125, 127, 277, 286
democracy   53, 63, 117, 142, 161, 167, 186 f., 198, 200, 219, 346, 387–390, 399
Demosthenes   88–91
Derrida, J.   13, 28, 32
Descartes, R.   337
Detienne, M.   41
determination   8, 31, 107, 276
determinism   251
difference
– d. between past, present and future   4, 12, 27–28, 37–38, 43, 45 f., 51–52
– d. of historical perspective   43 f., 101 f., 120, 143, 152, 157, 178 f., 207, 267, 353, 361 f., 387, 390
– temporal d.   43 f., 342, 353, 359–360, 390
digression   108, 110 f., 114–116, 317, 326
Diodorus   3, 5, 112, 116, 179, 257 f., 383
Diodotus   88
Dionysius of Halicarnassus   28, 62, 155, 312, 331, 336
divination, divine, the   124, 196, 271, 273, 294
Dodwell, E.   342–344
Doré, G.   339, 341
Droysen, J.G.   45
Dunkel, G.E.   221–223
Dunn, F.   6, 9 f., 229, 233, 294, 359

Echinades   339
Elmes, J.   347
empires, succession of   47–48, 187, 259 f., 331–338
ending   28, 36 f., 60–62, 64, 66 f., 96, 101, 116, 195, 209, 243 f., 247–250, 257, 263, 295, 376, 388
Epaminondas   146 f., 275
epistemology   136, 366
– Bayesian e.   366
– e. of testimony   368
eschatology   11, 48, 331
ethics   36

Index — 437

Eurocentric (time)   46, 335
Eustace, Rev. J.   344f.
exemplarity   11, 20, 34, 40f., 73f., 105, 164, 217, 225, 239, 290, 342, 360
expectation   5, 11, 18f., 39, 41, 44, 75f., 83, 102, 113, 123, 132f., 145, 201, 207, 212, 258, 273, 286, 288f., 292, 299, 316, 323, 333, 339, 364
experience   3, 5f., 12, 16f., 24, 29, 32, 36f., 45, 60f., 75f., 80, 83, 93f., 106, 109, 116, 120, 127, 136, 144f., 150f., 160f., 207, 212, 251, 256f., 268, 273, 292f., 301, 331f., 344, 363, 388

Fasolt, C.   55
fate   33f., 55, 112, 148, 157, 189–192, 196–199, 206f., 209f., 213, 237, 239f., 264, 324, 340, 344, 350, 354, 385
Ferrario, S.B.   22, 119
Finley, M.   215, 355
foreknowledge   3, 10, 15, 29f., 40
foresight   22, 27f., 88, 99, 141f., 146f., 150, 152, 159–161, 173, 260, 288, 326
forethought (πρόνοια)   21f., 193
Fornara, C.   6f., 67
fortune   3f., 8, 38, 43, 63, 65, 103, 135, 147–149, 151f., 171f., 185, 191–193, 201, 204, 208–210, 236, 254, 256, 258, 260, 262f., 269f., 275f., 291, 295f., 325, 342, 355
future   1–5, 7–49, 51–54, 57, 59–61, 65, 72–77, 79–100, 102–107, 109f., 116, 119–139, 141–145, 147f., 150, 153f., 156–164, 166–168, 170, 173, 175, 177, 180f., 183–188, 190, 193, 195–204, 207f., 210, 212–216, 218–237, 239–241, 243–246, 248, 250–253, 255, 257–264, 267f., 272–274, 276–279, 281f., 284f., 287f., 290–304, 306f., 309, 311–314, 316–318, 320f., 323–327, 329, 331, 338–345, 347–360, 362f., 385, 388, 391, 396, 398
– cultures of the f.   12
– diegetic f.   25, 79, 81, 83, 85, 87, 97
– extradiegetic f.   202f.
– fear of the f.   114, 197, 236, 320
– ideal v. actual f.   26, 132ff.
– intradiegetic f.   195, 202, 205
– planning the f.   279, 323
– plural f.   53
– polyphonic f.   3, 8, 13f., 16, 20f., 31, 44, 320
– probable v. actual f.   26, 67, 129f.
– real v. unreal f.   25, 79f.,
future past   24, 59–61, 65f., 68, 73, 75–77, 80, 218, 246, 259, 294, 364
futurity   25, 82, 91, 95–97, 99f., 244, 252f., 281

Gandy, J.   341
genealogy   48, 53, 378
Genette, G.   8, 19, 25, 31
genre   5f., 23–25, 33, 40, 46, 51, 82, 97, 99, 102, 119, 134, 136, 139, 178, 214, 218, 220, 229, 296, 303, 307, 316, 341
Geschichte   45, 278, 373, 397
Gibbon, E.   351, 357, 386, 394
Gillies, J.   46
Gomme, A.   86f., 226–230, 235, 237–240, 358
Graetz, H.   53, 397–399
Grafton, A.   336f., 365, 369–371, 374f., 378–380, 383
Grimm, J.   205, 291, 376, 378
Grote, G.   51, 354, 387

Hammond, M.   88, 342
Hannibal   143f., 146f., 149, 154, 245, 255, 286, 315, 317–321, 324f.
Hartog, F.   7, 52, 204, 294, 342, 343, 349
Hawthorn, G.   41
Hebraism   53, 397
Hector   261, 342
hegemony   43, 64f., 77, 107, 116f., 183, 253, 388
Hellenism   53, 397
Herodotus   3–7, 24, 26, 31–35, 48, 61, 66–68, 76, 79, 82, 92, 95f., 100f., 103f., 107, 112f., 115f., 119–122, 128f., 136–138, 167, 179, 181–184, 195–212, 214, 222–224, 229f., 233, 239, 258, 285f., 289, 295, 299, 331, 340, 355, 358, 363, 383
Hind, T.   46

Hippocratic corpus 91 f.
historia 2–6, 8, 10, 12 f., 17, 19, 23–27, 29–32, 35–37, 39–42, 44–46, 49–52, 54, 59–61, 63 f., 66–68, 75–77, 79 f., 85, 100 f., 103–110, 113–116, 119, 145, 153, 163, 173, 177–179, 215, 217 f., 220 f., 225, 228, 233–235, 239–241, 243, 246, 281 f., 296 f., 301–306, 311 f., 316, 321, 323, 334 f., 342, 345, 347, 361–365, 371, 382 f., 391, 394, 396
– *h. magistra vitae* 4, 44 f., 49–51, 221, 296, 342, 362, 364
– *h. perpetua* 36, 243
– h. rerum gestarum 44 f., 75, 77, 246
Historie 2, 10, 27 f., 33, 35, 37 f., 41, 43–47, 51, 53, 61, 64–68, 79, 82, 92, 95 f., 120, 141–143, 145, 154 f., 182, 195, 197–199, 201–213, 222–224, 230, 233, 240, 243–254, 256–258, 260, 263, 265, 267, 277, 282, 292, 312, 314, 323, 326 f., 376, 380, 383, 385, 394, 397 f.
historiography 1–11, 13 f., 19 f., 24–27, 30 f., 33, 36, 40 f., 44–46, 49–52, 54, 57, 59–63, 65 f., 68, 70, 74–77, 79–82, 92, 97, 99–107, 109, 115, 119 f., 137 f., 152, 155, 164, 177, 193, 197, 213 f., 220 f., 251, 256, 260, 277, 279, 282 f., 285, 289, 293 f., 296 f., 299–301, 305–307, 311–314, 316, 321, 323, 327, 338, 360–367, 371–373, 375, 378, 380–383, 385 f., 391, 398
– h. and medicine 82, 91
– poetics of h. 5, 20 f., 23–26, 30, 41, 44, 46, 54, 57, 60, 79
– scientific h. 5, 50–54, 91, 238, 260, 361, 364 f., 376, 378, 383, 394–396
Homer 120, 165, 170, 212, 217, 257 f., 300, 340 f., 351, 358, 375 f.
– H., *Iliad* 133, 170, 179 f., 217 f., 221 f., 224, 232, 257, 261, 263, 341, 374–376
hope / ἐλπίς 11, 43, 59, 66, 80 f., 84, 86, 96, 100, 106, 126, 132, 138, 145, 148, 159, 183, 213, 218, 236, 274, 279, 288–292, 296, 305, 316, 324, 352, 357
Hornblower, S. 5, 10, 18, 76, 79, 226 f., 230, 232, 235, 258, 261, 303, 340, 364, 383
Hughes, T.S. 49, 344 f., 348

human nature 16 f., 32, 49, 81, 91, 137, 145, 165, 181, 184 f., 193, 207, 233 f., 281, 302, 342, 359 f.

Ianziti, G. 42–43
immediacy 29, 164, 166, 168 f.
imperialism 52 f., 171, 203, 357, 385–388, 399
– i. and democracy 387 f., 390, 399
infinity 32, 36, 181, 189 f., 192 f.
invisibility 35 f., 216, 225, 232–234, 239, 241
irony 48, 127, 196, 227 f., 236, 241, 252, 319, 334, 352
– tragic i. 6, 15, 21–23, 42, 84, 112, 178, 197, 319

Jason of Pherae 108, 111
Jerrold, B. 339
Josephus 52, 385, 391–394, 396
– *Jewish Antiquities* 52, 391
– translator: Bradshaw, T. 393
– translator: L'Estrange, R. 391
– translator: Lodge, T. 391
– translator: Maynard, G.H. 392–393
– translator: Whiston, W. 391–393
Judaism 53, 372, 390–393, 395, 397

Kallett, L. 81, 91
Kant, I. 45, 361
Kathleen, K. 51
kleos / κλέος 358
– κ. ἄφθιτον 2
knowledge 3, 5, 8, 16, 18–21, 23–25, 27–30, 32, 36, 40–44, 46–48, 50 f., 54, 79, 84 f., 87, 89–94, 97, 102, 104, 107, 109, 120–122, 127 f., 139, 141–145, 149 f., 153, 184, 188, 196, 208, 210, 217, 228, 235, 249, 251, 254, 268, 277, 279, 329, 336, 340, 346, 351, 358, 361 f., 364–368, 370 f., 375 f., 383 f., 395
– k. from multiple evidence 367
– limits of k. 23, 27, 35, 96, 216, 226 f., 231, 237
Koselleck, R. 7, 12, 24, 40, 44 f., 51 f., 60, 68, 80, 207, 218–221, 293, 297, 301, 333, 342, 345, 356, 359, 362, 364

Index — **439**

Lakatos, I.   383
Lateiner, D.   198
leader   27, 43, 88, 97, 111, 115f., 120–124, 126, 134f., 138f., 150, 166, 181, 185–187, 210, 217, 251, 262, 269, 288, 290, 299, 325f., 340
– ideal l.   115–117, 120, 134f.
leadership   43, 96, 120, 129, 135, 144, 319
legibility   35, 215, 239, 241
Leonidas   343
liberty   52, 187, 269, 350, 385–390, 399
Livy   46f., 156f., 159, 162–164, 168, 290, 311–327, 343f.
Lloyd, G.E.R.   5, 7
logos   32, 177–180, 196, 205, 216, 223
– vs. *chronos*   177
Longinus   387
– on the sublime   387
Loraux, N.   2, 6, 230
Lorenz, C.   7, 11, 342
Lucian   39f., 59, 119, 293, 296–307
– *De Historia Conscribenda*   39, 296f., 299, 303, 305f.

Macaulay, T.B.   49, 339, 341, 343, 351f., 354, 356f.
Maier, F.K.   147, 150, 247, 251, 256, 291, 320
Mann, H.   77, 106, 109, 138, 143, 146, 187, 192, 204, 220, 232, 251, 278, 290, 297, 327, 340, 343, 350, 352, 365, 384, 392, 396
Mantinea (battle of)   106ff., 116
Marcellus   149f., 322, 325, 344, 352
Marincola, J.   6, 20f., 63, 76, 96, 119, 145, 155, 164f., 207, 227, 247, 260, 295, 316, 318
Meier, C.   6f., 359
Melanchthon, P.   334
mellonta / μέλλοντα   88, 236, 241
metaphor   35, 60, 64, 68, 95, 121, 209, 221, 223–225, 229–231, 233, 237, 239, 253–255, 270, 329, 363
microhistory   119
Milman, H. H.   53, 394–396
Mitford, W.   46, 351, 354

modernity   4, 12, 20, 27, 34, 44f., 47–49, 51f., 164, 221, 293, 335, 337f., 359f.
Momigliano, A.   10, 16f., 34, 48, 51, 54, 209, 331, 379f., 396
monologic   14, 20, 41, 44f. 54
Montesquieu, C.-L. de S.   342, 351, 386f.
moral law   11
Morrison, J.   7, 18, 81, 91, 235f.
motivation   124, 131, 287, 357, 364, 388
Mudie, R.   348
Müller, C.O.   394
multiperspectivity   320
Mycenae   225f., 231, 340, 343, 354–356, 359
Mynott, J.   1, 22, 80, 88, 339

Napoleonic Wars   347
narrative   2–6, 8–11, 13, 17–20, 22–32, 34–37, 39–47, 51f., 59–63, 66–68, 70f., 73, 75f., 79–81, 83, 85, 91, 96–98, 100–106, 108–111, 113, 115f., 119–121, 124, 126, 129f., 132f., 136–138, 141, 145, 153, 155f., 159–163, 171, 177–180, 182–184, 195f., 202–207, 212, 215f., 218–221, 223, 229, 233–238, 243–257, 261, 264f., 281–286, 288, 290–292, 294, 311–314, 316, 320f., 323–325, 327, 334f., 337, 341, 349, 357, 365, 370, 376, 380f., 391f., 394, 396–399
– n. and ethics   189, 193
– n. anticipation   26, 102, 104, 110
– historical n.   2, 6, 8, 11, 26, 29, 35, 37, 39, 44, 51–52, 59, 79–81, 91, 101, 103, 119f., 229, 235, 245–250, 256, 337, 391, 399
– n. pattern   6, 33–34, 49, 91, 124, 129, 137, 145, 147, 153, 164, 185, 204–210, 212–214, 259f., 272, 285, 313–314, 350, 359, 398
narratology   5, 76, 80, 218, 312
narrator   5, 8f., 18f., 28, 46f., 77, 83, 85, 97, 102, 113, 125, 130, 138f., 141, 195f., 200f., 208, 212, 217, 229, 245, 248, 250, 253, 255, 259f., 283f., 287–290, 292, 314–317, 322–325, 327, 339, 341

necessity   4, 11, 28, 31, 38, 41f., 130, 187, 203, 270f., 348, 390
Nestor   143, 341
New Zealand   339, 341, 351, 356f.
Nicias   20–23, 30, 100, 234–236
Nicolai, R.   87, 119, 139
Niebuhr, B.G.   361, 378–380, 394
Nietzsche, F.   34f., 38, 276–279
Nineveh   203, 353

Oakeshott, M.   80f.
Ober, J.   22, 226, 228–231, 233f., 240, 358
oikoumenē   188, 313
open-endedness   37, 251
openness   13, 37f., 77, 91, 172, 183, 243f., 252, 256, 359f.
opissō / ὀπίσσω   222–224
oracles   10, 100, 113, 182f., 196f., 200f., 286f., 293f.
Ozymandias   351

Parry, A.   229, 340
Patroclus   206, 341
pattern   6f., 33–34, 49, 91, 97, 124, 129, 137, 142, 145, 147, 153, 164f., 185, 195, 199, 204–214, 259–261, 272, 276, 285, 313–314, 350, 359, 398 (see also: narrative pattern)
Pausanias   343
Pericles   62, 103, 113, 121, 137, 226, 237, 275, 277, 294f., 299, 354, 357f.
permanence   33, 49, 193, 195, 207, 214
Perseus of Macedon   322, 325
philia / φιλία   122–124
Philip of Macedon   89, 316
picturesque   345, 352
piracy   356f.
Pisistratus   115, 375
Plato   16, 97–99, 102, 159, 167, 185, 190, 218, 275f., 293, 363, 389
– P., *Apology*   98f., 139
– P., *Laws*   159, 218
– P. on afterlife   97
– P., *Phaedo*   97
– P., *Theaetetus*   16, 98, 102
plausibility   29, 164, 166, 168f., 352

plurality   34, 38
– p. of worlds   279
Plutarch   3, 32f., 37f., 62, 111, 119, 157, 160, 165, 167, 188–193, 228, 267–279, 305, 383
– P. and cosmology   271
– Biographies   37, 267f., 274, 276f., 279
– Delphic Dialogues   271, 278
Pocock, J.G.A.   43, 333, 353
poetics   5, 15, 20, 23, 25, 29–32, 36, 40, 47, 54, 177, 218, 247
poiesis   17, 20f., 30–32, 35
polis   23, 63, 89f., 100, 338
politics   51, 54, 67, 76, 137, 144f., 251f., 267
Polybius   3, 5, 24, 28f., 32, 36f., 46–48, 59, 61, 63–66, 68, 70, 73, 75–77, 103, 141–155, 160, 166f., 170–172, 179–181, 185–187, 193, 243–265, 281f., 291f., 296, 304, 312–318, 320f., 323, 326f.
polyphony   3, 13f., 19, 25, 29f., 46f., 53f., 73
portents   129, 288, 321
possibility   3, 11, 15, 28, 30, 35, 45, 120f., 127f., 134, 139, 179, 198, 200f., 219, 226, 231, 233, 240f., 244, 249f., 257, 262f., 287, 289, 291, 300, 356f., 388, 392, 395
posterity   6, 29, 39, 74, 99, 155f., 170f., 173, 293, 295–299, 302f., 305–307, 346, 397
practical past   80, 82, 253
praxis   20f., 25, 30–33, 36, 54, 178, 191
predicting, prediction   47, 123, 132, 136, 142, 144, 201, 240, 287f., 296
premodern   4, 44
present   2–7, 9–16, 21–23, 25–29, 31–34, 36, 38f., 41f., 45, 49, 51–54, 60, 63, 71f., 74f., 79–82, 84, 86, 88–92, 94, 97, 99f., 109, 112, 114–116, 121, 126, 129, 132, 135, 138f., 145f., 148, 152, 156, 165, 171, 173, 179, 184f., 189, 193, 200, 204, 207, 209, 213f., 216–228, 230f., 233f., 239f., 248, 250f., 253, 260, 263, 267–269, 272–275, 278f., 281–284, 287, 292–295, 298–

Index — 441

300, 302f., 305–307, 313f., 331–334, 338f., 343, 345, 347–349, 351, 353, 355–359, 361, 363f., 366f., 374, 376, 381, 383, 385, 387, 392f.
Priam   170, 257, 342
probability, probable   16–18, 22, 27, 165, 366–368, 371f., 381
proem   29, 46, 64, 67, 70, 95, 101f., 104f., 109f., 156, 171, 173, 202, 212, 217, 224, 282f., 295, 313, 316f.
prolepsis   9, 18, 25, 39, 79, 95, 97, 101, 115, 136, 196, 203, 226, 261, 284, 292, 314–315
pronoia / πρόνοια   21, 149, 152, 190–192, 222
prossō / πρόσσω   221–222

Raaflaub, K.   7, 67, 281, 340
Rancière, J.   5, 23, 25, 30, 79
Ranke, L. von   50, 221, 306, 341, 351, 361–367, 370–372, 378, 380–383
reader   2–4, 6, 8–10, 13f., 18f., 21, 24, 26–29, 35–38, 40–42, 45, 47, 60, 62, 64f., 67, 70, 81f., 86–91, 94f., 97, 102–105, 108–114, 116, 119f., 130, 132, 136–139, 141f., 145, 147f., 151, 153–156, 166, 170, 173, 195–197, 201, 204, 206, 208, 212, 215, 223, 226, 228, 230–232, 235, 237–239, 243–245, 249, 251–256, 259–264, 268, 275, 277, 291, 295, 297, 304, 313f., 316f., 319–321, 323f., 326f., 349, 382, 392
– r. as participant   239
– r. as spectator   239
– r. response   103, 137, 173, 244, 252, 254, 281
regime (of historicity)   49, 52, 342
repetition, repetitiveness   13, 33f., 38, 184f., 204, 207, 209–212, 288, 302
res gestae (and *historia rerum gestarum*)   44f., 75, 77, 246
Ricoeur, P.   2, 5f., 34, 40, 80
Riegl, A.   215f.
Robert, H.   34, 124, 341, 348, 350, 393
Rollin, C.   46
Roma aeterna   29, 157, 388

Rome   29, 37, 52, 59, 64–66, 69–73, 75, 77, 146, 148, 155–159, 162, 166–172, 188, 244, 246, 249f., 252, 259–262, 264, 269f., 276, 279, 283, 286f., 312–315, 317–323, 326f., 329, 339, 344f., 352, 379f., 382, 385f., 391, 395
Rorty, R.   252
Rossetti, D.G.   353
Rothschild, L. de   393
Rubens, P.P.   47–48, 329f.
ruins   36, 49, 225–227, 230, 232, 241, 258, 339–360

Sallust   24, 61, 66, 68–74, 77, 158, 168, 248, 281f., 286f., 312
Second Punic War   163, 344
Shakespeare, W.   391
Shelley, P.B.   351
Sherman, W.T.   345
singularity   13, 44–45
skopein/σκοπεῖν   88, 229–231, 233
Smith, H.   16, 34, 351f., 399
Soane, J.   347, 352f.
Socrates   97–99, 123–125, 127, 130, 138f.
Sourvinou-Inwood, C.   205
space   41, 44, 73, 98, 121, 166, 189, 193, 251, 279, 283, 291, 302, 333, 336–337, 372
spatialisation   32, 187–188
Sparta   36, 41, 43, 49, 111f., 123–125, 135, 146f., 161, 172, 197, 211, 225f., 236, 240f., 258, 340–343, 345–347, 353–359
speech   14, 18–20, 22, 29f., 46, 62, 68–74, 88–91, 99, 111, 115f., 122, 128, 130f., 135, 159, 162, 168, 172, 181, 198, 201f., 208, 210, 217, 220, 232–237, 240f., 316–318, 320f., 339, 354, 364, 380, 385, 393
Stanyan, T.   46
stasis   105, 108, 168, 234
St Paul's Cathedral   352
Strabo   155, 188, 316, 343
strategy   47, 113, 119, 121, 138, 145, 316, 321, 323–325
Strawberry Hill   352

succession 6, 26, 46–48, 179–181, 187, 224, 259, 261, 331, 333–336, 338
suspense 103, 136, 145, 317, 321–323, 325–327
symplokē / συμπλοκή 247 253
Syracuse 102f., 239, 321, 344, 348, 383

Tacitus 24, 30, 61, 74–77, 173, 281f.
tarachē (kai kinēsis) / ταραχή (καὶ κίνησις) 37, 41, 65, 96, 107, 137, 243, 249f., 257, 264
technē / τέχνη 82, 92–93, 99
technologies of knowledge 25, 81f.
teleological 5, 24, 27f., 61–63, 66, 80, 255, 313, 363f.
teleology 5, 61f., 69f., 76, 80, 244, 255f., 294, 363
telesiourgema / τελεσιούργημα 249, 263
telos / τέλος 7, 10, 24f., 37, 41, 47, 53, 60f., 137, 153, 177–178, 248–250, 302
temporality 3f., 20f., 97f., 119, 177f., 195, 207, 212f., 256, 334f. 338
– cyclical t. 44, 46, 48f., 54, 142, 209, 251
– divine t. 10, 15, 32f., 86, 124–129, 182f., 190, 193, 230, 268, 283f., 288, 322, 338, 390, 395, 397
– elusive t. 2, 20f., 248
– mythical t. 10, 33f., 99, 195, 202, 204–207, 210, 212, 214, 300, 343, 378, 381
– teleological t. 5, 24, 27f., 61–63, 66, 80, 255, 313, 363f.
testimony 83–85, 366–369, 379, 381, 383, 394
Themistocles 87f., 113, 120f., 137, 203, 206, 235, 274, 277
Third Punic War 345
Thomas, R. 9, 49, 82, 94, 233f., 335f., 344, 348, 355, 360, 391, 393
Thucydides 1–4, 9–11, 13–27, 30, 32, 35, 39, 41, 49f., 59, 61–63, 66, 76, 80–83, 85–91, 94–96, 98, 100–107, 109f., 113–116, 121, 137f., 158, 165f., 168, 170, 179–181, 184f., 215, 221f., 225–234, 236–241, 258, 281, 285, 294–297, 299f., 302f., 306, 313, 333, 339–343, 346–348, 350, 353–366, 380, 383
– Archaeology 215f., 225, 228, 230, 339, 356f., 359
– Melian Dialogue 236f.
– Mytilene Debate 88, 237
– Sicilian Debate 20f., 62, 103, 234f.
time
– t. and death 48, 276, 329, 338
– cyclical t. 20, 44 46f., 54, 142, 190, 208f, 251
– eschatological t. 11
– exemplary t. 20, 34, 40, 44, 46f., 73–74, 225, 290, 342, 360
– future-oriented t. 14, 20, 23f., 44, 46, 81f., 91, 357
– linear t. 44f., 71, 187, 214, 219, 237, 267, 312, 314, 330f.
– monologic t. 20, 41f.
– plurality of t. 12, 14, 38, 207, 271f.
– polyphonic t. 3, 8, 13f. 44f., 45, 320, 327
– progressive t. 11, 33, 38, 46, 119, 195, 283
tragedy 5f., 9, 21, 23, 34f., 42, 177f., 197, 278
translation 13, 16, 42, 53, 60, 79f., 88, 98, 119, 141, 158, 188, 198, 213, 227, 233, 239, 244, 269, 293, 302, 311, 315, 317–320, 322–325, 339, 355, 391–394, 397
Trojan War 225, 340, 355f., 358
tychē / τύχη / fortune 3–4, 8, 38, 43, 63–65, 103, 112, 125, 135, 144f, 151–152, 171–172, 185, 191–193, 198, 201, 204, 208f., 236, 247, 250, 254, 256–260, 262f., 268f., 284, 291, 295f., 325, 342, 355

uncertainty 1, 4, 16, 18, 26, 28, 42, 83, 88, 96f., 106, 113f., 127f., 135–137, 142, 147, 150, 153, 233, 244, 247, 251, 259–261, 294, 325
unexpectedness 240, 254, 290
unity 3, 14, 19, 22f., 37, 54, 234, 243, 246–248, 255

Vernant, J.-P.   21, 205, 390
virtue   5, 74, 133, 138 f., 144, 168, 172, 185, 237, 270, 275 f., 290, 326, 346, 348, 386
visibility   35 f., 215, 225, 233, 239
voice   3, 8 – 9, 10, 13 – 15, 18 f., 21 f., 25, 27, 29, 31, 42 f., 47, 54, 79, 125, 157
anticipatory v.   3 f., 4, 15, 102, 109, 325
– apocalyptic v.   10
– authorial v.   8 – 9, 13 f., 19, 25 – 29, 31, 42 f., 47, 70, 79, 94 f., 102, 104 f., 120, 125, 130, 135 f., 243 f., 288
– v. of historical actors   3, 5, 9, 13 f., 17 – 19, 21 – 23, 25 – 29, 39, 43, 54, 75, 79, 228
Volney, C.-F. de   49, 349, 352

Walbank, F.W.   64 f., 142, 153, 244, 247, 249 – 251, 257 f., 260 f., 263 f., 313
Walpole, H.   350 – 352
Williams, B.   42

White, H.   73, 216, 233
Whitmarsh, T.   296
Wolf, F.A.   352, 372, 374 – 376, 379
Wood, R.   350, 375
Woodward, C.   341, 345 f., 350, 353
World War I   83, 85

xenia   122 – 124, 130 f.
Xenophon   3, 26 – 28, 37, 41 – 44, 96 f., 99 – 102, 104 – 116, 119 – 129, 131 – 139, 179 – 181, 295, 299, 350, 383
– *Anabasis*   26 f., 101 f., 119 – 121, 124 f., 127, 129, 132 – 136, 138 f.
– *Cyropaedia*   107 f., 112, 135, 138 f.
– *Hellenica*   26, 37, 42, 96, 102, 106, 108, 111 f., 114 – 116, 119, 123, 125, 127, 132, 137 f., 179, 295
– Polydamas (speech of)   111 f., 116, 222

Zeitgeschichte   60, 283

www.ingramcontent.com/pod-product-compliance
Lightning Source LLC
Chambersburg PA
CBHW070747230426
43665CB00017B/2275